RELIGION IN AFRICA

This book is volume 4
in the monograph series
of the
David M. Kennedy Center
for International Studies
at
Brigham Young University

This book is dedicated
to

Spencer J. Palmer

a distinguished scholar
of world religions
who first conceived of
this new look at
African religion.

cover design by
McRay Magleby

RELIGION IN AFRICA

Experience & Expression

edited by
Thomas D. Blakely
Walter E.A. van Beek
Dennis L Thomson

with the assistance of
Linda Hunter Adams
Merrill E. Oates

James Currey, LONDON
Heinemann, PORTSMOUTH, NH

David M. Kennedy Center for International Studies
Brigham Young University
Provo, Utah

James Currey Ltd
54b Thornhill Square, Islington
London N1 1BE

Heinemann: A division of Reed Elsevier Inc.
361 Hanover Street
Portsmouth, New Hampshire 03801-3912

01 02 03 04 VP 9 8 7 6 5

British Library Cataloguing in Publication Data
Religion in Africa.

1. Africa, Religions
I. Blakely, Thomas D. II. Van Beek, Walter E. A. III. Thomson, Dennis L
291.096

ISBN 0–85255–207–6 (Paper)
ISBN 0–85255–206–8 (Cloth)

Library of Congress Cataloging in Publication Data

Religion in Africa: experience & expression /
edited by Thomas D. Blakely, Walter E. A. van Beek, Dennis L Thomson
with the assistance of Linda Hunter Adams, Merrill E. Oates.
512 pp. 22.5 cm. — (Monograph series of the David M. Kennedy Center
for International Studies at Brigham Young University; v. 4)
Includes bibliographical references and index.
ISBN 0–435–08081–4. — ISBN 0–435–08083–0 (pbk.)
1. Africa, Sub-Saharan—Religion. I. Blakely, Thomas D. (Thomas
Dustin), 1945–. II. Beek, W. E. A. van. III. Thomson, Dennis L. IV. Series.
BL2462.5.R45 1992
291'.0967—dc20

Typeset in Provo and Philadelphia
by Sterling Augustine, Andrew Bay, Jesse Curtis & Merrill Oates
and Printed in USA

Contents

List of Plates

List of Tables and Figures

Photo Credits

Copyright for each photograph is retained and all rights reserved by the respective persons or institutions listed (with the exception of the photographers, artist, and scholars noted in parentheses).

Dan Ben-Amos: Plates 7–1 through 7–6.

Pamela A. R. Blakely and Thomas D. Blakely: Plates 20–1 through 20–4; 20–6 through 20–16.

Warren L. d'Azevedo: Plate 17–1.

Pierre de Maret: Plates 10–1, 10–5.

John M. Janzen: Plates 9–1 through 9–6.

Jon P. Kirby: Plates 3–1 through 3–3.

The Lamu Society, Lamu, Kenya (map designed and drawn by Francesco Stravo): Plate 2–1.

Azim Nanji: Plates 2–2, 2–3.

National Museum of African Art, Smithsonian Institution, Eliot Elisofon Archives (photography by Jeffrey Ploskonka): Plate 20–5.

Mikelle Smith Omari: Plates 8–1, 8–2.

Simon Ottenberg: Plates 18–1 through 18–6.

James E. Payne: Plates 1–2 through 1–4.

Maya Pejic: Plate 16–1.

Matthew Schoffeleers: Plates 4–1 through 4–3.

Verlon Stone: Plates 19–1 through 19–4.

Robert Farris Thompson: Plates 13–1, 13–2.

The University Museum, University of Pennsylvania, Photographic Archives: Plates 1–8 (neg. S4–140719), 10–3 (neg. 5005).

University of Iowa Museum of Art, The Stanley Collection (photography by Gene Dieben): Plates 6–1 through 6–3.

Walter E.A. van Beek: Plate 1–7 (caption information: Mirjam de Bruyn and Han van Dijk) and Plates 10–2, 10–4, 11–1 through 11–10.

Rob van Wendel de Joode: Plates 1–1, 1–5, 1-6.

Preface

A
READER—WHETHER SPECIALIST OR NOVICE in African studies—will
eventually become frustrated with a book by one author attempting to sum
up the tremendous diversity of religious experience and expression in
Africa. The thrill of great vistas glimpsed with a single guiding vision sooner or
later yields to disappointment when the author turns to subject matter that the reader
knows a bit better, or suspects the author has researched less deeply. The task
remains extremely difficult, and arguably impossible given current scholarly
knowledge, for one writer to master the complete sweep of this complex subject.

A common response to this realization has been to publish focused monographs
by individual scholars, especially in the decades since excellent field research on
religion in Africa has superseded the less well-grounded speculations from the
armchair. Similarly, most multiauthored collections of articles concentrate on a
relatively restricted scope geographically, theoretically, methodologically, or in
terms of topic. These strategies have produced superb scholarly work on many
aspects of religion in Africa.

The problem remains, however: where in one book can a reader find a high level
of expertise over a broad range of subjects and approaches in the study of religion
in Africa? One excellent book that helps fill this void is *Theoretical Explorations
in African Religion*, stemming from the papers read at a conference held in the
Netherlands in 1979, edited by Wim van Binsbergen and Matthew Schoffeleers
(1985). *Religion in Africa: Experience and Expression* provides a continuation of
some of these theoretical explorations, aiming for a similarly high scholarly quality
for each chapter in the book, while expanding the purview of the study of religion
in Africa a bit further.

This book stems from a conference entitled "Religion in Africa: The Variety of
Religious Experience in Sub-Saharan Africa" held at Brigham Young University
in Provo, Utah, 22–25 October 1986. Scholars from four continents who study
religious expression throughout all the major regions of Africa and in the African
Diaspora in the Americas gave presentations on a diverse array of topics. They
discussed research conducted in forty African nations, spanning a broad range of
religious traditions on the continent.

Though fifteen academic disciplines were represented, the contributions all had
in common—as do the chapters in this book—an emphasis on the solid grounding
of approaches and theories with in-depth archival and field research case materials.
The refreshing lack of a single dominant perspective at this conference—or
internecine struggles between competing scholarly paradigms—led Johannes
Fabian to remark in his closing statement to the hosts on behalf of the visiting
scholars that "it seems in this situation that a bit more of *Africa* has come through".

The conference chair was Spencer J. Palmer, of the David M. Kennedy Center
for International Studies and BYU professor of comparative world religions, to

whom this book is dedicated. We are also indebted to Ray C. Hillam, then director of the Kennedy Center for International Studies, which, with other groups at BYU, financially supported the conference. This book developed out of that conference. The Kennedy Center and the office of the Academic Vice President at BYU provided financial support for the book.

A number of conference participants made valuable contributions through presentations, papers, and discussions that assisted the authors in developing their manuscripts and the editors in constructing and completing this book, including Dan Andersen, Joseph E. Black, Alan Christelow, Gerald L. Davis, Virgie D. Day, Hasan El-Shamy, David J. Johnson, Marian A. Johnson, G. Wesley Johnson, William F. Lye, Carolan Pastma Ownby, Derek J. Thom, and, time and again over several years, Gordon C. Thomasson and P. Stanley Yoder. BYU Africanist and Latin Americanist librarian Mark L. Grover provided substantial help with the broadening and strengthening of the book's bibliography.

This book was produced by Linda Hunter Adams and her staff at the Humanities Publications Center, Brigham Young University. Her professional guidance has been invaluable in bringing this book to camera-ready copy. Extra special thanks go to Sterling Augustine for completing the design of the language diacritics and for expert and perserverant work on the galley and page-proof revisions. Chris Koller also helped with typesetting. Tim Hiatt and Andrew Bay made the final corrections. Andrew and Ana Maria Bay energetically helped clean up and format the bibliography, building on Amy Browning Crompton Rossiter's earlier work. Tory Anderson, Merrill Pugmire, Wai-Yiu Lo, Henry Miles, Carol Miles, and Kent Scadlock deserve much credit as well for their work on the manuscript. Thanks also go to Angela Adair, Kristin Clark, Steve Clark, Kristin Gebhart, Katherine Hamilton, Tami Larsen, Patricia Malouf, Catherine Moody, David Moore, Kenneth Nishimoto, Tory Perry, Alyson Taylor, and Dina Wakley for their assistance. Don E. Norton of BYU also did copy editing on early manuscript versions of the book. Carolyn Hone of the Humanities Research Center provided greatly appreciated help during the final editing phase. Also thanks goes to Charles Pope at BYU Press and Matt Schaepe and Renee M. Pinard at Heinemann Press.

Amanda King and Alessandro Pezzati (The University Museum, University of Pennsylvania), Christraud Geary and Amy J. Staples (National Museum of African Art), Christopher D. Roy, Jo-Ann Conklin, and Jeff Martin (The University of Iowa Museum of Art), and James E. Payne provided the editors very welcome assistance with photo research. Special gratitude goes to Dana Hagio and Elmer J. Reese for their impressively prompt and professional work in preparing some of the photographic prints for publication. The editors also wish to thank Frank Jan van Dijk for his detailed commentary on chapter 16 and Pamela A. R. Blakely for substantive editing work on several parts of the manuscript.

Merrill E. Oates particularly deserves praise for his many hours of hard work as editorial assistant for more than three years.

University of Pennsylvania
March 13, 1994

Thomas D. Blakely

Contributors

Wándé Abímbọlá recently retired as President of Ọbafẹmi Awolọwọ University, Ilé-Ifẹ̀, Nigeria. He has also served as head of the Department of African Languages and Literatures and Vice Chancellor at the University of Ifẹ̀. As a child in Ọyọ, Nigeria, he was apprenticed in Yoruba religious institutions. He received his advanced academic training at London, Northwestern, and Lagos. He has published extensively on literary and religious aspects of Ifá divination, including *Ifá: An Exposition of Ifá Literary Corpus* (1976) and *Ifá Divination Poetry* (1977).

Paula Girshick Ben-Amos is professor of anthropology at Indiana University, Bloomington. Her specialties include arts and anthropology, symbolism, social organization, and gender roles. She has done research and writing on Benin art and on African art more generally, including *The Art of Benin* (1979), *The Art of Power: The Power of Art, Studies in Benin Iconography* (1983, with Arnold Rubin), and "African Arts from a Social Perspective" (1987), and she authored the "Edo Religion" entry in *The Encyclopedia of Religion* (Eliade 1987).

Pamela A. R. Blakely received her Ph.D. at the Folklore Institute, Indiana University, and teaches "Health, Spirituality, and Womanhood in Africa" and other Africa-focused courses at the University of Pennsylvania. She has conducted five years of ethnographic field research with Báhêmbá in rural villages and urban eastern Zaïre concerning aesthetics of ritual, verbal art, material culture, sculpture, and culture history. She is editor, with Thomas D. Blakely, of the *Directory of Visual Anthropology* (1989), a reference volume of methods, topics, and publications in visual research and visual representation.

Thomas D. Blakely does research in anthropology, linguistics, and folklore and has taught at the University of South Carolina, Brigham Young University, Temple University, and the University of Pennsylvania. He is former President of the Society for Visual Anthropology and is currently an editor of the journal *Visual Anthropology*. His book *Hêmbá Visual Communication and Space* (forthcoming) and the article "Só'ó Masks and Hêmbá Funerary Festival" (1987), coauthored with Pamela A. R. Blakely, explore proxemic and semiotic issues that inform his current work on everyday and ritual speech and performance in Central Africa.

Warren L. d'Azevedo is professor of anthropology, emeritus, at the University of Nevada, Reno. His graduate studies were at the University of California at Berkeley and Northwestern University. He has conducted field research among the Washoe people of Nevada and California, as well as the Gola of Liberia. His published works include articles and monographs on social organization, ethnohistory, artistry, and religion. He is editor of *The Traditional Artist in African Society* (1973) and the Smithsonian Institution *Handbook of North American Indians,* vol. 11, on the Great Basin (1986).

Luc de Heusch is professor of anthropology at the University of Brussels and has done extensive field research in Central Africa. He is former Directeur d'étude associé at the 5th Section of the Ecole Pratique des Hautes Etudes, Paris. He is the author of *Why Marry Her?* (1971), *The Drunken King or the Origin of the State* (1972), and *Sacrifice in Africa* (1985).

Pierre de Maret is Dean of the Faculty of Philosophy and Letters and professor of archaeology and anthropology at the University of Brussels and is also affiliated with the Royal Museum of Central Africa in Tervuren. He has been conducting fieldwork in Central Africa since 1970. His main research interests are in Bantu origins and other topics in later prehistory, especially the Iron Age, as well as ethnotechnology, applied anthropology, and museology.

Johannes Fabian is Chair of the Department of Cultural Anthropology at the University of Amsterdam and has also taught at the Université Nationale du Zaïre (Lubumbashi), Wesleyan University, and Northwestern University. He has done research on Swahili language and on the Jamaa movement for over twenty-five years. Among his publications are *Time and the Other: How Anthropology Makes Its Object* (1983), *Language and Colonial Power* (1989), and *Power and Performance* (1990), and he is a major contributor to the current debates about anthropological writing and a criticial rethinking of anthropology.

John M. Janzen is professor of anthropology at the University of Kansas, in Lawrence. His research and teaching interests have concentrated on the sociocultural and medical anthropology of Africa. His most important work is a trilogy on African health and healing: *The Quest for Therapy* (1978), *Lemba 1650–1930* (1982), and *Ngoma* (1992).

Father Jon P. Kirby is a missionary and anthropologist in Ghana and is the Director of the Tamale Institute of Cross-Cultural Studies, which offers courses in cross-cultural orientation and in Ghanaian languages. The institute also sponsors and directs research on cross-cultural issues related to human development in Africa. He is author of *Jesus of the Deep Forest* (1981) and *God, Shrines, and Problem-Solving among the Anufo of Northern Ghana* (1986).

Asmarom Legesse is professor of anthropology at Swarthmore College and has also taught at Boston University and Northwestern University. He was born in Eritrea and received his doctorate from Harvard University. His research and writing have focused on the study of ritual, rites of passage, the life course, social change, human ecology, and indigenous systems of thought in Ethiopia, Eritrea, Kenya, and Jamaica. He is author of *Gada: Three Approaches to the Study of African Society* (1973).

Wyatt MacGaffey teaches social anthropology at Haverford College. He has written extensively on the history, politics, economics, religion, and art of Zaïre, especially on the Bakongo. His books include *Custom and Government in the Lower Congo* (1970); *Modern Kongo Prophets* (1983), a study of Kimbanguism; *Religion and Society in Central Africa* (1986); and *Art and Healing of the Bakongo, Commented by Themselves* (1991).

Azim Nanji is Chair of the Department of Religion, University of Florida, Gainesville. He formerly directed the Center for Global Studies at Oklahoma State University. He has done extensive field studies and writing on Ismaili Muslims in East Africa and in South Asia, including *The Nizārī Ismāʿīlī Tradition in the Indo-Pakistan Subcontinent* (1978). He has also published a number of articles on symbolic, ritual, historical, and social change issues involving Islam in African contexts.

Mikelle Smith Omari is associate professor of African art history and African-American art, University of Arizona, Tucson. She has researched Yoruba ritual and art in Brazil, the United States, and West Africa. Her research interests include images of power and the construction of gender, and other issues concerning women in religion. Her publications include *From the Inside to the Outside: The Art and Ritual of Bahian Candomblé* (1984) and *Manipulating the Sacred: A Semiotic Analysis of Art and Ritual in Africa and the Diaspora* (in press).

Simon Ottenberg is professor emeritus, Department of Anthropology, University of Washington, and recently was President of the African Studies Association. He has done extensive field research on political organization, social change, art, religion, and ethnicity among the Afikpo Ibo of Nigeria and the Limba of Sierra Leone. Among his numerous publications are *African Religious Groups and Beliefs: Papers in Honor of William R. Bascom* (1982) and *Boyhood Rituals in an African Society: An Interpretation* (1989).

Terence Ranger is professor of race relations and Chair of the African Studies Committee at the University of Oxford. He has worked on the history of Zimbabwe since 1957 and published extensively on his research and on other matters in the study of history, including the influential book *The Invention of Tradition* (1983, with Eric Hobsbawm). He is currently writing a history of the Matopos mountains and the High God shrines, to be called *Voices from the Rock*.

Lamin Sanneh is professor of missions and world Christianity and of history, and Chair of the Council of African Studies at Yale. He has previously taught at Harvard University, the University of Aberdeen, and at African universities. He is the author of *West African Christianity* (1983), *The Jakhanke Muslim Clerics* (1989), and *Translating the Message: The Missionary Impact of Culture* (1989) and has held editorial positions with the *Journal of Religion in Africa*, *The Christian Century*, and the *International Bulletin of Missionary Research*.

Matthew Schoffeleers, a Roman Catholic priest, read theology in the Netherlands and anthropology in the United Kingdom. He served for twenty years as a missionary in northern Malawi. He recently retired from the Chair in African Religion in the Department of Anthropology, Free University of Amsterdam. He has published extensively on religion in Africa, including the milestone volume *Theoretical Approaches to the Study of African Religion* (1985, with Wim van Binsbergen). His most recent work is *River of Blood: The Genesis of a Martyr Cult in Northern Malawi, c. 1600 A.D.* (1992).

Ruth M. Stone is professor of folklore and African studies at Indiana University, Bloomington, where she also serves as Director of the Archives of Traditional Music and head of the ethnomusicology program. Among her publications are *Let the Inside Be Sweet: The Interpretation of Music Event among the Kpelle of Liberia* (1982), *Dried Millet Breaking: Time, Words, and Song in the Woi Epic of the Kpelle* (1988), and *Performance in Contemporary African Music* (1988). She is also editor of the volume on African music in the forthcoming Garland *Encyclopedia of World Music.*

Dennis L Thomson is professor of political science at Brigham Young University, where he recently served as Associate Academic Vice President. A former U.S. Foreign Service officer in Africa, he has taught at the University of Arizona and the State University of New York at Binghamton. He did his graduate work at the University of California at Santa Barbara. He publishes on public policy, ethnicity, and religion and politics. His most recent books are *Private Exercise of Public Functions* (1985), *Ethnicity, Politics and Development* (1986, with Dov Ronen), and *Moral Values and Higher Education* (1991).

Walter E.A. van Beek is associate professor of cultural anthropology at the University of Utrecht, Netherlands. His first research, starting in 1971, was an ethnography of the Kapsiki and Higi of northern Cameroon and northeastern Nigeria. Since 1978 he has studied the cultural ecology of the Dogon at the Bandiagara escarpment in Mali. In recent years he has participated in several ethnographic film productions on Dogon culture and has produced a film on the pillage of African cultural patrimony by the international art market ("The African King"). He is coauthor with Jan van Baal of *Symbols for Communication* (1985), a textbook on the anthropology of religion.

Linda Hunter Adams is Director of the College of Humanities Publications Center at Brigham Young University. She teaches "Editing for Publication" in the English Department. An editor of numerous books and journals, she is currently associate editor of *Brigham Young University Studies*, editor of *Encyclia*, and production editor of the *Journal of the Rocky Mountain Medieval and Renaissance Association.*

Mark L. Grover is the African studies bibliographer at the Harold B. Lee Library at Brigham Young University. He received his Ph.D. in Latin American and African history from Indiana University. He has published in both Latin American studies and African studies, with his primary research focus being the study of religion in Brazil, Portugal, and Africa.

Merrill E. Oates is a Ph.D. candidate in cultural anthropology at the University of Pennsylvania. His research interests include religion and religious change in complex societies, nationalism, ethnicity, and transnational cultural flows.

Introduction

Walter E.A. van Beek &
Thomas D. Blakely

> *For now we see through a glass, darkly ...*
> (I Corinthians 13:12)

RELIGION, THE ELUSIVE REALITY

A COLLECTION OF ESSAYS on African religious experience and expression has to face two fundamental questions: what is typical of religion and what is so special about African religion? Religion is a difficult subject of inquiry, elusive by its very substance. Consequently, students of religion feel a recurrent need to define the nature of their subject matter and elucidate their own position in relation to it. This continuous taking stock of what one is dealing with reflects a major dilemma students of religion have to face.

Maurice Merleau-Ponty once characterized a person's dealings with any topic as a "*prise glissante*", a slippery, sliding grip (Merleau-Ponty 1945). whatever hold one deems to have on reality, on closer inspection the hold gradually vanishes. All the more so with the evanescent reality of religion. After all, religion aims to deal with phenomena beyond empirical reality, placing its core beyond the realm of any science. Most people do not claim that they can—at will—directly observe God, an ancestor, or a witch at work. However, this does in no way detract from the reality of widely held beliefs; in fact, the fundamental impossibility to falsify religious content is one major foothold of religion and a source of the bewildering variation and multiplicity of forms (van Beek 1982b). Furthermore, religion is hardly a phenomenon totally unto itself; it is inextricably bound to other aspects of culture and society. In the essays of this book the interrelatedness of religion with politics, economics, social processes, illness and healing, art, music, dance, and speech comes to the fore, among the many other ties that could be mentioned. So the difficulty in defining the subject matter stems both from the impossibility to define an empirical referent for its content and from the problems of boundary demarcation.

Granting these caveats, it still is useful to have a working definition of religion, since both the essentialist question (What is religion?) and the problem of boundary

1

demarcation (What is still religious?) will come up in our discussions. Starting from the dilemma of empirical research in dealings with the nonempirical, we propose as a working definition a mixture of van Baal and van Beek (1985), Spiro (1966), and Geertz (1966): religion as human interaction with a culturally postulated nonfalsifiable reality. This formulation combines both the insiders' view (religion engages in the *supernatural*—a term we shall shun, as it badly fits African religions) and the outsiders' etic view that we study the human side of the interaction only.[1] Important, for our purposes in this book, is the cultural angle: religion is expressed and experienced in ways and forms offered by culture or constituted as culture. In one approach to this, the question of the broader veracity of the beliefs studied is not posed; religious experiences and expressions are discussed within their empirical context only. This method, often called *methodological atheism* (Berger 1967; Towler 1974) has been standard procedure in social science for a long time, and for some good reasons. Most often in science, there is no way to choose between competing statements about nonempirical information.

Still, Mircea Eliade has pointed out (1969:62), such a stance gives research on religion a naturalistic bias: the researcher studies the religion of people somewhat like an entomologist focusing his binoculars on another insect. But in religion we humans deal with a very human phenomenon. In fact, there is no compelling empirical or analytical reason to do away *a priori* with the categories, interpretations, and explanations of the people studied, our informants and interlocutors. In other fields of interest we are not at all afraid of taking up insiders' categories, interpretations, and explanations: "Anthropological analyses, for all our fine talk, thus inevitably bear the stamp of the culture in which they have been forged" (Lewis 1986:11). A more cautious definition of method would suit us better, so we propose *methodological agnosticism*. Whatever the "patent absurdity" or the sympathetic *Selbstverständlichkeit* [self-evidentness] of the religious beliefs may be, or however much an ethnographer may heuristically *suspend disbelief*, or how the personal convictions of the researcher may influence his or her views (as they inevitably do), the empirical study of religion "just does not know".

One more reason for this more unassuming approach is that in the course of anthropological history the claim to "explain" religious phenomena has greatly diminished, moving from explanation towards interpretation (Fabian 1979a; Geertz 1984). The early masters of the field, like Tylor, Durkheim, or Freud, were bold enough to look for an explanation of religious phenomena whether based on reason, societal identity, or infantile illusions. Historically, the advent of phenomenology marked a growing questioning of these quests (Sharpe 1975). The drive of these early culture-heroes towards explaining *away* religion can be understood also as a reaction against religion, from their respective personal backgrounds (Sharpe 1975:240); personal backgrounds also influenced phenomenology, which aimed to preserve and protect religion (van Baal and van Beek 1985:202). In fact, some argue, the question as to veracity is itself slightly outdated, as it belongs to a positivistic philosophy of science that has run its course (Fabian 1979a, 1981). And of course the hermeneutics of postmodern anthropology have provided critiques of the construction of various kinds of "truth" (Clifford and Marcus 1986). Yet, this version of relativism is not what primarily occupies us here, as our discussion of translatability will show.

Nowadays few scholars in this subject venture into explanations, biosocial approaches being one exception (Wallace 1966; d'Aquili, Laughlin, and McManus 1979) and René Girard's revival of Freud another (Girard 1972, 1982). Today's students of religion focus on particular forms of religious expression and try to point out the consonances with other cultural and historical processes, while still trying to preserve the integrity of the religious experience-*cum*-expression. This is the core of the method and, in fact, closely resembles an answer (possibly apocryphal) that Carl Jung once gave. After a lecture on evil, people asked him whether he believed the devil existed. His answer: "No idea, but he works!" Thus, we study influences *on* religion and influences *by* religion, realizing that directly studying religious phenomena *per se* is at least very difficult. Religion is best studied in its sociocultural contexts, to be grasped by being human among the humans, which should make us modest—maybe even humble—trying to explore our deepest core.

> *How should I tell, or how can ye receive it?*
> *How, till He bringeth you where I have been?*
>
> (Hughes 1948:4)

TRANSLATION AND COMPARISON

From this general perspective of a shared human condition, two methodological problems are central to the authors of this book: *translation* and *comparison*. With translation is meant the expression of cultural meaning from one cultural system into a different cultural system, perhaps most interestingly when the two systems diverge greatly in preconception and reasoning. On several occasions E. E. Evans-Pritchard made a plea that the anthropologist's task was to translate. However, he limited the task just to that—translation—and shied away (at least in theory) from interpretation and comparison (Evans-Pritchard 1956:VI, 1965:120). His practice was better than his theory in this respect, as his book *Nuer Religion* shows. A leading theoretical question in the contributions here in the *Religion in Africa* book is whether and how a religious system can be "transculturated" into another culture. The fact that the latter culture can be a scientific-academic one, purportedly encompassing all known cultures, does not significantly alter the problem. The metalanguage developed for the description and analysis of religion and culture stems from individual cultures, not from a metacultural discourse, and is but little removed from the empirical observations (Lewis 1986:12). This translation-plus-comparison problem lies at the heart of anthropological theory. It is, in effect, the problem of cognitive relativity. Anthropology has long tried to set a course between the Scylla of universal categorization (ethnocentrism in disguise) and the Charibdis of extreme relativism. In the first case cultures have no fundamental differences; in the latter one they share neither rhyme nor reason.[2] Like most researchers nowadays, the authors in the volume chart a course of "relative relativism". Cultural expressions can be understood, but never fully, and can be communicated transculturally, but not without loss of meaning and the creation of new meaning. Our observations are interpretations, first of all, rendered understandable by both a shared humanity with all people and by a shared academic culture that hardly transcends the phenomena studied. This shared academic culture is both a major means and an important obstacle for understanding other cultures (Bruner 1986:10).

Our first section of chapters ("Religion and Its Translatability") deals with this problem directly. The authors focus on the effects of translation and translatability on religion and politics (Sanneh, Nanji), efforts to translate Christian concepts into African cultures and back (Kirby, Schoffeleers, Thomson) and translation and interpretation of core concepts in African cosmology from a massive literary corpus (Abímbólá).

Translatability of religion is central in Lamin Sanneh's contribution, in which he explores the effects the untranslatability of the sacred Arabic has had for both the uniformity in Islam (or the religious practice of Islam) and nationalism. Christian translation into vernacular languages is shown to be a springboard of nationalism, both political and religious. Islam makes a definite statement on the issue of "Arabic relativism": there is one sacred language (and culture) that cannot be expressed in any of the myriad of mutually interchangeable vernaculars. The effects are shown to be pervasive: unity in worship, supranational identity, and alienation from local culture for Islam, while Christianity with its definite translation stance leads to nationalism, diverging worship formats, and the prominence of local culture.[3]

In Azim Nanji's contribution, the relation between Muslims in East Africa and the bearers of other religions and cultures is termed an encounter. The encounter is not on any systemic level, but at a purely personal one. The interaction of people who have different beliefs in such a situation of cultural change generates new meanings as well as new opportunities. The three cases Nanji describes are, by design, quite heterogeneous: a king, an Indian Muslim trader, and a visionary leader of a liberation movement. Their lives (or stories of their lives) show that the complex phenomena of conversion and transculturation can in no way be reduced to simple categories or dichotomies.

Translation implies comparison—comparison in relation to the cultural categories of Western academia or to a background of Anglo-Christian culture or to another religio-cultural frame used by the researcher. Whichever way, the "relative relativism" of most of the chapters implies a prudent comparative stance. Three of the other authors of this section—Kirby, Schoffeleers, and Thomson—each engage in a cautious juxtaposition of notions from two kinds of religion. In conversion, the topic of Jon P. Kirby's contribution, this encounter seems to be one sided. Kirby shows both religious systems subject to changes, however, including the politically dominant Christian missionary one. The translation process results in a fascinating layering of religion that is not so much related to a duality in politics (as in MacGaffey's chapter on Kimbanguism), but to a duality in human experience, not unlike Horton's approach (1975). The processes of identity formation and problem solving appear to be sufficiently separate to have multiple religious systems being used at the same time by the same person. Kirby's main argument—religion as problem solving and therefore a layered institution—will be taken up later;

important here is that the African religious situation, even when seemingly simple, proves always to have more hidden dimensions and ingenious adaptations than may be evident or expected. As a consequence, Kirby pleads for a consistent multicultural approach (or at least bicultural), a plea that also implies translatability.

Matthew Schoffeleers's chapter is the most explicit on the issue of translation: his quest for an African model of the role of Christ in African Christianity is— among many other things—a dialectic translation effort. Looking at the *nganga* [medicine person] as a possible christological paradigm for Africa (though it does not seem to hold for West Africa, it still is wide enough for his purpose), he essentially engages in a double translation: the Western-imported Christ figure has to be translated into Central Bantu culture, and this evidently is difficult. So, the most feasible African model—the *nganga*—is translated back into the Christian setting, offering both new views on indigenous religion and a viable option for Africanization of Christian theology.

Dennis L Thomson's contribution centers on similar issues, on a broader African scale. Looking for commonalities between generalized African religion (a problem apart) and Mormon religious thought, Thomson, with all due caution, concludes a fair translatability of the systems into one another. His conclusion does raise the important question as to whether from common elements of religion a commonality of the religious systems can be concluded, a point to which we shall return later.

Wándé Abímbólá, operating more on the level of systematic theological notions, starts from Yoruba concepts: the wisdom and world vision in the gigantic corpus of Ifá divination texts. His treatment of Ifá systemic thought implicitly uses an Anglo-Christian grid as a comparative frame for his data, and discovers a relevant substratum of shared notions between the two. These remarkable parallels suggest a fair translatability of Western theological concepts to Yoruba culture and vice versa.

One fascinating aspect of these exchanges is that in the process new meaning is generated on both ends of the communication chain (cf. Devisch 1985). The *nganga* concepts and Christology—without merging—transform each other in a creative process of intercultural communication. This process does not generate a metalanguage through which a naturalistic study of religion would be feasible, but the result is a heightened sensibility for the subtlety and richness of both participant cultures, as well as an emergent new way of ascribing meaning. Similarly, in the blending of the "new missionary Christianity" with the local African religion that Kirby proposes, both are thoroughly transformed. In Sanneh's argument, the very fact of the translation endeavor inevitably compromises both religions, leading towards syncretic and separatistic idiosyncrasies. But this is the negative evaluation of the process, as given by a homogeneous religion, Islam. Viewed from "below", new expressions for new religious experiences are formulated through mutual translation, with new systems of meaning generated, and the whole process triggered by the dialectic nature of religious action (Leach 1969).

An important political aspect of the translation processes mentioned is the hierarchical relationship between religions. In Muslim, Catholic, as well as

Mormon instances, a hierarchy in translation is evident, maybe less obvious for the representatives of the "great" religions than for performers of the vernacular discourses. The newcomer religion is dominant whether or not it is translated into the subordinate culture. In most of the contributions mentioned, the authors try to break through this hierarchy and have the two religions express their concepts into each other. Kirby, Schoffeleers, and Thomson try to negate hierarchy. Sanneh stresses both the vulnerability and the strength of the Christian translation position. Still, the differences in power between the newcomers and the respondent religions are enormous and pervasive. Beyond the local African scene there is no real effort made to translate and utilize concepts such as *nganga*, ancestors, or *òrìsà* in Christian theology, let alone Muslim orthodoxy. Though the paths of adaptation may change the newcomers, the dialogue is held from quite unequal positions.

Comparison, and thus translation, can be performed in many ways. The second section of this book ("Comparisons over Time and Space") deals with a number of specific comparisons and contrasts: looking at the core, a closely related neighbor, and a diaspora extension of one culture; comparison on a large temporal and spatial scale of elements of religion; and finally comparison among carefully selected examples.

The first option, in fact, started with the subject matter of the chapter by Abímbólá: Yoruba and Yoruba-influenced culture. Paula Girshick Ben-Amos shows how for Edo women in Benin City the Olokun religious association is an autonomous road to power and greatness as well as an inverse mirror of male-dominated society. Both the female and the male side of society can be seen either as transformations (or translations) of one another, or as negations of the other's power base. Mikele Smith Omari examines an extension of Yoruba culture in the African Diaspora: Candomblé religion in Bahia, Brazil. Two aspects that strike the eye are the extent of preservation and incorporation of Yoruba elements and the reevaluation of Africanness in the Brazilian setting. In this case, too, the translation of Yoruba cultural elements to a different setting has resulted in something that is both old and very new, recognizably Yoruba, but invigorated and transformed, a phenomenon Felicity D. Goodman (1988) has drawn attention to on the individual level. The religiously motivated ideologies of identity lead to the acceptance of hierarchical relations in the surrounding society and to the inversion of societal values in Candomblé ritual and social organization.

There is a problem in this last formulation, however. The term *inversion* includes a primacy of the "outer system", the "official" society. However, from the principles of our methodological stance, we cannot assign priority to one power base over another. Standard explanation interprets religious social mobility as an *alternative* route, when political mobility is blocked by dominance. This explanation, going back to George Balandier's *reprise d'initiative* (1955), leads us astray from our methodological agnosticism and from the informant interpretations we prioritize and follow much more closely. To discern "what it is really all about" is to make a choice. Assigning analytical priority to the male-dominated power system is such a choice.[4] It is important to explore the mechanisms through which one power system is transformed into another, or how both political and symbolic power are articulated (Bourdieu 1979; van Binsbergen and Schoffeleers 1985). Since these mechanisms remain in the shadows of paradigmatic spotlights, students of African religious expression are still saddled with a premature choice. The claims for autonomous women's greatness through Yoruba/Edo/Candomblé religion thus induce rethinking of familiar preconceptions.

If a West African religion lends itself to such a long distance translation, why not some core concepts in Bantu culture? John M. Janzen explores the range of one core Bantu institution—the drums of affliction [*ngoma*]—with its cluster of elements (drum, divination, therapy, and definition of sacrality). How well does this cluster travel? Though his conclusion is somewhat tentative, the elements seem to travel remarkably well (see also MacGaffey 1980; Janzen 1992). There is some "random" as well as some systematic variation (e.g., per type of state organization) with its concomitant transformations of function; still, the polyvalent symbolism associated with the drums of affliction throughout appears to be at the meeting point between religious beliefs, problem solving, and professionalization.

Important in our context is the ease with which strands of meaning move from culture to culture. This kind of comparison is also the province of archaeologists. Pierre de Maret uses such comparison with great caution, circumspectedly shunning any premature conclusion. His very prudence, however, may give us some room for interpretation. The long distances over which African religious systems seem to have influenced each other strike the observer (Thomas and Luneau 1975:78 ff.). Also, the continuity of local forms in his Central Bantu case is a point to ponder; in counterpoint to documentation of rapid religious change, such a demonstration of tradition of long standing should give us pause (cf. Ray 1976:120 ff.).

A different kind of comparison is made by the next two authors. Walter E.A. van Beek compares two similar, but not geographically contiguous, cases. He gives a detailed description and analysis of the "world of magic" in two indigenous African religious systems. His "controlled comparison" explores the ways in which two quite comparable societies define and structure the less socially approved aspects of religion. Though in both cases the notions of "evil" concur with the characteristics of social structure, the common ground in the two contrast cases does stem from more than just societal structure. The two cases are shown to be transformations of one another, variant codes of a substrate message. Thus, by this comparison, an existential theme emerges: the ways of coping with evil reflect people's tension to live *with* and at the same time *without* others.

A similar theme—the problem of order and disorder, deeply hidden in the thickets of Bantu epics—leads Luc de Heusch in his quest for meaning in the strange tales of origin of the Bantu states and societies he has so productively studied. Here, the various codes not only express the fundamental dialectics of human life and interaction in society, they also reflect a structural logic immanent in the symbols themselves. Thus, humanity's dealings with evil (van Beek) or disorder (de Heusch) have their existential logic. They also serve as a springboard by which unconscious mechanisms for the creation of meaning are set into motion and over which the participants exercise only limited control: every human being is, in a sense, *un apprenti sorcier* (cf. Carlier 1974:259 ff.).

Above, we noted unequal positions in interreligious communication: the power bases of religious expressions can be very unequal. Our third section ("The Instrumentality of Religion: Process and Performance") houses responses towards this unequal situation and other issues concerning the dynamics between differing forms of religious experience and expression, both interculturally and intraculturally. Consequently, in this section the interweaving of religion with other spheres of action is central—the translation of religious notions into politics, social processes, artistic action, and vice versa. In order to gain a view on this instrumentality of religion, MacGaffey, Fabian, and Ranger use the asymmetrical relationship between religions as their starting point and show how—at least partly—balance is regained through the flexibility and creativity of African responses to external religious intrusion.

Wyatt MacGaffey, in his treatment of syncretism in Kimbanguism, explicitly starts from the hierarchical duality of the colonial and neocolonial Zaïrean situation. While rightly pointing out that "syncretism" is an awkward, redundant, and sometimes prejudicial term, MacGaffey relates "syncretic" tendencies to the continuing discourse between unequal partners: the Kimbanguist church and the Zaïrean state-plus-Western Christianity. This political duality or plurality in his view is important for interpreting tendencies towards religious stratification.

Johannes Fabian sketches the recent situation of the Jamaa movement, coming back to it many years after his first descriptions (Fabian 1971). He is in fact astonished to see the movement still alive in a social setting that seems no longer suited to it. Jamaa appears to have adapted to a competition in charisma between mainstream and marginal religious movements in Zaïre. Fabian's view of religious entrepreneurship, with a pervasive power symbolism (eating and ingestion, an important aspect of African corporal symbols [cf. Douglas 1973]), offers unexpected insights into Central African politics. His analysis of this symbolism could indeed be applicable well beyond Central Africa.

Terence O. Ranger's chapter on the American Methodist Episcopal Church in eastern Zimbabwe explores little known archival sources to chronicle how, over years and decades, important "theses" of AMEC missionary theology and practice were met by enthusiastic and deeply felt "antitheses" of African converts' beliefs and actions, producing new syntheses that simultaneously changed and energized the church. This fascinating case illustrates a key point made by Sanneh (vernacularization was a factor in the Africanization of the missionary Christian churches and marginalized the missionaries). It also highlights the creativity involved in the translation experience and the complexities of the conversion process.

Asmarom Legesse, addressing the issue of liminality and social change, gives some hints for a theoretical solution of how meaning is generated charismatically. After reviewing the well-established notion that though prophets rise, societal structures eventually prevail (Lanternari 1963:352)—structure in the end defeats communitas (Victor Turner 1969)—Legesse shows a causal chain among the seemingly disparate concepts of alienation, communitas, charisma, and prophetism and in doing so argues that the apparent victory of structure is a surface one only. Routinization may marginalize charisma, but this very process does change society: the traces of liminality and the whispers of communitas continue to operate in society and the sacrifice of the prophet can produce societal changes. Moreover, while a charismatic movement is on the rise, it embodies a strongly felt potential—however rarely such potential has been fully realized throughout history—to bring *sweeping* changes in society. Legesse then illustrates his thesis by showing how a movement can do without any prophet at all, at least without a self-claimed one (Rastafari and the Emperor of Ethiopia). Thus, in trying to bridge the gap between life cycle theory and theories of social change, he shows how translation processes can generate new systems of meaning, fresh definitions of the situation, and a changing traditionality.

Intracultural balances of power are just as important for societies and may find expression in religion. A crucial one is between genders, and this rarely finds a more cogent and complicated expression than in the male and female secret societies of coastal West Africa, where *poro* and *sande* institutions have been a continuing source of fascination and wonder for participants and researchers alike. For one thing, anthropological thinking about secrecy and culture almost hinges on these societies (Bellman 1984). Here in this book two contributions more directly address gender power balance as expressed through and conducted by male and female secret societies. In his chapter on the Gola of Liberia, Warren L. d'Azevedo works toward disentangling the webs of secrecy surrounding an important ritual that embodies female power. In his discussion of male views on the dangerous powers of femininity, some notions emerge that are common to many areas of Africa and part of a very African definition of humanity and fertility (see Jakobson-Widding and van Beek 1990). In the Gola view, religion is an instrument for harnessing the wild and destructive aspects of the female sex ("gender" would be less appropriate here), a taming of potential witches that never fully succeeds and then only for limited periods.

Simon Ottenberg addresses gender contrasts in a different vein with an intracultural comparison of a male secret society and a female secret society in Sierra Leone. Though part and parcel of the same Limba culture, the secret societies vary in function and the male version is considerably older than the female one. Still, as the author concludes with some surprise, they are remarkably alike, overall: a variety of societal factors have resulted in a twinlike pair.

Thus far, the focus has been on systemic interaction of religion and society. Some of the mechanisms for this interaction as well as the interaction of religion with other aspects of culture and society are in *performances*—that is, in the translation of notions into overt action—and the modification and emergence of such notions during aesthetically framed action. This aspect, present in several contributions, is the transactional side of religion. Ruth M. Stone, Pamela A. R. Blakely, and Thomas D. Blakely directly address these and related issues.

Ruth Stone, in her analysis of Kpelle music, shows how the layering of religion, domain demarcation, and problem solving—themes discussed previously in the book—are immanent in music and dance. She demonstrates ways in which performance of music and dance not only serves as an expression of religious notions and views, but how music and dance also add their own dimensions to religious experience and, while preexistent notions are utilized, new meaning is created (Geertz 1986:380). Stone's performance analysis further emphasizes that emotion—a neglected side of religion—is important in the creation of meaning through African music and dance.

Pamela Blakely and Thomas Blakely show how performances of intertwined kinesthetic and verbal art—as means to convey thought and emotion, to regulate thought and emotion in culturally and linguistically established patterns, and to contribute toward transforming these patterns—serve as important vehicles through which existential problems are translated and commented upon in transactional terms. Aesthetically valued speech acts by both women and men articulate meaning in a situation in which problems abound and answers are scant. The flexibility of the speech act (broadly conceived) in Báhêmbá men's oratory and women's song-dance—just like the musico-dance act in Stone's analysis—offers a way for the members of a society to reflect upon, engage in discourse about, reaffirm, and even change the society. Performance is at the same time experience, expression, reflection, discussion, affirmation, and emergent construction of new syntheses.

INTERACTION AND TRANSACTION: RELIGION AS AN INSTRUMENT

When comparing and translating religion, the authors concentrate on the instrumental nature of religion. With much respect for believers' opinions, solid fieldwork-based research should unravel the web of intricate relations that ties religion to politics, aesthetics, and social order. Not only is this elucidation revealing in itself, but eventually it runs parallel to informants' and interlocutors' views too. However firmly beliefs are held, or however minutely rituals are enacted, the goals of the participants are very much part of their daily world. Religion mostly for the sake of itself, ethics solely for the sake of a better afterlife, are actuality for but a few.

There is a clear contrast here between two academic traditions. The phenomenology of religion has a long tradition of concentrating on the higher echelons of religion, on the "official" religion (Vryjhof and Waardenburg 1979), on unadulterated forms, shunning syncretism (see MacGaffey's critique of Pye in this volume), avoiding witchcraft, and neglecting the link with power (Lewis 1986). This top-down strategy concentrates on texts and professionals. Even long before Otto (1917) defined religion as the interaction with the Sacred, Schleiermacher coined the phrase *das Gefühl der schlechthinnigen Abhängichkeit* [the feeling of complete dependency]. Here again we founder on the difference between a prescriptive and an empirical definition of religion. As an empirical definition, such a formulation would never do. An example: the Muslim mystic Rabia expressed his relation with Allah in the following terms: "O God! If I worship Thee for fear of hell, burn me in hell; if I worship Thee in hope of Paradise, exclude me thence; but if I worship Thee for Thine own sake, withhold not from me Thine everlasting beauty!" (North 1952:108). How many true believers would be able to formulate this, let alone live according to this lofty expression of worship? "How infinitely passionate a thing religion at its highest flights can be", William James remarked long ago (1902:14). True, but the intellectual and aesthetic pleasure derived from such a statement should not blind us to the fact that for most participants of a religion—in this case Islam—such a definition of dependency is but one among a number of factors influencing religious interaction. And the truly sacred can be a fearsome thing as well, a point many theologians and other academics tend to forget (Bateson and Bateson 1987); the "evil" (Parkin 1985) or "demonic" (Goodman 1988) are also important to take account of.

In the muddle of daily life, religion is much less lofty as well as less threatening, and the ideals of religion serve as goals for worldly ends. Mundane religious interaction is an essential part of a religion, of any religion. Not only is secularization present in any religious system (Douglas 1973): for religion to have any impact at all, some "secularity" is imperative. Legesse's remarks are apposite: no one is less secular than a prophet, but his influence is consolidated only through the inevitable mingling with the world. Besides, any religion counts its critics and sceptics, and they too should be included into the religious system as such. The case of Quesalid had been made famous by Claude Lévi-Strauss (1958). His position of shattering skepticism seems to have remained a part of Kwakiutl religion. But people do not have to take such extreme positions after all. One Dogon informant, an old man battered by a long and arduous life, once explained to Walter van Beek: "[Dogon] religion is a means for the old men to get meat". Still, he was fully within Dogon religion as one of the functioning clan priests of his village.

The notion of *instrument* usually is taken to imply a means to use for achieving a goal. However, we want to employ it in a much broader fashion, consonant with colloquial English (and Dutch). At least three elements can be discerned: the *means-to* instrument, the *monitoring* instrument, and the *performing* instrument. Religion, as shown in this volume, serves as all three of these senses of the term.

The means-to instrument might be the most obvious. Vernacularization, argues Sanneh, is an instrument (even if unintended) for national identity formation. Nanji shows how the interplay of religious conversion, ethnicity, and cultural values opens new vistas for individual merchants and political leaders. In the essays by Girshick Ben-Amos, Smith Omari, Ranger, Blakely and Blakely, and—to some extent— d'Azevedo and Ottenberg, religion is a means to power for women. Fabian analyzes how changes in Jamaa church practice contribute to the survival of the movement and foster adaptation to and construction of the "normal" Zaïrean situation of anarchy-*cum*-charisma. For Zimbabwe, Ranger describes the entrepreneurial options that were stimulated by American Methodists. Individual problem solving is at the heart of Anufo religion for Kirby, Janzen explores how dealing with affliction is a widespread Bantu religious theme, while van Beek shows how in two West African cultures the private rites of magic and other efforts to cope with evil serve to gain an acceptable integration of suffering in individual life. Finally, the promotion (and even the sacrifice) of communitas is a means to a mollified and potentially modified society in Legesse's view.

This, of course, is the classic structural-functionalist vision on religion, which may have lost some of its epistemological credentials (van Binsbergen and Schoffeleers 1985:15), but not all of them. And this perspective does remain an important tool in the fieldworker's tool chest (see Werbner 1989). The attempts at merging this more structural approach with a more transactional one are important, according to the program Van Binsbergen and Schoffeleers have outlined (1985:8). The gap they notice between the two approaches is still to be bridged, though several authors (van Beek, Fabian, Ranger, Stone, and Blakely and Blakely) try to combine them, and the discussions of performance-oriented approaches offer interesting possibilities. Thus, religion as a means-to instrument is analyzed on several levels at the same time: individual (Kirby, Abímbọlá), group (Ranger, Fabian, Ottenberg), the relation between individual and group (Janzen, van Beek, Stone, Blakely and Blakely), interdenominational situation (Fabian, Thomson, Schoffeleers), state formation and maintenance (Sanneh, Nanji, de Heusch, MacGaffey), and subordination in society (Girshick Ben-Amos, Smith Omari, d'Azevedo). The paradigm is as multifunctional as religion itself (van Beek 1985).

Religion as a monitoring instrument reads the interconnectedness of religion and culture in the other direction: not the impact *on* society but the impact *of* society is essential. Religion is seen as a sensitive instrument through which tensions, changes, and problems of human beings in society come to the fore. Two types of recording instruments are discernible. Religion may serve as an *archival* device for reminiscences of old political and social situations. In de Heusch's contribution this is a subcurrent, though his aim is in no way historical (de Heusch 1972): the folktales and myths echo old systems of kingship, even far beyond their cultural borders—echos remolded with poetic intensity so as to resonate with fundamental human concerns. A prehistorian like de Maret depends on another kind of archival element in religion for interpretation of his data. This historical aspect of religion is not the most prominent one in the chapters presented, but most authors in this volume do view the present religious situation as the outcome of a long and interconnected process of transformation and interaction (cf. Ranger and Kimbambo 1972). As Ranger shows in his chapter, these questions can be directly addressed diachronically too. Another example: Schoffeleers has shown that the myths of Africa tend to be more historical than the myths of, say, Amerindians and can be used as a commentary by the commoners on the "official" history of the elite (Schoffeleers 1985a:184).[5]

More central, however, is the monitoring of the *present*. In religion, the substrate of existential problems and interpersonal tensions emerge; van Beek's article concentrates on this issue, showing how the structural variations between the two systems of magic are based upon a shared definition of existential problems. Structural analysis, like de Heusch performs, aims at a similar goal: to establish the rules of logic immanent in human thought and interaction. In the d'Azevedo contribution, ritual highlights the ambivalence in gender relations. Ottenberg shows how male and female roles in society are reflected in both structural similarities and differences in detail between the two secret societies. Changes, moreover, can be equally evident through the monitoring aspects of religion. Power shifts in Zaïre become reflected in Kimbanguism (MacGaffey) and Jamaa (Fabian), while the intricacies of the Brazilian social environment show up in inverted form in the Candomblé Nago (Smith Omari).

A special synthesis that draws from both the means-to and monitoring instruments is quite important in this section—the performing instrument. Also, whereas the means-to and monitoring instruments relate religion to goals and aims beyond its borders, the performance paradigm stays closer to the informants' and interlocutors' definition of the situation. In the notion of performance the old adage of Marett that "Primitive [*sic*] religion is danced out, not thought out" (Marett 1909:vi) comes alive again, as the chapters by Stone and by Blakely and Blakely explicitly demonstrate in more current terms. Religion is something to do, if possible before an appreciating audience. The other people, either in their necessary presence or their noted absence, are essential. The notion of performance can integrate transaction and structure: the performing individual or subgroup in its performance sets itself apart from but at the same time defines itself as an integral part of society. Societal values are stressed in the same breath with the emulation of personal vanity (Kapferer 1986). Paul Stoller (1989a) shows in his discussion of Songhai possession troupes in Niger how the traumatic experiences of the performers are a vital element in their performance of problem-oriented plays.

In performance the gap between structure and communitas is temporarily bridged: ritual performances are expressions of communitas more than anything else; still, in these same performances individuality is expressed, people boast their prowess and skills, and the various layers of social identity are staged (e.g., the Gola Sande society performances discussed by d'Azevedo). So, the very ritual that defies structure, in its performance aspects fits the structure within communitas, thereby opening a way for communitas to become a lasting feature in structure—one of Legesse's main emphases.

Two important dimensions that, in practice, have fallen beyond the scope of most research on religion in Africa are *emotion* and *creativity*. In fact, emotion has been a sparse field for empirical cross-cultural research, mostly drawing attention in biological and psychological studies focused mainly on discovering species wide universals (Eibl-Eibesfelt 1972; Ekman and Oster 1979; Schechner 1986). A sociocultural anthropology of affect has only recently been shaping its tools (e.g., Lutz and Abu-Lughod 1990) and applying for respectability in academia. Here, the study of performance offers excellent opportunities for elucidating how emotion is channelled, formed, stimulated, structured, and expressed (Schechner 1986).

Creativity, even more difficult to deal with, in Africa is often closely associated with quality, which can be interpreted through the audience's evaluation of the performance (Bauman 1977). This aspect of performance is one of the most interesting ones in the context of religion. Performance is judged, in any aspect of religion (see Tambiah 1990). Of course, many rituals can be held, myths told, or epics wrought, without quality becoming a glaringly evident issue. The evaluation is always there, however. And effectiveness can depend on quality, such as when Báhêmbá prioritize a foregrounding of the [Jakobsonian] "poetic" during funeral ritual (Chapter 20, this volume). Religion is interaction, and in any interaction the partners continually assess the value and quality of their own and their partners' contribution (Kapferer 1986). The habitual judging of one's associates, a continuous flow in social interaction, is particularly concentrated during performance, mitigated and directed by the exigencies of the setting, its disruptive effects immunized by the liminality of the occasion (Karp 1988).

A final advantage of the focus on performance is that the notion of system as such fades to the background. As much as African religions are systems, they are systems in action, their systematic properties being the net result of social interaction more than individual or collective reflexivity. This aspect will occupy us later on.

Performance is central in Stone's analysis of the religious side of Kpelle music as she discusses the audience as an essential element, the transactional qualities of the proceedings, and the significance of emotions in the performance. Hêmbá artful speech and movement forms, subject of the fine-grained analysis by Pamela Blakely and Thomas Blakely, provide insights toward understanding Hêmbá religion both in its variety and its problem solving—the focus is on health, though "health" in this context has a very wide meaning, much more than just somatic health. Hêmbá religion (and maybe Bantu religion) focuses on individual and community health, using a host of alternative options and variations. Kíhêmbá speech shows how religion permeates daily life. Well-contextualized expressions of emotion, moments of reflexivity, creativity in symbolism (the "thorny plantains", for example), and the dynamic interplay between the ready-made and the emergent also can be grasped better from this performance angle.

Whereas these three authors concentrate on performance, in other contributions performance elements form an important undercurrent. In Edo women's religious associations and also in Candomblé the distinction between priestesses of diverging qualities is essential for vertical mobility. The very notion of "greatness" in effect is tied in with trance performance quality. This offers a fascinating angle on this kind of religious experience and its expression. Despite the seemingly individual nature of trance, it has to be learned in order to be performed before an appreciating and evaluating audience. Janzen stresses in his regional comparison of drums of affliction a third category in addition to divination and therapy (cf. Turner 1975 [1962]): entertainment. Where, in the first two, performance is crucial, in the third one it is absolutely essential. What binds the Bantu drums together might well reside in the commonalities of the performance as much as a shared therapeutic and diagnostic system (cf. La Fontaine 1985). Ottenberg shows how the performance of the initiation, both in dances and genital operations, may be an important factor in shaping the rituals, thus steering the individual's experience of religion. Not unrelatedly, the definition of gender is generated or re-created in the rites d'Azevedo describes. Ranger's description of the Africanization of the American Methodist Episcopal Church makes it clear that for the Africans involved the change was towards a better performance: African members, with their greater command of the language and culturally accepted symbolism and—above all—with their heightened sensibility toward spiritual experiences, easily topped the performance of the Western missionaries. The Methodist women's role is highly instructive here. Women came to the front of the flock on the waves of spiritual performance, to be dominated afterwards again when institutional performance began to count more.

Performance without spectators is highlighted in van Beek's discussion of private rites. There the notion of insufficiency is elaborated upon: in the field of magic no one is knowledgeable. This "groping in the dark" might be adduced to the absence of an audience: the rituals are performed without interaction with the audience that they do aim at. Thus, the uncertainty of individual rites, over-compensated in the belief system in order to make them foolproof (magic never fails; failure implies stronger magic elsewhere), might be called a "syndrome of the absent audience".

THE "AFRICANNESS" OF AFRICAN RELIGION

The last question to be addressed is not the easiest one: how "African" are African religions? We shall use the plural *religions* as there is certainly not just one African indigenous religion, let alone one African religion in general. The authors in our book, however, do elucidate two important characteristics widely shared by religions in Africa and in the African Diaspora: *variability* and *flexibility*. We shall first explore the parameters of variation, then those of flexibility, finally to arrive at the commonalities of "Africanité" that might be found and also the shared existential conditions that might be involved in the ways Africans have shaped their religions.

African religions operate at any social level or geographical echelon: the contributions of Kirby and van Beek show how religious elements keep the individual both within and outside his or her society. Clearly, the local community—the stage of most of the indigenous expressions of African religions—figures at the background of magic as it does in Hêmbá funeral performance (Blakely and Blakely), Gola ritual (d'Azevedo), or Limba initiation (Ottenberg). Urban local communities, with their diverging stresses and strains, are shown in the Edo and Candomblé cases (Girshick Ben-Amos, Smith Omari). A regional option is discussed in Ranger's chapter, one that transcends the region in Fabian's. MacGaffey ties Kimbanguism into the national Zaïrean system, while de Maret and Janzen explore the question of common Bantu religious elements for the whole of Central and Southern Africa, and de Heusch finds the codes embedded in Central African and West African myths to be similar. Finally, intercontinental options are sketched for Islam and Christianity by Sanneh, for generalized Christology by Schoffeleers, and in the African Diaspora by Smith Omari and Legesse. This variation of scale runs parallel to a variation in content: from magic, familial rites, village ceremonies, and lineage rituals to regional systems, national churches, and supranational creeds. African religions seem to have no privileged sociopolitical echelon, no particular level of group identity. This implies that religion in Africa has a very flexible and fluid interaction with the institutional environment in which it operates.

The second aspect of variability is that African religions never operate in a religious vacuum. There is a constant give and take between and among various religions. Of course, the incoming Islams and Christianities (plurals intended) have intensified the contacts. Some of the interaction is at the level of religion to religion: Fabian shows how the Jamaa maneuvered in relation to the mainstream churches in Zaïre. The continuous interaction between religions has created a paradox: a variety so big that people are tempted to speak of one religion (Mbiti 1969). On no other continent have so many religions interacted with one another.

Africa is the continent of political variation, too: centralized states, segmentary lineage polities, chiefdoms, acephalous gatherer/hunters, and empires; almost all the types and variations anthropology has discovered and devised are to be found in Africa. Whereas kinship theory developed in Oceania and South Asia, political anthropology flourished in Africa. Religion, as a sensitive monitor of political differences, shows its concomitant diversity. Religion also follows—and sometimes leads—the constant political unrest and upheavals, the shifting political and military centers. Africa is a continent in movement and turmoil, and has been so probably for the last two millennia. Political conquest, fragmentation, and redistribution of empires and kingdoms, all have resulted in a continent with a myriad of cultures in constant interaction. The colonizing, decolonizing, and neocolonizing processes, more obviously present in Africa than in almost any other part of the world, have generated additional parameters of variation: layered societies (MacGaffey's point), pluralistic religions (Kirby), and the whole spectrum from relatively unified national states to very amorphous ones.

Many more parameters could be mentioned, but these may suffice to draw a picture of bewildering variation. The very variety, however, is of course an expression of flexibility. Africans have managed to create and re-create expressions of religion in any situation, reacting to multiple changes, dangers, and possibilities. The long-term ecological changes such as the deterioration of the physical environment or the encroaching desert, as well as the short-term changes— political upheavals and colonization, nationalism, internationalization of relations—all have their responses in which religion played an important part. Whenever a new situation arises in Africa, Africans shower new problems and options with fresh meaning, firmly tying emergent orders into the previous ones.

Africans' mechanisms for this instant adaptation are various, rooted both in African situations and in indigenous African religions. Religions in Africa usually are—or eventually become more—pluralistic, nondogmatic, and action-oriented, combining ideological ambiguity with a "bricolage" of old elements into new patterns, characteristics that form an easy basis for permutations and combinations.

Pluralism in African religions is not an exclusive product of colonization; indigenous religions have had pluralistic aspects long before the advent of the "red people". And indigenous religions easily accumulate foreign influences and elements, accruing the new notions and religious associations into the previous amalgam. The wide variety of comparable *poro* and *sande* institutions offer an example. Divination techniques travel widely across cultural borders (Devisch 1985), "cults" spread from region to region (Werbner 1977), magical techniques are borrowed from the outer fringes of personal networks. Even on the local village level this results in multiple options for the individual: the various missionary and African Christian groups, semisecret societies, and healing associations among Báhêmbá (Blakely and Blakely), and the choice in divinatory processes among the Kapsiki and Dogon (van Beek), for example.

This pluralistic aspect is not at all necessarily a hierarchical one; it is frequently accumulative. The various options and notions often coexist without conflict. One major reason for the plurality and the absence of systemic conflict resides in the processes of oral transmission (van Beek 1988a), as well as in the nondogmatic character of indigenous religions. Ideological notions are not usually systematized or subjected to theological speculation. In fact, in many instances, it has been anthropologists and other scholars who played the role of the "native theologian" (e.g., Jules-Rosette 1975), bringing the various elements of indigenous religion into a complex, consistent web of representations and actions. Of course there is speculation, and there are people more interested in things religious than are their fellow human beings (Radin's favorite theme, 1927). The important point is that there is hardly a mechanism in indigenous religion to confront these notions and speculations with conflicting ones.

This absence is part of the action-orientedness of African religion. Most often, defining African religion from its belief system is putting it upside down. Religion is usually not thought out in the agora of theology, but lived out in the marketplace of Africa. Resonating with our point of departure, we allow the "everyday religion" (van Beek 1975) a large place in this book. In Africa, religion means performing or otherwise doing something: consulting a diviner, offering a sacrifice, praying, talking about a problem, enthroning a chief, falling into a trance, making magic, and dancing with masks at a funeral (Ìdòwú 1973:189). Indigenous African religion also often is a means to an end; people are often quite clear about why they do things and what they aim at: health, fertility, rain, protection, or relational harmony. Religion is part of a survival strategy and serves practical ends, either immediate or remote, social or individual. Religion as such, religiosity, carries no importance or status.[6]

Given the focus on actions, some degree of systematization is present. Some actions are clustered, focused on specific altars, sanctuaries, and deities. The relevant sacrifices, words, dances, and associated beliefs can develop into a system, with all elements geared toward one another. However, one system of worship does not greatly hinder another, and people not only are free to choose, they usually also can accumulate in their personal religious lives as many associations as they deem feasible. Thus, a religion usually is not one system, but an agglomerate of systems, some parts being more central than others, some elements quite isolated, while others are being integrated in existing ones. This is not to say that African culture and African religion cannot or should not be studied from a holistic perspective; they can and should be, provided we do not lose sight of two factors. First, the systematic properties (consistency, interrelatedness) should not be exaggerated. Secondly, African religions have been in constant change and adaptation long before the coming of the colonizers, even before the coming of Islam.

This propensity for continuous transformation (which might be the best definition of "tradition" in Africa) permeates the ways Africans have creatively acted upon the new options and possibilities opened by the various forms of Christianity and Islam. Familiar with the exigencies of performing and doing their religion and with religion as a means to an end, they are the essential "bricoleurs", who, in Lévi-Strauss's (1962) terms, use combinations of old meanings to reassemble them into new forms and meanings, in order to solve a practical problem.[7] For this, the religious option is the one most easily mobilized, a preferential channel for creating and re-creating meaning. Edo women create new meaning within an Edo hierarchy of greatness, their Bahía sisters reassess the meaning of their African heritage, drums of affliction take on new dimensions when performed in different social settings, independent Christians change their faith (and that of others) in an innovative way, while Methodist converts take missionary Methodism apart and reassemble it into a new prototype.

The religious action that is the core of African religion is group oriented, problem oriented, and closely linked to sociocultural context. The group can be relevant on any level of social interaction (e.g., Ottenberg's case), but there is always a group as a frame of reference. Even in magic, the most private of all religious action, the relevant group hovers in the background, as the Dogon and Kapsiki cases make clear. Healing too, as Janzen, Blakely and Blakely, and Kirby show, is a social process. The problems the actions aim to solve also are group related: definitions of illness tie the individual disorder to social problems; nobody has sketched a more convincing picture of this process than Victor Turner (1968). But the definition of problems is much wider than just individual problems: collective strains on women (d'Azevedo), on a movement as a whole (Fabian), on a newly developing class of entrepreneurs (Ranger), or of city emigrants (Stone) are just as well addressed by religion. As with any problem, the definition and solution depend on the total setting. Where indigenous religion at one time depended on the context of kin groups, political constellations, and religious specialists, there are now forms that depend on configurations of ethnicity, urbanization, transformation of social networks, competing religious groups, and labor-for-wages work environments.

It is time now to return to the main question of this section of the Introduction: what is the common denominator of African religions? Is there one at all? No single or generalized African religion, either modern or historical, can be pointed to, beyond speculations about the very distant prehistoric past. Still, a number of general characteristics have emerged throughout the bewildering variety of forms and expressions. Even if there is not only one African religious expression, there is an African "genius for religion", a shared creativity of Africans in expressing their individual and collective experiences through religion, a proclivity to find new expressions for old and new feelings, new answers for old as well as new questions. The notion of "bricolage" should not be viewed as "make do" or a messy compromise: this fabrication of new configurations of meaning is a highly creative process. After all, totally new answers, new symbols, and new ideas are scarce; the African expression of religious experience is geared to finding new clusters of meaning, embracing new concepts and religions, but in embracing them, reshaping them. Africans are translators, who by transculturating the incoming religious expressions, refit them for their own experiences and in so doing transform both expression and experience. African religious expression is a strong argument for "relative relativity". Africans show time and again that a transcultural translation *is* and at the same time *is not* possible: the understanding gleaned from the other culture, be it European, Islamic, or African, can be transformed into forms compatible with one's own culture, but the process of contact changes both partners in the communication. Understanding the other is possible after all, but perhaps only by changing oneself.

Turner's dichotomy *communitas/structure* suffers from an incompleteness, then. The absolute opposite of communitas is not structure, but solipsism: the idea of individual uniqueness and—consequently—solitude. Communitas and structure are the warp and woof of social fabric; the real antithesis consists of the solipsistic negation of the other. Africans cope in an interesting way with the problem of the individual's identity and nature. The balancing of a person to be both a conscious subject (the observer) and part of his or her world, his or her group, and his or her universe has been defined as one existential problem that finds expression in religion (van Baal 1981) or in Marc Augé's terms: "*l'homme et son double: la nécessité [et l'impossibilité] du social*" (1982:177). This perennial problem of a conscious observer to be alone in his or her *Anschauung* of the world, and still inevitably part and parcel of the same world, this fundamental quest for identity of the observing and experiencing ego on the one hand and gratification of his or her feelings of dependency finds a specific African expression. In the African definition, the subject becomes part of a *relation*, rooted in the dynamics of an evolving tradition, expressed through the corporality of African culture (Maurier 1985). The subject reasserts himself or herself in the dominance of the relation by shared communal roots on the one hand and by his or her options for agency on the other. Thus, in H. Maurier's terms, the basic experience that underlies African religious expressions, is the *je/avec* [I/with]: the antithesis of both the subject and his or her world finds a brittle but ever-to-be-regained synthesis in the sharing of identity with others.

This presupposes an anthropocentrism that is directed towards the person, the community (Maurier 1985;42), and the world at large. If the relevant other is not necessarily human, he or she is humanized. This anthropocenteredness, though not exclusively African, might be based on the shared experiences of Africans. Living in societies where, throughout history, humans were the prime asset, where wealth was and still is counted in terms of people, Africans were at the same time in constant danger and under continuous threat from outside human forces. Africans' life has been based on a paradox: living in a vast continent, where humans have been in continually short supply as an important asset, the dangers have stemmed from humans too. Africa is a continent of relatively few people, who are continually in each other's way. In religion, Africans have repeatedly found a way out of this paradox, defining the other—opponent or partner—in such a way as to change both the other and oneself, transcending the opposition *ego/alter* with the notion of *relatio*, a creative synthesis that is at the heart of both African religious experience and its expression.

NOTES

1. Sir Peter Buck's views are still relevant [with substitutions for the then-current generic masculine]: "As an anthropologist, I see religion as an essential part of the culture of any people. The things [humans have] created with [their minds] and worshiped in the spirit are as real to [them] as the material things [they have] made with [their] hands. The belief in the supernatural and in the immortality of the soul must be accepted as real facts that have led to action and results. I am not concerned as to whether they can be proved scientifically. As a student of the manners, customs and thoughts of people I am concerned with their beliefs" (Te Rangi Hiroa:1939:94).

2. This question is not without its philosophical fascination (see Hollis and Lukes 1982; Overing 1985) and will continue to be so for a long time to come. Research on universal

categories should not trivialize evidence of cultural variety and should take account of objections to the idea of universal categories raised by the sociology of knowledge and epistemology (Kohlberg 1971). On the other hand extreme relativism is glaringly inadequate as it not only denies the reality of cross-cultural communication, but even undermines the very method of reasoning by which the notion of relativity is formulated.

3. The Christian position articulated by Sanneh comes close to van Baal's analysis (1967) of the processes of decolonization, in which national identities were constructed by drawing from an array of local cultures.

4. An example from the discussions of the Religion in Africa conference may illustrate this point. Ranger told how a woman from England came to Zimbabwe and tried to convince Shona women that they were marginalizing themselves by opting for the religious route to power. The Shona women were not in the least impressed and made it very clear that "this was just what it really is all about" (cf. the Sudan *zar* cult described by Boddy 1989).

5. This historical relevance of African myths does not, in our opinion, invalidate a structural approach (de Heusch's chapter). Even within a historical framework, the leeway for variation in details relevant for structural interpretation is amply present. The logic of the mind can express itself through the data of history as well (Lévi-Strauss 1975).

6. The ambiguous role of religious mediators is a case in point: in many African societies the religious specialist is a man or woman of authority, but not the one really in charge. Though religion tends to support the status quo of political domination, religious officiators usually are outside the political mainstream.

7. The relevance of the term *bricoleur* for African religion does not imply that the distinction Lévi-Strauss posits between *bricoleur* and *ingénieur* holds as a fundamental difference in ways of thinking. In our view, all people engage in whatever type of thinking that can be found, depending on the time, topic, and circumstances.

Part I:

Religion and Its Translatability

Plate 1–1. Pupils at Qurʾān school in Djenne, Mali, learn to read and write the words of the Qurʾān on their polished wooden boards. The phrases of the sacred Arabic are learned by heart: recitation is important, not translation. Their teacher has jotted down texts on each of their boards and recited them for the students, who then repeat many times what they heard until the text as well as the writing of it are mastered.

Translatability in Islam & in Christianity in Africa:

A Thematic Approach

Lamin Sanneh

INTRODUCTION

RELIGIOUS EXPANSION IN AFRICA of Islam and of Christianity has raised intriguing comparative questions on the nature and character of Muslim and Christian communities on the continent. In several parts of West Africa—what the Arabic sources call *bilād al-sūdān* [the land of the blacks]— Islam is at least a thousand years old, whereas in the same areas Christianity is barely a hundred. This chronological disparity overlaps another disparity, that of attitudes toward indigenization. For Islam, in spite of its venerable longevity, vernacular languages were considered unsuitable for adoption as a scriptural and canonical medium, while Christianity adopted these languages as necessary and sufficient channels of biblical revelation and worship. This indigenous disparity far outranks its chronological counterpart in social effects and it primes the temper of reform sensibilities in the two traditions (Sanneh 1989b). Muslim reform in Africa tended to pit the hackles of nontranslatability against sluggish local accommodation, sometimes with thrones and empires at stake. Christian reform, by contrast, constituted the vernacular into a principle of renewal and national pride, usually one with non-African standards at stake. Throughout their spread and expansion in Africa, Islam and Christianity have reiterated their contrasting and distinctive forms.

In Christian reform, Africans have utilized the vernacular both for self-understanding and for appropriating Christian religion, whereas Muslim reform achieved the equally remarkable goal of alienating the vernacular by applying the progressive pressure of the nontranslatable Qur'ān. This contrast has major implications for how we view mission and vernacular pluralism in the two religions, as well as for the nature and purpose of conversion. And it is in the context of this contrast that I would like especially to examine the issues of religious "reform", "renewal", and "revival".

THE ISLAMIC PARADIGM

It is important to spell out the contrasting conditions before considering detailed local contexts for the principle of translatability. Muslims ascribe to Arabic the status of a revealed language, for it is the medium in which the Qur'ān, the sacred scripture of Islam, was revealed. In several passages the Qur'ān bears testimony to its own Arabic uniqueness, what the authorities call its *i'jāz*, or "inimitable eloquence" (Qur'ān x:38–39; xi:1–2, 16; xvi:104–105; xxviii:49; xxxix:24, 29; xli:41–42; xliii:1–3). The author of the Qur'ān, who is God, thus came to be associated with its speech, so that the very sounds of the language are believed to originate in heaven (see Guillaume 1962:74; Gibb 1974 [1963]:36–37). Consequently, Muslims have instituted the sacred Arabic as the language of canonical devotions. Given the lay character of Islam, these canonical devotions have brought the sacred Arabic to the ears of the ordinary believer, although normally only religious specialists understand this language in any satisfactory fashion (von Grunebaum 1962:37–59).

The active participation of lay Muslims in the ritual acts of worship [*salāt*], fasting [*sawm*] and, less frequently, the pilgrimage [*hajj*] to Mecca means that Arabic phrases, however imperfectly understood, remain on the lips of believers wherever and whoever they happen to be. Even in thinly or unevenly Islamized areas, the changes in perspective arising from use of the sacred Arabic provide the impetus for reforming local practice, rather than yielding to indigenous forms.

An intriguing situation arises in which the prestigious and revered status of Arabic acts to disenfranchise the vernacular. Mother-tongue speakers find themselves in the anomalous position of their languages being considered profane [*'ajamī*] for the decisive acts of the religious code, a consideration that bears little relationship to one's fluency in the Arabic. In fact, both the expert Arabist and the illiterate convert share a common veneration for the sacred language: the expertise of the one is the standard toward which the other aspires.

The success of Islam as a missionary religion is founded on the perpetuation of the sacred Arabic. As the religion arrived among the preponderantly non-Arab populations, its double blade gleamed with the pointedness of faith in one God and acceptance of the primacy of the sacred Arabic. In this situation it was often difficult to say which blade cut deeper, for often non-Muslim populations appropriated Qur'ānic phrases long before they converted to Islam. There is in fact an old tradition of non-Muslims venerating the sacred script. For example, the "Veil of St. Anne" is kept in a fifteenth-century bottle in the church of Apt, in the south of France. It turns out that the "holy" relic has an Arabic inscription containing the *Shahādah*, the Muslim creed, as well as the names of the Fāṭimid Caliph, al-Musta'lī (reigned 1094–1101) and his prime minister, Afḍal, with an indication that the textile was woven in Egypt in 1096–1097 (Schacht and Bosworth 1974:298).

The characteristic missionary institution of Islam is the Qur'ān school, where boys and girls are taught to memorize passages in Arabic from the sacred book (Plate 1–1). Rote memorization in school, rather than scriptural translation, has been the mode of Islam's expansion through sub-Saharan Africa and elsewhere. It is important to separate this matter from the question of adopting Arabic as the language of administration, business, and education. Sudan is the only black African country where one could say "Islamization" was accompanied by a thorough "Arabization". In the rest of the continent one may speak confidently of "Islamization" being accompanied by the enthronement of the sacred Arabic as the uncompromising standard of religious orthodoxy, even though Muslims have continued to use the vernacular in everyday life.

The famous Dr. Edward Blyden commented on the role that a nontranslatable Qur'ān came to play in Muslim Africa. His words have particular relevance to the theme of the displacement of vernacular pluralism by the force of a superior Qur'ān. Writing in 1875, he says that for Africans,

> the Koran is, in its measure, an important educator. It exerts … a wonderful influence. It has furnished to the adherents of its teaching in Africa a ground of union which has contributed vastly to their progress. Hauseas, Foulahs, Mandingoes, Soosoos, Akus [Creoles of Yoruba extraction] can all read the same books and mingle in worship together, and there is to all one common authority and one ultimate umpirage. They are united by a common religious sentiment, by a reverence and esteem. And even where the ideas are not fully understood the words seem to possess for them a nameless beauty and music, a subtle and indefinable charm, incomprehensible to those acquainted only with European languages. It is easy for those not acquainted with the language in which the Koran was written, and therefore, judging altogether as outsiders, to indulge in depreciating its merits. Such critics lose sight of the fact that the Koran is a poetical composition, and a poetical composition of the earliest … kind, and that therefore its ideas and the language in which they are conveyed cannot well be separated. The genuine poet not only creates the conception, but the word which is its vehicle. The word becomes the inseparable drapery of the idea. … Among Mohammedans, written or printed translations of the Koran are discouraged. The Chinese, Hindoos, Persians, Turks, Mandingoes, Foulahs, etc., who have embraced Islam, speak in their "own tongues wherein they were born", but read the Koran in Arabic. (Blyden 1967 [1887]:6–7)

It is this phenomenon that I wish to highlight as a contrast to the Christian case. One may argue that one effect of the preeminent, exclusive role of the sacred Arabic has been to discourage general Muslim interest in the languages of non-Muslims. This is not the same as saying that Muslims did not learn other languages, for they did, but that such languages, apart from their practical value, had no status in the Muslim dispensation. African Muslims who have only a nodding acquaintance with mosque Arabic feel proprietorial about it and are unwilling to allow non-Muslims to take responsibility for it. Ordinary Muslims have even in certain instances organized to oppose the teaching of Arabic by non-Muslim Arabic speakers in secondary schools. In their eyes the religion of Islam has a right to exercise proprietary control over Arabic, whether it is the Arabic of the Qur'ān or of the marketplace. Conversely, non-Muslims might also resist the introduction of Arabic for fear that Islamic conversion might be demanded as a price. In both cases we have a synthesis of language and religion, and it is surely one of the deeply interesting facts about Islam that in its remarkable missionary expansion it has preserved this synthesis, defying the forces of vernacular usage to carve a prestigious place for the sacred language.

Plate 1–2. The medieval Bet Giorgis stone church—one of twelve in Lalibela, Ethiopia—built below ground in the form of a cross and still in active use today. By A.D. 650, the Bible and much Christian literature had been translated into an early form of Amharic [Ge'ez], which became a vehicle for Ethiopian nationalism.

THE CHRISTIAN COUNTERPOINT

Christianity in Africa has been characterized by a vigorous vernacular process from the period of the earliest Christians on the continent. Thus, the Coptic church dates its founding to the period coinciding with religious upheavals in Upper Egypt about the middle of the third century A.D. In that upheaval, Coptic villages, long resistant to conversion, embraced the new Christian religion to the point of being prepared to suffer martyrdom in its defense (Eusebius 1984 [1965]:337 ff.). There soon followed, in the late fourth and early fifth centuries, the commencement of a vast and vigorous Coptic literature. This literature later enabled the Copts to long maintain a strong, if at times inhibiting, sense of identity, especially under Muslim Egypt from the seventh century A.D. onward (von Harnack 1905 [v. 2]:304–323; Butler:1884). In any case, Coptic translation work marked a genuine advance on the cumbersome hieroglyphic and foreign Greek writing systems of earlier times, which excluded ordinary people. Kenneth Scott Latourette agrees:

> In Egypt it was the successful effort to provide the masses of the population with a literature in the speech of everyday life which halted the exclusive use of the alien Greek for the written page and which stimulated the development of an alphabet which could be quickly and easily learned by the multitude in place of the ancient hieroglyphics which could be the property only of the few. Through this medium Coptic Christian literature came into being, largely the work of monks. (Latourette 1975:250–251; see also Frend 1984:577)

Plate 1–3. Ethiopian Orthodox priests—three of whom are each covered by a *tabot*—leave Bet Giorgis church for the processional of consecration at the annual Timkat festival. The parade proceeds around Lalibela town and to the river for feasting, returning the next day to place each *tabot* in its resting place inside the church.

Plate 1–4. A priest carries an illuminated Bible written in Ge'ez—for thirteen centuries the liturgical language of the Ethiopian Orthodox church—during Timkat at Lalibela.

Similarly, with the introduction of Christianity into Ethiopia, schools were established; and by the middle of the seventh century, most of the translation work into Amharic had been completed, with the Ethiopian Orthodox Church becoming the nerve center of Ethiopian nationalism (Tamrat 1972; Davis 1967:62–69). These and other materials begin to suggest that scriptural translation and similar linguistic efforts are a force in the rise of mother tongue aspirations—an early form of national sentiment. Also in modern Africa, mother-tongue aspirations have sometimes provided an impetus and vehicle for expressions of national sentiment[1] and certainly have been bulwarks in the fight against colonialism and against political, economic, and cultural imperialism. Literacy in the mother tongue has often been—and continues to be—a factor in indigenous renewal and the pluralist dispensation in Africa. And the missionary role in instituting mother tongues as part of Christianity has thus been important in all of these developments.

By contrast, we are confronted with a reverse picture for Islamic gains in Africa: Muslim orthodoxy holds to the principle of nontranslatability, which made vernacular self-understanding incompatible—this, notwithstanding the fact that Africans were themselves the preponderant agents in the dissemination of the faith and thus presumably free from external pressure to propagate prescriptive Islam. It is within this symmetrical framework that we have to ask about the status of linguistic and cultural pluralism under the decisive rubrics of faith and practice in Islam and in Christianity. An unconventional conclusion awaits our evaluation of the evidence.

REFORM, RENEWAL, AND REVIVAL IN THE ISLAMIC TRADITION

When we consider the nature and outcome of renewal movements in Islam and Christianity in Africa, we find a situation considerably affected by the translatability question. In the Islamic tradition the springs of reform and renewal were fed by the perennial premillennial figure who was to appear at the head of every Islamic century to set right the affairs of the people. In African Islam, an important occurrence of such messianic ideas was in the correspondence between the king of Songhay, Askiya al-Ḥājj Muḥammad Ture, and the itinerant North African scholar ʿAbd al-Karīm al-Maghīlī (d. ca. 1505–1506). The Askiya had inquired of al-Maghīlī, who was visiting Songhay in 1502, about the conditions under which religious reform might be necessary, a momentous question whose consequences extended into the nineteenth-century reform movements in other parts of West Africa. It is worth quoting this tradition in full. Al-Maghīlī acquainted the Askiya with the following authoritative opinion regarding reform:

> Thus it is related that at the beginning of every century God sends [people] a scholar who regenerates their religion for them. There is no doubt that the conduct of this scholar in every century in enjoining what is right and forbidding what is wrong, and setting aright [the] people's affairs, establishing justice among them and supporting truth against falsehood and the oppressed against the oppressor, will be in contrast to the conduct of the scholars of his age. For this reason he will be an odd man out among them on account of his being the only man of such pure conduct and on account of the small number of men like him. Then will it be plain and clear that he is one of the reformers [al-muṣliḥūn] and that whoso opposes him and acts hostilely towards him so as to turn people away from him is but one of the miscreants, because of the saying of the Prophet, may God bless him and grant him peace: "Islam started as an odd man out [gharīb] and thus will it end up, so God bless the odd men out". Someone said, "And who are they, O Messenger of God?" He said, "Those who set matters aright in evil times". That is one of the clearest signs of the people of the Reminder [ahl al-dhikr] through whom God regenerates for people their religion. (Hunwick 1985:66–67; Hiskett 1962:584)

In the hands of al-Maghīlī, reform and renewal are complementary. Reform may be more narrowly understood as undoing the harm that results from neglect of the religious code, while renewal may be taken to mean the level at which prescriptive standards are applied after the removal of impediments. The two parts are conjoined in the standard scriptural injunction: *amal bi-ma ʿrūf wa nahy ʿan al-munkar* [to enjoin good works and restrain from what is disapproved of] (xiii:21–22). "Revival" in the technical sense of religious enthusiasm is discouraged by Muslim religious authorities, for as they see it, the issue is alignment of conduct to make it conform to established prescriptions, not that of seeking the signs of the Spirit. Consequently, the opinions of al-Maghīlī on mixing Islam with African religion carry the mark of a rigorist. He is not satisfied with less than the explicit application of the code; it is not sufficient to imply in conduct acknowledgment of its authority. Thus he spells out what is to be done with those Muslims who also participate in non-Islamic rites. These, he says,

> are polytheists [*mushrikūn*] without doubt, because anathematizing [*takfīr*], according to the manifest meaning of the Law, is for less than that, and there is no doubt that Holy War against them is better and more meritorious [*afdal*] than Holy War against unbelievers who do not declare the witness of faith: "There is no god except God; Muḥammad is His Apostle". (Hiskett 1962:584, translation amended)

Al-Maghīlī is particularly severe towards those Muslims who continued to imbibe from a pluralist religious world, and their offense in his eyes is more serious than that of nonbelievers. Halfheartedness is more objectionable than nonmembership. In a similar way, the learned men implicated in religious compromise are the more reprehensible, for they ought to know better. Al-Maghīlī castigates them as "venal scholars" [*'ulamā al-sū'i*]. They make a career of frequenting the corridors of power, titillating the fancies of ignorant rulers, and bolstering their unjust authority. They add to the mischiefs of the land by doing the round of obscure villages and carrying, as a show of piety and learning, satchels that contain only cockroaches. Their charlatanry deserves no mercy, and a suitable example ought to be made of them. The Askiya put the following provocatory question to his mentor:

> And in spite of that [i.e., their lack of true understanding] they have books which they study, and tales which they utter concerning God's religion, and they maintain that they are the inheritors of the prophets and that it is incumbent upon us to imitate them. I seek from God Most High that He will help me to carry this burden which the heavens and the earth have refused to carry, and I seek from you that you will give me a decision, by what God has taught you, concerning these Qur'ān readers—is it lawful that we should act according to what they say concerning God's religion? (Hiskett 1962:581)

The reference in that passage of "the burden too heavy for the heavens and earth" is to the part of the Qur'ān in which human beings are entrusted with the stewardship of the world, whence the idea of *khalīfah* (xxxiii:72). Al-Maghīlī wrote back tersely: "It is said by the Scriptures and the *Sunnah* and the consensus of the learned that many of these Qur'ān readers of this community are only venal scholars, and they are more harmful to the Muslims than all the mischief-makers" (Hiskett 1962:581).

If the branches are in contention, then the root cannot be sound, and al-Maghīlī's diagnosis of the Songhay state is a radical view of the failure of political authority to uphold the religious code. He justified the *coup d'état* of 1492, which was an ideological revolution in which Askiya Muḥammad, a general of the imperial army and at that time at the head of the Muslim agitators, seized power from a ruler, Sonni 'Alī (d. 1492), who stopped short of applying the full rigor of the Islamic code. Such rulers are the scourge of right-minded Muslims, al-Maghīlī contends:

> There is no doubt that they are the greatest of tyrants and wrongdoers who sever what God has commanded shall be united, and make mischief in the land. The Holy War of the *amīr* Askia against them and his taking of the *sultanate* from their hands is the most meritorious Holy War, and the most important; and as for the people of the *Qibla*, are they infidels or not? No one from among the people of the *Qibla* should be anathematized because of sin ... and that which you have mentioned concerning the condition of Sonni 'Alī indicates unbelief without

doubt, and if the matter is as you have described it, then he is an unbeliever. (Hiskett 1962:585)

Several factors galvanized the reform impulse in African Islam: the concern with safeguarding the monotheist ideal against the sin of "association" [*shirk*], grievances over the unjust treatment of foreign Muslims in the state, the burdensome nature of levies and imposts, compromises in Muslim behavior and conduct, the threat of the organized state becoming the instrument of a well-coordinated traditional religious life, and the scandal of the nimble-tongued scholars pandering to the esteem of capricious rulers—all this increased the tension. By throwing in the idea of a messianic dispensation almost at hand, al-Maghīlī added an incendiary charge.

Yet the fundamental question has still to be asked: Why should such materials continue to appeal to African Muslims long and far removed from the Islamic heartlands? or, Why, given this distance in time and space, should the Islamic legacy be able to preserve its affinity with the Islam of first-century Arabia? The capacity of Muslims to invoke the ideal past as a model for their own time and place remains one of the most remarkably consistent features of the religion—and that without a "Vatican" or similar universal bureaucratic structure. By what principle, then, do African Muslims act to rescind the authority of indigenous tradition and practice and replace it with the prescriptive force of Islam?

THE NONTRANSLATABILITY OF MUSLIM SCRIPTURES: THE MOTIVE FORCE IN REFORM

A few provisional ideas are necessary on what is a large and complicated issue. We should dismiss outright the idea that Muslim opposition is forced by the nature of the inherent corruption and contradiction in indigenous traditions, for that accepts the verdict of a protagonist. Nor should we be content with looking for justifications in structural factors, such as the limitations of traditional political institutions when faced with the demands of a supratribal world of Muslims, foreigners, a cosmopolitan trading community, a literate elite, and the wider orbit of international diplomacy. All those factors are important, but they do not add up to the intense singlemindedness of Muslims cast in vastly different circumstances and time. We have a clue in the impatient outburst of al-Maghīlī regarding what he considered an incriminating defect in the scholars. "One of their characteristics", he charges, "is that they are not Arabic-speaking [*'ajam*]; they understand no Arabic except a little of the speech of the Arabs of their towns, in an incorrect and corrupted fashion, and a great deal of non-Arabic, so that they do not understand the intentions of the scholars" (Hiskett 1962:581).

Writers make relatively little of this complaint, even though it recurs in much of the standard literature. Its force stems from the nontranslatability of the Muslim scriptures, and it is, therefore, able to sweep aside local resistance and make capital of its foreign identity. Those African Muslims who begin their life with the obvious disadvantage of worshiping in a strange and foreign language will sooner or later reach, or be made to reach, the stage where practice, however imperfect, creates proximity—and culpability, as the words of al-Maghīlī prove. Our appreciating this point should help illuminate other areas of Muslim objection. In the sphere of its monotheist tradition, to take one example, Islam is able to act with effective authority because its judgment is enshrined in the material of a nontranslatable Qur᾽ān, which itself fosters a devotion and veneration bordering on the magical. In the area of worship, the reformers had the advantage of trying only to *reorient* and restrict a wide habit that encompassed worship at many shrines rather than having to invent the habit anew. The instrument of restriction was the mosque, and its responsibility for the prescribed acts of worship. Not even the high ground of kingly prerogative could allow Sonni ῾Alī to escape that restriction, though he judged it, correctly, to be antithetical to his power.

Other factors, such as limited literacy of the Muslim educational elite, the pressures of a foreign community, the impact of trading contracts, and the larger world

Plate 1–5. The mosque at Djenne, Mali: elders wearing the *grand boubou* of wealth and prestige to the Friday sermons here exit after the prayer. Many have performed their pilgrimage to Mecca, so for them Islam is not only a way of life in their city, but also a partnership in a worldwide community of scholars and believers. Djenne has been a center of Sunni Islam for centuries, its orthodoxy linking it to the Maghrib and the rest of the Arab world. This famous adobe structure incorporates architectural features widely used in West African mosques.

of dealing with other nations and their nationals, together build on a united front that presses hard against indigenous traditions—precisely at the point at which the sacred Arabic forces a choice. Al-Maghīlī and Askiya Muḥammad, two individuals ordinarily separated by what would be a huge cultural gap, had nevertheless found an enduring common ground, not just in a common religious attitude of pietism, but in how specifically such an attitude should properly be signified— namely in the primacy of Arabic in scripture, law, and devotion. The central task of the reformers was to *sacralize* in black Africa the cultural milieu that properly conveys the mission of Islam. They could argue that their case was made in heaven, with Africa as its footstool. The very strangeness of the Arabic of the Qurʾān adds to its religious authority and to its appeal as the blueprint for a righteous social order and therefore makes it more attractive for embodying the religious ideals.

The dilemma of Sonni ʿAlī under such circumstances is a classic one: he had adopted the religion, observed its tenets in a haphazard fashion, and encouraged its propagation under official direction. Yet, he perceived that Islam in its irreducible Arabic scaffolding raised the specter of being a state within a state. By the time he decided to check this incipient political force, it was too late. The foundations of indigenous institutions felt a violent shock with the charge of *ʿajamī* [foreign, or barbarous] which was levelled at them; in the case of Sonni ʿAlī even his pedigree was divested of legitimacy by a claim that his mother came from an outlandish country.[2] In spite of the violent turn of events in his relations with Islam, it was the achievement of Sonni ʿAlī in setting up the Songhay state that made it attractive enough for Muslims to want to control it, suggesting that coexistence was seen by Muslim leaders only as a means necessary to achieve the Islamic religio-political order. That scarcely warrants our elevating such a view of coexistence into a principle of genuine pluralism.

The reference by ʿUthmān dan Fodio (1754–1817) to the foreign origin of Sonni ʿAlī indicates that what happened in Songhay came to exert a powerful influence on Muslims elsewhere and in different times. Dan Fodio was the creator of the nineteenth-century Fulani caliphate in northern Nigeria. He was familiar with the writings of al-Maghīlī, invoking him as an authority for his own project of reform (Hiskett 1962:580, 591; see also Hiskett 1973).

The religio-political triumph of the Fulani *mujāhidīn* gave them a rare opportunity in the new conditions of Africa to articulate the significance of the Prophet's heritage. An ethnic minority themselves, the Fulani became the sponsors of an aggressive Islamization process that sought to overhaul completely African customs and institutions, replacing the *sarauta* chieftaincy system of the Hausa with state organs decreed by the Islamic religious code. In this process the employment of Arabic was a paramount duty. Following is a succinct account by ʿUthmān dan Fodio himself on the methodical regime of reform:

> Most of the people are ignorant of the Sharīʿa, and it is obligatory that there should be, in every mosque and quarter in the town, a *faqīh* teaching the people their religion. So also is it, in every village, obligatory on every *faqīh* who has completed his *farḍ ʿayn* [collective duty binding on Muslims] and has devoted himself to the *farḍ kifāya* [individual obligation without collective implication],

Plate 1–6. Praying inside the mosque at Djenne, Mali, where rigorous solemnity is expressed in the row upon row of large adobe pillars. Islam has been a vital factor in the creation of large empires in the African savannah between the Sahara and the forest for a thousand years. In empires such as Songhay, Ghana, Mali, and Masina, Islam served both as a unifying force and as a link with the wider Arab world. Old cities such as Djenne and old mosques such as this one served as centers of international learning with the sacred Arabic as the primary vehicle.

that he should go out to the people neighbouring on his town in order to teach them their religion and the obligatory parts of their Shar‘ [religious code]. If one person does this, sin falls off the remaining people: otherwise all of them will carry the sin together. As for the learned person, the sin will be because of his neglecting to go out [and preach]. But as for the ignorant, it will be because of his shortcomings in avoiding knowledge. Every layman who knows the conditions governing prayer is obliged to teach it to others. ... The sin of the *fugahā* is greater because their ability to propagate knowledge is more obvious and it is a duty more appropriate to them. (‘Uthmān dan Fodio, cited in Balogun 1975:74–75)

The Shehu then goes on to set out the missionary obligations of the ordinary Muslim: in teaching and propagating the faith, he said, the Muslim must begin with himself, then go to his family and relations, then to his neighbors, the people of his ward, the inhabitants of his town, the adjacent suburbs of his city, "and so on to the furthest part of the world" (Balogun 1975:75). In all the vicissitudes of worldly events and circumstances, Muslims must, in the Shehu's view, strive to realize the goals of an Islam informed by its inseparable Arabic milieu. It is by this standard that his own brother and the intellectual chronicler of the Fulani *jihād*, ‘Abdallāhi dan Fodio, assessed the Shehu's legacy. The following passage makes this clear:

> And many an error quenched while it was a live
> coal blazing fiercely
> And you rose up in a land whose customs
> became excessive,
> And which conflicted with the *sunna*
> of the joyous Prophet.
> . . . .
> You [‘Uthmān] overcame them as a strong man
> overcomes, as a stallion.
> And you broke them with the bright swords
> of His Qur’ānic verses,
> With spears of the *sunnas* of the
> dark-eyed Prophet,
> May God bless him as long as the
> east wind shakes
> The tips of the branches
> in pleasant meadows.
> (Fudi 1963:92–93)

‘Abdallāhi himself, an adept of the Arabic medium, nevertheless felt he had a permanent disability as a non-Arab. In words that Sonni ‘Alī could sympathize with, though from one he would not envy, he confessed:

> A poor slave, ignorant, drowning in a sea of sin,
> Confused in a sea of fantasy.
> Humble, speaking Arabic incorrectly, non-Arab in tribe,
> His mother and his father are from the family of ‘Al.
> (Hiskett 1963:97)

The Sokoto caliphate, which lasted from about 1807 to 1902, was a spectacular example of the success of prescriptive Islam without direct intervention from Mecca. Indeed, though he pined for the privilege of visiting the Ḥaramayn of Mecca and Medina, the Shehu and his principal lieutenants never knew Arabia from personal contact (Hiskett 1973:33). Yet that failure achieved its antidote in the resolve to replicate in black Africa the conditions of the Prophet's Mecca. The Shehu laments in a poem,

> I wept and tears poured down like heavy rain
> In longing for this Prophet, Muḥammad.
> I am as one afflicted with longing for him.
> . . . .
> Were I to visit Ṭayba, I would achieve
> the height of my ambition,
> Sprinkling myself with the dust of
> Muḥammad's sandal.
> (Hiskett 1973:33)

Although they wrote in the vernacular, the men of the Fulani Muslim caliphate looked upon Arabic as the preeminent standard of the religious and political life. Hiskett pinpoints this element in the Muslim reform heritage, saying it was the universal principle that guided the reform movement and inspired the leaders:

> These forces of Islamic ideology served to create in these men a sense of Islamic universalism. That is to say, they had a vision of a single, world-wide Islam, in which the way of life, the way of government and the morality and social behaviour of all individuals were regulated according to the Sharī'a and Sunnah, the Law and Tradition of the Prophet. They were determined that they would tolerate nothing less than this in their own countries. The *jihāds* were the practical expression of this determination. (Hiskett 1984:170–171)

The large stock of vernacular Islamic literature serves only as embellishment on the Arabic motif, and this function has been amply demonstrated in some recent works such as that of Haafkens (1983), who was writing mainly of Adamawa in the present Republic of Cameroon. It is intriguing to reflect on how the Fulani Muslim leaders came to lose most of their own language as the reform impulse strengthened under the caliphate. Thus it was that the headquarters of the reform order was constituted to reflect the ethos of a Middle Eastern Arabic-speaking environment (Hiskett 1975:136).

It must be stressed that accommodating religious functionaries, whom we class under the generic title "clerics", have continued to preside over a vigorous tradition of Islamic practice. For example, Patrick Ryan, in a dissertation at Harvard, has shown how Muslim Yoruba have ingeniously blended Yoruba tradition with their understanding of Islam (Ryan 1978). Certainly at that level a form of translation goes on, and no one who is familiar with Muslim Africa will question that. Ian Lewis for one has argued forcefully for a formulation that includes within mainstream Islam elements normally consigned to the periphery and outside the religious core as marginal or syncretic (Lewis 1983:55–67).

Plate 1–7. A *moodibo* [muslim scholar] in a small village in northern Mali. For an audience of fellow Fulani he reads from an Arabic manuscript history, translating it into vernacular Fulfulde as he goes. The books at his feet, inherited from his father, are old copies of law books from the Caliphate of Hamdallye in nineteenth-century Mali and copies of texts by ʿUthmān dan Fodio, the founder of the Sokoto Empire in northern Nigeria, also in the nineteenth century.

The Arabic writings provide a direct link with Muslim communities all over West Africa as well as an identification with a glorious past. For the listening audience, their lack of understanding of the foreign tongue—and the distances covered by the text in time and space—adds to the "beauty and music" of these written Arabic words and to the feeling of unity among all the "people of the book".

What remains fascinating in so many accounts of Muslim conversion, however, is how people begin their journey by embarking on the path of divination during a time of misfortune, for example, only to arrive at the point where, eventually, the unfamiliar, and for them modest, medium of the sacred Arabic becomes the operative medium of religious truth. Among the Mossi of Burkina Faso, barrenness among non-Muslim women may be treated by the divinatory diagnosis that the would-be children are refusing to be born except as Muslims. The obvious remedy is conversion to Islam. Among the Giriama of Kenya, to take another example, people falling ill are diagnosed as having been possessed by Muslim spirits for which the cure is, once again, conversion to Islam. In both cases, however, the destination is clear, or soon to be clear, even if the route is arcane. Every Muslim convert, however remotely located, must encounter Islam through the sacred Arabic. It is inconceivable to claim the Muslim name without sooner or later performing at least some of the mandatory five daily prayers. To do that, worshipers are obliged without exception to employ the Arabic of the Qur'ān. I have examined in detail one outstanding historical example of an African Muslim clerical tradition centered in the Jakhanke (or Jahanke) people of Senegambia. This group achieved a major transposition of Islam by repudiating for themselves—but not for others—*jihād*, and other forms of armed militancy, and by cultivating a reputation for political neutrality in which they refuse to hold political office. This pacific clerical tradition has a long history behind it; the accounts speak of its roots going back to the thirteenth century (Sanneh 1989a). Such peaceful dissemination of Islam inevitably implies a high degree of tolerance for mixing, and Jakhanke Islam is no exception. Yet both in the traditions concerning the founder of that clerical tradition as well as in the detailed work of the clerical center, what the Jakhanke themselves refer to as the *majlis*, Mecca remains the unwavering point of religious orientation, reinforced by observance of worship in the *salāt*, the standing reminder of the *ḥajj* pilgrimage obligation, and the use of Arabic in study, teaching and devotion (Sanneh 1976).[3]

THE COMPARATIVE CHRISTIAN EXAMPLE: REFORM AND VERNACULAR RENEWAL

The picture of mission and renewal in Christianity in Africa sharply contrasts with the Islamic one. For example, Henry Venn (d. 1873)—a nineteenth-century missionary statesman who was in close touch with the African situation—clearly saw that for Christianity to be successful, it must encourage national characteristics, for it utilizes the vernacular paradigm to express its message. The vernacular had particularly accompanied the spread and expansion of Christianity. So Venn argued that even if missions had a united view about the primacy of Jesus Christ, it was impossible that "distinctions and defects will vanish. ... But it may be doubted whether, to the last, the Church of Christ will not exhibit marked national characteristics which, in the overruling grace of God will tend to its perfection and glory" (Knight 1880:284, cited in Walls 1981:48; see also Warren 1971:77). The worldwide Christian mission was not, for Venn, the vehicle for propagating the universal values of Western political domination, but rather the commitment to

Plate 1–8. Mission schools in Africa have been important both in establishing Christianity and in promoting vernacular languages. Here a Presbyterian teacher talks with local residents using Bulu words and gestures at Efulen mission station, Cameroon, "about seventy miles southeast of Batanga behind the coast belt", ca. 1895. M. Henry Kerr, who lived at Efulen for six years in the 1890s, did linguistic research and translated the four Gospels and a hymnal into Bulu, in collaboration with another missionary, Dr. Adolphus C. Good.[4]

the "national" enterprise of the respective societies affected. Missionaries, he observed, were already "reeds shaken by the wind" of scarcity, and no statistical notion of their work does justice to what they are really about, which is to foster vernacular self-confidence. It is their job, he maintained, "not to supply an European pastorate, but to prepare native pastors, and to endeavour, by divine help, *to fix the spiritual standard in such Churches by securing for them a supply of vernacular Scriptures*" (Warren 1971:119, emphasis added). Thus Venn's formulations came pretty close to expressing the idea that might be considered the flagship of modern missions. As a principle this idea undercuts—whether intentionally or not—the idea of colonialism, at least in its obvious effects on indigenous cultures.

The vernacular principle had explosive consequences in the nineteenth-century mission in the Niger Delta in Nigeria. There, African Christians thought of "reform" in terms of greater indigenization, an orientation that rejects foreign models for the church in Africa. The paradox is that missionaries themselves were the foremost advocates of the vernacular principle, whether or not they intended its manifest implications. Some of the earliest protagonists in the struggle for an indigenous Christianity in Nigeria were local Baptists, and their movement was a by-product of the American Civil War. During that war, American missionaries were withdrawn from the Baptist Mission, leaving the work in the hands of local leaders. When these missionaries returned in the 1870s, they found a church that was self-governing, self-propagating, and self-reliant. After more than a decade of protracted negotiations, the missionaries and their African congregations decided to end their relationship. In March 1888, a group of disaffected Africans broke away to form the Native Baptist Church, taking with them all the great African pioneers of the cause in Nigeria. This secession "ushered in a new era of Christianity among the Yoruba. A spell was broken" (Webster 1964:61). In the meantime, growing restiveness among the Niger Delta churches stemmed from attempts by the [Anglican] Church Missionary Society (C.M.S.) to revise the terms of the Niger Mission, which was founded in 1841, and remove Africans from positions of leadership. Bishop Samuel Ajayi Crowther (ca. 1811–1891), a victim of raids by the Fulani Muslim forces and eventually rescued from the slavery into which his Muslim captors sold him, was the dramatic embodiment of the Niger Delta tensions (Ajayi 1969:206–273). In August 1890, following a difficult committee meeting, Bishop Crowther was dismissed from the Niger Mission to which Venn had appointed him as episcopal leader. A meek and mild man, Crowther continued to counsel conciliation right up to the end. However, his African associates and sympathizers felt he had been betrayed, and many of them—though not including his youngest son, Archdeacon Dandeson Crowther (1844–1938)—decided to strike out independently from the C.M.S. On the anniversary of Bishop Crowther's disassociation, a meeting was convened in Lagos to map out a strategy. A resolution was adopted that became the foundation statement of the United Native African Church (U.N.A.C.). It affirmed

> that Africa is to be evangelized and that foreign agencies at work at the present
> moment taking into consideration climatic and other influences cannot grasp the

situation; resolved that a purely Native African Church be founded for the evangelization and amelioration of our race, to be governed by Africans. (Webster 1964:68)

In making a conjunction between the Christian religious vocation and indigenous ascendancy, the U.N.A.C. had invoked a powerful theme in an environment primed to exploit it. Both the history of Christian mission and the indigenous aspirations it excited made the call for a "native" church inevitable. "Reform" in Christian Africa has, therefore, rested on the vernacular premise—a contrast to the meaning of "reform" in Muslim Africa. One of the most articulate proponents of Christianity as a vernacular movement was Bishop James Johnson (1836–1917), a long-time colleague of Bishop Crowther and a robust figure of his era. He grasped fully the implications of Christianity adopting the vernacular as an extension of Christian life. He commented that

> Christianity is a religion intended for and is suitable for every Race and Tribe of people of the face of the Globe. Acceptance of it was never intended by its Founder to *denationalize any people and it is indeed its glory that every race of people may profess and practise it and imprint upon it its own native characteristics*, giving it a peculiar type among themselves without its losing anything of its virtue. And why should not there be an African Christianity as there has been a European and an Asiatic Christianity? (cited in Ayandele 1970:304, emphasis added)[5]

It is clear that African Christian activity made the issues of "renewal" and "revival" important matters. "Renewal" was the re-awakening, in a Christian setting, of local impulse and bringing that to bear on Spirit-prompted vernacular participation. "Renewal" elicits a particular understanding of the local setting, while "revival" is the intense concentration on the life of believers, often manifesting itself in charismatic gifts. Both strands are represented in the prophet movements that swept across the face of the Niger Delta, Yorubaland, and beyond.

Beginning in about 1915, a prophet movement came on the scene in the Niger Delta in the person of Garrick Braide. Baptized in 1910, and then later confirmed in 1912 by Bishop James Johnson, Braide was to effectively utilize the vernacular issue. Barely literate, he mobilized masses of the citizenry in a bid to make Christianity more relevant to contemporary needs. He preached a fervent message of faith in one God, adherence to the religious code, including observance of the Sabbath, a heady clamor for indigenous leadership in the church, and the denunciation of trade and the consumption of alcohol—then the scourge of the Delta, where some three million gallons of rum, whiskey, and gin were consumed annually and where alcoholism was a major social problem. Braide was accused by the colonial authorities of economic sabotage, for his preaching caused a significant slump in the alcohol trade, with a corresponding loss to the colonial treasury in excise revenues. Braide was arrested and imprisoned. He died on 15 November 1918, shortly after his release. His followers formed a separate church, Christ Army Church, estimated from 1918 to 1921 to number some 43,000. The vast majority of those he affected were affiliated with the established denominations (Tasie 1978:166–201).

The language issue was absolutely pivotal to the rise of reform, renewal, and revivalism in the Niger Delta. From the 1850s, when Bishop Crowther was writing to Henry Venn, urging the development of Ibo, to 1909, when "Union Ibo" was concocted as a new amalgam of dialects, the language question ran like a deep fault in the hard crust of perceptions of European subjugation of Africa.

Many Western scholars have criticized missions for their heavy involvement in the vernacular, an involvement deemed to distort indigenous priorities by wresting control from local people in that sphere. Nevertheless, looking at the situation from the ground, we can see that there were only two possibilities. One was inadequate linguistic knowledge resulting in a flawed translation—numerous unflattering specimens of that exist. The other was linguistic competence and its outcome in works of unsurpassed brilliance, to which innumerable grammars and dictionaries belong, by general consent. In neither case, however, is the vernacular priority superseded, for a good translation aided the cause just as a bad one impeded it. Thus a good, successful translation vindicated indigenous claims, while a bad, unsuccessful one justified the charge of foreign incompetence. In both cases translatability made the vernacular framework the indispensable coefficient of the range and scope of Christian expansion, with a corresponding marginalization of foreign agents and their cultural norms. The operative standards for success and effectiveness were vernacular ones, not those of Home Committees and Mission Boards.

There is a fascinating discussion between Henry Venn and John Christopher Taylor, an Ibo who devoted himself to translation work. In his correspondence with Venn, Taylor challenged the position of Rev. J. F. Schön, the German-missionary partner of Bishop Crowther, asking whether Schön was better qualified to lead the Ibo translation enterprise than himself. "Let me as a subordinate", he challenged, "propound a question to you. ... Can I teach Mr. Schön German?" Venn did not answer that question directly, but in reference to the issue he accepted the necessity for indigenous leadership in the enterprise (Ogharaerumi 1986:212).

THE VERNACULAR IN CHRISTIAN REVIVAL

The vernacular principle was the pulse of the "revival" movements that swept across the Niger Delta and Yorubaland in the first decades of the twentieth century. One of the most spectacular of these movements was the Aladura revival of Yorubaland, which occurred between 1928 and 1930. One of its representative figures was the charismatic Joseph Babalọla. The manner of his preparation and call; his appearance when he first emerged as a prophet; and the stress he placed on the spiritual gifts of prayer, healing, and prophecy (what may be considered the golden charismatic triad) made "revival" a tangible, popular force in local Christianity. One account describes the manner of his call as follows:

> Joseph Ayo Babalọla was born in 1904 at Ilofa, a small town just inside Ilorin Province, Northern Nigeria, where his father was Baba Ẹgbẹ of the C.M.S. He attended various schools in Lagos (where a brother was a schoolteacher) and elsewhere, leaving in 1928 with Standard IV [grade 4] to become a steam-roller driver with the P.W.D. [Public Works Department]. He was working on the

Ilesha-Akure road in south-western Ekiti when, in October 1928, his roller stopped working, and a voice called his name three times, and told him to leave his work to go and preach the Gospel. There were three palm leaves stuck to the roller; one was dead and dry, one was turning dry, the third fresh and green with life. Towns which heard his gospel were like the third leaf. He was told to take a bell, and was given the message that prayer and *omi iye*, the "water of life", would cure all sickness; all "medicines" should be destroyed. (Peel 1968:70)

A little earlier than the dramatic experience of Babalọla, another charismatic figure with Creole roots, Abiodun Akinsowon, an eighteen-year-old girl, experienced a trance on Corpus Christi Day (18 June 1925). Her father, a clergyman of the African Church Movement at Porto Novo, Dahomey (now Benin), summoned the help of one Moses Orimolade, a charismatic leader, who enjoined prayer, asking people in the house to clap and call on the Spirit of God to heal Abiodun. People rushed to the place where Abiodun was, and after the spiritual ministrations, she recovered and subsequently joined Orimolade to found a spiritual society, called then the Seraphim Society, with Holy Michael the Archangel adopted by special vision as Patron or Captain of the Society. In 1927 the name of the society was expanded to Cherubim and Seraphim, an indication that the revival leaders were keeping very high company indeed. "All the major doctrinal and ritual developments were sanctioned by vision. Meetings were held in numerous private houses and parlours, as a widening circle of members became adepts in the spiritual activities which Orimolade and Abiodun had initiated" (Peel 1968:73). One active member confessed, "'Prayer was the object. In our [previous mission-founded] churches with their set services there was not sufficient time for us to develop spiritually. When you do a thing you must reap the benefits; what we were taught in church we do not experience in practice. We Africans are so low in everything, but by prayer we may win everlasting power in God's Kingdom. In a word, practical Christianity'" (Peel 1968:73).

What brought the Seraphim to people's notice more than anything else were the huge anniversary processions, involving thousands of people arrayed in white robes with special uniforms and adornments for different ranks and sections. A contemporary report describes how Moses Orimolade and "energetic assistant Captain Abiodun" sat together in a go-cart under a canopy very similar to that used at Corpus Christi and inscribed with a motto celebrating the power of the Trinity. Twenty-four elders with stars as ornaments on their clothes and long staffs accompanied them, followed by 3,000 members. They made their way to Balogun Square and as the moon appeared the leader "delivered the usual message of Christ and his love". (Peel 1968:75)

As the membership rapidly increased, the prayer sessions and processions were backed by a support network of Bible study groups, each under a leader. Orimolade acquired the sobriquet Baba Aladura, the "prince of prayer", while the spiritual elite who formed the backbone of the revivalist intercessory meetings was called the Praying Band, Ẹgbẹ Aladura, so important was that exercise in the entire revival atmosphere. The term *aladura* itself is of Arabic derivation, *al-du ʿa*, meaning invocatory or supplicatory prayer.

Beginning in July 1930, a series of remarkable occurrences in Aladura circles gave the movement a dramatic lurch forward. The numerous unconnected centers experienced an "outbreak" of revival showers, with spontaneous outpourings of charismatic powers and gifts and dramatic instances of personal conversion. The entire religious landscape in Yorubaland and beyond began to stir with the *sturm und drang* of the Aladura cavalcade. In this spiritual upheaval, St. Michael the Archangel "became an appropriate *Balogun*, or war-chief, leader of the Seraphim in their fight for victory over the forces of Satan" (Peel 1968:149). According to a popular teaching of the Christ Apostolic Church—considered an elite among the charismatic churches—prayer, which is the activating force of revival [*isoji* in Yoruba], is likened to gunpowder; and the Holy Spirit, that terror of the invisible enemy, is regarded as the gun, with the Bible as the ramrod. This is perhaps the closest that Christian revival came to the sphere of the sword of the Muslim reformers, though even here the revival theme made the believer both subject and object, agent and target, of the message. One leading convert, for example, spoke of participating in a "tarrying meeting", waiting for the manifestation of the Holy Spirit, when "there was something like a storm and I see that my tongue is changed; since then, ah! (he laughed)—there is a happiness in my life!" (Peel 1968:146). The "sword of truth", the Muslim *sayf al-ḥaqq*, had for Christian revivalists a recoiling effect, for it identified them as the unerring target. To that extent, translatability was itself a consistent force in transferring authority from the culture of the European missionary translator to that of mother-tongue speakers in Africa, with missionaries sooner or later becoming victims of vernacularization.

SUMMARY

This chapter has looked at the contrasting effects of religious expansion in Muslim and Christian Africa by using historical and religious examples. The emphasis in Christianity on vernacular translation fomented mother-tongue aspirations and thus helped to establish the indigenous context for "reform", "renewal", and "revival". The repudiation of non-African standards for religious appropriation is one dramatic effect of the vernacular translations of the scriptures. Consequently, Christian African pioneers came upon fresh boundaries and new forms of identity in vernacular self-understanding. From the earliest epoch, both Coptic and Ethiopian Christianity encouraged religious translation work, which became the main carrier of the sentiments of cultural autonomy, giving the forms of the religion their distinctive national flavor.

In the modern period an identical vernacular emphasis helped to bring into being the prophet movements in sub-Saharan Africa. The followers of these movements adopted the vernacular to embark on far-reaching innovations in church, ritual, and theology, considerably modifying Western forms of the religion while simultaneously introducing adaptations into local forms. What emerged was a fresh synthesis between a scripturally based religion and a newly envisioned African heritage. In the songs, testimonies, rituals, and polities of these new religious movements we encounter Christianity as it descends, at first unwillingly, but finally with gravity, from its chilly Teutonic rehabilitation, caught in the pulsating rhythms of its tropical vernacular expansion.

This chapter also draws a contrast between the effects of Islamic expansion in the nontranslatable Qur'ān and the pressure it brought upon vernacular resources. From the Arabic of scripture, law, and devotion sprang the roots of religious reform in Muslim Africa, guiding the sentiment and course of religious developments and bringing Muslim Africans much closer to the norms and prescriptions of orthodoxy. With the adoption of the Islamic religious calendar based on the lunar year, reform-minded Muslims appealed to the millennial theme to discredit the process of adaptation among their untutored coreligionists. Thus a messianic figure was designated who at the proper time would come to overturn existing practices and inaugurate the age of virtue and rectitude. Such teachings delegitimized the establishment and focused attention on ideas and agents uncompromised by indigenous identity. The idea of religion as a foreign intrusion was elevated to a prescriptive virtue by an appeal to Islam as *the odd man out*, essentially estranged from indigenous compatibility. The impressive gains of Muslims were threatened more by the breach of this rule than by its observance.

Muslims and Christians in Africa understood "reform" and "renewal" in contrasting ways, and such understandings connected with the religious status they gave to indigenization. Clearly, Islam engaged traditional languages and cultures at a point considerably distant from where Christianity encountered them. For Muslims thus oriented, the vernacular was the obstacle that reform overcame, whereas for their Christian counterparts it constituted the irreplaceable frontier of opportunity. The strength of Islam in making excellent capital out of its Arab character in Africa was the weakness of Christianity when Christianity failed to shed its European forms. And conversely, the strength of Christianity in making vernacular self-understanding and integrity the principle of religious vitality was Islam's weakness in denying to mother tongues the consecrated status of scriptural legitimacy. In their different ways, Muslim and Christian Africans have lived out the truth of these distinctions, although many Western scholars have tripped up badly by treating the two religions in an inverse symmetry, taking Muslim gains as proof of indigenous originality and Christian gains as the lack thereof. What I have suggested in this chapter is the particularity of religious distinctiveness that absolves neither community from the searching critique involved in making claims destined for indigenous adoption.

NOTES

1. For example, Kiswahili in Tanzania, Kirundi in Burundi, Somali in Somalia, Sesotho in Lusotho.

2. Noted in Sirāj al-Ikhwān, a nineteenth-century work believed to have been composed by 'Uthmān dan Fodio, folio 11, cited in Hiskett (1962:579).

3. For a continuation of this theme into the modern era, see Sanneh 1981a and 1981b; and for how the Arabic theme might work in other situations, see Sanneh 1979.

4. This photo and caption information come from the "Africa" files of The University Museum Archives, University of Pennsylvania, Philadelphia. Near the time of this photo, the Presbyterian Church (U.S.A.) had "foreign mission fields" in "Liberia, Kamerum, Corisco, and Gabon".

5. This is a topic dear also to the heart of Dr. Edward Wilmot Blyden. See his magnum opus, *Christianity, Islam, and the Negro Race* (1967 [1887]:164–168), and his work *African Life and Customs* (1908:62–64, 66).

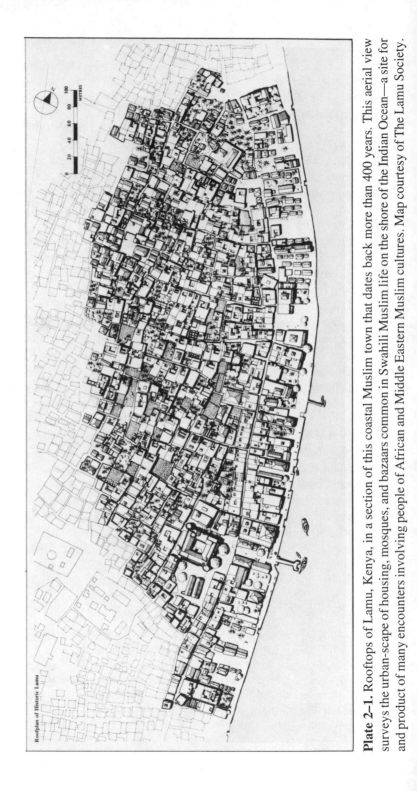

Plate 2–1. Rooftops of Lamu, Kenya, in a section of this coastal Muslim town that dates back more than 400 years. This aerial view surveys the urban-scape of housing, mosques, and bazaars common in Swahili Muslim life on the shore of the Indian Ocean—a site for and product of many encounters involving people of African and Middle Eastern Muslim cultures. Map courtesy of The Lamu Society.

2

Beginnings & Encounters:
Islam in East African Contexts

Azim Nanji

INTRODUCTION

THIS STUDY IS ABOUT beginnings and encounters—beginnings that mark a widening of religious identity and encounters between established religious identities and differing ones that have begun to intrude upon them. In order to explain these processes, this chapter focuses on the portrayal of three individuals, in oral, written, and dramatic literature. The first, a king, Kabaka Mutesa of Buganda, the second, a trader of Indian Muslim origin seeking to create a new home and ply his trade in East Africa; and the third, a visionary, Kinjeketile, the leader of the Maji Maji movement in then German-ruled Tanganyika. What links their lives are affiliations of time and of space. They lived and acted from the middle of the nineteenth century to the beginning of the twentieth century, and the geographical space, now called East Africa, became the stage on which their lives unfolded in quite dramatic fashion.

My purpose here is to portray their lives as ways of illuminating different facets of the history of Islam in East Africa. In choosing these three figures, I am aware that the allegiance of Mutesa to Islam was ambiguous and that Kinjeketile was not a Muslim. The focus on Islam, however, stems not just from the individual identities but rather from the source material and in Kinjekctile's case the representation of Kinjeketile and Maji Maji in a play by the Swahili Muslim writer Ebrahim Hussein. The projection of these individuals, whether in oral tradition or written form, takes place in a generative ambience in which the presence of Islam or affiliation to it is a critical factor.

In the recounting of significant individual lives, the narratives or the dramatic form in which they are presented do not focus on telling the history of Islam but rather portray personal experiences and encounters within the changing context of East African life. They help in this way to illustrate the times in which these individuals lived and the range of responses that their actions were able to generate. I hope that this approach combining literary material with political and social history can, at least partially, move us away from the narrower perspectives that have for so long dominated the perception of African religious history, and in particular the diverse and complex role of Islam in the wider religious history of nineteenth- and twentieth-century East Africa. Thus rather than follow the trend of thought that attempts to see the religious facet of Africa's encounter with modernity as essentially a one-sided impact that resulted in wholesale erosion and loss, I hope through these examples to convey some of the complexity inherent in these encounters and the confusing contexts in which protagonists had to live and respond to change.

ISLAM IN EAST AFRICA: CHANGING PERSPECTIVES

Coastal culture in East Africa had been undergoing a slow series of demographic and cultural shifts that, with the coming of Islam, created conditions for the development of a relatively homogeneous Swahili Muslim culture by the eleventh century. This coastal cultural zone extended from the Somali coast in the north to what is now the Mozambique coast in the south. Though it served as a base for the literary and public manifestation of Swahili Muslim religious and cultural life in subsequent centuries, it would be erroneous, as has occasionally been assumed, to regard the representations of Muslim culture on the coast as being primarily a wholesale adoption of Muslim modes of practice and ways of living imagined in their former Arab or "Shirazi" settings. As with other areas where Islam has spread, subsequent Muslim representations of the past tend to depict conversion and transition to Islamic modes of living as a dramatic and often total shift away from the local, domestic culture. Recent studies on East Africa, however, reveal that the "Swahili corridor" that evolved created conditions for a wide spectrum of Muslim expressions—the *waungwana* [indigenous "freed men and women"], the urban-style Muslims, and the Sufi modes such as the *Qadiriyya*, linked to the caravan trade. Subsequently in the nineteenth century, differing patterns were inaugurated by the establishment of the Omani-Busaidi Sultanate of Zanzibar and then by the incursion of colonial influence. But focusing unduly on the "learned", public, literary, and urban manifestations of East African Islam leaves untreated and unappreciated the wider processes of Muslim growth and development in the area. In addition, a polarized view of Muslim culture, in which the presumed "normative" and the "local regressive" are seen in disjunction, leads to a dichotomous representation of Islam in East Africa.

By the nineteenth century, the regional patterns already established on the coast had undergone dramatic changes. The new Sultanate of Zanzibar sought to impose greater control over the political and cultural affairs of the upper areas of the coast, challenging the largely regional evolution of Islamic life and organizations. The subsequent presence of the British and the development of links with the interior created conditions that allowed for even greater outside influences to penetrate from the coast inward, setting into motion a new phase in the Islamization of East Africa. This chapter is concerned with some of the new beginnings and encounters that took place in this most recent phase of the history of Islam in the region.

THE COMING OF ISLAM TO UGANDA

In the traditional account of *The Kings of Buganda,* recorded by Sir Apolo Kaggwa, mention is made of the first contact between Kabaka Sunna (d. 1854) and Muslim merchants in the middle of the nineteenth century (Kaggwa 1971). It is, however, during the reign of his successor Kabaka Mutesa I (d. 1884) that the initial encounter was translated into a deeper interest and subsequent conversion to and practice of Islam.

Kaggwa constructed his account from oral tradition, as were several other versions by Baganda Muslims and others. Subsequent scholarly attempts to locate the events and consequences that marked the conversion have been primarily concerned with showing how Kabaka Mutesa and his successor Mwanga learned, adopted, but often rejected or manipulated Islam or Christianity to further their own political power and to consolidate the primacy of the role of the Kabaka in the affairs of the Baganda people.

The coming of Islam can be said to mark an activity whose associations are set in time and in society. My assertion is that the coming of Islam and then Christianity to Uganda also marks the beginning of a new coherence in the history of religious change in Uganda, a coherence that has to do with the transition away from an oral culture. Such cultural change necessitates mediation. Whereas trading outside one's culture can be regarded as one form of mediation, the acceptance of an outside tradition marks the beginning of a far more radical effort to mediate change. It is noteworthy that Mutesa's interest in the text of the Qur'ān and his fascination with the notion of an afterlife (in which *recorded* human actions are decoded through reward or punishment) constitute an attempt to look beyond a defined oral culture to an alternative civilization, much of whose impetus came from the power of the written word. This is not to suggest that one should not affirm that social and historical influences and motivations prompted Mutesa's actions, but such influences reflect the linear impact of Islam on the lives of the Baganda people. The other level of influence involves Islam's opening up a whole range of new possibilities that Mutesa wished to affirm rather than reject for himself and his people, an enlargement that indicated his awareness of the new pluralistic and cross-cultural environment in which he would have to learn to wield his traditional power. Abdu Kasozi, for instance, has shown that the conversion of Mutesa and his encouragement of Islam and its practice led to his exercising much more authority over religious life in a shorter span of time than could have ever been done under traditional religion and that this can be viewed as one stage in the social and religious evolution of the Baganda (Kasozi 1981). The acceptance of the new faith was also accompanied by a certain ambivalence towards the past, an ambivalence that manifested itself simultaneously in the rejection of certain traditional practices, and in a great affirmation of the centrality of the institutional role of the Kabaka. For instance, Mutesa put an end to the practice of hunting with dogs, previously an important ceremonial occasion. He also abolished the tradition whereby the king ate alone, arguing that worship of One God implied that His creatures should sit together. On the other hand, when some other converts to Islam tried to excel at being Muslims, he had them put to death, lest they be perceived as showing that they were better Muslims than he was. Such ambivalence seems to indicate that anything new in Baganda society could only be mediated through the Kabaka and that while he may have understood the individualizing aspects of the relationship between human and divine inherent in Islam, such an aspect could not be permitted to overshadow the dominance of the Kabaka in the lives of his people. Religious affiliation had to be subordinate to ethnic identification and political hierarchy.

Whereas many elements marked discontinuity, they also represented beginnings generated by the encounter of two religious traditions. With the coming of Islam and subsequently Christianity, the nature of the discourse between the Kabaka and traditional Baganda religious authorities, between the Kabaka and his people, and finally between his people and the rest of the groups in Uganda was all to change in ways it would not have otherwise changed. The paradigmatic themes of the life of Mutesa as represented in the traditional account are change and ambivalence. These are illustrated at the most literal level in the enlargement of boundaries and identities but more profoundly as a disjunction between a life of oral culture and one marked by the recording and written expression of a historical consciousness. One manifestation of that change is an attempt by Kaggwa to record the history of the kings of Buganda. The growing power and significance of literacy, which is one aspect of the change ushered in by Islam, is important not simply in the mechanical changes it brings but because "it destroys the important function of 'structural amnesia' in oral cultures and makes available, through documentation, a specifically defined and limited past. Thus literacy displaces 'mythic' mentality and leads to the development of a historical consciousness" (Jan Mohamed 1983).

David Martin (1978) has argued that tradition "is based on a single universe of meaning". When that universe is fractured, its internal harmonies are lost forever. Martin goes on to argue that the possibility of choosing among alternatives implies "codification". This process involving choice and codification illustrates one of the new "beginnings" encountered by the Kabaka and the Baganda. The anguish and confusion expressed by Mutesa when faced with the rival and mutually villifying Christian and Muslim claims over his soul after death reflect this new movement towards codification. In the religious history of modern Uganda, this in turn would breed further encounters and alternative forms of being religious, in which some of the harmonies of past tradition would find a place.

Jaroslav Pelikan (1984) and Edward Shils (1981) have argued for a much more dynamic concept of tradition, an emphasis that has been carried further by Robert Bellah in his study *Habits of the Heart* (1985). Such a dynamic concept of tradition allows us to see discontinuities where and when they occur, but it also enables us to capture new tendencies that are mediated by tradition during periods of great change. The response of the Baganda rulers to the coming of Islam illustrates, in my view, the unfolding of such a process in East Africa's religious history.

ALLIDINA VISRAM: ECONOMIC ENTERPRISE & CROSS-CULTURAL ENCOUNTERS

One link in the vast chain of maritime trade that involved Muslim merchants and traders in late medieval times was that between the ports of the west coast of India and those of East Africa. Duarte Barbosa, the Portuguese traveller, saw many ships at Mombasa, Malindi, and Mogadishu that hailed from the Indian port city of Cambay, attesting to a flourishing exchange of goods. Until the middle of the nineteenth century, however, such trading contacts were confined to the coastal region of East Africa, and the visiting traders from India did not envisage settlement nor did they desire to go further into the interior, leaving that aspect to Arab or Swahili merchants who were principally engaged in the ivory and slave trades.

By the middle of the nineteenth century, drought and resulting famine had created such adverse conditions in the western Indian region of Cutch and

Kathiawad that migration to East Africa, rather than mere trading opportunity, came to be considered by many as the key to survival. For the purpose of this section, I have focused on one Muslim community, the Nizārī Ismāʿīlī Muslims (often referred to as Khojahs), and a pioneer migrant, Allidina Visram, to reflect the chapter's theme of "beginnings and encounters" across wider cross-cultural lines.

Plate 2–2. The entrance door to the "Ismailia Jamat Khana" building in Zanzibar. The Arabic-Persian building name and English inscription painted on the tympanum of this 1905 structure bear witness to the historic and ongoing process of intercultural encounters in East Africa, as do the tens of thousands of Arabic (and some Persian) loanwords incorporated into Kiswahili (similar to French and Latin loanwords into English) over the last 1,000 years. Jamat Khana buildings are used by Ismailis for congregational, devotional, educational, and social activities.

Allidina Visram came to Zanzibar as a young lad in 1877. He began his career as an apprentice in the business established by an earlier Ismaili trader, Sewa Paroo, whose trading activities and entrepreneurial skills were to serve Allidina Visram as a model. In 1897, on the death of Sewa Paroo, the apprentice—having risen in the esteem of his master—was appointed to take over the expanding business. His strategy was twofold. The first was to seek penetration of the interior in search for legitimate trade (that is, in contrast to those who still pursued the slave and ivory trades, even after the former had been abolished in 1833). The second was to diversify the nature of his business enterprises by opening branches as far as the Congo (now Zaïre) and along the new Uganda Railway and by moving beyond the retailing and importing of goods to the establishment of industries such as soda factories and cotton ginneries. In addition he also financed the ventures of others who were trying to establish themselves in trade. One key to his role as an entrepreneur was his connections in the Ismaili Muslim community to which he belonged. The then small community linked by ties of kinship and marriage, in addition to religious and communal solidarity, provided both a source of trained apprentices and individuals disposed to trading and a system of values that encouraged the quest for material prosperity, as long as it was balanced with a moral concern for the poor and the underprivileged.

Philip Curtin (1984) in his study of world trade has shown that cultural minorities use their commercial bent and community solidarity to establish a partial monopoly on the economic life of host societies. The migration and settlement in East Africa of people of Indian origin, including Muslims, reinforce this view while in some sense anticipating the antagonism and xenophobia that developed in the host society and that led, for example, to the expulsion of Asians from Uganda in 1972.

The thrust of the overall activity and purpose reflected in Allidina Visram's entrepreneurial exploits, and subsequently in the Muslim community to which he belonged, raises larger questions about how minority Muslim groups came to establish themselves in East Africa and furthermore how they sought to integrate their own particular vision of religious life with their role as cross-cultural brokers and traders. Given the fact that relations between Ismaili Muslims and other incoming Asian groups and the host society who perceived them as aliens were asymmetrical, how were the Ismailis to deal with sources of stress generated in what had now become a plural, colonial society and how were they to alleviate these stresses through their role as cross-cultural brokers and agents of economic change?

Allidina Visram, at the individual level, and the Ismaili community, at the collective level, provide instances of how these ambiguities were addressed. While concentrating on building institutions to strengthen community solidarity and religious identity, the Nizari Ismailis rejected the view that they should remain an ethnic enclave. In a colonial economy and society, their access to political power for promoting their own self-interest and that of others was limited, but they could use their sense of economic enterprise and private initiative to foster constructive change in their own community and perhaps among others as well. Allidina Visram's philanthropic activity is one illustration of this goal. He encouraged and contributed to the building of a school in Mombasa, which still bears his name, endowed a hospital, and even donated money for Namirembe Cathedral outside Kampala. It is easy to be cynical about the philanthropic activities of such tycoons, but it must be remembered that notions of "giving and sharing" are institutionalized in Islam and that Allidina Visram's efforts reflect a pattern almost continuous in Muslim philanthropic activity.

These efforts also were part of the wider corporate efforts of the Ismaili community to build bridges with other Muslims and peoples of East Africa, among whom they had established a permanent home for themselves. Elsewhere I have tried to show that in dealing as mediators and cross-cultural brokers, the Ismailis of East Africa were also coming to terms with mediating change within their own cosmological and sociological development (Nanji 1974, 1986). Their own boundaries were being enlarged as they sought to move away from purely ethnic self-identification towards a broader affiliation with the Muslim Ummah at large and a more local identification with their new homeland. In East Africa, they worked cooperatively with local Muslims through the creation of the East African Muslim Welfare Society, which was eventually responsible for building mosques and schools for Muslims in Uganda and elsewhere, to which the Ismailis contributed money as well as their talents for organization and local development.

Allidina Visram and the Ismaili Muslims are examples of mediation in the changing history of Islam in East Africa. While their own beginnings in East Africa required mediation between their own past and present, in time they came to play a far more important role as cross-cultural brokers, a role to which they brought their own religious and cultural values. It is this dual process of community formation and the contributions of individual Ismailis in broader spheres that represent one aspect of the significance of their history to the process of modernization and religious change in East Africa.

Plate 2–3. A *madrasa*—a school for young Muslim children that has an integrated curriculum—in Mombasa, Kenya. Here a Muslim woman instructs children in the Qu'rān, the life of the prophet, and other subjects, including reading and writing in Arabic, Kiswahili, and English.

THE DRUM AND THE VIOLIN

In a poem entitled "The Drum and the Violin", written when he was a student, the Swahili dramatist and poet Ebrahim Hussein expressed the conflict between Swahili Muslim values and those of the West, through the symbolism of two musical instruments, the indigenous drum and the foreign violin. The poem ends with the lines:

> I must worship Allah
> But will He listen to a divided voice
> The voice of someone who wears
> both a Muslim *kanzu* and a Christian cross?

In a dramatized rendering of the poem, the poet displays on his person the symbols of conflict, a black-and-white *kanzu* robe and a large cross. In his perceptions of cultural and religious conflict, he saw the drum as representing matter and desire and the violin as representing spirit and tranquillity. The rhythmic beat of life is thus contrasted with inner peace, where matter and spirit are dichotomized and the two traditions, indigenous and alien, are perceived as distinct and unbridgeable. From this simple dichotomy, reflected in the poem, Ebrahim Hussein moved in his later writings to the exploration of wider themes where religion, ethnicity, and nationalism are explored in the form of a drama, *Kinjeketile*, based on the events of the Maji Maji rebellion of 1905.

African writers who address in their fiction the impact of colonial rule find themselves defining the disintegration of a communal society and the discovery of one based on notions of individualism and its role in society (Jan Mohamed 1983). In his play *Kinjeketile*, Hussein is concerned with several important themes, most of which find an echo within a sensibility shaped by an awareness and participation in a wider Islamic heritage, but also a sensibility caught in an ambiguous pose between its own immediate ethnic heritage and the utopian goals of the future. The action of the play is set within an ethnic framework—that of the Wamatumbi. In the introduction to the play, Hussein clarifies the linkages in the religious cosmos of the Wamatumbi that he feels are relevant to his purposes as a dramatist: the belief in One God (Mungu), the presence of a mediating spirit (Hongo) between the realm of the divine and creation, and finally the human mediator (in this case Kinjeketile) between all these elements of the cosmos and the world of human beings. I would contend that some of the overarching metaphors necessary to his dramatization are derived from a larger Islamic framework, which in a sense provides the dramatic parallels Hussein needs for his theme.

The second set of metaphors, critical to the unfolding of the play, are those of an armed struggle against German colonial rule. Armed struggle is linked to the goal of establishing unity among the various "tribes". In one of his dramatic entrances, Kinjeketile speaks of the "rays of the sun" that will

> banish from your eyes
> clouds of smoke and fog
> that hid a brother from a brother
> that hid a tribe from a tribe. . . .
> Until the warmth of love will free us.
> We will expand, yes expand
> we will unite.
>
> (Hussein 1970)

Unity is to be followed by war. In his trance, caught by the power of the spirit, he speaks of everyone being the children of Seyyid Said, the then sultan of Zanzibar.

His "revelations" are in a strange form of Kiswahili—full of Arabic. As the medium between the two worlds, his revelations are couched in terminology reminiscent of Islam—of *jihād* [struggle], unity, and links with the Sultanate in Zanzibar. On the other hand, these notions cast a doubt in his mind about the genuineness of his experience and his role as a leader of the revolution, illustrating the conflict between the particularism of his people and the universalism of his goals.

The significance of these references from the play does not suggest that Hussein is arguing for an Islamic *jihād*. Rather, I would argue that the medium of Kiswahili, in which the play was originally written, and the literary tradition of Islam that has informed much of Kiswahili literature to modern times becomes, for Hussein, the most suitable vehicle for conveying the role of religion in the political process. Muslim literacy informs his own dramatic literacy, which in turn seeks to create a new historical consciousness through the portrayal of Kinjeketile. One of the problems in the play is that we never learn whether Kinjeketile ever becomes conscious as a character of the ambivalence in his role as a prophet or as a mere self-deluded visionary. This remains part of the ambivalence that Hussein is never fully able to resolve for himself. Though he allows Kinjeketile a prophet's role, he is unsure of how far the religious personality can bring about political change through a religiously motivated vehicle. For Hussein, as for many other East African writers who employ religious themes in their work, notably Ngugi wa Thiongo, religion is relevant only as a partial tool for expressing broader, national political goals. If it seeks universalism in and of itself, then religion as in *Kinjeketile* can only be a force for obscurantism, fanaticism, and even self-destruction. Kiswahili, English, and the representation of new hopes all ironically symbolize the eventual destruction of the narrower ethnic past. The play seeks the enlargement of the boundaries and capacities of the limited oral culture, and it also marks the beginnings of a new historical awareness in which a more broadly syncretic vision of African life is portrayed. In *Kinjeketile*, a Swahili Muslim sensibility is at its most ambivalent. The play is seeking to encompass wider themes: themes that involve encounter and struggle for independence from colonial rule and that articulate the goals of a united African society, and themes of past indigenous values and religion, including the role they might play in mediating the transition.

CONCLUSION

Charles C. Stewart (1985) and Ioan Lewis (1983) have both argued cogently against the misleading dichotomies that have marked studies of Islam in African contexts. These dichotomies seem to separate the various forms of Islam into "popular" and "establishment", rural and urban, Sufi and legalistic, and—of greater relevance to this chapter—pre-Islamic and presumed "normative" Islamic. Overly strict adherence to such dichotomies reduces the process of Islamization to caricatured polarities. An appreciation of the dialogic relationship between the notions of beginnings and encounters offers, in contrast, a less stratified approach to the study of Muslim East Africa and an opportunity for integrating sources and perspectives that chart a more dynamic and multiple process of diffusion of Islam in this region of Africa.

Plate 3–1. Newly ordained Father John Acheampong, SVD, in his parents' compound after saying his "first mass" in his home village of Assin Fosu, Ghana, 19 December 1977. Society for the Divine Word [Societas Verbi Divini] missionaries do not serve among their own people, so they learn other languages (and sometimes learn other cultures) for placement elsewhere, in contrast to Diocesan priests who serve in or near their home communities.

3

Cultural Change & Religious Conversion in West Africa

Jon P. Kirby

MISSIONARY SUCCESS STORY?

IN THE BRIEF SPAN OF EIGHTY-FIVE years Africa's Christian population has risen from about 10 million, or 9.2 percent of the population, to 237 million, and by the turn of the century, it is expected to reach 350 million, or about 50 percent, making it the missionary success story of all time. Yet there are indications that conversions to the Christian churches, especially the "mission-founded" churches,[1] are tapering off. Neither "the prognosis of the World Missionary Conference of Edinburgh (1910) concerning the so-called primitive peoples" that "most of these peoples will have lost their ancient faiths within a generation, and will accept that culture religion with which they first come into contact" (cited in Barrett 1982:5) nor the prediction of Roland Oliver, who, using the geometrical conversion progressions of South-of-the Sahara Africa beginning in 1912, said that by 1992 there will not be a "pagan" left, has hardly come true. "Despite vast numbers of conversions from their ranks to Christianity, Hinduism, and Islam, the absolute numbers of tribal religionists including shamanists have increased markedly and regularly in many countries [including Africa] from 1900–1980" (Barrett 1982:5). There are some indications that Christians are leaving the churches for traditional religions. And the dramatic increases in the close-to-traditional independent churches are, for the most part, due to the defections from the mission-founded churches, not traditional religions.[2] If we ask why the numbers of traditional religionists are increasing or why Christians are leaving the mission churches for churches more closely resembling the traditional patterns, the answer that immediately comes to mind is the contemporary search for identity and cultural authenticity. But there is also an increasingly hot debate going on as to whether or not there ever was a religious conversion of any consequence.

The question of Christianity's religious impact on traditional African religions is a thorny problem and a hotly debated issue today. Robin Horton (1971, 1975a, 1975b) has put forward the theory that neither of the two "world" religions is responsible for a recent change in focus from lesser gods to a commitment in Africa to the Supreme Being. Rather, he states, it would have happened anyway as a natural result of a widening of the political, economic, and cultural frontiers of African societies. In my opinion Horton's opponents (cf. O'Connell 1962; Fisher 1973) have rightly stressed that African societies have in fact always been aware of the "High God" and called upon Him when occasion demanded (e.g., times of territorial crisis). In this chapter, I stress that there must be a distinction made between cultural and religious conversion. Missionaries have tended to conflate the two while Africans have been highly selective. Thus, from the Africans' religious or problem-solving perspective, conversion to Christianity may mean very little or no change.

METHODOLOGY AND FRAME OF REFERENCE

What has been the Roman Catholic stance toward African traditional religion? What is it now? And what will it likely be in the future? These important questions, which offer a framework for this chapter, are not only based in linear, diachronic history but also involve processes within history such as the problem of faith and culture and the changing identity of the Catholic Church in our own time from a "Roman" to a "World Church".[3]

Citing examples and a case study (Kirby 1985) from West Africa, particularly Ghana, where I have spent the last twenty years as a missionary and anthropologist, I would like to stress not so much the interaction between Christianity (especially Catholicism) and traditional religion, nor how traditional religious beliefs were affected by the interaction—although there are many examples of this, from the more loosely structured independent churches to culture-contact religious associations such as Tigare.[4] I intend instead to examine the ways in which traditional belief systems and other traditional structural alignments have remained largely untouched by Christianity, though half the continent is nominally Christian.

I will look first at the past, at the strongly ethnocentric history of the mission churches in Africa. Then, switching over to the synchronic and emic approach of contemporary social anthropology, I will take a microcosmic glimpse at traditional beliefs and Christianity from the people's perspective by citing the case of the conversion experience of the Anufo of northern Ghana. Finally, I will return to the macro level and in light of what I have termed a "cultural identity crisis in Africa" examine a new approach to missionary work and a new understanding of the Catholic Church as "World Church".

A BRIEF HISTORY OF MISSIONARY ETHNOCENTRISM

To summarize four centuries of earnest toil in a few paragraphs is impossible and, in a way, it is quite misleading to characterize the bulk of it as ethnocentric. Nevertheless, it suits our purposes here to clearly discern the historical precedent for the dominance of Western culture within the church affairs of Africa. This will, I hope, explain, if not justify, a description more like a caricature than a portrait.

In the earliest phase (until 1800) Catholic missionary work in Africa achieved very little measurable success. Climate, a high mortality rate, few missionaries, the lack of indigenous clerics, the slave trade, and too close an association with

European politics, commerce, and culture all played a part. Missionary attitudes were also a part of the problem. Most missionaries saw themselves as chaplains to the forts or small trading communities and were much more interested in commerce than making conversions in the hinterland.

The Protestant churches entered the African scene in appreciable numbers only in the early nineteenth century. Although very few of the indigenous population were converted, communities of Christian settlers and recaptives were established in West Africa. Limited numbers of school children were also converted. But death rates were still very high, creating a personnel problem. There were few resources and not a great amount of support from the sending churches. The main problem, however, was that the indigenous rulers needed to be persuaded of the advantages—moral, intellectual, cultural, political, and economic—to be gained from conversion. The settlers set themselves apart from the indigenous peoples and didn't bother to learn native languages and customs. On the whole, missionaries knew very little of the culture, traditional values, and religious beliefs of the people, but rather stridently condemned everything in their way of life and religion.

By the middle of the nineteenth century a great rivalry arose among the various Christian denominations in implementing their common strategy—establishing schools and creating a Christian, Western-trained elite. The main Catholic presence in West Africa—the White Fathers, the Holy Ghost Fathers (founded in 1843), and the Society of African Missions—all concentrated on establishing schools. But the institutions they set up were not only under foreign control, they were also dependent on clergy and financial support from abroad. The organizations made little

Plate 3–2. Catholic Youth Organization member in Tafo, Ghana, wearing his uniform. The C.Y.O. is very popular in some rural areas, organizing sports, parades, and other large group activities for children. Non-Catholics attending Catholic schools also join the C.Y.O. and actively participate in its events.

or no attempt to adapt to African settings. Most missionaries were intolerant of anything that seemed to conflict with the form and content of the Christian tradition that they were bearing. In the last part of the nineteenth century, a new breed of more arrogant missionaries arrived, extinguishing any hope of a self-supporting, self-governing, and self-propagating African church. The determination was stronger than ever to rule over Africans, not to create autonomous churches. Although in theory the Catholics subscribed to an indigenous church with African clergy, they kept a tightly controlled system of provinces, extensions of a Roman church.

In the colonial period, education was again for all denominations the main source of converts and the main strategy for evangelization, though increasingly the purpose was to establish Christian families and, wherever possible, Christian communities. Although the Catholics were late arrivals, they made greater progress with schools. The Holy Ghost Fathers were successful schoolmen in eastern Nigeria, while the White Fathers in the French Colonies and in northern Ghana stressed communal evangelization and wide use of catechists. The White Fathers' strategy was remarkably effective in northern Ghana, especially among the Dagaaba. But as a whole, the Catholics were particularly slow in training sufficient indigenous clergy and catechists, and missionaries too often saw themselves solely as leaders, believing that there was little or nothing to be gained from an open, equal partnership with Africans.

The Christian emphasis on schooling had the intended effect of giving Christians a disproportionate influence. Senior positions open to Africans in the army, education, or administration during the colonial era were held by an African Christian elite who had been trained in mission schools (Clarke 1986:115).

In general, attempts to win over Muslims failed completely. Characterized by ignorance, suspicion, and hostility, the mission to West African Muslims consisted mainly of redoubled efforts to evangelize the "pagan" population in order to contain the spread of Islam.

The colonial period was especially characterized by denominational rivalry, recriminations, accusations, and counteraccusations based in narrow and rigid theological viewpoints imported from Europe. Each mission society believed itself to be in full possession of the truth to the exclusion of all others, and only in the late colonial era did anything resembling ecumenical cooperation emerge among churches.

ETHNOCENTRIC BIAS OF AFRICAN MISSIONS

Throughout its history, Christian missionary work in West Africa has displayed little cultural sensitivity toward African society. Catholic missionaries, like their Protestant brothers, were appallingly ignorant of African institutions and did not care to investigate them. Indeed, they were too busy suppressing traditional rituals and beliefs, thereby preventing an objective, balanced view of African traditional religions. With few exceptions, missionaries saw African traditional religions as a "morass of bizarre beliefs and practices" (Clarke 1986:221). This attitude prevailed not only among missionaries, but also among sociologists, explorers, and Western thinkers as a whole. According to the explorer Richard Burton, the African had "barely advanced to idolatry" and "had never grasped the ideas of a personal Deity, a duty in life, [or] a moral code" (Burton 1864:199).

There were some exceptions. A few extraordinary missionaries were among the first linguists and ethnographers of the people they were sent to evangelize. But until the 1940s there were few anthropological studies of African religion or philosophy, and thus little to challenge the widely held misconceptions. Indeed, even up until Vatican II, the post-1940s classical African ethnography had little effect on Catholic missionary policy.

In spite of a prevalent ethnocentrism and a paucity of ethnographic material, African culture was not wholly condemned by the Catholic Church during the pre-Independence, pre-Vatican II period. Polygamy was outlawed, but bridewealth was allowed, and in some areas mortuary practices were allowed in addition to the Christian rites. Oftentimes missionaries simply "looked the other way" when it came to certain traditional practices that native Christians felt constrained to perform. Some sought "pastoral solutions" to local problems and tried hard to distinguish between what was and what was not an indissoluble part of African religion. The extent to which these efforts were appropriate or misguided is now becoming clearer as we are beginning to understand the very little that is indissoluble in our own Western Christian forms.

As a general principle, however, we can say that before 1960 all mission-founded churches insisted that their converts abandon all contact with African traditional religions and cultures. These churches were poorly prepared theologically and culturally to accept any alternatives to their own way of praying, thinking, believing, or behaving. It was taken for granted that a new social order, a new political economy, and a new culture must accompany the change to a new moral order. Proper European civilization *was* Christianity, and the only way to bring about conversion was to establish this cultural framework. Indeed, anything else was unthinkable. Western law was Christian law; Western systems of organization, of government, of economics all formed the integral network of what it was to be a "Christian". These institutions were "church culture". What was Christian could, therefore, not abide with what was African. Thus confrontation between the "old" and the "new" continued right up until African independence, and that the "old" would eventually lose out to what was considered a "superior" Western way seemed to be a foregone conclusion. Even as late as my arrival in Africa in 1972, the veteran missionary who introduced me to my task explained that it really wasn't necessary for me to learn the local language well; I should be speaking English most of the time anyway so that through me Africans might perfect their use of that tongue.

Christian schools were established to demolish the "old" ways. Most missionaries considered the colonial administrations as allies in the essential task of destroying existing structures. Today an estimated 70 percent of all literate Africans call themselves Christians. But the question we will shortly ask is, how much are they imbued with Christianity and how much with a Western cultural veneer? This, of course, poses the further question of the relationship between faith and culture.

Since Independence, the foundations of the old mission strategies have gradually eroded. Mission-founded churches in Africa have witnessed the widespread nationalization of their schools, defections to independent churches, and less support from Western churches on the one hand, and on the other a steady increase in indigenous clergy, though there are still not as many indigenous clergy as are needed. Local African churches still request missionaries, but the emphasis is now on filling in the gaps—those areas that, for the moment, cannot be filled by indigenous clergy—not on missionary evangelism. African churches are still dependent on European or American missionaries for what cannot be provided locally—especially for the maintenance of the imported structures. At the same time there are fewer Western missionaries to do this work, which is being met with increasing resistance from both mission-sending and mission-receiving countries. But while all agree that the roles are changing, neither group is sure about how or in which direction missions should go, let alone how to get there.

I turn here to look at the religious life of an isolated ethnic group in northern Ghana, the Anufo. This group recently converted in large numbers to Christianity, and even more recently "unconverted". This case study cites the work of the Evangelical Presbyterian Church of Ghana, as well as the Catholic Church, and affirms that both Protestants and Catholics labor under unwieldy ethnocentric biases that prevent them from reaching the religious dimensions of African life. Their differences with traditional African values go much deeper than the denominational differences each imported from Europe. This study therefore exemplifies the present-day failure of traditional missionary methods and is prototypical of the ethnocentric model discussed above.

ANUFO RELIGION

Among the Anufo of northern Ghana, as with most other African peoples, there is no word for religion as such, for it is not objectified in their thinking but is rather an aspect of all of life. Religious belief and practice form an integral part of life and manifest themselves functionally in the modes of action and the apparatus for problem solving. Besides offering psychological reassurance, behavioral confirmation, social integration, an explanation for the unknown, and an explanation of origins, religion is—above all—a practical problem solver. Among the Anufo all of life is viewed as a problematic situation that must be kept in harmonious balance by using shrines to manipulate relations between persons, spirits, and things. Anufo religion is thus a "problem-solving" activity par excellence.

Anufo shrines provide a forum for intervention on three levels of problematic experience, each of which may involve social, political, economic, or religious relations. These are (1) the territorial level, where we find the earth shrines with their village custodians and congregations of whole villages; (2) the shrines of the kin groups or lineages, whose custodians are normally the heads of households and whose congregations are family members (these include ancestor shrines and those handed down by ancestors, e.g., divination shrines, shrines of the spirits of the wild, and fertility shrines); and (3) individual shrines, whose custodians include all adult males and whose congregations can range from one (the custodian himself) to a large membership. All problems can be divided into one of these diagnostic and therapeutic categories so that no matter what difficulty arises, there is an explicit format for a solution. Any ambiguities are sorted out by the diviner. But even so, one resorts to sacrifice or placation at the shrines only when problems become severe or when every known technical device has been unsuccessfully employed to correct them. So, religion is, in a sense, the dimension of everyday life that offers diagnosis and solution to severe problems, which, by definition, are those caused by imbalanced relationships.

There has been a strong Islamic presence among the Anufo, but although Arabic words dot their vocabulary and postures of Islamic etiquette, styles of dress, and artistic forms have influenced customs, Islam has not altered the Anufo tripartite problem-solving matrix. Rather, Islam here has adjusted to the traditional mode. Until quite recently, moreover, Islam has never really been a religious option: the three-tiered political system of Anufo nobles, Muslims, and commoners functioned as distinct caste-like social hierarchy groupings, such that neither commoners, slaves, nor lax nobles were allowed to convert to Islam.

In the past, the Muslims were a group of professional clerics who offered their services in making talismans, offering prayers for prosperity and success in battle, performing arcane magic, and offering secretarial skills to the nobles and commoners in exchange for prestige, high office, and the spoils of war. In the twentieth century, the growth of the more egalitarian Hausa Tijani Islam in northern Ghana and the subtle fostering of Islam by the colonial governments has caused class distinctions to blur. This has made Islam a convenient ladder for former slaves and commoners desiring to achieve positions of greater power and prestige, and it has created a legitimate alternative along with Christianity to traditional religion.

THE CASE OF THE ANUFO NONCONVERSION: PROBLEM SOLVING

In the 1960s a missionary named Al Krass inspired thousands of Anufo to convert to Christianity. By the time I arrived in Anufoland in the mid-1970s, most of these converts had either become Muslims or had reverted to their traditional beliefs. I couldn't help but ask: Why the dramatic change?

Certainly there had been an upset in the people's expectations. The Reverend Krass had established church structures, an agricultural program, health services, and a literacy program for the Evangelical Presbyterian Church of Ghana. He had improved the quality of life of the populace in a variety of small but important ways.

The people described the contact with Reverend Krass as *anyunu teke* [get your eyes opened]. This was their way of saying "here is an opportunity to move into the modern world". It was not, however, a spiritual "eye-opening", but a very secular and materialistic means of receiving the benefits of the "white man's world". When Krass left, all of these innovations and improvements seemed to disintegrate. The literacy instructors no longer received salaries, the evangelists weren't sent for further studies, and the village helpers did not receive bicycles and other perks. The buildings fell into disrepair and the programs stopped functioning. The converts felt abandoned. But this decline in missionary structures and services alone was not enough to explain the massive apostasy. Most importantly, how much of their conversion was a "religious" one—that is, how much did it touch the religious dimension of their everyday lives, particularly regarding Anufo religious problem solving—and how much of the conversion was cultural?

PROBLEM-SOLVING SURVEY

Later, while I was conducting anthropological fieldwork among these same Anufo, I came to see that the Christianity offered by the Reverend Krass and others bore little resemblance to the pragmatic brand of religious problem-solving mechanisms that the Anufo were used to. Nor did church structures and personnel address the kinds of problems dealt with by shrines. It occurred to me that one could "convert" to Christianity without having to change anything about one's traditional approach toward problem solving. Rather, Christianity offered a whole new range of options in addition to the former, not in place of them. It made sense, then, that when Western options no longer proved effective or viable, the converts shifted emphasis back to more traditional means, which they had never abandoned.

As a result of my studies in divination, I was able to devise a survey using fifty-eight standard Anufo problems (Kirby 1985, 1986) for which there were traditional solutions involving the placation of spiritual entities at shrines. I then asked 150 Muslim converts and 150 Christian converts what they do about these problems now that they have converted (see appendix).

The results proved very enlightening. All answers could be roughly grouped into three categories: (1) traditional solutions, (2) "syncretistic" solutions that were orthodox in appearance but traditional in aim, and (3) orthodox solutions (a West African orthodoxy). A majority of Muslims answered roughly one-third of the problems with orthodox solutions, one-third with syncretistic solutions, and one-third with traditional solutions. Not all of the problems were of the same weight, however. The preponderance of the more serious community-level problems were solved in an orthodox manner, while the less serious and more individualistic problems were solved in the syncretistic or traditional modes.

Almost all of the Christians solved fifty-four of the fifty-eight problems with purely traditional means. Four of the problems were solved syncretistically. But none of the problems were solved in a Christian orthodox manner. A minority of more school-educated Christians, however, did suggest orthodox solutions for problems that had a traditional Western ritual correlate, for example: what to do when building a new house, what to do when going on a journey, or what to do for good luck. However, these were often given only in addition to the traditional prerequisite activities for such situations.

In the light of these findings, one might ask: How do Anufo Christians express their faith? The fact that one could become Christian without ever confronting or redirecting one's religious problem-solving nexus indicates that such a conversion was never genuinely religious. Christianity was never presented as having its own special solution to any of traditional Anufo religious problems and thus was never perceived by them as religious. In fact, I was greeted with surprise by Anufo Christians and non-Christians alike when they found out that I had gone through the initiation rites of the diviner. It was not because initiation and divination were thought to be contradictory to my Christian religion, but because, as they said, "we did not know you were interested in our problems and the way we solve them" [i.e., "our religion"].

A REAPPRAISAL: FINDING AN AFRICAN IDENTITY

A significant change in the perspective of Catholic missionaries and the African Catholic churches has taken place since Independence and Vatican II. It is characterized by a limited dialogue and an ecumenical spirit toward other mission-founded churches, the independent churches, and Islam. But most importantly, traditional African religions have been gradually reevaluated. This reevaluation is being encouraged by a dual self-discovery: the Catholic Church is becoming aware of its identity as "World Church" and the African churches are evolving separate identities from a Roman church.

In this section, I examine the contemporary African missionary scene on a macro level to discern the nature of this dual evolution of identities, its theological roots, and its implications for mission work especially vis-à-vis traditional African rituals and beliefs.

In spite of the cultural imperialism of mission schools and the attempt to annihilate African culture and religion, we have seen that traditional religionists are actually increasing. While I was taking a public bus in 1975, after having introduced myself as *osofo* [priest] to some of the passengers, everyone began to say what church he or she attended. One middle-aged woman explained that she used to be "Presby" but now she goes to the "fetish" and feels much happier. Increasingly, the African cultural revolution is discovering its African roots. The new identity, while taking its past very seriously, is not solely a traditional or tribal one, but one that gels with the Western world without being a second-class imitation of it.

Since the church culture taught in mission schools did not penetrate African life but rather imparted a new and additional identity, the pastoral solutions offered by mission churches tended to relate to that identity, that is, to Western problems rather than to African ones. As these functions came to be identified with Christianity, it was assumed that Christianity was not supposed to deal with, indeed, was incapable of dealing with African problems and that any Christian who still had such problems really hadn't converted properly in the first place. Parallel institutions have therefore been maintained to meet the needs of a dual identity—one Western, the official one aligning itself with church culture, and one African, the unofficial one aligning itself with African traditional culture or what the missionaries called "paganism".

Today, according to one's African identity, an individual Christian or non-Christian might be required to enter into plural marriage; make sacrifices; pour libations to the ancestors; participate in rites of puberty and initiation; observe traditional laws regarding land use, taboos, and inheritance; and maintain certain shrines for one's own or one's family's good. On the other hand, an individual's new Christian identity may dictate that one attend Mass, have one's marriage blessed, receive the sacraments, and join charitable organizations. Except for the fact that prevailing marriage customs still stand in the way of sacramental marriage and therefore disqualify most Africans from full Christian church membership, the expectations of these two systems are not mutually exclusive. Rather, they are parallel.

The institutional churches' interpretation, however, still strongly favors the view that the two systems are mutually exclusive and that the African one is ignoble, sinful, and unenlightened, whereas the European one is the vehicle for light and nobility. Though this position is not so much vocalized nowadays, it is still embedded in the machinery of church organizational culture.

Institutions of Western culture are generically termed "white man" [5] by Ghanaians, which includes the borrowed structures *and* the elite corps of Africans who now run them. Ghanaians refer to the government, for example, as *aban* [literally: wall], which is a reference to the wall of the Cape Coast Castle, the seat of British power during the colonial era wars. Likewise the father of a newly trained catechist in northern Ghana joyously greeted me with the words "I'm so happy that my son has become a 'white man'". In such a situation it is quite understandable for generations of African Christians to simply remain silent about the things the "white man" wouldn't understand, thus ensuring the continuation of parallel systems.

GROWTH OF THE AFRICAN CHURCH: CONTINUITY AND CHANGE

Part of the reason Africa is now confidently striving for its own identity is that African clerics and prelates are sufficiently numerous to be able to manage their own church institutions. Although the Catholic Church has been late in responding to the need for indigenous clergy, it is now making considerable headway. From 1960 to 1975 the number of African priests grew from 1,661 to 3,650. During the late 1970s there was a startling increase and this trend continues today.

But in spite of their numerical growth, it is not the clergy, but the laity who are the real force behind the thrust for a new identity. In Ghana there are now almost 400 African priests, though these are still not nearly enough. The average diocese in Africa consists of about twenty parishes, each with one to three priests. But each of these parishes usually has around twenty village churches many miles apart from each other. The real ministry and evangelism exists on the village level and largely in the absence of the priest. Here are the praying communities, but they are eucharistic communities only once a month when a priest visits. The real ministry falls upon the catechists and other local ministers, associations of lay leaders, and women. The real pastor is therefore the catechist or untrained layman with whom he works. His locale is the local village as much as the church building, his consultors are the village elders as much as the parish council, and it is here that Catholic church culture defaults to local culture.

If the isolation of the laity is part of the problem, it may also be, as Adrian Hastings suggests, a part of the solution. But the solution offered by the laity may be quite different from the way the "official" Catholic Church describes itself. "The real pattern of worship, organization, and ministry already in operation in the villages owes remarkably little", Hastings says, "to the immediately preceding European experience; it has been moulded by the inherent exigencies of the local situation and is not markedly different from that existing either in Protestant mission-connected or in many of the independent Churches" (Hastings 1976:35).

Although seminaries are now bursting at the seams, the training offered does little to prepare young African priests for a ministry relevant in the parallel "unofficial" concerns of Catholic Church members. The majority of seminaries still teach little or no social anthropology, sociology, or missiology; they give only very

Western philosophical renderings of traditional African religions and are only recently adding courses in African theology that are very cautiously constructed to avoid any conflict arising from the still prevalent negative interpretation. African professors have been nurtured on Catholic Church culture in Rome. Courses in pastoral ministry therefore continue to stress sacramental administration in the Western style, and Western canon law is the final arbiter in all disputes. If there is to be a fuller cultural/ecclesial revolution in Africa, it would seem that its source is not going to be the clergy but the lay men and women who feel torn by the schizophrenia brought about by parallel systems of life and morality that seem to be fostered by the growing but very elite African clergy.

In fact, even the current "priest explosion" in Africa can in no way meet the needs of the growing Catholic population there. The priest to Christian ratio is continually weakening. And even if there were more priests, the local churches could not possibly give the financial support needed to maintain a priest in the Western institutional mold. Slowly the Catholic Church is facing up to the problem of a totally unviable system that needs reshaping according to the context of the local situation, society, and culture.

In any religious conversion there must be an enormous measure of continuity between the beliefs of the old and the new. Indeed, the new can be really grasped only in terms of old forms. And it might be said that to the extent that the old forms are ignored, repressed, or disallowed, one might question whether there ever really was a conversion in the first place. From the viewpoint of people who are undergoing conversion and people who are encouraging others to convert, however, the degree of rupture is emphasized more often than the continuity between the new religious beliefs and the old.

It is a truism that no group can conceivably change its deep religious beliefs and philosophy without noticeably changing its culture and that the degree of rupture is confirmed by visible cultural changes. But visible cultural changes, especially when the model comes from the outside, do not ensure a faith conversion. Cannot a group change aspects of its culture without changing its central religious beliefs or philosophy? Or is it not possible for a group to have two parallel philosophies and sets of religious belief, each relating to a different cultural persona?

Today the majority of Africa's 230 million Christians (half are Catholics) who were baptized in childhood and educated in Christian schools yearn for a return to their cultural roots and are fascinated by their traditional culture. A former generation would have never felt comfortable with giving such attention to traditional ways, for while they were unselfconsciously a part of these practices, they tried to repress them. The current generation no longer experiences the old life as a social and spiritual unity. However, many of the old problems and exigencies addressed by these systems still pertain. Although the problems are officially ignored by Christian structures, the people themselves are less rigid.

Youthful Christians are thus freer to revitalize old symbols and use them in new and creative ways. Over the past twenty years the Catholic Church has made great strides in adapting local songs and musical instruments, art and artifacts, to Christian worship. Liturgy has moved beyond the use of the drum and dance, from colorful vestments and the use of the vernacular, to more profound symbols and expressions of African belief. The independent churches have led the way, but traditional religion has provided the source for all these adaptations.

CONSEQUENCES FOR MISSIONARY CONGREGATIONS: BICULTURALISM AND DIALOGUE

The Anufo case offers us a new perspective on the history of African conversion and gives some clues about the future of religion on the African continent. If Africa has experienced a cultural conversion rather than a religious one, then we might ask how much has the Christian missionary mandate to preach the gospel really been accomplished there. And if this perspective is to be taken seriously, then missionary societies may, in the future, have to reorient themselves considerably. They may have to establish new identities, keeping before themselves and their church a vision of "World Church". It is quite probable that the extent to which they will be required to cross over cultural barriers, even in a shrinking world, will be much greater than ever before.

Cultural blind spots and biases obscure the most central myths of a culture from its own members—not just outsiders. These days when many missionary organizations are quite prepared to leave "cultural matters" to the African churches, the religious dimensions of traditional cultures may more profitably be understood and adapted jointly by the local church and by missionaries who are specially trained in crossing cultural barriers.

Plate 3–3. Ghanaian seminary students reviewing class materials in a garden at the Tamale Institute for Cross-Cultural Studies. A year at the institute augments their several years' training in philosophy and theology, preparing future Catholic priests for intercultural service and for applying their ministry to local cultural contexts.

If a new type of Catholic missionary is demanded for "World Church", whether clerical or lay, that person must be—or learn to be—bicultural. He or she will no longer be the one to "bring" the sophistication, power, and prestige of his or her own culture, nor of church culture, but he or she must be a person equipped to enter into the adopted culture to the point of being absolutely bicultural, taking on a different personality and identity. This means more than speaking and thinking in the indigenous language with all the nuances of a native speaker. That person must also come to experience life's problems arising out of this new orientation and bring to bear Christ's healing power on this experience.

Missionaries must be well trained for this cultural and religious learning—it does not simply happen by itself. How are they to be equipped for this new task? The present formation of Catholic missionaries and the African clergy, let alone the laity, is inadequate for these goals. Present structures stress the "clerical" aspects of formation rather than the cross-cultural and ministerial. It is still assumed that the ministerial formation policies of "mission-sending" churches can be applied univocally everywhere.

The bias of existing Catholic Church institutions in Africa must also be reckoned with. New missionaries and pastors quickly learn the unwritten rules of mission work once they are settled within a mission station, and so they focus mostly on building schools, clinics, churches, and establishing development projects. In the absence of any strong formation policies and programs, or "counterinstitutions", this unwritten agenda forms their attitudes and goals.

Finally, the bias against culture itself must be dealt with. Today, the dominant opinion of missionaries, and for that matter most Westerners, is that biculturalism is impossible, presumptuous, and unnecessary anyway. Where anthropology is taught in Catholic seminaries and formation houses, it is still most often "the handmaid of dogma, scripture, and Church history"—not their equal. Yet the coming of "World Church" will demand some fundamental changes, including supervised cross-cultural training in ministry-evangelism, for example. As the distinction between "mission-sending" and "mission-receiving" countries begins to blur, more centers where missionaries can be prepared to become language learners and bicultural candidates are likely to be established both in "mission-sending" and "mission-receiving" countries. Anthropologists, sociologists, and linguists will begin to take up a new role alongside theologians in helping to construct and guide "World Church".

ONE WHOLE "WORLD CHURCH"

Perhaps the most important consequence of "World Church" for African culture and conversion is the new mandate that each culturally distinct formulation of the gospel message has in forming a cumulative body of a fuller, more complete revelation—one that transforms the "mission-sending" church into a receptor of revelation. For whenever any culture encounters the gospel, if there is true interaction both the culture and the gospel change: the culture by being directed by a new message and new central symbols, and the gospel by being more fully articulated, thus allowing the whole Church to participate in a fuller version of the one revelation of the Holy Spirit.

The growing documentation of Christian prayers, proverbs, stories, and spiritual sayings reflecting a genuine African religious experience testifies to the existence of "World Church" and also enriches it. The prayers of Afua Kuma in Ghana (Kirby 1981:27–28), which glorify God using African historical imagery and the details of everyday experience, typify this rich store:

> He is the great Grass Hut, the Shed which shelters mice,
> the "Thump! Thump!" of the pestle, he beats down our hunger.
> Hard-wood hoe-handle, which brings us our food.
> *Onyankopon Amponyinam*: God the provider,
> who has medicine for hunger.
> *Oserekyi Sakyi*: the Elephant Hunter,
> whose family's cooking pots
> have no place for little mushrooms.
> Pencil of teachers
> which brings knowledge to the children!
> Spokesman of lawyers!
> Helper of police!
> Victorious Chief of soldiers!
> Food of prisoners!

Such modes of worship add to the recognition that current African Christianity has, in fact, two primary sources of inherited wisdom and continuity—Christian revelation and tradition on the one hand and African traditional religion, complete in its integral social context, on the other—living proof that "World Church" is alive and being continually enriched by the marriage.

APPENDIX

Selected Survey Questions with Commentary

7. What do you do when someone has sworn an oath?
   To swear an oath [*ta ndie*] is actually to defer the matter to the court of the ancestors, which means, of course, that all the persons involved must die and stand before the ancestors. For an oath to be undone the person who swore the oath must undergo a ritual of purification called *wulo no* [literally mouth-washing].
9. What do you do to protect yourself against witchcraft?
   Witchcraft is universally believed in and there are a great variety of antidotes and protections against it.
15. What do you do to make it rain?
   It is believed that normally rain should fall quite predictably, but when it doesn't it is because of some problem causing disharmony. In such cases rain medicine may be sought in addition to making attempts to find the cause.
20. What would you do to counteract poison?
   The Anufo believe that mystical and biological poisons are constantly being used in everyday life as a result of jealousy in particular and that they must be guarded against both mystically and biologically with antidotes.
27. What would you do in case of an animal bite?
   Bites of certain animals or of humans are thought to be especially dangerous and demand mystical remedies.

30. Would you use Muslim talismans?
    The Anufo have used Muslim magic, potions, and talismans for centuries, and it is a part of their general approach to problem solving.
33. What would you do about a child crying constantly in the night?
    Children are especially sensitive to disharmonies, and they express this by crying. Normally the cause will have to be divined and appropriate sacrifices made. Perhaps the child will have to have its name changed.
35. What would you do if you loved a girl?
    Young men often seek out mystical help to win the favor of a girl, especially if they are not distinguished by strength or are poor. Muslim talismans are a favorite.
40. What would you do if there were a sudden death in your household?
    Old age is the only death that is "natural"; all others are believed to be caused through poisoning mystically or biologically or through malevolent magic. Sudden death is always followed up by many divination sessions to determine the cause.
44. What would you do before naming your child?
    There are rites and procedures governing the task of determining the particular ancestor after whom the child should be named.
49. What would you do to ensure successful farming?
    Oftentimes farmers will seek out magical aids to ensure a good harvest, but the minimum is to make the annual sacrifices to the earth shrines and proper thanksgiving during the first fruits ceremonies.
53. What would you do in preparation for eloping with a girl?
    Many types of magical devices are popular to ensure a safe and successful elopement.

N.B. These questions were asked in conversational style by helpers whom I had trained. Normally each helper interviewed one person per day. Immediately following the interview my helper would report back to have the responses recorded.

NOTES

1. The term "mission-founded" churches is becoming widely accepted for the major Catholic and Protestant churches founded by missionaries. In this area almost any term has drawbacks and implies some sort of value judgments but this term seems to be far better than most.

2. The term "traditional religions" will here refer to tribal or indigenous religions in Africa as opposed to those imported through missionaries or by culture contact.

3. The concept of "World Church" was introduced by Catholic theologian Karl Rahner (1980:323–334) to indicate the present, post-Vatican II Catholic Church's understanding of its cultural identity. Rahner sees the Church as having progressed through three great epochs: an early period of Jewish Christianity; a period of the Mediterranean civilization, culture, and philosophy; and finally "World Church" in which the sphere of the Church's life is understood to be the entire world.

4. Tigare is a widespread religious association in Ghana and now in other parts of West Africa (e.g., the derived Tiga religious association in Nigeria). It is noted for its claims to control witchcraft. Originating in northern Ghana, it was incorporated and given structures and forms derived from mission churches by the Asante during the early colonial period. More generally, it is sometimes very difficult to distinguish between what is still a traditional belief and what is an indigenous church influenced greatly by traditional religion.

5. "White man" in common Ghanaian parlance refers to the police, the army, or any government official, or to the structures they work within and the duties they perform.

Plate 4–1. Zionist prophet blessing a sick child. Chikwawa district, Malawi, 1967.

4

Christ in African Folk Theology:
The *Nganga* Paradigm

Matthew Schoffeleers

> *L'ethnologie et la christologie sont-elles nécessairement exclusives?*
> — Richard Kearney (1985:44)

> All the separatist churches—and even the African sections of the mission churches—are syncretistic. ... All their Christian ideas are edited by the religious ideas they bring with them from their cultural upbringing.
> — Absalom Vilakazi et al. (1986:156)

INTRODUCTION

WE ARE REGULARLY TOLD BY MISSIOLOGISTS, social scientists, and African writers that Africans find it difficult to integrate Jesus Christ into their belief system, either because he is automatically associated with the West and the colonial past or because his very being is incompatible with indigenous religious conceptions.[1] This view seems implicitly confirmed by African Theology, which has remained relatively silent about this central symbol of the Christian faith.[2] It has even been authoritatively stated that in indigenous African cultures christological conceptions are nonexistent.[3]

All this has led some authors to conclude that African Theology experiences something in the nature of a christological crisis that urgently needs to be attended to (e.g., Setiloane 1979:64). Although several christological studies have appeared since (e.g., Udoh 1983; Christensen 1984; Kabasele et al. 1986), a feeling of crisis persists because those involved in christological research have been unable to reach even a modicum of consensus about a suitable African paradigm for Christ. Some prefer to cast him as Victor, others as Chief, yet others as Ancestor, without any party being able to establish a convincing claim (Shorter 1982; Kabasele et al. 1986). It has even been proposed to cast Christ as Guest, that is to say, as a stranger who is received with every possible honor, but who in turn is expected to conform to the customs of the house and submit himself to a process of enculturation. This "Guest Christology", as it has been dubbed by its creator (Udoh 1983), is a particularly graphic illustration of Christ's supposed strangeness to Africa.

The African christology problem that so many have struggled with is certainly worth probing. One question to be asked beforehand, though, is whether the intellectual elite stand isolated in this respect or whether this problem is shared by the population at large. This question suggests itself for the simple reason that it can easily be shown that—at the level of folk theology—at least one christological paradigm exists that is used over large areas of sub-Saharan Africa. That paradigm is the medicine person, known in many Bantu languages by the noun *nganga* or one of its cognates.[4]

If the *nganga* paradigm is valid, one must conclude that those who maintain that Africans have difficulty integrating Christ into their belief system may somehow be mistaken. On the other hand, the same people may be right if they refer to the Christ of the established churches, for it is imaginable that quite a few African Christians find it difficult to identify with a Westernized image of the Savior. The contradiction may therefore be solved if it is recognized that we are dealing with both Westernized and Africanized versions of the biblical Christ and if it is further recognized that the intellectuals are rebelling against the Westernized version.

Now, supposing the *nganga* paradigm is as widely used as claimed to be, then the question becomes why has it not been noticed, acknowledged, and utilized by African theologians, apart from one or two (Buana Kibongi 1969; Setiloane 1979) who have never been taken seriously by their colleagues on this particular point? G. M. Setiloane himself makes this clear when he mentions in his article "Where Are We in African Theology?" (1979) that a group of European theologians were shocked and scandalized when he addressed them on the subject of Christ the Medicineman. R. Buana Kibongi did not fare much better: although his article on Christ as *nganga* was published some twenty years ago in one of the most influential overviews of African Theology, it is virtually never quoted.

No doubt one of the reasons for this avoidance behavior vis-à-vis the *nganga* paradigm is that the paradigm is felt to be an intrinsic part of indigenous African religion and therefore—in the eyes of the official church—tainted too much with syncretistic connotations. Another reason is that quite a few Christian ministers, African as well as European, consider the *nganga* a rival who competes with them for the same clientele.[5] Those holding either or both of these opinions must of necessity consider it improper to construct a christology from that paradigm.

As revealing as this avoidance behavior may be to those interested in ecclesiastical policies, in this chapter I will discuss it only as a sideline and deal more directly with the question of why and how Christ is conceived of as a *nganga*: What parallels and contrasts do people perceive between one and the other, and in what sense are Christ and the *nganga* considered to be transformations of each other?

To answer these questions I will begin by briefly describing what the *nganga* role consists of and how it has been interpreted in anthropological literature. Following this I will provide evidence from different parts of Africa to show that not only Christ, but also the Christian pastor, is habitually regarded as an alternative *nganga.* I will also pay explicit attention to the reverse side of this process and show how the *nganga* role is being Christianized and occasionally even Christified.[6] By so doing, I hope to show some of the contrasting ideas and ideals that account for the dynamics of African folk christology.

Plate 4–2. Male diviner tending his medicine gourds. Nsanje district, Malawi, 1967.

THE *NGANGA* ROLE

Individuals referred to as *nganga* appear to engage in a wide range of activities, including the manufacturing of charms, the preparation and administration of herbal medicines, divination/diagnosis, ritual healing, witch detection, and witch-craft eradication. To these one may add a number of other activities not directly connected with health and disease: rainmaking and providing magical support for agriculture, hunting, fishing, and trading. The list could be extended, but such additions would only confirm the key note, which is that the activities of the *nganga* are centrally concerned with the promotion of good fortune and the counteraction of misfortune. What Victor Turner notes for the Ndembu of Zambia seems to hold for African societies in general: illness is conceived of as a kind of misfortune similar to bad luck at hunting, reproductive disorders, physical accidents, and the loss of property (Turner 1967 [1959]:300).

The *nganga* role is many sided, combining functions that in modern societies are fulfilled by specialists of very different kinds. Michael Gelfand, himself a medical practitioner and a lifelong student of numerous kinds of *nganga* in present-day Zimbabwe, describes these individuals as the kingpins of African communities, whose scope of activity embraces more or less everything affecting an individual or his family:

> European society has no one quite like *nganga*, an individual to whom people can turn in every kind of difficulty. He is a doctor in sickness, a priest in religious matters, a lawyer in legal issues, a policeman in the detection and prevention of crime, a possessor of magical preparations which can increase crops and instill special skills and talents into his clients. He fills a great need in society, his presence gives assurance to the whole community. (Gelfand 1964:55)

When categorizing the various kinds of *nganga,* most authors seem to favor a dichotomous typology distinguishing between herbalists and another role variously rendered as witchdoctor, diviner, or magician (Daneel 1971:143; Frankenberg and Leeson 1976:239; Janzen 1978:194; Maclean 1971:75).

The problem with these and similar typologies is that it proves impossible to demarcate the categories of *nganga* with any degree of precision, since they continue to overlap. In view of this it might be simpler and at the same time analytically more useful to distinguish between activities rather than persons. This requires a minimal division into three types of activity, namely: diagnostic, therapeutic, and prophylactic. The last category, however, would have to include not only activities to ward off sickness and misfortune before they have occurred, but also activities designed to prevent a recurrence of such events. Relevant examples of this kind of activity are witch-hunts and witchcraft eradication activities following a real or perceived increase of illness and misfortune in a community. The term *nganga* thus stands for an essentially fragmented role with a great many subdivisions, distributed over a large number of persons. On account of this, it is as polyvalent, open, and adaptive as African conceptions of sickness and healing (Neckebrouck 1983:226, 336, 359). It is also a role that, in contrast to some others in "traditional" societies, derives its authority from personal achievement rather than hereditary considerations. The successful *nganga* has to be alert and innovative and has to have a keen insight into what goes on in and around the community.[7]

When he or she is a diviner, a *nganga* is called upon to diagnose the nature and causes of any form of misfortune. It has been widely observed in indigenous African cultures that the more serious cases of misfortune tend to be ascribed to a variety of mystical causes, such as the evil wishes of witches and sorcerers, the anger of spirits affronted by neglect of themselves or of the sufferer's obligations toward kin, breaches of taboo and omission of ritual, and rightful curses by appropriate persons (Gluckman 1965:xxiii; Evans-Pritchard 1937:479; Turner 1967 [1959]:300; Maclean 1971:27; Janzen 1978:8).[8]

Plate 4–3. Consulting a female spirit medium. Nsanje district, Malawi, 1967.

What these causes have in common is that in one way or other they all refer to the system of values held by members of these societies and to violations of these values, either on the part of patients or someone close to them. The point therefore is that what appears on the surface as a system of *mystical* causation is really a system of *social* causation. The truth of this observation is brought out by a number of firsthand accounts of the diagnosis of disease (Turner 1967 [1959], 1975 [1962]; Janzen 1978:75–128) which show that diviners not only identify some mystical agent as the immediate cause of the affliction, but also relate that agent to specific disturbances in the patient's social environment. Divination, as Turner rightly observes, thus becomes a kind of social analysis (Turner 1975 [1962]:244), and the patient's treatment requires that tensions and aggressions in the group's system of relations be brought to light and exposed to ritual treatment.[9]

To be effective then, the *nganga* as diviner must have an acute perception of human frailties and failures. What is it that accounts for this perceptivity? Turner, for one, suggests that an influential majority of diviners must have paranoid tendencies:

> Many diviners are marginal men, through physiological abnormality, psychological aberrancy or social-structural inferiority or outsiderhood. It may be held that these disqualifications qualify the diviner to respond sensitively to stresses and strains in social relationships. Marginals and outsiders, since they possess little pragmatic power or influence, may be thought to be more objective than those involved in the struggle for goods and prizes. ... Diviners as a class may be said to exact a subtle revenge on a society which has rejected or belittled them as

individuals. They know that even the most powerful or fortunate are vulnerable to death, disease and misfortune, that they fear rivals and envy the more successful. In such crises diviners provide for the solid citizens a coherent if illusionary system which translates into cultural terms the mental structures of paranoia. Divinatory seances into the secret causes of outstanding misfortune provide a kind of resolution of the social relationships disturbed or broken by the crisis, but resolution is achieved only at the cost of a running total of hate, and sometimes of the actual ostracism or physical punishment of the secret plotter, "the witch". The diviner has now reduced the successful and orthodox villager to his own marginal position. The "reality" he professes to reveal is not communitas, but a secret war of all on all. (Turner 1975 [1962]:24–25)

I have quoted Turner at length because I consider this particular passage one of the most crucial in the entire literature on African diviners. Although one does occasionally come across references to the neurotic disposition of diviners (Sundkler 1961:115; Devisch 1975b:174–175; MacGaffey 1983:214, 255), nowhere is this disposition so insightfully described and accounted for: the diviner is someone who himself has suffered and who therefore understands suffering. At the same time, however, the diviner remains a human being, subject to feelings of greed and revenge.

The same passage is crucial also for the stark contrast it establishes with the healing activities of the *nganga*. If divination lays bare tensions, hostilities, and animosities, healing rituals reveal a different sort of human relationship, marked not by division, but by communitas.

I have frequently written about communitas, meaning by this relationships which are undifferentiated, egalitarian, direct, extant, non-rational, existential, "I-Thou" (in Ludwig Feuerbach's and Martin Buber's sense), between definite and determinate human identities. The empirical base of this concept was to some extent my experience of friendship during the war as a noncombatant private soldier in a British bomb-disposal unit. But it was mainly village life in Africa which convinced me that spontaneous, immediate, concrete relationships between individuals not only were personally rewarding but also had theoretical relevance. ...

Communitas is a nonstructured relationship, or, better, a spontaneously structured relationship which often develops among liminaries, individuals in passage between social statuses and cultural states that have been cognitively defined, logically articulated, and endowed with jural rights and obligations. Communitas, too, may provide the foundation for African explanatory models. Such models would not represent the cosmos as hierarchically arrayed, but as possessing a common substratum beyond all categories of manifestation, transcending divisible time and space, beyond words, where persons, objects and relationships are endlessly transformed into one another. ... The social experience underlying this model ... is an experience of communitas, the corporate identity between unique identities, the loss of the sense of number. (Turner 1975 [1962]:21–22)

Most kinds of *nganga* undergo complex initiation rituals. In two papers, which deal with such rituals among the Yaka of Zaïre, Renaat Devisch has shown how initiations contribute to a personality change and how they help legitimize the diviner's activities (Devisch 1975a, 1975b).

The unquestionable merit of Turner and Devisch is that they have developed a different line of analysis—different, that is, from the functionalist tradition summarized by Max Gluckman (1965: ch. IV) and the intellectualist position for which Robin Horton (1967) has become the principal spokesman. The difference is that Turner and Devisch have shown that the *nganga* is not only a social analyst, but also a creator of meaning and a potential prophet. They thereby confirm Peter Rigby's study of kinds of *nganga* among the Ganda which shows that a *nganga* may alternate between the role of prophet and diviner according to the demands of the situation (Rigby 1975).

A final characteristic of the *nganga*, or rather of a community's perception of the *nganga*, that needs to be mentioned is his ambiguity. E. E. Evans-Pritchard, for instance, notes as a general belief among the Zande that only diviners who themselves are witches are able to detect witches, and similar beliefs have been noticed among a range of other cultures (e.g., Crawford 1967:59; Haule 1969:44; Buxton 1973:276; Fry 1976:27; van Binsbergen 1979:210–211). Sometimes the diviners themselves seem to stimulate this belief, as among the Ndembu, where a category of doctors specializing in witch detection collect medicines from the interior of graves and on occasion even brandish human thighbones while dancing (Turner 1967 [1959]:137). Yet the matter remains important, for the Christian ritual healing, discussed in the next section, can be interpreted as a concerted effort to overcome the ambiguity of the *nganga*.

CHRIST AS *NGANGA*

In the catechesis and liturgy of African churches, Christ is often referred to as the one true *nganga* because this is an image that the audience intuitively understands and at the same time is seen as rooted in scripture. One of several testimonies notes:

> Among the Luo people in Mukoma diocese the medicine man has great power and influence. In the local catechesis and local language explaining Jesus Christ's work as "savior" is very difficult; so he becomes the Chief Medicine Man, who can cure all the sicknesses and problems of the people. Portraying Jesus as the supreme healer speaks to the Africans' cultural traditions. (Healey 1981:173)

One finds the same idea expressed in church hymns (cf. Ross 1969) such as the following one, which comes from a pentecostalist church in southern Malawi:

Yesu sing'anga;	Jesus, the medicine man;
Halleluya, bwerani!	Hallelujah, come!
Yesu sing'anga	Jesus, the medicine man
Amachiza matenda.	Cures diseases.
Yesu sing'anga	Jesus, the medicine man
Amachotsa ziwanda	Drives out evil spirits
Halleluya, bwerani!	Hallelujah, come!

(Schoffeleers 1985a:210)

In Zambia, members of the Mutumwa or Apostles' churches consider Christ "the true *shinganga* or healer whose work they continue" (Dillon-Malone 1983:207), a theme one encounters time and again among healing churches in the rest of Africa.

However, it is not correct to say that Christ is invariably compared with the *nganga* from the viewpoint of healing, since other aspects are drawn in as well.

Thus James Fernandez, after having noted that in the Bwiti church of Gabon Jesus is often referred to as *nganga*, makes the important remark that Jesus is called thus not only for his powers of healing, but also for his clairvoyance and his capacity to intermediate between the supernatural world and humans. Jesus is therefore often referred to by Bwiti adepts as *Eyen Zame* [He who sees God] (Fernandez 1982:210).

Again, Buana Kibongi, a Protestant theologian from the Congo Republic, notes that the *nganga* is to be considered a prefiguration of Christ, not only because of the healing powers of the *nganga*, but also because of his contact with the supernatural, which allows him to translate the divine into human terms. Christ, like the *nganga,* reveals God to humanity, the difference being that Christ does so much more adequately than the *nganga* (Buana Kibongi 1969:52–53). Note that this dual view of Christ as healer and visionary is mirrored in the anthropological literature reviewed in the previous section, where Turner, Devisch, and Rigby were introduced in connection with the prophetic or visionary role of the *nganga*.

THE PASTOR AS *NGANGA*

One frequently also comes across implicit as well as explicit equations of the Christian minister with the *nganga*. Thus in his classic on Zulu independent churches, Bengt Sundkler makes the insightful remark that the basic pattern from which Zulu Zionism is copied is that of the diviners and witchfinders rather than that of the historic Christian church (Sundkler 1961:242). Parallels between the two categories show up in many forms, from a common concern with healing and identical vocational experiences (Sundkler 1961:109–117, 350–352) to similarities in external appearance and personality structure; according to Sundkler, the ideal prophet should be thin, nervous, and high strung just as the diviner must be (1961:115). Sundkler is not the only one to perceive these parallels; they are also frequently commented on by the public, whether non-Christian or Christian (Sundkler 1961:109, 246). Much the same seems to be true of healing prophets elsewhere: they are commonly seen by outsiders and even by themselves as alternative kinds of *nganga* (Daneel 1971:104; Dillon-Malone 1983:211; Bucher 1980:173). Even the former archbishop of Lusaka, Emmanuel Milingo, who became famous as a ritual healer in the 1970s (Ter Haar 1991), was widely referred to as a *nganga*, although he himself would deny this (Milingo 1984:5).

The theologian Buana Kibongi, cited earlier, also states that in the Congo Republic the term *nganga* is applied not only to healing priests and prophets, but to other Christian pastors as well, including those who do not engage in healing:

> For good or ill, Christianity has not always escaped the heritage of *nganga*. The Christian missionary (minister, priest or Salvation Army officer) drew part of his authority, without knowing it, from the psychological state which *nganga* had created. The missionary was called *Nganga Nzambi* [God's priest] as distinct from the *Nganga mukisi* [the fetish priest]. It goes without saying that the missionary benefited from this respect, which was formerly due to the *Nganga mukisi*. Not only the *Nganga Nzambi* was respected, but because of the colour of his skin, his technique and his science, he was feared far too much. *Nganga Nzambi* was considered infinitely superior to the *Nganga mukisi*. ...

The Congolese priest or minister is also called *Nganga Nzambi*. He profits from the situation created by *nganga* and the missionary. *Nganga* has not only assured to some extent the social status of church workers; he has also left them the legacy of religious and moral conceptual tools. ... *Nganga*'s work partly enabled the Bible to be translated into Congolese languages. The Christian preacher consciously or unconsciously uses part of the vocabulary left by *Nganga*. This is where Congolese priesthood confronts Biblical revelation. (Buana Kibongi 1969:52–53)[10]

It must be noted, though, that Milingo and virtually all Christian ministers engaged in ritual healing object to the term *nganga* being applied to them. Thus Bishop Mutendi of the Zion Christian Church in Zimbabwe was of the opinion that the healing power of the *nganga* was derived from the ancestors, while that of the prophetic leader was received directly from Christ (I.A.M.S. 1985:76). Archbishop Milingo observed that one of the chief differences between himself and the various kinds of *nganga* was that the latter charged "a lot of money", something he himself absolutely refused to do (Milingo 1984:5). More statements of this nature by priests and prophets active in the healing ministry could be cited, but these are sufficient to make the point that most see themselves as radically different from the *nganga*. This is sometimes taken to disprove the supposed influence of the *nganga* paradigm. However, the opposite is true if one distinguishes between positive and negative identification.

Positive identification occurs when one approves of someone or something and especially when one tries to be like the other or acquire the thing approved of. Negative identification, on the other hand, occurs when one disapproves of someone or something and especially when one tries to be different from the person or thing disapproved of. Though these are opposite reactions, they are caused and shaped by the same source, and it cannot be maintained that positive identification is by itself a more powerful factor in shaping human behavior than negative identification. Thus Mutendi and Milingo, precisely because they keep asserting that the *nganga* is their negative point of reference, in fact affirm that the *nganga* functions as their model and paradigm. The interesting point, however, is that while Milingo denies that he is a *nganga*, others have no doubt that he is one, "perhaps more powerful and certainly cheaper than the rest" (Milingo 1984:5). The same goes, as we have seen, for the Zionist prophets, who are also seen by outsiders as resembling the *nganga* (Sundkler 1961:242; Daneel 1971:104; Bucher 1980:173; Dillon-Malone 1983:211).

One explanation of these contrasting and even contradictory attitudes is that the healing ministry of the Christian churches can be fundamentally understood as a transformation of the *nganga* role. It *is* that role because it addresses the same human problems; and at the same time it is *not* that role because it addresses those problems in a different way and by different means. Anthropologist Wyatt MacGaffey has perceived this transformation better than most and has written extensively about the Kimbanguist movement in Zaïre and its attitude toward indigenous medicine. After having summarized the similarities between the ritual practices of the healing prophet and the *nganga*, he goes on to comment on some of the differences: the use of plain water instead of medicated concoctions, the use of white ritual clothing and no body paint, and the insistence on not using any charms or equipment except his staff and the flag of the church. MacGaffey concludes his description:

> In prophetic practice whiteness is a powerful moral and philosophical statement of purity, clarity, transparency and sincerity; it symbolizes the prophet's commitment to openness and publicity, as opposed to the murky secretiveness of self-serving magic. As one prophet said, "The Holy Spirit in a man is like water in a glass, hiding nothing". (MacGaffey 1983:167)

This amounts to saying that the prophet tries to avoid the ambiguity we found to be characteristic of people's attitudes toward the *nganga*, and it is this avoidance policy that accounts for these complex transformations.

THE *NGANGA* AS PASTOR

Despite the disapproving attitude or even the active opposition on the part of some churches, many kinds of *nganga* nowadays are practicing Christians (Setiloane n.d.; Appiah-Kubi 1981; de Rosny 1986), and even some kinds of non-Christian *nganga* have occasionally borrowed ideas, symbols, and rituals from Christianity. According to J. R. Crawford, for example, whose research in Rhodesia (now Zimbabwe) covers the period 1956 to 1962,

> there has arisen a class of diviner who has adopted the method of divination of the prophets of the Pentecostal Churches [i.e., the prophetic healing churches], from whom, however, they may be distinguished, whether because they call themselves *nganga* (Shona), or *inyanga* (Ndebele) or because they charge fees for their services. (Crawford 1967:204)

A. P. Wendroff, who studied divinership in northeastern Malawi in the 1970s, notes the existence of a similar phenomenon, which he traces back to the proclamation of the Witchcraft Act of 1911. One of the effects of the Act was that, instead of continuing to make use of the poison ordeal or some other traditional technique, these diviners began to rely on guidance by ancestral spirits or the Supreme Being. In line with this, the ritual accompanying a consultation now involved the singing of hymns taken directly from the Christian liturgy (Wendroff 1983:256 ff.). It is clear also that this phenomenon is not confined to northeastern Malawi, since it has been observed in other parts of the country (Kankwatira 1975; Chakanza 1985:242).

Much of this borrowing apparently escaped the attention of the missionary churches, which explains why a Nigerian theologian recently expressed surprise at coming across practitioners in the Cross River State of eastern Nigeria who prayed "in Jesus' name" at the beginning of their sessions and even included readings from the Bible (Etuk 1984:83–85). The theologian in question is of the opinion that the most plausible explanation of "this new trend"—as he mistakenly calls it—may be that these diviners hope to attract churchgoers by making it appear that their trade is sanctioned by the Bible (Etuk 1984:87). As far as Zimbabwe is concerned, Crawford ascribes the same phenomenon to the competition between the various kinds of *nganga* and the prophets of the healing churches, who in parts of the country were already involved in nearly half of all divinations (Crawford 1967:221).

Finally, Wendroff, as stated earlier, regards it primarily as an adaptive development bringing traditional divinatory practices in line with the real or supposed requirements of colonial antiwitchcraft legislation. While it is obvious that these and other practical considerations have played a role, it is equally obvious that the Christianized *nganga* represents a specific form of mediation between Christian and indigenous ritual healing.[11]

THE *NGANGA* AS CHRIST

Although somewhere there may have been a living *nganga* who proclaimed himself to be Jesus Christ, I have not yet come across any explicit references to such a person in the available literature. What we do know of is a number of churches in which a mythical *nganga* is explicitly presented as the Christ or as an alternative Christ. At present we know of three such instances, namely, the Khambageu among the Sonjo of Tanzania, as described by Robert F. Gray (1963; 1965); the Mbona of Malawi, as described by W. H. J. Rangeley (1953) and me (Schoffeleers 1975, 1980, 1992); and the Bwiti of Gabon, as described by René Bureau (1985) and James Fernandez (1964; 1982), among others.

Although Gray's account of Khambageu contains interesting parallels with the Gospel narratives, I will leave it aside, since it is not altogether clear from his text whether it was he alone who noticed these parallels or whether they were perceived by the population as well. That objection cannot be made against Mbona and Bwiti, in whose studies there is no doubt that it is the public that notes the parallels between the local deity and Christ. Another reason for focusing on these two examples is that they have been extensively researched and that, with regard to the person of Christ, they appear to be mutually explicative. To demonstrate this, I will begin by highlighting a puzzle in one of Fernandez's publications on Bwiti.

Every week, we are told, Bwiti adepts engage in a night-long dance in which the mysteries of birth and death are celebrated. On practically all these occasions there is a central figure and leading dancer, called *nganga*, whom the participants identify with Christ, and who engages in a number of dramatizations, such as leading a witch-hunt (Fernandez 1964:288). This image of a *nganga* Christ cleansing the community of witches seems straightforward enough against the background of Christian-inspired witch-finding movements such as those of Tomo Nyirenda in what is now Zambia (Fields 1985). But this picture changes when we are told about a different ritual enacted at Eastertime, when

> several of the cult chapters put on an exciting chase and capture of the Saviour before the Crucifixion. Jesus is pictured like "Everyman", as trembling at the knowledge of His coming death. Thus, in fear and uncertainty about his compact with God, He takes off to flee through the village of the cult chapel. Other Banzie [adepts] take up the hue and cry. This chase goes on for nearly an hour, with the Saviour alternately hiding, then breaking out and fleeing again. In part, this interpretation of the time of fear and uncertainty before the Crucifixion expresses the Banzie tendency to humanize the Saviour and to have Him express every man's feeling. But anyone familiar with aboriginal Fang religion will immediately note the similarity between this chase and the chase that used to characterize the anti-witchcraft society ceremonies. (Fernandez 1964:287)

The puzzle, then, consists in the fact that these two rituals seem to present us with contradictory images of Christ. In the one case he makes his appearance as a witch-hunter and in the other as the innocent victim of a witch-hunt. This raises several questions: If the second representation implies a condemnation of witch-hunts (which is, one would think, the obvious inference to be drawn), how is it that the first representation casts him as being engaged in precisely that activity? Furthermore, if that question is legitimate, how does Bwiti solve the contradiction it raises? Since Fernandez does not provide us with any clues on this point—indeed, he seems unaware of the contradiction—the reader is left to his own devices. An obvious way to find an answer is to search for parallels elsewhere, and for this reason I now turn to the Malawian religious movement, whose titular deity, Mbona by name, is freely referred to by the congregation as their "Black Jesus" (Schoffeleers 1975).

Mbona is said to have been a *nganga* who was particularly gifted in rainmaking and who on that account enjoyed considerable repute among the population.[12] This reputation, so the stories tell us, led to a serious conflict between him and the local ruler, who, fearing for his position, ordered Mbona put to death on the accusation of witchcraft. However, after a long and tiring chase, when the chief's men caught up with Mbona and tried to stab him, they were unable to do so, for as soon as their knives and spears touched his body, they became limp and useless. In the end, Mbona himself had to tell them that if they wanted to kill him, they could do so only with a blade of grass or some other vegetal matter. Some versions add that the killing could be performed only by a child or that he had to be cut on the head "at the spot where a baby's fontanella is". This proved successful and Mbona was disposed of, but not for long, for soon after his death he manifested himself as a powerful deity and through the mouth of a medium made it known to the paramount that a temple had to be built and offerings made to him. The paramount had no choice but to obey, and thus it was that the movement came into being.

There is a similarity between this story and the Easter ritual of the Bwiti in that in both cases the protagonist is portrayed as the innocent victim of a witch-hunt. But the Mbona myth tells us something more: the victim is not just any individual, but a *nganga*. Supposing for a moment that this also applies to Bwiti, we are then in a position to contrast the two representations of Christ that we have note—the slaying *nganga* and the slain *nganga*. Now, the first suggestion is that these two representations refer to the two ways by which human communities try to eradicate witchcraft.

One method involves the elimination of all proximate causes of witchcraft, that is to say, the actual witches, by smelling them out and rendering them harmless. The other involves the elimination of all remote causes of witchcraft, in other words, everything in the social fabric that makes for greed, jealousy, lust for power, and hostility. This elimination of all the root causes of witchcraft would require a total transformation of society, and it is such a transformation, it appears, that the image of the slain *nganga* refers to. To clarify this point let us return to the Mbona story.

Mbona, it will be recalled, could not be killed until he himself taught his assassins how to do it. This is tantamount to saying that he was the master of his own fate, since it was he who finally allowed it to run its course. Not only that, but by making knives and spears shapeless and useless he renders all forms of violence powerless, and the salvific event of his death is brought about by symbols of peace and meekness in the form of a child handling vegetal matter. The outcome, according to the myth, is a new form of religious experience and expression representing a new social order in which the powerful (represented by the paramount) submit to and cooperate with the powerless (represented by Mbona and his medium). It is a social order in which witchcraft no longer exists and in which the role of the *nganga* is superfluous. In sum, it seems to be this chain of logic that finds its graphical expression in the *nganga* offering himself to be slain. I would hesitate to apply this interpretation to Bwiti, which belongs to a different culture, were it not that one of its students (Bureau 1985) has independently arrived at a similar analysis.[13]

What relation does this interpretation have to the *nganga* role in general? The second suggestion is that the images of the slaying *nganga* and the slain *nganga* are the ultimate expression of what Turner has called divination and revelation (1975), the two activities of the *nganga* that are inextricably linked with each other. Divination, as we have seen, refers to the *nganga* as the person who lays bare the sordid facts of life and whose task it is to neutralize the immediate causes of evil and misfortune. Revelation on the other hand refers to the *nganga* as a person who is able, by means of a ritual performance, to evoke a vision of society in its ideal state. Turner's merit is that he draws the attention of the anthropological world to this latter aspect, which is as essential as the first and without which it would be difficult to understand why the *nganga* may at times turn into a prophet (Rigby 1975).

CONCLUSIONS

Let me summarize my findings point by point:

1. In large parts of Black Africa the medicine person [*nganga*] provides a framework within which to conceptualize the person of Christ and the role of the Christian minister. Christ and the Christian minister in turn provide a framework within which to reconceptualize the *nganga*.[14]

2. The *nganga* is a folk paradigm, not a paradigm consciously constructed by professional theologians for the purpose of "indigenizing" the person of Christ. Though it is possible that the paradigms proposed by the professional theologians (such as Christ the Victor, Chief, Ancestor, and so on) may also be rooted in folk theology, so far the evidence to support such a claim is rather thin.[15]

3. Precisely because the *nganga* paradigm inherently forms part of folk theology, it offers privileged access to African conceptions not only of Christ and the Christian ministry, but also of sin and redemption. This is so because the *nganga* is the person who indicates which moral trespasses have caused his clients' suffering and what the clients must do to free themselves of that suffering. Like the biblical Christ, the *nganga* may thereby address proximate causes as well as remote causes, as illustrated by the dual image of the slaying *nganga* and the slain *nganga*.

4. We can now return to the question posed at the beginning of this chapter: Why has this *nganga* paradigm, which is so tangibly and extensively present in folk theology, not been exploited by the professional theologians? One of the reasons, I suggested, may be a conscious or unconscious fear of introducing syncretistic notions and practices. More specifically, the official adoption of the *nganga* paradigm would entail the established churches recognizing the objective existence of witchcraft and evil spirits and introducing pastoral techniques capable of dealing with these problems. They could not do this without giving their blessing to a theological system that would be fundamentally different from that of their mother churches, and that would put church unity under severe pressure. Such a blessing would also encourage the emergence of charismatic healers such as Milingo, who in their own way pose a threat to church unity and to the authority of the mother churches.

I must therefore conclude that the *nganga* paradigm will remain officially inadmissible as long as the established churches in Africa want to retain their links with their mother churches. These churches thus harbor two very different christologies, which stand in a dialectical relation to each other. Having established that African folk christology can be fruitfully studied in terms of the *nganga* role, our next task should be to study African folk christology in terms of missionary christology. It is not enough to state that the missionary Christ is alien to Africa: one must also establish in structural terms precisely why he is alien.[16]

NOTES

1. On this point, see Udoh (1983:passim) and Neckebrouck (1983:306-307), in which a number of relevant sources are cited; also Messi Metogo (1986), who discusses the person of Christ in Mongo Beti's novels.

2. The phrase "African Theology" refers to a school in Christian professional theology that sees African "traditional religion" as a foreshadowing of Christianity and as a source of paradigms for central Christian notions. African Theology is generally distinguished from Black Theology, whose frame of reference is not indigenous culture but existing forms of political oppression. For a discussion of these two traditions and the tensions between them, see Cone 1979.

3. Mbiti 1972. Much the same view is expressed by C. Kolié, who maintains that African peasants call Jesus only by biblical names, since they cannot or will not make use of African titles. The same author is of the opinion that African theologians are actually trying to introduce christological paradigms, which are unknown to the population at large (Kolié 1986:188).

4. A quick glance over my notes shows *nganga* or some cognate as occurring among peoples in South Africa, Mozambique, Zimbabwe, Zambia, Malawi, Tanzania, Uganda, Zaïre, Gabon, and Guinea Bissau. For a comprehensive overview of its occurrence in Bantu languages, see Guthrie 1970:209.

5. For example, Etherington quotes a missionary document that describes "witchdoctors" in Southeast Africa as "a competing priesthood composed of a few of the most crafty among the people who pretended to hold communion with the spirits" (Etherington 1978:209). Consider also the following statement by Robert Moffat, which seems quite typical of the classic missionary attitude: "Sorcerers and rain-makers, for both offices are generally assumed by one individual, are the principal [evil (?)] with which he [the missionary] has to contend in Southern Africa. They are ... our inveterate enemies and uniformly oppose the

introduction of Christianity among their countrymen to the utmost of their power. ... They constitute the very pillars of Satan's kingdom in all places where such impostors are found" (quoted in Setiloane 1976:108).

6. It is important to note that in African folk theology the person of Christ and the person of the Christian minister are sometimes almost indistinguishable. This has occasionally led observers to conclude that prominent healing prophets do in fact usurp the central position of Christ. Most missiologists, however, nowadays agree that it is more consistent with reality to understand the function of such prophets as "iconic", meaning that they "mirror Christ" or that they function "as windows through which Christ is seen by his followers" (I.A.M.S. 1985:77). This leads us to the conclusion, fully supported by this chapter: In Africa one cannot engage in meaningful christological research outside the context of both Christian and pre-Christian forms of ministry. Incidentally, this discussion is not confined to Africa, but also is found in the African Diaspora. Among the black population of Surinam, a similar discussion is taking place about the *bonoeman* [diviner/healer] as a christological paradigm (Jones 1985).

7. Melland (1923 [1967]:20) speaks of the people who fill the *nganga* role among the Kaonde as "encyclopedias of knowledge, who know the local 'Who's Who' by heart and who are by practice skilled in reading men's hearts".

8. The rule of mystical causation usually does not hold for minor or common ailments (Evans-Pritchard 1937:488; Horton 1967:60). Gillies, however, cautions that even in the case of more serious diseases, anthropologists have tended to exaggerate the extent to which those involved resort to mystical explanations (Gillies 1976).

9. Cf. Janzen (1978:9): "A feature of therapy management in Kongo society is the collective orientation of medicine. The whole diagnostic apparatus is sensitive to the social causes of physiological affliction". For a summarizing discussion of the technical and processual aspects of divination, see Gluckman (1965:229-235).

10. Consider the following text also: "Not only the missionary, but the Catholic priest in general—white or not—is perceived as '*l'homme du sacré*' [man of the sacred], intermediate between God and men. He is being 'set apart', which is accentuated by his perpetual celibacy. In defining his position, African people just use the categories which apply to men, who are set apart in their own society [diviners, healers, sorcerers, etc.]. Because of this notion of power, people may go to the priest to be healed, which in the eyes of less instructed people may happen in a semi-miraculous way" (Thomas and Luneau 1977:224; translated by Lagerwerf and cited in Lagerwerf, ed., 1985:17).

11. This mediation was made explicit by the famous healer Bwanali from Malawi (Marwick 1950) in a series of interviews given in the course of 1974 in which he declared that his ministry superseded both that of the traditional *nganga* and that of the Christian churches. He superseded the *nganga* because he prayed only to God, and he superseded the churches because, like his patients, he believed in the reality of witchcraft (Kankwatira 1975).

12. For an overview of the different versions of the Mbona myth, see Schoffeleers 1985a and 1987.

13. Bureau studied mainly the Christianized version of Bwiti, whereas Fernandez was more acquainted with the "traditional" version. See Schoffeleers 1986b.

14. J. Peel drew my attention to the fact that in West Africa Christ is conceived of as resembling a deity rather than a living person. See also Ray (1976:44-45) for an illustration of this principle. By itself this conception need not exclude the use of the *nganga* paradigm, because the divinity itself may have been conceived as resembling the medicine person, as we have seen in the Mbona case. However, my knowledge of West African religion is too slight to be more definitive on this point.

15. Although one occasionally hears African Christians refer to Christ as "Chief" or "King", I have not been able to find evidence that the chief's role has led to an elaborate christology the way the *nganga* role has.

16. For comments on earlier presentations of my ideas on African christology at Winnipeg (1980), Amsterdam (1981), Windsor, England (1982), and Provo, Utah (1986), I am indebted to Ben Ray, Michael Bourdillon, Jonathan Benthall, John Peel, Terence Ranger, Walter van Beek, and Wyatt MacGaffey. I also wish to thank Ms. Leny Lagerwerf of the Interuniversity Institute for Missiological and Ecumenical Research, Leiden, for her assistance in tracing bibliographic material.

5

African Religion & Mormon Doctrine:
Comparisons & Commonalities

Dennis L Thomson

T HERE IS NO REASON to consider the similarities and commonalities of
Mormon doctrine and African religions unless this comparison would yield
something different from a comparison of African religions with other
Christian churches. This chapter addresses how such a comparison can give us
something new and can potentially impact on our understanding of each of these
forms of religious experience and expression.

The Church of Jesus Christ of Latter-day Saints (the official name of the
Mormon church) has always been a missionary church. Believing that all people
must be brought to a knowledge of the gospel of Jesus Christ in order for the purposes of creation and life to be fulfilled, those who are knowledgeable of the gospel
have an obligation to tell others of it. Latter-day Saints (Mormons) believe that
Christianity had fallen into general apostasy and that all the keys of spiritual
performance and a fullness of gospel truths were restored to humankind by the
divine calling of a prophet, Joseph Smith, in 1820. For the next hundred years or so
the Church concentrated its missionary activity in North America, Western Europe,
and the Pacific islands. In the mid-1800s missionaries were sent to places such as
Siam and India, but little was accomplished and the missionaries were withdrawn
and put where success was more probable. While Europeans were missionizing
Africa, Latter-day Saints were missionizing Europe. In the last twenty-five years
new areas of missionary effort in South America and East Asia have produced
many new adherents to the Mormon message. The areas of missionary efforts of
the future will include South Asia and Africa. There has been some missionary
activity in both areas, but it has been limited. Missionaries have been in South
Africa since the middle of the last century and missions are also now established
in Sierra Leone, Ivory Coast, Ghana, Nigeria, Gabon, Congo, Zaïre, Uganda,
Kenya, Tanzania, Zimbabwe, Zambia, Botswana, Namibia, Lesotho, Swaziland,

Madagascar, and Mauritius. Interestingly, the missions in West Africa are there upon invitation of people who learned of the Church elsewhere and wanted baptism and the full church organization.

The Church, for all of its emphasis on public encounter in missionary activity, tries to be inconspicuous in public affairs. Possibly its own history of persecution has led it to concentrate on the spiritual aspects of religion rather than on social issues. Its concern for social and economic change aims for a private effect rather than a public one. It assumes that it is better to change individuals rather than overtly disrupt society. The Church is hierarchical, closely governed, practical, and demanding; and its doctrine and practice are heavily laced with Old Testament concepts. It is both prophetic and millenarian; and its focus and central concept is Jesus, his mission and redemption. It is open and receptive to new converts, yet it operates as a closed community with extensive and rigid demands on its members.

The Church has undergone persecution of its members and vilification of its doctrine as it has bumped up against historical Christianity. It is thus both interesting and instructive to look at some commonalities between Mormonism and indigenous African religions. Historical Christianity also came in contact with African religions in ways that were at times both inharmonious and disruptive of African society, something that has in part led to the extensive growth of independent churches in Africa.

As the Latter-day Saints extend their missionary activity in Africa, they may be just as unadaptive as some other forms of Christianity because of an insistence on universal practices in a hierarchical church. Yet there are aspects of its doctrine that make it more adaptive to, or accepting of, some of the African beliefs than other Christian faiths have been. African cultural practices and religious issues such as polygamy, ancestors, earth spirit, family worship, healing, divination, and even magic and ghosts (depending on how defined) can all be found to have correlates in Mormon doctrine. We could consider numerous issues relating to the family, and by extension to the community, as having commonality: the lack of a place traditionally for a single man or a single woman, the insignificance of a wedding ring, the naming ceremony in which both the child and the parent receive instruction, and the idea that a living person may be married to a dead one all are common to both Mormons and some Africans. The Baganda have a concept of *balubaale*, exceptional men who become gods, which has a Mormon correlate. There are similarities in ritual cleansing in addition to ritual birth, death, and resurrection. I will not discuss at length ghosts, or ancestral spirits, though the subsequent discussion of ancestors certainly gives a glimpse of a related concept. The same is true of divination, dreams, and visions: there is much more to be explored. The concept of lay leadership and the importance of the Old Testament would yield fruitful understanding. Then, finally, there is the role of healing techniques for curing illnesses, both real and imaginary; the integration of healing and medicine; and healing as an eschatological experience wherein the sick person tastes something of future perfection in the immediate experience (Shorter 1974; Becken 1975; Fernandez 1965).

I am fully aware of the fallacy of making "superficial adaptations" to African tradition. I agree with Shorter that "one must never begin with a Christian doctrine—for example the Holy Trinity—and then look for similarities in an African tradition. This is an entirely superficial adaptation, which turns it into a gimmick for making Christianity acceptable" (Shorter 1974:69). It may be no more legitimate to start with African traditions, but that is what follows here. I will discuss three concepts: spirits, polygamy, and ancestors.

SPIRITS

A wide range of thought about spirits can be found in African religions: in some places the subject is ghosts or ancestral spirits; in other places it is the attribution of spiritual life to rocks and trees; elsewhere it is the idea of "the earth goddess". David Barrett, moreover, says that thirty-one percent of all sub-Saharan peoples acknowledge an earth deity (Barrett 1968:121). In any case, African religions recognize the importance of these spiritual forces in the lives of people, acting with an independence that can be either troubling or beneficial to men and women. These forces have influenced and today influence people's lives. In some cases they are recognized as having an exceptional power and position.

Mormon doctrine on spirits is equally wide ranging—some aspects are regularly discussed and considered; other aspects are understood but not pursued. Spirit is seen as being something that animates all things. It is made by God, and in the instance of men and women their spirits are his literal offspring. Thus there is a direct familial relationship between humankind and God—humans are literally God's children and God is their father. In the Creation, a physical body was created into which was put the spirit, which God had begot. Beyond that, all living things were created first spiritually and second physically. All animals, trees, and plants have spirits, and especially the earth has a spirit and destiny. All animal life will be resurrected. Orson Pratt, a nineteenth-century Mormon Apostle, said that the beasts, the fowls, and the fishes "were so constructed in their nature to be capable of eternal existence" (O. Pratt n.d.:332).

The earth has a spirit that animates it and causes it to bring forth fruit. The earth was created spiritually before it was created temporally. "The earth itself, as a living being was immortal and eternal in its nature" (O. Pratt n.d.:333). It has a mission to perform and will also be judged and sanctified as it shall become the abode of the celestial kingdom. Brigham Young, an early president of the Mormon church, stated that "the earth is very good in and of itself, and has abided a celestial law" and that man should "strive to obey the same law that the earth abides, and abide it as honorably as does the earth" (Young 1954:101). Modern Mormon scripture states[1]:

And the redemption of the soul is through him that quickeneth all things, in whose bosom it is decreed that the poor and the meek of the earth shall inherit it.

Therefore it must needs be sanctified from all unrighteousness, that it may be prepared for the celestial glory;

For after it hath filled the measure of its creation, it shall be crowned with glory, even with the presence of God the Father;

That bodies who are of the celestial kingdom may possess it forever and ever; for, for this intent was it made and created, and for this intent are they sanctified. ...

And again, verily I say unto you, the earth abideth the law of a celestial kingdom, for it filleth the measure of its creation, and transgresseth not the law—

Wherefore, it shall be sanctified; yea notwithstanding it shall die, it shall be quickened again, and shall abide the power by which it is quickened, and the righteous shall inherit it.

(Doctrine and Covenants [D&C] 88:17–20, 25–26)

This same principle is asserted elsewhere in latter-day scripture (D&C 77:1; 130:9). Similar patterns of religious renewal are ascribed to the earth as are required of humankind. Of the flood in the days of Noah, Orson Pratt wrote: "The waters were assuaged: the earth came forth clothed with innocence, like the new-born child, having been baptized or born again from the ocean flood; and thus the old earth was buried with all its deeds, even as man has to be immersed in water to wash away his own personal sins" (O. Pratt n.d.:349). He goes on to explain that before the Millennium the earth will be baptized by fire, and after the Millennium the earth shall die again by fire and a "new" earth will come forth that will be the celestial kingdom.

Further allusion to an earth-being and to spiritual life in "rocks and trees" is found in Mormon scriptures, "Let the mountain shout for joy, and all ye valleys cry aloud; and all ye seas and dry lands tell the wonders of your Eternal King! And ye rivers, and brooks, and rills, flow down with gladness. Let the woods and all the trees of the field praise the Lord; and ye solid rocks weep for joy!" (D&C 128:23). Again Orson Pratt extends this concept:

Let creation speak; let the earth open her mouth and testify. Listen! What sounds are those I hear? Can it be the low murmurings of distant thunder? It cannot be! It proceeds as if from the bowels of the earth! But hark! Did I not hear words, articulated in a deep, low, mournful sound? Has the earth, indeed, a language? Can she also express her sorrows? But listen again! She sighs! She mourns! She exclaims; "Woe, woe is me, the mother of men! I am pained! I am weary because of the wickedness of my children! When shall I rest, and be cleansed from the filthiness which has gone forth out of me? When will my Creator sanctify me, that I may rest?"... Who could reflect upon the bitterness and anguish of our great common mother, and not weep over the untold miseries she has endured for six thousand years? (O. Pratt n.d.:453–454)

In this doctrine are similarities to the concept of an earth goddess found in African religion—an impersonal female figure that is seen as the giver of fertility. There is, however, no observance or rite attached to the Mormon belief. And the concept of guardian of marriage, family, and home that is found in some African religions is not present in Mormon doctrine. While this doctrine is sympathetic to African belief, it has never been extended in a way that makes African practice compatible. Still, while Barrett argues that there is no sympathy among most of the Christian mission church theologians for the earth goddess concept (Barrett 1968:121–123), the Mormons would prove an exception. Certainly the belief that the earth has a spirit that is the source of fertility would be compatible with Mormon doctrine.

POLYGAMY

Polygamy[2] has long been a problem for the historical Christian mission churches in Africa. Though polygamy is not an essential part of African religious belief, it has been a widespread cultural practice that has posed a dilemma to operational Christianity. Though in practice many African marriages are monogamous, the tendency has been for rulers, leaders, the wealthy, and certain energetic and competent people to practice polygamy, the requirements and positive attributes varying from society to society. Islam has sanctioned polygamy, with the only restriction being a limitation of four wives, so the indigenous practice of polygamy has produced no barrier to the spread of Islam, quite the opposite. The historical Christian mission churches have universally rejected polygamy. Some have gone so far as to deny baptism to polygamists while others have only barred polygamists from official church positions. This undoubtedly has been a factor that has promoted the development of independent churches in Africa (Ekechi 1976; Barrett 1968; Adejunmobi 1963; Asamoa 1955; H. W. Turner 1966; Appiah-Kubi 1974).

Christianity for all of its firm stance against polygamy is not without its own experience with polygamy, first among the Anabaptists in Münster in the sixteenth century, then among the Mormons in the nineteenth century (Cairncross 1974). The Mormon practice of polygamy was begun in the 1830s and endured until 1890 when it was discontinued under duress imposed by the U.S. government.

The Mormon doctrine of plural marriage is tied to its doctrine of eternal marriage. The family is an eternal unit formed on this earth but destined to exist in the hereafter by virtue of a marriage ceremony wherein husband and wife are "sealed for time and all eternity". By entering into this sacerdotal marriage the participants become eligible to obtain exaltation in the celestial kingdom of the hereafter contingent upon abiding the commandments of the gospel. It is in this context that the law of polygamy was espoused—the creating of an eternal patriarchal family.

The practice of polygamy by the Church was not passive in only giving assent to the practice; it was active. The modern scriptural admonition says:

> I am the Lord thy God, and will give unto thee the law of my Holy Priesthood, as was ordained by me and my Father before the world was.

> Abraham received all things, whatsoever he received, by revelation and commandment, by my word, saith the Lord, and hath entered into his exaltation and sitteth upon his throne. ...

> This promise [of posterity to Abraham] is yours also, because ye are of Abraham, and the promise was made unto Abraham; and by this law is the continuation of the works of my Father, wherein he glorifieth himself.

> Go ye, therefore, and do the works of Abraham; enter ye into my law and ye shall be saved. ...

> And again, as pertaining to the law of the priesthood—if any man espouse a virgin, and desire to espouse another, and the first give her consent, and if he espouse the second, and they are virgins, and have vowed to no other man, then he is justified; he cannot commit adultery for they are given unto him; for he cannot commit adultery with that that belongeth unto him and to no one else.

> And if he have ten virgins given unto him by this law, he cannot commit adultery, for they belong to him, and they are given unto him; therefore is he justified.
>
> (D&C 132:28-29, 31-32, 61-62)

Not all Mormons were polygamous. Estimates range from two to fourteen percent of the men were engaged in plural marriage at any one time (Reimann 1974:133). There is no evidence that those who did not practice it were ostracized, nor was it just limited to the leadership—there were many common members of the Church who were polygamous. The practice of polygamy, however, was proscribed in 1890 by the prophet of the Church at that time, Wilford Woodruff—himself a polygamist. He declared:

> Inasmuch as laws have been enacted by Congress forbidding plural marriages, which laws have been pronounced constitutional by the court of last resort, I hereby declare my intention to submit to those laws, and to use my influence with the members of the Church over which I preside to have them do likewise. ...
>
> I now publicly declare that my advice to the Latter-day Saints is to refrain from contracting any marriage forbidden by the law of the land.
>
> (D&C Official Declaration 1)

The general conference of the Church voted unanimously to "accept his declaration concerning plural marriages as authoritative and binding" (D&C Official Declaration 1). Many members of the Church had been imprisoned and disenfranchised. The harassment by federal officials had continued for several years and the property of the Church had been confiscated. Even then President Woodruff asserted that "I should have gone to prison myself, and let every other man go there, had not the God of heaven commanded me to do what I did do [i.e., stop new polygamous marriages]" (D&C Official Declaration 1). Note that the law was not rescinded, but the practice. Since that time the Church has been as zealous as any other Christian denomination in dealing with polygamy. Anyone entering into a polygamous marriage is excommunicated from the Church.

Though the declaration to cease the practice of polygamy was given in response to American law, the prohibition is upon all the Church. Joseph Smith once said that "no man shall have but one wife at a time, unless the Lord directs otherwise" (Joseph Smith 1938:324). It is not probable that the Church would condone new polygamous marriages in Africa where it may be legal and prohibit it in America where it is not. That would only invite non-Africans to go to Africa to contract plural marriages. Presumably, the law of polygamy will be in effect again sometime in the future, possibly during the Millennium or at least through eternity.

After the ban neither husband, nor wives, nor children born of polygamous marriages suffered any stigma in the religious or social life of the Church. In my lifetime I have known devout and respected Church members who were husband, wife, or child of polygamous marriages entered into before this century. My grandfather was such a child of a plural wife. Indeed, I believe most Mormons who can claim polygamous ancestry do so with a bit of quaint pride or at least distinction. So long as polygamous family units existed legally in the country of their residence, were constituted prior to the ban, and did not further teach nor advocate polygamy, in the generations of the recent past they lived out polygamous lives in the arms of the Church. An African who was polygamist prior to joining the Mormon church would not likely be prohibited from being sealed to his wives "for time and all eternity" in the sacerdotal marriage ceremony in a Mormon temple; this would constitute an acceptable family unit in the life hereafter.

ANCESTORS

The African family is the focal point of the concepts discussed above, as is the Mormon family. Indigenous religion and the family are closely connected in Africa. In fact, African religion can be seen as "a system of rites, rules, and practices that aims at preserving and strengthening the fellowship of the people, the tribe and the family, and at increasing its power" (Barrett 1968:123, fn. 32).

The concept of the family is a unity of the living members, the dead ancestors, and the unborn posterity, to paraphrase Kenyatta. The concept is a complex one. How far the clan or lineage extends varies from one society to another; but it virtually always includes both the living and dead descendants of its founder or apical ancestor. Still, generalizations about ancestor veneration are difficult because of the considerable variations across Africa in the degree of importance of ancestors and of the nature of the interrelationships between ancestors and other beings and forces. Nonetheless, some commonalities generally accepted for indigenous African religions are the following: (1) Ancestors are associated with the soil or place of residence; (2) involvement with ancestors implies considerable interactions with the spirits of the dead; (3) ancestors are a major "source and sanction of morality in dealings between kinsfolk" (Banton 1963:49); (4) the individual's concern is mainly for ancestors of one's own lineage (Pauw 1963:34) or the lineage of one's spouse; (5) the relationship with the ancestors is generally one of love rather than of fear, though both or either may be the case; (6) the living have need of the ancestors, and the ancestors have need of the living; there is a kinship obligation that does not stop at death; and (7) the ancestors are mediators. How these commonalities are manifest with different people changes, but the scope of interaction remains broad across most societies (see Pauw 1963 on the Usia, Taylor 1958 on the Baganda, Little 1965/1966 on the Mende, Wilson 1963 [1951] on the Nyakyusa, and Shorter 1974 on the Shona). As Berthold A. Pauw has argued, "The stress is on fulfilling one's obligation to members of one's own lineage, and ... the fact that death does not sever the existing kinship relationships. Although the quality of the relationship may be somewhat changed through death, the essential relationship endures" (Pauw 1963:40). This kind of enduring relationship is also characteristric of Mormon belief and practice.

For Mormons, there is certainly a close relationship between the living, the dead, and the unborn. Again this concept depends on an understanding of the spirit. All spirits of people are begotten of God in the premortal existence; there they await birth into an earthly family. The earthly family is then formed by an "eternal marriage". People thus fit into a patriarchal chain that began with Adam and continues through all generations. Mormons understand that this collective family is referred to in Ephesians 3:14–15: "For this cause I bow my knees unto the Father of our Lord Jesus Christ, Of whom the whole family in heaven and earth is named".

Harold B. Lee, a Mormon Apostle and later prophet of the Church, said that marriage was "for the purpose of the organizing of spirits before the world was formed" and to have children upon this earth. He then said there is a divine purpose in marriage being continued after the resurrection that is for "a continuation of the seeds forever and ever" (Doxey 1978:428; Lee is citing D&C 132:19). This position is also sustained in Mormon doctrine by Isaiah, speaking of the inhabitants of the "new heavens and new earth": "They shall not labour in vain, nor bring forth for trouble; for they are the seed of the blessed of the Lord, and their offspring with them" (Isaiah 65:23). There are numerous accounts in which we see the connecting link of the dead, the living, and the unborn.

Latter-day Saints find significant the last two verses of the Old Testament: "Behold, I will send you Elijah the prophet before the coming of the great and dreadful day of the Lord: And he shall turn the heart of the fathers to the children, and the heart of the children to their fathers, lest I come and smite the earth with a curse" (Malachi 4:5–6). In response to this, Mormons search the genealogy of their dead ancestors to identify them so that the saving ordinances of the gospel can be performed for them. This, they believe, is alluded to in 1 Corinthians 15:29, "Else what shall they do which are baptized for the dead, if the dead rise not at all? Why are they then baptized for the dead?"

Thus the dead rely on the living to accomplish this baptismal work for them while the living must do it in order for the living to fit into the patriarchal chain. Neither can succeed spiritually without the other. The epistle to the Hebrews says of the dead "that they without us should not be made perfect" (Hebrews 11:40). Modern scripture says:

> And now, my dearly beloved brethren and sisters, let me assure you that these are principles in relation to the dead and the living that cannot be lightly passed over, as pertaining to our salvation. For their salvation is necessary and essential to our salvation, as Paul says concerning the fathers—that they without us cannot be made perfect—neither can we without our dead be made perfect.
>
> (D&C 128:15)

This is not unlike some Africans, such as the Shona of Zimbabwe, who believe that the dead are doomed to eternal wandering unless they are called home to the ancestral lineage by a special ceremony. The ceremonies amongst the Mormons by which the dead's concerns are laid to rest take place in the temples wherein the vicarious saving ordinances are performed.

Though discussion of interaction with the dead is not direct nor extensive in scripture, Mormon doctrine of spirits comprehends and anticipates a potential involvement of the living with the dead. In 1 Corinthians 13:12 it says, "For now we see through a glass, darkly; but then face to face: now I know in part; but then shall I know even as also I am known". This is accepted as the opportunity for partial knowledge and acquaintanceship to be had with those who will be fully known in the afterlife. The deep Mormon belief in prophecy, visions, and revelation—which has not been discussed here—both implies and requires belief in communication with the departed. The doctrine is specific that revelation is not limited to the Church hierarchy but may be received at all levels by all people on matters for which they are responsible. Therefore, the president of the Church receives revelation for the Church, a bishop for his congregation, a father or mother for the family, and an individual for himself or herself. Accounts of a dream or visitation of a dead ancestor may be greeted with skepticism, but it is never denied that such a visitation is plausible. These encounters are sometimes attested to publicly. One of the Apostles of this century, Rudger Clawson, told in a sermon to the Church of his experience with an elderly Church member who had become diligently engaged in searching genealogy and performing ordinance work for his ancestors:

> He further said, "I saw in vision … my father and mother, … who had not received the Gospel in life, and I discovered that they were living separate and apart in the spirit world, and when I asked them how it was that they were so, my father said: 'This is an enforced separation, and you are the only individual that can bring us together; you can do this work; will you do it?' " … he informed me that he had attended to the work, and I rejoiced with him and congratulated him. (Conference Report 1908:74)

This is an accepted occurrence among Mormons and is not seen in any way as unusual. Parents report that dead children have assured them that they are all right and widows or widowers tell of receiving counsel from a departed spouse on raising their children. President Wilford Woodruff related this story:

> Perhaps I may be permitted to relate a circumstance with which I am acquainted in relation to Bishop Roskelley, of Smithfield, Cache Valley. On one occasion he was suddenly taken very sick, near to death's door. While he lay in this condition, President Peter Maughan, who was dead, came to him and said: "Brother Roskelley, we held a council on the other side of the veil. I have had a great deal to do, and I have the privilege of coming here to appoint one man to come and help. I have had three names given to me in council, and you are one of them. I want to inquire into your circumstances". The Bishop told him what he had to do, and they conversed together as one man would converse with another. President Maughan then said to him: "I think I will not call you. I think you are wanted here more than perhaps one of the others". Bishop Roskelley got well from that hour. Very soon after, the second man was taken sick, but not being able to exercise sufficient faith, Brother Roskelley did not go to him. By and by this man recovered, and on meeting Brother Roskelley he said: "Brother Maughan came to me the other night and told me he was sent to call one man from the ward", and he named two men as had been done to Brother Roskelley. A few days afterwards the third man was taken sick and died. (cited in Lundwall 1966:313–314)

Parley P. Pratt, an early Church Apostle, told of a time when he was in prison during the early period of persecution of the Church. He wondered if he would ever be free again. After some days of prayer and fasting, his wife, who had died two years previously, told him he would be freed. "I was made to realize that she was sent to commune with me", he recalled (P. Pratt 1874:206–207).

Another Church leader, Joseph F. Smith reported a vision he had while reading 1 Peter:

> As I pondered over these things which are written, the eyes of my understanding were opened, and the Spirit of the Lord rested upon me, and I saw the hosts of the dead, both small and great.
>
> And there were gathered together in one place an innumerable company of the spirits of the just, who had been faithful in the testimony of Jesus while they lived in mortality. (D&C 138:11–12)

He said on another occasion:

> We begin to realize more and more fully, as we become acquainted with the principles of the gospel, as they have been revealed anew in this dispensation, that we are closely related to our kindred, to our ancestors, to our friends and associates and co-laborers who have preceded us into the spirit world. We cannot forget them; we do not cease to love them; we always hold them in our hearts, in memory, and thus we are associated and united to them by ties that we cannot break, that we cannot dissolve or free ourselves from. ... [They] can see us better than we can see them—they know us better than we know them. ... I claim that we live in their presence, they see us, they are solicitous of our welfare, they love us now more than ever. (J. F. Smith 1939:430–431)

Joseph Smith said in a funeral sermon that the dead "are not far from us, and know and understand our thoughts, feelings, and motions, and are often pained therewith" (J. Smith 1938:326); and Brigham Young elaborated that the spirit world is here on the earth. People "are brought forth upon this earth for the express purpose of inhabiting it to all eternity". On another occasion he said, "Can you see the spirits in this room? No. Suppose the Lord should touch your eyes that you might see, could you see the spirits? Yes, as plainly as you now see bodies, as did the servant of Elijah" (Young 1954:376–377). The spirits here are those of the deceased, rather than of the unborn.

Parley P. Pratt said:

> The Spirit World is not ... heaven ...; but it is an intermediate state, a probation, a place of preparation, improvement, instruction, or education, where spirits are chastened and improved, and where, if found worthy, they may be taught a knowledge of the Gospel ... a place of waiting for the resurrection or redemption of the body; while, to those who deserve it, it is a place of punishment, or purgatory or hell, where spirits are buffeted till the day of redemption.

> The Spirit World is here on the very planet where we were born, or, in other words, the earth and other planets of a like sphere have their inward or spiritual spheres as well as their outward, or temporal. The one is peopled by temporal tabernacles and the other by spirits. (P. Pratt 1978:80)

Certainly in the constant presence, the interaction, and mutual obligation between the living and the dead the belief of many Africans and most Mormons is very close. The nature of the great family that extends both into the past and into the future is also similar. There are aspects of ancestor veneration that are not similar, however. Worship of the dead—sometimes claimed by European and American observers to be an African practice—is not found in Mormonism nor is there in Mormon belief a sense of ancestors punishing the living. But historically where Christian missionaries have in general required their converts to reject indigenous beliefs and ritual relating to ancestors it should be evident that much in Mormonism requires ancestors to be a significant factor in one's religious practice and belief.

CONCLUSION

For the Latter-day Saints the explanation of the similarities between indigenous African religions and Mormon doctrine is of divine origin. In the Book of Mormon it states, "For behold, the Lord doth grant unto all nations, of their own nation and tongue, to teach his word, yea, in wisdom, all that he seeth fit that they should have; therefore we see that the Lord doth counsel in wisdom, according to that which is just and true" (Alma 29:8).

Orson F. Whitney, another Apostle, commented on this passage of modern scripture:

> God's truth has been taught all down the ages by men bearing the Priesthood, the authority to represent Deity. But other men, not bearing that authority, wise and worthy teachers, have been raised up in various nations to give them that measure of truth which they were able to receive. ... Men not wielding divine authority, ... but nevertheless endowed with wisdom, with profundity of thought and learning [have delivered],each to his own people, that portion of truth which the all-wise Dispenser sees fit that they should have. (Whitney 1917:27)

In addition, common traditions have been handed down from common sources. Peter observed that "God is no respecter of persons: But in every nation he that feareth him, and worketh righteousness, is accepted with him" (Acts 10:34–35). This belief is strongly held by Mormons. People who have lived the "law" that has been given them will be taught the fullness of God's law in the afterlife, and they will be judged according to the law which they had. All people receive God's truth to some extent and indeed many receive revelation that in reality is holy scripture. The Book of Mormon itself is such a document given to ancient inhabitants of the Americas, ancestors of American Indians. Mormons fully expect that other scripture exists which has been given to other peoples and that all people possess some eternal truths.

Aylward Shorter has written that "Christianity comes both to complete and to challenge what traditional religion teaches" (Shorter 1974:71). I like that. In light of Whitney's statement, Mormons must assume that indigenous African religion cannot be rejected out of hand, because much of it may be based upon the same spiritual sources as Christianity or its Mormon manifestation. On the other hand the practices and beliefs indigenous to Africa cannot be assumed to demand indiscriminate acceptance. For Mormons, the central role and mission of Christ must be accepted without compromise or the effort of the Christian mission is without avail. As we have seen, however, there are several concepts upon which Mormons and members of indigenous African religions can approach an understanding and mutual appreciation.

NOTES

1. Mormons believe that God's word is given to people in different times and places throughout history; thus in addition to the Holy Bible their scripture includes the Book of Mormon (given to ancient inhabitants of the Americas), the Doctrine and Covenants [D&C] (modern revelation), and the Pearl of Great Price (assorted writings from the past).

2. "Polygamy" (and "plural marriage") as used here refers specifically to polygyny, with one husband married to more than one wife concurrently. The other kind of polygamy—polyandry, with one wife married to more than one husband concurrently—does not occur among Mormons and is rare in Africa.

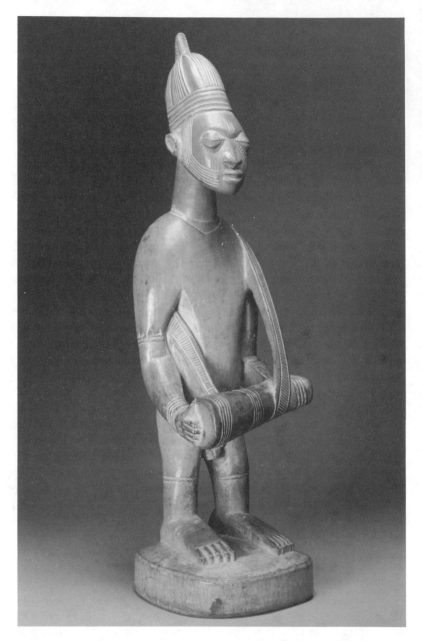

Plate 6–1. Figure for a Ṣàngó shrine. Yoruba (Ọyọ, Erin): Nigeria. Wood. H. 81 cm. (33 in.). The University of Iowa Museum of Art, The Stanley Collection. This musician, wearing his hair in the style of a Ṣàngó priest, plays a "*bata* drum ... said to have been introduced by Ṣàngó to increase his prestige and terrify his opponents" (Roy 1985:71). In Yoruba history and cosmology, Ṣàngó was the fourth king of Old Ọyọ who later became the *òrìṣà* [benevolent supernatural power] of thunder and lightning.

6

Ifá:

A West African Cosmological System

Wándé Abímbólá

INTRODUCTION

A GREAT DEAL OF SCHOLARLY ATTENTION has been devoted to the study of Ifá during the last fifty years. Prominent among these are the works of Bernard Maupoil (1943), Melville J. Herskovits (1958), William Bascom (1969), and myself (1975a, 1976a, 1977). These works have concentrated on anthropological, literary, and linguistic studies of Ifá. Little work has been done so far toward a study of Ifá as a thought system.

Ifá as a literary and divination system is found in many parts of West Africa, including Nigeria, Benin, and Togo, especially among the Yoruba, Ewe, Fon, Igbo, Edo, Ijo, as well as many other ethnic groups of West Africa. During the slave trade, Ifá was exported by African slaves to many parts of the Americas, especially Cuba. There, an important community of Ifá priests existed for hundreds of years before they dispersed to other Caribbean and American countries because of the Communist revolution in Cuba in the late fifties and early sixties.[1] Today Ifá as a divination system is very active in the United States, Puerto Rico, Venezuela, Brazil,[2] Cuba, and Trinidad. It is, however, among the Yoruba of West Africa that Ifá has reached its greatest degree of excellence to the extent that Ifá is today "the cornerstone of Yoruba Culture" (Abímbólá 1976a).

In spite of increasing Christian and Islamic evangelical activities in West Africa, Ifá remains a prestigious and popular system of divination among the Yoruba. The reasons for this prestige and popularity are not hard to find. For hundreds of years Ifá has made a great contribution to Yoruba culture. In indigenous Yoruba culture, Ifá has governed almost every aspect of Yoruba life from the birth of a child through his or her childhood days to marriage and old age and finally death. Even today many Christians and Muslims consult Ifá during all the important events of their lives. All known Yoruba towns and settlements have their own *odù* or chapter of Ifá which appeared to the diviners during the divination exercise that usually accompanied the foundation of all Yoruba settlements.[3] This is what Ifá priests have in mind when they sing in praise of the contribution of Ifá to the development of Yoruba cities:

Ifá ló tẹlè Adó o o.	Ifá is the founder of the city of Adó.[4]
Ifá tẹ Ìdó-Ọṣun.	Ifá is the founder of Ìdó-Ọṣun.[5]
Ifá tẹlé Ẹdẹ	Ifá is the founder of the city of Ẹdẹ.[6]
Ilú tẹ́ ẹ múrun tẹ́,	The towns that you founded through Islam,
Ẹ jẹ́ á gbọ́.	Kindly let us know.[7]

In the following pages, I will attempt a short exposition of some of the important ingredients of Ifá as a literary, ritual, and cosmological system. It is my intention to demonstrate that Ifá is a coherent, self-consistent system of belief par excellence, with a heritage that all peoples of the world could take pride in calling their own. Ifá contains an immense volume of traditions, consisting of 256 chapters [*odù*]. Each *odù* is believed to contain from six hundred to eight hundred poems known as *ẹsẹ Ifá*, totaling as many as 204,800 poems. If all these oral texts were tape-recorded, transcribed, and published as books, it would result in hundreds of books, thus making Ifá one of the most extensive literary texts ever developed. I will use some of these texts in our exposition of Ifá as a cosmological system.

THE ÒRÌṢÀ AND THE AJOGUN

According to Ifá texts, the Yoruba believe there are two pantheons of supernatural powers who compete for the domination of the universe. They are the *òrìṣa*, who are also known as *irinwo 'mọlẹ̀ ojùkọtún* [four hundred supernatural powers of the right], and the *ajogun*, who are known as *igbaa 'mọlẹ̀ ojùkòsì* [two hundred supernatural powers of the left]. The *orìṣà* are by their very nature benevolent to human beings while the *ajogun* are malevolent. By employing Portuguese terminology, I will speak of the *orìṣà* as "Deus de Bem" and the *ajogun* as "Deus de Mal".

The *òrìṣà* were the first inhabitants of this earth [*aye*], which they created from a primordial molten substance. They were actually sent from *ọrun* [heaven] by Olódùmarè,[8] the Yoruba High God, to create dry land from the primordial watery matter. The *òrìṣà* who was charged with that responsibility and who led all his colleagues out of *ọrun* is Ọbàtálá, otherwise known as Òrìṣàńlà. They descended from a chain in the sky and landed on top of a mountain in Ifẹ̀—Oòdáyé, which became the original Ifẹ̀ of ancient times. On top of this mountain they found palm trees from which they tapped palm wine. Unfortunately, Ọbàtálá, the leader of the team, drank so much palm wine that he slept at the time appointed by Olódùmarè to create dry land from water. So his younger brother, Odùduwà, got hold of the sacred objects of creation—a parcel of sand from *ọrun*, a hen with five fingers on each foot, and a chameleon—and with these objects he created dry land from the watery substance. Wherever the hen spread the parcel of heavenly sand, dry land appeared. The chameleon was later let loose to feel the surface of the earth to find out how solid it was before the *òrìṣà* descended from the mountain onto solid ground on earth.

Each *òrìṣà* was charged with his or her own responsibilities before departure from heaven. Òrìṣàńlà had responsibilities for creation—to create all living things on behalf of Olódùmarè. Ifá has responsibilities for divination and wisdom. Ògún is the divinity in charge of war, hunting, and all heroic deeds. Òrìṣà-oko is the

Plate 6–2. Staff for Ṣàngó. Yoruba: Nigeria. Wood. H. 39 cm. (15 in).
The University of Iowa Museum of Art, The Stanley Collection. Over
the female figure's left shoulder is an "emblem of Ọya … wife of
Ṣàngó" (Roy 1985:72, citing personal communication: H. Drewal
1984). An *òrìṣà*-possessed devotee, holding this thunderax in his or
her hand and "dancing to the piercing, crackling sounds and staccato
rhythms of the *bata* drum", graphically embodies and conveys the
"sudden, overwhelming, and seemingly capricious power of Ṣàngó"
(Roy 1985:72, citing Pemberton in Fagg and Pemberton 1982:74).

divinity responsible for agriculture. Ṣàngó is the producer of thunder and lightning. Olókun is the divinity of the ocean, while Ọlọ́ṣà is the divinity of the lagoon. Odùduwà, who created dry land, became the greatest ancestor of the Yoruba. Only his descendants can wear beaded crowns and are known as kings [ọba]. Oya is the divinity of the river Niger. Ọ̀ṣun and Ọbà, who together with Oya are wives of Ṣàngó, are also divinities of the rivers bearing those names. As a matter of fact, all the rivers and streams of Yorubaland are regarded as òrìṣà. All the important mountains and hills are òrìṣà. Some of the notable trees, such as Ìrókò and Osè are regarded as òrìṣà. The belief is that when the four hundred òrìṣà finished their work on earth, they changed into mountains, hills, trees, and so forth. Others entered into the earth's crust and disappeared.

The ajogun, as mentioned before, are two hundred in number, but the most important among them are the eight warlords—Ikú [Death], Àrùn [Disease], Òfò [Loss], Ègbà [Paralysis], Ọ̀ran [literally, Big Trouble], Èpè [Curse], Ẹ̀wọ̀n [Imprisonment], and Èṣe [a generalized name for all other human afflictions].

DEUS DE BEM VS. DEUS DE MAL

The sacred literature of Ifá portrays the universe as a cosmos in which there is an eternal and relentless struggle between the Deus de Bem and Deus de Mal. While the former are interested in blessing human beings with all the good things of life (money, children, and good health), the latter are interested in completely destroying people and their work. It is this fundamental difference of interest that causes conflict. As a result, many verses of Ifá deal with this all-important issue of conflict in Yoruba thought. Let us now consider an example of a verse that tells the story of conflict between the òrìṣà and the ajogun.

Àtàtà tan-ìn tan-ìn	The Ifá priest named Àtàtà-tanìn-tanìn
A díá fún Ọlọmọ,	Performed Ifá divination for Ọlọmọ[9]
Ìyan, ìyan gìdìgbí.	The mighty one.
Gbogbo ajogun gbogbo ní ń dòòyì ká Ọlọmọ	All the ajogun surrounded Ọlọmọ
Tí wọn ń fẹ́ ẹ́ pa á.	In order to kill him.
Wọ́n ní ẹbọ ní ó rú.	He was instructed to perform sacrifice.
Ó sì rú u.	And he performed it.
Ní ọjọ́ kan.	It happened one day,
Ikú, Àrùn, àti Òfó dìde	Death, Disease, and Loss stood up
Wọ́n ń ṣígún lọ sílé Ọlọmọ.	And went to attack the house of Ọlọmọ.
Wọ́n sí bá Èṣù lójúde.	They met Èṣù outside the house.
Bí wọ́n bá ti fẹ́ẹ́ wọlé Ọlọmọ Èṣù ṣá ń bu ìyẹfun èlùbọ́ sí wọn lẹ́nu ni.	As they were trying to enter the house, Èṣù was pouring yam flour into their mouths.
Bẹ̀ẹ̀ ni gbogbo ajogun kò gbọdọ̀ fẹnu kan ìyẹfun èlùbọ́,	Since the ajogun must not eat yam flour,
Ìgbà tí ìyẹ̀fun èlùbọ́ kan àwọn ajogun lẹ́nu,	When yam flour touched their mouths,
Omíìí kú, òmíìí sì ṣàárẹ̀ nínúu wọn.	Some of them died and some became sick,

Sùgbọ́n kò sì èyì tì ó leè	But none of them was able to enter
wọlé Ọlọmọ nínúu wọn.	the house of Ọlọmọ.
Ìgbà tí inú Ọlọmọ dùn tán,	When Ọlọmọ became happy,
Orin awo ní ǹ kọ.	He started to chant the song of Ifá priests.
Ó ní, "Àtàtà tan-ìn tan-ìn.	He said, "The Ifá priest named
	Àtàtà-tanìn-tanìn
A diá fún Ọlọmọ,	Performed Ifá divination for Ọlọmọ,
Ìyan, ìyan gìdìgbí.	The mighty one.
Ikú tó lóun ó pawo,	Death, who had boasted that he would
	kill Ifá priest,
Kò leè pawo mọ́.	Can no longer kill him.
Ikú ti yẹ̀ lórí awo.	Death has shifted away from
	the head of Ifá priest.
Ikú è é jèlùbọ́;	Death does not eat yam flour;
Bíkú bá póun ó jèlùbọ́,	If Death attempts to eat yam flour,
Ẹnuu rẹ̀ a kù,	His mouth would collapse.
Ẹnuu wọn a fún tuuru.	His mouth would be tightly compressed.
Àrùn tó lóun ó sawo,	Disease, who boasted that he would
	attack Ifá priest,
Kò leè sawo mọ́.	Can no longer attack him.
Ikú è é jèlùbọ́.	Death does not eat yam flour.
Bíkú bá póun ó jèlùbọ́,	If Death attempts to eat yam flour,
Ẹnuu rẹ̀ a kù,	His mouth would collapse.
Ẹnuu wọn a fún tuuru.	His mouth would be tightly compressed.
Ajogun gbogbo tó lóun ó sawo,	All the *ajogun* who wanted to attack Ifá priest
Kò leè sawo mọ́.	Can no longer attack him.
Ikú è é jèlùbọ́.	Death does not eat yam flour.
Bíkú bá póun ó jèlùbọ́,	If Death attempts to eat yam flour,
Ẹnuu rẹ̀ a kù.	His mouth would collapse.
Ẹnuu wọn a fún tuuru".	His mouth would be tightly compressed".

(revised from Abímbọ́lá 1976a:162–164, 1977:50–53)[10]

In this story, Ọlọmọ the mountain is attacked by the *ajogun* but is saved by Èṣù, who uses yam flour to render them powerless. No reason is given by the *ajogun* for their attack on Ọlọmọ. The enmity between the Deus de Bem and the Deus de Mal is so intense that one need not commit an offense to be attacked by his or her opponent.

Below is another example of conflict between two supernatural powers, but this time it is Òrúnmìlà (another name for Ifá) who is on the offensive against Ikú [Death], whom he shoots and kills with an arrow on a farm.

Pómú pómú sigi sìgì sigi	The Ifá priest named *Pómú pómú sigi*
pomu pómú.	*sìgì sigi pomu pómú.*[11]
A diá fún Òrúnmìlà	Performed Ifá divination for Òrúnmìlà
Ifá ó tafà	When he shot an arrow,
Yóó pakú lóko.	And killed Death on a farm.
Nǹkan ló dẹrú ba Òrúnmìlà,	Something frightened Òrúnmìlà on his farm.
Ló bá wálé	He therefore returned home
Ó bi òkè Ìpọ̀rúi rẹ̀ léèrè wò.	And inquired about it from his
	Ifá divination instruments.

Wọ́n ní ẹbọ ní ó rú.	He was told to perform sacrifice.
Ó sì rú u.	And he performed it.
Ìgbà tí ó rúbọ tán,	After he had performed sacrifice,
Ni àwọn awoo rẹ̀ bá fún un ní ọfà mẹ́ta	His Ifá priests gave him three arrows
Wọ́n ní kí ó máa ta á káàkiri okoo rẹ̀.	And asked him to shoot them all about his farm.
Ìgbà tí ọ̀kan nínú àwọn ọfà náà ó lọ,	When one of the arrows was shot,
Ló bá kọlu Ikú.	It hit Death.
Láyà ló gbé bá Ikú.	It hit Death on the chest.
Gbìì tí Ikú lulẹ̀ bàyìí,	Death fell down with a loud noise,
Ló bá jáde láyé.	And he went out of the earth.
Láti oko ni Ọ̀rúnmìlà ti kó ijó wálé,	It was from that farm that Ọ̀rúnmìlà danced homewards.
Ó ní bẹ́ẹ̀ gẹ́gẹ́ ni àwọn awo òún wí.	He said that was exactly what his Ifá priests predicted.
Pómú pómú sigi sìgì sigi pomu pómú.	The Ifá priest named Pómú pómú sigi sìgì sigi pomu pómú.
A díá fún Ọ̀rúnmìlà	Performed Ifá divination for Ọ̀rúnmìlà
Ifá ó tafà	When he shot an arrow,
Yóó pakú lóko.	And killed Death on a farm.
Olónìímoró tafà,	Olónìímoró shot an arrow,
Ó pakú lóko.	And killed Death on a farm.
Pómú pómú sigi sìgì sigi pomu pómú.	We praise Pómú pómú sigi sìgì sigi pomu pómú.

(Abímbọ́lá 1977:106–107, cf. Abímbọ́lá 1976a:172–173)

Èṣù AND THE NOTION OF Ẹbọ [SACRIFICE]

Interestingly, every conflict in the Yoruba cosmos can be eventually resolved by the use of sacrifice [ẹbọ]. Sacrifice is the weapon that brings about resolution and tranquillity in a universe in which conflict is the order of the day.

Due largely to the dual role of Èṣù among the supernatural powers, the Yoruba are able to achieve resolution in the universe. Èṣù is believed to be an òrìṣà. So instead of 400 supernatural powers, the Yoruba often speak of 401, Èṣù being the one divinity on top of the 400. Èṣù, who is still actively worshiped in Yorubaland, is regarded as one of the most powerful òrìṣa. He is capable of changing his form at will. If you meet him in the morning, he could be a giant but in the evening he could have changed himself to become a dwarf. Each odù is governed by its own Èṣù. Hence there are 256 different forms of existence that Èṣù can assume. But Èṣù is also a kinsman of the ajogun; the eight ajogun warlords are his errand boys, as is noted in a saying popular among Ifá priests:

Ikú, Àrùn, Ọfò, Ẹgbà, Ọràn,	Death, Disease, Loss, Paralysis, Big Trouble,
Èpè, Ẹ́wọ̀n, Èṣe	Curse, Imprisonment, Affliction
Ọmọ ọ̀dọ̀ Èṣù ni wọ́n.	They are all errand boys of Èṣù.

Èṣù is like an impartial judge who mediates between the Deus de Bem and the Deus de Mal. He is able to do this by using a sacrifice provided by a would-be

Plate 6–3. Staff for Èṣù. Yoruba (northern Ekiti): Nigeria. Wood, indigo dye, beads. H. 41.8 cm (17 in.). The University of Iowa Museum of Art, Stanley Collection. Èṣù, the only Yoruba *òrìṣà* portrayed in sculpture, is powerful yet ambiguous, can rapidly change form, and appears to humans in a variety of often-contradictory images. Here Èṣù is manifest as an impertinent boy disruptively blowing a whistle but also as a calmly reflective, wise old man.

victim. When Èṣù presents sacrifice to a warring *ajogun,* the *ajogun* allows his victim to go away unhurt. But if a would-be victim does not perform sacrifice, Èṣù is not in a position to help him. This is the meaning of the saying

Ẹni ó rúbọ ni Èṣù ú gbè   Èṣù supports only he who offers sacrifice.

(See also Abímbọ́lá 1976a:187)

In the following verse of Ifá, Èṣù succeeds in saving Ọ̀rúnmìlà from Death because Ọ̀rúnmìlà performs sacrifice. Death had sent Àgbìgbò, an evil bird who was a former pupil of Ọ̀rúnmìlà who had turned against his master, to carry a coffin to the house of Ọ̀rúnmìlà in order to kill Ọ̀rúnmìlà. But through the offering of sacrifice, Èṣù is able to persuade Àgbìgbò to take the materials offered as sacrifice instead of Ọ̀rúnmìlà, whose dead body Àgbìgbò had planned to put inside the coffin.

Omii ṣẹ́lẹ̀rú ò mu kèǹgbè.	Spring water cannot cover up a water gourd inserted in it.[12]
A díá fún Àgbìgbònìwọ̀nràn	Ifá divination was performed for Àgbìgbònìwọ̀nràn
Tí í ṣe ọmọkùnrin ìgbépósí.	The strong man, carver of coffins.
Bí Àgbìgbò bá gbẹ́ pósí kalẹ̀ tán,	After Àgbìgbònìwọ̀nràn had finished carving a coffin,
Ojúde ẹni tí ó bá gbé e sí,	He would go and place it outside a person's house.
Ikú ní lá tí pa olúwaarẹ̀.	The result would be that that person would die.
Ìgbà tí Àgbìgbònìwọ̀nràn gbẹ́ pósí tán,	When Àgbìgbò finished carving a coffin,
Ló bá gbé e,	He carried it,
Ó di ọ̀nà ilé Ọ̀rúnmìlà.	And went to the house of Ọ̀rúnmìlà.
Ọ̀rúnmìlà lálàá ikú mọ́jú ojọ́ náà	That night Ọ̀rúnmìlà dreamt of death.
Ló bá gbé Ifáa rẹ̀ kalẹ̀,	In the morning, he took his divination instruments
Ó bi í léèrè nípa àlá tí ó lá.	And inquired about his dream.
Ifá ní kí Ọ̀rúnmìlà ó sáré rúbọ.	Ifá warned Ọ̀rúnmìlà to perform sacrifice immediately.
Ìgbà tí ó rú u tán,	After Ọ̀rúnmìlà had performed sacrifice,
Wọ́n gbé ẹbọ náà lọ sí ìdí Èṣù.	He carried it to the shrine of Èṣù.
Láìpẹ́, Àgbìgbò gbé pósí dé ojúde Ọ̀rúnmìlà.	Before long, Àgbìgbò arrived at the house of Ọ̀rúnmìlà with his coffin,
Ó bá Èṣù lójúde.	And he met Èṣù outside the house.
Èṣú ní kín ni Àgbìgbò ó kì sínúu pósí náà.	Èṣù asked him what he intended to put inside the coffin
Àgbìgbò dáhùn pé Ọ̀rúnmìlà ni.	And Àgbìgbò replied that he intended to put Ọrúnmìlà there.
Èṣú wáá bi í léèrè pé	Then, Èṣù inquired further from him
Kín ni ohun orò tí ó gbà	What he would like to take
Tí kò fi ní í mú Ọ̀rúnmìlà lọ.	instead of Ọ̀rúnmìlà.
Ó ní òun ó gba eku àti ẹyẹ àti ẹran.	He said that he would take a rat, a bird, and an animal.

Èṣú dá a lóhùn pé gbogboo rè náà	Èṣù replied that all those things
Ni Ọ̀rúnmìlà ti fi kún ẹbọ rú.	Were included in the sacrifice of Ọ̀rúnmìlà.
Ni Èṣú bá kó gbogboo rè jáde fún Àgbìgbò.	Èṣù then brought those items out for Àgbìgbò
Hàùn tí Àgbìgbò kó gbogboo rè,	Who hurriedly gathered the materials,
Ló bá gbé pósí i rè ǹlè,	Lifted up his coffin,
Ó sì kọrí sí ọ̀nà ibòmíì.	And went to another place.
Ìgbà tí ó lọ tán,	When he was out of sight,
Èṣú ní kò gbọdọ̀ sọ pósí náà kalè mọ láéláé.	Èṣù decreed that he must never put down the coffin from his head.
Títí di òní olónìí,	To this very day,
Pósí náà ń bẹ lórí Àgbìgbò.[13]	The coffin is still on the head of Àgbìgbò.[13]
Ìgbà tí inú Ọ̀rúnmìlà dùn tán,	When Ọ̀rúnmìlà became happy,
Ijó ní ń jó,	He started to dance.
Ayọ̀ ní ń yọ̀.	He started to rejoice.
Ó ní bẹ̀ẹ̀ gégé ni àwọn awo òún wí.	He said that was exactly what his Ifá priests predicted.
Omii sẹ́lẹ̀rú ò mu kèǹgbè.	Spring water cannot cover a water gourd inserted in it.
A díá fún Àgbìgbòniwọ̀nràn	Ifá divination was performed for Àgbìgbòniwọ̀nràn,
Tí í ṣe ọmọkùnrin ìgbẹ́pósí.	The strong man, carver of coffins.
Béku lo ó bà á gbà,	If it is a rat that you would like to take,
O gbeku,	Take the rat,
O múu yáu lọ.	And go away.
Àgbìgbòniwọ̀nràn,	We implore you, Àgbìgbòniwònràn,
Gbérù ẹ,	Carry away your load,
Gbẹ́rù ẹ.	Carry away your load.
Àwa ò rà.	We will have nothing to do with it.
Béja lo ó bà á gbà,	If it is a fish that you would like to take,
O gbẹja,	Take the fish,
O máu yáu lọ.	And go away.
Àgbìgbòniwọ̀nràn,	We implore you, Àgbìgbòniwọ̀nràn,
Gbérù ẹ,	Carry away your load,
Gbẹ́rù ẹ.	Carry away your load.
Àwa ò rà.	We will have nothing to do with it.
Béran lo ó bà á gbà,	If it is an animal that you would like to take,
O gbẹran,	Take the animal,
O máa yáa lọ.	And go away.
Àgbìgbòniwọ̀nràn,	We implore you, Àgbìgbòniwọ̀nràn,
Gbérù ẹ,	Carry away your load,
Gbẹ́rù ẹ.	Carry away your load.
Àwa ò rà.	We will have nothing to do with it.

(Revised from Abímbọ́lá 1977:88–93; 1976a: 212–215)

In the following example, the would-be victim refuses to perform sacrifice. Instead of helping him, Èṣù turns against him. As a result, the would-be victim cannot achieve his heart's desire. But when he later changes his mind and performs sacrifice, things change once again, but this time in his favor. The full story is as follows:

Gbòngbò ṣe wọ̀rọ̀kọ̀ fi
   wọ̀rọ̀kọ̀ jánà.
The crooked wooden stump crosses
   the road crookedly.

A díá fẹ́kùn
Ifá divination was performed for Lion

Níjọ́ tí ń lọ oko ọdẹ.
On the day he was going ahunting.

Oko ọdẹ tí òun ń lọ yìí,
He inquired if his hunting expedition

Òún le ríṣe bọ̀ ńbẹ̀?
Would yield for him abundant reward.

Ni ẹkùn dáfá sí.
That was why he consulted Ifá

Wọ́n ní kí ó rúbọ elénìnì.
He was asked to perform sacrifice so as to
   triumph over his enemies.

Ẹkùn ní ta ní ó ṣelénìní
   òun ẹkùn?
But Lion boasted that nobody was bold
   enough to antagonize him.

Ó ní òun ò níí rú.
He said that he would not perform sacrifice.

Láìpẹ̀, ẹkùn kọrí sóko ọdẹ.
Before long, Lion went into the forest
   to hunt.

Èṣú di atégùn,
Èṣù turned himself into wind,

ó tẹ̀ lé e
And followed him.

Ìgbà tí ẹkùn dé oko ọdẹ,
When Lion got into the forest,

Ló bá rí ìrá,
He saw an antelope,

Ó sì pa á.
And he killed it.

Ńjẹ́ kí ẹkùn ó máa dá írá
   ní inú lu,
But as he was trying to open up its abdomen,

Ni Èṣú bá já èso igi àfọ̀n kan,
Èṣù plucked a fruit of an àfọ̀n tree,

Ó sọ ọ́ mọ́ ẹkùn ní bàrá idí
And threw it against Lion's hips

Bí ó ti bá ẹkún ní bàrá ìdí tán,
As soon as it landed on his hips,

Ẹsèkẹsè ni ẹkùn sá lọ.
Lion ran away.

Kí ó tóó padà dé,
Before he returned,

Èṣú ti gbé ẹran lọ,
Èṣù carried away the animal.

Ìgbà tí ẹkùn padà dé,
When Lion returned,

Tí ó wá ìrá títí,
And searched unsuccessfully

Tí kò rí i,
Without seeing the animal,

Ló bá tún wá ẹran mìíì lọ.
He looked for another animal,

Ṣùgbọ́n bákan náà ló já sí.
But the same thing happened.

Ìgbà tí ebi wáá bẹ̀rẹ̀ sí í
   pa ẹkùn
When Lion became hungry,

Eré ló sá rúbọ.
He hastened to perform sacrifice.

Ìgbà tí ó rúbọ tán,
After he had performed sacrifice,

Ó tún padà lọ sí oko ọdẹ.
He then went back into the forest to hunt
   for animals.

Èṣù kọ̀ sì dẹ́rù bà á mọ́.
And Èṣù did not frighten him again.

Ijó ní ń jó,
He started to dance,

Ayọ̀ ní ń yọ̀.
He started to rejoice.

Ó ní, "Gbongbo ṣe wọ̀rọ̀kọ̀
   fi wọ̀rọ̀kọ̀ jánà.
He said, "The crooked wooden stump crosses
   the road crookedly.

A díá fẹ́kùn
Ifá divination was performed for Lion.

Níjọ́ tí ń lọ oko ọdẹ. ...
On the day he was going ahunting. ...

Kèè pẹ̀ o,	It will not be a long time,
Kèè jìnnà.	It will not be on a distant journey,
Ẹ wáá bá ni ní tìṣẹ́gun".	Before you meet us in victory".

(Revised from Abímbọ́lá 1977:102-105)

ORÍ: THE PRINCIPLE OF PREDESTINY[14]

This exposition of the Yoruba cosmos is in terms of the supernatural powers who dominate that universe, but one may ask: What about the human beings? How do they relate to these supernatural powers? An important place is reserved for human beings in Yoruba cosmological thought. Each human being has a physical and a spiritual aspect. The physical part of the human is the *ara* while the spiritual aspect consists of *ẹmí* and Orí. It is the business of Òrìṣàńlá, the Yoruba High God, to mold *ara* with clay. This is why Òrìṣàńlá is regarded as:

Alágbẹ̀dẹ ọ̀run.	Blacksmith of heaven.
Ọkọ abuké.	Husband of hunchback.
Ọkọ arọ	Husband of lame.
Ọkọ aràrá borí pẹ̀tẹ́.	Husband of dwarf with a big fat head.[15]

It is Olódùmarè who supplies the soul [*ẹmí*] by breathing the breath of life into the would-be individual. Orí [the inner or spiritual head] is provided by *Àjàlá alámọ̀ tí í mọrí* [Àjàlá the porter who molds heads]. The interesting thing is that Àjàlá is not a divinity. As a matter of fact, he is an incorrigible debtor, a drunkard, and a completely wretched and irresponsible man. But his house is part of the abode of Olódùmarè (Abímbọ́lá 1976a:116–131).

I do not have the space to tell in full the interesting story of Àjàlá and how human beings select Orí for themselves before they are born into this world. Suffice it to say here that once chosen in heaven, Orí becomes the element that determines the fortunes of each individual on earth. A person who chooses a good Orí that has no defects readily succeeds on earth, while she or he who chooses a defective "inner head" has to make sacrifice ceaselessly to improve the quality of this inner head and to repair any damage to it that might have been responsible for her or his misfortunes in life.

Orí is therefore an important link between human beings and the spirit world, since Orí is the spiritual aspect of humans. The principle of Orí transforms human beings into spiritual entities, thus making divinities out of human beings. Orí is regarded as one of the 401 *òrìṣà*. Whatever has not been sanctioned by a person's Orí cannot be given to that person by any other *òrìṣà*. In this sense Orí is the most important *òrìṣà* as far as human welfare is concerned. A verse of Ifá expresses this as follows:

Orí pèlé,	Orí, I salute you.
Atètè níran.	Orí, nicknamed *atètè níran*.
Atètè gbeni kòòṣà.	He who first blesses a man before any other *òrìṣà*.
Kò sóòṣà tí í dáni í gbè	No divinity blesses a man
Léyìn Orí ẹni.	Without the consent of his Orí.
Orí pèlẹ́	Orí, I salute you.

Orí àbíyé.	You who allows children to be born alive.
Ẹni Orí bá gbẹbọọ rẹ̀	A person whose sacrifice is accepted by his Orí
Kó yọ̀ sẹ̀sẹ̀.	Should rejoice exceedingly.

(Revised from Abímbọ́lá 1976a:137, 142)

In spite of the importance of Orí, however, a place is still reserved for free will in Yoruba thought: a good Orí is a *potential* for success. Hard work and good character, among other things, are still required to make the potential bear fruit.

ẸSẸ̀: THE PRINCIPLE OF STRUGGLE AND SELF-HELP

Ẹsẹ̀, which literally means "leg", is the symbol of struggle and self-help in Yoruba thought. No matter how good may be the quality of the Orí an individual brought from heaven, that person must struggle and work hard to bring the potentialities of her or his Orí to fruition. Ẹsẹ̀ is therefore the symbol of the activity that must accompany any successful human endeavor.

The following verse of Ifá tells the story of how the many Orí [inner heads] make a proposal without consulting Ẹsẹ̀. The result is that there is no means of executing the plan, and, as a result, the proposal fails.

Ọ̀pẹ̀bẹ́ awo Ẹsẹ̀	Ọ̀pẹ̀bẹ́, the Ifá priest of "Legs" [struggle, self-help],
Ló dífá fún Ẹsẹ̀	Performed Ifá divination for Legs
Níjọ́ tí ń tìkọ̀lé ọ̀run bọ̀ wáyé.	On the day he was coming from heaven to earth.
Ní ọjọ́ kan,	One day,
Gbogbo awọn orí ṣa araa wọn jọ,	All heads called themselves together,
Wọn ò pe Ẹsẹ̀ sí i.	But they did not invite Legs.
Èṣú ní, "Ẹ ò pe Ẹsẹ̀ sí i,	Èṣù said, "Since you do not invite Legs,
Bí ó ti ṣe gún náà nù un"	We will see how you will bring your deliberations to success".
Ìjà ni wọ́n fi túká ńbẹ̀.	The meeting ended in a quarrel.
Ni wọ́n tóó wáá ránńṣé sí Ẹsẹ̀.	They then sent for Legs.
Nígbà náà ni ìmọ̀ràn tí wọn ń gbà tóó wáá gún.	It was then that their deliberations became successful.
Wọ́n ní bẹ́ẹ̀ gẹ́gẹ́	They said that was exactly
Ni àwọn awo áwọ̀n wí.	What their Ifá priest had predicted.
Ọ̀pẹ̀bẹ́, awo Ẹsẹ̀,	Ọ̀pẹ̀bẹ́, Ifá priest of Legs,
Ló díá fún Ẹsẹ̀	Performed Ifá divination for Legs,
Níjọ́ tí ń tìkọ̀lé ọ̀run bọ̀ wáyé.	On the day he was coming from heaven to earth.
Ọ̀pẹ̀bẹ́ mọ̀ mọ̀ dé ò,	Ọ̀pẹ̀bẹ́ has surely come.
Awo Ẹsẹ̀.	Ifá, priest of Legs.
Ẹnìkan kì í gbìmọ̀ràn,	No one makes a deliberation
Kó yọ tẹsẹ̀ẹ́ 'lẹ̀.	Without reckoning with Legs.
Ọ̀pẹ̀bẹ́ dé ò,	Ọ̀pẹ̀bẹ́ has come,
Awo Ẹsẹ̀.	Ifá priest of Legs.

(Revised from Abímbọ́lá 1976a:148–149)

ÌWÀPÈLÈ: THE CONCEPT OF GOOD CHARACTER

One expectation of the Deus de Bem when they bless and support human beings is that human beings will cultivate good and gentle character [ìwàpèlé]. Good character will prevent an individual from colliding with the Deus de Mal, as well as keep that person in harmony with his or her fellow human beings and the total natural and supernatural environment in which the individual lives. In a universe peopled with so many supernatural and human powers, it is certainly a good policy to cultivate good character (Abímbólá 1975a).

The Yoruba regard *ìwàpèlè* as the most valuable accomplishment of any human being. Good character is the element that allows one to fully enjoy the good things of life—hence the Ifá verse that says:

Ọgbón inú, awo Alárá,	Wisdom of the mind, Ifá priest of the house of Alárá,
Dífá fún Alárá,	Performed Ifá divination for Alárá,
Èjì Ọsá,	Nicknamed Èjì Ọsá,
Ọmọ amúrin kàn dógbòn agogo.	Offspring of those who use one iron rod to make thirty gongs.
Ìmòràn, awo Ajerò,	Great understanding, Ifá priest of Ajerò
Dífá fún Ajerò,	Performed Ifá divination for Ajerò.
Ọmọ ògbójú kòrọọ jà jálè.	Offspring of the brave man who refused entirely to engage in a fight.
Níbo ló gbé ríwà fún un o,	Where did you see *ìwà*, tell me,
Ìwà, ìwà là ń wá o, ìwà,	*Ìwà, ìwà* is the one I am looking for.
Ó ní bó o lówó,	If you have money,
Tó ò níwà,	But if you do not have good character,
Owó olówó ni.	The money belongs to someone else.
Ìwà, ìwà là ń wá o, ìwà.	*Ìwà, ìwà* is the one we are searching for.
Ọmọ la bí,	If one has children,
Tá à níwà,	But if one lacks good character,
Ọmọ Olómọ ni.	The children belong to someone else.
Ìwà, ìwà là ń wà o, ìwà.	*Ìwà, ìwà* is the one we are searching for.
Bá a nílé,	If one has a house,
Tá à níwà,	But if one lacks good character,
Ilé onílé ni.	The house belongs to someone else.
Ìwà, ìwà là ń wá o, ìwà.	*Ìwà, ìwà* is what we are searching for.
Bá a láso,	If one has clothes,
Tá à níwà,	But if one lacks good character,
Aso aláso ni.	The clothes belong to someone else.
Ìwà, ìwà là ń wá o, ìwà.	*Ìwà, ìwà* is what we are looking for.
Ire gbogbo tá a ni,	All the good things of life that a man has,
Tá à níwà,	If he lacks good character,
Ire oníre ni.	They belong to someone else.
Ìwà, ìwà là ń wá o, ìwà.	*Ìwà, ìwà* is what we are searching for.

(from Abímbólá 1975a:396–399)[16]

The following verse—a popular Yoruba proverb—expresses the individual's responsibility to develop good character:

Ọwọ́ ara ẹni	Each individual must use his own hands
Là á fí í túnwà ara ẹnií ṣe.	To improve on his own character.

The Ifá corpus features a detailed explanation of what Ifá regards as good character and its opposite—hence, the following verse that upholds the value of honesty and condemns wickedness:

Òtítọ́ ni mo ní ńnú,	It is honesty which I have in me,
N ò níkà ń nú ...	I do not have any wickedness. ...

(Abímbọ́lá n.d.:207)

In another verse, Ifá speaks of the value of sùúrù [patience]:

Ìbínú ò da ǹkankan fún 'ni,	Anger does not produce a good result for any man.
Sùúrù baba ìwà,	Patience is the father of good character.
Àgbà tó bá ti ní sùúrù	If there is an old man who is endowed with patience,
Ohun gbogbo ló kó já.	He will be endowed with all good things.

(Abímbọ́lá n.d.:255)

NATURE AND THE ANCIENT COVENANT

In traditional Yoruba thought, there is a deep respect for nature as an important part of the universe. When the òrìṣà finished their assignment here on earth, most of them turned themselves into objects of nature such as trees, rocks, hills, mountains, rivers, lagoons, and the ocean. This is the reason the Yoruba have such an important place for nature in their thought system. Furthermore, they believe that there was an ancient covenant between human beings and nature; this covenant compels mutual respect. The Yoruba believe that each object of nature has an ancient name that is used to communicate with it and to command it to do our will. The Yoruba base their use of spells, chants, and incantations against any human or nonhuman creature on this belief.

At a certain level of understanding in Yoruba thought, therefore, there is no such thing as a nonliving thing. Every object and creature of this earth can be made to come alive and participate in an important endeavor. This is why Ifá personifies all so-called nonliving things and speaks of them in human terms as if they are all human beings (Abímbọ́lá 1976a:195–235). The Yoruba indeed believe that there are many aspects of nature, especially those linked with the òrìṣà, that are higher than human beings, aspects of nature before which human beings must bow in appreciation of their eternal qualities. The following verse speaks about the longevity of Ọlọmọ [the mountain]:

Àgbà yẹkú yẹkú orí ìgbá:	The old immortal man on top of a locust bean tree:
Ìgbá ò wó,	If the locust bean tree does not fall down,
Àgbà yẹkẹtẹ̀ ò sọ kalẹ̀.	The fat old man will not descend therefrom

A dífá fún Ọlọmọ, àwáyéèkù.	Ifá divination was performed for Ọlọmọ, the immortal.
Wọ́n ní ó rúbọ àìkù,	He was asked to perform sacrifice so that he may become immortal.
Ó ṣe é	He performed the sacrifice,
Ikú ò pa á.	And he became immortal.
Ogún ọdún òní o,	Twenty years from today,
Òkè ń bẹ láìkú gbọin gbọin.	The mountain is alive with good health.
Gbọin gbọin ni tòkè.	Good health and immortality are the attributes of the mountain.
Òkè, òkè gbọin gbọin.	The mountain remains forever immortal.
Igba ọdún òní o,	Two hundred years from today,
Òkè ń bẹ láìkú gbọin gbọin.	The mountain remains immortal with good health.
Gbọin gbọin ni tòkè.	Good health and immortality are the attributes of the mountain.
Òkè, òkè gbọin gbọin.	The mountain remains forever immortal.
Ìgbà gbogbo lòkè ń bẹ láìkù gbọin gbọin.	For all time, the mountain remains immortal with good health.
Gbọin gbọin ni tòkè.	Good health and immortality are the attributes of the mountain.
Òkè, òkè gbọin gbọin.	The mountain remains forever immortal.

(from Abímbọ́lá 1968:25–26)

CONCLUSION

I have attempted in this chapter a short analysis of the Yoruba worldview, explaining the Yoruba cosmos in terms of the supernatural, human, and nonhuman elements that inhabit it. Constant conflict is the order of the day in the Yoruba universe. Thanks to Èṣù and the role of sacrifice, human beings are able from time to time to achieve resolution and peace in the midst of conflict. It is through the intervention of sacrifice that warring human and nonhuman forces are brought together and compelled to take part in a resolution for peace—even if this peace may turn out to be temporary.

In Yoruba thought human beings are raised to a divine level through the Yoruba belief in Orí [inner or spiritual head] as a spiritual entity who dwells in every person. But this concept of predestiny is counterbalanced by an equally salient belief in free will. It is a good combination of predestiny and free will that makes for success. Here again, the importance of sacrifice is paramount, since a bad Orí can be repaired by the offering of sacrifice.

The most important aspect of free will, however, is good character. It is the duty of every human being to strive to cultivate good character. This will allow that person to be at peace with all neighbors encompassing the supernatural, human, and nonhuman. The importance of good character is summed up in the following Yoruba saying:

Ìwà lẹ̀sìn.   Good character is the essence of religion.

Nature is also important in Yoruba thought. For the Yoruba, both the living and the so-called nonliving things are coinhabitants of the universe. The Yoruba therefore do not support any unbridled exploitation of nature for materialistic purposes. Nature also has its divine aspects, since most of the òrìṣà turned themselves into objects of nature at the time of their departure from the earth. Nature must be nurtured and respected rather than seen as nonliving and therefore shamelessly exploited.

Yoruba cosmology is a profound and coherent thought system codified in the Ifá literary corpus. In spite of in-depth studies of Ifá by many scholars in recent decades, this profundity and coherence has been largely neglected. Much greater attention should be directed to the study of this complex, extensive, and important African system of thought.

NOTES

1. When Fidel Castro took over the reins of power in Cuba in 1959, among the many Cubans who fled the country were priests of Ifá who went to other parts of the Caribbean, Central America, and the U.S., spreading Ifá divination to these other areas of the Americas.

This chapter employs a widely used Yoruba orthography: sharp accent (á, é ...) equals high tone; no diacritic over vowel (a, e ...) equals midtone; grave accent (à, è ...) equals low tone; dot under "s" (ṣ) equals aspirated "s" as in *sugar* or *short*; dot under "o" (ọ) equals low midback vowel as in *caught*; dot under "e" (ẹ) equals low midfront vowel ɛ as in *bet*.

2. What is practiced in Brazil is a simplified version of Ifá known as Dílógún Ifá. This form of divination also originated from West Africa and can be found elsewhere in the Americas. Instead of the sacred palm nuts and the divining chain, Dílógún Ifá makes use of sixteen cowries.

3. These odù are known as *odù tó tẹ ilú dó.*

4. There are several towns known as Adó. There is Adó Àwáyé, which is believed to be a town sacred to Ifá; Adó-Ekìtì, where Ondo State University is located; and Adó-Odò, which is near the coast.

5. Ìdó-Òṣun is a town near Oṣogbo in Òṣun State of Nigeria.

6. Ẹdẹ is also near Oṣogbo in Òṣun State of Nigeria.

7. This is a popular song among Ifá priests during their worship ceremonies.

8. For a full account of Olódùmarè, the Yoruba High God, see Ìdòwú 1962.

9. Olọmọ is another name for the mountain that is an important Yoruba divinity.

10. The sixty-four poems in Abímbọ́lá 1977 were collected between 1963 and 1970 from a renowned Ifá priest, Oyedele Ìṣọ̀lá of Bẹẹṣin Compound, Pààkòyí, Ọ̀yọ́, Nigeria. Other Ifá priests have helped in the interpretation of this material.

11. This is an imitation of the sound made when shooting arrows.

12. "The Yoruba use gourds or clay pots to draw water from rivers and springs.... Since spring water flows out gently and in small quantities" and "is usually very shallow, it is not possible to immerse a water gourd completely in it when drawing water" (Abímbọ́lá 1977:162; 1976a:251).

13. Àgbìgbònìwọ̀nràn, or simply Àgbìgbò is a bird believed to be a former pupil of Ọ̀rúnmìlà. Àgbìgbò later turned against Ọ̀rúnmìlà and became an ally of the *ajogun* on whose behalf he was carrying coffins about to kill human beings. When Èṣù cursed him, the coffin got stuck to his head. The coffin is now represented by a tuft of hair that can be found on the head of Àgbìgbò today. For a full story of Àgbìgbònìwọ̀nràn, see Abímbọ́lá 1975b:208–234.

14. For a full discussion on Orí, see Abímbọ́lá 1976a:113–149, 156–160.

15. This is a popular praise chant of Òrìṣàńlá.

16. Collected from Oyedele Ìṣọ̀lá, Bẹẹṣin Compound, Ọ̀yọ́, December, 1973 (Abímbọ́lá 1975a:419).

Part II:

Comparisons over Time and Space

Plate 7–1. Priestess Eduzemegie Eweka in a state of possession at the weekly meeting of her congregation in Benin City, Nigeria. While in a trance she diagnoses social and medical problems and relays Olokun's demands to his devotees.

7

The Promise of Greatness:
Women & Power in
an Edo Spirit Possession Cult

Paula Girshick Ben-Amos

STUDIES OF SPIRIT POSSESSION cults in Africa have been concerned to a large extent with the status and role of women, who are the main participants. Spirit mediumship is seen as a way for women, who are "existentially inferior… and jurally subordinate" (Kilson 1972:173), to resolve their emotional problems, whether they be frustration at male dominance (Lewis 1971), lack of avenues to gain self-esteem (Walker 1972:7), or ambivalence about maternal roles (Kilson 1972:171). Whatever psychological resolution that they achieve through mediumship is temporary and rarely translatable into real social power because the ritual roles of mediums and healers are subordinate and the cults in which they operate peripheral (Gomm 1975; Kennedy 1967; Kilson 1976; Wilson 1967).

These assumptions about the status and functions of women's religious associations are increasingly being questioned (see, for example, Berger 1976; Constantinides 1979; and Karp 1990). My study of the Olokun cult among the Edo in Benin City, Nigeria,[1] suggests that women's religious associations are not necessarily peripheral or low in status. On the contrary, worship of Olokun is at the very center of Edo cosmology and has a major part in ongoing religious practices. Women play primary religious roles as priestesses in both the urban and rural areas, that is, within Benin City, the royal capital of the Edo Kingdom of Benin, as well as in the numerous Edo villages that are part of that kingdom.[2] (Benin City is also the capital of Edo State.) The status that urban Edo women achieve in this cult is permanent, not temporary, and the psychological benefits of participation are not temporary outlets but a real redefinition of self.

In order to understand the centrality of the Olokun cult and, ultimately, how women achieve high status through participation in it, we must first look at Edo cosmology. In the cosmology, there is a basic contrast between two realms: the dry land and the deep waters. Water is considered the primordial substance that once covered the world and from the center of which land first emerged. The deity Olokun is identified with these great waters that surround the land. More specifically, he is associated with the Olokun River (called Ethiope in English) in the southeastern part of the kingdom, which the Edo believe is the source for all the rivers and oceans of the world. The path to the spirit world lies across the waters, and the souls of those who have died as well as those about to be born must pass over the waters. This last association explains why Olokun is considered the bringer of children. He is similarly considered the source of wealth and good fortune, since before one makes the crossing Olokun may choose to bless the soul, thus insuring luck, wealth, and success (Ben-Amos 1973).

Olokun is conceived of as a king[3] living under the waters in a magnificent palace, a scene that, as we will see later in this chapter, is the theme of elaborate mud shrines erected in his honor. This palace in Benin thought is a paradise of purity, beauty, and joy. According to the Edo adage, "In the palace of the king there is never silence"—referring to the songs of praise, sounds of drumming, and shouts of children that fill this underwater world.

All the wealth of the everyday world abounds under the sea, especially coral beads, cowrie shells, and brass. As he sits on his throne, Olokun is surrounded by his wives, chiefs, and courtiers, who are the multitudinous rivers that cut across the kingdom. These wives and chiefs are the focus of their own village worship and are considered to be vivid individual personalities. I was told that "the Olokun gods have human nature. Some of them are hot-tempered, others calm and kind. Some are selfish, others very serviceable" (personal communication: Imade Oriza 1976).

Above all, the kingdom of Olokun is the epitome of all that the Edo consider to be ritually pure and undefiled. Ritual purity is symbolized by the color white, which predominates in all aspects of Olokun ritual and art. Olokun priestesses are expected to dress in pure white ritual attire and to observe very stringent taboos regarding pollution.

Like Olokun, the Oba [ruler of the Benin nation] is a king living in a magnificent palace surrounded by wives, chiefs, and courtiers. As Olokun rules over the waters, so the Oba presides over the land. But these parallel realms are not equal in Edo thought; rather, the realm of the land is but a reflection of the greater realm that lies under the sea. Neither are the rulers of these two realms equal. This is clearly stated in the adage "The king of the waters surpasses the king of the land". It is assumed that the king of the land derives his wealth from the sea. According to oral traditions, the prototypical monarch, Oba Ewuare, who brought the structure and substance of divine kingship to Benin (Bradbury 1969:139) is said to have gone down to the riverbank, where he found all the coral beads, brass, and cowries of Olokun lying out to dry. Ewuare stole these royal materials and brought them back to the palace in Benin, where until today they form the foundation of the king's royal treasure house.

This distinction between two parallel but unequal realms is the key to understanding the position and power of Olokun priestesses. The implication of this inequality is that those who establish links with the superior realm become themselves superior. The linkage with the god—often starting in the devotee prenatally—continues and intensifies throughout the course of a devotee's life. By means of this connection, Olokun offers his devotees a model of achieved greatness that is irrespective of gender. This model is presented in the mythology, the ceremonies of initiation, and the life experiences of the priestesses themselves.

In mythology, Olokun is the senior son of Osanobua, the creator god. Like other West African high gods, Osanobua has removed himself from everyday life. In contrast, his senior son—a position of significance in Edo lineage structure—is concerned with the most crucial issues of everyday life: fertility, health, and wealth. In Edo thought, Olokun has surpassed his own father in importance, a notion expressed in the adage "One can indeed bear a child greater than oneself as Osanobua bore Olokun". This adage suggests the theme of achieved greatness to the devotees of Olokun, who—significantly—are considered to be his children, not his wives as is so common elsewhere in West Africa. The implication of this filial relationship clearly is that they, too, can aspire to success and prosperity.

Olokun is worshipped by traditional women generally because of his role in providing children. It is common for parents of a young girl to install a small shrine to Olokun for her protection and well-being and when she marries this shrine is transferred to her husband's house. The shrine consists of a whitewashed mud altar upon which are placed pieces of kaolin—a white symbol of purity and good luck—and a ritual pot containing fresh river water. Throughout her life, this shrine will be the primary contact point with the deity. She can approach it actively or infrequently, according to her needs, interests, and commitment to Olokun.

Some people, however, are especially selected by the god to be his devotees. Priestess Azaigueni Aghahowa explains:

> On their coming to earth, Olokun asks some people to worship him. Olokun sends his children, both men and women, to earth in order to promote his name and make people know of his existence. As he sends them, he gives them a name. If on arrival, the child finds a good priestess to establish an Olokun shrine, and the priestess pronounces that name, it will be peaceful for the child. (personal communication:1976)

In order to know if a child is destined to be a devotee of Olokun, or any other deity for that matter, the parents can consult a diviner to determine if there is a "calling in the womb", though not all parents do this. Upon birth, the appearance of divine calling can be marked by special curly hair, called *ihiagha* (Plate 7–2). There are many different types of curl and a diviner has to ascertain which deity is involved. According to the priestess Ekuase Odigie (personal communication:1976), if the curl is in the shape of a blacksmith's hammer, the child belongs to Ogun, god of metal; if the hair is a single very tight curl, the child belongs to Eziza, the whirlwind; and if the curl is in the form of a royal ceremonial sword [*eben*], it is the child of Olokun.

The most common type of recruitment in Benin, however, is through suffering. As I talked to priestesses, I heard story after story about periods of disassociative states, disturbed pregnancies, failed marriages, marketing disasters, and terrible diseases, all experienced because someone did not realize that the sufferer was really a child of Olokun. Often this was because families did not have the money to pay a diviner to reveal the identity of the deity or to pay a priestess to install the proper shrine. Sometimes even if they did pay, the specialist who was consulted utterly failed to recognize the truth or misled the sufferer out of ignorance or greed. As the years went by with no resolution or relief, these women experienced great misery. From their descriptions an interesting pattern emerged: those very illnesses that Olokun inflicted on his recalcitrant children were the symbolic opposites of the benefits and glories of his kingdom—lameness from a god who loves dancing, blindness from a god who demands beauty, barrenness from a god who blesses humans with children.

Such a long period of illness and altered states of consciousness is a common phenomenon associated with spirit mediumship. Lois Paul, in an analysis of Mayan midwives, sees this as a time when the sufferer undergoes a process of redefining herself, a period of turning inward and reformulating her identity. In Paul's words, "As her feelings and thoughts take shape in templates provided by her culture's cosmology, she is doing the 'dreamwork' necessary to bring about the isomorphic coherence between the subjective woman and the objective role" (Paul 1978:147).

Plate 7–2. Edo girl born with special curly hair [*ihiagha*], the sign of a divine calling by Olokun.

After years of suffering, these women in Benin eventually did contact the proper priestess, who installed their Olokun shrine without mistake. From then on, they began to prosper. Indeed, the description of their "before" and "after" lives fits the Edo paradigm of greatness. The king himself is expected to suffer before attaining the throne. The prototypical king, Oba Ewuare, mentioned earlier, was said to have wandered for years before successfully winning the throne. In the coronation ceremony, the about-to-be crowned monarch must climb a special palm tree before entering Benin City. The ascent of this tree symbolizes the difficulties and obstacles he must overcome before reigning. Significantly, the name of this tree is the proverb that encapsulates the meaning of his life and, by extension, that of the priestesses: "If one does not see suffering, one will never see prosperity".

The initiation ceremony continues and intensifies this process of linkage between the devotee and the realm of Olokun. There are generally two parts of the ceremony. On the evening of the first day, just as the sun begins to descend into the sea and its rays reflect on the initiate, she undergoes ritual purification (see Plate 7–6). She stands between chalk marks, indicating the path to Olokun, while a baby chick tied on a string is whirled three times around her head; at each whirl, a different source of pollution is driven from her body.[4] Then a bowl of water mixed with chalk, salt, cowries, and leaves is sprinkled on her head. After the purification, the initiate begins to dance and is expected to go into a trance in which she calls out her name in the spirit world (failure to do this is a bad omen). The name she calls is not that of Olokun himself but of one of the myriad rivers who are his wives and chiefs. It is significant that gender is not a basis for establishing this linkage: women can call out the names of male rivers and men of female ones. As Priestess Azaigueni Aghahowa, who initiated me, explained:

> The names are not given to people on earth because of complexion or stature; it is exactly what the person is in the kingdom of Olokun. As you are working on earth, so Ezenughegbe [my Olokun name] is working over there, moving around, doing serious work that concerns her. (personal communication:1976)

This name is of great significance because it establishes a bond between the individual and one particular personage in Olokun's kingdom. The nature and character of this personage becomes a model after which the devotee patterns her behavior. The goddess Igbaghon, for instance, is said to be hot-tempered, while Ezenughegbe is flashy and loves beautiful clothes. Thus, the attributed personalities of the different deities establish sets of expectations for behavior and character for the devotee.

On the second day, the initiate goes to the river with her priestess and an entourage (Plate 7–3). At the river she is bathed and fills her pot with fresh water to be placed on the newly established shrine. She throws into the river gifts for Olokun; these gifts are explicitly seen as a down payment on future returns she will now begin to receive from Olokun. As Priestess Azaigueni Aghahowa explained, the river is the source of these benefits:

> If you go to the river at a quiet time, you will hear the sound of drums and dancing from Olokun's kingdom. Olokun will be bringing up brass plates, beads,

Plate 7-3. Priestesses going to the river for a ceremony.

and other materials and will put them on the riverbank to dry. If someone brave goes there he can run and take some. This is how Olokun gives out things from the water to the earth. (personal communication:1976)

This visit to the river replicates that of Oba Ewuare, who first brought all the riches of earth from Olokun's kingdom.

Once her shrine has been installed, the initiate is firmly linked to the world of Olokun both spiritually and physically. Her shrine, with its pot full of fresh water, representing the river itself, is a meeting point between the realms of the sea and the land. Her immediate and intimate contact with Olokun's realm is one of the major sources of her growing status and power. The trances that first were the signs of her calling now become the sources of her information as she moves from spirit possession to mediumship. In mediumship (see Plate 7–1), as I was told, "the god comes down on the woman's head and she can see everything. Anything that she says is directly from Olokun" (personal communication:Osarenren Omoregie1976). Trance is a central feature of the weekly meetings of congregations. During these meetings one or more priestesses go into a trance and in this manner convey the requirements of Olokun to his followers.

Trance, however, is not the only way to obtain direct communication with the deity. The second most common means is through dreams. In Benin, dreams are not conceived as subjective expressions but as actual situations of contact with super-natural reality which can be predictive or instructional. Chief Osahon gave me the following account:

> In my mother's womb it was predicted that I would be an Olokun priest and so my shrine was installed. I am now 82 years old and I started worshipping Olokun 82 years ago. Each time I slept I found myself in very deep water. When I went inside I saw another country; I saw a king sitting on a dais with courtiers, wives with beaded anklets and necklaces, and pages with ceremonial swords.... I was dressed like a chief in grand regalia and two people supported my hands. A big drum was sounding behind me. I found myself dancing and tossing a ceremonial sword. I celebrated the festival very well. At daybreak I went to the oracle who told me that I was going to be a titled chief in the same shape and pattern that I was in the water in my dream. Four years later the king invited me to the palace and gave me a chiefly title, a ceremonial sword, and coral beads. (personal communication:1976)

Among the fifty or so priests and priestesses whom I interviewed, there were three—Priestesses Azaigueni, Imade, and Eruba—who claimed to have experienced Olokun's world in a very different way: they had fallen into the river and actually visited Olokun under the waters, staying from five to seven days. This experience, considered rare in Benin, confers upon these three priestesses a very special authority. Priestess Eruba describes this event:

> Once I started to neglect worshipping Olokun and became a Jehovah's Witness for seven years. I was a transporter and carried things from Benin to Onitsha. When I was crossing the river at Asaba in a canoe I began hearing voices in the water, calling my name, saying, "Have you forgotten your name in the spirit world?" When I looked back I saw someone calling me, asking me to come back. It was there that I experienced that as you look at the environment here, so there is

an environment under the water, another world. I was able to recognize what Olokun really is in his kingdom. (personal communication:1976)

Imade Oriza, who was born in the 1880s, told me that "it is not common nowadays for people to go under the water because Olokun's taboos are violated all the time. You cannot find people who are ritually clean" (personal communication:1976). The claim by these three priestesses to have made this voyage, then, has double authority: it proves the inherent moral worth of the voyager, who is "pure enough" to be allowed to make the trip, and it provides a very special kind of knowledge, as Priestess Eruba claimed, of what Olokun "really is" in his kingdom. While most traditional people in Benin know in general about that kingdom through stories and myths, these women know through direct experience. Such experience legitimizes their positions and provides them with a cosmological seal of approval.

Bearing one or more of these types of experiential knowledge, the priestess is qualified to perform her ritual duties. In addition to purification and sacrifice, priestesses practice healing and divination. In advanced stages of initiation, priestesses learn precisely which leaves found by the riverbank can be used to give ritual baths and can be prepared into medicinal potions to cure those diseases related to Olokun's areas of concern. When I first met Priestess Azaigueni she showed me her photo album with snapshots of those whom she had successfully cured; these included a girl with a closed vagina, a man unable to impregnate three wives, a woman unable to conceive, an unlucky and unstable man, a woman who was pregnant for several years without being able to deliver, and a child who was dumb. Each of these diseases has a cause related to disturbances in the world of Olokun. For example, Priestess Odigie described the cause of lameness:

> In the kingdom of Olokun it is traditional that one has to kneel and touch his forehead to the ground when greeting Olokun. And, one must put some cowries down [give some money]. There are some people who cannot fulfill these conditions in the palace of Olokun but still want to come to earth. When one is born this way, without paying tribute to Olokun, he will remain on his knees for the rest of his life. (personal communication:1976)

Olokun priestesses, having in many cases experienced the very same illnesses as their patients, are devoted to curing and even make house calls. If successful, they can become wealthy from their practice.

Divination is another skill that provides an income (Plate 7–4). Priestesses either use materials such as cowrie shells or kola nuts or "predict" from a state of trance. People come from far distances to find solutions to problems. Divinations are incorporated into regular rituals or can be done privately by appointment.

Divination and healing are the bread-and-butter activities of most Olokun priestesses, but calling by the deity can also introduce women to a range of artistic activities. Olokun is a deity who demands beauty [mosee] in many forms: singing, dancing, personal attire, and adornment for his shrines. Certain devotees are called by the deity to go farther and become specialists in the creation of chalk designs, pottery, and life-sized mud sculptures (Plate 7–5). The recruitment of these artists

Plate 7–4. Priestess Aiweroya Ukurebo divining with cowrie shells. Many ceremonies are performed in front of an *ikhinmwin* tree [*Newbouldia laevis*] such as this one, the type of tree that was at the center of the world at the time of creation.

Plate 7–5. Priestess Iyahen Olaye seated before her personal shrine that she molded.

follows the general pattern for Olokun priestesses, involving intense suffering. The story of Iyahen Olaye is typical:

> My parents lost many children before I survived. My mother was instructed by a diviner to install an Olokun shrine when I was still in the womb. It was predicted by the diviner that I would become a priestess but when I grew up I became uninterested in worshipping Olokun. I was moving with Europeans and civilized people, playing the social life. At that time I started violating the taboos of Olokun; I was committing every ritual violation. And the reaction was incredible! The carnal part of my body became closed entirely. I became neither man nor woman. For a period of eight years no man was able to cross me [have sexual relations with me]. I became sick. I began to trace out the cause of my trouble. How can a woman having no sex ever hope to have a child? As a result I decided to commit suicide by drowning myself in the river. One evening I prepared all my property packed together with the aim to carry it to wherever I would kill myself. That very night when I was sleeping I had a dream. In it I discovered that my gold necklace was lost and began searching for it. As I was searching, I met a man who came out of the water and asked me what I was looking for. I told him. The man told me his name was Olokun, and he warned me to go home and worship him, for he understood all my difficulties.
>
> During the time of my suffering, my main occupation was molding pots. Each time I put them in the fire they got broken. When I dreamed about this man I found all my broken pots and my lost necklace there by the river. The man told me that all my property is on the ground waiting for me. He advised me to continue molding pots and to use that very pattern with figures to make molded shrines [shrines with mud sculpture]. He showed me the molded shrines in the river. He gave me the right to do this without being harmed and promised me that if I install my Olokun shrine properly, life will be well with me. I will have children, get money, and never lose property again. (Iyahen Olaye: personal communication 1976)

In her dreams, Olaye was not only called to be a molder but later even received her training that way. It is common for artists, whether they have inherited their profession through guild membership or learned it through apprenticeship, to get innovative ideas through dreams, but it is only artists who are called through divine inspiration who get their actual training in that manner.

Within each congregation, at least one woman is chosen by Olokun to make abstract chalk designs out of powdered kaolin. These designs decorate the ground around the entranceway and in the courtyards of shrines. The creation of these designs is the crucial temporal marking that "opens the day for Olokun in the water", a ritual that must be performed daily. Both kaolin and clay, the other substance used to create art forms for Olokun, are found at the riverbank, the contact point between the realms of earth and water. Clay is used to make the ritual pots all initiates must put on their shrines and also to create large scale figurative tableaux (Plate 7–5) in shrines in the homes of chiefs and priests and priestesses in Benin City and in numerous villages in the southeastern part of the kingdom. These tableaux represent Olokun in his underwater palace with all his chiefs, wives, and retainers. All of these artistic forms and activities, including dancing, are seen as attempts to replicate on earth key features of Olokun's kingdom (for a discussion of these art forms see Ben-Amos 1973 and 1986).

While deriving from cosmological modes, the varied activities of the priestesses, especially curing, divination, and sculpting, have concrete effects in everyday life. Over time, the more successful priestesses begin to gain a wide reputation. Men and women come from other parts of southern Nigeria, from as far away as Lagos and Calabar. With this recognition comes economic success, and priestesses begin to acquire considerable amounts of money, which they commonly invest in real estate around Benin City. Such investment entails the purchase of a plot of land upon which a large building is erected. Rental of rooms in these buildings brings in tenants over whom the priestess as landlady potentially can have influence. She may resolve disputes between tenants, act as broker between them and other members of her network, and generally act as patroness to clients. The rental money she acquires from them goes into the purchase of additional plots of land, the continued embellishment of her shrine and support of weekly and annual rituals, and status purchases such as coral beads, gold jewelry, refrigerators, and tape recorders.

When a new ontological status as ritual specialist also includes economic success, this combination can be translated into two major (and ultimately related) achievements: individual autonomy and high social status. Judith Hoch-Smith and Anita Spring have suggested that "through ritual roles women may become autonomous persons, no longer recipients of 'reflected glory' " (Hoch-Smith and Spring 1978:14). This is certainly true for the most successful priestesses in Benin City—they do, indeed, become autonomous persons. In the traditional Edo family structure, women are subordinate to men, first to their fathers and older brothers and then to their husbands. As R. E. Bradbury points out, "At all levels, personal relationships are conceived of in master/servant terms. In the elementary family a man's wives and children are his servants" (Bradbury 1969:155). But when Olokun priestesses begin to earn significant sums of money they tend to move out of their husbands' compounds and set up their own residence. Whatever money they gain on their own has always belonged to them and in their separate households with their own sources of income they are quite independent of their husbands. The movement away from her husband's domination is expressed in the idiom of divine demands; that is, the priestess claims that Olokun has demanded that she live apart from her husband.

The shift to her own residence usually occurs after the priestess has ended her childbearing years. The cult of Olokun is, after all, focused on childbearing. Most recruits are drawn to it with the hope of curing barrenness or increasing the number of offspring. Yet those who go on to become priestesses are career women who must devote increasing amounts of time to their ritual activities. Younger priestesses often feel a conflict between the desire for more children and the push to autonomy. For example, one highly accomplished young priestess was in love with her husband and felt quite distressed that her Olokun was demanding that she live separately. Whenever she and her husband were in the vicinity of her altar they addressed each other as "relative", in order to throw the deity off the trail. But for older women, the separation is generally welcomed. As Priestess Eweka explained:

> The idea of marriage is out entirely. My seven children are quite all right. What I am trying to do is fix my Olokun shrine properly. Olokun has warned me not to be wandering about with men. I am settled down with my Olokun now and my Olokun has satisfied me beyond what any husband can do. (personal communication:1976)

Once a priestess like Eweka has decided that she has had enough children, she feels free to leave her husband's house. In so doing, she is taking control over her own sexuality, making her own reproductive decisions. For a woman in Benin society this is truly autonomy.

With economic success and personal autonomy, the priestess moves beyond the level of commoner and propels herself into the elite. She is now on a par with men who hold chiefly titles and women who are born or married into the royal family. As a result, she acquires the various trappings of status, including deference behavior appropriate to high rank. Women, children, and junior or untitled men kneel before her and address her with the honorific greeting "*domo-o*". She in turn need not kneel before any man, including—and especially—the king of Benin. Those who meet her speak to her respectfully, often calling her "*iye*" [mother]; they do not look her directly in the eyes, and they must listen attentively to any advice she may give. As a leader she is entitled to weekend and evening visits from her followers, clients, and others who wish to show her respect and curry favor. When the priestess goes out on "official business", she travels with an entourage, a sure mark of high status. No self-respecting chief or important politician would dream of going out officially without such accompaniment to demonstrate his capacity to gather followers. Indeed, an Edo expression to describe a situation of utter humiliation is to compare the subject to a chief going out without an entourage. On these outings the priestess dresses in chiefly attire—the same attire she wears when performing rituals—which consists of a white wrapper and numerous strands of coral beads around the neck, wrists, and ankles. She is treated like a chief by those whom she visits: placed in the seat of honor, she is presented with choice food and beverages, sometimes even gifts and money, and is given the privilege of breaking and distributing kola nuts, a rite that should be conducted by the most senior person present.

Within her circle of devotees, the priestess functions like a Benin chief. She is at the center of a group of followers who are drawn from various social and geographic backgrounds. Although members of her family sometimes participate, her cult group consists mainly of people who came to her on the recommendation of friends, successfully treated patients, and diviners and priests who have ascertained that she is the appropriate priestess for treatment of their problems. In addition to her regular coterie, there are clients who come periodically in response to crises in their lives. These various followers come for regular weekly services and special annual rituals. Ultimately, the size of her congregation will fluctuate with her ability to attract people through successful cures and personal charisma.

The shrine is the center for most of her activities. It is located in her residential compound, where she lives with her younger children, as well as married daughters who have left their husbands to join her, wards left in her care, tenants, and patients who are staying with her on a temporary but often extended basis while they

Plate 7–6. Priestess Azaigueni Aghahowa and some of her followers performing an initiation ritual in front of her shrine to Osanobua, the father of Olokun. The shrine (lower left) includes an *ikhinmwin* tree.

undergo treatment. All of these persons are considered her dependents: she is in charge of their behavior and they owe her service. Cult followers who are not resident nevertheless also owe her service. They run errands, such as carrying messages or going to the market to buy ritual materials, and help with the cooking and the maintenance of the cleanliness of the shrine.

The priestess is responsible for settling disputes, giving advice, and guiding decision making for this varied group of residential and nonresidential clients and followers. In this she is acting exactly like a Benin elder or chief. But even more, she has the added prerogative of granting titles to the participants in her religious association, an extremely significant political function in Benin. Indeed, her religious association is set up like a court, with a hierarchy of title holders, who hold the very same titles that chiefs have within the royal palace, and a number of retainers and functionaries. Although on a smaller scale, this parallels the court of the Queen Mother and various feudal chiefs.

Like a chief, the priestess is at the center of a network of economic redistribution. As mentioned earlier, she is the recipient of fees paid for her medical services and of gifts given by people as signs of respect. She also is paid handsomely for conducting initiations of new priestesses. Much of this money is channelled back into the upkeep of the shrine, the purchase of regalia (costumes, coral beads, and the like), and the acquisition of ritual materials such as animals for sacrifice and food for participants. Money she receives for the initiation of novices and other ritual activities in which her followers participate must be redistributed among them on the basis of seniority. As Herbert Lewis points out for male Shoa Galla mediums:

> His wealth provides the material means to fulfill his functions. This is not to say that a *k'allu* may not become a rich man, but rather, that the aim, the end that brings esteem and influence is not accumulation alone but successful organization and manipulation of ritual, judicial, and social activity. (Lewis 1970:178)

Beyond their households and religious associations, Olokun priestesses do not have the official political authority of chiefs, but they can attain unofficial power. Through their financial resources they can act as patrons, taking care of dependents, giving out money in return for services, settling disputes within their neighborhoods and sometimes beyond. They can act as brokers, setting up contacts between people whom they have come to know through their varied ritual activities. And, lastly, they can have access to the Oba. Priestesses visit the king with their entourages on festival days and consult with him on medical matters. A well-known priestess commonly acts as midwife to the royal wives in the palace. In these ways an accomplished priestess can acquire some influence and power in broader public and political arenas.

In the introduction it was suggested that the cult of Olokun presents a model of greatness to its devotees. But how do people in Benin define greatness and can these priestesses in fact achieve it? The concept of greatness in Benin involves at least three aspects: fame (having one's name known while alive and remembered afterwards); high political rank, expressed through acquisition of a title; and control over resources, whether economic or ideational (special knowledge and magical powers). In these three regards, Olokun priestesses can indeed attain greatness. Their fame can be spread throughout the Benin area and beyond. Modern communication has facilitated the gaining of renown. Some priestesses have appeared on Nigerian television with their dancing groups and a few have managed to get coverage of their activities in the Edo State newspapers. Their rituals are announced regularly in radio spots on current events. Second, these women do acquire chiefly titles, albeit within their own limited cult circle, but they are known outside as *igieohen* [titled priestesses], and they do attain the trappings and some of the powers of high rank outside that circle. Lastly, priestesses obtain economic resources that they use as patrons in the same manner as others of elite status, and they control knowledge and occult powers in crucial areas such as healing. While not every priestess obtains all three of these attributes of greatness or even a high degree of each, the hope and the potential for such achievement exist. Looking around them, aspiring priestesses can see colleagues who have already attained these desired goals of fame, prestige, and power, and they can know that the promise of greatness is theirs as well.

NOTES

1. My research on this topic in 1976 was supported by a Fellowship for Independent Study and Research from the National Endowment for the Humanities, for which I am very grateful. The late Oba Akenzua II was very supportive of my research then, as in previous years. It would be impossible to thank individually all the Olokun priestesses and priests who gave so generously of their time and knowledge, but they will understand if I single out my Chief Priestess, Azaigueni Aghahowa, for special gratitude. Lastly, I am indebted to Warren d'Azevedo for his careful reading and insightful comments on this chapter.

2. In the urban center, Olokun worship is carried out by congregations scattered throughout the city and varying in size from groups of perhaps a dozen devotees to several hundred, each of which is headed by a chief priestess and a group of titled priestesses. Men participate as well in similar capacities as congregation leaders and devotees but are fewer in number in comparison to women. Village worship is concentrated in the district of Iyekorhionmwon in the southeastern corner of the kingdom. There the cult is a community affair headed by a priest and priestess, both elderly, selected by virtue of seniority or by divination.

3. In Edo belief Olokun is unambiguously male, in contrast to the neighboring Yoruba where Olokun is a female deity.

4. The special taboos imposed on Olokun priestesses include prohibitions on wearing a costume that is not pure white, touching a shrine without undergoing purification, and having sexual relations in broad daylight.

8

Candomblé:

A Socio-Political Examination
of African Religion and Art in Brazil

Mikelle Smith Omari

INTRODUCTION

R ELIGION AND ART CONSTITUTE the cultural spheres most clearly demonstrating the significant, pervasive impact Africa has had on Brazil. The obvious conduit of this impact historically was transatlantic slavery. The objectives of this chapter are to discuss critical repercussions of this impact through a socio-political examination of the religious institution known as Candomblé and to briefly review the art forms integrally supporting this religion. An initial consideration of the nature and meaning of Candomblé in general will precede a discussion of the ritual and art of Candomblé Nagô, which has close connections with Yoruba *òrìṣà* religion in Nigeria.[1]

"Candomblé" is the Portuguese term most commonly used in Bahia to describe Afro-Brazilian religion.[2] In the singular, it denotes the large body of ritual practices brought to Brazil by African slaves; in the plural it refers to individual sects or temples of the religion. "Candomblés" also in the past referred to huge festivals and parties held on the slaves' free days that provided opportunities for honoring African deities. In current Bahian usage, the term "Candomblé" includes the ideological corpus of the group—its myths, belief system, worldview, cosmology, values, rituals, and ethics—as well as the physical locality where deities are enshrined and the ceremonies are held.

Candomblés may be viewed as extended family units with descent traced through initiations. Frequently allegiances are formed that even supersede biological family ties (Costa Lima 1967:65–83; personal communication: Oṣunlade 1982a). Ideally, initiation is seen as a rebirth, a creation of a new being. In this context, the officiating priest or priestess is considered to function in a creative capacity, which may be compared to the biological state of female parturition. Even when the initiator is a male, the same analogy is made. During my participation in initiation rituals, I have frequently overheard congratulations on the successful *parto* [birth], much in the manner as would be extended a woman who had just recently terminated a successful physical birth.

The numerous ethnic "nations" formed during the period of slavery gave rise to the various different types of Candomblés. Gege [Jeje] Candomblés derive from the Ewe or Fon rituals brought from Dahomey (now Republic of Benin).[3] Their deities (known as *vodun* or *vodu*), dances, languages, and rituals vary only slightly from those derived from the Yoruba. This similarity is due to socio-religious amalgamation in Africa that reflected the frequent contact and wars between the Yoruba and the ancient kingdom of Dahomey (Mercier 1954:210–234). The striking Yoruba ascendancy in Brazil may be attributed to the great number of slaves of this ethnic group brought to Brazil during the mid-nineteenth century (Verger 1981a:55; Nina Rodrigues 1977 [1905]:107).

Angola and Congo Candomblés are derived from slaves speaking a variety of Bantu languages from areas now within the borders of Zaïre, Cabinda, Angola, Mozambique, Zanzibar, and other Central, East, and Southern African countries. The grammar and vocabulary of these Candomblés' ritual languages are basically Bantu yet also exhibit influences from Portuguese and from Amerindian languages such as Tupi or Tupinamba. Deities in these Candomblés have Bantu names although many of their attributes and ritual paraphernalia are derived from the Yoruba models (Carneiro 1948: 60, 77–78, 86–88, 97, 109). Dance and music differ from the Yoruba in these Angola and Congo Candomblés, although they clearly pay homage to Yoruba patterns. At every festival I attended in Bate Folha and Bogum—two very old, highly respected Angola Candomblés—all of the Yoruba gods had to be summoned, danced for, and sent away before the festival could end successfully. Another factor that distinguishes Angola ritual is the corporate manifestation of Exu [Èṣù, the Yoruba god of chance and unpredictability]. Although Exu manifests in indigenous Yoruba religious ceremonies in Africa and the United States, Exu never manifests in Yoruba-derived Candomblés in Brazil. My research indicates that the most frequent mode of Afro-Bahian ritual representation of Exu is by means of a conical clay form. This image varies from three inches to approximately four feet in height, with the eyes, nose, and mouth made of cowrie shells, with sacrificial materials inside and out.[4]

Caboclo [Indian] Candomblés are the only ones clearly inspired by Amerindian or Brazilian deities, but even these are frequently mixed with Angola, Gege, or Yoruba cosmology and ritual. Their deities are called *encantados* [enchanted or conjured ones], and all their ritual songs are in Portuguese. Surprisingly, the dances performed in these Candomblés and the national Brazilian dance (*samba*) are very similar (personal communication: Ijaola 1981). The *encantados* are the only gods manifested in the Caboclo Candomblé, which I visited in Bahia, who demonstrated the non-African traits of dancing with their eyes open, smoking cigars, and giving consultations and advice with the intention of healing during public festivals. Feathers and brightly colored costumes of Amerindian derivation dominate their annual festivals, while the yellow and green colors of the Brazilian national flag predominate in liturgical garments and house decorations. Fruits and vegetables are the most common sacrifices, rather than the animal sacrifices most common in Yoruba and Angola Candomblés. These fruits and vegetables are present in abundance during public ceremonies for Caboclos and are distributed to the spectators near the end of the celebrations by the possessed Caboclos. According to Edison Carneiro (1948:88–89), *encantados* are mere duplications of the Yoruba *orixá* [gods]. Carneiro cites, for example, the amalgamation of Sultão das Matas [Sultan of the Forests] and Caboclo do Mato [Pure-blooded Indian of the Forest] with Oxossi, the Yoruba god of the forest and the hunt. My research indicates, however, that Caboclos exhibit more original, possibly Amerindian, traits than Yoruba ones and may therefore represent valid attempts to preserve aspects of indigenous Brazilian religion that have not been adequately studied.

CANDOMBLÉ NAGÔ IN BAHIA

Candomblé Nagôs are the most numerous of Candomblés and appear to be the most influential religious associations in Bahia. Major portions of their ritual and cosmological systems and mode of liturgical vestments have been adopted by the Gege, Angola, Congo, and, to a lesser extent, the Caboclo Candomblés. The word *Nagô* is derived from *anago*, a term applied by the Fon to Yoruba-speaking peoples residing in the Republic of Benin. *Nagô* is now used in Brazil to designate all Yoruba, their Afro-Brazilian descendants and Yoruba myth, ritual, and cosmological patterns. However, distinct Yoruba nations in Brazil such as the Oyo, Ketu, Egba, Jebu [Ijẹbu], Jexa [Ijeṣa], and others from Lagos and Ibadan were noted by Raimundo Nina Rodrigues as early as 1890, two years after the abolition of slavery (Nina Rodrigues 1935 [1896]:104), and are still discernible or operative today.

The first securely dated Candomblé Nagô in Bahia was founded in 1830 in Barroquinha, an area now in the town center, by three African women: Iya 'Deta, Iya Kala, and Iya Nasso (Carneiro 1948:63–65). This Candomblé, named Ilé Iya Nasso [the house of mother Nasso], was moved sometime in the late nineteenth century to its present location in Vasco de Gama near the gasoline station São Jorge. It is currently called Casa Branca, the White House. Quarrels over the leadership succession of two chief priestesses led to the subsequent formation of two additional houses: the Candomblé of Gantois in Engenho Velho [the old (sugar) mill] where Nina Rodrigues conducted most of his research; and the Beneficent Society of São Jorge, more commonly known as Axé Opô Afonjá [the sacred force of the staff of (the *orixá* Xango) Afonjá]. This later Candomblé was founded in approximately 1918 by Aninha in São Gonçalo do Retiro and is where I conducted a significant proportion of my field research in Bahia.[5]

Although there are a few rural Candomblés Nagôs (e.g., in Cachoeira, Santo Amaro, and Feira de Santana), it is essentially now an urban phenomenon. As we will see later, however, a symbolic, ideological connection is maintained with rurality. An estimate of more than five hundred Candomblés Nagôs existing in 1983 is probably conservative (personal communication: Vicentio 1983); and these were especially concentrated in the metropolitan area of Bahia. This number included both the older, elite founding houses made famous by numerous researchers since the late nineteenth century, as well as the almost anonymous, proletarian, neighborhood Candomblés. The elite Candomblés command more prestige and attract more adherents than the proletarian ones and therefore have a larger economic pool available for ritual expenses. I found that among these elite Candomblés, the temple area, *terreiro*, usually encompasses numerous acres of land and includes large areas of virgin forest and one or more brooks and streams. Elaborate separate buildings were built for each individual *orixá* honored in the *terreiro*. Each building (known as the *ilé orixá* [shrine of the god]) was constructed of mud and covered with cement or stucco. Roofs were composed of curved, elongated tiles, and the interior as well as exterior were painted in the appropriate symbolic colors of the *orixá* owner of the shrine.

The basic plan of the entire structure consisted of a sacred inner core room where the key objects and implements embodying the sacred force, *axe*[àṣẹ in Yoruba] of the *orixá* were located and an outer room where sacrifices and other rituals were conducted. Among these *axe* were various types of ceramic and porcelain pots and dishes containing the stones, bits of iron, brass, silver, lead, or other metal representing the natural essence of the *orixá*. Next were liturgical implements, which are type-motifs and are specific to each separate *orixá*. Last are numerous plates and dishes containing the remains of liquid and solid offerings, which are considered to have been the preferred food and drink of the *orixá* during their former existence on earth. The natural elements and liturgical implements all receive a portion of blood and food sacrifices, which are offered during daily, weekly, monthly, and annual rituals. Entrance is forbidden into this inner core shrine room except to the Iyalorixá [chief priestess], Bablorixá [chief priest], and Axogun [male official charged with sacrificing animals], the incarnated *orixá*, or a very few senior, elderly adepts who are initiates of the specific *orixá* owner of the shrine. All others must remain in the outer room of the shrine area during ceremonies. This outer area usually has photographs of the illustrious deceased dedicated to the *orixá* owner of the shrine or liturgical implements displayed on the walls. Some of these outer areas contain normal furnishings one would find in any domestic house, such as chairs, armoires, and so forth.

In contrast to the elaborate structures of the elite Candomblés, I found that the proletarian ritual spaces usually consisted of only one or two tiny rooms in a small house. However, even in one of the *terreiros* in Jardim Lobato, where I lived, a separate area to be used as an arena for the large, public annual festivals was incorporated. These proletarian Candomblés were frequently built near areas of trees, shrubs, and other forms of vegetation. This choice in location is undoubtedly linked to the central role that leaves, herbs, and flowers played in all of the rituals I observed.

At Axé Opô Afonjá, and Terreiro Omolu Xapana, where I also lived, many of the initiates live in the Candomblé during the annual festival and initiation cycles, which last from a few weeks up to several months. Initiates sleep in the Candomblé overnight for the weekly or monthly rituals. They commonly refer to this residence as the *roça*, a Portuguese term meaning country, rural region or backwoods plantation. It was recently pointed out to me that this term is also colloquially used to refer to the "interior" of Brazil, the vast, expansive rural area outside of any metropolitan city (personal communication: Augustinho 1984).[6] The frequent use of the term *roça* when discussing Candomblé activities and the fact that a special uniform is worn while one is in the sacred space support the interpretation that for the initiates, Candomblé is viewed as a separate reality or microcosm, or minisociety. There is a sense of leaving the profane, urban openness and entering a rural, cloistered, sacred physical and spiritual space where different norms exist. During the ceremonial periods at Axé Opô Afonjá, the chief priestess also moves to the *roça* and lives in the major shrine, which incorporates her special official living area known as the *ile xango* [shrine of the *orixá* Xango Afonjá], patron of the *terreiro*. This building now also contains a basement museum. The residence of the Iyalorixá in the *roça* during the annual festivals signifies a heightened collective spiritual force that adds to the general excitement and sense of community. Located on the grounds is a school that teaches the resident and neighboring children the traditional history, music, dance, mythology, and songs of the gods. It is known as the Comunidade Oba Biyi, the community of Oba Biyi (the initiate name of Aninha, the founder of this *terreiro*).

The *roça* is permanently organized around older, committed initiates—usually Candomblé officials—and devotees who are destitute or infirm. Each permanent resident is provided with at least a private room or, if means permit, a separate house. Rooms are equipped with all the basic accoutrements, though all washing and bathing and some cooking are done in communal areas. Sometimes rooms are shared by relatives, close friends, or members of the same initiation group called a *barco* [literally, a small open boat]. Temporary residents will be given a separate room or share with someone else. My own residence at Afonjá was a sleeping room in the Casa de Oxala, a large, long, rectangular building serving multiple purposes, where the shrine of this god was also located. I shared my room with Oşunlade, an Iyalorixá visiting from Brasilia. Although Oşunlade had been given her own room, she preferred to share with me, regarding my room as "better". Because Oşunlade was unusually expansive and garrulous, this fortunate situation resulted in the collection of significantly rich and substantial research data by virtue of our almost continuous, close association.

AFRICAN MICROCOSM AS INVERSION OF LUSO-BRAZILIAN MEGACOSM

Two tenets of Candomblé Nagô are the preservation of "pure" African ideas and the meticulous maintenance of the esoteric religious ritual processes of the Yoruba-speaking peoples of West Africa. The tropical climate in Brazil was similar to that in Africa, moreover, and it was thus possible to find the same or similar vegetable substances that played a central religious role in Africa. Candomblé sacred herbology may have been further augmented by knowledge gleaned from Brazilian Indians (personal communication: Abímbọlá 1990). The transatlantic crossing led to some unavoidable alterations in other domains because of the oppressive conditions of slavery and the requirements and restrictions of a new socio-political environment. Many changes that occurred in the art and religion were adaptive and defensive; the amalgamation of African gods with Catholic Saints is just one example of this type of accommodation.[7] In some sects, conflicts caused by the pressures to assimilate into modern Brazilian society led to the incorporation of Catholic altars into the ritual dancing space of the public Candomblé area.[8]

Field observations, however, indicate that values and behavior characteristic of the upper and middle classes (mimicked in the lower classes) in Luso-Brazilian society at large—in the megacosm—are *inverted* in the Afro-Brazilian religious realm, or microcosm. Thus, some of the criteria that accelerate upward mobility in Candomblé Nagô are the values placed on direct descent from Africans (especially the Yoruba, including the fact that black skin is prestigious), mastery of Yoruba language (used in chants, songs, and esoteric rituals), the ability to dance well, and familiarity with medicinal properties of herbs and the spiritual force contained in leaves and their proper combinations and uses.

In the megacosm of mainstream Brazilian society it is ideologically desirable to be as far away from the gods as possible except when asking for favors, whereas in the microcosm of the alternative Candomblé culture, closeness to the gods is desired and highly valued. Proximity to the gods is achieved through the performance of certain tasks, a prodigious investment of time as an active member, and the experience of trance. Careful and consistent attention to one's *orixá*, willing performance of *tarefas* [ritual duties] necessary for the efficient maintenance of the temple, and active participation in the preparation for annual festivals also affect how rapidly one moves to the top of the Candomblé hierarchy. Authority and permissible activity depend on length of initiation. Tasks associated with the initiatory rituals of novices, the collection and treatment of herbs and leaves, and responsibilities in the shrines of specific gods are seen as privileges to be earned, and they bestow substantial prestige and honor upon the recipient. Someone who is not permitted to work in the sacred space is relegated to the spiritually valueless status of a visitor. It is also deemed an honor to be able to offer a sacrifice—whether animal, vegetable, or material, including art—to an *orixá*.

Most people participating in the Candomblé Nagô *terreiros* that I investigated are of African descent.[9] Devotees are primarily from the lower socio-economic classes and generally hold blue collar or service-oriented jobs. A small but slowly rising number of members hold white collar jobs or are training to be professionals.[10] Such examples are usually encountered in the older, wealthier, more prestigious ritual houses such as those of Menininha de Gantois, Axé Opô Afonjá, and Ile Moroailaje. Robert F. Thompson (personal communication: 1981) has suggested that these Candomblés occupy the apex in the hierarchy of Candomblés[11] and thus constitute an elite.

In the *terreiros* I studied, only persons of clear African descent held important ritual posts.[12] Significant numbers of whites, however, do observe public ceremonies and participate in the secular aspects of the Candomblé organization. This is especially true of well-known temples, although it applies to lesser-known ones as well. The attraction of whites to Candomblé was first noted in 1896, only eight years after slavery was abolished in Brazil (Nina Rodrigues 1935 [1896]:155).

In contrast to the Europeanized capitalistic sectors of Bahian society that emphasize private property, individualism, and conspicuous consumption in the secular realm,[13] Candomblé emphasizes the welfare of the group as a whole.

Material display and embellishment are a form of sacrifice to the *orixá*, who dispenses spiritual (and, it is believed, material) rewards and benefits in return for these sacrifices. Rituals and large public festivals are financed primarily by members and affiliates, although money for extraordinary expenditures, such as the repair or erection of a shrine or other construction, may be solicited from wealthy or famous secular officials and patrons of the Candomblé such as Ogans or Obas (see Costa Lima 1977). While there is no cost for initiation into Axé Opô Afonjá, clothing, animal, and vegetable sacrifices are provided by the novices. These items are usually obtained only after saving for years, through loans, or with the help of extended family, friends, and patrons. My observation of Candomblé members during an interval of three years revealed that their greatest expenditures were in the service of the gods and not for personal secular needs. In fact, the startling simplicity of their Western type of daily dress provided a dramatic contrast to the rich, often extravagant, opulent luxury of the public ritual dress of the *orixá*.

Land belonging to the Candomblé is held in common, and it is dispensed by the head priestess to those who need it to build houses, pending civil approval. This practice may have its roots in Yoruba principles of land ownership and allocation. Food and economic aid are provided for devotees who experience unforeseen need. In this respect, Candomblé Nagô functions as a mutual aid organization.[14]

The overriding focus of the Candomblé is communal rather than individual. Indeed, one of the highest compliments that can be paid to an initiate is that he or she is obedient, meaning that he or she places the interests of the group in the service of the *orixá* above himself or herself. Candomblé Nagô also offers Afro-Bahians a channel through which they can achieve a significant measure of self-esteem, social solidarity, prestige, and social mobility within a system that celebrates African values, behavior patterns, ideas, and dark skin color. Thus Candomblé provides an important alternative to the megacosm and fulfills a critical need for its members, who are otherwise denied full participation in Luso-Brazilian society.

CANDOMBLÉ NAGÔ INITIATION

Candomblé Nagô is characterized by belief in and worship of a pantheon of divinities of which Olorun [Olódùmarè in Yoruba] is the supreme, although nonworshipped, head.[15] The seventeen major *orixá* are regarded as spiritual forces based in Africa who can only be manifested or expressed by certain human beings of the deities' choice. The will of the *orixá* is ascertained through divination sought by individuals when persistent misfortune or illness is experienced. Dreams are also important indicators of the need for initiation.

If the outcome of the divination indicates the necessity to initiate, the individual begins to make preparations by amassing funds to pay for the clothing, food, animal and vegetable sacrifices, pots, liturgical implements and other items that will play an essential part in the extensive and complex series of required rituals. Because of the characteristically low economic status of the majority of initiates, it may take years to accumulate the necessary resources. I personally witnessed the initiation of one individual dedicated to the *orixá* Yansan who had saved for ten years to fulfill her initiation obligations (Itaparica Island, 1 July 1981). In order to defray some of the expenses, a chief priest or priestess will frequently wait until a number of individuals can be initiated as a group. The group can then share some of the major expenses.

There are a number of levels of initiation and all of them involve similar learning procedures. They vary only in depth of learning and the degree of esoteric ritual detail involved. Common to all types is a specified period of seclusion during which the initiate is taught proper ritual procedures and behavior, the use of virgin and special symbolic clothing, and rituals involving the "inner head" [ori; Yoruba orí]—the seat of the sacred force and the god. The performance of any ritual act involving the head, botar a mão na cabeça [lit. "to put the hands on the head"], is believed to create a spiritual link and bond between the officiant and the recipient that can be dissolved only by death. The only way this link can be broken is by a ceremony similar in purpose and concept: tirar a mão da cabeça [lit. "to withdraw the hand from the head"]. Submission to this ritual incorporates the individual into the familia de santo [spiritual family group] of the temple in which it is performed (personal communications: Crispim 1981b; Kayode 1982a). Ndolamb Ngokwey (1984:50) noted that ritual manipulation of the head serves not only to "fix" the orixá in the head but also to "seal the asymmetrical relationship between the novice and initiator, a relationship patterned after the parental/filial model characterized by authority and dominance of the parent and the submission and dependence of the children". Ngokwey further asserts that "this same asymmetricity characterizes the relationship between the filho-de-santo and his orixá, as well indicated by the coercive power of the orixá" (1984:51).

The first and primary initiation in Candomblé Nagô that I experienced is the ritual procedure known as bori [borí in Yoruba: to "feed", "propitiate", or "worship" the inner head]. This generally consists of a ritual inside the sacred shrine precincts in which the individual is seated on a ritually prepared, natural straw mat and dressed totally in the sacred liturgical costume. All the colors of the garments and implements must be white or light colored, because it is believed that the orixá Obatala [Obàtálá] governs all rituals dealing with spiritual creation, rebirth, or death. In these contexts, the color white symbolizes the sacred force and presence of Obatala. The basic ritual consists of the sacrifice of a white dove or pigeon, whose neck must be wrung in a special ritual manner rather than cut. The blood is placed on the head of the individual along with other sacred items such as kola nut and some of the favorite foods of the orixá owner of the individual's head. Special songs and dances are performed throughout the ritual that can last from one to three hours. These are performed by the Iya Kekere (the assistant to the chief priestess and the second in command) and by any other elderly initiates or Candomblé officials who happen to be in the temple area at the time and who wish to participate. Divination with a kola nut cut into four pieces is performed periodically throughout the ritual to ascertain the will of the orixá being fed. Tiny portions of all the food and the sacrifice are placed on the tongue, palms of the hand, soles of the feet, and forehead of the novice before finally being placed in tiny bits in the center of his or her head and in the food receptacles of the orixá. Finally, a long white cloth is wrapped around the head of the individual and tied tightly. This head-tie serves to secure the items placed on top of the head during the night-long seclusion of the individual after the ceremony. In the morning, the items are removed from the head and disposed of. The head priestess asks the novice to reveal any dreams that occurred during her or his night in the shrine and uses this information combined with the results of divination to ascertain the will of the deity. Finally, the individual is washed with a special herbal bath and the initiate's clothes are changed.

The next level of initiation, known as *assentar santo* [lit. to seat the *orixá*], consists of a series of rituals designed to localize the dynamic, immaterial force of the *orixá* into a material foundation such as a bit of metal, wood, or various types of stones according to the perceived nature of the deity. The stones, metal, or wood are placed inside lidded jars in water, honey, palm oil, vegetable oil, or any combination of these, according to the preferences of the deity symbolized by the specific material. The novice is secluded for seventeen days, fed special food, and is not allowed to speak except by means of a series of special handclaps. She or he is taught the special songs, history, and peculiar characteristics of her or his *orixá*. In the Candomblé I investigated, at this stage of initiation the head is not shaved nor are cuts made in the occiput of the initiate's head. *Assentar santo* can be seen variously as a means to an end or merely a preliminary step in the initiatory process usually reserved for those who will eventually become mediums of the *orixá*. During seclusion, the novice is cared for by a senior initiate of the same *orixá* owner of the initiate's head. This person is known by the title of 'Jibona. After this ritual procedure is terminated, the pot or receptacle containing the material symbol of the initiate's *orixá* is placed in the common shrine for all initiates of that level.

The most elaborate, lengthy, expensive, and intense initiation is that intended to prepare an individual to serve as a medium [*cavalo*, lit. horse] of the *orixá*. This procedure usually occurs just once a year, beginning in June or August, in the Candomblés I studied. Before scheduling this ritual into the annual calendar, the head priest or priestess will ordinarily wait until there are at least five or more persons who need to be initiated as mediums. The motives are largely economic, so the members of the initiation group and their families can absorb many of the costs collectively. If there are not sufficient novices, this type of initiation will be postponed until the following year. In an initiation cycle in which I participated at Afonjá (August to November 1982), there were six novices. Two were dedicated to Omolu, two to Oxala, one to Yemanjá, and one to Ogum. In smaller proletarian Candomblés, the number of individuals initiated at one time can vary from one to ten or more. The exceptions to the usual procedure of initiation are occasioned by urgency on the part of the novice, insofar as initiation is seen as a solution to extreme mental, psychological, physical, marital, or economic problems or pressures (personal communications: Hilda 1981; Crispim 1982a).

In this third type of initiation, the novices must make arrangements to live in the temple grounds for the entire period of seclusion, which can vary from seventeen days or three months to a year, depending on the outcome of the divination. This divination is usually performed twice, once with the *'dilogun* [a Portuguese abbreviation of *eerindinlogun*], the sixteen cowrie system, and once with four pieces of kola nut. Before entering the seclusion room, the initiates stay in various private homes of initiates who live permanently in the *terreiro*. During this period the initiate is dressed in a simple, white liturgical costume. Each initiate is interned in the seclusion room [known variously as *ronco* or *camiarinha*] on the sacred day of Oxala, Friday. Beginning before sunup on early Friday morning, each novice is submitted to a special herbal bath and *bori* according to the hierarchical rank of the *orixá* owner of the individual's head. Afterwards, each novice is led to the seclusion room, which has been ritually purified by washing the walls with special water containing pulverized leaves sacred to the *orixá* of each novice. The walls were subsequently freshly whitewashed. Each group of initiates remains in this one room, which may be windowless and usually contains only one door. At the top of the door frame, fringes of fresh, young palm leaves are placed and serve as protective devices against the spiritual intrusion of deceased ancestors and other negative influences that might impede the successful conclusion of this process of rebirth. Each of the novices must sleep or sit on his or her own personal mat [*esteira*], which must not be used by anyone else. Except in special cases, such as prostrating to honor an *orixá*, no novice's body can touch another mat or use the mat owned by one of the initiation group. Each initiate has his or her own white enameled tin plate and wide-mouthed cup [*caneca*] on which is painted a special symbol. This must not be touched or used by anyone else except the 'Jibona of each initiate. All the members of the initiation group spend the majority of their time isolated in this room. All eating, sleeping, and learning is accomplished there and the initiates are not permitted to talk except by means of the special handclapping that functions as a special ritual language called *karake*, whose name is of unknown linguistic origin. The novices leave the seclusion room daily before sunrise and after sunset to be bathed in special ritual herbal water. They may sometimes be walked around the interior of the *terreiro* close to their cloister room, in order to obtain a minimum of exercise, but this must be accomplished only when the eldest initiates are in the vicinity. The only relief available to the novices during this extremely regimented period is by means of the trance-state known as *ere*, a form of infantile trance to be discussed more fully later. In this form of trance, the novices laugh, joke, tease, and generally behave like boisterous, mischievous children.

During the first few days of seclusion, the novices undergo many rituals during which their hair is cut, the scalp is shaved, and they receive a necklace made of *kele*—large, tubular beads in the sacred color(s) of their deity. They also receive an anklet, known as *xaoro,* made of braided raffia palm fiber to which small metal bells [*guizos*] are attached; in Africa these ornaments are used for children (personal communication: Rubin 1984). Both the *kele* and the *xaoro* symbolize the complete submission of the novice to the Candomblé as a general entity, to the *orixá*, to the head priest or priestess, and to the 'Jibona.

During this time, the novice also receives protective devices made of virgin, braided raffia palm fiber: a long necklace[*mocã*] used to force trance and armbands known as *contra-egun* that provide protection against ancestral spirits.

The most important portion of this type of initiation, that which specifically prepares the novice to enter into trance and incorporate his or her *orixá*, takes place in the restricted confines of the sacred shrine of the Candomblé. If the *terreiro* is an elite one that encompasses many different separate shrines for the *orixá*, the novices are led, completely covered from head to toe in white cloths, to the main shrine; in the case of Afonjá, the main shrine was that of the *casa de Xango*. In the case of Dona Hilda's Candomblé, where all of the *orixá* are kept in one common room, the inititates are taken there. During this phase of the ritual only the Iyalorixá [chief priestess], the Babalorixá [chief priest], a senior cult official who functions as assistant, and the 'Jibona of the novice can be present.[16] During this portion, ritual songs recalling the role of Oxala, the creator *orixá*, are sung and cuts are made in the occiput of each novice's head. During the period in which cuts are being made, the novice is seated on a small stool made of virgin wood and painted with the symbols of his or her *orixá*. This stool is then placed on top of the individual's personal sleeping mat or a new mat. It is only during the period when ritual incisions are being made that the Brazilian novices sit on the stool (personal communications: Crispim 1981c, 1982e), contrasting with Santéria initiations in Cuba and the United States. Specific combinations of leaves, herbs and other natural ingredients are placed inside these cuts, made with a new, previously unused razor blade. These cuts are subsequently activated by placing sacrificial blood on the occiput—blood from two- and four-footed animals preferred by the *orixá*. The initiate then enters into the state of *orixá* possession trance. Feathers from the fowls are taken from the mouth, leg, and tail areas and placed on the initiates' heads. The initiates are then led out of the shrine area to dance the dances of their *orixá*. They are then led back into the shrine room and cuts are placed on the back (in the manner of the parallel Yoruba scarification marks), upper arms, and chest of the initiate. Into these are rubbed ingredients believed to contain sacred force. The initiates come out once again to dance and are led, entranced, back into the shrine room to pass the night.

The following day, initiates undergo rituals in which they receive necklaces [*ileki*, Yoruba *ilèkè*] of their *orixá* as well as of any accompanying *orixá* participating in their "road, destiny or direction of new life after initiation". At this time, they are given new initiation names symbolizing the rebirth [*sundide*], but these names may not be uttered publicly. During this portion of the ritual, the head is painted as a symbolic artistic and cosmic map that simultaneously evokes all the elements of the Yoruba concept of the cosmos and the specific type-motifs of each *orixá*. These motifs are painted on by the head priestess according to the patterns indicated by the results of divination. The colors most often used are those obtained from natural pigments imported from the West Africa Yoruba: *efun* [white chalk], *osun* [red camwood powder], and *waji* or *elu* [powdered blue indigo]. This design is used for subsequent rituals in the initiation process and especially on days of public presentation of the novices. These days are called *saidas* [lit. coming out or public appearances].

During the long period of seclusion, the novices are trained in the history, esoteric ritual language, mythology, and aesthetic and sacrificial preferences of his or her own personal *orixá*. Another crucial portion of this new learning involves the ability to control the state of trance in the proper ritual circumstances. In this manner, the possession trance does not occur spontaneously, but rather in response to certain internalized cues such as the specific drumbeat, music, or songs of the *orixá*. In all the situations I observed, all the initiates exhibited the faltering, half-unsteady behavior of little children while learning these new concepts. Even those who had grown up inside the socio-ritual arena of the *terreiro* appeared to require teaching of the special dances of their *orixá* and I observed a number of these "practices" [*xire*] at Afonja, Curuzu, and Itaparica at which this learning took place. These "practices" were held during the weeks preceding the *saída*, the official public coming out party of the new initiates, also known as *orunko* or *dia de dar o nome* [the day of giving the name] because it is the first public utterance of the initiate's new name. During *orunko* the new initiate wears a conical pack of protective leaves, herbs, and sacrificial and natural ingredients on top of the occiput, where the ritual incisions of the *orixá* have been made. The conical pack is known as *oxu*; the initiate is subsequently known as *adoxu* or carrier of the sacred cone on the head. After this ceremony, the new initiates, also known as *iyawo* [wives of the *orixá*] or *filhas/filhos de santo* [daughters or sons of the saint], are considered to be adequately ritually prepared and are permitted to end seclusion. The ceremony that marks this transition is known as *panan* or *quitanda*. It consists of a symbolic relearning of the daily procedures of life, such as cooking, ironing, washing, and getting married. This ritual underscores the belief that the *adoxu* are new beings. From this point on, they are subject to new laws and ritual obligations and are incorporated as members of the extended spiritual family of the Candomblé.

ORIXÁ IN CANDOMBLÉ NAGÔ RELIGION

One of the most important keys to understanding Afro-Bahian art and ritual is to become cognizant of the preliterate, preindustrial worldview that characterizes the microcosm of Candomblé. In this respect, the regulation of life is regarded as emanating not from the individual or even the community (as is the case with Western technological society), but rather, in the microcosm, life controls emanate from a complex hierarchy of deities [*orixá* and *exu*], ancestors [*egun*] and other spirits.

The *orixá* form the most crucial components of the cosmological system of Candomblé Nagô. They are regarded as personifications of the forces of nature. Xango [Şàngó], in Yoruba], for example, represents thunder, lightning, and fire; others incarnate socio-political and economic forces. Ogum [Ògún] is the god of war and iron or other metals, while Oxossi is the god of the hunt. Other *orixá* are considered to have been actual heroes, persons of extraordinary force and abilities who were subsequently deified after death: e.g., Obatala [Ọbàtálá] is regarded as the "real" king of Ilé-Ifè the holy city of the Yoruba, and commemorated annually in this role, while Xango was once also a king [*alafin*] of Òyó, capital of the largest and most powerful of the Yoruba city-states. *Orixá* are also thought of as possessing human characteristics. They are honored and characterized by dance, music, and costume during public festivals. Their behavior is reenacted by means of mythical dramas or presentations that take place in the dance arena: for example, the quarrels and amorous rivalries of the male *orixá* (Ogum, Xango, and

Oxossi) for the female *orixá* Oxum [goddess of fresh water and sensual love]; or the jealousy of Oxum for the *orixá* Oba (another of Xango's wives), who was tricked by Oxum into cutting off her ear and serving it to her husband in a soup, thereby causing the eternal separation of Oba from Xango. These brief scenarios are typical of the complex store of lore associated with the character of each individual *orixá*.

An intricate symbolic system identifies each *orixá* by special songs, drumbeats, series of dance steps, beads, color combinations, costume, liturgical implements, leaves, herbs, food, and sacrificial animals. Each *orixá* governs certain geographical features (such as crossroads or bodies of water), and days of the week are consecrated to one or more distinct *orixá*. On this special weekday, a liturgical observance that is somewhat more elaborate than the daily worship takes place. This weekly ceremony is named *ossé* from the Yoruba word for week.

According to Claude Lepine (1981:13–23), each *orixá* possesses a distinct personality and characteristic mode of behavior that gradually becomes integrated with (or superimposed upon) the devotee's personality and behavior. Thus, an *adoxu xango* becomes forceful, noble, jealous, impulsive, unfaithful, proud, and stubborn according to the mythological prototype supplied by the *orixá* Xango. It is believed that the longer an individual has been initiated, the more his or her personality and behavior modes reflect those of the god, rather than his or her own. This phenomenon can be observed in general daily life but becomes more pronounced when the individual enters the possession trance of his or her *orixá*, known as *estado do orixá* [the state of being (in) the god].

The relationship between the initiate and the *orixá* who is the owner of his or her head is intense, personal, and reciprocal. The *orixá* is viewed as simultaneously possessing unlimited capabilities for coercive and punitive powers as well as supportive and beneficial powers. The concept that the *orixá* (and other supernatural forces) possess the power to intervene in a positive manner in all human affairs is counterbalanced by the idea that if they are offended, negative intervention is the unfailing result.[17] Candomblé members sincerely believe that the *orixá* possess the power to punish not only initiates and affiliates of the *terreiro*, but anyone who offends them, the initiates they protect, or the values they represent.

The Candomblé members with whom I interacted essentially viewed themselves as "powerless" in relation to the wider Brazilian society, and to life in general. This perspective is not surprising in light of the historical pattern of persistent adversity and socio-economic and political marginality that has characterized the Afro-Brazilian experience. This sense of fatalism and onerous destiny seems to be counterbalanced by the concept of the *orixá* and other spirits as possible providers of order, meaning, hope, and control over life inside the microcosm as well as out in the megacosm. In this worldview, it is interesting that art plays a central role in the attainment of positive goals and controls on life.

Each *orixá* (as well as each initiate and ancestor) possesses an aspect characterized by chance and unpredictability. This spirit or aspect is known variously as Exu or Elegba [from Yoruba Èṣù or Ẹlégbára] and is defined by Bastide (1978a:170–198) as a seventeenth *orixá*.[18] Exu can act out of greed or perversity, with approval of the *orixá* owner of the victim's head, or at the behest of sorcerers. There are Exu that cause specific illnesses (e.g., tuberculosis, alcoholism); others cause marital, financial, employment, or mental problems.

Within the shrine [*peji* or *ile orixá*] each *orixá* is localized and ritually consecrated in a stone, seashell, piece of metal or some other natural element containing his or her sacred force. The liturgical implements symbolizing the *orixá* are also kept here along with an image of Exu, which must receive the first bit of any sacrifices offered to the *orixá* or their symbols. All of these objects remain permanently in the shrine. They are only taken out when the shrine is cleaned or (in the case of the liturgical implements) when they will be used by the incorporated *orixá* during the annual public festivals.

Among the West African Yoruba, there are separate temples and a specialized priesthood for each god. In Bahia, however, each temple space is used to house and worship all of the *orixá* honored by the particular Candomblé. The head priestess and devotees, therefore, become familiar with symbols, esoteric rituals, songs, rhythms, and costume elements of many *orixá* while remaining in command of those belonging to his or her own *orixá*. In contrast, a Yoruba devotee of Oṣun in Africa [Oxum in Brazil] is likely to be completely ignorant of the ways of Yẹmọja [Yemanja] (Abímbọ́lá 1976b:14–15).

There seems to be no consensus among Candomblés Nagôs regarding the hierarchical ranking of the *orixá*. As a rule, however, public festivals begin with celebrations of the youngest, most hot-headed *orixá* (e.g., Ogum) and progress to the increasingly cool-headed ones. They usually end with celebrations of Oxala, who is the oldest and regarded as father of all the *orixá*.

POSSESSION TRANCE AS CENTRAL NEXUS OF CANDOMBLÉ RELIGION

In my opinion, features that distinguish Afro-Bahian Candomblé as a religion, in contrast to being considered "merely" as folklore (in the colloquial Brazilian sense of "folklore" as less serious than "religion") are (1) the consistent, systematic, and active worship of a number of gods and the activation and maintenance of their combined sacred forces; (2) the ritual feeding and manipulation of sacred liturgical objects representing and imbued with the force of these gods; (3) the wearing of private and public ritual garments *always* confined within the physical and spiritual limits of the sacred space of the Candomblé;[19] (4) the continuous initiation of new recruits, who insure the continuity of the traditions; and, most importantly, (5) the phenomenon of trance, which is the critical determining qualifier of Candomblé as a religion, and in fact is the key means by which the religion has continued in the New World throughout the centuries of separation from Yoruba religion in Nigeria.

During possession trance, a human medium is possessed and serves as a vehicle through whom an *orixá* or saint [*santo*] corporalizes.[20] Possession trance is the central nexus of the religion, because it is only through trance that the gods "physically" come from Africa to the private shrines and public ritual dancing spaces in Brazil and bring with them the sacred force necessary to revitalize and

Plate 8–1. Senior initiates in trance, possessed by their respective *orixá*, Candomblé of Dona Hilda, Bahia, 1981.

sustain the religion (Plate 8–1). Ideologically and in reality, there could be no Afro-Bahian religion without the spiritual and ritual transformation of the possession trance.

The achievement of trance is communicated by visual signals easily recognized by Candomblé Nagô members: special body posture, specific behavior, and changes in key elements of the possessed person's costume.

As soon as Candomblé devotees enter trance, their eyes close. Conscious members then remove the possessed persons' shoes and head-ties. This allows their bare feet and bare heads to contact the earth and the air that members believe contain the sacred force and vital essence of the *orixá*. The devotees' clothing is loosened and a head-tie is arranged over each torso, the head-tie ending in a large bow at the small of the back in order to signal the change from normalcy to possession trance.

The hands of each entranced devotee are positioned to communicate the changed state. Specific positioning of hands while in trance varies from *terreiro* to *terreiro*. For example, at Axé Opô Afonjá, the *orixá* place their hands left over right at the small of the back, while in Curuzu the hands are placed on the left hip. As a final indicator of the state of possession trance, each devotee assumes the characteristic behavioral patterns of his or her gods during the dance. These behavioral patterns are supplemented by pacing back and forth while "at rest" (not dancing).

In all the Ketu "nation" Candomblés where I participated and observed, each incorporated *orixá* further communicated the state of possession trance by assuming his or her particular yell or shout [*ika*]. For example, all initiates possessed by Yansan [Oya] shout something like "Hayeeeeee!" The *ika* further serves to identify both the state of possession trance and the type and quality of *orixá* present. The congregation in turn greets each *orixá* by a specific individualized salute, such as "Epa Hei!" to salute or honor Yansan.

At the great annual festivals, during an intermission in the ceremony, the *orixá* change completely from the generic festival garments into elaborate clothing appropriate to each deity. The *orixá* are then led back in a row into the dancing arena to the accompaniment of the constant ringing of a special ritual bell [*agogo*]. They then reenact through dance the detailed myths and stories associated with each *orixá* present.

Trance functions emically as a religious communion for the Candomblé members and reinforces the solidarity of the group in addition to having cathartic, emotional compensation, or social power functions for individual devotees (Lepine 1981:27; Bastide 1978:259; Verger 1954:337–338; Ngokwey 1984: 54–55). Great prestige and admiration accrue to an individual who can easily become entranced by his or her *orixá*. The facility of trance is interpreted as evidence of the satisfaction of the *orixá* with the rituals and sacrificial offerings.

On the other hand, if trance is delayed, it produces great anxiety for the group: I have witnessed numerous occasions when an initiate desired trance but it would not come or was delayed. The usual reaction to this occurrence was increased group support expressed by louder singing in a more rapid rhythm than usual. In addition, enthusiastic handclapping to the accompaniment of an extremely rapid drumbe at [*adarrum*] designed "to bring the *orixá* to the initiate's head" was observed. In the event that all efforts to achieve possession failed, everyone was disappointed, and the ceremony was ineffective.

BASIC CANDOMBLÉ COSTUME

Required Candomblé dress for all women[21] except the most casual visitors, suppliants, or visiting dignitaries is a ritual uniform composed of five elements: the *camizu*, the *saia*, the *oja*, the *ileki*, and the optional *pano da costa* (Plate 8–2).

The *camizu*, the name of which is derived from the Muslim burial tunic (Nina Rodrigues 1935 [1896]:152), consists of a short-sleeved blouse trimmed in lace and attached to a plain cotton slip. The *camizu* is a basic element of dress whether the devotee is in trance or conscious.

The *saia* is a full ankle-length skirt gathered at the waist and fastened by long ties extending from a narrow waistband. The material of the *saia* varies in accordance with the status of the wearer; increasing opulence is associated with increasing status. The *saia*—except for the universal white worn at funerals and at sacrifices or ceremonies for Oxala—is also an important visual communicator of which *orixá* the wearer serves (e.g., blue and white for Yemanja).

The *oja* or *torço* is a long narrow piece of cloth, approximately 12 inches by 72 inches, that serves as a head-tie in the African fashion when the initiate is in a normal state of consciousness. The *oja* is usually white, made of varying materials, and trimmed in lace. It is this costume element that is immediately taken off the head and placed on the torso when possession trance first occurs. The repositioned *oja* indicates not only the changed state of being but also the identity of the *orixá* possessing the initiate. For instance, incarnated female *orixá*—known as *ayaba* or queens, including Yansan, Yemanja, and Oxum—have their *oja* tied over their breasts and under their armpits into a big bow at the small of the back. Oxossi, a male *orixá*, has two *oja* crisscrossed front and back ending in a bow at each side of the waist. Oxala, another male *orixá*, has two *oja* crisscrossed in the manner of Oxossi but ending in bows at each shoulder. These symbols allow one to immediately identify the *orixá* possessing the devotee.

Ileki (or *eleke*) bead necklaces form the fourth important component of the daily liturgical uniform and indicate identity of the *orixá* by the color(s) and sequential arrangement of individual beads. The specific type of beads and length and type of necklaces used indicate full, partial, or noninitiate status.

All initiates are *adoxu*—carriers of *oxu*, the conical pack of ingredients that protected the sacred cuts on their heads during the initiation ceremonies discussed earlier. Recently initiated novices who are still in ritual seclusion, however, are known as *iyawo*. After *iyawo* leave ritual seclusion, they are *Filhas/Filhos-de-Santo*. While *iyawo* are still secluded, they are distinguished by a special necklace called a *kele*. The *kele* is also worn during seclusion for the transition ritual from Filha-de-Santo to Ebomin, a ceremony symbolizing the completion of seven years of initiate status.[22] The *kele* consists of large tubular beads worn close to the neck in choker fashion, the color(s) and material of which indicate the type of *orixá* who is master of the new initiate's head. The name *kele* as well as its essential form seems to have been appropriated from the type and name of necklace associated with the West African *orixá* Şàngó, which is generally a choker type of necklace made of large round or tubular beads in red or red and white, the sacred colors of Şàngó (personal communications: 'Mogba Şàngó 1982; Baba Şàngó 1981). In Bahia the *kele* is a sign of submission to the *orixá* and is taken off only after the initiate's first public appearance [*orunko*], which is also the first day he or she utters his or her new sacred initiate name. Removal of the *kele* marks the end of strict ritual seclusion and total submission to the *orixá* and the initiating officials (personal communication: Crispim 1982b). The removal of the *kele* may also symbolize the initiate's newly acquired sense of power, since a major part of initiation is devoted to teaching control of trance so that the *orixá* will not come arbitrarily but rather only during specific rituals and in response to definite "cues" or "summons". Once the *kele* is off, the *adoxu* places the necklace in her ritual core of sacred objects along with the stone [*ita* or *ota*] in which her *orixá* is localized and consecrated. This complex of objects is commonly known as *assento* or *assentamento*, meaning "seat" or "foundation" in Portuguese.

Firma, a tubular bead or shell slightly larger than the other beads on the *ileki*, symbolizes the initiatory status of the wearer who has completed ritual seclusion. The *firma* also communicates the relationship between his or her patron *orixá* and other *orixá*. For example, an *adoxu* of Yansan would always have a *firma* for Xango, her principal husband, while an Omolu devotee would always have a blue-and-white striped *firma* for Nanan, his mythological mother. Thus, only someone who actually had ingredients containing the sacred force of his or her *orixá* placed in slits in the head would technically be entitled to wear a *firma* bead or shell on his or her *ileki* necklace. The absence of a *firma* indicates either an initiate at the lowest stage [*abian*] or someone who wears the beads as a protective device.

The fifth and optional costume element is the *pano da costa*, a wide, rectangular piece of cloth, 24 inches by 36 or 48 inches, depending upon the wearer's girth. The *pano da costa* is derived from the Yoruba strip weave cloth made by men and known as *aşọ oke*.[23] It is customarily worn wrapped around the torso and over the breasts during annual public festivals. During the one formal ritual that I observed taking place outside of the sacred space (the annual gift-giving to Yemanja formally marking the end of the Candomblé ritual cycle at Afonjá, November 1982), many participants were allowed great license regarding the use of the *pano da costa* and wore it draped over the left shoulder in the manner of an Iyalorixá. *Pano da costa* vary in quality and color depending upon the nature of the ritual, the patron *orixá* of the initiate, or the *orixá* for whom the festival is held [*dono da festa*], and the economic means and tastes of the initiate.

Sacred implements also form an integral part of the costume. These belong to and symbolize individual *orixá*. They are kept in the shrine of the *orixá* and and are brought out for use only by an incarnated *orixá* during an annual festival, a three- or seven-year obligation [*obrigação*],[24] or at the first public festival of a recent initiate [*saída de iyawo*, literally the coming out of the *iyawo*].

Plate 8–2. Iyalorixá [chief priestess] wearing basic costume elements—
camizu lace-trimmed blouse, *saia* ankle-length skirt, *oja* head-tie, and *ileki*
bead necklaces—plus *pano da costa* over her left shoulder as a sign of her
status. Visitor to Maninha Gentas, Bahia, 1983.

COSTUME AS AN EXPRESSION OF STATUS IN CANDOMBLÉ

Each level in the Candomblé hierarchy (Iyalorixá, Ebomin, Iyawo or Filha/Filho-de-Santo, etc.) is distinguished by a special mode of social behavior. Within each level, status accrues with length of membership: even a few minutes' difference in time between processes of actual full initiation—such as cuts in the head and implantation of the god's sacred forces—confers seniority and, by extension, prestige. All high officials of ritual rank are selected from the high initiate class of Ebomin. Marked deference is paid by all initiates to the Iyalorixá when addressing her: the heads are bared, and bowing or prostrating full length on the floor is required in a manner similar to the Yoruba mode of paying respect to their kings. Within the sacred space of the Candomblé, priests and priestesses hold status that is—at least conceptually—on the royal level. This contrasts to the ambiguous status previously noted for priests and priestesses in traditional Yoruba society.

Socio-religious positions are communicated by modes of dress. During public and private rituals, the Iyalorixá traditionally wears a *pano da costa* folded into a rectangle and worn over her left shoulder. This costume item is a special prerogative of the chief priestess's station and distinguishes her from the others even in the proletarian Candomblés in which economics do not permit an elaborate and more formal mode of dressing as is characteristic of the larger Candomblés such as Afonjá and Gantois. In one proletarian Candomblé that I studied in Curuzu, the daily use of the *pano da costa* by the Iyalorixá was entirely dispensed with and reserved for only great ritual occasions. In the richer "elite", more "traditional" Candomblés, the Iyalorixá will frequently use for her *pano da costa* the highly prestigious *aṣo oke* cloth imported from Nigeria, and the colors of her personal *orixá* dominate.

The dress of the Iyalorixá in all Candomblés that I have studied is composed of special rich and unusual fabrics, and these cannot be duplicated by lesser members. These elements of costume are frequently gifts from clients who solicited divination that is given free of charge at Afonjá. Special necklaces and beaded bracelets or other materials of unusual size, shape, and combination form part of the entire complex.

Another special element of dress signifying status is the *bata*, a loose over-blouse resembling the West African Yoruba *buba* but with flaring sleeves of medium length, worn alone or loosely over the *camizu* and the upper part of the *saia*. It is usually made of a richly embroidered transparent material, predominantly white or in various pastel colors according to the wearer's *orixá*. The *bata* is trimmed in handmade or machine-made lace according to the status and economic means of the wearer. The *bata* is a symbol of the completion of the seven-year *obrigação* ritual marking the transition from the junior initiate state to the senior initiate state of Ebomin. As a senior initiate, the Iyalorixá is entitled to a *bata*, but one that marks her rank by the quality of material used. Senior initiates can wear the *bata* tied at the waist with the *oja* head tie or under their *pano da costa*. Most frequently, in public festivals, both junior and senior initiates wear their *pano da costa* wrapped around the torso over the skirt and under the armpits. A tied *oja* secures the *pano da costa*.

OBJECTS AND SPACES AS MARKERS OF SOCIAL STATUS AND RITUAL LEVEL

In principle, upon fulfilling the seven-year *obrigação*, any initiate with sufficient money, spiritual powers, a small following of potential clients, and the blessing of the Iyalorixá may undergo a ritual to prepare her or him to open her or his own Candomblé. The new temple and shrines must contain sacred items, including the consecrated sacred elements of the initiate's particular *orixá*, in order to implant sacred forces in the new *terreiro*. The complete grouping of ritual objects is known as *deka*. This process requires the help of many ritual specialists and elder priests and priestesses of other Candomblés[25] (personal communications: Oṣunlade 1982b; Crispim 1982c).

Public rituals take place in the sacred space known as *barracão*—a large, square or rectangular, whitewashed building made of cement-covered mud. In the past, roofs were thatched, but they are now covered with red half-cylindrical tiles. In Afonjá and other major Candomblés, the *barracão* serves as a dancing arena during public festivals as well as a storage area for the ritual clothing of each *orixá*. Every full initiate stores the special clothes for her *orixá* in one of the three special rooms isolated from the major public area.

When the *barracão* functions as an arena for the drama of the *orixá*, seating is hierarchically arranged. Against the wall opposite the entrance is the throne of the Iyalorixá, the highest authority in the Candomblé. This chair is larger, taller, and more elaborate than any other in the *barracão*, befitting and symbolizing her status. At Afonjá, there are two smaller chairs on each side of the others. They are reserved for the Obas of Xango, the highest positions in the civil hierarchy.[26] Near the west wall is an area designated for initiates, furnished with long narrow wooden benches and square wooden stools. Directly opposite, along the east wall, are several tiered rows of chairs for officials and distinguished guests. Along the north wall are bleachers for spectators. Men sit on the left side of the public entrance and women on the right. On either side of the entrance is a reduced version of the bleacher seating. Immediately behind the dance arena, drummers are situated on a raised area in full view of the audience. Everyone pays careful attention to seating arrangements.

Inside the sacred space, ordinary material possessions also indicate status and ritual level. In her own home, an initiate uses whatever utensils she prefers, but in the sacred space, only the Iyalorixá uses fine china, or crystal, or chrome plates, cups, and glasses. A senior initiate is entitled to medium-quality dinnerware, while other initiates must content themselves with inexpensive enameled tin cups, of the wide-mouthed type known as *caneca*, and enameled tin plates signifying their low status. Usually lower-status initiates are required to eat with their hands.

Architectural form and setting also reflect ritual status. The Iyalorixá lives in the largest, most well-appointed house, usually located at or near the implanted sacred force in the shrine of the Candomblé's patron *orixá*. Other living areas are hierarchically arranged.

In the megacosm, the head priestess may possess the social status, dwelling, and clothing of the elite or she may come from the lower socio-economic class. Some, such as Mae Estella[27] and Olga do Alaketu, are well educated and well traveled. Nevertheless, Candomblé imposes its own status, and within its parameters, the position of the Iyalorixá as the keeper, manipulator, and activator of the sacred force makes her status paramount.

CONCLUSION

African religious expression and experience are impressively encapsulated in the African Diaspora religious system known as Candomblé Nagô, most pervasive in Bahia, Brazil. Candomblé Nagô operates as a minisociety or microcosm, based on a preliterate, preindustrial worldview, initially transported from precolonial Africa to the New World through the transatlantic slave trade and still maintained today within the sacred space of Candomblé Nagô. This religious microcosm helps regulate the lives of its largely Afro-Brazilian participants through the dynamic preservation and manipulation of a complex ritual system based on West African Yoruba deities and buttressed by African as well as Afro-Brazilian art forms.

While Afro-Bahian religions such as Candomblés Nagôs affect and are affected by Luso-Brazilian society, they constitute autonomous psychological and behavioral spheres. Afro-Bahian ritual art developed in this context and thus contrasts with the macrocosm because it sustains and mirrors internal "African" social and religious values. Afro-Bahian ritual art originally was and still is multifunctional. For Candomblé initiates, it recalls the legendary past and thereby maintains conceptual and formal historico-ritual links with Africa (personal communications: Crispim 1982d; Kayode 1982b). Rituals and symbols associated with religious ceremonies further reinforce the connection to the "mother country". Afro-Bahian art also serves as a system of nonverbal communication that conveys internal messages or cues concerning social status, appropriate social behavior, or spiritual states.

Candomblés Nagôs can be viewed as "political entities" in the sense that they directly or indirectly operate as "centers of cultural resistance" based on African precepts in the face of persistent and vigorous attempts by the wider Luso-Brazilian society to force the adoption of Western- or European-oriented ideas, values, and behavior patterns. African experience and expression are further maintained by placing emphasis on the welfare of the group and religious community, rather than on single individuals.

NOTES

1. I am indebted to Wándé Abímbọlá for critical commentary and a close reading of this chapter.

2. *Kandombele* is a Bantu root word meaning "African musical presentation or festival" (Castro 1976:144). Castro's dissertation is essentially a dictionary tracing the etymology of words used in Afro-Bahian religions.

3. "Gege" is a corruption of "Ewe".

4. Another frequently encountered image of Exu is a horned, iron humanoid figure with a long tail, probably a result of the Catholic syncretization of Exu with the devil (a phenomenon that also occurs in West Africa). Each initiate, ancestor, and *orixá* has

a personal Exu that must be propitiated first in any rite. The Exu serving the *terreiro* as a whole is frequently housed outside near the gate entrance in a separate shrine (e.g., at Lobato). In others, Exu has a separate shrine within the temple grounds proper (e.g., at Afonjá, where it is located next to the Xango shrine).

5. Although these are reputed to be the first Candomblés of Nagô origin, Chief Priestess Olga do Alaketu asserts a 1635 founding date for her *terreiro*, Ile Moroailaje in Luis Anselmo, Matatu de Brotas. This date is engraved on a plaque that hangs over the door leading from the public dancing area into the sacred shrine, but I could find no historical data corroborating this claim.

6. This usage was just recently confirmed by Annette Bird by whom I had sent a present to the Iyalorixá of Afonjá. On Bird's return, she indicated her unsuccessful attempts to telephone Mae Estela, being repeatedly told that she was not at home, but rather at the *roça*, shrine area (personal communication: 13 May 1984, Venice).

7. The Bahian brand of Catholicism seems to feature an intense personal relationship and identification with a particular saint on the part of the believer [*crente*]. Specific saints are prayed to for specific requests, for example, Santo Antonio for successful marriage; Cosme and Damião for jobs, luck, or removal of obstacles. The majority of households appear to maintain separate altars for one or more saints and regularly replenish them with lighted candles and fresh flowers. Thus it was an easy transition for slaves to identify their *orixá* with a personalized saint possessing similar capabilities, for example, Saint Lazarus (the saint of leprosy and oozing sores) with Omolu/Obaluaiye (the god of smallpox, AIDS, and other virulent diseases).

8. Casa Branca in Engenho Velho has a Catholic altar to the right of the entry of the building [*barracão*] where public festivals are held.

9. Based upon my observations, African descent is evidenced by extremely curly hair and dark skin color.

10. In September 1982, I participated in the initiation rituals of an office worker, a university student, and a medical intern. One woman undergoing *santo assentado* was a lawyer from Rio de Janeiro.

11. It is my opinion that the "status" of some houses was achieved from the attention focused on them by scholars (e.g., Raimundo Nina Rodrigues, Artur Ramos, Edison Carneiro, Pierre Verger, Melville Herskovits, Roger Bastide, and Ruth Landes). Jorge Amado (a writer) and Carybe (a famous artist) are celebrities of international importance who hold prestigious secular positions in these old houses (specifically Axé Opô Afonjá). They have contributed substantially to the reputation and renown of certain Candomblés. Thus the ceremonies in these older, elite *terreiros* attract huge numbers of tourists, eager to observe the "exotic" public rites.

12. This pattern of clear African descent did not hold true for every house. For example, the Candomblé of Menininha de Gantois was alleged to be a house full of white and foreign initiates (personal communication: Ebomin Detinha of Xango, numerous conversations, 1982). Among the *terreiros* I researched, there was only one white full initiate [*adoxu*] and that was Djalma of Yansan at Afonjá.

13. *Webster's Ninth New Collegiate Dictionary* (1983) defines *capitalism* as "an economic system characterized by private or corporate ownership of capital goods, by investments that are determined by private decision rather than state control, and by prices, production and the distribution of goods that are determined mainly by competition in a free market".

My interpretation of capitalism emphasizes large-scale ownership and production of goods for profit. I do not think that any Candomblé I studied would fit this description. Concomitant with a capitalistic economy are Western values and consumption patterns, which generally extol private rather than communal property.

14. During my stay, I met many destitute people who were given land, food, and money by the Candomblé, usually in exchange for the performance of regular ritual duties.

15. Olorun [Olódùmarè] is rarely worshipped in Africa as well, although he is clearly recognized as the High God (Ìdòwú 1962:30–37).

16. As a junior initiate I was not allowed to enter the shrine during this restricted phase, although all the details of the procedure were related to me later. These details were confirmed by a Zaïrean colleague of mine, Professor Ndolamb Ngokwey, who, because he is an African, was allowed to assist and witness this portion in a Candomblé in Feira-de-Santana. Ngokwey was researching in Feira-de-Santana at the time I was conducting field research in Bahia.

17. One example (among many): a cousin of YedaMaria, the well-known Bahian artist, suffered frequent and intense headaches over a period of years. Despite frequent advice by a number of divinations to initiate, she consistently refused. Finally, when she was close to death, her parents took her to a Candomblé, where she was initiated: she subsequently recovered and prospered (personal communication: YedaMaria, July 1982).

18. Exu has been described as the "slave" of the *orixá* by some scholars but is more accurately defined as an ubiquitous dialectical principle functioning as a go-between, mediator, catalyst or activator, and messenger. Bastide's information was gathered as an Ogan in a Candomblé (Bastide 1978a:49). He participated simultaneously in the civil hierarchy and sustained the *terreiro* through his regular contributions. Exu is neutral, positive, or negative, depending on the ritual context and other factors.

19. This space is defined as the physical area inside the fences or walls of the *terreiros*. During the ritual season, the sacred space could conceptually be extended to include the mental or spiritual space of the participants.

20. Since an *orixá* requires a medium in whom to manifest, many *orixá* known in Africa are not found in Brazilian Candomblés. Ewa (the *orixá* of the Yewa River in Ogun States, Nigeria) is an example of a deity rarely worshipped in Brazil, because the ritual link has been all but lost. Any medium who can serve as a vehicle for a rare *orixá* (such as Ewa, Oba, or Inle) is immediately initiated into the Candomblé regardless of the expense, as in the case of an Ewa initiation I recorded for Axé Opô Afonjá.

21. Men also wear a special uniform, consisting of a white tunic and trousers. Men who perform animal sacrifice [*axogun*] wear special white caps.

22. *Iyawo* are initiates with less than seven years' membership or more than seven years without the completion of the expensive required ritual for advancement. I have found this term most frequently used to refer to novices during their seclusion throughout initiation. After they are released from seclusion and begin to assume the more normal Candomblé functions and to participate in the public annual festivals, there is a tendency to use the term *Filha-de-Santo* rather than *iyawo* for this category of initiates. This status may persist for many years (even up to twenty or more) if the initiate (or sponsors she may solicit) cannot finance the ceremony. The title of Ebomin [from the Yoruba *ęgbon mi,* my elder relative] is conferred upon completion of the ritual.

23. This cloth consists of extremely long, narrow strips sewn together to make a prestigious and very expensive cloth worn by the Yoruba for very "high" occasions (e.g., marriage, presentation to a king or an important party). In Bahia *așo oke* has comparable prestige value. Since Yoruba imports are expensive, the majority of initiates must be satisfied with machine-made pieces.

24. Colloquially, any ritual in Candomblé is called an obligation [*obrigação*]. Every initiation involves an elaborate series of taboos [*ęwọ,*], for example, avoidance of certain foods, curfews, restrictions on clothing, and physical contact at certain times.

25. A series of sacred items are necessary to enable a senior initiate to open a *terreiro*: the assent of the initiate's *orixá*, seventeen cowries for *eerindinlogun* [*dilogun*] divination, new razors for shaving the head, and a cutting container in the parent *terreiro*. The new priest or priestess is still regarded as a member [*filha, filho,* lit. son or daughter] of the parent

terreiro and is required to participate in all major private and public rituals for his personal *orixá* and the *orixá* of his *mae* or *paidesanto* [mother or father of the saint]. I observed Moacir of Ogun, an initiate at Afonjá and an Oje at Ile Agboula, actively and regularly participate in the rituals at Afonjá although he was head priest of his own *terreiro*. Further, as a mark of respect, he was obliged to wait until the ritual cycle was completed at Afonjá before beginning his own. In turn, Afonjá begins public festivals for a particular *orixá* only after its parent *terreiro*, Casa Branca, has completed its ritual activity.

26. At the time of my research these positions belonged to Pierre Fatumbi S. Verger, Oju-Oba [the eyes of Xango]; Jorge Amado; Carybé; and Vivaldo Costa Lima.

27. Mae Estella graduated as a nurse in 1945 from the federal university. She accepted the responsibilities of spiritual leadership of the Candomblé of Axé Opô Afonjá only because divination forcefully dictated this path, and she feared the consequences of ignoring the instruction.

PERSONAL COMMUNICATIONS CITED IN THE TEXT

Abímbólá, Wándé. 1990. 7 November.

Augustinho. 1984. Los Angeles, California, 6 May.

Crispim, Pai. 1981a. October.

Crispim, Pai. 1981b. 5 October.

Crispim, Pai. 1981c. Various.

Crispim, Pai. 1982a. October.

Crispim, Pai. 1982b. Bahia, Brazil, 13 November.

Crispim, Pai. 1982c. 21 November.

Crispim, Pai. 1982d. November.

Crispim, Pai. 1982e. Various.

Hilda, Dona. 1981. February.

Ijaola, Philip Taiwo. 1981. Salvador de Bahia, Brazil, March.

Kayode, Ode. 1982a. 23 June.

Kayode, Ode. 1982b. July.

Osunladc. 1982a. 12 September.

Osunladc. 1982b. October.

Rubin, Arnold. 1984. 2 July.

Sàngó, Baba. 1981. Ketu, Republic of Benin, April.

Sàngó, 'Mogba. 1982. Ibadan, 16 May.

Thompson, Robert F. 1981. 15 April.

Vicentio, Seu. 1983. (Assistant Director of the Bahian Federation of Religions.) 26 July.

Plate 9–1. An initiate of *ngoma* Zebola, in Kinshasa, seated before a medicinal pot. The white outlining of her person, eyes, and the pot helps visually constitute and denote her seclusion "in the white" for a process of purification and healing.

9

Drums of Affliction:

Real Phenomenon or Scholarly Chimaera?

John M. Janzen

CHIMAERA AND ORTHRUS

ALTHOUGH THIS CHAPTER is about African religion, the Greek myth of the Chimaera provides a poignant analogy with which to set up the main point of inquiry and argument. Since antiquity, Chimaera has stood for a combination of incongruous parts and therefore of an illusion or fabrication of the mind. I will use the incongruity of the Lycian and Athenian calendars and their mythic personages to represent competing paradigms in the understanding of an important dimension of African religion, the "ritual of affliction".[1] The first concern is a methodological one, that of identification and comparison of examples of the institution over a wide area. The second concern has to do with how the institution has been understood and interpreted, from the vantage point of a range of both indigenous and scholarly paradigms. But first the Greek myth.

Chimaera, a fire-breathing goat with lion's head and serpent's body, was one of the "dreadful brood" of Echidne and Typhon. Also included were Cerebnerus, the three-headed Hound of Hell; the Hydra, a many-headed water serpent; and Orthrus, the two-headed hound of Geryon, who lay with his own mother and begot of her the Sphinx and the Nemean Lion. The monstrous Chimaera was killed by Bellerophon on a winged horse, just as Perseus killed the Medusa with the help of winged sandals.

According to classicist Robert Graves, these narratives reflect the Hellenic conquest of Lycia and the replacement of the moon-goddess with figures from the Hellenic region (Graves 1955:244). The Chimaera, according to this interpretation, was a calendar symbol of the tripartite year of which the seasonal emblems were lion, goat, and serpent. When the goat emblem disappeared, the Chimaera gave place to the Sphinx, with a winged lion's body and serpent's tail, and Orthrus, or Sirius, represented in the Dog-star, which inaugurated the Athenian New Year. Like Janus, Orthrus had two heads, corresponding to the reformed Athenian year with two seasons. Orthrus's son, the Lion, emblemized the first half, and his daughter, the Serpent, the second. Since the reformed New Year began when the Sun was in Leo and the Dog Days had begun, Orthrus looked in two directions—forward to the New Year and backward to the Old (Graves 1955:133).

Thus the two mythic paradigms stood apart, the one negating, redefining, and supplanting the other: Chimaera vs. Orthrus; three-season vs. two-season calendar; Lycians vs. Greeks; them vs. us; strange vs. familiar.

However, unlike the Greek mythic setting in which Orthrus's dualisms became normative, killing off the Chimaera's pluralism, in our application of this problematic to African religion it is not clear that one supplants the other. One set remains "chimeric" to the other, conversing past one another in the epistemological and ontological night, so to speak.

PARADIGMS UNFURLED:
A BRIEF HISTORY OF SCHOLARLY DISCOVERY

The Sub-Saharan African interpretation of adversity, paradox, and change has widely occurred within the framework of cults, specialized communities, cells, or networks, often with a therapeutic dimension. In Central Africa they have been best defined by Victor Turner, still the major author on them, as the cultural interpretation of misfortune in terms of domination by a specific deceased human or nonhuman agent and the attempt to come to terms with the misfortune by having the afflicted individual join the cult venerating that specific agent (Turner 1968:1–24). In some areas the rites have come to be called by a more colloquial term—"drums of affliction"—reflecting the significance of drumming and rhythmic song-dancing, and the designation of the whole gamut of expressive dimensions by the term *ngoma* [drum]. The drumming is considered to be the voice or influence of the ancestral shades or other spirits that possess the sufferer and give the treatment. A brief review of some of the major works on cults or rituals of affliction in East, Central, and Southern Africa will reveal the diversity of ways they have been seen and understood.

Hans Cory, in the 1930s, studied the constellation of *ngoma* groups among the Sukuma in colonial western Tanganyika and on the Islamized coast. His work for the British colonial government was concerned with the potential of *ngoma* for instigating social unrest (Cory 1936, 1955).[2] Turner in the 1950s worked among the Ndembu of northern Zambia, introducing the term "drum of affliction" as a translation for *ngoma* in the title of his book on Ndembu religion (Turner 1968, 1975 [1962]). Turner's in-depth studies of twenty-three Ndembu rituals of affliction showed their inner workings and social contexts, their intricate ritual symbolism, therapeutic motivations, and societal support systems. At the same time, although he put forth his portrayal of the Ndembu as universal persons with believable aches, pains, and expressions, his accounts are almost totally ahistorical, localized in their coverage to the villages in which he did fieldwork, and presented in a largely static analysis characteristic of the structural-functionalist paradigm of the time.

Later work on *ngoma* was done by Terence Ranger (1975) in coastal and historic trade-route Tanzania. The revivalist and dance dimensions of *ngoma* were shown to follow the trade routes and population movements between early colonial settlements. J. Clyde Mitchell (1956) studied the labor migrant associations of the copperbelt, the *beni-ngoma* [people of *ngoma*], casting them as cultural revival movements. Wim Van Binsbergen, Gwyn Prins, and Anita Spring studied *ngoma* in Zambia. Spring's work added comparative epidemiological and ethnographic work from the "*ngoma* mode" of healing and fertility among Lovale women (Spring 1985). Prins and Van Binsbergen contributed to the history of western Zambian *ngoma*, the first to the cognitive framework of therapeutic ritual (Prins 1979), the second to the linkage between numerous cults in the history of a region as an expression of differing modes of production and forces of historical change (Van Binsbergen 1977, 1981). Harriet Ngubane (1981), Monica Wilson (1961 [1936]) and others studied *ngoma* in Southern Africa, where it was perceived as having largely to do with divination (especially among the Nguni-speaking societies). Vera Buhrman and Nqaba Gqomfa (1981–82) depicted the *ngoma* novices as psychotics and explained the rituals as psychotherapy.

Each of the foregoing authors has presented the ritual of affliction in a slightly different perspective and theoretical orientation. Therein lies the challenge. Not only is each couched in a different paradigm, be it ritual symbol or epidemiological data, either resistance to change or innovation, it is not apparent from these authors' work precisely how widespread this institution may be. Luc de Heusch and Jan Vansina have been among the few to attempt broader surveys of religious movements, groups, and features in Central and Southern Africa. Willy De Craemer, Jan Vansina, and René Fox (1976) offered a summary profile of Central African religious movements, which they suggested was a culture reaching back a millennium or more. De Heusch (1971) established a structuralist comparison of types of possession cults and relationships throughout the West African and Central African regions. These latter authors, however, utilize mainly the analytical language of structuralism and speak of individualized spirit possession. With the exception of the later work of Vansina (although not in therapeutics) and Theophile Obenga, their models do not incorporate African languages.

On the basis of these foregoing disparate approaches to a presumably single institution, we are clearly dealing with not just one, but a series of scholarly chimaeras that may be characterized by the following contrasting paradigmatic sets:

1. *Time and scale perspective*: Ahistorical, ethnographic present, static, and local accounts of rituals (Turner 1968) vs. historical or developmental perspective, understanding of the rise and decline of a *ngoma*; the movement character of a ritual form, and the way it routinizes or becomes folklorized (Schoffeleers 1985a; Ranger 1975).

2. *Institutional identity*: Institution as a relatively new form responding to change brought by colonial era (Van Binsbergen 1981; Swantz 1970) vs. perspective that it is a classical institution, several millennia old, reflected in a common cluster of indigenous vocabulary terms across wide region (Janzen 1982, 1992; De Craemer, Vansina, and Fox 1976).

3. *Etiology of misfortune*: Analytical language about individual "spirit possession" and trance behavior as a core feature of institution (Zaretsky and Schaumbaugh 1978) vs. "spirit" considered to be an ideology, or hypothesis, invoked by diviners and diagnosticians to interpret misfortune or change in social environment (some healers).

4. *Character of knowledge*: Spirit possession seen as a kind of purely religious phenomenon in and of itself (Lambek 1981) vs. possession as an ideology or

hypothesis that can be a vehicle of any type of knowledge channelled for any and all kinds of domains within the institution (Janzen 1982, 1992).

5. *Efficacy of intervention*: Therapeutic ritual of the institution is considered to be expressive of experience and reality, that is, symbolic behavior with little or only placebo efficacy (Turner 1968; Lambek 1981) vs. perspective that it has an identifiable impact on the epidemiology of pathology (Spring 1978, 1985; Janzen 1992).

Before we can look at the consequences of these paradigmatic differences upon the study of affliction rites, we must examine the evidence.

POINTS OF COMMONALITY

First, we will seek to identify the central elements of an institution over a large area, then test or demonstrate the proposition that this institution exists throughout Central, East, and Southern Africa. We know that many of the features may vary locally. Can we reason effectively that local differences are really variations of a common core?

A COMMON LEXICON FOR RELIGION AND THERAPEUTICS

The demonstration of a common vocabulary for Central, East, and Southern African religion and therapeutics is enormously facilitated by Malcolm Gutherie's voluminous *Comparative Bantu* (1967–71), in which proto-Bantu cognates are reconstructed from an inventory of available Bantu language vocabularies.[3] The current wisdom is that the Bantu family of languages, a subgroup of the Niger-Congo language group, originated in the region of eastern Nigeria and Cameroon about 3,000 years ago. Theophile Obenga's recent *Les Bantu: Langues, peuples, civilisations* (1985), on a somewhat less systematic basis, constructs domains of language and culture from core lexica, most of which are "Western Bantu". Together with several local dictionaries, these works allow a quick profile of key religious, health, and healing terminologies in the Bantu-speaking world (Janzen 1983; 1992).

An initial common vocabulary feature of the medicine of Bantu-speaking Africa that is at the basis of our inquiry is *ngoma*. I have previously translated it as "ritual", "cult", "drum of affliction", or simply "drum". However, this connection between the term and the phenomenon is far from being a neat single referent. We are here led to the center of the Bantu controversy since, although there are some widespread referents of the term, few if any are present everywhere. Also, not all rituals of affliction are called *ngoma*, especially in the western region.

In the belt across the middle of the continent—from Kikongo in the west (near the Atlantic coast of Zaïre, Angola, and Congo) to Kiswahili in the east (on the Indian Ocean coast of Kenya and Tanzania)[4]—where Gutherie finds the greatest convergence of common terms, *ngoma* refers first to the elongated wooden drum with a single membrane attached at one end with pegs. It is usually also identified as a dance drum, although in societies where possession and therapeutic cults are present, *ngoma* more than any other drum is used in this therapeutic setting, in accompaniment with shakers, other types of drums, and singing.

Where there is therapeutic cult activity, the *ngoma*-inspired dance ritual is central to this therapy. It is widely stated that the sound of the *ngoma* is the voice of the ancestors or other spirits. However, not all *ngoma*-accompanied or *ngoma*-led dancing is for therapeutic purposes. *Ngoma* drums are also used for dance entertainment and competitions, as well as in the sacred drumming of state. As one moves south, *ngoma* drums become less common. They are present in Venda possession cults, in Swazi and Shangan possession rituals, and in some areas royal settings. But among the southern Nguni peoples (Zulu, Xhosa) they are absent from both royal and cult settings. Here, *ngoma* refers neither to the drums used (cowhide over stretched sticks or oil drums), nor to the dancing, but exclusively to the singing, divining, and with prefixes, to those who carry out these tasks. Thus, the Zulu

Plate 9–2. Mganga Botoli Laie of Dar es Salaam exhibits paraphenalia of *ngoma* Mbungi: five *ngoma* drums, shakers, medicine, and his costume.

isangoma diviner is literally "one who does *ngoma*"—that is, sings the songs. In Xhosa, much influenced linguistically by the Khoisan "click" languages of Southern Africa, the role term for the *ngoma*-singer becomes *igqira*.

Across the entire region, recognition of sickness is signalled by numerous local or regional terms such as the Northwest Bantu *-okon-*. Throughout the region the cognate term *-duad-*, or *-duadi*, whose verb form is *-luala* in Kikongo, or *-halwa* in Kindembu, expresses the existential quality of suffering injury or misfortune. This is differentiated from physical injury or sore, for which *puta* or *pute* is used.

Health is identified by numerous metaphors, including "balance" [*-lunga*, in both Isizulu and Kikongo], "purity" [*veedila* in Kikongo], "strength" or "force" [*ngolo* or *ngulu* in Western Bantu]. The one pan-Bantu concept is "coolness", the most widespread cognate of which is *-pod-*, "to become cool, or cool down" or "to become well, healthy". In Kikongo, this root is used in the term for the cupping horn, *mpodi*, which is also seen as a purifying treatment.

The widespread dichotomy that distinguishes misfortunes or afflictions stemming from "natural" or God-given causes from those stemming from human involvement is recognizable throughout the region. Although the terms for God vary from Nzambi or Nyambi in the western region to Mungu or Mukulu in the east and Umkhulane in the Zulu south, everywhere these terms are associated with misfortunes that are apparently "in the order of things". By contrast, unnatural and inauspicious misfortunes are said to be caused by "other people" [*kimbevo* or *kia muntu* in Kikongo; *ukufa* or *kwa bantu* in Isizulu]. The cognate stem used here, *-ntu*, is of course that from which the name *bantu* was drawn by nineteenth-century linguists.

One of the most common and widespread action terms in spelling out human-caused misfortune is that describing the use of powerful words and intentions—whether good or evil—with the cognate stem *-dog-*, *-doga*, or *-dogo*. In Kikongo in the west, *-loka* is the use of powerful words in oath and curse, and *kindoki* the process of using them to bewitch. In Kiswahili in the east, *kuloga* means to bewitch, to use unchantment on, to place under a spell or charm, *mlozi/walozi* denotes wizard(s) or sorcerer(s), and *ulozi* refers to witchcraft or sorcery. In Isizulu in the south, *-thak-* is the verb root and *ubthakath* is the process or state of ensorcelling. In short, the impact of words and thoughts upon the state of others defines a major concept in the Central, East, and Southern Africa worldview. It is also the type of cause that *ngoma* therapies are the most efficacious against. Just as words or intentions are often channelled within the community, especially the lineage community, so the networks and orders of *ngoma* song-dance can offset them.

Ancestors [*-dimu* in proto-Bantu or Eastern Bantu] extend the roles of humans in causing misfortune as well as providing protection in African society. Venda and Shona call their rituals of affliction *ngoma dzavadzimu* or *bira dzavadzimu*. The generic term *-kulu* [elder] is also used to refer to ancestor.

Moving from the etiological and worldview terms to those defining therapeutics, we may note that *-ti* [medicinal plant] is pan-Bantu. Others are Eastern or Western Bantu, suggesting later and specialized derivations. White clay, a basic purificatory ingredient associated with the spirit world, is found everywhere as a basic ingredient of health care and ritual. Its verbal referent is *pemba* or *pembe* in Western Bantu and *ikota* in some Eastern Bantu societies. In Western Bantu *-kag-* or *-kay-* is a term for leafy plant. These ingredients are often the basis of more complex compounds [*bilongo* in Western Bantu] that form the material ingredients of the sacralized medicine bearing nonmaterial dimensions such as physical, social, and symbolic techniques, including the series of features that constitute a full *ngoma* ritual. Such compounds, especially when spoken or sung over, become powerful medicines invoking the attributes of ancestors and spirits. *Pingo* and *mpungu* in the west, and *kango* in the east and south of the Bantu-speaking region represent this. Regionally localized equivalents, such as *-kiti* or *-kisi* in Western Bantu and *-dawa* in the Arabized east, similarly have this connotation.

In the same way as the formulation and naming of the sickness or its agent may generate the treatment mode, through control of that agent, so the therapeutic technique and the specialist are often described by the same term. Thus, in regions of the Bantu-speaking area tonal or contextual emphases separate the cognate stem *-ganga*, meaning medicine, from *-ganga*, meaning doctor, according to Gutherie. Whereas the former emphasis is sporadic [e.g., *buganga* in Kihemba in eastern Zaïre], the latter is nearly universal in the region, ranging from *nganga* in western Kikongo to *nganga/banganga* in Kihemba to *mganga/waganga* in East Africa to *inyanga* among the Zulu (see also in this volume: Schoffeleers, ch. 4; de Maret, ch. 10; Blakely and Blakely, ch. 20). Other terms for practitioner include *buki*, a Western Bantu term whose cognate stem *-buk-* suggests the combination of curing and divination/diagnosis; *-dagud-* in the northeast, meaning to practice medicine or to divine; *mbanda* in Southwestern Bantu, referring to specific types of doctors. These general terms for doctor or healer are given more specificity in a compound word in combination with another term.

A CHARACTERISTIC WORLDVIEW

Beneath the diversity of cults of affliction is a characteristic worldview regarding misfortune and how it is classified and dealt with. Adversities that are regarded as the natural order of things are dealt with through the use of straightforward remedies, techniques, and interventions that are often individual and private. Adversities that are extraordinary, or attributed to spirit or living human forces, need to be dealt with through the placation of these forces, or through coming to terms with them by intervening in that same sphere. Cults of affliction address this second level of adversity, or its avoidance. Thus, a hunter's chronic failure, a worker's chronic loss of a job or failure to find one, accidents despite every precaution, or misfortune juxtaposed with social conflict, all characterize expressions of the second level of causation.

The worldview that inspires cults of affliction includes, as an axiom, the idea that ancestral shades and spirits, ultimately expressions of the power of God, may influence or intervene in human affairs. The shades may be either direct and identifiable lineal ancestors or more generic human spirits. Other spirits of the Central, East, and Southern African pantheon may include more distant nature spirits, hero spirits, or alien spirits that affect human events in many ways. Old as well as new knowledge tends to be related to the shade and spirit forces, as events are interpreted and adversities dealt with. Thus, in recent decades, there has been a tendency for lineal ancestors to be supplanted by more generalized spirit forces in cults of affliction, as common social problems occur, increasingly, outside the domestic community.

DIVINATION AND DIAGNOSIS

The demonstrable presence of spirits is not automatic and pervasive in rituals of affliction. The character and role of spirits is more like a hypothesis in which relationship to concrete events in individuals' lives needs to be established. An important dimension of all rituals of affliction is therefore the intellectual, or analytical and diagnostic, function of evaluating the nature of life and the reasons for misfortune. A distinction is often drawn in the community, in this connection, between divination (the intellectual analysis of a situation) and ritual therapy (the attempt to intervene in the situation to change it). This distinction accounts for some of the diversity of affliction cult types. Where social change is intense, the need increases for cognitive clarity. Thus, in eighteenth-century coastal Kongo, during the decline of the kingdoms with the increase of trade, including the slave trade, divination cults were in great profusion, particularly those relating to adjudication and conflict resolution. In Southern Africa today, the term *ngoma* is identified almost exclusively with divination, because of the pressing need for analysis and interpretation of life in the land and region of Apartheid. Closer examination, however, shows that the functions of divination and network-building are related in a complementary way.

Divination or diagnosis thus always accompanies rituals of affliction, either independent of the healing role or as a part of the specialized techniques and paraphernalia of a particular cult. Divination must be thought of as a continuing query into the "whys", "whos", and "wherefores" begun in the family therapy management setting and carried through by specialists with expert judgment and training, specialists who may have had their own profound individual dilemmas, who have been recruited to a particular mode of ritual life, and who have been initiated to the spirit world. As a technique, divination may be based on a mechanistic system of signs and interpretations, such as the southern savanna *ngombo* basket filled with symbolic objects signifying human life, the bone-throwing technique of Southern African Nguni society (Plate 9–3), or the recitation of scripture from the Bible or the Koran. Alternatively, and by some observers increasingly, divination is done by direct recourse to possession, in which the diviner, as medium, speaks the words of the ancestral shade or spirit in answer to a query. Some diviners use a combination of both techniques or a selection of hierarchically arranged types. In Swaziland, master diviners today train novices in the arts both of mechanistic bone-throwing divination and also in the mastery of possession-divination. In any case, these divined diagnoses, representing a type of analysis or interpretation of daily life, offer the basis for the more synthetic, ritualized follow-through of the cults of affliction.

IDENTIFIABLE INITIATORY THERAPIES

Therapeutic attention to affliction often entails elements of initiation of the afflicted into membership in the order, ideally resulting in the elevation of the afflicted to the status of priest or healer. Whether or not this actually happens, there being many "drop-outs", depends on the novice's progress through early stages of therapy and counselling, on the novice's or kin's means, and on the extent to which the cult is controlled by an elite that restricts access to its basic resources. Throughout the wider cult of affliction region, initiation is marked by two distinct stages: an initial therapeutic purification of the affliction and, if the novice progresses through counselling and further therapy, a second stage, a "graduation" to the status of fully qualified priest, healer, or professional.

The efficacy of the therapy, regardless of its specific techniques, is partially assured because of support from fellow afflicted members of the community, who are usually not the sufferer's kin. In most instances of prolonged sickness in African society, diagnosis and decision relating to the course of healing—"the quest for therapy"—are in the hands of a kinship-based therapy managing group. In the cases that come into the orbit of cults of affliction, the support community broadens to become that of the cult members. The quality of support shifts from ad hoc kin aid to that of permanent involvement with a wider network in the initiate-novice's life, corresponding to the long-term involvement of the individual with the affliction, or as a healer-priest over it.

Some cults of affliction, such as Nkita among the Kongo peoples of western Zaïre, are situated within lineages. Nkita responds to the unique circumstances and symptoms of children's sicknesses and barren women amidst the stresses and fears of lineage segmentation. The appearance of a cluster of Nkita afflicted within a lineage segment provides the rationale and the setting for the regeneration of lineage organization whose members are reaffiliated with the ancestral source of their collective authority. Most cults of affliction, however, occur outside the kin setting, functioning as a replacement for kin relations and giving the individual lifelong ties with others along the lines of the new affliction or occupation-specific community. This feature has led some to hypothesize that cults of affliction may even proliferate where kin-based social units are in disarray. In the urban setting of South Africa, for example, there appears to be a prevalence of recruitment to affliction cults among those, especially women, who carry the burden of being single parent household heads.

Plate 9–3. Sangoma Ida Mabuza, of Betani near Mbabane, Swaziland, reads the constellations of "bones" on the mat before her, in one of the many divination techniques related to the *ngoma*.

THE CORE RITUAL: "DOING *NGOMA*"

The rituals of initiation, healing, and celebration have common core features throughout the area, although they vary tremendously. Although the use of the pharmacopeia is available in *ngoma*, song and dance are at the heart of the initiate's or celebrant's participation. The "song-dance" [*ngoma*] is the product of the initiate's personal pilgrimage, and its lyrics mirror dreams, visions, as well as more mundane experiences. What I translate as "doing *ngoma*" has common verbal reference in societies across the region: *kusika ngoma* in Kikongo referred in the past to striking the big *ngoma* drum that performed the song-dance of the major *nkisi* medicine; *kuyimba ngoma* in Kindembu of northern Zambia referred to the singing of *ngoma* songs in the rite; *sangoma* in Nguni languages referred to "doing *ngoma*" and *isangoma* was the one who does *ngoma*.

Throughout the region the performance brings together a group of individuals all of whom, whether novices or fully qualified healers, take turns presenting themselves. Their initial prayer or confession-type exclamations are followed by the confessor intoning a song, which is then met by the choral response of all other performers. Thus the heart of "doing *ngoma*" is the characteristic African call-and-response done so that a circle of individuals together brings out of one another the personal self of each in turn.

These sessions may punctuate events of any type within the network of an order—the first initiatory therapy of a new novice, the purification of novices or healers following a death or a polluting transgression, a counselling session, or at the time of the graduation and "coming out" of a graduate.

These songs, and their rhythms, create a framework of reality within which the affliction or condition is defined and the mode of relating to it—the remedy—is formulated. Thus, despite the collective setting, a great deal of individualized attention is given. The moving, pulsating context of ritual celebration is conducive to cognitive dissociation and restructuring, lending affliction cults a psycho-therapeutic, even conversion-like quality, although they are not sectarian—that is, mutually exclusive—in their membership. The need to define and redefine experience continues throughout the career of the initiate and priest-healer; seasoned elders continue to deal with their own dilemmas and life transitions. Thus, for example, grief over the death of a close kinsman, put in terms of being polluted, requires the priest-healer to suspend healing activities until the time of mourning is over and purification can take place (Plate 9–4).

POINTS OF VARIABILITY

Beyond these core features, the content and format of affliction cults vary greatly. The scope of issues addressed may range, as we have seen, from treating epidemic or chronic disease, to deformities, to occupational roles that require specialized knowledge or that may be dangerous to individual practitioners yet necessary to society. In one setting the range of issues may be put into a single ritual format; in other settings, issue-specific communities may grow into numerous named orders and dances. These communities may in turn be organized as a decentralized series of local cells or of overlapping networks. Alternatively, the prevailing structure may become tightly hierarchical and territorially centered in a fixed shrine or central administration. Economic and political factors often play a role in shaping the structure of affliction cults. However, the taxonomy of issues addressed usually arises from unique environmental conditions or from unique leadership of individuals who see the opportunity to interpret to others a vision of solutions to human need.

The institutional and behavioral variations beneath the terminological commonality of Central, East, and Southern African religion and therapeutics are due to differing climates, differing political and economic formations, differing colonial experiences during the seventeenth to twentieth centuries, and differing responses to diseases and stressful environments.

PRESENCE OR ABSENCE

The first point of variability has to do with the presence or absence of the affliction cult in a society. Although the vocabulary for the ritual institution of health is very widely present, a "roll call" of *ngoma*-type institutions at a given time and region reveals an uneven pattern. For example, the neighboring cultural regions of the Sotho-Tswana and the Nguni speakers of Southern Africa offer a striking illustration of this. Although the vocabulary of the spirit possession hypothesis, *twasa*, is present in both languages, as are the term *ngoma* and other vocabulary items for health and illness, the institution is highly developed in Nguni society and absent in Sotho-Tswana society.

Plate 9–4. A group of *amagqira* in Guguleto township, Cape Town, "do *ngoma*" in the street to "throw out the darkness" of one of their members polluted by the death of a kinsman.

CENTRALIZED AND ACEPHALOUS SOCIETIES

Since the most concentrated region of linguistic homogeneity among Bantu-speaking societies is in a belt across the midcontinent from Kikongo speakers in the west to Kiswahili-speakers in the east, that the cults of affliction here also reveal a significant concentration of common features is not surprising. A brief comparison among the coastal north Kongo, the Ndembu of Zambia (on the periphery of the Lunda empire), and the Sukuma of the Lake Victoria region of Tanzania—all societies that may be characterized as having been segmentary or decentralized—illustrates these common features.

Cults of affliction in these societies, while they were associated with individual affliction in the narrow sense, also related to the sacralization and organization of technical knowledge and its relationship to the legitimation and reinforcement of the social order. Divination played a role, either specific to each cult, as among the Sukuma, or as a more specialized set of techniques, as among the Ndembu and Kongo, both of whom practiced the *ngombo* basket divination technique. Some cults related explicitly to the prevailing economic activity of the society, both the techniques and those who failed to succeed in practicing them. Thus, in Ndembu and Sukuma society, hunting was the focus of several *ngoma* orders, with specific organization around the mode of hunting (whether bow and arrow, or gun), and the type of animal (elephant, snake, porcupine). The Sukuma snake-handling order was, and is, a prime example of a cult devoted to the control and reproduction of technical knowledge. Known for effective snake-bite treatments, the snake dance society members also possess effective antidotes against the numerous poisonous snake venoms of western Tanzania. In coastal Kongo as well as Tanzania several cults dealt with trade and commerce, an appropriate focus for this important economic activity that brought divisive mercantile techniques and attitudes into lineage-based societies, as well as several contagious diseases. On the Kongo coast, where formerly centralized kingdoms had featured appeal courts, the cult of affliction format emerged in the seventeenth and eighteenth centuries as the vehicle for judicial affairs and conflict resolution. I have written at length on the Lemba cult, which arose between the coast and the markets of the Pool region near today's Kinshasa to reconcile conflicting demands of mercantilism and lineage redistribution among the area's mercantile elite. Similarly, in nineteenth-century Sukumaland, antiwitchcraft medicine cults were introduced from the Congo Basin in response to rising social disorder that accompanied the early colonial period. Among the Ndembu, the response to early colonialism took the form of cults of affliction focused on new diseases, including "fevers", "wasting", and "disease of the paths", and other suspiciously colonial and contagious diseases, such as malaria, tuberculosis, and venereal diseases that would have entered through migrant laborers. Everywhere, twinning, breach births, and other dangerous or unusual conditions of reproduction were prime categories for cult of affliction attention.

The picture of cults of affliction within, or in relation to, centralized states contrasts markedly with the acephalous, decentralized settings. In centralized states, cults of affliction appear to be less influential, or may be entirely absent, as in the Tswana chiefdoms where strong historic chiefship has provided social continuity, a format for the juridical process, and some means of material support to otherwise marginalized or needy people. Cults are known to have provided the impetus for the emergence of centralized polities, as in the case of the Bunzi shrine of coastal Kongo. In other settings the cults have also emerged in the wake of historic states, picking up the aura of royal authority and the trappings of sovereignty. A prime example of this is the cult of Ryangombe and the Bacwezi of the lake region of eastern Central Africa, found in Tanzania's major cities, whose spirits are said to be the royal dynasties of the ancient Cwezi kingdom (Berger 1981). The same model has been applied to the possession cults of Mayotte off the coast of East Africa, whose spirits are ancient Saklava kings of Madagascar (Lambek 1981:152).

The dynamic relationship of cults to centralized polities has been accompanied by changes in the way spirits and shades are focused in consciousness and ritual. As the scale and function of a cult expand, narrowly defined ancestor shades may give way to nature, alien, or hero spirits. In a few instances, centralized shrine cults have persisted over centuries, defining primary values and social patterns for generations of adepts. The Bunzi shrine of coastal Kongo, Mbona of Malawi, Korekore and Chikunda in Zimbabwe are well-studied examples that continue into the present. Some authors have made a distinction between these centralized "regional" cults and topically focused cults of affliction (Werbner 1977). But the orders, taken in their entirety, suggest more of a continuum along several axes: centralized to segmentary, inclusive to specialized, controlled by state sovereignty to independent (or even opposed to state sovereignty). Cults have crystallized opposition to states, both in precolonial, colonial, and, to a lesser degree, post-colonial settings. Thus, the Cwezi cult channelled opposition to hierarchicalized structures in the interlacustrine states such as Rwanda (Berger 1981). Cult leaders organized opposition to Rhodesian labor recruitment practices in the early twentieth century and inspired early strikes in the mines (Van Onselen 1976). The role of *ngoma* networks in popular resistance in South Africa may be substantial.

Where states have been absent or attenuated, rituals of affliction have provided a format for calling positive attention to people who are marginalized or afflicted, such as women, or the handicapped, or people who are struck with misfortune in economy-related tasks such as hunting, women's reproductive capacity, or commerce. In some settings, the model of the cult has provided the basis for normative social authority, defining and organizing economic activity, social organization, and more esoteric religious and artistic activities.

In colonial and postcolonial Africa, the logic of using affliction and adversity as a focal point for organizing social reproduction has contributed to the perpetuation, even the proliferation, of cults of affliction, often in a way that has baffled governmental authorities and outside observers. Cults have arisen in connection with epidemics, migration and trade routes, shifts in modes of production, responses to changes in social organization, and the deterioration of juridical institutions. Colonialism itself undoubtedly generated many of the cults of affliction appearing in the twentieth century. Post-independence conditions have continued to provide grist for the mill of cult formation.

UNITARY AND DIVERSE MANIFESTATION

The midcontinent provides a striking contrast to the southern part of the continent in the extent to which rituals of affliction are specialized and multiple. Across the southern savanna in Zaïre, Zambia, Malawi and in eastern Tanzania many locales feature separate rituals to deal with women's disorders, reproductive problems, physical deformities, work-related disorders of various kinds, and those pertaining to various types of spirits. In the Nguni societies of the south, rituals of affliction are one-dimensional, with all types of dilemmas being channeled into a single network of ritual experts and their novices.

SACRALIZING AND FOLKLORIZING

The distinction between "therapeutic" and "entertainment" *ngoma* is an important one in understanding the larger dynamics of religion and ritual in Dar es Salaam. This distinction already seems to have existed in the early twentieth-century Sukuma *ngoma* described by Cory. It was implicit in the observation of Botoli Laie, a Kilwa healer with whom I spoke (shown exhibiting ritual paraphernalia in Plate 9–2), that the *ngoma* drumming-dancing is distinct from the medicines and is done for the exorcistic or therapeutic initiatory seances by hired musicians. The sacrality or secularity of the *ngoma* depends on its function or use, that is, the context and not the music or dance form as such. *Ngoma* performances in nightclubs and "folkloric" entertainment events put on by the national dance troupe will not differ in their form from possession or exorcistic rituals conducted by *waganga*.

The profile for Dar es Salaam holds to some extent throughout the *ngoma* region. Although there are few good studies of the full "career" of a ritual of affliction, the stages of transformation might go something like this. Initially there would be a crisis or societal perception of impasse. Then would emerge the response to crisis with its visions, insights, dreams, and charismatic leaders. The ritual form, matured, would become a routinized ceremonial held within a community of adepts to which therapeutic initiation is the mode of entry. Successful, a recognized ritual with its characteristic songs, dances, and performances would become widely represented in the society. Finally, long after the crisis or the precipitating circumstance has passed, the ritual would become a customary set of actions that is picked up, even for commercial use, by a dance troupe (Plate 9–5).

The character of such a cycle may be cast as a tension between the sacrality of the original solution and the gradual and eventual secularization of the rites and their legitimation. Initially, the rite is set apart from the mundane; its contextualization in the focal point of crisis, affliction, or adversity gives it an aura of danger. As the crisis is dealt with by society, or overcome, or disappears, the ritual no longer has this aura. Yet, as art, it may be appreciated as an important feature of the culture.

The duration of such a cycle—emergence, florescence, decline, "folklorization" as "entertainment"—depends on the nature of the issue addressed, the degree of specificity of the focus, and the breadth of its representativeness in the society. In the western Bantu area, the Nkita rite, which relates to lineage organization, factionalism, and reproductive problems, has continued for at least five centuries and is rooted in the very nature of lineage structure. Lemba, also western Bantu, addressed the contradictions of public authority and became very influential during the coastal trade. Its rise in 1650 and its demise in 1930 was related directly to the character and location of the trade caravans between interior markets and the coast. New urban rites today address the issues of individuals and households in mass society and will offer new transformations of the cycle.

CURRENT TRENDS

In the capitals of Zaïre, Tanzania, Swaziland, and South Africa—representing the arc of Bantu-speaking societies across Central, East, and Southern Africa—the historic cults as well as new adaptations are represented by part- and full-time healers and priests and their adepts.[5] Ethnic communities of the hinterland have usually brought their religious institutions to the city, where they have undergone important shifts of function and signification. So indigenous an African form as the *ngoma* has not always been tolerated or accepted; thus it exists alongside, and beneath the surface of, new Christian and Islamic religious communities.

KINSHASA

In Kinshasa, a city of three million inhabitants, covering over two hundred square kilometers alongside the Zaïre River, local scholarship speaks of the "grands rites", representing numerous regional and ethnic traditions from around the Zaïre River Basin (Bibeau et al. 1979; Janzen 1992). Nkita, of Lower Zaïre and Bandundu origin, concentrates on the dynamics of the matrilineage and the individual affliction, believed to originate from lineage problems. The cult cell is within the lineage itself, frequently originating in the crises of segmentation and the need to renew leadership. The mode of affliction in Nkita is often one or another form of threat to the continuity of the lineage, either in children's illnesses or deaths or in the barrenness of women or couples. These problems are often associated with inadequate leadership. An individualized therapy concentrates on particular cases; a collective therapy seeks to renew leadership through the reestablishment of harmonious relationships with ancestors and nature spirits.

Zebola, originating in the Equator region upriver, manifests itself in physiological and psychological sicknesses of individual men and women. In its historic rural context, the Zebola affliction was traced back to possession by nature spirits. A regimen of seclusion, counselling, and ritual therapy brought the individual—mostly women—back to health through therapeutic initiation in the Zebola order (see Plate 7–1). In its urban setting, especially Kinshasa, Zebola possession is frequently diagnosed in cases of women who are pathologically affected by household entrapment. Becoming a Zebola sufferer and neophyte puts the individual into permanent association with a peer group of fellow sufferers and, through therapeutic initiation, eventually gives the individual a leadership role in the wider community and network of the Zebola order. In Ellen Corin's penetrating study of Zebola in Kinshasa, the women and (a few) men who enter Zebola are increasingly from a variety of cultural backgrounds other than the Equator region (Corin 1979).

Mpombo and Badju (Bazu) originate from the Mai-Ndombe area a few hundred kilometers upriver. Zaïrean psychologist Mabiala, who is studying these cults, notes that a variety of vaguely defined signs and symptoms are the modes of affliction here, including dizziness, headaches, lack of mental presence, skin rashes, lack of appetite, difficulty in breathing, heartburn with anxiety, rapid or arrhythmic heartbeat, fever with shivers, sexual impotence, dreams of struggles or being followed by threatening animals, weight loss or excessive weight (especially if accompanied by spirit visitations), and a variety of gynecological and obstetrical difficulties. Therapeutic initiation characterizes the entry into the cult of afflicted by women suffering from these ailments.

Mizuka in Kinshasa is a cult of affliction brought to the city and continuing largely in the Islamized Kiswahili-speaking community. Men and women are initiated following psychic crises, hallucinations, nervousness, thinning, weakness, dizziness, and bad luck (Bibeau et al. 1979). Other cults of affliction in Kinshasa include Nzondo, Bilumbu of Luba origin, Nkundo or Elima of northern pygmy influence, Mikanda-Mikanda, and Tembu.

Plate 9–5. A "folklorized" entertainment rendering of *ngoma* Msewe of Zanzibar by the national dance troupe Mungano in Dar es Salaam.

DAR ES SALAAM

Dar es Salaam, a city of a million or more on the Indian Ocean coast of East Africa, has numerous ritual communities representing its multiple cultural regions and groups, as does Kinshasa. The indigenous designation for cult of affliction is more homogeneous in Dar es Salaam than in Kinshasa, in that *ngoma* is a local term recognized widely to include ritual therapeutic communities. *Ngoma* itself has the loose meaning of drumming, dancing, celebration. The medicinal use of *ngoma* is quite detached from the ritual, given the distinction between *ngoma* of entertainment and of therapeutic ritual.

The dominant community of *ngoma* therapies in Dar is that of the coastal Islamized Zaramo people. Local scholarship identifies the indigenous Zaramo rites of Rungu, Madogoli, Killinge, and Ruhani (Swantz 1970; Janzen 1992). Many other distinctive rites have been identified among immigrants to Dar from coastal cities and the islands. A Kilwa *mganga* practiced *ngoma* Manianga and Mbungi. Another *ngoma* cell group of *waganga* practiced Msaghiro and N'anga.

The particularlism of naming suggests that there is much innovation and adaptation in the overall idiom of *ngoma* ritual. What is more helpful in understanding the Dar es Salaam *ngoma* scene is to note that these names refer to spirit classes involved in possession of afflicted individuals. Whereas the cult names particularize, spirit classes are generalized into two or three groups. Among the coastal Islamized peoples, spirits are called *masheitani* and *majini*, both Arabic-Kiswahili words. The distinction is not as important, apparently, as that distinguishing spirits of the water from those of the land, with some occasionally identified with the beach or coast. Thus, Msaghiro is an *ngoma* for sufferers of chronic and severe headache caused by a combination of Maruhani, Subizani, and Mzuka spirits, all coastal or beach spirits. Each of these classes is further subdivided. The Subizani, of whom there are ten—some male, some female—are rock or beach spirits who affect children, both making them ill and helping to raise them healthily. *Ngoma* N'anga is a manifestation of Warungu spirits of the land, hills, baobab trees, and mountains whose mode of affliction is in chronic severe headaches. Frequently each spirit type will be "played" in an *ngoma* ritual by a particular type of instrument.

In addition to the *ngoma* of coastal societies, one also finds *ngoma* of inland groups in Dar. The Bucwezi cult of the lake region is found in the city, as are those of other regional clusters such as the Nyamwezi, the Sukuma, and even some Nilotic groups such as the Maasai. The Sukuma cluster of various kinds of *ngoma* was described earlier. Of interest here is the manner in which they exist in the modern city.

The distinction between Islamic and indigenous African therapeutic music and dance and the role definitions of healers also remains somewhat ambiguous and fluid. One *mganga* who identified himself as Muslim said he practiced *ngoma* therapy as a medicinal rite; it had nothing to do with religion. His Muslim devotion was not compromised by practicing *ngoma*. Another said *ngoma* was pagan religious ritual and he did not practice its therapies. But he was a member of a Sufi community within which prayers, singing, dancing, and Koranic reading were regarded as therapeutic.

There are many common features in the cults of affliction of Kinshasa and Dar es Salaam. For the most part they are rituals imported by immigrants from across their countries. A proliferation of cults around themes or issues has made them adaptable to the urban setting. This specificity has shifted somewhat in the city, both in the ethnic identity of adherents and the type of affliction addressed.

MBABANE-MANZINI AND CAPE TOWN

Ngoma in Mbabane-Manzini and in Cape Town, by comparison, is far more unitary in its institutional organization; it is not as frequently, nor as extensively, used for entertainment; it is caught up, in this unitary structure, with both divination and network building. The decision to include Mbabane-Manzini and Cape Town in the survey was made partly out of an interest in understanding the Nguni cluster of societies (Shangani, Thonga, Ndebele, Swazi, Zulu, Xhosa), partly to compare the setting for *ngoma* inside and outside of South Africa within Southern Africa. These sites were selected because of the strong representation of *ngoma* in Nguni societies in contrast to its marked absence in Sotho-Tswana societies.

Zulu diviners [*isangoma*] have been described by numerous authors. However, they are midway on a continuum of features present in all the Nguni societies. For one thing, "spirit" here is represented almost entirely by either lineal ancestors or evil spirits. In Zulu divination, the mechanistic bone-throwing techniques prevail. Among Xhosa, undramatic meditative techniques are most common. Among the Swazi *sangoma*, however, although the same holds true for a part of their work, they may have recourse regularly to far more demonstrative, even violent, possession behavior as a series of increasingly powerful and distant nature and alien spirits dwell inside them. Reasons for this contrast of possession mode across the Nguni spectrum are too involved to deal with in this chapter. However, they point to societal values and structural issues with very different outcomes in superficially similar, and historically related, settings.

One of these external factors bears on the contrast between South African and Swazi society. In the Republic of South Africa, laws are rigid and oppressive. The impact of this upon the *ngoma* ethos, along with the orientation upon lineal ancestors, is that things are all rather clear-cut, albeit oppressive. South African laws, work restrictions, and hardship have not succeeded in eroding the basic African worldview; it has hardened it, so to speak. Whereas in Swaziland, which has an intriguing mixture of ancient kingdom and modern bureaucracy, and a per capita income that is near the highest in black Africa, there has been a middle-class revolution of rising expectations and realizations. The middle-class work force of both men and women is in an upwardly mobile current that has shaken family and religious values to their core. Thus divination regarding work opportunities, social crises resulting from individual decisions, and marital or nonmarital arrangements, all lead to an enormous clientele for the *sangoma* (or the *takoza*, as they call themselves). This is the setting in which *ngoma* roles and activities are associated almost exclusively with divining.

In the townships of Cape Town—Guguleto, Langa, Nyanga—the scene of much disorder in recent years, the work of the *amagqira/sangoma* is to a far greater extent that of providing solace and encouragement and network support to the many who come to them. African society of the townships has very little true centralized authority. In a survey taken in Guguleto, one in four households was involved in one way or another with a *ngoma* network: as sufferer-novice, midcourse-novice, or graduated and practicing healer-diviner. In addition to the churches, trade unions, legal or illegal political groups, and the increasingly irrelevant and mistrusted township committees, the *ngoma* structure is one of the most pervasive dimensions of the social fabric. As already noted, the institutional structure of *ngoma* in Cape Town is unitary, that is, without a variety of named *ngoma* orders, as in Kinshasa or Dar es Salaam, despite the varied ethnic backgrounds of the Xhosa, Zulu, Sotho, and Tswana participants.

Participants of *ngoma* in Cape Town, when interviewed about their own histories, reveal the usual accounts of headaches, weakness, disorientation, other afflictions and dreams of ancestors or of healer-dancers with furred and beaded costumes. It is clear that despite the high numbers of novices, not all make it through the therapeutic initiation to become builders of personal networks. Yet for those who do make it through the therapeutic initiation, the "course through the white" (Plate 9–6), far from being the classic image of the psychotic healer, members of Cape Town's *amagqira/sangoma* networks strike one as very strong individuals who have overcome psychological and social contradictions to fulfill their calling as pillars of society.

CONCLUSION, OR PARADIGMS REVISITED

This chapter opened by asking whether the case can be made for the existence in Central, East, and Southern Africa of an institution that has been called variously "ritual of affliction", "cult of affliction", or "drum of affliction". The main evidence in favor of such a proposition is the widespread cognate "*ngoma*" [drum], and its range of related meanings, assumptions regarding misfortune, and patterns of action. Yes, there is something like an institution out there. The differences of interpretation have to do with the way social and historical sciences see this institution and its core features.

The Central, East, and Southern African "affliction cults" do not correspond readily to the post-Enlightenment Western definition of disease and medicine. In the language of our initial explanatory analogy, they are certainly chimaeric in the light of Occidental institutional structures and the ways in which individuals are supposed to become sick and are healed. They represent a paradigm of organization and of problem solving that is "other" to Western positivistic medicine and modes of social control. Western social science seems to have reified this otherness into a closed set of propositions, as suggested at the outset of this chapter.

As the reader may have perceived, the first of each set of contrasting paradigms (pages 163–164) I hold to be misconstrued. These would see rituals of affliction in a largely ahistorical and static light, relatively new forms of response to colonialism and industrialization, mainly identified by overt trance behavior due to psychopathology, and expressive of aberrant social and personal conditions.

Rather, I regard as closer to the reality of rituals and cults of affliction the second set: a historical perspective in which particular rituals emerge, rise, have their day or duration, and then decline, to be replaced by others; that this is part of a classic (proto-Bantu or West African) institution as witnessed by the cluster of cognates that everywhere correlate with it; that the "spirit hypothesis" is a secondary ideology or interpretation that must be connected to individuals' and groups' misfortunes; that any type of knowledge may theoretically be channelled through these rituals, rather than merely "spirit" knowledge; that this knowledge, applied through techniques and behaviors, may in fact alleviate the distress that has been addressed.

In the historic examples known to us, that is, turn-of-the-century, colonized societies alluded to above, the affliction cult groups provided a means of buttressing

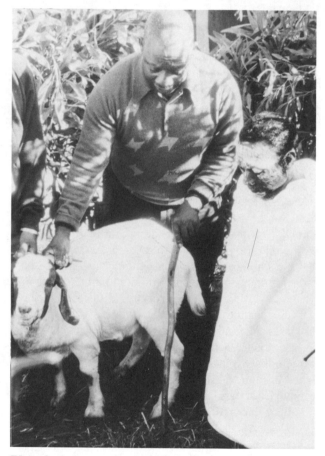

Plate 9–6. A man dressed in a white blanket and whose face is smeared with white, entering his novitiate in a weekend ritual in Guguleto township, Cape Town. He kneels beside the sacrificial animal, before pots of beer and medicine. The goat is said to give its life in exchange for the "dirt" of the novice's sickness. Later, the animal will be consumed in a community feast.

and celebrating social categories of economic pursuit (land, hunting, trade), social order and justice, as well as the very fabric of society (marriage, authority, women's health, reproduction), and specified areas of sickness in a narrower sense. Perhaps the underlying characterization of the historic *ngoma* orders would be that they ritualized key points of the social and cultural fabric where it was highly charged or highly threatened. Affliction and misfortune merely served as the signal, the trigger, for spiritual sanctioning, as a mode of recruitment to leadership and a means of reproducing specialized knowledge.

In the twentieth century, new rituals of affliction have tended to be short-term movements of panacea, of desperation. They have provided expression to the pains and social problems of wide segments of the populace. There has been a great deal of interpenetration between these rituals and independent Christian churches and with Islamic orders. New permanent cults have arisen around characteristic ills such as the isolated nuclear household in the urban setting; epidemic diseases such as tuberculosis and the chronic problems related to it; the divination of problems such as unemployment in a proletarian setting; success in business; retention of a job; or protection of wealth once it is acquired. Many cults focus on the alienation and entrapment so common in the African urban setting. Through psychiatric and comparative religious models, we come to see an ontological bridge to them.

Affliction cults in Central, East, and Southern Africa have taken the classic themes of marginality, adversity, risk, and suffering to energize or renew society in the face of profound economic and social change in the past century. They exist and are real, but we must make certain that we understand them for what they are.

NOTES

1. I shall use "cult of affliction" as a substitute term when speaking of specific instances of the ritual of affliction because it has become a widely used scholarly convention.

2. In addition, my study has benefitted from several archival manuscripts written by Hans Cory, deposited at the University of Dar es Salaam: Sukuma Secret Societies (Mwanza), East African File Cory 191, 1938; Baswezi (Disciples of Lyangombe), East African File Cory 45, 1949; Sukuma Songs and Dances, East African File Cory 192, n.d.; Sukuma Dances, East African File Cory 192, n.d.; Migabo, East African File Cory 138, n.d..

3. Guthrie's theoretical work on linguistic history has been superseded by a new generation of analyses, research, and writing. The lexicon found in *Comparative Bantu* is still the best tool in print for this type of work, although it is not comprehensive in its listing of cognates and in the set of languages covered.

4. A *lingua franca* related to Kikongo, called *Kikongo de l'Etat* or "Kituba", is today spoken widely in the capital city Kinshasa and throughout the Bas-Zaïre and Bandundu regions in western Zaïre. Kiswahili also has been spoken well beyond the East African coast for over 150 years and is now spoken by 30–50 million people throughout Tanzania, Kenya, Uganda, Burundi, Rwanda, and in the eastern Zaïre regions of Shaba, Kivu, and Haut-Zaïre.

5. This chapter, and other essays I have written on this subject, are the products of extended research in western Zaïre over twenty years, in particular of a 1982–83 field project in the four capitals described in this section. I am grateful to the Senior Research Fellowship program of the Fulbright (CIES) Fellowship Program, to the University of Kansas sabbatical fund, and to the University of Cape Town. Many individuals, especially scholars and healers, helped me understand the reality of *ngoma*.

Plate 10–1. Classic Kisalian grave (radiocarbon date: A.D. 1180 ± 95) at Sanga i
eastern Zaïre (Shaba) containing numerous objects: 1. a copper necklace, 2. irc
and copper bracelets, 3. ornaments made of shells, 4. iron pendants on a bel
5. animal bones, 6. a copper ribbon decorating a staff, 7. more animal bones, ar
8. many ceramic pots. The arrow points north. Atypically for this period, th
woman's legs are *not* pointed downriver.

10

Archaeological & Other Prehistoric Evidence of Traditional African Religious Expression

Pierre de Maret

I T SEEMS THAT MOST ARCHAEOLOGISTS are afraid of religion. So, when first asked to contribute to the conference leading to this book, I declined the offer, feeling that I had nothing relevant to say, or very little at best. Somewhere in the archaeologist's subconscious, the religious dimension is associated with failure. Indeed when the archaeologist has in front of him or her an artifact or an archaeological structure, the tendency of certain functionalist and neopositivist methods is to seek ecological or economic explanations. The archaeologist resorts to spiritual interpretation only when all else fails. As so many farfetched speculations have been made about prehistoric religions, today's archaeologist prefers any other explanation to a *deus ex machina*: "it must be symbolic" or "it must be for ritualistic or symbolic purposes".

Since Leroi-Gourhan's classic *Les Religions de la Préhistoire* was published in 1964, no other general work has appeared on that topic. During the 1980s, general works and textbooks have included, at best, only a very brief mention of religion. This lack of interest corresponds to a particular stage of the epistemological evolution of archaeology but is also due to the nature of the archaeological remains themselves. Remains from the environment and material culture lend themselves better to the reconstruction of ecology, technology, and economy than to that of political, social, and religious structures. Thus, in the search for a rigorous scientific approach, the interest of the "New Archaeology" has been in the former rather than in the latter. Ethnology on the other hand, through the structuralist school, has gained greater knowledge of symbolic thought.

The reincorporation of symbolic study into the field of archaeology has taken more than a decade. In the 1980s, mainly under the impetus of Ian Hodder in England, an approach has developed critical of the functionalist archaeological thesis that shape is determined only by the function (Hodder 1986). Contrary to what is imagined by some, archaeology remains pretty much a human science rather than a natural science: one must take into account the symbolic structure characteristic of each society, because such structure has a direct bearing on every aspect of life. This line of approach remains difficult because the relationship between the object and the symbol is variable and, by definition, arbitrary.

"Ethnoarchaeological" research in current societies on issues interesting for archaeology is an attempt to resolve this problem—e.g., studying material culture (Plate 10–2) or the way different groups currently living in Africa use adornments as symbols of ethnic membership. Africa, with its extraordinary diversity and continuity, offers exceptional opportunities for this type of study (Atherton 1983).

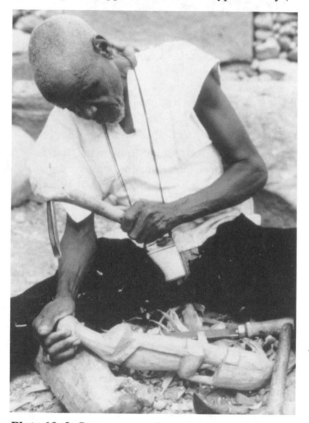

Plate 10–2. Statues are an important part of the material heritage of African religions. Though metal, ceramic, or stone statues may last longer, wooden statues can span several centuries. Interpretation of old statues is helped by the study of recent carvings and the function and significance of sculpture in present-day religions. Here a Dogon blacksmith carves a statue for a client to use at an altar to reinforce his sacrifices. The figurine represents the owner, and—contrary to the usual interpretation—does not depict an ancestor.

It seems likely that archaeology will reappropriate the symbolic and religious dimensions of culture in its quest to understand prehistoric life as a whole. The African experience is likely to be highly significant in this process.

In preliterate societies, religious behavior is manifested through verbal and non-verbal communication and, fortunately for archaeologists, through material culture. The latter category includes remains of ritual behavior: offerings or sacrificial remains, altars or larger religious structures, burials, and things we call works of art (whether or not they are identifed as such in the societies where they were made and used) such as sculpture, engraving, and painting.

But where is the boundary between a purely decorative purpose and meaningful symbolic expression? Why is pottery shape and decoration seldom considered as religiously significant when rock art is generally viewed as the most obvious manifestation of religious life? Briefly, the problem exists on two levels: first, how do we know that an archaeological remain is meaningful in the symbolic or religious sphere; second, how do we interpret a symbol, as it may have several senses of meaning, have been a multiple metaphor, or have been known originally only by a handful of initiates? Even if we sent ethnographers back in time, they would not necessarily be able to decipher that symbolic structure. What then can an archaeologist hope for when left only with a handful of rubble?

It is clear that we touch here on the very nature of archaeology, its paradigms and its limitations. But after this cautionary tale, my intent here is not so much to discuss the finality and the power of archaeology as to provide some background on the most recent aspects of research on prehistoric African religion. To do so, let us examine four areas in which cases of religious reconstruction have been attempted, using a direct analogy between ethnographic and historic situations—rock art, sculpture, burial rituals, and monuments.

ROCK ART

Rock art is one of the areas in which recent progress in interpretation has been the most exciting. This work has been well summarized by Whitney Davis (1984). According to Davis, rock art "refers to an extended network of ritual acts and beliefs, to out-of-the-ordinary perception and knowledge, and to adaptively significant local information".

There are in Africa two major traditions of prehistoric rock art: one in the Sahara and the Nile Valley, the other in Southern Africa. Although ritual events are often thought to be the major subject of Saharan rock painting, there is no external means of verifying this, as we have no evidence other than the paintings themselves. Nonetheless, the most recent of these paintings are detailed enough to allow some comparison. Thus, Griaule (1934), Dieterlen (1966) and Lhote (1966, 1967) were able to suggest a connection between rock painting and some myths and rituals practiced among the Peul that have been documented ethnographically (Davis 1984). In the Nile Valley, a parallel between predynastic painted pottery and rock art representing dancing or mourning women associated with papyrus boats also exists (Murray 1956).

So far, the most exciting evidence of a connection between rock art and ritual has come from Southern Africa. The oldest dated evidence of naturalistic animal painting has been found in southern Namibia in the Apollo XI cave. Three detached slabs bearing the painting of a human figure and the outline of a rhinoceros occur in levels dated some 28,000 years ago (Wendt 1976). With few exceptions it is generally extremely difficult to date rock art that remains unburied on the walls. It is believed to be much more recent and to be made by the direct ancestors of the present-day San "bushmen". This provides a good opportunity to compare the iconography of that art with the abundant ethnographic and historic data on San "bushmen" (Lee and De Vore 1976; Richard B. Lee 1979; Marshall 1969; Tobias 1978). This comparison has been attempted by Patricia Vinnicombe, Harold Pager, and especially J. David Lewis-Williams. Vinnicombe showed that San rock art was overwhelmingly concerned with the image of the antelope and especially the eland, although the eland was not the most important element in their environment and diet (Vinnicombe 1972a, 1972b, 1976; see also Pager 1971, 1975). She concluded:

> It is significant that eland painting is characterized not only by dominance in number and size but by the systematical rendering of proportion, action, and color division and by the fact that they are superimposed and juxtaposed in relation to other subjects according to a set pattern. The eland [herd animals that periodically amalgamate into large groups] epitomized more than the regulated unity of the Bushmen band: it served as a link between the material and spiritual worlds. (Vinnicombe 1976:352–353)

Plate 10–3. Rock painting of five antelopes, Macumbe cave, Chinamura Reserve, Zimbabwe (after L. Frobenius: *Erythräa*). The brown of the better-painted older paintings shows through the yellow of the more recent ones. About one-tenth natural size; copied by J. Lutz.

Even more interesting is the recognition by Lewis-Williams (1980, 1981) of the essentially shamanistic nature of San rock art as he wrote:

> The trance dance itself, the capture of the rain animal and the experiences, symbols, and metaphors of trance were prominent among the artists' subject matter. I believe further that the trancers and the artists were, for the most part, one and the same. (Lewis-Williams 1982)

This discovery led him to investigate San metaphors and symbols of trance experience as well as the cross-cultural features of trance. Because the nervous system is common to all people, certain hallucinations—neurological rather than cultural in form—are the same for all people. In the early stage of trance, subjects "'see' neurologically produced geometric forms, one of which is catenary curves" (Lewis-Williams 1986). Indeed, catenary curves and zigzags appear in San rock art, as well as bees whose buzzing is explicitly associated by San to what one can hear in trance.

In my own area of research, Central Africa, rock art is present only on the periphery of the Zaïre River central basin. It is consistently overlooked in any of the general syntheses done on African rock art. Almost completely abstract, it often eludes interpretation even after extremely careful studies, as exemplified by Bidzar petrographs in Cameroon (Marliac 1981). In the Kongo area of Lower Zaïre, rock art is at times more naturalistic and combines indigenous and Christian themes (Mortelmans and Monteyne 1962; Raymaekers and van Moorsel 1964). Once again, although this rock art could well have started during the Late Stone Age, a strong degree of continuity has been suggested between those signs and contemporary Kongo signs and cosmograms (MacGaffey 1978b; Thompson 1981). Kongo informants explained the meaning of many of these signs; some of them are still used in decorating various objects. They can symbolize, for example, the moon, mountains, or stars. This type of motif is widespread and one may question the validity of the interpretation given by the informants who, although Kongo, came from other areas and are separated from the artist by several centuries. Nevertheless, these caves played an important role in Kongo religious ritual and belief. This usage may well date back two thousand years, as I have been able to show that neolithic remains were encountered very deep in those caves, suggesting a special purpose, probably ritual (de Maret 1986). Their names reflect also their ritual function: for example, the "Secret of the country" or "Mbenza Cave". Mbenza appears to have been an ancient chthonian divinity related to a fertility cult. Besides caves, its name was also given to rock outcrops, such as Ntadi dia Mbenza found near Biongo and engraved with an extremely elaborate but mysterious geometric design. Across the Zaïre River in Mayombe, on Seke Mbanza territory, I visited a rock shelter also called Ntadi dia Mbenza, which, unlike all the other known rock art in the Kongo area, is decorated with white and red dots and lines. According to an old informant who was taken there by his father while he was a child, the cave was regularly repainted and while doing so the people used some of the paint to paint themselves. Only men who had children could be initiated in this manner. The meaning of those drawings was known only by the Ngudi a Nganga. Similar Ntadi dia Mbenza rock shelters are to be found in the same region.

Sculpture

Besides rock art, other forms of artistic expression carry a symbolic message, including sculpture. Only sculptures made of terra-cotta, stone, or metal have been preserved long enough under tropical conditions to testify to very old religious practices, with at least one remarkable exception: a carved wooden animal with a snout, dated in the eighth century and found buried in gravel of the Laviela River in central Angola. In the Kongo area, there are notable examples of stone sculpture, the Mintadi, which were put on the tombs to honor the dead (Shaje 1986). The Christian influence since the late fifteenth century in that area can be seen in the brass or copper crucifixes and in statues of the Virgin cast locally, also in copper or brass.

It is not possible to cover, in a single chapter, all the sculptures discovered in sub-Saharan Africa. Some of the most recent and most remarkable discoveries are

- two terra cotta heads probably used for ritual occasions, such as initiation school, by Early Iron Age farmers (circa A.D. 500) near Lydenburg in eastern Transvaal
- the heads of the Aowin style, from an ethnic group in southwest Ghana
- the heads from the south of Lake Chad, circa tenth century A.D.
- the Nok sculptures from central Nigeria
- the Djenne Djeno sculptures from the inner delta of the Niger, circa twelfth century A.D.

In some cases, by combining ethnographic data and observations from careful excavations, one may hope to reconstruct the context of the social and economic ritual of that art. Unfortunately the aesthetic quality of some sculptures makes them victims of art dealers who organize their systematic pilferage. Torn away from their archaeological context, these objects—which could tell us so much about the symbolic system of those who created them—are condemned to be only works of art. In this way, hundreds of terra cotta statues from Djenne Djeno were sold into the international art market, a situation deplored by Roderick and Susan McIntosh, who have conducted careful excavations in that region (McIntosh and McIntosh 1986).

Burial Rituals

The largest known graveyard in sub-Saharan Africa was discovered in the Upemba depression, in the center of Shaba in eastern Zaïre. Excavations carried out on six of the forty known sites led to the establishment of the first complete Iron Age sequence, precisely dated by more than fifty radiocarbon and thermoluminescence dates. After a Late Stone Age occupation, the Iron Age in this area started around the sixth century A.D. with the Kamilambian phase, which was replaced by the Kisalian phase around the eighth century. This Ancient Kisalian gave way to the Classic Kisalian in the eleventh century. A third tradition, the Kabambian, makes a distinction between Kabambian A and B, the latter ending around the eighteenth century. This is approximately when the famous Luba state emerged (Reefe 1981:107–114); vestiges of this period are characteristic of Luba practices, as described by ethnographers and still seen today. The continuity and density of the occupation as well as the persistence of certain customs and aspects of material life (pottery, basketry) from the Kisalian to the present indicate that the mass of the population remained much the same through time (de Maret 1978, 1985a).

The changes that occurred could have resulted from the presence of newcomers as well as from the growing political and economic influence of the outside world. The fact that the numerous lakes could have been used as refuge areas would also

Plate 10–4. Knowledge of the past often has to be gleaned from objects that are no longer found in their archaeological context. This terracotta statue (of a king?) from the Djenne area of the inland delta in Mali comes from an illegal dig and subsequent attempts to sell the statue on the illegal art market. Such dealings severely hamper scientific archaeological research in Africa.[1]

have favored continuity. An anthropometric study of the skeletons shows strong affinities with today's Luba people.

Let us examine the ritual aspects of this remarkable continuity. Since the Early Iron Age, the body of the deceased was placed in the grave, oriented towards the cardinal points. From this period onward, grave goods were put with the deceased, first only iron tools and weapons that were indicative of the importance of funerary practice. The Kisalian graves contain numerous objects (see Plate 10–1). There was a relationship between age and the burial ritual: adults were buried deeper than children and children deeper than infants. The body was generally interred lying on its back, its feet placed downstream in relation to the Zaïre River. Among the Luba, waterways played an essential role in funerary rituals and in relation to the afterlife. For example, the dead chief was usually buried at the bottom of a river.

Much of the pottery found in the graves was made solely for burial. In children's graves the size of the pots is proportional to the child's age. It is obvious that much of the pottery was symbolic, constructed on a small scale and therefore not suitable for normal use. Among grave goods are cannon bones from goats and antelopes, especially frequent in children's graves, which were apparently used as dolls along with anthropomorphic bottles. The base of one of these bottles was engraved with a scene of copulation, suggesting that those dolls were used in some fertility rituals. This would explain their presence not only in children's but also in women's graves.

It is possible that people were sacrificed to accompany the body of an important person. This practice was found in Katoto, a cemetery belonging to a tradition roughly contemporaneous with the Kisalian in the southern part of the Upemba rift (Hiernaux, Maquet, and De Buyst 1972). The Katotian pottery is very different from the Kisalian and very little pottery found in the graves could testify to any episodic exchange. However, both cultures achieved similar levels of social organization, as evidenced in both cases by the presence of ceremonial axes and anvils in the richest graves. These axes, perforated and finely engraved, their handles decorated with nails, are much like those found recently among the Luba as a symbol of authority. It is certainly not by chance that the only Kisalian iron anvil so far collected comes from one of the three Kisalian graves out of 163 where a ceremonial axe was discovered. The two Katotian anvils were also associated with ceremonial axes.

Early this century, there is at least one case of a major chiefdom in the Upemba where the chief's regalia included an iron anvil. There is a strong symbolic connection between the chief and iron working among Bantu peoples generally, and the ritual metaphor for a chief was often an iron anvil. Throughout Central Africa, two anvils are often struck together during a crucial stage of the enthronement ritual (de Maret 1985b). It is very interesting to note that the anvil in the Kisalian grave was lying like the dolls in the women's graves, oriented like the skeleton, its "head" in the same direction as the skull and next to it (Plate 10–5). The same was true for the anvil found in an identical position next to the skull of a Rwandan king who died in the seventeenth or eighteenth century (Van Noten 1972). Another example of this practice was found in Zambia at Ingombe Ilede, a fourteenth-century cemetery (Fagan, Phillipson, and Daniels 1969). In all of these cases, the anvil was the symbol of leadership rather than the indication of a true blacksmith (de Maret 1985b).

The Kabambian A is characterized by a change in most of the pottery and rituals. At Sanga, the best-known site, the orientation of the skeleton is systematically reversed, the head instead of the feet being oriented downstream. With the appearance of the Kabambian B the burial orientation once again changed, reverting back to that of the Kisalian. During the Kabambian B, only a few pots, still functional, were placed in the grave around the head. That also changed with the more recent Luba graves, where strings of blue beads are the only grave goods to be found. Unlike the preceding rituals, the deceased is buried in a contracted lateral decubitus with hands brought back to the face. This practice corresponds to the Luba ritual of this century.

During the Kabambian and Katotian periods, conus shell disks were also used. Usually worn by the chief, these are another well-known symbol of power. For example, Allen Roberts (1985) informs us that among the Tabwa east of the Upemba, the shell's spiral structure symbolizes the moon, while its central point and inner spiral symbolize human origin and dispersion.

These examples show how the study of burial rituals helps to decipher symbolic structures. They confirm the great antiquity of some of the current rites and myths of Central Africa.

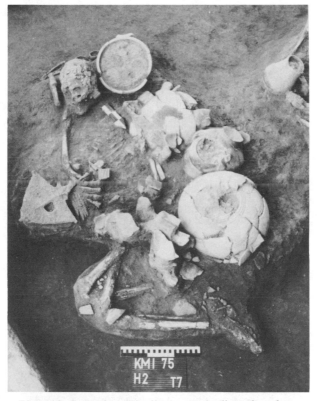

Plate 10–5. Ancient Kisalian grave (radiocarbon date: A.D. 845 ± 150) at Kamilamba, eastern Zaïre. Note the cylindrical anvil near the skull.

Monuments

When we speak of monuments, the famous ruins of Zimbabwe are the first to come to mind. The Shona word *zimbabwe* means "venerated house, the dwelling of a chief". Great Zimbabwe is interpreted as the residence of a sacred chief, with some spaces and structure designed for ceremonies. It became the central settlement of an oligarchy that had grown out of the peasant stock around the thirteenth century. According to Peter Garlake:

> Archaeology at present allows no precise interpretation of religion in Great Zimbabwe's growth and power structure. There is no doubt, however, that many structures reflect it. Turrets, towers, monoliths, altars, and a series of soap stone sculptures of birds that were set both on walls and altars, must all have had a supernatural significance. (Garlake 1978:84; see also Garlake 1973)

Zimbabwe is a monumental illustration of the way that political and religious power were intimately intertwined in the rituals of many African sacred kingships. Overshadowed by Zimbabwe are various other monuments in sub-Saharan Africa. In Central African Republic near Bouar, megalithic structures dated around 500 B.C. were found. They were most probably built for ritual purposes by a sedentary group using polished tools (David 1982). Other megalithic structures are known in the Grassfields of northwest Cameroon, an area considered by linguists as the homeland of the early Bantu. So far, it has not been possible to date those structures, but their age may well be similar to their Bouar counterpart (de Maret 1980).

In Senegal, megalithic monuments, generally tombs, are dated between the sixth and ninth centuries but also possibly earlier (Thilmans, Descamp, and Khayat 1980).

A catalogue of all other monumental evidence of religious behavior in sub-Saharan Africa is impossible to establish here. Nigeria alone has yielded a wealth of data, especially in Yoruba country, where altars were generally built in the courtyard. Spectacular evidence of this practice comes from Ife, where some of the famous terracotta heads have been recovered in a very old courtyard. A pot or a pot neck, probably receptacles for libation, were usually embedded in the center of a potsherd and pebble pavement. There are numerous other aspects of archaeological evidence found both in Benin and Ife that echo traditional Yoruba religious practices (Garlake 1978:132–134).

Linguistics

Besides archaeology, linguistics may also serve as a means of reconstructing ancient religious practices; it is a very promising field in which only limited research has been done. Two different approaches are possible. The first is to reconstruct terms related to religion in protolanguages.[2] For example, in the Bantu world, throughout Central, East, and Southern Africa, one may conclude that the word meaning "god" in the various languages could not be reconstructed at a common proto-Bantu level. There are two roots with a general meaning of "god": one is *–*jàmbé* (9/10),[3] which is present in the western half of the area, and another is *–*dùngù* (1/2), attested in the eastern half (Figure 10.1). Those terms have often been used to designate the Christian god, but this is the result of a recent shift in meaning. *–*Dùngù* may well

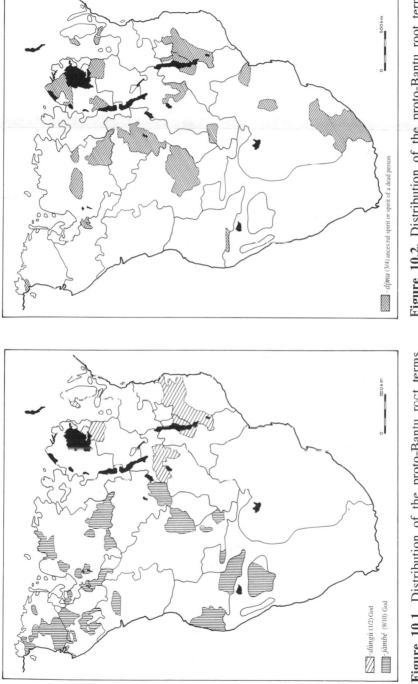

Figure 10.1. Distribution of the proto-Bantu root terms —*dùngù (1/2) [God] and —*jàmbé (9/10) [God].

-*dùngù (1/2) God

-*jàmbé (9/10) God

0   500 km

Figure 10.2. Distribution of the proto-Bantu root term —*dímu (3/4) [ancestral spirit or spirit of a dead person].

-*dímu (3/4) ancestral spirit or spirit of a dead person

0   500 km

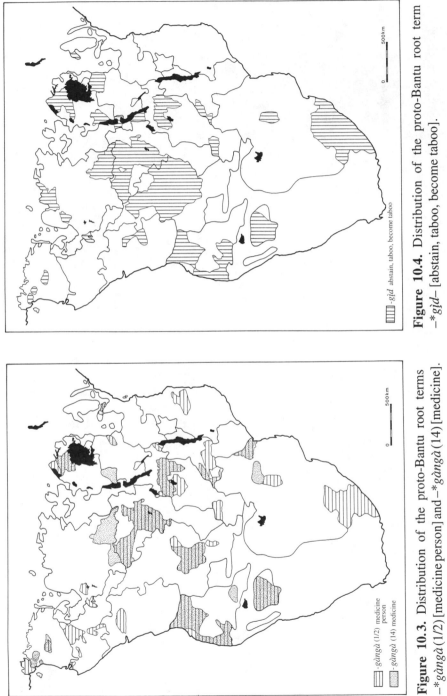

Figure 10.3. Distribution of the proto-Bantu root terms —*gàngà* (1/2) [medicine person] and —*gàngà* (14) [medicine].

- *gàngà* (1/2) medicine person

- *gàngà* (14) medicine

0   500 km

Figure 10.4. Distribution of the proto-Bantu root term —*gìd*– [abstain, taboo, become taboo].

- *gìd* abstain, taboo, become taboo

0   500 km

have meant "a divinity among others", a spirit, and may well be related to the root −*dùngà*, which means the afterworld, the place where the dead go.

On the contrary, the term for ancestral spirit or the spirit of a dead person is present with that meaning throughout the Bantu area and is easily reconstructed as −*dímu* (3/4) in proto-Bantu (Figure 10.2). The opposition between the medicine man or simply medicine [−*gàngà* (1/2) or −*gàngà* (14)] (Figure 10.3), and "bewitch" (or "curse") [−*dòg*−] and its derivatives, mentioned by Luc de Heusch (1970), is probably very old. Since these terms are present throughout the Bantu area, they may be reconstructed as proto-Bantu. Similarly, "to refrain from something because of a taboo" or "to be taboo" [−*gìd*−] is also very old and attested throughout the whole Bantu area (Figure 10.4).

The second possible line of inquiry is a close and careful semantic analysis of metaphors and other semantic shifts. This is a domain that has hardly been touched, but I am convinced it could be very useful, particularly in the structuralist analysis of rites and myths, in unveiling very old symbolic connections.

CONCLUSION

I have attempted in this survey of prehistoric evidence of traditional African religions to give a general overview of our knowledge on this topic. I have particularly sought to indicate the direction of future research. To do so, I have emphasized some of the lesser-known examples.

Whether in the realm of archaeology or linguistics, Africa offers both great diversity and numerous examples of a remarkable continuity. It offers many occasions for a fruitful joint effort in which, starting from ethnographic data, one can attempt to bring life, through archaeology and linguistics, to these ancient religions. I am convinced that the African experience can play a decisive role in the integration of the analysis of religious phenomena into the archaeology of preliterate societies. In so doing, it can significantly further the progress of archaeological science as a whole.

NOTES

1. A documentary film—*The African King*, by Walter E.A. van Beek and Nigel Evans (Nigel Evans Productions, 1990)—addresses these and similar issues.

2. I am grateful to Claire Grégoire for collecting and mapping the attestations of the various terms throughout the Bantu world.

3. A term such as −*jàmbé* (9/10) should be read as follows: the hyphen " − " prior to the root indicates that there may be a prefix that varies depending on the particular Bantu language (or a suffix if the hyphen follows the root). The asterisk " * " indicates that this is a reconstructed root in a hypothetical reconstructed ancestor language (protolanguage). The tone marks over vowels are à = low tone, é = high tone, and no diacritic = mid tone. "(9/10)" indicates that the singular of this root is in the Bantu substantive class 9 and the plural is in class 10. Bantu languages have about 18 substantive classes that determine concordial agreement among pronominal, adjectival, and adverbial prefixes and infixes throughout a sentence.

Plate 11–1. Amaga, a shaman, performs the *bulo*, the main new year festival of the Dogon, in Mali. An outsider in some ways in Dogon society, his divinatory and diagnostic expertise, and his contacts with the spirits make him a necessary intermediary for his village in guarding against and warding off evil. During this large communal ritual, aimed at cleaning the ritual slate for the next year, his role is very prominent—even to the point of conspicuously "showing off ", as he does here.

11

The Innocent Sorcerer:
Coping with Evil in Two African Societies (Kapsiki & Dogon)

Walter E.A. van Beek

CASE 1: THE INFERTILE WIFE (KAPSIKI)[1]

TERI KWATCHA EXPLAINS his problems to his friend, the blacksmith/diviner Cewuve. "You know my second wife, Kwaberhe Kwampa, the one from Rhumsu (a neighboring village). I married her some ten years ago, as a *kwatewume* [run-away-wife] and gave a lot for the bridewealth already, as the first husband claimed his orignal bridewealth. She is a good wife; she ran away to another village only once, and she returned after two weeks. She finds no rest here, as she is still not pregnant, and never has been. We have consulted the crab [divination] many times and got various answers. Can you tell us why her belly stays empty?" Cewuve puts the crabfish in the pot, inside the neat arrangement of straws and calabash sherds, and asks the little animal: "Crab from the pot, crab from the pot, do tell us why this woman is sterile; tell the truth". The answer is distilled from the havoc wrought by the animal in the small confines of the pot. Several sessions are needed to come to a more or less clear answer, and finally the smith concludes: "Maybe they told you that someone near her was responsible, a woman [*mete*, "witch"] blocking her fertility or so, or that the jealousy was the cause. Not so. Your wife is *ndegema* [not in harmony with the supernatural world]. It is not a person who harmed her nor a *ndebeshèngu* [sorcerer]; it is *ndrimike* [badness]. Her *shala* [personal god] has done it, so a sacrifice is called for. Take a black male goat, and have her leave for the bush with a blacksmith. Out in the bush the blacksmith breaks the legs of the goat and leaves it there. Then she returns home. You may hold a house sacrifice then [a ritual in which red beer is brewed, a goat slaughtered, and a meal held with the neighbors and clansmen]".[2]

Teri Kwatcha goes home in a pensive mood. Usually Cewuve shows himself a very cautious diviner, quite pessimistic in his outlook and his forecasting. He always predicts bad things to happen, and that is good. Bad things not only do happen, they are the only real things, the real events. This cautious optimism gives food for thought.

Teri decides to see Kweji Xake, one of the principal healers of the village. Kweji agrees with the crab (of course) that *shala* may be the cause but suggests another possible explanation. "Maybe, Teri, not your wife but you are *ndegema*. A long time ago you came to my father (Vandu, now deceased) for *rhwè* [medicine, magic] to marry a wife. He gave you the one to "catch" a wife, and the manner to keep that wife at home. But he never gave you the *rhwè* that comes with it. For anyone who marries his wife with "means" runs the risk of making her sterile. So you come with me and I will give you *rhwè* to heal that sterility". Teri accepts Kweji's medicine, which he must apply to his wife without her knowledge. The small bundle of grasses has to be buried at the doorstep of her hut, as well as under the spot she puts her jars.

Back home Teri ponders his own protective *rhwè*: his protection in war, against burglary in the compound (the thief will forget to steal once he is in the house) and—most important of all—his *sekwa* [a ritual means of enforcing the payment of debts]. All these "means" of protection may "attack" the people in the house, and his second wife's sterility may stem from the dangers inherent in *sekwa,* too. Teri decides to remove his *sekwa*, as the most potent of all *rhwè,* from the house. After putting Kweji's medicine on the spots indicated by the specialist, he leaves the house with his *sekwa* bundle of medicine under his clothes and hides it somewhere in the bush.

When his wife returns home (she had been to the market of Rhumsu, her native village, to sell some beans), he tells her about his visit to the diviner Cewuve, promising her a black billy goat for the sacrifice and a house sacrifice later on.

Teri's wife, after all these attentions, in fact did get pregnant. About a year later she gave birth to twins, one of which died.

Plate 11–2. Sacrificial jars, center of rituals for Kapsiki who live in northern Cameroon.

CASE 2: PROTECTING THE HOUSE (DOGON)[3]

In the village of Tireli, at the foot of the Bandiagara escarpment, Dogolu Say pays a visit to Mèninyu, his father-in-law. Leaving his shoes outside the gate, Dogolu cautiously enters the compound; Mèninyu not only is the father of his second wife, but also a renowned ritual specialist. After the lengthy salutation, Dogolu waits till Mèninyu has finished a chiropractic session on a neighbor who just had a nasty fall, all the while chatting with the patient. When alone with Mèninyu and following the usual small talk, Dogolu comes to the point. He is building a new house for Atimè, his friend from abroad who has come to live in the village. "You know, people will come and look in the house, maybe will dream about it. They will speak about him and me. Words will be there, words will rise, and as you know the words of the mouth [*anga tĩ*] you may help me". Of course, Mèninyu knows exactly what Dogolo means: people will be jealous and even give vent to their jealousy, so the harmony between Dogolu and his clanbrothers will be disrupted. "I will give you some *ginu dom* [means to protect the house]", he assures Dogolu, "but be sure that you and your guest do the "guard the head" [*ku domonu*, sacrifice for protection] later at my altar". Dogolu agrees and asks also for special protection for the open space of the compound; for many visitors will come there, and many words will be spoken in the open air.

A few days later after sunset Dogolu buries the protection of the house at the spot where the threshold will be. It is a piece of cord with three strands, white, blue and black, with twenty-eight knots, for which he will give Mèninyu a gift of 3,000 CFA (about $12) later on. He knows Mèninyu well enough to be sure nobody in Tireli will be aware of the proceedings. If not, he would have gone to another village. In fact, he does have a second protection, bought in Nakomo (a neighboring village), which will be put just above the door inside the main hut. It has cost him 10,000 CFA, money he considers well spent. He knows how to make some protection himself, but only against a specific threat: against a special kind of *dugugonu* [sorcerer]. What he needed here is a more general protection that also works against Christians and Muslims. The various diviners he consulted did agree on the villages where he could find materials to protect his house: Tireli and Nakomo.

When Atimè arrives, Dogolu takes to Mèninyu a cock, a hen, some other foodstuffs, and seasoning. On Amagoro, a powerful altar that has been served by the lineage of Mèninyu since times of old, the father-in-law of Dogolu then performs the sacrifice "to guard the head". This specific sacrifice is not eaten: after being grilled and seasoned, the meat is stacked away under a heap of stones. If anyone should even taste it, he or she would drop dead instantly. Mèninyu tells Atimè of a Fulani herdsman who did not believe this taboo. He partook of the meat, started down for the valley, and died within the perimeter of the village. Mèninyu also explains that the secret of the magical means does not reside in the things one uses—like the three-stranded string—but in the words spoken into it. One has to know the *anga tĩ* [words of the mouth] in order to be effective. Anyone who knows the words can perform it.

Now the house is well protected against intruders, against a great variety of dangers: witches [*yadugonu*], who will put poison [*dugo*] in the water; sorcerers

Plate 11–3. Mèningu, the Dogon father-in-law in "Case 2", invokes the supernatural world to "protect the house". He strikes a small iron adze on the rock and intones the long ritual text that exorts the gods, spirits, and ancestors to care for and look after the owner of the altar.

Plate 11–4. Yèngulu, a friend of Mèningu, following the intoned text (Plate 11–3), performs the sacrifice with the blood of a chicken.

[*dudugonu*], who will send their chains to poison food or drink; Muslim marabouts, who are considered very potent; and Christians, who may have evil eyes. Nobody knows specifically which person is dangerous. With a good protection nobody is worried any longer; but the danger can stem from anybody, especially someone very near. Lest the protection abates, Dogolu and Atimè never speak about it (though they may indicate its presence with a small bronze plaque on the threshold) and should beware of menstruating women stepping over it: one of the two *ginu dom* is of the kind that is spoiled by the presence of menstrual blood. Still, it would be a good idea to have one's own *ama* [altar] in the compound. A regular sacrifice on an often-used compound altar will reinforce the protection gained elsewhere, since an altar that is frequently used for sacrifices becomes a protective power in itself.

KAPSIKI: EVIL FROM ALL SIDES

Evil has many faces. In the next two sections, I explore the threats the Kapsiki and Dogon perceive in their social environment and their notion of evil. For the Kapsiki, one should discern between those ills and evils that come from people and those that come from *shala* [god]. The first source usually is called *ndrimike* [badness], but in the problems stemming "from god" this term does not apply. The notion *shala* has many meanings besides that of the "personal god"; it can also imply a place, a mythical snake, or a certain kind of illness, all closely associated with "god" (van Beek 1987). As usual in African religion, the main supernatural being is ethically neutral. No evaluations are ever made concerning the events that are deemed his work. *Shala menete* ["God has done it"] is a standard phrase of resignation. The Kapsiki are confident that ultimately their interest and that of their *shala* will run parallel, but at a given moment one can never be sure of the positive influence of their *shala*. Even more ambivalent is the relationship between an individual and someone else's *shala*: the Kapsiki, with their individualistic orientation, consider the well-being of someone's *shala* as potentially a threat towards another person.

An individual can fall out of grace with his or her personal god in many ways, but some kinds of falling out can come from breaking taboos. A fair number of actions are taboo, ranging from forbidden sexual relations to slaughtering a pregnant goat or having a cock crow on one's granary. Not all these actions can be prevented, but they still call for reparation. Without reparations, several kinds of bad things can happen: illness, infertility (as in our example), bad luck in trading or in cultivation. No specific threat is associated with *shala*. Protection as such is not possible—careful living is called for. If mishaps occur, divination should indicate the source of the trouble.

Shala-related beings may be dangerous too: Va, the personification of the rain, and Veci, the sun, can be encountered in person, which calls for a sacrifice. These beings are relevant in very special situations only, like drought, and then are dealt with collectively, either in a rain-sacrifice or in communal rituals. Also related are the spirits that roam in the *gutuli* [bush], which can possess a person, leading to insanity. Against these, special *rhwè*, known only to very few specialists, must be applied (van Beek 1978:394).

Apart from *shala*, some other dangers lurk in the "other side of the world". Death and some illnesses (measles and smallpox) are conceived of as persons. However, against these, practically no *rhwè* exists. Some specialists claim *rhwè* against smallpox or measles, but no one can resist Mte[death]. In fact, the futile fight against Mte and the failure of the many ruses to escape from him form the backbone of Kapsiki mythology. Just as the people of old tried in vain to escape or conquer death, no contemporary Kapsiki can hope to put it off. And so against these three no real protection exists, only acceptance.

A second category of mishaps coming from outside bears no close relationship to *shala*. Included here are the many epidemics, which are not personified, such as malaria, meningitis, or dysentery. Against these, various *rhwè* exist, some of them well known, others secret knowledge for the specialists. Sometimes women's sterility is considered among these epidemics, but more often this has other origins (as in Case 1). Usually the symptoms are clear and well known. In addition, the many ways in which *rhwè* and other ritually important objects can attack people are considered a threat from beyond, like the threat the *sekwa* posed for the people in Teri's compound. These objects, like neolithic remains of former populations, may be used in a variety of ways for the well-being of the owner. All of them, however, may present some danger to the owners. In Kapsiki, no blessing is ever free; what one gains in a special way beyond the average situation will have to be paid for elsewhere. Usually these "blessings" shorten one's life span.

Far more important as a focus of ritual attention are the many ways evil can stem from human beings. No clear distinction can be made between natural and supernatural threats, but three human sources of evil can be discerned: bad characters, people with the "evil eye", and "spirit walkers".

First, there are people who have a bad or special *mehele* [character or spirit]. The witches [*mete*] are the clearest example. A witch is someone (male or female) who inherits a special deviant type of *shinankwe* [shadow]. At night it leaves the sleeping body through the anus and roams in the bush, red like fire, as a kind of wild cat. It eats the shadows of sleeping children's hearts. The victims, when waking up, feel weak and become ill. Unless the *mete* drops the shadow of the heart, the victim will die.

Witchcraft is deemed to be inherited matrilineally (in a strictly patrilineal kinship system). The Kapsiki on the whole are well aware of who are *mete*. Most witches, however, are not "active"; jealousy, ire, or lust for vengeance set the involuntary processes of the witchcraft in motion. So witches are more or less responsible for their vile acts; it is their *fete* [fault]. However, not every witch is known as such. One major risk for the village resides in strangers coming. These strangers, because of virilocal residence, tend to be women. Often, in-marrying women are hardly known at all, so it is possible for a witch to be among them. This is probably one reason that women are deemed to be witches more often than men. Many folktales warn the young and eager man against the dangers of the beautiful but unknown wife coming into the village for marriage.

Kapsiki divination may indicate that a certain illness is the result of *mete* activities but cannot indicate which activity. There are no high-status diviners in

Kapsiki society, as there are elsewhere in Africa. This lack of pronounced hierarchy among diviners ties in with the acephalous juro-political organization of the Kapsiki, in which pronouncing a judgment over other people is very difficult to do. The usual reaction, after the crab has indicated witchcraft, is to cry into the dark of the night, "Let go, let the heart go". It is hoped that the witch will then fear detection and return the shadow of the heart.

Essential in these matters is that the *mete* in question be someone close, either a close kinsman, a wife, or co-wife. Witchcraft, as nearly always is the case in Africa, is the "enemy within the gates". If someone, either a known witch or a newly arrived wife, is suspected of taking the shadow of a child's heart, the sick child is put before her in the full presence of as many people as possible, saying: "Here it is. Do eat the rest now". Formerly, if the child died, the witch was chased from the village and her ears were cut off. Since colonial days, the government no longer allows this, and so the witches proliferate. (In recent years, however, accusations of witchcraft have regained acceptance to the Cameroonian courts.)

Although treatment of *mete* infliction may be limited, protection is normal and easy to obtain. Everybody knows some protective medicine, and each blacksmith can furnish the *rhwè* needed for a newborn baby.

Kapsiki society is not a witch-ridden society; the number of accusations is very small and relatively few illnesses are attributed to witches. Children are deemed to be about the only possible victims for *mete*, and of children's plights only the combination of diarrhea without blood, fever, and much urinating (more or less the symptoms for a Western medical diagnosis of bacterial dysentery) point to *mete* influence.

Another kind of harmful people are the men or women with the "evil eye" [*hweteru*]. Their spirits roam the village at night—in no specified form—and suck blood from people and animals. These victims do not die, but become unproductive. These *hweteru* act so from sheer spite and jealousy; they are deemed to be in command of their bad shadow, inherited matrilineally. In this case, people generally do not know who is *hweteru* in the village. There is no known cure, only protection against them, that is very easy to obtain: a common plant species gives fair protection. However, it remains important not to foster jealousy: anything nice or beautiful must be hidden from view.

A third kind of special people, though much less harmful, are the "spirit walkers" [*kelèngu*]. Their shadow leaves them at night, in their own image, and joins colleagues in the village. Together, their shadows are believed to go on noble exploits like stealing sorghum in enemy fields or waging war against the spirit walkers of neighboring villages. When they steal the shadow of the harvest, they put it with their own crops; as a result their supply of grains seems interminable. Their main thrust is against other villages, so people do not consider the *kelèngu* as shameful or evil and therefore freely speak about them. This *mehele* [character] is inherited from father to only one son, and the spirit walkers can be recognized by their thin linear somatic type; they explain their own thinness by their overdose of activity: "We are never at rest; we work during the day and steal at night". As protection, one must shield one's fields from the *kelèngu* of other villages. Some medicinal plants offer this protection, as does a thorn hedge or a row of a black sorghum variety around the field. The *kelèngu* sometimes are aware of future events, a domain in which their authority is uncontested, which is one reason they are sometimes dubbed "clairvoyants" in the literature. Whatever they see happen in the spirit world will happen shortly after in the daily world. When they kill people among themselves in their battles, that spirit walker will die within a few days. No medicine will help. Women may be walkers too, for any war has to have its spectators.

Special circumstances at birth may indicate a threat too, usually not for any specific individual, but for the whole community. Twins, breech birth, a child born with the caul, or one conceived without preceding menstruation, all imply their specific threat for either the parents or the whole village, ranging from drought to the death of the father before the child's initiation. In all these cases a small ritual is indicated to take away the bad luck or danger; though all these rites are different, they all are well known and relatively simple.

It is not only people who are inherently different that pose a threat to the individual. A large danger comes from overt actions of people, whether they are specialists or not. The most harmful people are those who practice *beshèngu* ["black magic"], the epitome of evil in Kapsiki society. This magic is practiced by someone who aims at harming others, killing, or rendering infertile. It is evil because it harms and because it intrudes. The term *beshèngu* denotes not a specific object or combination of things, but a great number of different ways of harming other people. Some of those are well known (for example, the whiskers of the leopard); others are very secret and known to the specialist.

Beshèngu is a specialist's job, done professionally by blacksmiths mainly, the ritual intermediaries par excellence in Kapsiki culture. A number of ways to make the *beshèngu* itself are recounted by the Kapsiki, all in the most general terms, because everybody emphatically wants to disclaim having any such knowledge. The main fascination centers on the distribution of *beshèngu*: sorcerers are reputed to train flies to bring the *beshèngu* over to their victims, they bury it in the footpaths, or they change themselves into flying creatures in order to administer their wares. The Kapsiki are sure that all "important" men do have such a *beshèngu* bought from a specialist in another village. However, it is not the possession of *beshèngu* that is evil, but its use. One may defend oneself against possible attack; some kinds of *beshèngu* can be used for protection. In many ritual texts and public discussions, curses are formulated against the users: "Anyone who walks with *beshèngu* [i.e., who carries it with him in order to use it], let him drop dead in his tracks". Still, according to some informants, those curses were often mouthed by the very people who at least owned the stuff.

The threat of use does not come from inside the compound, as does witchcraft; people think of this kind of sorcery as coming from outside; however, it does not really come from far away either. *Beshèngu* is, in the ideas of the Kapsiki, sought after by people who are kinsmen, probably agnates, who are jealous of their clan- and lineage-brothers or interested in their misfortune. A large inheritance may trigger the use or accusations of *beshèngu*, usually between the agnates competing for the inheritance.

Treating the resulting illness is difficult and must be done by the same type of specialist who can perform the harmful magic. These rites are very secret. The information available on this protection indicates that the content of the rites is highly idiosyncratic, varying from specialist to specialist. It also is independent of tribal identity: knowledge of magic easily transcends the tribal boundaries; in fact, specialists far away always are deemed more powerful and potent than those nearby.

Protection against *beshèngu* is more important than treatment, and it constitutes an important focus of daily Kapsiki religion. One must live carefully, especially when one has gained some social prominence, in order to minimize the dangers. Protection against this threat, which is difficult to realize in any way, focuses on the protection against infection: how to keep the trained flies away, how to protect the compound against flying creatures. Constant vigilance is needed, and the protection against *beshèngu* must be kept in good shape.

As with any activity aimed at the supernatural, the use of *beshèngu* carries a risk. When an untimely death occurs, people may suspect a sorcerer, in which case the *wuta*-ritual is performed, a complicated affair that takes one of the relatives of the deceased to a village far away. The culprit is ritually killed in a large pot [*wuta*]. Afterwards the relative lets the village know that he has "gone to *wuta*" and waits for the culprit to die. The next death is interpreted as the result of this ritual. The culprit then is buried without any public mourning. However, there

Plate 11–5. Pulling out evil (blood): a blacksmith's client. Kuafashe has been suffering from headaches and has gone to see the blacksmith Cewuve, who, like most of his professional colleagues, is considered an able herbalist and doctor. Based upon a standard Kapsiki definition and diagnosis of her illness, he has applied a small heated bottle to her chest in order to rid her of excess evil blood.

is danger of contamination. Close kin of the culprit are considered in danger too, for the death by revenge resembles an epidemic, which will attack them also. A special ritual is performed to protect the culprit's kin from the rightful vengeance.

This epidemic nature of death by revenge, or death by one's own *fete* [fault], is central in another ritual, the *sekwa* mentioned in the example. In principle, *sekwa* is a means to ensure the repayment of debts: when someone refuses to repay a debt, the creditor may put his *sekwa* in the debtor's compound. Then death will strike that compound like an epidemic, wiping out the debtor's household as well as anyone who has ever eaten there. This *sekwa* is often used as a threat, but the threat is seldom carried out. It is considered a perfectly legitimate means for enforcing repayment, and neither its manufacture nor its possession or use bears any social stigma. *Sekwa* consists of a bundle of objects; its composition is well known to everyone. There is no remedy against its use except to pay the debts immediately. When *sekwa* is applied, it is put in the middle of the courtyard, visible to everyone. But things rarely go that far.

Another threat that has its origin in one's guilt is the curse *bedla*. When a close kinsman or kinswoman does not behave according to the rules of conduct—for example, does not show the proper respect for a mother's brother or a father—one may resort to a formal curse. This curse does not entail a great deal of ritual but is simply spoken: "If such and so has misbehaved against me in that manner, then she may not get pregnant anymore". A wide variety of afflictions can be administered in this way, and the closer the relationship between the parties, the more dangerous the curse is, the most feared curses coming from the mother and her brother. As the formula indicates, the curse is only effective in cases of factual and serious misbehavior. It can be eradicated by a simple ritual of blessing.

A final type of danger from people is the threat of war and theft. Both were rampant before the colonial pacification of the area, and protections against them are still important today. Magic for war, a prized possession of a few, is made by some specialist blacksmiths and has had to prove itself in battle. It usually consists of horns or an iron receptacle filled with an assortment of magic odds and ends, and it must be kept active by sacrifices. Famous war protection is known throughout the village.

Magic against theft is much more widespread and varied. Some plants offer protection, but sometimes complicated ritual patterns are needed. Here protection means attacking the culprit. A normal protection makes the thief forget his thieving intentions when he enters the compound; a better and more expensive one ruins the "head" of the thief, making him lose his way completely inside the house. The strongest medicine, however, kills the thief once he enters the house, especially if he climbs over the wall instead of entering through the only gate. After a theft, the thief may be cursed, and a fair number of afflictions are attributed to this retaliation. However, such curses may prove dangerous, as some close kinsmen may have appropriated the object in question and will be attacked by the curse.

DOGON: EVIL UNDERGROUND

Compared with the Kapsiki, the Dogon face a nameless, anonymous evil that has neither face nor familiarity[4]. Their supernatural world is populated by capricious gods. Ama, the main deity, is depicted as essentially good, but not reliable: he always changes things. The many sacrificial texts at the communal rituals invoke this capriciousness, deploring the way Ama changes happy people into mourners, puts villagers in the bush and bush people in the village. Still, when asked, people insist that Ama is "good", even though the concepts of good or bad in fact do not apply to Ama. A number of spirits are associated with the sky and with rain; they share Ama's characteristics without his capriciousness.

Lèwè (in most literature "Lèbè"), represented as a snake in most myths, is Ama's earthly counterpart and receives a lot of ritual attention during the communal rites. Lèwè is both beneficial and dangerous; he is the adversary of Ama, but people do swear at his altar, for he can be severe in cases of false oaths. A group of spirits is associated with this chthonic aspect. The *atūwūnū*, the *yebā,* and *yènè* and *yènèū* each belong to a certain aspect of the physical environment: rocks, dunes, bush, and trees. They are described as spirits of diverse form, either as small human beings or as one-legged creatures. The first among them, the *atūwūnū*, are considered the first inhabitants of the scree; animosity characterizes their relationship to the Dogon: they hit people with clubs and steal children. Protection is offered by simple sacrifices at certain spots, though the threat is not very prominent. The other spirits may also present a danger—often conceived in the form of insanity when people are attacked by them—but have contributed to Dogon life: for example, the ritual language of Dogon masks is of such spirit origin.

The most menacing Dogon deity is Nòmò, the water god. Feared as no other being, he does not command a great deal of ritual attention but is the main inspiration for some ritual specialists in Dogon, the shamanic priests [*binukèju*]. He too is a capricious god, ever changing his appearance and eager to trap people in the water. The fear of drowning is great in Dogon society, astonishingly so when one considers the dry Sahelian climate and the virtual absence of water during most of the year. Still, Nòmò and his familiars, like the crocodile, the sheath-fish, and water serpents command a deep respect. There is no known protection against this threatening side of Nòmò, but some small offerings are made to make him release his prey. Larger sacrifices and offerings are made by his people, the shamanistic priests.

The ancestors [*tire anaū*] do not represent an important category in Dogon belief. They are invoked collectively in the communal rituals and do not represent any threat. Mishap does not stem from the ancestors, but from the gods or from living people. As intermediaries between man and Ama, the ancestors are of some importance, but Dogon religion cannot be properly termed an ancestor religion. Specially mentioned among the ancestors are the people who built the steep stairways that scale the high Bandiagara escarpment bifurcating Dogon territory, a great feat that is wholly positive. Without those stairs the Dogon would be bereft of half their communication with other villages.

Protection against Ama is impossible and not really necessary; against Lèwè, correct behavior and just oaths are sufficient; and against Nòmò protection is impossible. Ritual protection, however, is needed against the evil that stems from one's fellow humans. Compared with the Kapsiki, the threat from other people is vague and diffuse in Dogon society. A general uneasiness characterizes Dogon interaction with strangers, though this uneasiness may never show through the outward veneer of hospitality and cordiality. Theirs is a harmony-oriented society, and any obvious breach in harmony is a serious problem. A central term is *dògò* [shame, loss of face]. Having to admit a fault in public; being exposed as a liar, a thief, or a witch; admitting that someone is not welcome; using the wrong term of address; not returning a greeting; or showing lack of respect for an elder—all these mistakes and transgressions cause *dògò*. This type of shame is unbearable for Dogon and may incite someone to suicide (often by jumping from a cliff); though not actually recommended, this action does meet with some approval.

The kind of evil that brings *dògò* is *sò* or *tī* [speaking, the word]. The word is the most powerful magical element among the Dogon. Speaking ill about someone means loss of face for him or her, as one should be "unspoken of". One who knows the world knows "his words" and keeps his tongue. In our Dogon example we saw Dogolu worrying about the possibility of being spoken about and taking measures accordingly by sacrificing on a powerful altar. Of course, people do gossip, but they are very careful in their actual wording as well as in their audience.

In theory this caution in speaking should not imply that people hide their thoughts. Hiding one's thoughts and feelings is also frowned upon. People who hide their feelings, never "declare" themselves, and do not really mingle with equals have a *bèrè gè* [a black belly]. Such people are not really concerned about their fellow humans: if they see a stray animal belonging to a neighbor, they will not warn the neighbor. The ideal is to have a "white belly and a white liver", that is, to have just and unshameful thoughts and be free with their expression. Severe *dògò* comes from being found out in public for shameful acts, so judgments are important and very sensitive events. The ultimate shame stems from being wrongly accused in public; in such a case, the "word is reverted", or suicide follows, or the person emigrates.

The word can hurt in yet a more insidious way. Though many words are used to describe magic in Dogon, a central term is *anga tī* or *anga sò* [the words of the mouth]. Protection or harm is done mainly by the words of the mouth: by reciting the spells one seals the words into the ritual object. Knots, locks, thongs, and other objects symbolizing the tying of words are important among the many objects used in Dogon magic. Despite the large number of material means, it is the knowledge of the words that counts. The words of the mouth can offer protection—mainly against similar magic—but, even without accompanying objects, they can be a threat; when directed against other people these words can make them ill (symptoms of desiccation and general apathy can be ascribed to this kind of magic) or make them fall from the mountainside. However, most applications of these spells alone are ethically neutral. Examples include enabling people to change their appearance when pursued by enemies or when stealing a wife from another village, winning a court case or preventing someone from lying, or winning a wrestling match. This whole complex usually is called *dauru*, and though people do hide their knowledge of it, they are not ashamed of it.

When the words are combined with objects, their effects multiply for good and evil. The regular sacrifices of the Dogon, which are a part of the great rituals of the community, are words spoken over an altar (the word *ama* means both "altar" and "god"). Protection against evil, as in our example, consists of words spoken over a pot with objects or over a slaughtered chicken. The general term for the objects used in this kind of private ritual, and in fact a central term in Dogon religion, is *òmònò*. It has a wide range of meanings, from simply a sacrifice (also a communal one) to an object or bundle of objects used in private rituals and sacrifices. It is neither good nor bad. The *òmònò* can be a thing (e.g., a statue) sacrificed together with the regular *ama* altar or an object sacrificed separately to harm other people.

The rites in question are almost identical to the regular sacrifices: the *òmònò* is used together with the altar. Sometimes the actual *òmònò* is buried in the mud cone that forms the altar. The private rites among the Dogon do form a continuum with the communal ones. Likewise, *òmònò* that has been given much ritual attention becomes more potent, thus making the termination of its use difficult. The constant combination of words and objects, plus a long history of sacrifices, multiplies the efficacy of these procedures.

Evil also multiplies this way. The general Dogon term for an evil object, *dugo*, often is translated as "poison", but without words it would be powerless. *Dugo* is private, secret, and bad, aimed at killing people. Of what objects it consists is quite unclear. In fact, it is so evil that nobody can claim knowledge of it—it is of no use for protection. Two kinds of people use it, the male *dudugonu* ["sorcerers"] and the female *yadugonu*, which we will translate as "witches".

Sorcerers [*dudugonu*] are manipulators of evil. They have their *òmònò* objects on which they sacrifice often. Applying the "poison" to a chain with a set of pincers (see Plate 11–6), they send the appliance away with their "words". This chain proceeds on its own force and nips the victim, who then dies. Sometimes footpaths are infected with *dugo*, but this is not a threat that is widely felt. Another way of administering *dugo* is putting it under one's thumbnail, which can be put in the beer just before offering the calabash to some stranger.

Some protection against *dugo* is offered in politeness or in ritual. When offered a drink, one always lets the offerer drink first, a rule that is explained to outsiders as politeness but that has a protective value as well. Further protection is offered by

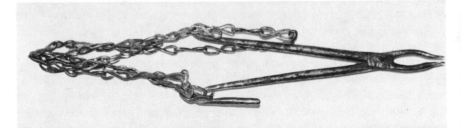

Plate 11–6. The "creeping evil": iron pincer and chain used in sending "poison". Collection: Herman Haan. A sorcerer, Dogon say, puts some of his strongest stuff on the pincer and then speaks the "*anga tĩ*" [words of the mouth]. Propelled by the power of the words, the pincer and chain are believed to creep through the bush towards the victim.

special objects in which the words of the mouth are knotted, like bracelets made of plaited cord. This kind of protection, again, is produced by specialists. In Dogon society these specialists are not the blacksmiths, but the ritual elders who are responsible for the regular religious practices. Among them, the shamanic *binu* priest can offer some protection through his sacrifices.

Dugo can be bought, though it is expensive (prices of 20,000 CFA [$40] are mentioned). According to informants, it is not even hard to obtain, but it must be bought in another village. Against *dugo* no treatment is known; a few medicines may give some initial relief, but eventually the victim will die. The main symptoms are a swollen abdomen and high fever.

Witches [*yadugonu*] work with *dugo* too, but in a wholly different way. They do not manipulate evil objects with words and other conscious acts; they are less than consciously subject to the evil when they do evil deeds. Witchcraft in Dogon could be partly defined as a proclivity to poison other people; a *yadugonu* feels compelled to put poison in other people's drinks or food. She thus presents a constant danger to strangers, kith and kin. According to the Dogon, children are the victims of witches' poisoning; child-rich mothers are very careful with their less fortunate sisters and, consequently, older childless women may be viewed suspiciously when they give attention to another woman's children.

Witches are ascribed another bewildering trait. Besides administering poison, they roam at night in the bush and jump on people who inadvertently come their way. Flying through the air with burning sticks in their hands, they land on the victim's head, sometimes urinate on him, paralyzing him for some hours, and rendering him incapable of speech (most victims are thought to be male). It is not the shadow of the witch that does this, but the witch herself. After a victim consults the shamanic priest, a ritual is performed as a remedy, of which an emetic is the central part. The patient then vomits a hairy worm, an act that immediately loosens up his tongue. Some people are reputed to be stronger than those flying witches and can stay on top of them for the whole night. In such cases the witches remain their friend. As witches, however, they may pass on his name to their colleagues who might try him out.

Dogon do not discuss or speak aloud the names of *dudugonu* or *yadugonu*, though some people may be suspected. Accusations are not voiced, nor does any kind of divination reveal their identity. According to the Dogon, the fox (the main intermediary for divination) would be afraid to do so lest the diviner be killed. The male sorcerers, who aim mostly at enemies, teach their trade to their sons, selecting the one who "knows his words". Female witchcraft is passed matrilineally from one *yadugonu* to her daughter or younger sister—not at birth but at the death of the old witch—and may lead to an unbroken chain of ten generations of witches. If a mother seeks to end her witchcraft, her daughters become infertile. Tales are told about rituals by witch collectives, similar to the communal sacrifices done by a family, in which both the witches and the sorcerers participate. The passing on of the witchcraft, consequently, is not deemed to be wholly involuntary; witches have to wish to become so. Once they have chosen the path of poison, and once the *dugo* resides in their granaries, the way back is very difficult.

As with the Kapsiki, Dogon society is not witch-ridden. The threats of evil are well concealed and do not figure prominently in communal life. Given the openness of the Dogon community and the demand for constant accessibility of everyone at any time, this is hardly surprising. The ties within and between the patrilineal and residential units are strong enough to put a firm lid on suspicions, tensions, and whisperings. Characteristically, "odd people", the ones with special potential and capacities, are either harmless or beneficial. The two endogamous groups within Dogon society, blacksmiths and tanners, have a ritual function couched in terms of blessing, never of harming people. The shamans, either male or female, have their own special niche in the great rituals, even if they do associate more closely than others with the dangerous elements of the supernatural world. An occasional clairvoyant who foretells the future is highly respected and is considered a welcome complement to the foretelling powers of the shaman or the fox and cowri diviners.

Besides these human-borne threats, the Dogon know their illnesses and environmental risks; however, these are not personalized. The treatment of illnesses is clearly differentiated from the protection against evil. Illnesses can be treated—evil cannot. The specialist in illness treatment, *jòjòngunu*, usually is not considered a *dudugonu*, though some suspicions may surface. General risks, such as drought, plague, or war, are not considered an evil from outside but are things with which the capricious supernatural world plagues its underlings.

COMMUNAL RITES AND THE NEGATION OF EVIL

Our cases show how individuals among the Kapsiki and Dogon regulate their relations with each other as well as with a particular part of their perceived supernatural world. To understand and interpret these two encounters with evil, we must gain some insight into the structure of ritual and belief.

The concept of evil, a central notion in this chapter, is not a very common one in anthropological discourse. This concept stems from the phenomenology of religion (cf. Sharpe 1975) and has only recently been introduced into anthropological debates (Parkin 1985). The assumption is, of course, that the notion of evil is applicable outside the Judeo-Christian context, beyond the sphere of the "great traditions". As an emic theological or philosophical concept (Ricoeur 1969) it has to prove its cross-cultural validity. Here I am testing the productivity of this notion of evil in the indigenous African religions of the Kapsiki and Dogon. We will see that both religions feature notions analogous to the concept of evil; even where no generic local term is present, a cluster of notions purveys the same message. An opposition between good and evil, defined in whatever form, has been shown by structuralist studies (Schwimmer and de Josselin de Jong 1982), as well as structural semantics (van Beek 1975), to be present in many religions and worldviews. Given the near ubiquity of the opposition, it is probable that a notion or a cluster of concepts with the denotation of "evil" can be found in most religions.

Though we will focus on notions and rituals pertaining to protections against evil, Kapsiki and Dogon religions are not limited to this aspect. Both have a great number of important communal rituals that have attracted a fair amount of attention in the literature. In these rites, too, people occupy themselves with the problem of evil (van Beek 1988a), but the focus is not so much on protection. Among both the Kapsiki and the Dogon the ultimate message of, for example, new year festivals and "rites of passage" is one of harmony, belonging, and group solidarity; differences between groups are played down in favor of unity. However, the two religions are not identical in this respect and their differences will be relevant for the protective rites too.

The great rituals among the Kapsiki stress this kind of togetherness very explicitly, strongly condemning any antisocial act or attitude that the participant may foster, like quarrelling. In this way endemic social problems will never show in ritual, for they might threaten the fabric of ritually induced harmony. For example, the great insecurity of men over the presence of their wives never surfaces in the rituals. Though the acquisition of wives is the dominant issue in the main new year festivals (van Beek 1987), the performance of the ritual gives the impression of an indissoluble link between husband and wife. Also, individualism is played down in ritual. While the ability to fight and to stand for one's own rights—to show fierceness combined with cunning—is highly appreciated in daily life, it is not during the special festival time of the ritual.

In the case of the Dogon the sense of harmony is very strong; overt harmony has absolute priority in interaction within the village. Individual differences are muted in daily life in favor of the smooth relations. However, in the rituals differences are accentuated: the young men parade before their own village half or ward, competing with their peers from the other half.

Thus the rituals are geared toward harmony and unity by controlling expressions of disunity. Types of behavior that threaten disunity vary between the two cultures. Against the Kapsiki trend of social fragmentation, the need for unity must be voiced by denying some central values concerning the right of expression, mainly by curbing individualism. For the Dogon the all-too-human desire to stand out among one's peers, to show off in front of an appreciating audience (Plate 11–1, p. 196), is to be curbed in daily life but finds expression and its catharsis in ritual (van Beek 1991c). So in its rituals the society shows itself as it is not, in order to reaffirm and revitalize its perceived model. In this way the great rituals are comparable to theater: they conjure up a vision of society with the inherent bias and distortion (and counterpoint) that are essential for its functioning. They reproduce society by redefining it, negating some of its basic premises (van Beek 1991b).

In this dialectical process one major element seems to be lacking: the notion of evil. The rituals mentioned above refer to harmony with the supernatural world and to the disturbance human action may create, but they do not point at any outside agent of evil or at any inherent notion of evil as incorporated in human beings. The human faults and mistakes referred to are of a fairly innocent nature: people following their idiosyncratic needs and wishes, putting individual interest above the common good. In both religions, however, a notion of independent evil does exist—in human nature or from outside agents, or of a more vague notion of damaging influence. And, as our two opening cases show, this influence can be fairly important. The antinomial side of social life does not surface in the great rituals of the Kapsiki and the Dogon; in fact,

Plate 11–7. Teri, the mother's brother of the newly initiated Tizhe, spits some beer on his nephew's shoulder to bless him at the end of his seclusion period. As part of Kapsiki boys' initiation, Tizhe has not been out of his hut for eight days. As a new adult, he is vulnerable to evil influences, so he must be protected against them.

it is almost totally suppressed. The wicked people and the evil emanations are not mentioned, nor are any countermeasures against them indicated or ritually reinforced. It is as if evil does not exist, as if neither Dogon nor Kapsiki believes in anything evil. Evil is a kind of double negation, where a part of the supernatural world is denied presence as well as existence.

CONTRASTS OF "EVIL"

The societies of the Kapsiki and Dogon are comparable in ecological setting, social and territorial organization, and historical experiences, yet, they differ consider ably in the way they cope with evil. In earlier sections, I reviewed evil and threatening influences, and in the preceding section, I sketched some commonalities of the major rituals in the shadow of which these involvements in and with evil take place; I also discussed systematic differences between the two cases. I will do the same now with the protective ritual and the notions of evil, moving from the contrasts between the two religions to the resemblances.

The threats the Kapsiki perceive stem from an ambiguous supernatural world that can have positive or negative import but is in the last instance dependable; people can in the long run rely on the gods, who behave in a more or less orderly fashion. Problems stemming from the supernatural world arise mainly in the form of illness (van Beek 1992a) or infertility and are couched in terms of guilt. A vague and general "badness", mainly nonobjectified and nonpersonalized, is brought about through specific individuals or personified illnesses. Evil, or "badness", is part of everyday village life and must be chased away periodically. Despite its vague nature it does have a precise location (even Death or Epidemic has its proper, well-known village; see van Beek 1978:293). If evil attacks, treatment is possible.

The same holds for evil of human origin: some specific people may be bad, but they are predictable and the problems they inflict can be treated by their equals. Witches are born with a deviant shadow (the manner of birth is important for the ritual status of the individual) and are fairly well known; they can deactivate their own inborn proclivities if they wish to, without harm to themselves. Witchcraft is limited to "normal people", that is, to those who are not differentiated by birth (like blacksmiths or twins), and is not thought to have any collective aspect. The types of witchcraft vary in range, badness, and importance, but all are relatively easy to ward off. Witches and sorcerers are clearly differentiated, and sorcerers have a protective as well as an aggressive aspect. Knowledge of objects, mainly not human-made, is crucial; spells are not very important. Blacksmiths form an important segment of society in this respect. Divination is specific, indicating precise sources of suffering and very precise ritual treatments, though some loopholes are preserved in the divinatory process; specific accusations about individual people are not voiced.

Guilt between individuals is an important source of problems too. Misdemeanor between kin, refusal to repay debts, or suspicion of black magic can lead to several ways of cursing; guilt leads to revenge, often with the explicit aim to kill the culprit. These deaths-by-guilt are contagious for co-residents and close agnates. Apart from the evil of sorcery, the epitome of interhuman badness is theft, because it encroaches on the cherished twin values of property and privacy.

In contrast, the Dogon supernatural world is not dependable, but highly capricious. In the relationship between humans and gods, transgressions against the supernatural world are not important to explain misfortune; the taboos that exist are few and easy to comply with. The essence of evil is precisely identified (poison), but imprecisely localized, and illnesses are not personalized. This vague evil, which is predominantly of human origin, is not thrown out in rituals, but immobilized and suppressed, mainly by negating its existence and stressing the harmonious side of life. Evil is not a part of normal village life, but something of the night and the bush. Once evil is inflicted, treatment is virtually impossible; whatever efficient treatment is given is meted out by a specialist who is not associated with evil.

Ritual—and evil—power lies in the knowledge of words, backed up by objects that are usually human-made. Spells are the most important part of the procedure. Objects can be bought, and they derive their power from constant use. Once one is on the road to ritual use of objects, it is difficult and dangerous to turn back and to stop it, both for the regular altars and for the strictly private ones.

With witches, it is not the shadow but the whole personality that is important, and among the several types of witchcraft one is paramount. Characteristics of birth are relatively unimportant (the castes have no specific function in this). Neither is the proclivity of evil inherited at birth: inheritance occurs at death. The identity of poison people is unknown, and they may operate in groups. Divination is unspecific and general, never clear about causes or treatment. Accusations, specific or general, are never voiced.

Shame—not guilt—is the main focus of ritual, and revenge killings are not allowed and are practically unknown. Between humans one should bless, not curse, avoiding the degradation of the fellow Dogon. In relation to evil, these blessings aim not at harming or killing culprits, but at strengthening the social bond, in fact at immobilizing evil—it should be suppressed. Between equals, the epitome of evil—apart from poison—is lying and false accusation. Protection against this is difficult and can be done only by strong affirmation of the value of sociability and constant accessibility. Loss of face affects kith and kin too and easily involves the whole community.

Table 11.1, an overview of the complex differences in these societies shows important characteristics of Kapsiki and Dogon notions of evil and their context. The commonalities resulting from these differences (the right-hand column) are treated in the next section.

THE NATURE OF EVIL

The supernatural world for both the Kapsiki and the Dogon is not trustworthy in the short run, which may threaten the individual but in itself is not a source of evil. Water plays an interesting part in both instances: places with permanent water feature prominently as the danger spots, yet water is also crucial for life. Water seems to share the life-giving as well as the dangerous sides of the gods. Still, though the gods can be quite unreasonable, their inflictions can and must be

	Kapsiki	**Dogon**	**resemblance**
"supernatural world"	ambiguous, + or − but eventually dependable	capricious and not dependable	no immediate trustworthiness
supernatural threat	guilt punished by one's personal god [*shala*]	punishment for neglect of altar to Ama	inherent, but marginal; inflictions must be endured
theory of normal humans	one-dimensional	dependable	antithetic to supernatural world
origin of evil	special persons (deviant shadow)	unspecified persons (whole personality)	humans
known persons?	mostly, but the way they harm is vague	identity is vague, but means are known	limited specification
inheritance of evil	at birth	at death	inherited
relation with ego	close, lineage based	vague but close	close
specialization	protective and aggressive	protective	expensive
definition of evil action	theft (encroaches on property and privacy)	false accusation (causes loss of face)	antithesis of communal value
evil essence	object	poison	artifact
locomotion	evil flies	evil crawls	self-propelled
contagion	epidemic	taints person	contagious, lasting
diagnosis/ divination	specific sources and treatments	unclear on causes or treatments	specific humans not named
treatment?	yes; + protection and revenge	no; protection and oaths; not revenge	protection is important
prevention	careful behavior	careful speech	circumspection

Table 11.1. A comparison of Kapsiki and Dogon notions of Evil

endured. If the gods are reasonable, the problems they send are one's own fault. In both societies, the supernatural world should be kept at a distance and not mingled too closely with human affairs. In neither Kapsiki nor Dogon are ancestors of prime importance in the religion. This in fact offers the possibility of keeping the other world at arm's length.

Evil originates mainly from fellow humans, and it carries a limited identification. If evil humans can be pointed out, the way they harm is vague; or if a specific poison is the main instrument, then the identity of the culprits is vague. There is a dialectic relationship with evil: it should be known somewhat, but without an overly close association. If the bad individuals are vague, illnesses will probably not be personified. In ritual, evil is partly—but never completely—overcome or suppressed; it stays just inside or beyond the perimeter of the village. The individualized Kapsiki culture associates evil more easily with particular beings, makes a sharper distinction between involuntary and self-willed evil, and tolerates the background presence of evil more easily than the Dogon culture, which is more oriented toward communal harmony. For Dogon, evil has to be defined outside the boundary of human existence and is always somewhat voluntary. An impersonal evil renders treatment very difficult and does not specify a section of the human being most vulnerable to the absorption of evil. Manifest differences between people, like manner of birth, then, are not used to implicate the persons in question.

In either case, once evil is started, it is hard to stop. It proceeds at its own force and impetus, whether it is guilt-triggered or stems from the object. The objects used in the protective rituals become tainted with the enemy. In both cases, Kapsiki as well as Dogon, human-made artifacts are professed to be used, and eventually they all must be discarded, lest they grow too strong. This may take one or several generations, but eventually one has to get rid of protective magic.

The definition of what is the most evident evil in society is consonant with the (inverted) main values of each society. In fact, the concept of what constitutes the main internal threat to society is much more clear than the positive values themselves. The Kapsiki abhorrence of theft and the morbid fascination of the Dogon with false accusations and lies are manifest in many ways. Consequently, one can more easily characterize these cultures by their chosen evils than by their definitions of good. One reason for this may be that much evil is considered to be of human origin, coming from the people very close at hand. Afflictions coming from abroad, be they from outside enemies or from environmental risks, are not evil; they are just there. No one argues with the climate. Instead, a quiet and dignified suffering is called for (similar to when evil for which there is no protection comes from the gods)—a kind of suffering that is most clear in the Kapsiki culture, where showing affliction does not elicit help. But when evil comes from nearby, the culture in question offers a frame for selecting what aspect of possible interaction is defined as evil. The societies concur that killing within the group is always evil. The life of the individual is considered vulnerable, and a sharp focus on health is discernible in both cultures. The other aspects in which a human being is deemed vulnerable vary much more. The privacy and autonomy of the Kapsiki is vulnerable to theft, just as the integration into society of the Dogon is vulnerable to loss of face and credibility.

A second reason that cultures may be characterized by their chosen evils is more dialectic. The notions of evil for the Kapsiki and the Dogon carry some independence. Evil is defined as a substance and as an artifact; "the absence of good" would never do as a definition of evil. The notion of good is more dependent on the notion of evil than vice versa. A good person usually is defined as someone who follows the rules of his society. Following the rules implies for a Dogon different things than it does for a Kapsiki, as the positive values vary. But in both cases following the rules primarily means not trespassing them, abstaining from faults and mistakes—in short, the absence of evil. Of course, positive values can be defined—sociability or autonomy—and strived for in an active, positive way. Still, being sociable means never refusing someone, and autonomy or relying on oneself means not leaning on another person. The proof of good is abstention from evil. There may be a sound reason for the inequality of good and evil. Evil is within reach. Good is not. Both cultures harbor an ideal for human beings that cannot be reached. The "white belly and liver" of the Dogon is a good example: everyone should be open toward the other as well as ready for inspection at any time—a goal very imperfectly realized in everyday life. The vaunted autonomy of the Kapsiki is both a psychic and an economic impossibility also. So, good as such is definitely out of reach in practice and is best defined as the relative absence of evil.

PRIVATE RITUAL: THE INNOCENT APPRENTICE

The private rituals that protect against evil (or generate it) are markedly different from the communal ones discussed earlier. These rituals do not rally scores of people, nor do they occupy a special place on the ritual calendar. Performed alone, with a minimum of publicity, sometimes even furtively, they seek to protect against evil influences, aiming at isolating the person in question from the dealings of his fellow humans, instead of participating in group identity. Here the individual shields himself or herself against certain elements or aspects of the society at large, putting individual interests before those of the group. In these rituals the individual is on the defensive: he or she inevitably faces a whole society of people with conflicting ambitions and unknown but large reservoirs of knowledge and power. It is, in a sense, the down-to-earth part of religion that fits in with the lowest echelons in social organization, the (nuclear or extended) family and the individual. After the dialectic euphoria of the great community rituals, this is the complementary, sobering alienation inherent in daily existence. "The religion of Monday" I have called it elsewhere (van Beek 1975:60), but maybe the term "rites of Monday" is more apt. After all, both aspects are part of one religion.

In these "rites of Monday" the focus, as mentioned above, is on the individual. What picture of the individual emerges from these rites? In the Kapsiki case, the individual is a self-evident social entity, connected with the immediate family (most often the nuclear one) but in fact alone. This aloneness is clear in divination in which the individual faces the whole village and any other group relevant to the problem in question as opposites, not as fellows. Fundamentally, a Kapsiki has to rely on himself or herself, on his or her own resources and characteristics. Most of these cannot be changed; one has to live with oneself. Thus, the general social situation of a man or women is accepted as given, and only minute details can be changed. In ritual and divination those problems are addressed that may stand between an individual and his or her potential existences. The sterility of a woman, illness, or an overdose of bad luck are problems that can be actively addressed and are situations one can change. The same holds true for any supernatural or other aggression directed against the individual; active protection is called for. But on the whole the individual is accepted as he or she appears to be; a rich man will always be rich, a poor man poor: his personal god [*shala*] has made him so. A dangerous man or woman, a known witch or harmful sorcerer, will be expelled from the village, since in no way can one change such a fundamental trait of personality. If it is their character, they will remain so. That implies that in daily life Kapsiki make a clear distinction between those wrongs, mishaps, or transgressions that are one's fault and those that are not (one's *shala* did it). In the first case, it may be possible to redress the wrong, such as in those cases in which the individual is himself responsible for being *ndegema*. This term implies the vertical relationship between the individual and the supernatural world: if a taboo has been broken, or if sacrifices have been neglected, then one is out of harmony with *shala*. The relationship between ego and *shala* is quite independent from the one between the individual and the rest of the village. If the individual is not responsible, then a quiet acceptance [*kanewe le ntsu*, literally "to look with the eyes", meaning a quiet resignation of suffering] behooves a truly mature person.

The Dogon have a more active theory of personality. In their view the individual is not a self-evident social unit but exists mainly in relation to kinsmen and peers—in social context. This shows in divination, where the individual is symbolized as surrounded with his or her equals vis-à-vis the opposite entities, the supernatural world—god, the grave, and the relevant problem. In general, their relationship with the community at large is less problematic than for the Kapsiki, so their defenses against their fellow human beings are less specific than in our first example. What they want to protect themselves against is being talked about, the "words", which implies a falling-out with the community and being out of harmony with other people. So the Dogon "rites of Monday" convey the impression of the individual as a part of a larger whole, in one of its many social echelons.

Given the existing and reinforcing social context of the individual, a Dogon feels sure that he or she can change some aspects of his or her personality. The environment is considered "manageable" (van Beek 1992b) and personal riches a result of conscious and deliberate efforts. Of course, a lot of things are beyond control, like fertility, illness, and death. But since these are completely beyond control, they are left to Ama [God] (van Beek 1988b). The Dogon term for personal mistake, *liri*, reflects this emphasis. The term refers to the relation between humans, not between a person and Ama. Redress of wrongs must be sought in interpersonal relationships, by asking forgiveness and by trying to forget the existence of friction. People who are bad have chosen to be so; they are not born that way. So they must be changed, mainly through public exposure and loss of face.

Despite these obvious differences, some resemblances between the two societies' "rites of Monday" can be discerned. The individual is portrayed as a vulnerable being who is an obvious prey for the (supernatural) predators at large in the more or less direct environment. Still, that same individual has his or her defenses and can rely on outsiders; many of these private rituals do involve asking for professional assistance, an aspect notably absent in the great community rituals. In our examples, a diviner/blacksmith (Kapsiki) and a general ritual specialist (Dogon) are consulted. Individual rites also often call for divination, a professional service only a few qualified people can offer (Plate 11–8). The rites performed may be simple, but often are not, and in any case their application calls for specialized and secret knowledge. Even if the rites are simple, it may be much safer to have a specialist perform them.

Thus, the moves to establish oneself as an individual and the processes involved in maintaining the boundary between ego and community reinforce the social ties of the individual, making him or her more dependent on others. These social relationships are not to the same persons the individual seeks protection for or against (kith and kin or outsiders); on the other hand, the specialists are the same that may help threaten the individual supernaturally. A specialist in protection is also a specialist in aggression. To guard oneself, one must deliver part of the independence to those people who may be most dangerous to one's very existence.

In the protective ritual the individual works in a state of partial knowledge, both in the diagnosis of the problem and in its treatment. Divination does not offer a clear answer to one's questions—at least not as clear as many clients wish (van Beek

Plate 11–8. Adiyè, a Dogon of the village of Amani, consults the cowrie shells in order to know what dangers the future holds for him. He is one of the few who "really knows the words" [*anga tĩ*] both to protect from and to inflict evil. Cowrie shell divination is widespread in West Africa.

1978:367). Reasons for this reticence, to be specific, are obvious from the point of view of the diviner/specialist, but the system of divination itself may preclude precise answers. Compared with the Kapsiki, whose divinatory system allows for straightforward answers (van Beek 1982a), the Dogon system (Pern, Alexander, and van Beek 1982; Paulme 1948) is intended to furnish only general answers to broad questions: Will there be "peace" in the near future? How will the next cultivation season turn out?

Among both Kapsiki and Dogon, people rely on more than one divinatory system at the same time, partly to overcome the limitations of one system and partly because they may lack trust in the personality and the craftsmanship of the diviner. In any treatment too, this ambivalence shows. In the Kapsiki example, a problem arises from the partial knowledge of a series of coherent magical applications: starting one magical means (how to marry a wife) implies changing the "natural" course of events. A wife who is magically induced to stay may remain barren. The *rhwè* to restore fertility may result in the death of the firstborn. The medicine against this threat may stunt the growth of the child or prevent the youngster from ever marrying. When dabbling in the realm of magic, one has to be very knowledgeable to avoid serious mishaps.

Serious mishaps can also happen with the power emanating from the ritual paraphernalia themselves. If the Dogon has been sacrificing on a certain altar for a long time, it will become dangerous to stop the sacrifices. The altar demands its sacrifices, or else.... In the Kapsiki example, *sekwa*, while in itself without any social stigma, has the same qualities: it may attack people, especially vulnerable people like children and pregnant women, the very people it is deemed to protect or help. Magical means, the paraphernalia of the "rites of Monday", are inherently obstinate in character. The individual never really masters the unruliness of the supernatural world, nor can he or she be sure that the chosen specialist can master it. The individual, in fact, is a little helpless against the vast reservoir of unseen enemies and specialists that are potentially against him or her. The individual, and even the specialist, is in an apprentice role, sometimes literally "*l'apprenti sorcier*". There is no security in these rites, no guarantee of effectiveness.

The general attitude seems to contradict this "working in the dark"; when performing magical ritual, people exude a great confidence. The very instant the rite is performed or the medicine taken, the problem is said to be solved. There is no discernible doubt about its efficacy if people feel sure the medicine taken is the right one. Still, there is a lurking suspicion about its effect, for people are not surprised when the "right stuff" does not work. This contradiction is worth investigating. In the Kapsiki example, Teri keeps a number of options open; he does have faith in his diviner but still considers other possibilities and checks other "authorities". Nevertheless, each separate ritual act will be executed with a clear show of confidence. A scene from the Kapsiki may illustrate this.

> Zera Mpa has a magical protection against "war" that he wants to show to his friend. It is a complicated object, consisting of several goat horns and a cow's horn full of unknown but potent things: herbs, roots, and objects like owl balls, claws of various beasts, toucan beaks and the like. His father long ago "found"

it in the bush, meaning that he once spotted an enemy who wore it; after a long vigil Zera's father stole it when the other took a bath. It is a potent *rhwè* that offers a secure protection against the intrusion of iron: no iron object can ever pierce your flesh when you wear it. But it might have lost its strength, so Zera tests it. He takes a huge melon, puts the *rhwè* around it and thrusts a knife into it, burying it to the hilt, the juice splashing him in the face. Zera, his face glowing with confidence, tells his friend: "You see, it does not work any longer. But if it would have had its *berete* [force], the blade would have broken off immediately; not even the tip would have entered the melon". (personal communication:Mogodé, 23 August 1973)

This confidence in part is trust in the specialist, or in the case of Zera, in the powers of the people of the past. And the unshaken belief people show after *disconfirmation* is even more astonishing than the confidence people exude after performance of any magical rite. Failure of magic strengthens belief in it. The reason for the failure always lies within the sphere of magic itself: the powers have leaked away, elsewhere people have even stronger powers, or rites have not been performed properly. Magical ritual is a closed system in which the observable has no bearing on the belief in efficacy. Of course, the tenacious belief often is a strong factor in helping make a ritual procedure efficacious, as has been demonstrated and argued convincingly (Tennekes 1982).

A final picture emerging from the private rituals of our two cases is one of feigned innocence. All people seeking protection against evil seem to approach the field not only as apprentices but also as people for whom working with evil is an alien occupation. When they come to the specialists to search for supernatural

Plate 11–9. In some Dogon villages, terracotta figurines [*toũ*] are fabricated that represent illnesses and deformations. Though the people making them claim that they help in healing, many other Dogon are convinced that they are harmful and represent evil. (H. 18 cm.; terracotta. Collection: Herman Haan.)

protection, they tend to suggest that they do so for the first time (this is one reason the Kapsiki tend to switch specialists after consultation), that they do not know the character of evil. They pretend to be unaware of the enemy, having gathered only recently some vague rumors about its threat. The language used is vague and full of evasions. One central reason for this approach is to disclaim any knowledge of harmful magic and—even more emphatically—to deny that one would ever use it against a fellow being. The clients appear to be free of all evil, full of benevolent innocence, and reticent to learn anything specific about this dark side of the world.

Thus, in these "rites of Monday" another pious lie is performed: the adults act as if they are children. With just a glimmer of knowledge, they act as if they believe unquestioningly, fully accepting the authority of their specialist, while they themselves are innocent of all evil. As the group in the great communal rituals disclaimed even the existence of evil, the individual having these magical rites performed disclaims any identification with evil, even when dabbling in it. In both instances, Dogon and Kapsiki, the execution of these magical rites runs counter to some central values in society. Kapsiki society is pervaded by a strong sense of privacy and respect for the autonomy of the other (van Beek 1982a); for them *rhwè* is essentially an intolerable intrusion into the private lives of other people. For the Dogon, with their highly valued harmony, the very notion of malevolent people is an affront, which can be tolerated if these people are far removed and anonymous. The negation of individual association with evil helps to reproduce a society in which evil "knows its place" and is kept in check, reinforcing the priority of social values over individual interests, helping to reproduce an evil-free society of fully socialized adults.

SYMBOLS OF EVIL

So far, our analysis has proceeded along more or less structural lines, aiming at the systematic oppositions on the basis of a joint frame of reference. The content of the belief about evil, the collective suppositions accompanying the systematic choices highlighted above, is also worth examining.

The images evoked by Kapsiki and Dogon show a similar systematic contrast. Evil in Kapsiki culture is stable and unchangeable. It is associated with carrion and dung, and the Kapsiki suppositions about evil show a definite anal side: the witch's shadow leaves and reenters the body through the anus, while in stories Death is mastered by poking a hot iron into his anus. The spirit when descending from on high waits on the dung heap of the house for a suitable time to enter a woman's womb. So a certain association can be found between the aggressive spirit and human excrement. The mouth is the antithesis of the anus for the Kapsiki: from the mouth blessings emanate, either by talking or by spitting (see Plate 11–7, p. 214). Evil resides in the heart or the shadow, good in the mouth and the head.

Protection focuses either on the wall of the house or on the skin of the body; the two are homologous for Kapsiki (van Beek 1986): what the skin is to the body, the wall is to the house. Danger should not enter past the compound wall at all lest it attack the family and should not enter the skin either, the last protective barrier.

The blade of the enemy's knife breaks at the skin, just as the thief will drop dead when climbing over the wall. Even when the flies imbued with black magic have penetrated the house, they cannot find an opening into the protected body. Children are protected with medical anointments and medicine, rendering their skin tough, leathery, and less susceptible to evil. Both mouth and anus have to be guarded against intrusions, too, but the skin as such is especially vulnerable for attack. Protection aims at killing the bringer of evil in his tracks.

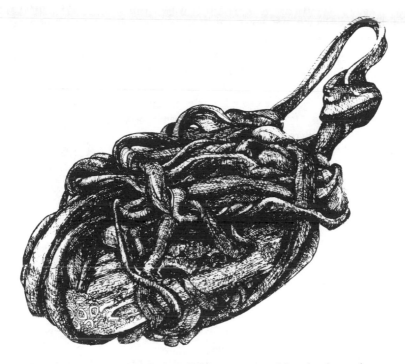

Plate 11–10. The hoof of a wild boar, wrapped in a leather string, is used by Kapsiki as a protection in war. If used with the proper words, it will keep the bearer from being wounded by any iron object such as arrows, spears, or throwing knives.

Evil flies through the air: it floats, not really flying like a bird but hovering like an insect, with a smooth and unpredictable movement like that of a cat. If associated with a color, it is red. It is not so much created (cf. Macfarlane 1985:90) as omnipresent. It can be anywhere, and it can absent itself for a time; thus, chasing it is a way of coping with it.

In Kapsiki society, evil does not manifest itself as an organized group of people or counterculture (Thoden van Velzen and van Wetering 1988b). The bad people do not represent a counter society nor do they follow an alternative set of norms that negates the mainstream value system. Although those people who are different, slightly abnormal, or subnormal—special births, twins, blacksmiths, etc.—are dangerous, they do not form a group on their own as such. The personified dangers (Death and some epidemics) share that aspect. They are in some ways subhuman (half a body, one leg and one arm, etc.) and in some ways quite human. They can be tricked and led astray, even if only for a short time. These abnormal people, however, do form an integral part of society, like the foreign wives who cannot be trusted, but are indispensable.

The Dogon notion of evil is more capricious and changeable. Though some scatological aspects are discernible (the witch urinating on her victim), the Dogon focus is more oral: the main gate of evil is the mouth. The evil is produced by the mouth (triggered by the condition of the liver) and enters it too. Purification is done in the mouth, either in the absolute form of an emetic or by chewing some special roots and barks. In this case, both blessing and evil stem from the mouth. Protection and attempts at treatment are delivered in the mouth; medicine has to be chewed, often without ingesting it. Protection has to be given in the vicinity of the body, before evil actually touches or enters, and the protection does not aim at killing but at immobilizing evil. "Poison people" cannot enter or are attacked by an irresistible itch; witches remain outdoors, scratching.

Evil creeps, crawling around the perimeters of the living space, either in the form of objects or in the form of people, and may jump on others when they are close by. In the form of words, evil is omnipresent and can be generated at any time from the liver, but in its artifact shape it encircles the village and then suddenly attacks. Its color, if any, is black. Red is associated with capriciousness, such as with the gods—not with evil.

There is somewhat of an organized-group side to Dogon evil; a sense of a countergroup, a secret society of "poison people", keeping the normal society under a limited siege. The norms and values in that counter society are inverted: women are more dangerous (stronger) than men, and normal society's main values (harmony and accessibility) are transformed into random killing and secrecy. The strong sense of identity from group membership in normal life is negated by a total anonymity, a nonidentity of bad people.

Consequently, evil does not stem from abnormal or subnormal people, but from very normal ones, who cannot be discerned as being evil but who secretly gather together to do it. The harmful spirits are the ones that most closely resemble the Dogon themselves, while the tree spirits, or the spirits with a half body, have been helpful in the past.

The symbols used for evil and the collective representations shaping these symbols show the systematic contrast between the two cultures discussed earlier. Evil in both cases is localized within the human body (cf. Douglas 1966, 1973), and in a specific part of it. The Kapsiki body symbols—anus, heart, and skin—and the Dogon ones—mouth and liver—in themselves are not symbols of evil alone, but of beneficial action as well. Also, the mouth, heart, and liver are the central seats of emotion in the respective cultures. In the Dogon case, blessing and evil stem from the same source, while among the Kapsiki, defensive symbols are different from offensive ones. This is consonant with the anonymity versus the specificity of the definition of evil in both cultures; in these respects the symbolism of evil is simply a part of the general symbolic system. The Kapsiki do not have notions of a community of sorcerers; this fits in with their general tendency toward individualism, like the social interaction among "poison people" fits in with the community-oriented Dogon.

In some other ways, however, the body symbolism presents the diametrically opposite focus compared to daily behavior: the Dogon, who are very tactile in daily interaction, easily and frequently touching each others' bodies, have a magical defense that does not center on the skin, while the much less tactile Kapsiki do concentrate protection on the individual's skin. The evil coming from outside the Dogon community is not brought about by abnormal persons, but by unidentifiable normal people, while in the Kapsiki case the supernatural danger comes from abnormal people who are fairly well known. In the great rituals as well as in daily life the reverse holds: danger comes for the Kapsiki from the normal strangers outside the community, and for the Dogon from the "abnormal" ones who are well known. So the notion of evil, while firmly entrenched in the whole of the culture's symbolic universe, is an important part of a transformation of norms and values of the "normal" society. This systematic difference is shown in Table 11.2.

In both cases evil has a sufficient degree of vagueness. One who becomes too involved in it can be caught in its web and perish. So the individual, who has his social identity and the models of his culture imprinted and reinforced in daily life and in the great rituals, has to chart a cautious course between good and bad, between the unattainable ideal of good and the prison of evil (cf. Ricoeur 1969). However, the very vagueness of these concepts associated with evil enables one to cope with it. Evil fits in with the rest of religion, and its definition allows for a substantive middle ground between extremes. The definitions of both good and evil imply that in any phase and aspect of life, one must always live with both of them; coping with evil implies coping with good too (Willis 1985). The show of innocence, mentioned above, is a viable solution. The model of the child in the

	proceeds from	resides in	characteristics
Kapsiki "evil"	anus	heart	flies, floats, darts; red; not created; individual subhuman
Kapsiki "good"	mouth/head	skin	protection can also kill
Dogon "evil"	mouth	liver	creeps; black; created; humans in group
Dogon "good"	mouth	liver and intestines	protection immobilizes

Table 11.2. Contrasts of Evil and Good among the Kapsiki and the Dogon.

face of good and evil keeps the options open both to make mistakes and to use the power of evil to avoid their consequences. The possibility of this charade may be essential for living in any culture. If the space between good and evil is reduced, one tends towards a puritan system (Thoden van Velzen and van Beek 1988), in which the slightest slip from the ideal is considered a grave sin and where innocence is no longer possible. Kapsiki and Dogon cultures allow ample room for individual maneuvering between the two poles of good and evil, and each in its own way manages to shape not an easy way of life but a life that is feasible.

NOTES

1. Research among the Kapsiki of northern Cameroon and the Higi of Nigeria; carried out in 1971, 1972–73, 1979, 1984, and 1988; was made possible by grants from the Netherlands Foundation for the Advancement of Tropical Studies (WOTRO) and the University of Utrecht.

2. Orthography of Kapsiki and Dogon words

h	voiceless velar fricative f	
c	voiceless alveo-palatal affricate	Church
j	voiced alveo-palatal affricate	John
y	voiced alveo-palatal halfvocal	Young
dl	voiced alveolateral fricative	
rh	voiced velar fricative	
ĩ	nasalized i	
ũ	nasalized u	
ò		god
e		the
è		that

No tones are indicated.

3. Research among the Dogon of Mali; carried out in 1978, 1979–80, 1981 and followed up by repeated fieldstays in 1982, 1983, 1985, 1986, 1989, 1990, and 1992 financed by the Netherlands Foundation for the Advancement of Tropical Research (WOTRO), the University of Utrecht, Time-Life, and Agence Aigle.

4. On the Dogon a considerable body of ethnographic literature has been produced by the French ethnographer Marcel Griaule and his collaborators (Griaule 1938, 1948; Dieterlen 1941, 1982; Griaule and Dieterlen 1965; Calame-Griaule 1965). The data as presented here do not stem from this literature for two reasons: first, almost no reference to any religious expression that could be dubbed "witchcraft" or "sorcery", let alone "evil", has been made by the Griaule school. Second, a large part of that literature has come under severe ethnographical criticism by the present author (van Beek 1991a).

12

Myth & Epic in Central Africa

Luc de Heusch

FROM THE ATLANTIC COAST to the mountainous areas of the African Great Lakes, marvelous fictional narrations have been passed on from generation to generation.[1] My intent is to analyze how these epics are related to the processes that have taken shape in the accounts of the deeds of the heroes who founded states among the Luba in Zaïre or among the peoples of Rwanda. In two books devoted to Bantu myths and rituals, I have tried to show that these tales—although they do have historical pretensions since their function is to lay the foundations for sacred kingship and to legitimate this key institution in the social and cosmic order—nonetheless have to be treated throughout as myths (de Heusch 1972, 1982). Under this assumption and in the light of this previous research, I would now like to examine the series of epics about Lianja, the legendary hero of the Zaïrean Nkundo, who form an acephalous society organized in lineages without any kind of sacred chieftaincy.

Like many of the Central African epic heroes, Lianja had a very unusual, indeed fabulous, birth: he sprang, fully armed and accompanied by a twin sister, from the lower leg of his mother, whose pregnancy had been overlong. Having pointed out this essential characteristic, Pierre Smith (1979) has qualified these exceptional heroes who spring out of the same imaginary pattern as "overconceived" [*surconçus*].

Specialists in full costume sing the epic of Lianja around a fire; their faces and bodies are painted with asymmetrical drawings; they wear feather headdresses and hold spears. The performance lasts several successive nights. This prose epic has several variants. I refer to the version collected by Edmond Boelaert (1949). For the sake of clarity, I have divided it into several sequences.

1. All the wives of the ancestor Wai were pregnant and gave birth except for one, whose pregnancy drew out so long that everyone made fun of her. In secret, an old woman took an egg out of this wife's womb; and the next day, a handsome boy hatched from it. Bokele, this son, managed to be accepted by his father Wai. To bring the sun nearer to the village, which had always been plunged in darkness,

Bokele set out on a canoe trip. With the help of wasps, a turtle—the "magician of war"—and a hawk, Bokele stole the sun from the people who were keeping it.

2. From the land of the sun, Bokele brought back a wife, Bolumbu. They had a son, Lonkundo, who could not be given any order other than to come to eat. During a visit to his mother's family, he died twice because the grandmother broke this forbiddance. The first time, Lonkundo came back to life because of the "medicine of immortality" that his father had entrusted to his mother; but the second time, there was no more medicine because the grandmother had burned what had been left over! Lonkundo's corpse was brought back to Bokele, who became furious. He killed Bolumbu, whom he held responsible, and he brought his son back to life. Lonkundo sprang up onto the roof, attacked his father, and dealt him a fatal blow. He left his father's village. However, Bokele appeared in his dreams and taught him the art of building traps. With this know-how, Lonkundo captured much game. One night, he dreamed that he had caught the sun; in fact, he had caught Ilankaka, a shining woman who had lost her way while following a spirit. Lonkundo married her straightaway.

3. During her pregnancy, Ilankaka wanted to eat only bush rats, which she was given in abundance. At night, Itonde, who was already an adult, stealthily left Ilankaka's womb to devour the smoked meat she had stored away. When his parents were about to catch him, he spat a stinging substance onto their faces. As he tried to take some of the meat, he became mixed up in the nets around it. Meanwhile, his parents, temporarily blinded, crawled away into the dark of the forest. Coming to a village where Lonkundo's family was living, they recounted their misfortunes and advised the villagers to poison any stranger who would come along.

When daylight came, Itonde freed himself from the nets. He began knocking animals out by throwing palm nuts at them. He then had the meat cooked and ate it. Having begged to be spared, a first bird sent him another bird that gave Itonde a magic bell fulfilling all his wishes. The name of this bell means "the world", for the signs of all things were drawn inside it. Itonde struck the bell, and it showed him the path to follow to his father's village. He tried to be accepted as Lonkundo's son but succeeded only after passing the ordeal of poison. Lonkundo then organized a big feast in his honor, blessed him, and gave him a new name—Ilele.

Now an old man, Lonkundo decided to pass his authority on to his son. He exhorted him to take a wife. However, Ilele refused every beautiful girl whom his father presented. He left to look for a wife himself. He finally met an aggressively virtuous virgin, Mbombe, who made suitors wrestle with her. She had always managed to make them slip and fall in an oil puddle. Ilele was the first person to come out of this match a winner. He married Mbombe, and they set out for his place. They were accompanied by eighty men loaded with bride-price for Mbombe's father. Although Mbombe had told her husband not to reveal his identity during the trip, Ilele told his name to an ogre. The ogre struck him in the heart, but Mbombe used the medicine of immortality that her father had given her and brought him back to life. The same episode recurred, but this time, Mbombe rebuked her husband and threatened to leave him. They continued their journey. Ilele forgot the way to his father's village, but using her magic, Mbombe led him there. Her relatives were asked to come take possession of the bridewealth. Ilele praised his father for his generosity.

4. Pregnant and long overdue, Mbombe would not eat anything until the day that a hornbill [*calao*] dropped an unknown fruit called *safou* in front of her. After boiling it, she tasted it and liked it very much. She even wanted more. To satisfy his wife, Ilele let himself be led by the hornbill to the forbidden *safou* tree, which belonged to Sausau. In spite of the protests of the keeper, Ilele climbed the tree and picked the fruit. He went back several times. He had to confront the birds that Sausau had ordered to keep anyone from approaching the tree. Ilele threw the fruit at them, thus marking their feathers in the ways that characterize the various species. To chase away one of these birds, he struck his magic bell and made it rain. During another attack when a blue pheasant flew into his face, Ilele rang the bell again, but it cracked, and the two opponents fell to the ground. The hero was captured in a net stretched out by the turtle, who then cut him up with a piece of wood. Back in the village, Ilele's death was mourned, and the women bitterly criticized Mbombe.

5. Mbombe's pregnancy had reached a critical point. Her womb swelled enormously. She bore ants, then other insects, new kinds of birds, and human beings grouped in tribes. Mbombe went into labor again, and someone inside her womb started talking. Refusing to be born like the others, this being, Lianja, sprang, fully armed, tall and handsome, from his mother's tibia. He jumped up onto the roof. Nsongo, his twin sister, who shone like sunlight, soon came and sat next to him. The people gathered around and greeted them. The twins jumped down, flew up into the sky, and came back. By rudely questioning his mother, Lianja forced her to stop hiding the truth about the circumstances wherein his father had died. The very day he was born, Lianja decided to revenge his father's death.

Sausau made fun of the newly born Lianja and showed the messenger the head of Ilele, whom he had killed and had eaten. Helped by flies and hornets, Lianja fought Sausau. Protected by the magic bell that Nsongo rang during the fight, Lianja could not be beaten. He cut off his opponent's head, but Nsongo, who had fallen in love with Sausau, persuaded her brother to bring him back to life. Lianja revived Sausau as well as other enemies who had been slain. He had the *safou* tree cut down.

With his companions, Lianja set out on a long trip toward the river. On the way, he captured several men. He met up with Indombe, a python roosting at the top of a tree that shone like the setting sun. Nsongo ran away scared. Lianja asked Indombe to come have a talk, but the python refused to crawl down. Lianja even offered to carry him, but he managed only to make the python angry. When Indombe finally uncoiled and settled onto his shoulders, Lianja was crushed under this unbearable weight. Becoming very hot, he lost consciousness. When he came to, he took the magic bell and began ringing it until his force came back. Meanwhile, Indombe had climbed back up into the tree. Lianja ordered the sun to slow down. The sun refused, so he captured it in a trap. When he approached the sun, he was burnt. Darkness fell. Striking the bell with his arm, Lianja once again came to. The morning sun was shining. Indombe decided to go with Lianja, who, now aware of the danger, placed the bell as protection upon his shoulder. The python settled thereon. Under this load, Lianja sank into the earth, but he took on force by striking the bell. He thus managed to go forward. He walked for a long time in silence. When he came to a pool, he wanted to get rid of his companion in order to take a drink. Furious, Indombe burnt Lianja, who fell down. While uncoiling, however, the python struck the bell, and Lianja came back to life. Together, they set out again. Lianja now thought himself strong enough to enslave the python. When Indombe resisted, Lianja decided to kill and eat him. Indombe agreed on condition that Lianja should eat all of him. The next day Lianja, who had left the python's head under the bed, once again met Indombe roosting in a tree. Changed into a spirit, Indombe vanished into the forest.

Lianja, Nsongo, and their people continued on their way toward the river. Various tribes, including the Nkundo, parted company and settled in their present dwelling places. Their animal companions also parted company with the humans. When he finally came to the river, Lianja told his people to settle in Indombe's forest while he and his sister would stay on the bank. Indombe's curse befell the farms planted in the forest. When Lianja stretched out his arms, however, the curse was raised and plants could grow. On the riverbank stood a tall palm tree with branches reaching up to the sky. Lianja took leave and climbed it. He took his sister, Nsongo, on his hips and his mother, Mbombe, on his shoulders. They vanished into the sky, and the people scattered to attend to work.

MYTHS AND EPICS

This text is remarkably coherent even though Boelaert put it together from various sources. As given, it can be submitted to the same structural analysis as a myth. Like a myth, it takes place on several levels, each of which follows a specific code. The story ends as it started, with an ascent. Whereas this undertaking is fully successful at the start (Bokele's solar quest), its outcome is less certain at the end (even though Lianja was able to capture the sun). We know nothing about what happened to Lianja after he climbed the world-tree. According to other versions, his fate is symmetrical and opposite to his great-grandfather's. Accordingly, at Nsongo's request, Lianja too tried to get the sun, but he was burnt and died. Let's look more closely at this variant:

> Armed with spears and a shield, Lianja set out alone up river. After a long journey, he came to the fountainhead and to the dry land of Bongila, where the only inhabitant was a patriarch, the son of God, who tried, in vain, to persuade him not to pursue his baneful journey. Lianja set out on a lake and headed still farther westward. He came to the Old Woman of the West who refused to receive him into her house. She warned him to flee before sunrise. When the sun came up, it was already too late: Lianja died burnt. The Old Woman set the hero's corpse adrift on a raft. It came to the land of Bongila where the patriarch changed the mat around the corpse. As it continued drifting eastward, the various tribes of mankind, one after the other, accepted it. (Boelaert 1962)

This episode, which can be taken as the end of the epic even though the foregoing version left it out, has the ring of an authentic myth. It helps us understand the periodic ceremony that the Nkundo perform in honor of Lianja. Once a year, villagers chase sicknesses and epidemics toward neighboring lands by carrying, in procession, a bunch of leaves to the border and throwing them into the forest just before sunrise. Through this ceremony, Lianja, this fictional character, steps out of the realm of literature.

This variant, which enriches this epic's cosmological code, helps us understand the topology of Lianja's trip toward the river. At the journey's end, on the riverbank, the hero came to the palm tree with branches joining heaven and earth. This journey does not figuratively represent the migration of the Nkundo under a charismatic chief. Nothing in the symbolism lets us suppose that this epic has stored up in memory the events that occurred when the Nkundo settled in the forest, as Boelaert has suggested. Quite clearly, Lianja's journey is a mystical trip toward the west, the land of the sun. The river he reached after having left the Nkundo and other tribes along the way literally marks the skyline, the border between heaven and earth. This migration serves to explain both dispersion (the spatial dispersion of peoples) and speciation (the separation between humans and animals): "Beasts, people, insects, all were thus left in place". Bokele, Lianja's distant solar ancestor, also took a river trip in order to bring the sun toward humankind. There is no doubt that the river marks the border between two cosmic realms.

The same holds true for another Central African tale that, in many ways, resembles Lianja's epic. This tale is the account of the founding of the Luba state. Elsewhere (de Heusch 1972:ch. 1) I have shown that this epic, which legitimates the Luba sacred kingship, also follows a cosmological code. A first king, Nkongolo, a python who rules earth and the dry season, is set opposite a hunter, who rules heaven and rainfall. This hunter's son, the warrior Kalala Ilunga, founded a new dynasty after having put an end to the reign of Nkongolo, his mother's brother. Like Lianja, Kalala Ilunga leapt about and apparently defied the law of gravity. He moved easily between earth and sky.

The presence of a mighty snake in the Nkundo epic leads us to make comparisons that abolish the differences between myths and epics. Lianja, like Kalala Ilunga, had to measure up against a python. Whereas, on his journey to heaven, Lianja was crushed under the animal's weight, the Luba python personifies the rainbow, which stops rain from falling. In both cases, the python was beheaded and then reborn as a spirit. According to the Luba, the python king's head was carried upwards by a termite mound whereas, according to the Nkundo, the beheaded python was reborn at the top of a tree. The magic bell protected Lianja from contact with the shining python, an animal associated with the rays of the setting sun. How strange to discover that the Luba epic sets up the same likenesses between the sun and the rainbow python, who rules the dry season! (de Heusch 1972:ch. 2). In his fight with Indombe, Lianja also had to deal with the sun. He was burnt by both the python and the sun.

There is an obvious, major difference between the Nkundo and Luba epics whenever they are compared from a sociological viewpoint. Kalala Ilunga, a celestial being through his father, took the royal power from Python, a chthonian being, whereas the outcome of the match between Lianja and Indombe was uncertain. Unlike the Luba, the Nkundo have formed a lineage society without any sacred kingship. Lianja vanished into heaven without founding a dynasty. In contrast, Kalala Ilunga rose to heaven in order to be legitimated by his father before overcoming the python king, his maternal uncle, and founding a new dynasty on earth.

The python is the ruler of the forest in the Nkundo epic. He kept the hero from quenching his thirst, and he stopped plants from growing. Like his Luba equivalent, Nkongolo represents the principle of dryness. How can there be any doubt that the Luba and Nkundo tales use, each in its own way, similar mythical material? In the second case, this material has been grafted onto the theme of the "overconceived" hero who is both a magician and warrior.

WARFARE, HUNTING, AND MAGIC

A code of functions, in Dumezil's terminology (1949:65), structures Bantu thought. Epics with a historical mission, in that they relate the founding of states, are structured on a strong opposition between a hunter hero who brings the mystic part of sacred kingship and a warrior hero. Let us look at this problem in the Nkundo epic.

Only the first and last heroes, Bokele and Lianja, fulfill the warrior function: the first in heaven, the second on earth. They are also, as we have seen, "solar" heroes. Bokele victoriously—with the help of the turtle, the magician of war—fought against the celestial people who controlled the sun. His son, Lonkundo, was a hunter with no military deeds; he was satisfied with having his warrior father killed in order to avenge the murder of his mother. He excelled at trapping animals, however, and thus obtained a "shining" wife who, in a lesser form, brings to mind the wife whom his father had brought back from heaven. Lonkundo, the happy hunter, was extraordinarily generous, as he proved during his son's marriage. He symbolizes both wealth and abundance. In the next generation, Ilele inherits his father's function but also takes on a magical dimension. This hunter's son was a born magician. Just after his anomalous birth, which occurred through his own will and without his parents' knowledge, he freed himself from the hunter's net and captured animals by stunning them with palm nuts. Thanks to the bird whose life he had spared, he came to possess a magic instrument that could fulfill his wishes. Unfortunately, the bell cracked when he confronted the birds that were protecting the forbidden *safou* tree. Ilele was killed through the devices of the turtle whose magic had ensured his grandfather's (Bokele's) military victories. Ilele was thus a hapless magician. Lianja, the son who avenged him, was both a magician and warrior. He owned the same magic bell as his father, but he was also an invincible warrior like his great-grandfather. He brings together two functions that have been, till that point, separated.

These "functions" succeed each other over time as follows:

1. Bokele, the warrior.
2. Lonkundo, the hunter.
3. Ilele, the hunter and magician.
4. Lianja, the warrior and magician.

Warfare, hunting, and magic are three distinct, pertinent terms. Hunting represents the abundance of food and the generosity of exchanges in opposition to military conquest whether in heaven (Bokele's solar quest) or on earth (Lianja's adventures). Magic "overdetermines" these opposing functions. The hunter's (Ilele's) magic had no power over death. The turtle, the magician of war who was Bokele's ally, caused the death of Ilele, whose magic could not work against the attacks of birds, which were celestial creatures. However, Lianja, a magician and warrior as well as a light, airy being who held up under the python's crushing weight, is presented as being invincible. He came back to life several times.

THE QUEST FOR IMMORTALITY

Protected by the birds, the *safou* tree from which Ilele stole fruit obviously mediates between heaven and earth. From the start, the epic attempts to establish this mediation: Bokele undertook a solar quest, assisted by aerial creatures—wasps and a hawk. The episode about Lianja's mother, who bore new species of insects (some of which would become the allies of her triumphant warrior son), is not included by chance. The *safou* tree is the equivalent of the palm tree uniting heaven and earth. Ilele perished at the trunk of the first tree and his son Lianja climbed the second one to disappear forever. It is said that he is still alive, that people may meet him in the forest or on the river; but it is forbidden to talk about these meetings (Boelaert 1949:73). The epic leaves the question of Lianja's death, or immortality, open: this alternative is the central mystery. When he climbed the *safou* tree in order to satisfy his wife's whims, Ilele went to meet his death. In the case of Lianja, we'll never know whether, when he climbed the palm tree in Indombe's forest, he became immortal. The episode about the meeting between Lianja and the python that was roosting in a treetop and shining like the sun reproduces in weaker terms the opposition between heaven and earth that the tale's cosmological axis has established since the far-off beginning. Significantly, the python, when he finally crawled down out of the tree, crushed the hero under his weight: Lianja sank into the earth. Clearly, Indombe resisted with all his might Lianja's celestial quest just as he would later hinder farmers from settling in the forest. Sausau, the master of the mysterious *safou* tree, is, in all due consideration, but a double of the fabulous snake, humankind's enemy. Sausau caused the father's (Ilele's) death, whereas the python was a major hindrance on the triumphant son's (Lianja's) journey toward the river, this borderline between heaven and earth. The fates of Sausau and of Indombe are perfectly alike; the one repeats the other: beheaded by Lianja, each of them came back to life. Let's suppose that, by acting in this way, Lianja was trying to introduce a new principle of discontinuity into the universe, that he was trying to end the excessive conjunction between earth and sky that had been established by the python, this enemy of water and of agriculture who roosted in a treetop, like a flaming sun too close to the earth.

Lianja, the "overconceived" hero, stands in a strange relationship with time. At first, time had been, we might say, suspended inside his mother's womb as he participated in the cosmic time of creation. In a variant tale, God created Mbombe directly in the beginning of the world and destined her as spouse not for Ilele but for Mbongu, the unique son of his own daughter (Boelaert 1949). I will not delve into this new genealogy, which transforms the epic into a myth about the origins of the world, but I would like to point out how this variant changes Lianja's solar quest: the hero successively commanded various animals to lay hold of the sun, but they all declined except the eagle, who went straight to the Creator. Herein, Lianja resembles his forefather, Bokele: he introduces the alternation of night and day by establishing the sun as a mediating term between heaven and earth. Nonetheless, by rising into heaven and vanishing toward the west, Lianja also abolishes this mediation. Maybe his is a quest for immortality. Do not forget that Bokele, who had brought the sun from the firmament, had a medicine with which he could bring people back to life. Mbombe, the cosmic mother, had the same medicine, which she used to bring her obviously weak husband, Ilele, back to life twice. Lianja, her son, had the same power as his mother: he came back to life thanks to the magic bell during his match with the python, and he generously resuscitated his enemies.

The quest for immortality runs like a thread throughout the Nkundo epic. From this point of view, a strong opposition exists between Lianja and his father, Ilele, a magician with waning powers, whose death, after his losing fight with the birds, is described in full.

Variations upon the Theme of Paternity

The epic's code in familial matters holds other surprises. The relations of paternity undergo a strange tension that is resolved in the end. Two heroes had to be accepted by their genitor: Bokele, because of his hidden birth after a long overdue pregnancy, and Ilele, because of his strange birth. Whereas the former was born out of his father's sight, the latter blinded his parents to keep them from learning about his ability to leave his mother's womb at night. The abnormal birth of Lianja, the last hero, is also characterized by his separation from his father, since his mother was a widow. The descent of these children raises problems. Filiation is one of the moving forces in the epic's plot. The initial separation between father and son sets in movement the process that brings them closer to each other: whereas Bokele and Ilele finally managed to be recognized by their genitors, Lianja, the orphan, wreaked vengeance by slaying his father's murderer. The fourth case is especially interesting: Lonkundo, who was born normally, killed his father to avenge his mother's death. Nevertheless the epic insists upon the positive nature of the paternal function: Bokele protected his son and entrusted his wife with the medicine of immortality. The maternal grandmother is at the origin of the tragedy. The violent separation between father and son is followed by their meeting in the realm of dreams: though slain by his son, Bokele appeared to him in dreams in order to teach him how to hunt with traps and snares. In the case of Lianja, his only thought since his birth was to avenge his father, and he did not even draw back from bullying his mother.

The same thread runs through the account of the heroic deeds at the origin of the Luba state. Kalala Ilunga, a warrior, a magician, and also an airy being who leapt about like Lianja, received from an absent father (a hunter) the force to fight against an abusive maternal uncle. In the Nkundo epic, Lonkundo's maternal grandmother fills the same negative function: she twice caused the death of the hero whose calling was to be chief, for he could not be ordered about.

A TEMPORARY CONCLUSION

Lianja's epic is like a daydream about a sacred kingship that could not be put into effect. A fantastic story is arranged like a myth. This tale differs radically from classical epics—such as *La Chanson de Roland* or the tales of the Bambara kings of Segou, based on military deeds. On the other hand, it could be proven that the legend of Sunjata is entirely based upon the structures of mythical thought processes. This story about the founder of the Mali Empire deals with origins, the origins of a new dynasty. The most remarkable traits of heroes in the Bantu epics are also those of Sunjata, this mighty warrior whose historical existence cannot be doubted. In particular, he was born after an overlong pregnancy. According to a version collected in Gambia, Sunjata, after having stayed in his mother's womb for seven years, was unable to walk for seven other years! (Innes 1974:35). According to a version from Guinea, he had a hard time of it during childhood: at the age of three, he was still crawling; his head was so big that he seemed unable to hold it up; and he would be still and silent inside the house all day long, much to his mother's regret (Niane 1965:15). Unlike the "overconceived" heroes of Central Africa, however, his extraordinary vital force was hidden for a long time. Still, in this version, though his birth occurred at the normal time, it was marked by strange events: lightning flashed across the suddenly darkened sky, thunder rolled, and a sheet of rain swept by along with a tornado (Niane 1965). The hero's cosmological associations are made obvious since, at his birth, the rain stopped and the sun came back out.

This marvelous child's magic force suddenly became manifest to all. However, the "waking of the lion" did not occur before his father's death. The structural pattern is similar to that of Lianja's epic wherein the hero's extraordinary fate apparently entails his genitor's disappearance, as though the account were a variation upon the Oedipus complex. Whereas Lianja's fate was to avenge his father and set up a sort of imaginary royalty, Sunjata's destiny was to take possession of a realm and extend the domain inherited from his ancestors. When he turned seven years old, one of his half-brothers was appointed crown prince, against the will of the deceased king. Sunjata, the cripple, then managed to kneel for the first time and pick up an enormous iron bar that the smiths had made for him. Standing up with much effort, he began taking giant steps, went and pulled up a baobab tree (Niane 1965:20-22).

A second major characteristic of this hero deserves attention. This mighty warrior-to-be is presented initially and exclusively as a hunter. As a teenager, he never stopped hunting. His forefathers, the first kings of Mali, who are not remembered as mighty conquerors, did however excel in hunting. In this respect, they stand in a special relationship to the natural forces at the source of magic power. One of them, Mamadi Kani, who invented the hunting whistle, could communicate with the spirits of the wild (Niane 1965:3). His many followers were merely clients whom their master had brought together in the forest in order to teach them the secrets of hunting and of medicine. *Simbon*, which means "hunting whistle", is an honorary title that Sunjata would later bear (Niane 1965:86). The same holds true for Mamadi Kani's four sons (Niane 1965:3). Sunjata's mother was a monster, as was the enormous Mbombe, Lianja's mother, who belongs partly to the animal realm and to nature. An ugly hunchback, Sunjata's mother was the human double of the dangerous (wild) ox that was ravaging the country. Two hunters brought her to Sunjata's father, who married her because a diviner had predicted that she would bear his successor. The diviner, who was also a hunter, claimed the "great Simbon" as master (Niane 1965:4). He had prophesied that Sunjata would be the seventh conqueror of the world, more powerful than Alexander (Niane 1965:6). Indeed, this hero, though at first a hunter, did not wait long to become a warrior. The warrior function, in fact, supplies the very stuff out of which the epic is made.

This symbolic linkage of hunting (as a source of fecundity, at the juncture between the cultural and natural orders) and warfare also characterizes the accounts of the heroic deeds at the origin of the Luba and Lunda kingdoms in Zaïre, even though the historical context was quite different. Such a convergence is not fortuitous. It expresses the symbolic rationale of a common institution, sacred kingship.

Epics as a literary genre are, when all is said and done, only the product of an illusion, of a stylistic effect. At least one firm conclusion can be drawn: whether written or spoken, an epic is not built upon the wreck of memories about history. Instead, it gives real or imaginary history a poetic depth and density that makes it unfit for positivistic analysis.

Notes

1. This chapter is translated from French by Noal Mellott.

Part III:

Instrumentality of Religion

Plate 13–1. This tombstone cross with a hole through the middle only margin denotes the Crucifixion of Christ, for Christian Bakongo, partly since they do see Christ as a scapegoat but instead as a renowned healer and mediator. Resona with ancient Kongo thought, the cross especially signifies "the parting of the wa one arm being the boundary between this world and the afterlife, the other representing the path of power between the worlds, and the hole at the junct referring to the grave itself (cf., MacGaffey 1986:116–120ff).

13

Kimbanguism & the Question of Syncretism in Zaïre

Wyatt MacGaffey

LTHOUGH THE WORD "SYNCRETIC" is commonly applied to religions, little thought has been given to the origins and specific features of syncretism. The term is in fact ambiguous, since it is taken to indicate a particular kind of religion or religious situation, characterized by the combination of heterogeneous elements; yet on the other hand, all culture, and *a fortiori* all religion, continually draws upon foreign elements. Citing a study of syncretism by J. H. Kamstra, Michael Pye observes that "to be human is to be a syncretist" but that "most practitioners of the study of religion are strongly influenced by Christianity and tend to see syncretism as an illicit contamination, as a threat or a danger, as taboo, or as a sign of religious decadence". Ambiguity in scholarly usage thus conceals an implicitly adverse judgment: "syncretism" has become a pejorative term, applicable only to situations of which one disapproves (Pye 1971:83–93).

Such usage is conspicuous in the history of European comment on Kimbanguism, one of the world's best-known religious movements, initiated in Lower Zaïre (then Lower Congo) in 1921 by the Kongo prophet Simon Kimbangu. This region was the object of intensive Protestant and later Catholic mission work from the 1870s onward. In 1908 it was incorporated into the Belgian Congo. The movement of 1921 aroused widespread popular enthusiasm but was rapidly suppressed by the Belgians, who imprisoned Kimbangu and his followers (Andersson 1958; MacGaffey 1983). Repression continued until 1959, when the sons of Kimbangu were recognized by the government as the leaders of the Church of Jesus Christ on the Earth by the Prophet Simon Kimbangu (EJCSK). This organization, now reputedly the largest African-founded Protestant church, belongs to the World Council of Churches and is one of the three publicly recognized churches of modern Zaïre, the others being the Catholic and the united Protestant Church of Christ in Zaïre (ECZ).

EJCSK, however, though the largest, is by no means the only church claiming the spiritual legacy of Kimbangu. Conspicuous among the many others is a group of similar movements centered in Manianga, in the northern part of the province: in the literature on Kimbanguism this tradition is called *ngounziste* in French ("Ngunzist" in English), from the Kikongo *ngunza* [prophet]. Its constituent churches have usually called themselves by some variant of the term Church of the Holy Spirit [Dibundu dia Mpeve a Nlongo, or DMN].

The history and internal variation of Protestant Christianity in Lower Zaïre therefore present us with three kinds of churches, which we may think of as three concentric circles: First, at the center, "orthodox" churches controlled until recently by the American Baptist, British Baptist, and Swedish Evangelical missions, now united with other "communities" in the ECZ. Second, the independent EJCSK, the major organized result of the Kimbanguist movement of 1921. Third, a number of lesser offshoots of Kimbanguism, of which (for the purposes of this chapter) the Ngunzist DMN group are the most important.

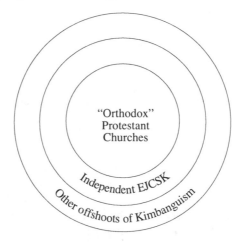

Figure 13.1. Protestant Christianity in Lower Zaïre [Bas-Zaïre].

Relations among churches in these three categories have always been political, both in the sense that they are schismatic and competitive and in the sense that they have been rivals for the favor of the government, colonial and postcolonial, upon which they all depend. Political discrimination (intended, that is, to defend the boundary of a particular corporate organization) is evidently a factor in the attitude of two of the principal commentators on Kimbanguism, Efraim Andersson and Marie Louise Martin, though their interests differ (Andersson 1968:77, 131–142, 158–161; Martin 1975). Andersson, though acknowledging and effectively documenting "the legacy of popular religion" among practicing members of the Swedish mission church in northern Kongo, still asserts that he can identify the "essential difference between paganism and Christianity". The difference is especially elusive when the mission church is compared with what Andersson calls "the sects", that is, the cluster of movements that eventually gave rise to EJCSK and the DMN churches. Within the Swedish mission church itself, especially in 1947 and 1955, individuals and movements emerged—bearing all the characteristic signs of ecstatic prophetism—who are nevertheless accepted, by Andersson at least, not only as Christian but as having brought special benefits to the rest of the church.

In 1921, some missionaries of the Baptist Missionary Society, to whose church Kimbangu originally belonged, had a good opinion of his work, although it is doubtful, given the strength of Belgian and Catholic sentiment at the time, that the mission as a whole, even if it wanted to, could have embraced the new movement (Desroche and Raymaekers 1946:117–162). In 1969, however, EJCSK was admitted to the World Council of Churches, as a result of reports rendered by Martin, among others, whose own religious background (Moravian) is similar to Andersson's evangelical Lutheranism. Martin's defense of EJCSK constantly distinguishes between it and "Ngunzism", which means in effect all the features of Kimbanguism in general of which she disapproves because they are "syncretic". Once again, the distinction is difficult to maintain and requires sustained special pleading: speaking of EJCSK, she says, "I myself was amazed to see how extensively ancient patterns of thought were transformed on the basis of the Gospel and vested with new content without succumbing to the danger of syncretism" (Martin 1975:x, 73).

It is easy to illustrate the difference between "ancient patterns" and the gospel, as both Martin and Andersson do, the latter with the benefit of extensive knowledge of the language and of the indigenous religion. Personal familiarity with Ngunzism would enable them to cite many examples of moral benefits and deeply thoughtful Christian piety there too, however. And of course scandalous misuse of the gospel can be documented in any European Christian mission or church by anyone disposed to do so.[1] A weekday evening service at EJCSK's holy city of Nkamba, birthplace of the prophet, or in some little congregation remote from the hoopla of the church's special festivals for foreigners can be an impressive and moving display of the austere dignities of the Protestant faith, but so can the equally disciplined early morning service of an Ngunzist church at its own holy city. It is equally impressive to listen to the advice given to a woman in distress by a DMN elder, into which is woven his knowledge of the Bible, of humanity, of oppression (the walls of his house bear the mark of Belgian bullets), and his belief in spiritual guidance and relief. In their unorthodox and often spectacular rites the DMN churches worship God with a vitality and exaltation that many a Protestant pastor of unimpeachable orthodoxy would envy, combining worship with concern for the social and psychological well-being of individuals.

It is not my intention, however, to extend the benefits of special pleading more generously than others have done. I wish to argue that the inadequacy of "syncretism" is derived from the inappropriate theory of meaning implicit in it.

In the article previously cited, Pye advances the view that the distinctive feature of syncretism is ambiguity of meaning (e.g., as exhibited in the situation studied, not in the usage of scholars). With reference to Shinto-Buddhist syncretism in particular, he says: "The elements under consideration became ambiguous. They were able to bear two distinct meanings: depending on the different points of view of the people involved with them" (Pye 1971:92). Such syncretism he thinks must necessarily be temporary. Since the traditions move all the time, meanings are continually refashioned. Pye's explanation for this dynamism is animistic ("the urge which many religions have to move out and to move on"), but he also postulates that within the individual consciousness "the ambiguous clash of meanings demands some resolution" (Pye 1971:92). He anticipates three possible resolutions of the ambiguity: assimilation, by which one meaning eliminates the other; fusion, in which a new religion emerges; and dissolution, a drifting apart of the two meanings. Such resolution, though effective for individuals, may not prevent other individuals from experiencing in turn the clash of meanings, so that "syncretistic situations may persist for a long time and even indefinitely, even though they are ... intrinsically temporary" (Pye 1971:92–93).

The assumption that clashing meanings demand resolution, formally known as the theory of cognitive dissonance, remains unverified. In practice, people seem to tolerate high levels of cognitive cacophony. In retrospect, the theory (as applied to the study of religious change) can be seen as profoundly ethnocentric: our civilization has been so much influenced by the technology of literacy that we have come to think of the activity of the human mind itself as being like that of the scholar confronting the printed page (Greenwald and Ronis 1978:53–57). Jack Goody points out that widely disseminated books, archives, and records of every kind have made science itself possible, precisely because they intrude upon our discourse and force us to take note of discrepant statements (Goody 1977). Pye writes as though meaning were defined, for a believer, by something akin to a dictionary of his faith; the syncretist, finding the same "word" given different meanings in the "dictionaries" of Shintoism and Buddhism, feels compelled to seek some resolution.[2] In general, believers who are not scholars are uncertain of their beliefs and are inconsistent in their responses to questions about belief. The sense they have of "meaning" in their religion may develop at several levels of consciousness but certainly includes as an important element the sense of satisfactory communication with others in ritual. Ritual itself is a social event, takes place in a wider social context, and presupposes the values and meanings constitutive of community life in that place and time. It presupposes, for example, a certain routine to the week or the year; a certain allocation of resources; a division of social labor between men and women, adults and children; and common assemblages of visual and verbal symbols in which these distributions are signified.

The linguistic philosopher John R. Searle argues that "large tracts of apparently fact-stating language" depend for their meaning on the constitutive rules of the institutional context in which the utterances occur. The actors' sense of communicated meaning is at least partly a function of their ability to produce an intended effect, action consistent with pertinent institutional conventions. The parties to communication may not in fact share, "in their heads", exactly the same sense of what has been communicated (Searle 1969:50). As Edmund Leach says, "Just as two readers of a poem may agree about its quality and yet derive from it totally different meanings, so, in the context of ritual action, two individuals or groups of individuals may accept the validity of a set of ritual actions without agreeing at all as to what is expressed in those actions" (Leach 1954:86).

SYNCRETISM AND SOCIAL PLURALISM

Although syncretism of some kind is a universal property of culture, religious situations that most often attract the label are particularly likely to occur in plural societies, that is, societies in which two or more institutional sets ("societies") exist within a single governmental framework. All colonial and postcolonial states are plural societies, although not all plural societies are colonial (Smith 1974).

The Belgian Congo, created in 1908, incorporated a large number of indigenous societies in a new political framework of European bureaucratic type. Kimbanguism arose in one of these, that of the Bakongo of the Atlantic coastal region. Kongo society was characterized by matrilineal descent, an economy of subsistence agriculture on which was superimposed a considerable volume of trade between the coast and the interior, and a cosmology in which the influence of the spirits of the dead upon the living was mediated by chiefs, priests, magicians, and witches. Institutions of this kind are not readily understood by Europeans, who expect anthropologists to interpret them (MacGaffey 1970a). The institutions of the colony itself, on the other hand, were relatively familiar; they included Roman-Dutch law, capitalist industry, bureaucratic government, and Catholic and Protestant Christianity. The dominion of this second or bureaucratic sector over the first or "customary" sector was governed by a policy known somewhat misleadingly as "indirect rule", whereby customary institutions were tolerated and even strengthened, provided that they conformed to what the Belgians described as universal moral norms. In fact, since the political and economic conditions of existence of customary institutions were entirely different from what they had been before, these institutions represented the social adaptation of the Bakongo to colonial rule in the twentieth century. What is important about them is not that they were "traditional", since they were no more so than those of the bureaucratic sector, but that they were maintained in their difference and subordination by the colonial regime, as a matter of policy.

Each of these sets of institutions presupposed a distinct cosmology and employed its own group of cultural codes. The bureaucratic sector was predicated upon a linear concept of time and, during the colonial period, on the reality of race. The cosmology of the customary sector presupposed a repetitive cyclical or spiral concept of time and included the belief that blacks, when they die, go to Europe or America, where they become white, and whence they may return to Africa as ancestors or ghosts, for good or evil purposes. The cultural codes included contrasting rules about such things as gestures, social precedence, and proper dress for men and women; the most important communicative resource was of course language, whether French or Kikongo, in each case closely tied semantically and practically to the respective institutional sets. In neither of these cosmologies are such concepts as the unilinear course of time, the reality of race, or Europe as the land of the dead, scientifically necessary or transcendently true. In each instance, the content of the cosmology can be related to the organization of the society, in conjunction with which it shapes the experience of the members, "formulating conceptions of a general order of existence and clothing these conceptions with such an aura of factuality" that the moods and motivations it establishes "seem uniquely realistic" (Geertz 1966; MacGaffey 1978a).

Between 1908 and national independence in 1960, Bakongo were progressively assimilated into the bureaucratic sector. They were converted to Christianity, educated in the European fashion, induced to work for wages, and subjected to taxation. They participated in state, church, and industry, however, on an entirely different footing from Europeans and remained subject, in their private lives, to Kongo institutions connected with matrilineal descent and the "customary" codes regulating marital, interpersonal, and local relationships. That is to say, the Bakongo under colonial rule belonged to two societies, not one, in which "meaning" with respect not only to matters of religion but to all matters of social purpose, identity, and ontology were expressed in different languages (Kikongo and French) and with different assemblages of symbolic practice.

It follows that whenever Kikongo speakers and French speakers interacted in contexts other than those in which only the most perfunctory or practical meanings were at issue, a high level of shared misunderstanding was institutionalized. A special colonial vocabulary, neither French nor Kikongo, was developed to mediate this noncommunication; in religion, some of its most useful words were *nlongo*, which meant "holy" to Europeans and something like "taboo" to Africans; *sumuka*, "to sin" or "to violate a taboo, to pollute"; *nkadi a mpemba*, "the Devil" or "a vengeful ghost"; and so on (Janzen and MacGaffey 1974). Since communication consists as much of interaction as language, a like ambiguity also characterized action, including ritual, but extending into all institutional contexts, not just religion (Doutreloux 1967:261).

The real semantic dissonance that inevitably arises in plural societies is part of a more general conflict of purposes arising on the political level. The separation of the sectors and the dominion of one over the other are maintained by continuous political activity. As Pye observes, the possible resolutions of the tension include assimilation (one meaning eliminates the other), fusion (a new religion emerges), and dissolution (drifting apart of the two systems). The fact that syncretic situations may persist indefinitely (even though, according to the concept of cognitive dissonance, they are "intrinsically temporary") is due, Pye explains, to the continual recurrence of syncretism in the minds of new individuals. According to the sociological perspective, however, ambiguity can be expected to persist in plural societies as long as the plural constitution itself persists, and its resolution depends on political rather than cognitive processes.

SYNCRETISM AND EJCSK

The social context of Kimbanguism is the structural pluralism of a colonial state in which two separate institutional sets are maintained, one of them politically and economically subordinate to the other. The form of this relationship persisted after independence, although the class structure of the population changed: the African foremen and clerks of companies, missions, and government replaced Europeans as the managers of these organizations, and thus of the state. Meanwhile, almost all Zaïreans continue to live by two sets of rules, consciously and visibly segregated; in all public contexts, the truths of the bureaucratic institutional set dominate those of the customary set, which are only tolerated insofar as they can be represented, in French, as conforming to the categories of the bureaucratic world.

Religion among the Kikongo-speaking peoples in Zaïre can be represented diagrammatically as two overlapping circles, B and C, with a common area, X. The language of B is French; and its institutional structure, which gives meaning to both language and behavior, is "bureaucratic". The language of C is Kikongo, and its institutional structure is "customary". Items of belief and practice that fall in the common area, X, can be interpreted in either French or Kikongo and therefore have alternative meanings; items belonging to B or C but not falling in X are those that can readily be described only in French or in Kikongo, respectively. EJCSK, which began as a popular movement located in C, so to speak, has moved since 1959

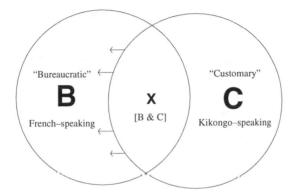

Figure 13.2. "Bureaucratic" vs. "customary" religion among Kikongo-speaking peoples in Zaïre.

increasingly into B (arrows in Figure 13.2). This movement was largely forced by political considerations and has had its costs as well as its advantages. The leadership is conscious of the ambiguities involved, and its propaganda apparatus has been outstandingly successful in manipulating them before both Kikongo- and French-speaking audiences. These manipulations are socially and politically necessary and cannot be reduced to either theological ignorance or dishonesty.

Let us consider a concrete example. The rules of the church (EJCSK n.d.), in addition to the Ten Commandments, are

1. Respect the government (Romans 13:1–3).
2. Love everybody, even your enemy (Matthew 5:43–45).
3. No smoking, whether tobacco or hemp.
4. No alcohol.
5. No dancing or attendance at dances.
6. Do not bathe naked or sleep naked.
7. No quarreling.
8. No use of charms or magic.
9. Pay taxes.
10. Do not harbor resentment.
11. Everybody must admit his or her illdoing, before witnesses.
12. The only food taboos forbid eating monkey or pig.

All of these rules can be seen as making sense in either European (Francophone) or African (Kikongo) terms, but some fit much more easily into the one than the other, and the meaning of all of them changes according to the perspective. Rule 1, respect for government, is the least ambiguous and might seem to entail Rule 9, payment of taxes. In fact, taxation is a bureaucratic practice, to which the people have become accustomed in this century, but which they continue to resent, commonly (and with some justice) seeing it as a forced levy benefiting the governing class; they contrast it with personal, "voluntary" presentations, as to a chief or patron. Rules 3, 4, and 5 conform to Protestant (Baptist) morality but also make sense in indigenous terms; dances in particular are recognized, not as immoral in themselves, but as occasions for immorality. Rule 8, against magic, makes sense either in European terms ("no superstition") or in Kongo terms ("no self-seeking truck with the occult"). Rules 2, 7, 10, and 11 seem to be merely good moral advice but attract attention by their redundant multiplicity; in fact, in Kongo perspective, they are prescriptions against witchcraft, or against the attitudes from which witchcraft can unconsciously arise.

Rules 6 and 12 cannot easily be justified in French, and Kimbanguist attempts to do so are notably unsatisfactory. As to not bathing or sleeping naked, Kimbanguists say that persons of the opposite sex may pass by the bathing place or the house might catch fire, forcing the unprepared sleeper to expose himself or herself to the public. To the extent that these are real dangers, everybody confronts them, and there is no reason why commonsense precautions should be made into rules of the church. Members of other churches observe the same rules and more readily explain that in the reflecting surface of water one can see and be seen by the people of the other world, "the angels", some of whom are of the opposite sex; likewise, religious people expect to be visited by "angels" in their sleep. As a high-ranking minister of the Church of the Twelve Apostles said, describing a remarkable experience, "I had just lain down to sleep when the angel of the Lord appeared before me in a great shower of sparks; fortunately, I was wearing a good pair of underpants". In Kikongo, these "angels" are the dead [bafwa].

The taboo against pork is explained by Kimbanguists variously as based on Mosaic law, the story of the Gadarene swine, the filthy eating habits of pigs, or the risk of parasites and disease. The inadequacy of these explanations is obvious. Closest to the real reasoning is the story of the Gadarene swine, into which evil spirits fled from Jesus; domestic pigs are favorite repositories in which witches imprison the souls of their victims, and to eat domestic pork is to risk involuntary participation in witchcraft feasts.[3] Kimbanguists are allowed to eat wild pig. Likewise, as the head of the church, Joseph Diangienda, explained to me, "There are two kinds of monkey; one of them is forbidden, but the other we can eat". He did not elaborate, but Andersson explains that, of the two kinds, makaku (or nsima) monkeys live in bands, whereas nsengi monkeys go in pairs, as man and wife, and are believed to be human beings in disguise [bituzi] (Andersson 1958:176).

Kimbanguist theological accounting is not just a matter of keeping two sets of books. The church must participate in one or both of two institutional sets, each of which requires certain adaptations of organizational form and practice, and of interpersonal behavior, as well as language. For EJCSK to survive it had to develop a bureaucratic structure, a fiscal system, a school system, and various formal protestations of faith. More recently, the expectations of Protestant theology, upon which international and local support for the church is to some extent conditional, have pushed it to adopt a communion service, celebrated for the first time in April 1971. Such a move could be costly if it violated popular conceptions. As Andersson explains, the communion, even in its Baptist form (commemorative rather than sacramental), is inconsistent with popular notions of sin, grace, and salvation, even as they are found within the mission churches (Andersson 1968:148–153, 169–171). Popularly, the kingdom of God "on earth" is a matter of freedom from affliction. Affliction is caused by breaking cult rules [*sumuka*] or by witchcraft, although orthodox Protestant pastors struggle to convince their congregations that afflictions are in fact caused by "Satan", who has become a kind of aggregate, all-purpose witch. Communion, even within the mission churches, is often regarded as an ordeal to detect and punish witches, and like all such ordeals can be misused by the clergy, should they themselves happen to be witches. In 1966, certain Kongo pastors who were vigorous upholders of mission orthodoxy against all forms of prophetism regarded the communion as an item of European culture not necessary to true Christianity and thought that in an age of increasing independence from missionary control it should be abolished.

The EJCSK's introduction of communion had therefore to be carefully prepared, though we do not know what considerations occupied the thoughts of the leadership. In the domain of bureaucratic discourse, the church first uttered a theological explanation, written by the Secretary General. Less readily intelligible to the foreign observer was the performance, once only, of a special preparatory ritual, in which M. Diangienda himself or one of the priests [*sacrificateurs*] "sealed" each of the faithful on the forehead with the sign of the cross in Nkamba water (Martin 1975:161, 179–182). No explanation for the ritual or its origin was made available to outsiders, but the gesture, of Catholic origin, has long been used by Diangienda as a blessing and is popularly understood as having a beneficial effect on the recipient's *lusunzi* [his soul or life-chance], situated in his forehead [*ndunzi*]. The soul itself is often represented, in indigenous art, by a cruciform design.

Communion is supposed to be received three times a year: April 6th (the feast of the prophet's manifestation), October 12th (the date of his death), and Christmas. The omission of Easter, for which April 6th effectively substitutes, is interesting. The feast is celebrated only by the head of the church, Diangienda. In practice, Kimbanguists partake only if they are in Kinshasa (the capital), Nkamba (the New Jerusalem), or Kisangani (the third city of Zaïre); by 1980, communion had been celebrated only twice.

After 1960 the church lost much of its popular support by curtailing ecstatic and healing practices incompatible with its organizational needs; people began to say that it was nothing but another mission church. In 1972, in an effort to renew its spiritual vitality and discipline, EJCSK introduced a new observance—the retreat. Biblical precedents were cited for this new institution, which Kimbangu was also said to have foretold. Retreats took place deep in the forest, or at another place free of distractions. Kimbanguists were supposedly required to attend once in a lifetime, but members of other churches and faiths were welcome. A retreat lasted from Tuesday to Saturday and was marked by frequent prayers, a fast of three days' duration, Bible study, confession of sins, and other exercises expected to renew contact with the Holy Spirit as in the old days at Nkamba in 1921.

Every night, men and women slept separately at their camp in the forest, and watches were appointed of nine men and nine women (or 3, 5, or 7, but not an even number) to pray in turn throughout the night. Public confessions were heard throughout the morning, and then the participants, in odd-numbered groups, moved still deeper into the forest to pray and sing hymns. Everybody made the sacrifice of not eating, drinking, or washing for at least one day, some for two or three. Now and again someone would become possessed [*lauka*] and run shrieking to one of the pastors to confess something he or she had kept back; not to confess was to risk mental illness or even death. In the forest, people began to see visions [*mambu mamanene mangitukulu*]: "the crucified Christ, or you might see a huge eye which was perhaps the eye of God, we don't know". People spoke in strange tongues, such as English, which were intelligible to others though not to the speaker. The reports of visions were written down and transmitted to the central office of the church.

The institution of the retreat testified to the church's capacity for adaptive renewal but entailed its own risks. The closer the church reached towards the energy locked up in the real authenticities of indigenous culture, the sharper its rivalry with competing systems of spiritual guidance necessarily became. It is not surprising, therefore, that dealing with magicians and resorting to charms ("fetishes") were important and frequent themes of the confessions (MacGaffey 1976:40–43).

SYNCRETISM AND NGUNZISM

Though prayers and dreams may remain private matters, the process of healing intrudes into the public domain in any society. Where life or social competence is at stake, therapy is subject to supervision in more than one public context; it is accordingly difficult for the practitioners, while it affords privileged opportunities to observe the structure of pluralism.

In Zaïre, as also in much of Africa from Nigeria to the Republic of South Africa, the rituals of prophetic churches commonly reveal two phases (see Kiernan 1976:356–366). The first phase consists of an ordinary Protestant service: hymns, prayers, Bible reading, and sermon. The second phase, marked by the appearance of the prophet himself, and by other changes of personnel, music, and spatial organization, is devoted to specifically prophetic activities and is highly ambiguous. The usual prophetic activities include oracular prediction and revelation [*mbikudulu*], ecstatic manifestations, prophylactic blessings, spiritual healing, "war" with hostile spirit forces, and, in Ngunzist (DMN) churches particularly, a form of spiritual testing and confirmation known by the French word *bascule* [weighing] (Janzen and MacGaffey 1974, no. 48). All of these practices are justified by reference to biblical texts, as are the practices of American Protestant churches. The participants think of themselves as Protestants or Catholics (the theological differences between the two mean little to most Zaïreans). When asked why their practices differ from those of mission-related churches, they argue that they have restored elements that the missions have improperly excluded. From their point of view, "true Christianity" is coterminous with the C sector of Figure 13.2, and all elements of B, or mission Christianity, that fall outside of X, the common area, are "syncretic" (improper) European additions.

Nevertheless, the contents of DMN rituals also closely parallel those of indigenous Kongo priests [*nganga*, singular]. One individual observed in Matadi in 1970 would enter in solemn procession with six or seven acolytes, most of them women dressed in white as nuns. He himself wore a white soutane and carried a staff resembling a crozier. The hymns sung by the congregation described the activities in progress:

> He is awake, has put on his robe,
> See the dawn!
> The lost sheep I seek,
> The white and the black,
> God's prophet is awake.

As the prophet invoked a blessing on water contained in a number of clear glass bottles, he and his acolytes trembled spectacularly and uttered ecstatic cries. Evidently imitating Catholic communion, the prophet poured a little water from a cup into the mouth of each acolyte, remarking that "all those who have received water to drink shall be saved" and afterwards rinsing his hands and drying them on a napkin that was folded and placed on top of the cup. He would then proceed to divination, saying, "Hark! The time for prophecy has come!" (Janzen and MacGaffey 1974, no. 22; MacGaffey 1983:159–177).

The glossolalia, trembling, and divination while in a state of possession can all be matched in the nineteenth-century rituals of *nganga manga, nganga ngombo, nganga ntadi*, and others intended to "sniff out" [*fyela*] witches. The Matadi prophet even referred to himself as *mfyedi* [diviner]. In the past, the ecstatic acolytes were called *mintombo*, from *tombula* [to raise up] spirits. The list of parallels also includes treatment by means of blessings, potions, and ablutions; divinatory inquiry proceeding through a series of alternatives (natural causes or witchcraft; if witchcraft, from the maternal or paternal side of the family?, etc.); the use of songs describing the proceedings; and the techniques of raising excitement by an increasing volume of music and the interpolation of increasingly specific revelations alternating with glossolalia. A Kongo anthropologist describes the work of *nganga ngombo* as follows:

> After a while one would see trembling and changes of behavior among those present, especially in the case of the one holding the pot of fetishes [medicines]. These signs manifest that at that moment the *nkisi* dwell in everybody who is trembling. And that is a good thing, because this is the means whereby the possessed (*habitées*) do whatever the possessing spirit tells them to do or say. If the *nkisi* tell them to go to the river in the middle of the night, they will run there. Being possessed, their voices change quality, and some of them speak Lingala or some other language instead of their own Kindibu dialect of KiKongo. Under

the influence of the *nkisi* they reveal the names of witches and the history of witchcraft in the family in question, and also what should be done to effect healing and restore peace, prosperity, and fertility. (Buakasa 1968:153–169; cf. Cavazzi da Montecuccolo 1965:181–183)

In the basic healing technique of DMN churches, the healer circles the patient, flapping a towel and laying hands on the head or afflicted part, with invocations and much trembling. Some healers puff and blow, to add to the wind [*mpeve*] created by the flapping towel, or spread the towel over the sufferer. The towels used have been specially blessed for the purpose. Such towels and other cloths, including flags, have replaced animal skins and raffia cloths formerly used in the same way. In 1700 a Capuchin missionary described healing procedures he had observed:

> Then they take the skins of certain animals with which they touch the patient all over, and from time to time they shake him and strike him, saying that these skins will draw out the evil that has seized upon him. To signify this, the fetisher snaps and shakes the skins to shake out the evil adhering to them. (Cuvelier 1953:131)

In the nineteenth century, similar rituals were performed by *nganga mvutudi*, *ntombodi*, or *ntadi* to "return the soul" of a patient, the sign of success being that the priest was able to lay a raffia cloth on the patient's head [*tensikisa lubongo ku ntu mbevo*] (MacGaffey 1986:239). More examples of similar parallels could be given, and they form the basis for arguments that the modern prophet is merely a witchdoctor in Christian clothing. The prophets themselves, however, continually draw a sharp distinction between themselves and the *nganga n'kisi* [peddler of charms and magic] (Andersson 1958:3). Prophetic ritual practice, in contrast to that of the magician, stresses the use of plain water instead of herbal concoctions in palm wine. In this connection the whiteness of enamel vessels and the clear glass of the bottles used is important. Ritual clothing is plain white, with at most a few touches of red and an occasional embroidered sign. This whiteness is a powerful iconoclastic statement of purity, clarity, transparency, and sincerity, symbolizing the prophet's commitment to openness and publicity, as opposed to the particularism and murky secretiveness of self-serving magic. As one prophet said, "The Holy Spirit in a man is like water in a glass, hiding nothing".[4]

The resort to whiteness is no doubt partly an accommodation to censorship— holy water and white robes are acceptably Christian, whereas body paint and animal skins would declare their origin—but it is not simply protective coloration for covert "paganism"; a distinction is being made, within the implicit structure of indigenous religion, between beliefs and practices associated with the pursuit of personl advantage and those that assert the priority of public interests and values. Trance, glossolalia and the like are metaphorical expressions of the prophet's direct commission from God [Nzambi], in whose name and with whose power he purports to act. The charms of the magician, on the other hand, are bought and sold and stand for the pursuit of self-interest, which Kongo thought associates with witchcraft. This tension between public and private values is fundamental to the religion of most of Bantu-speaking Africa and can be discerned in Kongo history at least as far back as 1700 (MacGaffey 1970b:27–38, 1977:177–193).

Plate 13–2. This tombstone combines a Christian cross with an indigenous figure of a *n'kisi*, which is often anthropomorphic with a mirror on the belly. In Kongo thought in general, less distinction is made between animate and inanimate than in European thought; a *n'kisi* is invoked as an animate agent that has power to heal diseases and solve other problems. The animation of the *n'kisi* is attributed by Bakongo to the presence of the dead (sometimes an ancestor) in the figure in the material form of medicines (c.f. MacGaffey 1986: ch. 6).

OTHER CHRISTIAN CHURCHES

In effect, Bakongo assimilated the missionary condemnation of indigenous religion, described as "sorcery", "superstition", and the like, to their own standing distrust of all dealings with the occult not subject to public discipline. This misunderstanding persists to the present day and does not differentiate Kimbanguists or Ngunzists from other Kongo Christians, Catholic or Protestant. Collectively resolving in the name of Christianity to return to the right way, they enthusiastically adopted the moral prescriptions, rituals, and scriptures brought by the missionary, to the extent that they could read in them values they already respected. In the era of decolonization, the ambiguity of this conversion is much debated, notably by Catholic intellectuals in Zaïre. On the one hand, Zaïreans feel that they have always known God; as a government spokesman put it, "The missionaries expected to convert us to a faith, whereas they merely converted us to a kind of rite different from our own". On the other hand, as one of the leading intellectuals has written: "Catholic, universal, whatever you like, the problem remains: Catholicism is a religion marked by the West even in the understanding of the message. Carried, sustained as it is by European structures, it is hardly possible to love it without committing oneself in the history of the world" (Mudimbe 1973:35). From this dilemma arises the active contemporary movement towards an "African theology" (Inongo 1973:216; Mudimbe 1973:35; Tshibangu 1974).

According to Cardinal Malula, archbishop of Kinshasa, "Eight tenths of the life of our people is governed by the belief in witchcraft, divination, and dreams. This is a fact. After 80 years of 'evangelization', and despite all the condemnations of our 'civilizing masters', this sole fact should give us pause" (Malula 1977:5). Lufuluabo, a Franciscan priest, in the book to which the Cardinal prefaces these words, explains that the faithful, despite all the sermons they have heard, believe firmly in sorcery; to escape its effects, they turn not to their priest but to a diviner. The clergy are thus isolated from their flock in their moments of greatest spiritual need. "I know that we will make no true progress until we question the [European-derived] massive and summary condemnation of so-called superstitions, in which practically all African values are included" (Lufuluabo 1977:8).

Lufuluabo later got into trouble with the Catholic Church for practicing divination himself, and the problem continues to vex the best theological minds in the country. The respected scholar Vincent Mulago argues that for those who truly understand the essence of Christianity and African tradition there can be no contradiction between them (Mulago 1981:41). In the same issue of the same journal, Bimwenyi, Secretary-General of the Episcopal Conference of Zaïre, contradicts Mulago and gives sophisticated expression to Lufuluabo's point of view. He vigorously asserts that the Church as at present constituted is fundamentally alien to Africa, where Christian communities

> pray to God in a liturgy that is not their own, live according to a moral order which is not a transformation, by the grace of God and the breath of the Spirit, of their own former order. They are ruled by a canon law which is not a law born of the conversion to Christ of the socio-juridical realities immanent in the universe to which they belong.... If they reflect, they do so according to philosophical and theological systems generated by the meditation and reflection

of other Christian communities that have evangelized them. (Bimwenyi 1981:49, English translation mine)

Protestant churches, on the other hand, traditionally emphasize individual inner redemption ("finding Christ"). In principle, the cultural embeddedness of the gospel is irrelevant to this view of salvation and pastoral practice. Insofar as the mission elements of the Protestant churches have identified a theological problem in the events of recent years, it seems to be that of "ecumenism"; having undergone enforced unification in the Church of Christ in Zaïre, some of them are worried that they are being drawn into excessively close contact with others whose sense of salvation does suffer, in their view, from its cultural embeddedness.

CONCLUSION

The issue of syncretism in Zaïrean religion is thus more complex than at first appears. All of the several organizations calling themselves Christian show the results of centuries of cultural diffusion; but that is not what the issue is about. "Syncretism", with the implicit meanings of "deviance" and "covert paganism", has been used pejoratively by groups in a position to make the accusation effective against African-founded or "independent" churches. The members of those churches, contemplating the theology and practice of established Christianities, find them, too, to be syncretic in the same sense but lack the power to make their accusation stick. So far, then, we have the B and C of Figure 13.2, with the area of agreement, X, but this diagram represents only the conscious, reciprocal evaluations of the parties.

My thesis, grounded in the analysis of the social pluralism prevailing in Zaïre, is that the difference between Christianity as apprehended in bureaucratic and customary terms, respectively, goes far deeper than conscious evaluations, subjectively perceived differences, and cognitive dissonance. It is a matter of radically different cosmologies experienced not as theories of time, life, race, and the like but as the lived realities of contrasting institutional systems.

Secondly, I have argued that these incompatible cosmologies are entertained by the same people, no matter what their religious affiliation; they refer to the two contrasted social contexts in which all Zaïreans are to some extent engaged. The incompatibility of the two emerges most clearly in discussions by intellectuals of the intractable problem of witchcraft.

Only if belief and meaning were entirely independent of social practice and institutional context could Christianity ever be diffused without changing in form and content, and thus giving rise to new syncretisms. This is not evidence of human weakness, but the paradox of "the Word made Flesh". It may be a valid question in comparative ethics or Christian theology to discover whether the same truths are compatible with different forms, or the conditions in which members of different societies can share the same transcendent meanings, but inquiries of this kind must not be directed invidiously towards selected churches or religions. The orientations and commitments of the ordinary membership of all these churches, whether mission-related or not, are generally similar, no more and no less marked by syncretism than churches elsewhere.

Neither the debate about syncretism nor the practices to which the debaters variously refer are likely to be abolished by argument or preaching. The problem, I have argued, is political, as are the forces that created it and will put an end to it. The government of Zaïre has been struggling by legal and administrative means to abolish institutional pluralism, which it describes as a racist legacy of the colonial past. According to the letter of the law, all "traditional" forms of kinship and land tenure have been replaced by uniform national institutions; in practice, not the law but the uncertain progress of capitalism is slowly bringing about a society divided no longer by pluralism but by class (Axelson 1970:274–289).

A corresponding cultural homogenization of Kimbanguist doctrine and practice is taking place. The mimeographed *Essence de la Théologie Kimbanguiste*, circulated in 1980, aligns EJCSK with evangelical Protestantism in its theology of baptism and salvation, but explicitly dissociates itself from that tradition in accepting the doctrine of the Real Presence of Christ in the Eucharist (although, as we have seen, the Eucharist is not central to Kimbanguist worship). On the other hand, the new doctrine omitted most of the features, conspicuous in earlier versions, that could be traced to ancestral Kongo religion.

NOTES

1. Early American Baptist (ABFMS) correspondence provides an example of what surely should be called syncretism: "Divine Providence has evidently placed the Anglo-Saxon (perhaps Teuton) race in the forefront of the battle to be pioneers of the Gospel" (Harvey to Duncan, 11 October 1893; cited by Kimpianga kia Mahaniah, 1975). Surely the battle was to spread the gospel, not to be pioneers.

2. In fact, according to recent studies, most Japanese are unaware of the theological incompatibility of Shintoism and Buddhism, treating "ancestors" and "buddhas" as two different names for the same thing (Newell 1976).

3. Western Kongo legend says of the *basi kintiemuna*, "the wide-awake people", that is, those who are awake at night, or witches, that "if they speak of eating pork they have a cannibal feast in mind". *Kintiemuna* literally means "firefly", a sign of witchcraft (Bittremieux 1936:19).

4. The same values are explicit in the religions of many other Bantu-speaking peoples. "What is good, for Ndembu, is the open, the public, the unconcealed, the sincere" (Victor Turner 1975:239; see also Fry 1976:27).

14

Jamaa:
A Charismatic Movement Revisited

Johannes Fabian

M OST OF WHAT I WILL HAVE to say is an attempt to disentangle some complex and confusing developments in and around a Zaïrean religious movement, the Jamaa.[1] When I first came in contact with it, more than twenty-five years ago, I called it a charismatic movement because it seemed to confirm Max Weber's notions of charisma as a "major force of revolution" in "traditional" societies (Weber 1964; Fabian 1971). In the years that followed I repeatedly revised my views on both the Jamaa movement and the theory of religious enthusiasm (see Fabian 1979d and 1981, for summaries). While I had tried to keep up with changes in the field, I was not prepared for what I found during two brief but intensive periods of research in the summers of 1985 and 1986. Some of the structural principles that Weber summarized in his concept of routinization have certainly been operative. But more striking have been developments that cannot be subsumed under that notion. These will require further revisions. In the concluding section of this essay I shall tentatively sketch my current view by formulating some thoughts on power, or rather *pouvoir*, a term that has the advantage of embracing the English "power" and the German *Herrschaft*.

FATES OF CHARISMA

The project on which I am about to report is a new look at the Jamaa, more than forty years after its emergence. I shall assume that this movement has by now a certain notoriety.[2] Nevertheless, it will be useful to recall what, to me at least, have been its most striking characteristics.

When the Jamaa appeared in 1953 near the mining town of Kolwezi (then Katanga Province, now Shaba) it was in many respects an extraordinary phenomenon. Its membership was almost exclusively African, but the founder, Placide Tempels, was a Belgian missionary (Tempels 1945). In Central Africa, and probably beyond, it was at the time also the only important religious movement to arise from a Roman Catholic background. Although it diverged in doctrine and organization from the mission church, it understood itself as a kind of revival (without using that term) within the Catholic church. In that respect, the Jamaa was perhaps comparable to the Balokole revival among Anglicans in East Africa.[3] Theoretically, the Jamaa was interesting because it seemed to make the case for "endogenous" social change, being creative and innovative rather than reactive or nostalgic.[4]

At first, the Jamaa was acclaimed as a genuinely African form of Catholicism. Yet, as it elaborated and consolidated its own distinctive identity, a confrontation with the hierarchy and clergy (then still largely expatriate) became inevitable. The tensions came to the surface as early as in 1967 in Lubumbashi and 1970 in Kolwezi, after years of internal conflicts among factions in the clergy. By chance—I was working on another, unrelated project—I was in Shaba in 1972–74 when a Jamaa, weakened by dissent from within, with little support from the clergy (the founder was still alive but had returned to Belgium in 1962, where he was under ecclesiastic censure in a convent) and afflicted by self-doubt and a kind of fatigue, was given an ultimatum by the Zaïrean conference of bishops: either to abjure in a public ritual its doctrinal errors and practices considered deviant, or to be excommunicated.[5] Because I was preoccupied with other matters, I could not do systematic research at the time. Informally, I was in close and frequent contact with leaders and members of the movement. I noticed that reactions to the ultimatum were by no means as clear-cut as the hierarchy had hoped. Large portions of the Jamaa simply refused to be put, collectively or individually, in an either/or position. They insisted that they had nothing to abjure and continued to attend church services even after the bishops' decisions had been read from the pulpits. Frustrations among the more authoritarian pastors and bishops mounted and made some of them resort to legal action and appeals to the government, to the army, and to the largest employers of the region. Jamaa members were psychologically and physically brutalized, thrown out of churches, fired from mission-funded jobs, even accused of supporting antigovernment rebels.[6] Using an expression from Weber, I described the outcome of the 1973–74 campaign of suppression as a "castration of charisma". A concerted exercise of spiritual and political power and outright coercion had, in my view, more or less disabled a once vigorous movement.

I concluded that "there is a good chance that oppression will succeed in adding the movement to the long list of sectarian groups which vegetate as interesting but largely inconsequential by-products of colonization and decolonization" (1979:200). I had hoped that this essay would be my last word on the subject. When I resumed contacts with the movement in 1985 and was thinking about a title for my report, I came up with something like "Goodbye Jamaa". I am now convinced that the Jamaa is not likely to leave the scene, although it no longer occupies the central place it once did. Nor do I think any longer that the movement should be dropped as a subject. I found it changed in unexpected ways. Friends and acquaintances I had made many years ago are still involved with Placide Tempels's ideas, some showing signs of fatigue, others being fired by renewed enthusiasm. Still others, many of them born after Tempels had left for Europe, are attracted by his teachings; both members of the first hour and latecomers seem determined to carry on, even if it means that the movement must be transformed. "Survival through change" is a suggestive and handy formula for such a situation. Applied to the Jamaa in Shaba, it would have to cover many interrelated forms and levels of change. Before I can sketch the outcome—the present shape of the movement—I must report on some of the events and conditions that provided the frame in which individual members and groups of the Jamaa have been making their choices.

CONCENTRATION VS. DISSIPATION OF POWER

Even if we started with the mistaken assumption that the Jamaa since the mid-1970s has done little else but stagnate and decline, we would have to relate its internal development to some spectacular changes that occurred in its religious, political, and economic environment. An explanation of the movement's career based on some sort of internal logic (be it structural, evolutionary, or both) seems less plausible than ever. The same goes for reductions to external pressures or causes. Both temptations are easier to resist now than twenty-five years ago, if only because the Jamaa has by now acquired a "history". It can no longer be made to accommodate the atemporal systemic approaches that were fashionable in the 1960s. At any rate, I feel that I must first situate my report in a historical context.

When my writings on the Jamaa, together with those of others, contributed to its public image—six to ten years after Zaïrean Independence in 1960—several things converged to create the impression of charismatic vigor, of intellectual originality, and of social innovation. The movement's political context in the second half of the 1960s was marked by Mobutu's rise to power, by consolidation of his "revolutionary" regime, and by a modest economic boom linked, symbolically perhaps more than actually, to the nationalization of the mining industry—Zaïre's principal source of wealth. The religious climate was one of optimism and experimentation encouraged by the Vatican council; the mission church was moving toward Africanization and Catholic Zaïrean intellectuals contributed to an official ideology of national pride, the famed doctrine of *authenticité*. The Jamaa, being the heir to "Bantu Philosophy", could appear to contribute to these processes. Even though it remained aloof from party politics and had few followers among the new elites and cliques, the Jamaa took part in a society-wide struggle for cultural independence.

Experts in the field will remember that an optimistic outlook on innovative and integrative contributions was characteristic of the study of religious movements in Africa during that period. In part this outlook was justified by situations such as the one I just described; but it was also, in varying degrees, the artifact of a certain kind of social theory that owed more to Talcott Parsons than to Max Weber, and very little to Karl Marx and other more pessimistic theorists of religion and politics. Be that as it may, in Zaïre, after a period of divisive ethnic conflicts following independence, the general tendency appeared to be one of concentration of power and efforts. Even rapid, indeed rabid, urbanization manifestly did not result in the predicted disintegration of culture and society. Instead, Zaïre became one of the African countries most remarkable for the rise of a new popular culture expressed especially in music and painting (see Fabian 1978).

In the 1980s, some of the external forms of that remarkable period continued to endure on the surface—Mobutu still was the sole ruler of the country (although no one was sure where his power ended and that of the new Zaïrean technocrats and multinational interest groups began); mining was still the pivot of the economy and somehow managed to keep the country afloat; the Catholic church seemed to have consolidated its power (in some respects there was a return to privileges enjoyed during colonial times, especially in the fields of education, social services, and health care). Still, the economic crisis that began in the mid-1970s had become endemic. Shortages of fuel, food, and basic consumer goods were constantly felt; pauperization was rampant even among those who still held jobs; apathy and despair had replaced the optimism of the period between 1965 and 1975.

According to a widely held opinion, this should have been just the situation to encourage the rise of religious movements, and if one does not probe too deeply, this seems in fact to have happened. Repression succeeded in removing the threat once posed by the Jamaa to the power of the Church. However, at the same time the urban and rural areas of Shaba witnessed a great proliferation of independent churches and other religious groups.[7] Further research will determine to what degree the legal confrontation between the Church and the Jamaa served as a catalyst in this process. My guess is that it did to a great extent.

From the mid-1970s up to 1986, there was a liberalization of the tough policies toward religious groups (other than Catholics) that the Zaïrean government had inherited from its colonial predecessors. Religious independence had for some time spread in the Protestant context and could, at any rate, be predicted in Zaïre, considering the recent history of other African countries. Little or nothing prepared the Catholic church in Zaïre, which was used to docile "lay" movements, for the emergence of a pentecostalist revival, locally most often referred to as *groupes de prière* [prayer groups]. From all available evidence, two things happened almost simultaneously around 1973–74: a turn among African Catholics to forms of worship and rituals hitherto considered typical of Protestant or traditionalist churches, and the importation of the international charismatic revival led, in Lubumbashi, by a small group of missionaries (mainly Jesuits) and other expatriate Catholics.[8]

All of a sudden, the environment in which the Jamaa had arisen and developed was changed, especially within that core of ardent practicing Catholics that was at one time the domain of the Jamaa (with some competition, admittedly, from the Legio Mariae, another international organization that had come to Africa earlier). From then on, the Jamaa's problems were no longer competing leaders and factions within, and a more or less united adversary without, but a new kind of religious fervor all around. No wonder that leaders of the Jamaa, and not only they, experienced this new situation as a dissipation of charismatic power. All the persons with whom I discussed these recent developments, including followers of the charismatic revival, deplored the proliferation of religious groups; most of them blamed the economic and political situation, that is, misery and a special kind of organized anarchy.

The charismatic revival had one immediate effect on the Jamaa. It recruited many of its followers and leaders, especially from among those Jamaa members who had put their loyalty to the Roman Catholic church above their attachment to Tempels's movement, at least publicly. My own observations show that this, while syphoning off some membership, has in fact contributed to a further spread of Jamaa ideas, perhaps not so much on the level of doctrinal content as in the form of discourse or discursive praxis. The style and rhetoric of the Jamaa *mafundisho* [teaching, instructions] can easily be detected in the prayer meetings of the charismatics. To determine this more exactly will be a principal task for future work on the tape recordings of services and conversations that were made recently.

The new situation also brought about important changes on the level of organization. In the past, the Jamaa had been remarkable for its ability to maintain local groups (usually attached to a parish)—as well as regional and supraregional links—with a minimum of organizational means. Until the 1970s the movement functioned without bylaws, membership roles, or even written material for instruction. Networks of spiritual kinship and orally transmitted teachings were considered sufficient to safeguard the identity of the Jamaa. This changed when the decisive confrontation with the church hierarchy came. For different reasons, loyal as well as dissident Jamaa groups were forced to adopt a complicated bureaucratic organization and to codify the doctrine in written manuals. Loyal groups were ordered to conform to the organizational pattern of other religious associations recognized by the church; the dissidents had to show a *règlement intérieur*, official representatives, financial statements, and information on membership in order to satisfy government regulations regarding "cults" and churches.[9] Although this is a hunch that will have to be checked later, in both cases the *Mouvement Populaire de la Révolution*, the unique political party of Zaïre, may have served as a model. A party-like organization quite likely increases the chances for recognition and survival, given the fact that, until recently, official policies prohibited all nonparty associations, from Boy Scouts to veterans' clubs.

It would be a mistake, however, to take this surface trend toward more formal and more centralized organization as evidence contradicting earlier observations on the dissipation of power. The Catholic charismatic groups of Lubumbashi, for instance, also had to conform to church regulations. From local to national levels they are officially headed by "shepherds" and steering committees presided over by priests; pastoral directives formulate doctrinal guidelines and rules of conduct.[10] But it is doubtful whether these manifest structures are more than tokens of transparency calculated to satisfy the church hierarchy. Pentecostalism resulted in a multiplication of groups that are more or less independent of each other, oriented toward individual prophets or small groups of leaders. As we know from its long history in the Protestant context, this development tends to multiply units of basically the same pattern; its potential for innovation is small. Religious entrepreneurship, centered on a founder-prophet-healer, creates highly localized and often shortlived congregations. People move around among these groups; in fact there is a kind of shopping around for the most satisfying results. This is evident in the biographies of adepts. The situation may be experienced as a new kind of freedom; it also causes frustration and disaffection.

In sum, the Jamaa faced in the 1980s conditions which no longer resembled those existing in the years immediately before and after Zaïrean independence. A veneer of overt organizational structures may suggest hierarchization, centralization, hence concentration of power. Charisma seems to be transformed into bureaucratic structures. In reality something much more complex may be happening. In order for us to understand the changes that are visible on the surface, I must now back up and point out some facts that are less obvious but all the more important.

CHARISMA AND EMBOURGEOISEMENT

Originally, the Jamaa in Shaba had its demographic basis among young married adults. Socially it drew on what might be called a "captive population" (as we speak of a captive audience). These were the mine workers and other wage earners who lived in the company settlements of the *Union Minière du Haut Katanga* and of the BCK railroad, the two largest employers in the area. Various factors contributed to a rapid spread of Jamaa throughout Shaba and beyond: the mobility of workers who transferred between work sites or worked on projects such as the electrification of the Lubumbashi-Angolan border railway, the return of employees to rural areas after retirement or termination of contract, and the upheavals of the Katanga secession and later invasions. In spite of such frequent movement, however, the official labor policy was to discourage short-term migration of the kind that still serves the mines of South Africa. Since the 1920s the economics of labor recruitment and the exigencies of labor management in Shaba had favored stable, long-term contracts with workers who lived with their families. These labor policies entailed company responsibilities for feeding, housing, and entertaining workers and keeping them and their families in good health. They also favored cultivation of moral values thought to be guaranteed by stable nuclear families. Early on, this invited close collaboration between companies and missions. Since the 1940s Catholic missionaries were on the company payroll, not only as teachers but also as pastors. In Katanga, and not only there, the policies of labor stabilization served as a model for native policy in general, especially when the creation of an African middle class became an actively pursued goal (e.g., through the creation of urban zones called *centres extra-coutumiers*).[11]

Jamaa doctrine, with its emphasis on Christian marriage and the couple, expressed the experiences African workers had with labor stabilization and endowed them with deeper meaning. No wonder that in the eyes of church leaders and company managers the Jamaa first appeared as a harmless "family movement" that could help to defuse the danger of "deracination" and proletarization among the urban working masses.

By the 1970s, the policy of stabilization had done its service. The industry had created a labor force that was more than self-reproductive and could envisage cutting down on costs for the services it had to provide under a paternalist regime. This was at least one of the reasons for a weakening of the bonds between mission and industry. It also removed some of the means by which the Church could exercise direct control of the movement and its sympathizers. At the same time it became apparent that accelerated urbanization did not inevitably result in proletarization, which would have endangered economic and political objectives. Rather, what occurred was in fact a sort of petit-embourgeoisement. Although living conditions remained precarious, especially for those who were not directly employed by the mining and railroad companies, a majority of the urban population developed aspirations to a modicum of the good life. That process dates back almost to the beginning of Belgian colonization; it became visible on a large scale as soon as direct controls on styles of living, leisure activities, and patterns of consumption were removed after 1960.

In the 1970s "Africanization" seriously got under way. There was, in 1973, a rather short-lived scheme of Zaïreanization of all small- and middle-sized business and industry owned by expatriates. Even if it was economically disastrous, it gave Africans experience in areas that had been closed to most of them. There has also been a steady increase of African personnel in the higher echelons of government, industry (especially in the technical branches), health services, secondary and higher education, and the clergy. These new elites form a substantial part of the urban population, not so much numerically (although each "bourgeois" tends to have a large retinue of relatives and clients), but economically, politically, and culturally. Unlike their predecessors in colonial times, then called *évolués*, they adopt a life-style that suits them without having to attach themselves to expatriates. It is therefore no longer appropriate, if it ever was, to view African middle-class life as a mere imitation or importation of Western culture. The towns and cities of Zaïre now have a *petite bourgeoisie* that, albeit with certain restrictions imposed by a depressed economy, has direct access to globally available goods and ideas—from video recorders to Rosicrucianism. Zaïreans are reached by the world system much more quickly and directly than during the days when most of them belonged to a colonial labor force sheltered from outside influence by employers and authorities.

Among the "commodities" that circulate globally are, I am convinced, phenomena such as Catholic pentecostalism, a form of movement which confounded earlier theories that sought religious enthusiasm mainly among the oppressed and disenfranchised.[12] I am not about to declare the spectacular rise of Catholic prayer groups in Zaïre a mere side effect of the formation of a middle class. But that such connections exist cannot be doubted, and a comparison with the Jamaa brings out some of the salient characteristics of that new movement.

The vast majority of Tempels's followers were workers. If there has recently been an upward social trend, it reflects the rise of members who first joined the Jamaa when Africans were barred from higher positions. Charismatic prayer groups appeared when such restrictions no longer existed. From the beginning they attracted larger numbers of "intellectuals"—members of the teaching professions, including university professors, physicians and other professionals, higher government officials and politicians, and especially young graduates of the university, academies, and training schools. Teachers, nurses, and technicians joined these groups, often when they were still students. This would have been impossible in the Jamaa because it admitted only married couples. In fact, the integration of young people and adolescents is one of the outstanding characteristics of the pentecostalist revival. These youths may even occupy positions of leadership, because the spiritual gifts that confer high status are not a matter of achievement or seniority. In the Jamaa, where seniority played a central role, leaders had to rethink their positions, and many have begun to follow the charismatic example in paying more attention to the young. At any rate, among the past mistakes now generally admitted in the movement is the neglect of children by parents too deeply involved in the marriage- and couple-centered activities of the Jamaa.

My account seems to suggest that a worker-based religious movement, formed during colonial times, is being bypassed by socio-economic developments of the postcolonial era. The Jamaa must keep up with these progressive forces or disappear. Leaving aside the question of how meaningful the term "postcolonial" may be, especially as it relates to the economy, there are reasons to be dissatisfied with a straight tale of progress. I now want to offer some evidence for what, to me, signals regressiveness, or at least elements of regressiveness, in the process of (petit-)embourgeoisement to which I linked the emergence of the Catholic charismatic revival in Zaïre.

REGRESSIVE PROGRESS?

One effect of embourgeoisement on religious orientations and attitudes should be a greater individualism, a privatization of beliefs and activities, perhaps something along the lines known from the history of Protestantism in Europe and America. Only a very superficial contact with the charismatic revival in Shaba could lead one to believe that such is happening in this case. True, as elsewhere in the world, prayer groups in Shaba seek uncontrolled inspiration by the Holy Spirit. Hierarchical power and functions reserved to the clergy usually are not contested (although there have been dramatic cases of just that[13]), they are relativized. More than offices inherent in an institution, the charismatics value the "gifts" of individuals such as speaking in tongues, discernment of spirits, faith-healing, rapture, and trance. All this I found in Shaba, and it conforms to pentecostalist practices all over the world. But in groups that have only indirect connections to the international movement, if any at all, spirit possession and the detection of witchcraft and its exorcism seem to have become the foremost preoccupation. Some observers perceive similarities between these Catholic prayer groups and indigenous antiwitchcraft movements. Even some insiders are troubled because they realize that to combat witchcraft is to affirm its existence. It would be too easy, however, to qualify these preoccupations as a return to, or relapse into, "tradition". This is not what I mean by regressive progress. Tradition does not remain constant—it cannot simply be returned to. The complex of ritual practices to which the charismatics resort is a recent construct, certainly in this Catholic context. To cope with the vicissitudes of urban life is one of its functions, and in this it shares motivations with old escapist movements. New as a source of frustration is the widening gap between the aspirations of a middle class and the economic and political means to satisfy them. In fact, the links that do exist to the international charismatic revival may indicate that assumptions regarding economic deprivation and political oppression are not sufficient; somehow the Zaïrean bourgeoisie experience dissatisfaction or need similar to that experienced in affluent Western societies.

Compared to the optimistic, humanist, and universalist outlook of the Jamaa twenty years ago, the ritualization of problems of personal well-being and interpersonal relations that seems to occur in the charismatic revival looks regressive; again, not as a return to pre-Christian forms but as an abdication from searching for solutions to societal problems that are larger than the difficulties experienced in the middle class.

There is yet another way to illustrate what I meant by regressive progressiveness. Again, compared to the Jamaa of the 1960s, a characteristic of the prayer groups of the 1980s has been an emotionalization, or perhaps better a de-intellectualization, of religion. As far as I could detect from written sources and conversations, charismatics did not develop anything that could be compared to the elaborate philosophical-mythical system of *mawazo* [thoughts] that the Jamaa had inherited from Tempels's struggles with Bantu philosophy, little also that could be compared to the Jamaa's practice of graded initiatory teaching. These *mafundisho* [instructions] found their palpable expression in a distinctive oral discourse, recognizable as typically Jamaa on all levels, from lexical innovation to the creation of oral genres.

To me at least, it has always been its language-centeredness that made the Jamaa a creative contributor to social processes that started around Zaïrean independence. In the beginning, I was inclined to overemphasize the self-centered, even esoteric, functions of Jamaa ways of speaking. With the years I have come to recognize the impact it made on the popular language of Shaba and on moral and political discourse, including that of the MPR. As I noted before, Jamaa doctrine continues to be articulated in content and style by leaders of charismatic prayer groups who had their religious formation as Tempels's disciples. This constitutes a situation that is of special interest because it allows us to test, as it were, some of the sociolinguistic assumptions regarding the determinants of speaking. Even without much detailed analysis of recordings, it is already clear that something changes when Jamaa teaching is no longer embedded in practices of progressive initiation. In the mouths of charismatics, Jamaa ideas are edifying but no longer vital, life giving.

Predictably, as the charismatic movement turns away from oral and initiatory teaching to the scriptures, a personally "inspired" reading of the Bible becomes more important. My first impression from witnessing such readings is that they are not only emotionalized but take on a divinatory function. That again would not be exceptional if one considers the use of the Bible made by fundamentalist Christians. But here the divinatory element seems to carry more weight. It may be linked to the discernment of spirits or the detection of witchcraft. During prayer meetings, choosing a passage from the scriptures to be commented on seems to be the privilege of those that are recognized as visionaries. They make their choice usually according to the inspiration of the moment, not following a preset schema (although the liturgical calender of the Catholic church is frequently an occasion to select a chapter or episode). In the Jamaa, use of the scriptures was in the past very restricted. Certain, but few, events from the Old and New Testament were selected to serve in initiatory teaching; some favorite passages of Tempels's were often repeated. But there was no sustained study of the Bible and very little individual or divinatory reading. The scriptures were foundational, but any kind of Bible-fundamentalism was foreign to the Jamaa.

Finally, I should like to mention another point of contrast between prayer groups and the Jamaa. Paradoxically, the charismatics who place so much value on spontaneous, uncontrolled expression of feelings and experiences conduct their group activities with a degree of ritualization that never had an equivalent in the Jamaa. True, initiation was an important ritual in the Jamaa; its members, as ardent Catholics, regularly participated in the rituals of the Church. But the weekly *mafundisho* of local groups, the monthly meetings of the fully initiated, and the occasional supraregional events were striking because they lacked the colorful actions, paraphernalia, and attire present in other religious movements in the same environment. Jamaa rituals include some singing, of a rather subdued kind; prayers and instructions in a certain sequence; and some typical ritual gestures. But these could not be compared to the elaborate rituals, the special dress and other accoutrements, the use of percussion instruments and choirs to lead the singing and dancing, the frequent shouting of Alleluia-Amen, ululations, clapping of hands—all this for two or three hours once or twice a week— found in the seances of the charismatic groups. Some charismatic groups also ritualize space within and around their meeting places.[14] These groups participate in frequent retreats, fasting, obligatory prayers at home, and special prayers that may have to be said over a period of several months. This, in addition to attending mass and other church events, adds up to an amazing degree of ritualization. Of course, it takes middle-class leisure for this to happen, limited as it may be nowadays in Zaïre where even university professors have to spend much of every day with nonacademic activities to provide for their families.

SURVIVAL OF THE DOOMED: THE JAMAA IN THE 1980s

To sketch some of the salient characteristics of the charismatic revival in Shaba is necessary because, apart from outright repression by ecclesiastic and political authorities, nothing affected the Jamaa more than the radical change in its own Catholic environment and, as it were, on its own ground, charismatic enthusiasm. In my account so far, when comparing the Jamaa with the charismatics, I have been referring to the Jamaa I knew in the 1960s and early 1970s. I now turn to the shape of Tempels's movement in the 1980s.

First of all, I think it is correct to use the term "movement" in the singular. All groups I had direct or indirect contact with during my recent visits claim succession to (or identity with) the Jamaa of the 1960s. Even though divisions among them are great and likely to be of a permanent nature, it is not for the anthropologist to pass judgment on conflicting claims. One should also avoid, as much as possible, a typological or taxonomic approach in comparing groups or clusters of groups. Difficult as it may be to avoid such terms, one should not speak of branches and factions. This would lead to stating hierarchical relations between more or less authentic varieties of Jamaa. Rather, each of the recognizable varieties should be regarded as one current manifestation of the movement. Incidentally, this perspective reflects attitudes I found among leaders and members of different and sometimes opposed orientations. No one saw in these oppositions within the Jamaa a proliferation of sects. Sectarianism in and around the Catholic church is deplored; discord in the Jamaa is experienced as a vital threat. It is something that does not just affect or modify the movement; discord endangers *umoja* [unity], and in the classical teachings of the Jamaa, unity has never been just a means, but an end in itself.

Because it held an ontological conception of its own identity, organization, and activities, the Jamaa has been able for a long time to resist or ignore outside pressure to behave like just another pious association. If, as its doctrine asserts, to be Jamaa is not only to be a good Catholic but a complete human being—in fact, the only way to be a complete human being—then the movement is not experienced by its members as a "voluntary association", to use a term that at one time had much currency in African studies. To express this, Tempels and other Jamaa leaders often denied that a movement called Jamaa existed. Self-identification as a specific movement would have been incompatible with the universalist logic of their humanism.

Ironically, the same ontological conception of identity that previously made the Jamaa immune to outside threats and temptations caused internal problems it was incapable of resolving. Because of these unresolved problems, the movement became weak and vulnerable so that the confrontation with the Church in the early 1970s had the effect it did. This statement requires some explanation. In the classical Jamaa, doctrine and organization were inextricably one. Both were realized as initiatory teaching/learning. I once expressed this as "becoming Jamaa is being Jamaa" (or the other way round). Ritualized teaching, the ritual of initiation—in fact all manners of participating in the activities of the movement, relating to one's spouse and to other couples—were considered realizations of *mawazo*. "Realization", that is, living these thoughts, was not conceived as applying moral rules to conduct—in this sense the Jamaa was an amoral movement—but as manifestations, proofs of life, fecundity, and love [*uzima, uzazi, na mapendo*]. These were the "three great *mawazo*" that made up *bumuntu*, what it means to be human, the central tenet of all Jamaa teaching.

Almost from the beginning, problems were caused by this ontological conception. It was not able to separate organizational forms or means from intellectual ends. If, as it was postulated by the Jamaa, initiation through teaching was to "give birth" to new member-couples [*kuzala*], hence a proof of fecundity [*uzazi*], then it became almost inevitable that leading members would be tempted to out-teach each other in order to maximize the proofs of their fecundity. At first this occurred as friendly competition, as demonstration of extraordinary fervor applauded by all. But then some leaders began to elaborate and intensify the ritual of initiation and to increase their lineages of spiritual kinship [*kizazi*] by actively recruiting candidates away from others. At any rate, the lineage concept, even in its spiritual interpretation, was inherently segmentary. Already in the 1960s the necessity was felt to counteract these tendencies that threatened to explode the movement.

In retrospect it seems likely that the willingness or unwillingness to meet that danger created the major line of fission that separated the orthodox Jamaa from a heterodox form then called Katete. The orthodox groups, urged by sympathizers among the clergy, began to create a new kind of forum in which leaders could meet and settle their differences above the level of local groups and kinship lines. These meetings were also used for the first attempts to codify *mafundisho* in writing (around 1961 in Kolwezi and 1967 in Lubumbashi). The documents that were composed then had little immediate effect on the oral practice of teaching, and the meetings were not successful in counteracting competition for fecundity. For outsiders and potential candidates, these struggles were difficult to understand. They further contributed to an image already tainted by suspicion of esoteric practices.

Thus the repressive measures that were eventually taken struck a Jamaa that was internally weakened. It had probably also passed the peak of its attractiveness to

African Catholics. As it turns out, repression, by forcing groups and individuals to face their commitments, actually helped the Jamaa to survive. Survival had its price, though. Painful choices had to be made and important changes accepted. Because a common basis for common response no longer existed, different leaders were taken into different directions.

In 1985–1986, there were at least four kinds or manifestations of the Jamaa movement in Shaba; elsewhere, especially in Kasai and Kivu, the situation may have differed slightly. However, the reports I have gathered suggest that Shaba remained the model for other areas.

First, there were groups in Lubumbashi and Likasi whose leaders and members submitted to abjuration and accepted a formal organization imposed on them. Under the supervision of clergy they abstained from activities banned as deviant and followed written and approved documents in their teaching. These "loyal" groups, as we may call them if we adopt the perspective of the mission church, were in communion with the hierarchy and were admitted to the sacraments and services. They called themselves *Jamaa Takatifu Katolika* (JTK) ["The Holy Catholic Jamaa"].[15]

Then there were groups in Lubumbashi and Kolwezi (and probably elsewhere) whose leaders and members either never submitted to abjuration or later recanted, claiming that they were misled. Technically, they were excommunicated by the Church, but they refused to accept this. Privately, they continued Jamaa teaching and initiation as before, while individuals and small groups quietly resumed attending mass and other church activities. They did not seek a clandestine continuation of the Jamaa and thought of their situation as transitory. In some cases they acted with the approval of individual pastors. By avoiding submission and continuing Jamaa activities without accepting new forms of organization or codification of doctrine, this cluster of groups had remained closest to the Jamaa of the 1960s; they called themselves simply *Jamaa*.[16]

In Lubumbashi and Kolwezi, leaders in this second category had at one time been associated with a third option, which eventually led to the foundation of an independent church called "The Holy Jamaa in Africa" [*Jamaa Takatifu mu Afrika,*] abbreviated JTAF, conforming to Zaïrean law regulating cults and churches. JTAF was represented in Kolwezi and Lubumbashi and many other places but had its headquarters outside industrial Shaba in the northern town of Kalemie. As far as I could tell from the materials gathered during my trips, this group had remained entirely faithful to Tempels's teachings (it stayed in contact with the founder until his death in 1977). It viewed its independent status as a necessity forced upon it by the Catholic church hierarchy, and it categorically denied being a sect or a form of Protestantism. To the outside observer interested in the history of Tempels's movement, JTAF is the most interesting among its recent manifestations.[17]

Finally in 1985–1986 there was a residual category of groups with little or no contact among themselves. It contained individuals and groups that continued to be inspired by Tempels's ideas. Among them were persons or couples who submitted to the Catholic church but chose not to continue actively with the loyal Jamaa. Many of them found a new social frame in the charismatic revival. According to some information I received, but was unable to confirm, the heterodox Katete of the 1960s also was surviving. Their most prominent leader had returned from Kolwezi to his rural home base, where his followers resurfaced as part of the Kitawala, one of the influential movements of the colonial era. In fact, several persons to whom I spoke recently insisted that the Katete was never anything else but Kitawala. Because the latter was banned during colonial and early postcolonial times it used the Jamaa and other religious groups as a cover.

CONCLUSION: PARADOXES OF POWER

Needless to say, this sketch of the situation in the 1980s gives little more than the barest outlines of the sociologically most conspicuous features that await deeper anthropological analysis. Survival through change and continuity through diversification are—apart from being commonplace—figures of speech that may give our account a certain plausibility without telling us much about the nature and content of that which is said to survive and continue. Moreover, the fact that the Jamaa took the road of diversification still requires explanation. How does diversification within the Jamaa relate to the proliferation of religious groups in its immediate and wider contexts?

In looking for answers, it is tempting to relate our observations on religious enthusiasm to events and behavior in the economic sector. Several of my Zaïrean interlocutors pointed to similarities between religious leadership and the development of small- and middle-sized business in Zaïre. The typical Zaïrean entrepreneur, it was pointed out to me (and I had some occasion to verify this), prefers to operate on his or her own. Business associations are relatively rare and short lived; exclusive control seems to be more important than the possibility to spread risks and divide the profits. What are the reasons for this? Are they simply a matter of economic constraints, endemic lack of trust in a sick society, or should one consider that they express cultural preferences and therefore choices rather than failures?

If these observations are correct, they must have some bearing on the question of power/authority/*pouvoir*. So far, we have asserted or implied the following: charismatic processes (in the sociological sense of charismatic), as illustrated by the Jamaa, have been involved in the emergence and legitimation of a certain kind of power. Whether or not certain laws have been operative (Weber's routinization, for instance), historical developments in Shaba during the last generation suggest that the principal change was not so much from enthusiasm to routinization, from charisma to a more formal *Herrschaftsform*, but from a concentration of charismatic authority to its dispersal or diversification. Must we regard this as just another instance of the decline in Zaïre, the same sort of decline that other observers have seen in the crisis of the state, of education, of ecclesiastic authority?[18] In other words, must we regard diversification as failure to assume power and responsibility, perhaps as an expression of the general economic and political powerlessness of Third World nations? When I noted that diversification assured the survival of the Jamaa, I implied another possibility. Dispersal of power certainly could be a matter of political strategy; it might also be a culturally specific way to conceive of power. At this moment, Zaïre lacks both a clearly defined external enemy and a truly antagonistic internal structure. The dispersal of power that can be observed in almost all areas where power can be exercised is therefore not likely to be a matter of strategy in fighting internal and external enemies. A different interpretation is conceivable. Since what I really have in mind is a self-interpretation of Zaïrean culture, I prefer to introduce it ethnographically rather than in abstract theoretical terms.

Because there are images illuminating intricate connections, and keywords capable of unlocking semantic spaces, there may also be communicative events that suddenly open up insights into a complicated praxis. In anthropological writing, such events, when reported, show up as anecdotes. As such they are suspect because, according to rigid canons, science needs cases, not anecdotes. Even if one does not subscribe to such rules, there is reason to be careful with anecdotes. Often it is difficult to tell whether it was the event that forced a new view on us or whether it was the story told of that event that convinced us. I fully agree with recent discussions in which the role of rhetoric in ethnography is stressed.[19] If we want to take rhetoric seriously, we must preserve the difference and tension between experience and account.

Having said this I shall now tell an anecdote, recalling an event that at first seemed rather insignificant but has since given me much food for thought. It will, I hope, throw some light on the situation we are trying to understand.[20]

About halfway through my 1985 visit to Shaba, I found myself one evening in the company of three Zaïreans, an electronics engineer, an architect, and an agronomist. The latter was a colorful person who had turned from government official into big cattle and grain farmer. In the course of that transformation, he had also become the founder and leader of a small independent church.[21] We all had met a few days earlier, and I was invited every evening to join this group of friends when they made their rounds, eating, drinking, and talking in their houses and in those of their women friends. That night, having already eaten a copious meal in one home, we went to a house belonging to Lukasu (meaning "the hoe" in Kiluba), as the farmer and prophet was called by his friends. In a large, barren, and ill-lit room whose walls and ceiling still showed the damage done by bullets and shrapnel during the last Shaba war, we settled down at a low table before a bowl of chicken, a huge *bukari* (the maize and manioc staple of the area), and a small wooden mortar of crushed peppers. An enamelled basin filled with water was placed on the floor next to the table. A young man and several women were ready to wait on us but kept themselves in the dark at the far end of the room. Earlier we had gotten into an animated discussion about religion, Bantu philosophy, and Placide Tempels and his Jamaa movement. We went on talking as we approached the table. Just as we sat down before the food there was a moment of tension. I had the feeling that, unlike the earlier meal that had been served in a bourgeois fashion—with plates, forks, and knives—this one was offered to me as a challenge or test. This was not just food, it was material for some kind of communion (a feeling that was confirmed later when our host announced that this was a very special occasion). My companions watched me. I wetted my hands in the water, asked for a towel, took a handful of *bukari*, kneaded it into shape, dipped it into the sauce accompanying the chicken and took the first bite. Immediately the tension broke; I had performed the appropriate acts in proper sequence and passed the test.

One of the men then reached out to the bowl of chicken and offered me the gizzard. This, he told me, is the piece reserved to the person of the highest rank.

Somewhat confused and embarrassed, I offered to share the choice piece. All three protested. The one who had offered it said, rather curtly, either you eat it or give it to me. It must have been obvious that I did not understand their reaction, certainly not its strength and unanimity. The explanation was quick and concise: *Le pouvoir se mange entier*. Power is eaten whole. That this dictum was pronounced in French took nothing away from its significance and authority. Its Luba origin was obvious even to me, and it became an occasion to return to our discussion of African philosophy. The meal continued pleasantly.[22]

Two things are striking about the saying that was quoted to me. First, it makes a connection between acquiring power and eating. The fact that in this case a meal was the occasion to invoke this cultural axiom only added force to an image long established. In the Kiluba language "to eat" is frequently used to denote access to power [*kudia bulopwe*]. It can also signify the conclusion of a special relationship or pact of friendship [*kudia bulunda*].[23] Indirectly, the image is operative in honorific titles or when, for example, the elephant is said to symbolize chiefly power, not only because of its strength, size, and so forth, but "because it eats more than other animals".

In sum, these are images that depict access to power as ingestion/incorporation rather than occupying a position or territory, or imposing order. Once ingested, as it were, power is internalized; it becomes like a person's weight, a property rather than a function. Of course there have been Luba potentates in the past (and there are Luba politicians in the present) who were also strategists of power. Still, it can be said that the dominant connotation in the cultural image we encountered comes close to Weber's notion of charisma as a personal property. What we catch in these societies with our sociological category of charismatic authority should therefore perhaps be regarded as the routine and not as an exception. It would then follow that to postulate in societies where *le pouvoir se mange entier*, logical or actual opposi-tions between charismatic authority and the forms designated as traditional or rational-bureaucratic may be an ethnocentric projection on our side.

But our axiom has another implication that requires interpretation. This is the stress laid on the *wholeness* of power. A paradoxical thought—because eating entails destruction (or digestion), and incorporation in one body means separation from other bodies. Power is here tied to concrete embodiments rather than to abstract structures. The point in this is not that power cannot be shared, but that one refuses to acknowledge disembodied "divisions" of power of the kind that charac-terize Western political thought.

Stress on incorporation and on the notion of wholeness—ontological ideas in the last analysis—creates a cultural logic in terms of which "concentration of power" will be tied to personal carriers. It will not meet expectations that we express, to cite Weber one more time, in the quasihistorical law of "rationalization", that is, an accumulation of power envisaged on the model of the accumulation of wealth and its attendant problems of organization (Weber 1964). Therefore, what looks to us at first like dissipation in the stronger or diversification in a weaker meaning may not be indicative of forced adaptation, much less of disintegration and decline. It may be the very form in which a particular cultural notion of power realizes itself. What looks paradoxical or simply confusing from the outside—the pursuit of power as ingestion and the insistence on its wholeness—expresses a cultural preference for a kind of anarchy, be it in religion, economics, or politics. When, in the area that interests us here, secular and religious authorities try to remedy a state of anarchy perceived by them as dangerous, they impose controls from the outside, often acting for outside powers. Such measures are not likely to "ameliorate" anything; they only oppose different theories of power. When the Zaïrean government, which after all must operate in its own cultural context, alternates between repression of, and tolerance toward, the proliferation of religious groups this may be interpreted by outsiders as a sign of weakness (or yet another instance of corruption, since large sums of money are involved when groups apply for official recognition). It may also indicate that the Zaïrean state, other than the Catholic church, enacts a culturally valued anarchy based on notions that encourage the ardent pursuit of power, as well as the proliferation of its embodiments.

NOTES

1. Earlier versions of this chapter were presented as conference papers at the Colloque Franco-Allemand, Paris, November 1985 (a meeting of French and German Africanists) and the Variety of Religious Experience in Sub-Saharan Africa conference at Brigham Young University, Provo, Utah, 23–25 October 1986. Travel to Zaïre was supported by a grant from the Subfaculty of Social Science, University of Amsterdam. I am grateful to J. Dassas for the hospitality he offered in Lubumbashi and to Kitenge M. and Tshunza M., who made possible the trip to Kolwezi. Members of the Jamaa and of the charismatic prayer groups, too numerous to be named here, generously contributed their time, energy, and thoughts to this project. I must insist that this paper is a first attempt to construct a sociological frame for further anthropological questions. It is based largely on firsthand information and impressions; little attention is paid at this point to the vast literature that could be cited. Also absent from this account is most of the ethnography that will eventually be part of a fuller report (documents, printed and oral texts, taped conversations, and so forth).

2. As far as I know, De Craemer 1977 and Fabian 1971 remain the only book-length studies of the Jamaa. There have been several memoirs and dissertations of which only Zabala 1974 was based on sociological inquiry in Lubumbashi.

3. Lloyd Fallers was the first to make that connection (see his preface to Fabian 1971). To my knowledge it has not been followed up systematically. For a more recent article on the Balokole, including references to the existing literature, see Winter 1983.

4. My own attempt to place research on the Jamaa into the context of social change theory was published in 1969. For a thorough revision of these views a decade later, see Fabian 1981.

5. For the full text of the list of abjurations compiled by the conference of bishops of the Shaba and Kasai regions (at a meeting in Lubumbashi, 15–20 January 1973), see Zabala 1974:113–119 and Tshibangu 1974:46ff. (French version only).

6. I first reported these events in Fabian 1979b:201–203. On my recent trips I was given more detailed information. I realize that my account makes or implies grave allegations regarding the violation of human rights. I therefore must insist that, at this time, I merely report testimony by members of the Jamaa whom, for obvious reasons, I cannot name. I should also note that, within the possibilities given to them by the Zaïrean system, Jamaa groups and individuals have engaged in legal action to protect their rights.

7. Several of these entities have been the subject of mémoires de licence at the University of Lubumbashi. There has also been an attempt to construct a typology based on an inventory of more than 100 "churches" and "communities" in Lubumbashi. The author dates this

proliferation to 1971 (promulgation of *l'ordonnance-loi No. 71/012*, December 21) when the Zaïrean government first defined conditions for the recognition of "cults" and churches; see Lukanga Dende 1983. At least one other legal text seems to have been published in 1979 (*ordonnance-loi No. 79002*, January 3). In June 1986 the local press reported, "There are 227 religious sects in Lubumbashi of which 75% operate illegally"—leaving an impressive number of "legal" churches, movements, communities, and so forth.

8. Two texts on the history and nature of the charismatic renewal in Zaïre were available locally: Verhaegen 1983 and *Le Renouveau, une Chance pour l'Eglise Africaine.* Important indirect information, especially on the problems this movement poses for the Church hierarchy, is contained in a pastoral letter by Archbishop Kabanga (in French and Swahili, printed in Lubumbashi, no date). He also seems to have appealed to his confrere, Archbishop Emmanuel Milingo of Lusaka in Zambia, probably the most prominent African Catholic charismatic. Milingo visited Lubumbashi around 1974 (I was unable to get the exact date) but did not leave much of an impression on local leaders, mainly because of language difficulties. On his ideas, see Milingo 1984. One example from the vast literature on charismatic renewal in which its worldwide impact is reviewed is Martin and Mullen 1984.

9. For the loyal Jamaa (JTK), see their *Règlement d'ordre intérieur* approved by Archbishop Kabanga on 9 June 1974. This was published as part of the officially approved text of Jamaa teachings (Comité ya Jamaa 1975:1–3). In 1986 a further step toward formalization was taken. A project of "statutes" formulated with the help of a jurist, member of JTK, was formulated and submitted to the hierarchy for approval. It was discussed at a conference of the local clergy in Lubumbashi that failed to come up with an official response. JTK leaders interpreted silence as approval and organized a national congress to discuss the project. It took place after my departure in July. For the dissident, independent *Jamaa takatifu mu Afrika* (JTAF), the "Holy Family in Africa", see their detailed "Outline of functions in our Church, the Holy Family in Africa", JTAF 1984–85.

10. In the Archdiocese of Lubumbashi, a pastoral committee officially supervises all prayer groups. That committee was involved in formulating the pastoral letter cited in note 8. Some of its members inform me that it has been more or less inactive since mid-1985.

11. Two important sources on the history of labor economics and urbanization in Shaba are Fetter 1976 and Perrings 1979. For an account of connections between labor history and linguistic and other cultural policies, see Fabian 1986.

12. One of the most encompassing works demonstrating the middle-class roots, individualism, and entrepreneurship in many religious movements of the type to which the international charismatic renewal belongs is still the collection of essays edited by Zaretsky and Leone 1974. Notice also that in the document on Zaïrean pentecostalism that I cited in note 8, this movement is traced back to the so-called Cursillo (Verhaegen 1983:12). On the Cursillo see the 1982 study by Marcoux. When Marcene Marcoux, then a student of mine, began her investigations around 1970, she was very much aware of the Jamaa. We did not know then that scholarly comparison would one day be overtaken by actual confrontation— thanks to "global circulation". See also on that notion, Fabian 1981.

13. The most notorious case is that of Abbé Pius Kasongo, one of several African Catholic priests in Shaba who, in the early 1970s, began to exercise charismatic gifts. Kasongo became the leader of one of the largest prayer groups in Lubumbashi and had great success as a healer. When he defied orders by his bishop to return to Kolwezi, he was eventually suspended from his rights and duties as a priest (in 1983). He nevertheless continued to live at a Catholic parish (in the compound of the mining company) and to use adjacent grounds for his mass meetings. His political support among the middle class and elites of Lubumbashi has been strong enough to make the hierarchy back away from legal action. Kasongo, although we had become acquainted years ago, was the only important religious leader who refused to talk to me during my 1985 trip. Finally it came to a meeting

at the end of my stay in 1986. Kasongo refused a recorded interview but gave me a published documentation of the activities of his group, Alimasi and Kasongo 1985.

14. For instance, in one of the groups that invited me to several meetings, participants took off their shoes before entering the room. This interior sacred space (called *Mont Olivier*) has an exterior counterpart in the form of a small enclosure called *Israel*, which serves for preparation and meditation. Another classical opposition I encountered was that between inhabited space and the "desert" or bush [*jangwa* or *pori*]; the latter seems to play a role especially in the quest for visions and experience. All this awaits detailed analysis before we can determine whether these notions are simply taken over, as ready-made elements—partly from Protestant churches and related groups and partly extending the use and meaning of autochthonous spatial configurations and concepts (see also T. Blakely, forthcoming)—or whether they were developed independently within the prayer groups.

15. Information gathered in the form of documents, taped meetings, and conversations with leading members, most prominent among them Baba Seba (Nkondo), who had been a leader of the Jamaa in Lubumbashi twenty years ago. In 1985, I met with Baba Seba and his wife at least once a week. In 1986, our meetings were somewhat less frequent. Baba Seba died in 1989.

16. Information based on several meetings with members of that group at Kolwezi. Some of the leaders I had known since 1966. I found them rather intransigent then (see Fabian 1971:93ff.) and they don't seem to have changed much since. More than other groups they also showed signs of age and weariness. In 1986 I met with B. Kaumba V., the most prominent leader in Lubumbashi. The attitudes I had found in Kolwezi were confirmed. The reception was as polite as the refusal to discuss detail was adamant.

17. Information based on contacts (taped conversations, meetings, services) with JTAF groups in Musonoi (near Kolwezi) and Ruashi (Lubumbashi). In these groups, too, I found old friends from the 1960s and was given a rather overwhelming reception. Important information was added in 1986 when I met with the leader of JTAF, B. Lutema Kapiteni (of Kalemie), and was given a copy of the church's catechism (see JTAF 1984).

18. Three publications document the agonies of Zaïre—and those of the experts trying to understand what is going on: *Canadian Journal of African Studies* 1984; Young and Turner 1985; and Nzongola-Ntalaja 1986.

19. To cite but one example, see Clifford 1983, also a source for further references. I myself have tried to make the case at some length in Fabian 1983.

20. While this essay was awaiting publication, I completed a study of conceptions of power in Shaha in which the anecdote to be told also plays an important role (Fabian 1990).

21. Called *Sifa lwa Bwana* [roughly: Praise to the Lord]. As I learned from another source, most or all of his followers are small peasants and agricultural workers who are employed or otherwise dependent on the church leader's farms.

22. Incidentally, I gave the piece back to him and he ate it.

23. I had heard the expression in a persiflage of a speech made by one of the politicians of the first hour (J. Sendwe, I believe), who began his discourse with "*Depuis que j'ai mangé mon pouvior*". Regarding the rich semantics of *kudia* in Kiluba, the language of the Baluba of Shaba, see Van Avermaet and Mbuya 1954:106 ff. The meaning of *le pouvoir se mange entier* took on a new dimension when in 1986 a group of actors, the *Troupe Théatrale Mufwankolo*, chose it as the topic of a piece. I was able to assist and document its production through all the phases from group discussion to rehearsal and the performance filmed in a village near Lumbumbashi. The results of this sort of "performative ethnography" confirmed my intuitions regarding the importance of this cultural axiom (see Fabian 1990).

15

Protestant Missions in Africa:
The Dialectic of Conversion in the American Methodist Episcopal Church in Eastern Zimbabwe, 1900–1950

Terence O. Ranger

INTRODUCTION

W E ARE BEGINNING TO realize that during the missionary period the foundations of a vigorous African Christianity were laid. We are also beginning to realize that these foundations were laid in a concealed and mysterious manner. Very little developed as the missionaries planned or hoped or feared. Hence historians of the Christian Movement in Africa have to read between the lines of missionary records, passing by apparent but illusory triumphs in order to locate real but unperceived successes. It is tempting to seek for true sources of African Christian history outside missionary archives altogether—in the oral reminiscences of the African Christian creators of the church. Indeed, if we had to choose between one source or the other, such personal reminiscences would no doubt get us closer to the truth. Yet the emergence of an African Christianity was a dialectical process, an interaction between missionary and African consciousness. We need sources of both missionary and African provenance and we need to learn how to read the one in the light of the other.

Between 1980 and 1983, in my research on the history of eastern Zimbabwe, I collected missionary records of the three main mission churches—the Catholics, the Anglicans, and the American Methodists. I also collected oral testimonies from African members of those churches. I became fascinated by the different atmosphere of the three African popular Christianities that had grown up in eastern Zimbabwe. All had grown out of the same eastern Shona cultural context and all shared a recognizable common Africanity. None were reproductions of the parent mission church. Yet each seemed quite distinct from the others. Plainly there now exist an African popular Catholicism, an African popular Anglicanism, and an African popular Methodism.

In a number of papers I have tried to explain why some eastern Shona have drawn upon Catholicism, others upon Anglicanism, and yet others upon Methodism. I have advanced some more or less crude (if effective and so far as they go true) socio-economic correlations. I have also tried to show how Anglican and Catholic ideas of the pilgrimage and of the holy place were drawn upon by missionary and African convert alike (Ranger 1984, 1987a). But this leaves me with the problem of popular African Methodism. Methodists tried hard not to develop holy places and frowned upon pilgrimages. They possessed no doctrine of the saints that might have made a connection with African ideas about the continued significance of the dead. Methodists possessed, in short, none of those resources of theology, ritual, and symbol that seem to have offered for both Catholicism and Anglicanism such natural points of contact with eastern Shona ideas and practices. Yet there is no doubt that a committed, even a passionate, African popular Methodism did arise.

It is my aim in this chapter to explore the dialectic between American Methodist belief and practice and the uses made of these by groups among the eastern Shona. I am assisted in doing so by the very Protestantism of the American Methodist Episcopal Church (AMEC). Many Protestant churches in Africa have laid a particular emphasis on the autobiographical testimonies of their converts. They have also possessed a keen historical consciousness, wishing to put on record the dispensations of Providence. Hence from the beginning, Protestant publications have printed African conversion testimonies and these, however stereotyped in form, can nevertheless provide a way in to the African side of the dialectic. Moreover, even if published Protestant mission histories have almost always offered nothing but an external and misleading account of the rise of the African churches, the archives established by Protestant missions often include material of a very different significance.

THE AMERICAN METHODIST EPISCOPAL CHURCH
AS AN EXAMPLE OF PROTESTANT MISSION

Missionaries of the American Methodist Episcopal Church (AMEC) recognized themselves the mysterious and hidden nature of the processes of growth of African Methodism. They insisted, of course, on the centrality of their own contribution. In 1932, for example, Mrs. John Springer repudiated the idea that the missionary methods of St. Paul had been vastly superior to those of evangelists in Africa:

> Paul had no need to start schools to teach ABC's; the schools were already in existence. He did not need to start Bible Schools for the training of pastors, for there were those at hand who had already been taught the Scriptures from their youth up. ...
>
> [Can] we expect [Africans] to accept the Gospel and immediately to set out to evangelise their own people with no Bible, no primer, no hymn book, no school? I do not say that it cannot be done but I do not know of any place where it has been done. ...
>
> The usual method of most missions in Africa has been to get a few teachers or workers from other tribes to go with one in the starting of a new Mission. ... Schools are started and the process of evangelisation begins. Sometimes it takes years ... to even get a nucleus of native Christians. But with the advance of trade and the opening up of the country, results have come sooner owing to the fact that the Natives have been more open to the Gospel teachings. Then as the groups of

Natives come to the missionary for schools, they are first induced to build their own chapels and later on to feed their own teachers. (Mrs. Springer 1932)

Yet this gradualism was really foreign to the spirit of the AMEC. "God is in a wonderful way pouring out His Holy Spirit on our native work", wrote the missionary Robert Wodehouse from Umtali in July 1903. "It is just wonderful how rapidly God does the work of conversion and enlightenment".[1] "Three years ago there was nothing", wrote Wodehouse in April 1904. "We have had many conversions, genuine old-fashioned conversions. I think we ought to look for and expect conversions. It does not take God's Spirit long to do this gracious work in a dark heathen heart".[2] Wodehouse and other missionaries noted that most of these rapid conversions were achieved by African Christians themselves. "The boys I have talked with", wrote T. A. O'Farrell in a report on evangelisation in 1911,

> very frequently mention some native preacher who seems to have helped them very much. The boys seldom said that they had been helped by white missionaries. I suppose these spiritual matters require the close heart to heart talks that are more likely to occur between two natives than between a native and a white man. ... There is also a considerable number who profess Christianity in the isolated kraal thru the preaching of boys who have been to the mines or to schools. How far these people can go without more careful teaching it is hard to say.[3]

The same pattern recurred in Mozambique. In 1909 W. C. Terril, the superintendent of Inhambane District, reported a rapid increase in converts despite the small numbers of white missionaries.

> The work propagates itself, according to laws of the Kingdom of God. A native comes and wishes permission to go out and start a station. We give him a few school supplies ... Many are leaving their heathen lives. ... I am puzzled to know why there has been so much success with such a lack of qualified men. My only answer would be that God has blessed and is blessing the work of His people.[4]

These seem rather like the methods of dozens of black St. Pauls.

In the years that followed, the missionaries established central institutions that provided "more careful teaching" and turned out more "qualified men". Yet there remained an awareness, at moments at least, that the rhythms of church growth had little to do with the intensities of missionary activity:

"And he said, So is the Kingdom of God, as if a man should cast seeds into the ground; and should sleep, and rise night and day and the seed should spring and grow up, he knoweth not how. Thus cometh the Kingdom of God in Rhodesia. Time after time during the past Conference year", H. I. James told the AMEC Conference in 1932,

> this short parable of our Lord has come to my mind in the events of the work. For a number of years our missionaries have been growing less in number and funds from the Home Church growing less to an alarming extent, but the work goes on and the seed sown springs up and grows—we know not how. After three years of economic depression acutely touching the members of our Church, I feel confident in saying that the Native Church was never so strong as now. What wonders God hath wrought. The Native Church has been established. It has its own ministry ... all strong virile Christian men.[5]

AMEC missionaries knew that this rapid Christianization, carried out by black pastor-teachers, must inevitably produce something new and different. Sometimes they compared what was happening in Africa—with a sort of nostalgic envy—to their own past:

> In many cases one has been reminded of Methodism's early days. A quarterly conference at Bokisi [in Inhambane, Mozambique] furnishes an example. ... While the sermon was being preached a solemn hush came on the audience and soon weeping was heard, and in a few moments there was a coming to the altar. It was not long before the whole audience was on its knees before God in earnest prayer, some for pardon, others for cleansing and still others for power with God and man. Heaven was very near and the Spirit came in power. ... These experiences teach us that the African can be converted, blessed and kept the same as any other people, by the power of the Gospel of Christ.[6]

But this was still too much to domesticate African popular Methodism. Others were aware of its peculiarity. "We must not think", wrote E. L. Sells in 1936, "that everyone who hears the Gospel is immediately changed into a Christian of Western culture and civilization. We would not want it so if it could be true. Christ deals with the Black man in Black man's ways" (Sells 1936:21). Similarly, in 1944 the superintendent of Mtasa/Makoni District, Per Hassing, told the Annual Conference:

> My work among the African population has shown me the power of the Gospel of Christ. My six brethren in the ministry have been travelling and working faithfully among the people. The longer I work with them, the greater becomes my respect for them. ... At some places we have seen something of a revival among the people. ... The message of Jesus Christ shows its power wherever it is spoken in the Holy Spirit, and where man does not interfere with it. Things that are strange to our western trained eyes are surely happening in many of our meetings. But very many strange things indeed were happening in the early Church as it is pictured in our New Testament. It always follows when the Gospel enters a new culture and environment.[7]

I have been highly selective in these citations, of course. Most missionary reports emphasized the need for close white supervision and stressed the "savagery" out of which they thought African Christians had so recently come. When a "historical" section appeared in the Rhodesia Mission Conference's official journal from 1917 onwards, it consisted of lists of missionaries "with the dates of entering and leaving the work". Despite fugitive glimpses of another dynamic of growth, official AMEC history was a chronicle of missionary endeavor. Several factors accounted, however, for a constant reflection in mission publications of the African Christian experience.

African Public Testimonies and Sermons as Historical Sources

One factor was the insistence within American Methodism upon public confession and testimony. At the first session of the East Central Africa Mission Conference, for example, the assembled missionaries shared in a Lovefeast led by Bishop Joseph Hartzell and "the different members of the Mission related the dealings of

God with them in their conversion, their preparation and their appointment to service". In the printed minutes of the conference many of these testimonies are given. The testimonies follow an established Methodist idiom, telling of the darkness or coldness in which the testifiers had previously lived, the way in which they had struggled against the promptings of the Holy Spirit, their eventual surrender to the inner voices and dispensations of Providence. In the testimony of Wodehouse there is even an African dimension, directly parallel to the experiences of many subsequent black converts:

> It was at a Methodist revival meeting in Grahamstown, South Africa, that I found Christ when a lad of fifteen; I, with some companions went forward to the penitent form; we did not find peace there, but went out into the Bush to pray, and before we returned that night we settled the matter and accepted Christ.[8]

At this first conference African agents of the mission also testified:

> Tizore Navess, the native pastor of the Makodweni Church of the Inhambane District, was called forward and he gave a statement of his conversion and work. ...George Mpondo, the interpreter and teacher employed at the native church in Umtali, gave a statement of his conversion.

On this occasion the actual text of these testimonies was not published, but readers were told that Navess had "made an extempore address of much merit. Among the things which he mentioned was the early coming of the Missionary, his surprise and joy on learning of the possibility of unending life, his early interest in religion and his sound conversion".[9] Soon African testimonies were being published in full and became a consistent feature of AMEC publications. The minutes of the Sixth Session of the East Central Africa Mission Conference, held in 1909, include no fewer than thirteen African testimonies, some of which I shall quote later in this chapter. These conversion narratives were reassuring evidence of the true Methodist character of the infant African church. At the same time, however, they did not follow exactly the conventional forms of the American testimonies, and there is much to be learnt from them of the specificities of the African Christian experience.

Public testimonies by African Christians certainly did not take place only at formal annual conferences. These testimonies constituted an essential part of the spread of popular Christianity by Africans themselves. As Wodehouse wrote in 1904:

> Several members gave most interesting accounts of their reception at the heathen kraals where they were brought up. ... We have always urged them to pray aloud during their devotions—especially at heathen kraals, as the natives come out and listen and in many cases are brought under conviction. We have some most interesting cases where the young converts have not been ashamed to confess Christ and their friends have been saved as a result.[10]

Such public confessions and professions became so much a feature of popular African Methodism that in 1909 the missionary Shirley Coffin claimed that "the methods of Methodism" were "wonderfully adapted to work among these people. The evangelistic service, the Class meeting, the voluntary testimony and prayer customs which obtain among us, our hymns ... all seem to be just what fits the need in our efforts to Christianize the people".[11]

African testimonies were so useful, indeed, that large collections of them were made and many still survive at the Old Umtali archives.[12] They were printed in the vernacular broadsheet *Umbowo Hwe Ukristu* [Witness of Christianity], which was published from 1917 on as a vehicle for African pastor-teachers and which mixed accounts of the wonders of popular African Methodism with articles on "Hygiene ne Sanitation". They were also published in the English-medium *African Advance*, produced at Old Umtali for supporters of the mission in the United States. In October 1916, for example, *African Advance* carried accounts by two "Twice-Born Men", Nathan Gwizo and Furness Chatepa, and commented:

> These men tower as do the mountains, mighty examples and effective agents of the Saving Grace of God. It is upon such that the seed time and harvest of this great field depends. ... There is no support for these men for 1917. Long-time shares are needed or work abandoned. Two to four 25 dollar shares will support a station for a year, and ten to twenty villages will be reached.[13]

African testimonies were published separately as little fly sheets, such as *Read What Three Twice-Born Men of Africa Have to Say Concerning Their Experiences*, in which the missionary Sells followed revealing accounts by Murumbi Makoni, Moses Razunguzwa, and Gibson Chikungwu with the comment that readers will have been able to see from them "how the fear and grip of the witch-doctor and the slavery of superstition takes hold upon the African. ... No advance can be made socially or economically until he is spiritually converted and delivered from such domination. Economic betterment cannot take place until fear and superstition are removed from agriculture and health".[14]

African Christian testimonies—made use of and interpreted in all these ways—constituted a major genre of both official and popular Methodism in eastern Zimbabwe and Mozambique. Nothing similar survives for eastern Zimbabwean Catholicism or Anglicanism. AMEC missionaries not only had a particular interest in testimonies, they also had a particular interest in sermons. The enunciation of the Word was sometimes enough in itself to produce saving effects. Wodehouse wrote in 1903 of one of his African pastor-teachers, "Charles is a powerful preacher and it is no unusual thing for the heathen to drop as if struck by a rifle ball under his preaching".[15] In 1913 Bishop Hartzell described an assembly of a thousand Africans at Old Umtali:

> The sermons and addresses by missionaries and natives were of a high order. ... As I was describing the return of the prodigal son, the native leaders and people started a movement forward and fell on their faces around me. In a moment, the great audience was prostrated on the grassy ground. There was no noise except one universal subdued sob.[16]

In 1913, too, the Committee on the State of the Church found that "among the natives we are seeing fulfilled that prophecy as is recorded in the Psalms, 'As soon as they hear they shall obey me'".[17] Since the Word was so powerful, missionaries were naturally interested to learn what African pastor/teachers were saying in their sermons. Thus we have several records of African preaching. In the AMEC Archives at Old Umtali, for instance, there is a packet of material collected together in 1916 by H. N. Howard, with a note by his wife: "Monday mornings when older boys came in from their teaching assignments of the day before, Mr. Howard would inquire about their experiences, their sermons, their illustrations. I would take them down for future use. Mr. Howard considered these to be of special value".[18] Some of the sermons in the packet, and these the most illuminating, were written down in English by the men concerned. In this way a good deal was recorded about the early African Methodist experience at the time.

RESEARCH FOR THE HISTORICAL SOCIETY: SELLS AND MACHUMA

More was recorded as the AMEC in eastern Zimbabwe developed a historical consciousness. The African edition of the AMEC *Discipline* laid it down:

> In each Annual Conference there shall be a Historical Society, to be appointed or elected in whatever manner the Conference may decide, whose duties shall be to preserve the records of the Conference, gather all data referring to its organisation, its past history, its former members, and to collect all data of interest from the memories of elderly persons and to preserve these for future generations ... and to keep before the minds of our people the glorious deeds of the heroes of the past.[19]

The Rhodesia Conference set up a historical committee in 1935. The committee was mainly interested in formal written records and in collections of missionary correspondence, but from the beginning it appealed to "Native Ministers, as well as to missionaries".[20] In 1937 four of the most senior African ministers were added to the committee. In 1941 it was reorganized as a historical society, with a commitment to hold public meetings on topics of interest to Methodists.

The moving spirit of the society was E. L. Sells, who served for some thirty years as custodian-archivist. Sells was interested, as we have seen, in African testimonies and he deposited collections of them in the archives. But he was still more interested in the "objective" written record. It was the aim of the society, he wrote in 1952, to make "accurate information" available, since "it was long realized that the traditional information was not all based on facts but hearsay passed on from one to another with such personal interpretation as best fitted the story". Insofar as Sells was interested in the oral tradition, his emphasis was still on missionaries. "The Old Missionaries are about all gone and with them will go the historical information".[21]

As the church became more and more dominated by African ministers, however, the emphasis changed. In 1966 the society noted that "materials by, from, and about African Christians themselves are greatly needed".[22] The real change came in 1969 when a full-time African archivist was appointed. The position went to Shepherd Machuma, who in the two or three years that the AMEC funded the post brought quite another dimension to the historical consciousness of the church. In 1973 Machuma declared his credo to the annual conference: "Since we should be proud of our church and of our tribal history—the cornerstone of our character and behaviour—I want to lay greater emphasis on the *importance of our people learning the worthwhile teachings of our Church and of our tribal life and of putting them into practice".*[23] The pre-Christian past was no longer to be seen as "savagery", but as a source of character. Machuma had already presented this new view of the African Methodist past in the columns of *Umbowo*. In May 1972 he asked rhetorically: "Why do we so often work and talk like our parents? We are made of the past". He then added: "To some people history is not history unless it is written down. ... Memory has always connected people with the past". He busied himself in the collection of black African Methodist oral tradition from surviving pioneers of the church and from their descendants. These transcribed traditions—now in the AMEC Archives—often relate the precolonial status and achievements of the pioneers to their subsequent role as Christian leaders.[24]

In October 1972 Machuma contributed to the *Umbowo* issue honoring the 75th anniversary of Old Umtali. Machuma noted that the site had been given to Bishop Hartzell by Cecil Rhodes and that this act had always constituted the starting point of official AMEC history. Machuma added, however, that prior to the Rhodes gift, the "great leader and *n'anga*" Mutiaera had lived on Chiremba mountain facing Old Umtali, thereby establishing a sort of spiritual tradition. Machuma's account of the subsequent history of the church, while giving all too much space to the missionaries, nevertheless emphasized especially the emergence of the two African lay associations, the male Wabvuwi in 1918 and the female Rukwadzano in 1930.[25] In the following months Machuma told the history of the church in more detail in a "From the Archives" series in *Umbowo*, beginning with two conventional narratives of the doings of the first missionaries but at once following these with two articles on "How the Mutasa Tribe was founded" (Machuma 1972–73).

Machuma's published material amounted to a very cautious revision of the official history. But his collection of oral traditions, still available at Old Umtali, amounts to a full-fledged alternative version of the rise of popular Methodism in eastern Zimbabwe. No doubt some of this material was influenced by the emotions of African nationalism and is to that extent anachronistic. But if we use it to throw light on those early African testimonies and sermons, and vice versa, it is possible to reconstruct a good deal of the African side of the dialectic of conversion. We can see how particular groups among the African peoples of eastern Zimbabwe responded to and drew upon AMEC thought and practice.

I have written of a "popular" Methodism, but it is important to note here that Machuma's oral traditions and the records of African testimonies do not represent "the people", however we might define them. We are dealing here with groups of past or future privilege—chiefs or the sons of chiefs, evangelists who emerge as the real local leaders of a powerful new movement, agricultural and commercial entrepreneurs. Even when we come to see the way subordinated and exploited women found a weapon in Methodism, we must note the elite and exclusive character of the leadership of the women's Christian association. Though evidence for the atmosphere of African Methodism in eastern Zimbabwe is abundant, this evidence does not extend so far as to throw much light on the experience of the ordinary villager.

THE THEOLOGY AND PRACTICE
OF MISSIONARY AMERICAN METHODISM

A further advantage of the AMEC to a historian of the dialectic of conversion is that its missionaries made frequent and explicit theological statements. They believed, first, that God had given a special commission to Methodism in Central Africa:

> Paul had a great overmastering desire to lay Rome at the feet of Christ. Why? It was the heart of the world at that time and he longed to seize that heart and lay it at the feet of the Master. ... Africa in a very true sense is the heart of the world today. ... I purpose for myself to join with my fellow workers in the grace, strength, and power of Almighty God to do my best to save America by saving Africa and laying this great continent at the feet of our Master.[26]

AMEC IN AFRICA: BLACK EMANCIPATION, NON-CATHOLICISM, AND INDIVIDUAL RELIGIOUS EXPERIENCE

For three reasons, the AMEC had a special role to play in winning Africa. First was its record of work for blacks. The Committee on the State of the Church wrote in 1916:

> Twenty years ago when talk was rife of giving up the work in Africa, when Africa had few friends ... Bishop Hartzell was elected as Missionary Bishop for Africa. In all other respects it was a dark hour for the Dark Continent. But Bishop Hartzell had been born for hard places. For the previous thirty years he had been standing in hard places for the black man of the Southern States. Thrown into that seething cauldron of the reconstruction days ... his was the duty to shield, cultivate, and bring to fruition the seed of civilization among the blacks of the South.[27]

The AMEC stood for black emancipation and progress. "The spirit for freedom and desire for Truth is abroad. The Methodist Church stands essentially for these two things".[28]

The second reason the AMEC was peculiarly equipped to work in Africa was its opposition to Roman Catholicism. In 1911 AMEC missionaries in southern Mozambique rejoiced at the proclamation of the Republic in Portugal: "With it came the expulsion of the Jesuit—the power of Rome as a state church was broken. We are certain that God's hand is in it all, and that these His people shall no longer sit in darkness but shall behold that 'Great Light'. Ethiopia is literally stretching out her hand to God". The people of southern Mozambique were calling for missionaries—"Here are more than a million souls who are under no Christian influence, that is, they are not touched by Protestant Missions".[29] The AMEC personnel at Old Umtali looked yearningly across the border into central Mozambique: "Portuguese East Africa is stretching out its appealing hands to East African Methodism, and lifting its pagan, ignorant heart to God, the God of Methodism. God hears, but Methodism seems to be deaf".[30] It was a tremendous opportunity, believed the committee on the state of the church. For centuries, they thought, Catholicism had done nothing but deepen the darkness in Mozambique. Now the revolution in Portugal had opened the door "for the preaching of the 'sincere word'". The Portuguese authorities had been impressed by AMEC work at Old Umtali and Kambini. "We are the only church that is doing the work on sane and fundamental lines. If we could at this time go into the Portuguese country we feel sure that we could establish ourselves there so firmly that we could claim that vast empire for Christ under the Methodist banner".[31] In Southern Rhodesia [Zimbabwe], too, the AMEC saw themselves as engaged in confrontation with Catholicism. In 1919, H. N. Howard urged an expansion of the work in Mrewa district, where Catholicism had shown "marked activity":

> We do not believe that the native is being helped as he should be by the ministrations of this Church. The medieval attitude of this denomination with its dogmatism and the great amount of licence allowed the native appeals to the undeveloped mind, and the native, who relies on magic in his own customs, is not greatly elevated by the new kind of magic which he imbibes in the name of the living God.[32]

The third reason the AMEC felt it had a special commission from God was that it was part of what Bishop Hartzell called "the advancing waves of Anglo-Saxon civilization northward toward the heart of Africa".[33] In 1917 a special conference called "Committee on the World War and America's Responsibility Therein" set out the AMEC view on the balance in the world:

> "The alignment today is the free, peace-loving peoples against despotism and war. ... God has given to us of His stores that liberty might not die. The individual is still fighting against collectivism". Once Protestant England had stood out against collectivist Catholic Spain; now the Anglo-Saxon world stood out against "perfidious, frightful, ruthless trouble-making Prussianism". "God is on the side of the development of the individual. ... The Spirit's work is with the individual".[34]

The centrality of the individual experience of the Spirit was the main theological proposition of the AMEC in eastern Zimbabwe: "In common with all the churches", wrote O'Farrell,

> we have Jesus Christ, The Holy Spirit, and the Word to feed upon. But we also have a religion of experience, the observance of which has meant much to Methodism. The very power of Methodist Christianity has been such that in a comparatively short time we have become a world church. ... Our people everywhere are grounded upon religious experience.[35]

THE VERNACULAR WRITTEN WORD: BIBLE TEXTS AND HYMNS

All the work of missionaries and African pastor-teachers was directed towards precipitating religious experience in individuals. As we have seen, the sermon was a key instrument for achieving this; so also was public testimony. But the AMEC did not believe that the spoken word was enough:

> And He said unto me write. And John was able to say: "These things have I written". And John wrote many things. Indeed he has written enough to form the basis for a complete code of morals and a justice that would regulate all human relationships and a perfect code for four-square manhood and highest spiritual

attainment. But what would the world be today without "What is written" ? ... King Josiah when he began to clean house, after his father and grandfather, found "The Books of the Law". When he caused them to be read terrible fear took hold upon him for he saw how woefully Israel had strayed from the path God had directed them in. They had been without the writing.

For the whole of the dark unwritten past of the African races there is not a single sign of a written page. ... The highway to constantly rising levels of human life and living is paved with good books. ..., Africa must have books. The situation is imperative. The supreme need is for religious and educational literature in the vernacular. These are not only absolutely essential to permanent missionary work in building up an all-round religious, social and industrial order, but in view of such a shamefully inadequate missionary force on the field it is essential to even the slightest progress.[36]

So the early missionaries worked with their first converts to create a written vernacular, and a press was set up at Old Umtali, "putting ink into missionary and Gospel messages at twelve-hour-a-day pace".[37]

What was translated and printed first was, of course, *the* Book and the pastor-teachers carried with them printed vernacular passages of the Bible from which they read the saving Word. As early as 1901, E. H. Richards described his teachers in Inhambane district None could pass an examination in any subject, he wrote: "But he has the true Spirit, prays a great deal and knows the Gospels very well indeed He is fairly well read in the Zulu Bible and in the Tonga Testament. ... Our teachers are only capable of teaching to read through the Gospels, and add or multiply a trifle. ... [Yet] our evangelistic work has been tremendous considering the agents at work".[38] Soon there were conversion testimonies that stressed either reading the Bible or hearing the Bible read as the key to their salvation experience. Furness Chatepa described in 1916 how he had begun to read "an English Bible" when "I was not a Christian yet". Later "I had good time to read about God". When he was asked by a missionary to become an evangelist he at first refused but then remembered from his reading that "Jesus said in the Gospel if you refuse me in this world I will refuse you before my Father which is in Heaven and I told the missionary now let me go anywhere". Nathan Gwizo described how:

> In his preaching the African teacher said there was a man this man was Noah. God told him to tell the people that they are not living right but when Noah talked to the people they did not listen and God destroyed all ... and I was not know what to do, because he said there was no place for anyone to run to it. Then he said so at this time if you don't repent God will destroy you with fire and when I heard that I like kneeled down to the altar. Thus how I was repented.[39]

Another vehicle of the Word and instrument of conversion was the hymn. The AMEC hymnodist was E. H. Greeley, who aspired to "give these people such hymns and tunes as will set them all singing the truths of the Gospel" and who believed that "there is no part of the pastor-teacher's work more important than the singing".[40] Indeed, the hymn came before the sermon in the process of evangelization. Groups of African Christians would enter a kraal singing, thus attracting a curious crowd to whom they then taught the words and tune: "My tent was near a great rock", wrote E. L. Sechrist in 1909, "which overlooked the whole village. Here I often sat and chatted with the old men ... while my boys interested the pickanins and younger people. In a short time phrases of Gospel songs were to be heard here and there all over the kraal".[41]

One of the AMEC's most significant converts, Thomas, son of Chief Maranke, testified to his conversion by hymn: "They came in our village. They sang and preached and the song which they sang was very sweet in our ears but we did not understand what it meant. ... In 1906 again just the hymn was sung, it says, come to Jesus, come to Jesus, just now, just now. He will save you, save just now. He will help you, he will help you just now. By hearing these words they opened my heart and drew me to the altar".[42]

A RELIGION OF LOVE AND REASON

AMEC missionaries believed that sermons, testimonies, Bible texts, and hymns could have an almost instantaneous effect. But there was nothing "magical" about this effect, which was achieved solely through the immediate and obvious truth of the Word. Methodism was a religion of emotion—the emotions of the repentance of sin and of the joy of salvation—but it was also a religion of reason. Once Africans had come to believe in the benevolent power of God, they would be open to his plan for rational and progressive development. Once Africans had been baptized, they were sustained in the fellowship of the church, not by efficacious sacraments or veneration of the saints but by comradeship and instruction. They attended "old-fashioned Methodist Love Feasts"; they attended Sunday School, which in Africa mounted "superlative sum-mits" of significance.[43] Instead of learning about the saints, African evangelists were given "studies in the life of John Wesley, History of Methodism, and the Discipline".[44] In 1938 the missionaries of the Umtali district "emphasized the conversion of John Wesley" in their teaching, thus stressing "the transforming power of the Lord Jesus".[45] A sermon preached by H. N. Howard in 1918 expresses perfectly the complex significance of the memory of Wesley in the AMEC—a lesson in love, in providential dispensation, in divinely ordained progress:

> The money that we get has come from America. But who started the gospel? John Wesley started the gospel in America. He started it with his friends and they gave in a collection. Many people in America were believing now and much money came to John Wesley. John Wesley preached much from the text, "Love your neighbours". And soon God made him sorry because of these words. They troubled him and he said, Who is my neighbour? ... Every nation is your neighbour.
>
> But how was he to get there? This troubled him much. By and by God gave the white man advice and iron. He made of these the railway. ... Then he came to Africa on the train and on the ship which God had taught him to make. God had made a straight path to come to Africa. ... So the train and the ships brought the man sent here from John Wesley's Church. He came to Cape Town. He preached there and the people believed and took up a collection. Then one was sent to Natal. From there one was sent by the believers to Johannesburg. ... Those of Kimberley sent the gospel to Bulawayo, Bulawayo sent the gospel to Gwelo. Those of Gwelo sent the gospel to Salisbury. Salisbury sent it to

Umtali. It reached Old Umtali. Then it came to Manyarara (our oldest station). Now many people of Manyikaland believe. All this came to pass because of the collections that the people who have believed have taken. So it is necessary for you to cast your collections, my people. (Howard 1918:19)

Now that Wesley's gospel *had* reached Manicaland, God would give Africans "advice and iron". Becoming a Methodist opened Africans to scientific rationality. Once again it is Howard who most clearly expresses this. In a somewhat condescending article entitled "The Primitive Mind and the Natural World", Howard set out how to wean Africans from superstition to science. Rain is crucially important to the African:

> The only god that he recognizes is the rain god. The rain god lives on the top of a high mountain. From thence he sends the rain. There the yearly sacrifices are resorted to. There the entranced woman will conjure up the spirit of the departed chief who is powerful to prevail on the rain god Mwari to send rain on the land. So the question where does the rain come from gives us a chance to dig away foundation from the superstitions that gather around the coming of the rain. (Howard 1916)

With a teakettle and a slate one can show a class how steam condenses into rain. "This of course dispels at once those ideas of a god of rain living on the mountain". Similarly, Africans are concerned with the causes of disease. They explain it in terms of possession by evil spirits. But "we have a microscope and show to our classes in hygiene the small animals that live in some of their drinking water. ... So we are breaking down the power of the witch doctor and taking disease from the realm of the supernatural and placing it increasingly in the realm of the things that are explainable".

SPIRITUAL AND MATERIAL IMPROVEMENT

With gospel enlightenment and rational education, the way was open to material improvement as well as spiritual. The AMEC missionaries were insistent that their God-given responsibility was to the whole man: "Poverty is the word that perhaps best describes the lives of these people. Poverty of material comforts; poverty of social ideals; poverty of religious conceptions. Richness must be poured into their lives ... to bring regeneration to the entire economic, social and spiritual life".[46]

From its earliest days the AMEC station at Old Umtali was called an Industrial Mission. It was not expected, of course, that God's gift of "advice and iron" would enable Africans to build railways and steamships, except as laborers for white contractors. But it was hoped that while the convert was "being Christianized he is being civilized and is being put in a position where he is an actual producer instead of being always a labourer and relying on someone else for his daily being". In 1907 E. L. Sechrist set out the aims of industrial training:

> In all this work the main thought is not to make the boy a skilled workman but to advance him to the limit of his capacity. He should have work in Mechanics, he should have work in agriculture, and in the care of a house and home. ... He should have such training in Agriculture as will enable him to cultivate to the best advantage with the help of his wife and children and perhaps some oxen his own

garden plot and farm. The exceptional man will advance farther and will receive by actual experience the training which will fit him for manager on some farm belonging to a white man and in the years to come an estate of his own. In mechanics the same holds good. Every boy should learn to do the work of his own house and the exceptional student will become a trained mechanic.[47]

Increasingly the AMEC's emphasis was on agricultural development as they came to believe that Gospel Christianity could flourish better among a prosperous peasantry than among labor-migrants. The gospel liberated Africans from the control over agricultural production that spirit mediums exercised—"Economic betterment cannot take place until fear and superstition are removed from agriculture".[48] But once a cultivator no longer had to observe communal restrictions and obligations, he was free to develop into a rural entrepreneur, to adopt the plough and to produce for the market on as large a scale as he could manage. The AMEC preached "The Gospel of the Plough" and it was often said that the most important conversion in Manicaland had been the conversion of the first cultivator to use a plough. "Exceptional men" soon emerged. Abraham Kawadza, that first plough-user, bought a farm and competed directly with whites. Many others produced on a large scale in the African areas. The mission agriculturalist wrote in 1923:

> The success of our native people in agriculture is really wonderful. ... At present there are hundreds of ploughs owned by natives and the crops grown are really wonderful. Some of our best stations like Gandanzara are a wonderful demonstration. At this particular station every person who has any cattle has a plough and there are forty-three ploughs owned by the people there. These people who own the ploughs are no longer poverty stricken. They are the foundations of progress in the village.[49]

OTHER SPECIAL CONSTITUENCIES: CHIEFS AND WOMEN

This mixture of old-time conversion experience and development exhortation was directed to *individuals*, and to some sorts of individuals more than to others. The AMEC was particularly concerned, of course, with its pastor-teachers and with the "exceptional men" who were to constitute a rural economic elite. In addition, however, there were two other groupings to which the missionaries paid special attention. One was the chiefs of eastern Zimbabwe. For practical reasons early missionary work sought to base itself at the large central kraal of a chief and to work out from there. In addition the missionaries believed that the children of chiefs made especially good leadership material. The two factors in conjunction meant that a school was first established at the kraal of the chief; the chief's sons and daughters had early access to education and many became agents of the AMEC, pastor-teachers and ministers. They then headed the work of evangelization throughout the chief's territory.

One striking example was the country of Chief Maranke, who lived on Mount Makomwe. In 1907 it was reported that Maranke, "one of nature's gentlemen", had allocated a site for a church and school just below his kraal. God had given the missionary, Greeley, "seals to his ministry even in the household of the chief".[50] In 1909 Greeley himself described how "aspiring preachers and teachers" had taken "the Gospel to every kraal in Maranke's kingdom", fanning out from the chief's mountain: "I hope I will not be called Jesuitical", wrote Greeley, "when I tell you that I have 10 sons of the King in school and all are praying. I am diligently seeking for every possible heir to the throne. May the time soon come when the land between the Sabi and Odzi Rivers shall be a Christian Kingdom".[51] The April/June 1918 issue of *African Advance* contained a photograph of old Chief Maranke, "anxious for his people to know the True God" and flanked by two of his sons. "The father calls the one with a beard 'King of the Christians'". The beardless son was Thomas Maranke, now "a pastor of the Church": "Through personal work he has led scores into the new way. Through his preaching—strong, eloquent, persuasive and tender—he brought hundreds to the altar of repentance unto salvation. He can repeat from memory most of the Gospel of John. He can repeat whole chapters in many other parts of the Bible".[52] In 1923 it was reported that Chief Maranke "has refused permission to other missionary societies to enter his reserve. ... He looks to us to meet the needs and demands of his people along missionary lines".[53]

The other, and very different, special constituency to which the AMEC missionaries addressed themselves was the women of eastern Zimbabwe. Male missionaries long bewailed their failure to work among African women: "We are doing scarcely nothing for the women of Africa, and I tell you it is a *shame*, it is APPALLING: ... Our Native evangelists are calling for special work among the women. ... It seems impossible for us to undertake it".[54]

The same writer expressed continued frustration—and revealed many of his assumptions about "womanhood"—seventeen years later, in 1928:

> One of the greatest channels of dynamics for Church work lies broken and obstructed. The Woman's soul is the very chariot of beauty and the finer attributes of God's own Soul. And the World has yet to learn of the fulness of her precious cargo. Certainly Christ-possessed Womanhood is one of the most powerful assets of the Church. A woman was the sole custodian of God's own Holy Son.[55]

The AMEC believed that African women had been the most oppressed part of an oppressed race, enslaved or bartered and crushed by unremitting physical labor. The liberating message of Methodism might be especially directed towards women. Freedom for women meant the opportunity to realize their divinely intended potential as makers and guardians of "the [among the heathen] unheard of blessing—a home".[56] In 1946 the mission agriculturalist looked back on what he believed the gospel had achieved among rural women in eastern Zimbabwe. Predictably he linked the change in the position of women with the introduction of the plough. The result had been "the emancipation of the women from the drudgery of digging". Instead they had been able to earn money by vegetable gardening and so buy themselves books and pay their children's school fees. They had become partners of their husbands. "The home, God's word, and the church" provided all necessary purpose in life. "In the Ransomed Home where father and mother believe in the word of God and live in the faith of the Lord Jesus the children have a chance for the first time to live without the fear of witches".[57]

American Methodism had little symbolic space for the female principle within the very male Trinity. In 1944, addressing the Methodist women's organization, the Rukwadzano Rwewadzimai, O'Farrell was reduced to telling them "about the mother of John Wesley who had 19 children".[58] Nevertheless, by the 1930s African women had become the mainstay of the church; devout Christian wives, mothers, and homemakers held office in the Rukwadzano.

CAMP MEETINGS AND REVIVALS

Later in this chapter, I shall take these four special constituencies—pastor-teachers, entrepreneurs, chiefs, and women—and explore what they contributed to the dialectic of conversion. But before doing this, I will conclude this examination of the ideas and practices of American Methodism by discussing the camp meeting and the revival. I have been stressing that the missionaries sought to follow the emotion of the conversion experience with rational education and practical training. But they knew that faith had to be sustained and that "the fervent emotionalism of the people" had to be channelled.[59] The instruments for renewal of faith and channelling of emotion were the camp meeting and the revival.

In the early days the camp meeting could be used for evangelical purposes as well as for Christian renewal. In 1915, for instance, more than a hundred Christians under six teachers came together "in a large thickly populated valley" in Chief Mutambara's country for a two-day camp meeting: "The enthusiasm of the Christians was indescribable. In the evening when the camps had been prepared all fell to singing and for the first time in their experience the hills resounded with Christian songs. At first many were frightened. But soon young people began following the crowds who went about preaching. They hung around the camp fires in the evenings".[60]

By the 1920s camp meetings had become a regular, even an annual, event in established Methodist areas. In 1928, for instance, M. J. Murphree reported:

> A number of Revivals have been held, but the outstanding event of the year was the Camp Meeting held near Gandanzara in July. Since coming to Africa I have often thought that Camp Meetings, after the manner of some which I have attended in the Homeland, would be of great power and influence among our people here. We meet with the people often in Quarterly Meetings and Conferences, but there is usually so much business to attend to, that there is little time for prayer and preaching. ... This Camp Meeting resulted not only in Spiritual Blessing to those who attended but the revival fires have been started in practically all the stations represented at the Camp. One of our Native Ministers writes of the Camp Meeting in the following words: "Another thing which gives me great joy to testify is the Camp Meeting at Gandanzara, when the Holy Spirit of God came with great power".[61]

AMEC missionaries were not quite certain, however, in how much power the Holy Spirit should descend. Their theology was pentecostal—they spoke of "spirit-filled Christians"—but pentecostal with some reserve. They did not teach or accept that Africans filled with the Spirit were thereby given the gifts of prophecy or tongues or discernment or the power to exorcize demons. Some AMEC thinkers chided their brethren for such caution. In 1927, for example, Susan Wengatz wrote from the Congo Mission to urge Methodism "Back to Pentecost":

> God stands ready to give the old time power to all who will meet the conditions of consecration and faith. We have always preached this Pentecostal power but we have not always "expected" our people to receive it. But we have found that while we doubted their ability to really understand what full consecration to God meant, God has found them free from any prejudice or teaching that hinders a full and complete surrender to Him in much less time than it takes us to make a like transaction. (Wengatz 1927:10)

In eastern Zimbabwe, however, missionaries preserved what they thought of as a proper sense of caution even in the midst of the most spectacular and desired revivals. The missionaries at Old Umtali, for example, longed for "a strong influx of the Spirit" to deepen the faith and experience of their pupils. They heard in 1915 reports of astonishing manifestations of the Spirit at the South African General Mission at Rusitu. In 1918 they invited Reverend Hatch from Rusitu to pray with African teachers at Old Umtali.[62] The result was a spectacular descent of the Spirit, which is remembered to this day as "the greatest revival of all".

The missionaries were delighted. But they were anxious not to allow African Christians to be carried away on waves of sheer emotion. And they were all too aware that local Anglican clergy and the native commissioner at Umtali were scandalized by what they saw as "the abandonment of the native who considers himself to be under a spiritualist influence over which he has no control".[63] Hence their comment was at once joyful and guarded:

> Last June there came upon our native teachers a baptism—a Pentecost. We were not impressed with the gymnastics that some went through, but a large number of our men became flaming fires with a heavy burden for their people rolled upon them. They received such a baptism as Paul, who said, "Woe is me, if I preach not the Gospel". This spirit followed them to their out-stations, and hundreds of our members were turned from being weaklings and became strong upstanding men and women of God. Lives were cleaned up. It was a marvellous and blessed experience.
>
> The emotional side of life is indeed the great dynamic and does erupt some out of deep pits and turn them right about and set them on new paths. But the emotions were never made to become dominant over the intellect. We do not want to lose any part of the blessing by dissipating its power into sentimentalism. Nor do we want anyone to get the idea that he is not saved if he takes the work of grace quietly.[64]

Thereafter missionaries constantly sought to eliminate "the extreme phases which have always been associated with a revival among an emotional and primitive people". [65]

AFRICAN INTERACTIONS WITH AMERICAN METHODIST THEOLOGY AND PRACTICE

For me two questions insistently arise from this review of the thought and practice of the American Methodist church in eastern Zimbabwe. I am struck, first, by the contrast between what this Methodism was offering to and demanding from

Africans and the teaching and activity of Anglicanism and Catholicism. I am struck, second, by how much the AMEC missionaries saw themselves as the active principle. Under God, of course, they innovated spiritually, socially, and economically; and Africans responded, sometimes with astonishing rapidity and enthusiasm and sometimes slowly and gradually. The overwhelming picture given by AMEC publications is one of white agency, however, despite the fugitive insights into another process I have been examining here. I want to ask, therefore, why it was that some Africans responded to Methodism rather than Anglicanism and Catholicism. I also want to ask how, in their response to Methodism, they seized upon it and made it their own.

LITERACY AND LEARNING

These two questions can mostly be answered simultaneously—many Africans responded to Methodism rather than other forms of Christianity because of what there was in Methodism in particular that they could seize upon and make use of. But at one level the two questions have to be answered separately because some of what was attractive in Methodism arose out of its similarities to rather than its differences from other churches. Thus all three churches emphasized the teaching of literacy through the village school—and the grassroots movements towards Christianity in eastern Zimbabwe were above all else a popular demand for the capacity to read and write. In the 1910s all three churches reported a rush of adult men and women into kraal schools. In 1911 the AMEC missionary O'Farrell described how five "old men" had come to school at Mutambara's: "These old men got right down to work. They all learned to write their names the first day. One could notice a change in them almost immediately. We gave them Chimanyika primers. ... Personally I am willing to receive all the old men in school now".[66] This account might just as easily have been Catholic or Anglican. So also might have been O'Farrell's slight uneasiness about the process:

> A question I have worried about very much is whether the people are not more attracted by such things as learning, improved dress, food and standard of living than by the Gospel itself. Often the boys and girls have said that they wanted to go preaching in crowds. They say "When we stand up to sing they will see that we look different from them and our faces are different and they will say 'We want to be like that'".[67]

O'Farrell's and similar Anglican or Catholic anxiety over the rush for "learning" was justified since the rush was certainly not to mission Christianity as such. As O'Farrell himself went on to say, "There were a considerable number who profess Christianity in the isolated kraals thru the preaching of boys who have been to the mines". In this early period many village schools and churches were started by returned labor migrants who had picked up literacy at the mines and who used their new skills to become founders and leaders of new villages on their return home. These men had no affiliation with any of the three churches competing for influence in eastern Zimbabwe, and it was almost by accident that one of these churches succeeded in recruiting them. In the Chiduku Reserve in Makoni district, for example, the first Methodist and the first Anglican school/church had both been founded by returning labor migrants.[68]

The founder of what became the AMEC station at Muziti's in Chiduku was Nehemiah Machakare: "I started to preach the Gospel among the villages 1907", Nehemiah told his new AMEC colleagues later.

> I was preach the Gospel in kraals there I been born. I was thinking to build the Church of God, then I build the small hut. Then I saw the people came so many. ... I build the large church. ... Then I hold the 4 services every Sunday there came great congregations. ... Then I have visited among the kraals ... to spread the Gospel among the heathen and preach pray day times and night times. I thank my God has been with me where I preach the Gospel among my friends.[69]

In 1909 Wodehouse described how Nehemiah's work had been discovered by Greeley "on one of his pioneer trips":

> Here we have an established mission, with a good native church to seat 600 or 700 people, built entirely by Nehemiah and the heathen boys who assisted him. There was no organisation or church behind him. ... We were glad to receive this faithful man into the Methodist Episcopal Church with the native Christians, and we appointed him one of our workers. So that a running mission station with 226 probationers passed into our hands, giving us access to the whole district.[70]

Nehemiah had been "converted in the Wesleyan Church at Salisbury" so it was perhaps predictable that he should choose to join the American Methodists rather than the Anglicans. Still, the Christians at Muziti's and the villages around it must certainly have felt their church and school to be self-founded rather than given to them by missionaries.[71]

BENEFITS TO CHIEFS : KEEPING COMMUNITIES TOGETHER

All three main mission churches in eastern Zimbabwe also made approaches to chiefs and tried to recruit their sons and daughters into their schools. There was little that was specifically Methodist in what the AMEC could offer to Chief Maranke and the other chiefs with whom they interacted. It happens, however, that the AMEC data provides particularly clear examples of what it was that chiefs got from cooperation with missions.

In the 1890s the settlement pattern everywhere in eastern Zimbabwe was one of large chiefs' kraals surrounded by stretches of more or less empty country. Sells, in an unpublished manuscript, described as typical Chief Mutasa's kraal, which was "divided into sections composed of smaller kinship groups each ruled by an Induna, whose hut was in the centre of the group". At the center of the whole village was "the enclosure of the Chief's court, where he conducted his council and in which his large number of wives lived". The chief controlled agricultural production and was given a tenth of the crops produced. But with the rise of the colonial peasant economy these centralized large villages broke up and the people started living in a more dispersed settlement pattern:

> The small kinship groups built their huts a little away from the main village. The site was nearer the cultivated lands. As the new land for breaking became

scarce these small groups moved on and even sub-divided as they multiplied. ... The summer huts by the gardens soon became the permanent living quarters.

To the chagrin of both chiefs and missionaries, there was a danger that the imperatives of agriculture and commerce would be heeded too enthusiastically and that the trading store would supplant the chief's enclosure as the focal point of rural life:

New methods of agriculture are giving a larger production. Things have almost become the god of the day. ... Commerce had pushed into the village and stores were soon to be found within reach of every village. ... In many sections these became the centre of social life and a convenient meeting place for neighbours and friends. Small villages were built around many of these stores.[72]

The one alternative to commerce as a means of holding rural communities together, and one more acceptable to some chiefs, was the church. "Along with commerce", wrote Sells, "churches and schools have come to occupy a central place in community activities". And his argument was illustrated by a photograph of headman Muziti's village, now grouped around the church and school originally built by Nehemiah and contrasting completely with the companion photograph of Mutasa's village in its prime, organized around the chief's enclosure. In fact, headman Muziti was considerably disconcerted by the sudden rise in his village of Nehemiah's influence and for some time resisted this spatial and symbolic reorganization.[73] But other chiefs—Maranke among them—made a wholehearted use of the church network as a means of holding their territory together. As Superintendent John Springer reported in 1923:

The seven stations of Marange Circuit [ran its Superintendent's report] in 1923 are located rather compactly, six of them forming an irregular circle around Mt. Makomwe, the mother station. They are from nine to fifteen miles apart. ... The paramount chief, Marange, is reaping some marked benefits from our work. With the decay of the former authority of the native chiefs ... the people are no longer compelled to live at the chief's capital as of old and have moved away to where they have fields and farms. This has greatly weakened the power of the chief and has meant the breaking up of much of the former social life. There are no longer any large kraals and we were impressed as we passed from one station to another that the paths were very dim and often no paths at all, showing how little travel there was among the people themselves. But these monthly meetings are bringing the people together again from the different sections. ... We found that even the main trails leading to Mt. Makomwe on which is the capital of the chief gave evidence of infrequent travel. At the first of these circuit meetings at Mt. Makomwe nearly two years ago there was not a large number present. At the last meeting in May there were over four hundred ... probably more than had assembled at one time on the hill for some years.[74]

The superintendent described how active a role chief Maranke himself played in this church network, though not himself baptized. He received and exhorted delegations of young people coming to ask for teachers. "Several of his sons" had inherited his "gift of speech" and were now teachers themselves. In many ways, Greeley's hope of "a Christian Kingdom" had come true: "For several years there has been no foreign missionary residing within the precincts of the circuit and the work is carried on with very little foreign supervision".[75]

CHURCH SUPPORT FOR "PROGRESSIVE" SUCCESSION AND "METHODIST CHIEFSHIP"

Chief Maranke and his teacher sons illustrate another advantage to be derived from alliance with the mission. Among the Shona the position of chief did not go from father to son, but to the oldest qualified claimant in a rotation among chiefly houses. So when Chief Maranke called one of his sons the King of the Christians, he was making an entirely new claim. No matter who succeeded him as chief, his sons would command the Christian Kingdom. Mission-educated Africans often pressed a further demand—that the customs of succession should themselves be changed so that old fathers could be succeeded by young "progressive" sons. In general the Native Department repudiated such demands and backed precedent. But in at least one case the patronage of the AMEC did bring about such a father/son succession.

This was the case of chief or headman Gandanzara, whose people took vigorously to the AMEC gospel of the plough. Philip Gandanzara's testimony describes what happened:

> My father was a chief of Makoni. He was a heathen man who feared the evil spirits and used charms. One day a missionary came to my father's home. ... He called my father and said to him , "I want to tell you and your people about God". ... The people replied, "We are taken care of by the spirits of our ancestors who died a long time ago, but this God that you tell us about we do not know him". Then the missionary began to tell us about the God of Heaven. ... Then the missionary gave my father a book of St. John's Gospel and went away. ... My father sent me to school. When I was able to read my father gave me the book. ... I gave my heart to God and was baptized and later I was made a steward in the Church. When I became of age I married my wife in the church. My father was now becoming old and feeble. He made me his assistant to help in his work as a chief. When he died I was made the Chief in his place. (Sells 1936:31–32)[76]

Yet the Gandanzara chiefly story not only shows us what that family got from the AMEC that they might have got from any other mission—protection from white land owners and a father/son succession; it also shows how a specifically Methodist chiefship could arise over the years. To begin with, the evidence is ambiguous. The Gandanzara father/son succession, after all, depended upon undercutting the belief in the ancestor spirits who legitimated the usual Shona rules of successsion. So it is not quite clear how we should read the report published in *Umbowo* in 1923, written by the AMEC teacher at Gandanzara, Daniel Chipenderu, describing a metaphysical debate there over the 1922 drought. "The heathen" came to Philip, now acting as headman on behalf of his aging father, and pressed him: "Allow us to be given spirits that the rain comes, behold we die of hunger". The drought affected only Gandanzara and not other villages where sacrifices had been made for the ancestors. But Philip refused. Instead: "All the people of the Church continually prayed to God until God heard the prayers of His people. Then it rained hard and the gardens of the people have good crops".[77]

Similarly ambiguous was the request of the old man just before his death in May 1926 and Philip's succession. "Before he died", wrote another teacher, "he asked whether he might be buried in consecrated ground with the Christians. They agreed and they sang hymns at his funeral".[78] Under Philip's long rule all indigenous ceremonies died out in Gandanzara.

But there is less ambiguity about Philip's second conversion experience in 1935: "This work as a Chief among heathen people tended to make my heart cold. I was a Christian in name only. But at a meeting of the women held in the church at my village this year I felt that I was a sinner. I confessed my sins to God and I gave my heart to Jesus who forgave me". Philip experienced a descent of the Spirit. He had a vision of the devil burning the villages and was given a divine commission to "tell other chiefs and headmen about Christ". Thereafter Philip Gandanzara became the very model of a new Methodist style of chiefship. He was a regular attender at the great pentecostal meetings organized by the Methodist women's Rukwadzano and came to be revered by the women as a truly Christian chief. In 1951, for instance, he attended the Rukwadzano annual convention in Zimunya: "Ishe Gandanzara, who even his appearance meant more than his words to the crowd, encouraged the younger christian men to stand as soldiers of the cross, and save our country from sin".[79] "By this time the tables had been turned on 'heathen' chiefs. They no longer received the traditional voluntary labor from their people. But the women of the Rukwadzano worked annually in the fields of Philip Gandanzara".[80]

Philip's eldest son, Naboth, was senior lay Methodist leader in the Umtali region and a successful politician, becoming a senator. When his father died in June 1972, after forty years rule over Gandanzara, Naboth claimed the succession according to the new rules of Methodist chiefship. His candidacy was vigorously supported by African Methodist progressives. T. Gwatidzo wrote from Gandanzara in 1975:

> The late headman was a christian; his influence did spread to the village that we were all brought up under church. To prove this, he refused the brewing of beer in his area up to now which has lessened crimes of thuggery and all sorts of political commitments. His village became the centre of civilisation and attraction.

Naboth would ensure "that the standards of the area may not go down".[81] And the Rukwadzano women of Gandanzara also wrote to say that their movement had been established there by Philip and his wife, who became life chairwoman. They had been assured by Philip that Naboth would succeed and that the church would be safe: "our church will perish" if he did not.[82]

Methodists as Entrepreneurs: Entrepreneurs as Methodists

This Gandanzara story proves exemplary when we turn to look at the other three groups whom I identified above—entrepreneurs, pastor-teachers, and women— and ask what American Methodism specifically offered to each. Like Philip Gandanzara, each group pursued its own interests through Methodism; as they did so they became steeped in Methodist beliefs and involved in Methodist practices. There were certainly African entrepreneurs in eastern Zimbabwe who were not

Methodists; nevertheless, Methodist entrepreneurs constituted a special and important category. For one to understand this special connection it is necessary first to correct the impression given by printed AMEC material. Africans in early twentieth-century eastern Zimbabwe were not sitting about, idly toying with a mere subsistence agriculture, and waiting for an American Methodist missionary to come and suggest that it would be a good idea to produce for the market. In fact, as Africans adjusted to colonial conquest and the demands of the colonial economy, a great majority chose the peasant option rather than the migrant labor option. Throughout eastern Zimbabwe African men were putting their energies into cultivation for the market and turning themselves into peasants (Ranger 1985:ch. 1). The question was not *whether* African families would produce for the market, but on what scale. Since the market demand was for cereals and other food stuffs, it was possible to continue to cultivate the same sort of crops in the same sort of way as in precolonial times, but just to hoe more land in order to produce a regular surplus. It was also possible to make moderate innovations, acquiring literacy in order to deal with traders or using wheeled carts in order to facilitate carriage. But in addition to this "small peasant" and "middle peasant" response, there were men who wanted to go further and to innovate both technically and socially. Such men wanted to use ploughs to open up much more land, to invest both family and wage-labor in production. They also wanted to break away from communal obligations, to ignore the commands of chiefs and spirit-mediums about when to plant and where and what, and to ignore the demands made upon them by the extended family and the clan. In short, just as with the rush for "learning", agricultural innovation was in the air anyway and would have taken place without any Methodist, or even any mission, input. Mission Christianity shaped the style rather than the fact of entrepreneurial innovation. In other writings I have argued that at least in Makoni district, the part of eastern Zimbabwe I know best, "small peasants" made a natural interaction with Catholicism, with its ideal of the egalitarian *community*; "middle peasants" made a natural interaction with Anglicanism, which in its Anglo-Catholic Zimbabwean variety also stressed community but which encouraged the local Christian leaders of producing peasant communities. And I have argued that although there were both Catholic and Anglican entrepreneurs, nevertheless aspirant "large peasants" made a natural connection with American Methodism with its emphasis on "richness", on the plough, and on the individual "ransomed home".

There is abundant data in AMEC reports on the emergence of these entrepreneurs, so abundant that after a while the tone ceases to be triumphalist and becomes rather anxious. It begins to dawn on the missionary commentators that what they are recording is the emergence of a new class, whose class interests are often dominant over their religious commitment. The missionaries begin to feel that rather than the church having brought all these progressive marvels to birth maybe the church had been used by entrepeneurs in their own interests. In 1917, still in the triumphalist period, G. A. Roberts noted that

> regarding the boys who have gone out from Old Umtali during the last three or four years, their success and enterprise as native farmers has been wonderful if not phenomenal. Out toward Makomwe you can find Solomon Zwo, Shilling,

Peter Mundondo, Feradzayi, Samuel Pendeke, Jaz Tedzwa, Mutendi, Matikiti, all doing vegetable gardening and farming in a larger way with plow and cattle. ... Further afield you can find Jeremiah Boki with fifty cattle and two ploughs, while a score of others up through Makoni's country are waking up to better methods.[83]

In 1922 John Springer, returning to the Rhodesian mission field after fourteen years away, noted a transformation around the AMEC stations, beginning with an expression of concern:

I was surprised to find that quite a large number of my old pupils who had given several years to the pastorate, had gone into farming on their own. ... Where a man has cattle of his own, and not belonging to his chief, and where he ploughs and scatters his own broad fields, he cannot live in a kraal with many others. ... These same farmers have bought wagons. (Springer 1922:11)

In 1929 O'Farrell, when attending the first session of the Native Christian Convention of the AMEC, was struck by the attainments of the laymen:

Andrew Matlyukira is a building contractor, runs a successful market-garden and is General Secretary of the Native Agricultural Society. ... Another has two wagons, three plows, a motor car, more than a hundred cattle, thirty donkeys, and last year raised nearly three hundred bags of mealies.[84]

It was hardly surprising that in 1937 O'Farrell commented that it "was not difficult to see the emergence of a favoured class among the natives. All too frequently this group loses sight of the masses and their needs". Perhaps the AMEC ought to turn to the "submerged classes: We forget that still, many laborers live for months in very inferior huts, that hours are far too long, and often Sundays are also work days".[85] Maybe it was less appropriate than had hitherto been thought to have successful entrepreneurs such as Abraham Kawadza address conventions and camp meetings as a living example of the material success that Methodist piety could bring.

In view of the scale of the success of the Methodist entrepreneurs, it is hardly surprising that Shepherd Machuma's oral archive reveals that they did not at all share the missionary's view of their "conversion" to progressive prosperity. Missionary accounts stressed the darkness of their previous existence and their dependence on the mission for their achievements. Entrepreneurial family traditions emphasized instead the status of the entrepreneurs before conversion and the glories of their wealth after it. The point is readily made if we contrast two accounts of that most famous of all economic "conversions", Kawadza's adoption of the plough, both in the AMEC archives.

The first is among Sells's papers. Entitled "When Savage Africa Goes on Evangelistic Trail", it was written by E. B. Caldwell in February 1920:

Kawadza was a naked, low-type African filled with superstition and fear of the white man. ... He lived his life in nakedness and shiftlessness, as most natives do, content to live on whatever of a living his two wives were able to make for him. ... I think old Kawadza is one of the homeliest mortals I ever looked upon. He does not look as though he had sense enough to come in out of the rain. The missionary was not at all enthusiastic over the thought of taking such material into his church but as soon as he became a Christian he began to try to cover his nakedness. ... He began to desire better methods of farming than the hoe, and he borrowed a plough from one of the missionaries and got a span of oxen and began to plow and plant and it seemed as though every time he put seed into the ground God blessed it. He built large huts to hold his grain and stored it. Then he began to buy stock and in a little while he was by far the wealthiest native for many miles around.[86]

Very different are the values expressed in Kawadza family tradition. This tradition emphasizes that Kawadza had fought bravely for Chief Mutasa against Chief Makoni at the great battle of Mhanda and been given a wife as a reward. Indeed Kawadza came from a renowned warrior family. The picture given by family tradition of Kawadza's relationships to the missionaries is also very different. "Since Abraham Kawadza was a very gracious man, he had many friends. Some of his friends were Bishops Springer and Johnson. Kawadza would help them whenever they had a conference. He would even give them a cow for meat or sheep or goats". It frankly rejoices in his wealth:

> Abraham Kawadza was one of the richest men of that time. He had a lot of property ... cows, goats, sheep, horses and waggons. It is said he had a lot of oxen and used to travel on horse back. ... Abraham Kawadza used to go to town [Umtali] on horse back to go and order his things for his business. ... He fed his workers on milk and meat.[87]

WEBERIAN CAPITALISM AND ENTREPRENEURIAL PENTECOSTALISM

Yet, this consciousness of class and this consciousness of status did not mean that Methodism was unimportant to the entrepreneurs. On the contrary, they would have agreed with the missionaries that "material and spiritual development go hand in hand".[88] O'Farrell noted in 1929 that "the vast majority" of his successful laymen had "found Christianity very satisfying". Indeed, a mixture of religious and commercial metaphors came as naturally to the entrepreneurs as to the missionaries. Four AMEC Africans expressed their tribute to the missionary H. I. James in 1940 in characteristic terms: "Fear not, we Africans seem to be unsensible sheep and yet we sell well at the market if well looked after and guided in the right way of Godliness and civilisation".[89] Kawadza family tradition stresses Abraham Kawadza's practical piety: "Though he had many workers he could not allow them to go for work before they had a prayer. ... For his Thanks Giving he would bring a cow or a goat or a sheep or a lot of bags of maize here at Old Umtali Mission". It is clear though that Kawadza's piety was more than merely practical. He was a constant attender and exhorter at camp meetings, especially at the very enthusiastic and pentecostal gatherings organized by the Rukwadzano. Kawadza seems to have been, in short, a classic example of the Methodist entrepreneur who harnessed pentecostal ecstasy through discipline and industry. The Weberian Spirit of Capitalism hovered over American Methodist eastern Zimbabwe.

This Weberian spirit came down on communities as well as on individuals. The village of Gandanzara was one such community. In 1924 Roberts wrote:

> The advancement in the matter of growing of field crops has been wonderful. ... If any person is disposed to doubt the progress in agriculture let him come with me in the Makoni District. Going in the most direct bee-line to Gandanzara, you will pass through and by a number of fields plowed with cattle and American

steel ploughs. Old men by the score have copied the younger generation and are also yoking up their cattle to the ploughs, making use of their cattle as I believe God intended they should be used. The day of prosperity has passed the dawn. Gandanzara, with its adjacent little villages, has sold many wagon-loads of maize this year and is still marketing the surplus crop. These sales spell prosperity.[90]

Philip Gandanzara himself, that model Methodist chief, was an enthusiast for agricultural innovation, underwent some training at the government agricultural school, and worked with African agricultural demonstrators to introduce new crops on his fields at Gandanzara. Philip was supported enthusiastically by the plough-owning family heads who were the mainstay of Methodism in the village. Gandanzara thirsted for education—in 1924 the director of the Rhodesia Mission Press reported a symbolic scene from the village:

> In November I carried a trunk full of books and some grain bags to the quarterly meeting at Gandanzara. When the announcement was made that books would be given in exchange for grain the children scattered in every direction. Presently they returned, each laden with a basket of grain. ... After the purchase little groups could be seen here and there about the village, the proud owner of a new Catechism, asking questions and the other children chiming back the answers.[91]

But if, like Philip, the Methodists of Gandanzara were enthusiasts for entre-preneurial farming and for education, like him they also underwent "the revival fires". In 1928 at the camp meeting in Gandanzara "the Holy Spirit of God came down with great power. The work that was done there is indescribable. God alone can understand the joy and peace which came to the new born souls". In 1931 the Methodists of Gandanzara circuit spent ten days at a camp meeting at Nyatande, which thereafter became "holy ground". In 1935 a "revival was con-ducted at Gandanzara". The Methodists of Gandanzara would have been very much at home with the agricultural spiritual metaphors of Rush Wagner:

> I hope to do some farming for God in Rhodesia that will gladden the heart of the Father more than all the prize cattle or grain show farming. ... I intend to do some farming within the hearts of the people. ... How much they need to have the weeds of sin, superstition, doubt and fear dug out! How much they need to have the fruits of the spirit cultivated![92]

Sells's pamphlet, citing the experiences of three "Twice-Born Men", springs out of this entrepeneurial pentecostalism. One of the three men, Murumbi, son of Chief Makoni, was converted by Abraham Kawadza in 1931. Another, a spirit-medium and rainmaker for Chief Makoni, was converted at the Nyatande camp meeting in 1930: "I found that I had a new heart. When I was a heathen I was not happy because I was living a life of fear. I could not have a garden to grow my food and the fear of the spirits made me a slave". Sells's conclusion that "no advance can be made socially or economically until he is spiritually converted" was as much a deduction from the experience of Gandanzara circuit as it was a statement of AMEC dogma.[93]

PASTOR-TEACHERS: NOT THE CREATURES OF METHODISM

I argue, then, that Christian chiefs and entrepreneurs were not the creatures of Methodism, however much they took on its coloration. But what of the pastor-teachers, many of them "new men" and occupying a role that had not existed before? Surely they were the creatures of the mission? I believe not, and for three reasons. One I have already remarked upon—the fact that there were many self-appointed and successful teachers and preachers before the mission churches absorbed them. The role sprang from the situation of labor migrancy and rural expectation as much as from missionary strategy. Another is an extension of this. These self-appointed teachers were men of particular independence of mind. This was particularly striking in Mozambique. Here the returned labor migrants—literate in English and also Protestant after their experience in the mining compounds of the Rand—stood out against the Catholic state-feudalism of the Portuguese. The AMEC's "spirit for freedom" was attractive to these men so that from the beginning American Methodism was an opposition religion in Mozambique. Yet despite this—or because of it—the early pastor-teachers in Mozambique made their prickly sense of self-worth very clear to the AMEC. E. H. Richards's report from Inhambane in 1901 brings out the independence of the Mozambique teachers very well.

Richards described the lack of opportunities for returned labor migrants in the colonial economy of Mozambique as being "as mean as any under the Turkish government". He described forced labor and the difficulty of raising "any sort of product for sale". In such a context the missionaries expected that the prospect of paid employment as a teacher would be very attractive, but the perspective was different from the African pastor-teachers' side.

> The most terrific conflict ever indulged in between the missionary and the native was on this question of wages. The teachers all struck before they ever received a wage. They struck before they became teachers. ... They had heard that in Natal, in the Transvaal, and even in America that "preachers" got more than the Inhambane wage, and they stood on their dignity as "preachers" and not as citizens of Inhambane. ... The mission never gave in a hair's breadth, nor did the teacher. But with stoical sagacity he took the wage offered to him, but not as "wages"; he looks at it to this day in scornful contempt ...takes it as a mere mouthful, not a sweet morsel at all, but nevertheless as aidful to his present needs.

Still, in the chaos and famine of late nineteeth-century Mozambique, "every one of our teachers has divided over and over again his living and all his salary for the salvation of his friends and relatives who have come upon him, nor is he a whit less generous to downright strangers".[94]

There was little prospect that any political "spirit for freedom" would attract teachers in eastern Southern Rhodesia. The AMEC much admired the British South Africa Company regime, with its "Anglo-Saxon" commitment to economic development. In April 1909 E. L. Sechrist went so far as to tell the native commissioner at Umtali that "we wish to teach the boys here a uniform salutation to white people. Will you kindly let us know if you favor the military salute?"[95]

In Southern Rhodesia the "independence" of teachers was going to have to be a matter of asserting status and leadership both within the church and within Africans' own societies. And here we come to the third point to be made: In the AMEC records the status and power of the missionaries are shown as infinitely greater than that of the teachers or even of the later ordained African ministers. The missionaries are shown as the masters of literacy, of the gospel, of science, to all of which the teachers can obtain only limited access. However, I shall argue that in fact African teachers and preachers acquired an ensemble of powers that made them, in the local rural context, men of more influence than the missionaries.

PASTOR-TEACHERS' INFLUENCE: MASTERY
OF THE SPOKEN AND WRITTEN WORD

As we have seen, a disproportionate number of early teachers were the sons of chiefs and while they testified to their conversion from "heathen" darkness, they were proud of their traditional status. But to this they added a formidable command of the Word. As preachers they had two advantages over the missionaries. They were, of course, fluent in the spoken vernacular and masters of its oral techniques. As *African Advance* noted in October 1916, "The method of teaching by parables is a practical method in Africa. Our native pastor teachers not only use the parables of our Lord but many others of local import that are readily understood and with telling effect". Offered as an example were some of the parables of pastor/teacher James Chikuse: "The caterpiller leaves his coat on a tree. He does not go back for it. It should be so when we leave our sins with Jesus".[96]

The sermons collected in 1916 by H. N. Howard also reveal a powerful capacity to draw on indigenous images. One plays on the basic activity of cooking meal porridge, *ufu*:

> The water and the ufu were talking together one day and the water said to the ufu we together are greater than the fire. For when I am stirred into you we make the food for the people. Now the red fire he is small. He is of no use. So they spoke these things to the fire and boasted of their greatness. But the fire said do people eat food without cooking it? No; they will make me burn. ... If the people will eat you without bringing you to me to touch they will be sick. ... They will vomit. They will not receive strength. ... Now, the water of which I speak is the Devil, the ufu is man and the fire is Jesus.

Another makes use of ideas of bridewealth. A man does not give his daughter for nothing—merely for food—but for cattle that will enrich the family. So God gave his son "for something of consequence", not merely to feed us for "we must get food ourselves by our own work", but "to save men; to give them life". Another presents a marvelous pantheist image of the power of God.[97]

The African pastor-teachers did not lose their advantage with the development of vernacular literacy. After all, they were centrally involved in the creation of the literary vernacular. The missionaries freely admitted their dependence on their converts, and it was the African pastor-teachers who became the real masters of the new instrument of communication rather than the missionaries. Their control of literary Chimanyika, as eastern Chishona came to be called, made them the arbiters of identity.[98]

It was the literate teachers, rather than the oral mediums and elders, who now became masters of history. It was they who created that sense of tribal identity to which Machuma later attributed so much importance. One among many such Methodist historians was Jason Machiwanyika, author of a very influential account of the Mutasa chiefdom. His obituary by Greeley gives some idea of his significance:

> I want to make a little tribute to one of our native teachers, Jason Machiwanyika. He perhaps did not follow Jesus as closely as we should have liked, yet I feel that he was an exceptional native in some ways and worthy of more praise than blame. No native I know spent more of his spare time for the good of his people. ... He was very conversant with native customs and history of the Manyika people. I have hundreds of pages of history and folk lore stories written by Jason. Since last January he brought me a volume of material concerning the kings and their wars, and the native customs and a number of hymns of merit.[99]

The AMEC believed that each people needed a literature. Men like Machiwanyika were creating it.

In all this the teachers were taking full advantage of Methodist opportunities—the Methodist emphasis on the Word, whether in oral or written form. They also took full advantage of the Methodist emphasis upon the Bible. Here the teachers made the Bible their own in a way that the missionaries no longer could. Early twentieth-century Zimbabwe was biblical ground—an Old Testament country of Prophets throwing down idols, a New Testament country of Pauline conversions. I can return to my favorite village of Gandanzara to make the point. Here, first, is an Old Testament hero from Gandanzara, Isaiah Mupepwa. Isaiah was born in Gandanzara and spent three years in the AMEC school there. He served in his home village as assistant teacher. Then he was sent to carry Gandanzara Methodism to the still "heathen" Nyatsanze. At Nyatsanze's—so Isaiah's report runs—a powerful *n'ganga* had guarded against Christianity by warning the people that if they "hear any new words other than I spoke to you a great pestilence will break out among you". So Isaiah went into the cave where the *n'ganga* had left his *magona* medicine receptacles. He carried the fearful objects down and set them in his house. Then, as *African Advance* tells the story:

> One day the people came to him in a body. They said, through their speaker, We have come, teacher, to say that we think that that old witch doctor was a liar. Your God He is the God. A great revival began. ... I believe that as truly as the Spirit of God came on Elijah of old and made him stand alone against the superstition of the people of Israel so the Spirit of God came on Isaiah Mupepwe.[100]

And here is a New Testament hero from Gandanazara, Benjamin Katsidzira, pastor-teacher there in 1926. Katsidzira's work at the outstation of Nyamukwarara had been disrupted by people moving away: "But something tells me that God is still having his work in this place. Something like a vision of Old Paul to Corinthians, when God said to him, Fear not Paul, but preach, I have much people in this city. To me it seems the same thing".[101]

METHODIST PENTECOSTALISM:
EMPOWERMENT FOR PASTOR-TEACHERS

The major difference between American Methodism and the other two missions of eastern Zimbabwe, so far as the pastor-teachers were concerned, was its pentecostalism. The descent of the Holy Spirit upon them could confer full power and legitimacy. Nor did they seek to restrict Pentecost. They sought the whole range of gifts of the Spirit—prophecy, tongues, exorcism, healing, rainmaking. So in the Machuma oral traditions it is the great Revival of 1918 that stands out as the key moment of transition from a missionary church to an African church:

> In 1918 people were gathered at Old Umtali for a revival meeting. ... As they were on their knees praying, the Holy Spirit came down upon them. ... The whole room was in bright light of which they had never seen before. Everyone of them spontaneously said, Amen, Amen, Haleluya, Haleluya. Zachariah Mukombiwa walked on top of people saying, Haleluya, Amen. ... Many many people were convinced that the Holy Spirit had come down upon them as it did to the Apostles when they were in the Upper Room. No sooner did they come out of the church than they found themselves in twos going to pray in different places in the mountain nearby. Josiah Chimbadzwa and his friend Samuel Chieza went to a place in Chiremba Mountain to pray. When they came back Josiah could not even eat for the Holy Spirit had filled his heart. ... He saw distant places when he was up this mountain ...and he wished if the people of these places had witnessed what the people of Old Umtali had seen.[102]

So from Old Umtali the spirit-possessed teachers spread out. Josiah Chimbadzwa went to bring the Holy Spirit down at Mutumbara; he was arrested by the police, but when they tried to beat him the Spirit held back the whip "before it had reached John at all". Two other of the spirit-possessed teachers, John Cheke and David Mandisodza, performed a miracle of healing. Ishe Muredzwa, sister of Chief Mutasa, guardian of the tunnel to his hut and maker of rain, had a crippled daughter on whose behalf she had consulted twenty-five n'ganga(s) in vain. Now John Cheke laid hands on her, commanding her in Jesus' name to walk:

> Dorcas sprang up and shouted "Friends I am healed, Jesus Christ has healed me, I am no longer a cripple—Haleluya, Haleluya". All the Ziyembe people saw her jumping up in rejoice. ... After all people had seen this miracle, they started forming prayer groups and thus Chibvuwi started. ... The Chibvuwi people then started visiting villages to pray with people together. These Vabvuwi were nicknamed Marombe—seekers of Christ, because they were seeking lives of people to Christ.[103]

Thus in the oral tradition was the major male Methodist lay association legitimized in the miracles of "the greatest revival which the Methodist Church of Rhodesia has ever seen". The missionaries also reported the healing of Dorcas and the conversion of her mother Muredzwa, but they portrayed Muredzwa as a monster of heathen cruelty and darkness before her conversion. The oral tradition emphasized much more her spiritual power—wherever she travelled "rain would follow behind her to rub out her footprints so that enemies would not follow".[104] Her conversion was not just another instance of the coming of light into pagan darkness. It marked the moment of transition from one African spiritual authority to another.

Inevitably the 1918 message arrived in Gandanzara, carried there by one of the revival's most remarkable figures, Johanne Mafuta, a *n'ganga* who had experienced "another Damuscus Road" and "like Saul, turned right about".[105] We can see the descent of the Holy Spirit on Gandanzara through the alarmed eyes of the Native Department. In August 1918 the native commissioner called in the teachers from Gandanzara to examine them:

> From what I can gather they had prayers from Sunday to Wednesday; one Johanu visiting them from Umtali. A kopje in the vicinity was called "Sinai" and that the commandments came from this kopje. ... The natives were told that the Holy Ghost descended from it. ... Dougwa Pass was called "Galilee Pass" and that the Lord Jesus came through that pass to bring the Holy Ghost to the Hill Gwidza.[106]

In this way, in a church that did not encourage shrines and pilgrimages, the very landscape of Gandanzara, to this day dominated by Gwidza Hill, was seized upon for African Methodism.

In the aftermath of such a pentecost it was hardly likely that even the entrepreneurial ploughmen of Gandanzara would rest content with explanations of rainfall that depended upon steam-kettles or of disease that depended on microscopes. Methodist pastors at Gandanzara had greater powers than those that sprang from mere rational analysis. In 1935, for example, Silas Pambayi Kasambira was posted to Gandanzara:

> It so happened that they had a terrible drought in his circuit. He asked people to go out to the mountains to pray for rain. Those at Gandanzara went to a hill in Wilson Chikuruwo's field. Then Silas said to the people: "Why have you not brought your raincoats, we may have rain today". As they were praying one of them stood up and said: "There is rain at Mukahanana". No sooner did they get down the mountain than they were in torrential rains [107]

One Sunday as he was preaching, a woman came to the altar and knelt. When the service came to an end, Silas asked the stewards and stewardesses to remain behind with the woman. Silas came near this woman and asked her what she wanted done to her. She said she wanted a child. Then Silas said to her, "In Jesus' Name, He will give you a child". After a time, this woman gave birth to a boy. These were not powers available to the missionaries.

The Rukwadzano Methodist Women's Organization

I have left little space in this already over-long chapter for the important question of African women within the Methodist church. In 1918 the revival empowered African *men* to operate within a missionary-dominated church. In the 1930s a further revival empowered African *women* to operate within a male-dominated church. By the 1930s the peasant option had been undermined in many parts of eastern Zimbabwe, and while the plough entrepreneurs of Gandanzara could weather economic depression, many Methodist men were driven into labor migration for long periods. Women increasingly became responsible for cultivation and they considerably outnumbered men in Methodist congregations. But instead of this numerical majority resulting in increased authority and independence for women in the church, the reverse happened. Both missionaries and African men feared that rural stability would collapse if women were allowed too much freedom. "We acknowledge our sins of ignorance", confessed the AMEC missionaries, "in preaching this very liberty in which the women have too quickly come for their own good at this transitional period in their lives, and we recommend that we preach to them Paul's injunction: 'Let wives be subject to their husbands'".[108] Thus as male African pastor-teachers and leaders of the Vabvuwi entered into new legitimacy and influence after 1918, African Methodist women saw their own status and opportunities decline.

It is in this context that we must understand the rise of the Rukwadzano Women's Organization. Official mission history sees this as the fruit of missionary concern. In 1928 J. R. Gates had stressed that

> woman was the sole custodian of God's own Holy Son and that woman was true to her trust and gave to the world her full portion of an unmarred Redeemer. But this power must be given effective means of expression. Some suitable and simple organization should be worked out so that the Soul of mothers may give concerted expression to its God-given power.[109]

Thereafter the annual reports record the working out of a constitution for the Rukwadzano, modeled on the already existing Wesleyan Methodist women's organization, the Manyano. But matters were not so simple. There had already been friction over the Wesleyan Manyano, one of the African ministers accusing missionaries of "trying to take for themselves from the natives the glory which was theirs in the Manyano work".[110] And in the development of the AMEC Rukwadzano we can see similar tensions. The pastor-teachers' wives and other devout monagamous pillars of the church were determined that their organization should not be merely a tame business of jumble-sales and tatting. They were determined that Rukwadzano should indeed give concerted expression to their "God-given power".

METHODIST AFRICAN WOMEN: PENTECOSTAL EMPOWERMENT

Machuma's oral tradition reveals their claim to pentecostal legitimacy:

> In 1930 at Old Umtali, men and women were filled with the Holy Spirit. They started going to the forest to pray. Mai Wanetsama started going to pray in the forest. ... She used to go to these places at night. At Gandanzara ... a group used to go in the forest to pray. Baba Katsidzira came and told the women to start the organization since others had already started on it. After a very short time these women elders went to different places to do the Lord's work.[111]

> Mrs Kanyangarara started the Rukwadzano. ... It is said she died for 12 hours and during her trance, she was told to come back to earth and carry on God's work. She visited almost every church giving her testimony of what she had been shown in heaven by God.[112]

This prophetic foundation and spirit-filled power gave the Rukwadzano great self-confidence and also led them more or less to take over the camp meeting and revival traditions. They became the major force in evangelization and they made their own—and very effective—approaches to chiefs.

The proposed constitution of the Rukwadzano Rhwe Wadzimayi in 1938—drawn up by a committee dominated by African men—proposed for the women a set of tasks drawn from Titus 2:3–5:

> Teach the aged women likewise, that they may be in behaviour as becometh holiness, not false accusers, not given to much wine, teachers of good things; that they teach the young women to be sober, to love their husbands, to love their children, to be discreet, chaste, keepers at home, good, obedient to their husbands, that the word of God be not blasphemed.[113]

Rukwadzano activists, however, while sober and holy, turned out not to be "keepers at home" nor obedient to husbands who wanted to keep them there instead of going on evangelizing tours and organizing night-long pentecostal meetings. By 1941 missionaries were remarking that "there are indications that this organization is going to need careful instruction and guidance if it is to operate effectively and efficiently" and that "the manner of holding great meetings could be improved upon". The largely African male Committee on the State of the Church was worried about the "decline of the Wabvuwi work" and made a series of recommendations designed to revive male evangelical activity. They also criticized the Rukwadzano's "habit of all-night singing" and their "extravagance of money in the buying of food".[114] To all this Mrs. Titus Maranke made a magnificent reply in presenting the first of the formal Rukwadzano reports to the annual conference, beginning with her own more radical text:

> "The hand of the Lord was upon me, and carried me out in the spirit of the Lord, and set me down in the midst of the valley which was full of bones, and caused to pass by them round about: and, behold, there were very many in the open valley; and, lo 'they were very dry'. Ezekiel 37:1, 2".
>
> The women of Africa were scattered about just like the bones on an open valley. They used to be sold to far countries for life. They used to be stolen by robbers. The Matabele people used to carry us off by thousands. The women of Africa were ... like slaves. The chief work of women was in the fields and the cooking of food and beer. Sometimes they used to receive beatings. The men had no thought that the women could do anything. ...
>
> God saw that the hope of the women of Africa was lost like the hope of the dry bones on the open valley and he sent us His Living Word. Today "there is a noise and behold a shaking and the bones come together, bone and bone". The source of the RUKWADZANO RWEWADZIMAI is the Word of God, which is preached to us and brings us together. The aim of the Rukwadzano rweWadzimai is to seek the lost women of Africa. ... That is why we are having these big Rukwadzano meetings which seem to be much expense but the soul is more worthy than any expense in the sight of God.
>
> There is a saying among our people, "There is a secret power in a woman by which she can send a king to fetch her a cooking stick". We believe that that power is used of God now. In all our meetings that power by the help of God is drawing our chiefs to come to our meetings. ... We plead with you, our missionaries, to be patient with us and give us a chance to bring our African people into the Kingdom of God.[115]

Thereafter, as attempts to revive rural male Methodist associations failed, the Rukwadzano exercised its pentecostal powers. In 1944 its southern section began its report to conference with a text from Luke about "women healed of evil spirits" and exorcisms became a feature of Rukwadzano mass meetings.[116] Bishop Abel Muzorewa, first African head of Zimbabwean Methodism, describes in his autobiography attending a camp meeting with his mother:

> In addition to the large gathering for singing, preaching and prayer, people used to go apart in small groups to confess their sins, to share their faith and to pray for each other. One day while in one of these groups with my mother, I was astonished to see a woman fall down as we were singing. ... This woman is being possessed", my mother explained. "As we pray with her, we are doing what Jesus did—casting out demons from people who were possessed by the evil spirits". ... I sensed the great faith of my mother that God is as present today to overcome and heal as he was in the time of Jesus. (Muzorewa 1978:11–12)[117]

We have already seen how headman Philip Gandanzara was "re-born" by means of his encounter with the Gandanzara Rukwadzano and how the women came to be a major support of his Methodist chiefly authority. Much the same happened in other places so that rural Methodism came to depend on an alliance between those two "stay-at-home" powers, chiefs and women. One example from the 1949 report of the Rukwadzano annual convention at Mutambara may suffice. Mrs. Titus Maranke wrote in her report of the great gathering:

> My mind went back to Rukweza's convention when one bright morning a man who was a Sikiro (a man whose spirits of departed forefathers talk through him) stood up and shout with a voice beyond his own. This is the great God. This is the Might God. This is powerful God. After a pause he said we had power we are feared by all the people but we never had glory together a large gathering like this or half of this, and in my heart I say "King of Kings and Lord of Lords". ... Myself I came to understand the words at the huge multitude gathering at Mutambara.
>
> The happiest thing in all our conventions is that men came with desire to see the womens meeting, but instead they see their Saviour. Chief Mutambara said ... "I am going to greet you by firing my gun, don't be afraid it is my greeting. The word of God have come to change things and things mean what they didnt mean before. ... It is through you, Rukwadzano, when we were scattered bones the word of God through Rukwadzano brought us together".[118]

In a maternal metaphor the women of Rukwadzano rejoiced that they had overcome their enemies. The association was "like a baby born from a small group of women"; this "baby was sought to be killed, but like Moses it was saved by some other Wakurus [elders] who thought it was a nice-looking baby. ... Now the baby is growing in every station. ... It is even crawling towards its neighbor's yard".[119]

With a marked lack of enthusiasm, the male clergy of other denominations watched the crawling baby approach their backyards. The Anglican priest Fr. L. S. Machika wrote from Makoni district in 1949:

> I think that if people are really converted in *their hearts* they should tell the priest *privately* not publicly. ... Methodists encourage these sort of behaviours a

lot ... since 1918. Their position worries them now, because they have a sort of two churches, a women's church and men's church. Women bring charms to be burnt often almost weekly, and they weep a lot; men wait anxiously, rather doubtful of the women's behaviour in church and public. I know what goes on in these great gatherings of the Methodists.[120]

CONCLUSION

This long chapter requires only a short conclusion. I have been seeking to explore the dialectic of conversion in eastern Zimbabwe. To do so I have set out thesis—the theology and practice of AMEC missionaries. I have also set out antithesis—the beliefs and actions of African converts. This has meant presenting the question in too conflictual a way, giving a literally black-and-white picture. But, of course, the dialectic results in a constantly shifting and negotiated synthesis. At any one time, and even today, popular Methodism is the result of an interaction between both missionary and convert contributions. In 1925, E. H. Greeley, the missionary whose humility and dedication I find the most impressive, expressed his millennial dream:

> ... a vision of the future inspired by God's unfailing goodness and care for man ... a vision to which I have aspired and planned and worked. A vision of being able to think in black and so feel as these people feel.[121]

As a result of the processes described in this chapter, any scholar who aspires today to "think in black" about many of the people of eastern Zimbabwe has to learn also to think Methodist.

NOTES

1. R. Wodehouse to Reverend E. D. Kohlstedt, 28 July 1903, Wodehouse Letter-book, April 1902–April 1905, AMEC Archives, Old Umtali.
2. R. Wodehouse to Thomas Kennion, 26 April 1904, Wodehouse Letter-book.
3. T. A. O'Farrell, Evangelisation, January 1911, green file, Early District Conferences, AMEC Archives, Old Umtali.
4. W. C. Terril Reports, Inhambane District, *Official Record: Minutes of the East Central Africa Mission Conference, Methodist Episcopal Conference, Sixth Session*, 1909, 24.
5. Report of H. I. James, Superintendent of the Rusapi District, *Official Journal of the Second Session of the Rhodesia Annual Conference* 1932, 36–37.
6. W. C. Terril Report of the Inhambane District, *Official Journal* 1915, 4.
7. Per Hassing, Report of Mtasa/Makoni District, *Official Journal* 1944, 28.
8. Report of Rev. Robert Wodehouse, *Minutes of the First Session of the East Central Africa Mission Conference* 1901, 42.
9. Ibid.:12, 58
10. R. Wodehouse, April 1904, Wodehouse Letter-book, vol. 2.
11. Report of Shirley Coffin, *Official Record* 1909, 57.
12. For example, material collected by E. L. Sells and now in green files, "Early District Conferences", "Early Christians", and "E. L. Sells" in the AMEC Archives, Old Umtali.
13. Twice-Born Men, *African Advance* 1(2) (October 1916): 6.
14. E. L. Sells, *Read What Three Twice-Born Men of Africa Have to Say Concerning Their Experiences*, Umtali, n.d., 3. See also the use made by Sells of African testimonies in his *On Trek with Christ in Southern Rhodesia* (Sells 1936), especially pp. 30–33, "Two Chiefs Find the Way".

15. R. Wodehouse to Bro. Scott, 28 July 1903, Wodehouse Letter-book.

16. Bishop Hartzell, Mission Work in Portuguese East Africa and Rhodesia, *Official Journal* 1913, 7.

17. Report of the Committee on the State of the Church, *Official Journal* 1913, 88.

18. Capital File, Miscellaneous Correspondence, AMEC Archives, Old Umtali.

19. Methodist History Society, *Journal of the Rhodesia Annual Conference the Methodist Church,* 1958, 288.

20. Report of Historical Committee, *Official Journal* 1936, 71.

21. Report of the Methodist Historical Society, *Journal of the Rhodesia Annual Conference* 1952, 75.

22. Methodist Historical Society, *Journal of the Rhodesia Annual Conference* 1966, 76.

23. Italics in the original. The Report of the Conference Archivist, *Official Journal of the Rhodesia Annual Conference of the United Methodist Church* 1973, 58.

24. Among the files made up by Machuma, I have found most useful "Revival", "Healing of Dorcas Muredzwa", "Evangelism", "Outstations", "Life Histories", "How Rukwdazano Began", "Makoni". I should make it clear that my research was directed especially towards the history of Makoni district and that there is much in the Machuma deposit concerning other districts which I did not note and hence have not used for this chapter. Nor was I in any sense focusing especially on the history of Methodism but was working towards a general agrarian history of Makoni. This chapter is more intended to draw to the attention of African historians of Methodism the potential of the Old Umtali archives and of *Umbowo* than as a definitive statement. It is odd and I think regrettable that the African historians who have worked on the AMEC have depended almost entirely on the formal records of the church.

25. *Umbowo Hwe Ukristu* [Witness of Christianity] 55 (10 October 1972).

26. W. C. Terril, Report of the Inhambane District, *Official Journal* 1913, 12–13.

27. Report of the Committee on the State of the Church, *Official Journal* 1916, 61.

28. Report of Your Committee on the State of the Church, *Official Record* 1910, 69.

29. Limpopo District, Report of District Superintendent, *Official Journal* 1911, 11.

30. Ibid., 16.

31. Ibid., 49.

32. H. N. Howard, Mrewa Circuit, *Official Journal* 1919, 45.

33. Notes from Bishop Hartzell's Address at The Opening of Conference, *Minutes of the First Session* 1901, vii.

34. Committee on the World War and America's Responsibility Therein, *Official Journal* 1917, 65.

35. T. A. O'Farrell, Report of Nyadiri District, *Official Journal* 1946, 238.

36. And He Said unto Me Write, *African Advance* 2(2) (April/June 1918):13.

37. Umtali District, Report of District Superintendent, *Official Journal* 1911, 15.

38. E. H. Richards, Annual Report of the Inhambane District, *Minutes of the First Session* 1901, 27.

39. Twice-Born Men, *African Advance* 1(2) (October 1916):6.

40. Mrewa Circuit, *Official Journal* 1917, 36.

41. Report of E. L. Sechrist, *Official Record* 1909, 51.

42. One Thing I Know, *African Advance* 1(3) (January 1917):5.

43. Report of J. R. Gates, *Official Journal* 1928, 38.

44. Report of the Committee on Native Course of Study, *Official Record* 1910, 72.

45. Report of the Umtali District, *Official Journal* 1938, 235.

46. T. A. O'Farrell, Report, *Official Journal* 1926, 28.

47. E. L. Sechrist, Report, *Official Record* 1907, 38.

48. E. L. Sells, *Read What Three Twice-Born Men of Africa Have to Say Concerning Their Experiences*, n.d., 3.

49. G. A. Roberts, Report, *Official Journal* 1923, 67.

50. R. Wodehouse, The Umtali District, *Official Record* 1907, 25.

51. Report of E. H. Greeley, *Official Record* 1909, 44.

52. Pastor-Prophet to the Pagan People, *African Advance* 2 (2) (April/June 1918):15.

53. Report of J. M. Springer, *Official Journal* 1923, 41.

54. J. R. Gates to Dr. Leonard, 28 January 1911, Box File "Gates et al.", AMEC Archives, Old Umtali.

55. Report of J. R. Gates, *Official Journal* 1928, 37.

56. Report, The Inhambane District, *Official Record* 1907, 19.

57. Report of Mutambara District, *Official Journal* 1946, 227–228.

58. Report of the Rukwadzano, *Official Journal* 1944, 52.

59. Report of W. Bourgaize, *Official Journal* 1922, 4.

60. T. A. O'Farrell, Mutambara, *Official Journal* 1915, 32.

61. Report of J. M. Murphree, *Official Journal* 1928, 35.

62. Ranger 1987a gives an account of the Rusitu Revival.

63. Native Commissioner, Umtali, Monthly Report, July 1918, File N 9/4/35, National Archives, Harare. The AMEC missionaries would not have liked his further comment that "the inherent spiritualist tendency of the native mind readily responds to the mysticism of religious ritual".

64. Report of the Committee on the State of the Church, *Official Journal* 1919, 37.

65. Old Umtali Circuit, ibid., 45.

66. T. A. O'Farrell, Evangelisation, January 1911, green file, Early District Conferences.

67. Ibid.

68. The Native Department noted the grassroots enthusiasm for literacy. In 1909 the native commissioner at Umtali recorded that "the natives in this district have a craze for learning reading and writing not confined to the younger people only—old women, wives and mothers may be seen daily struggling over almost indecipherable characters scrawled on a slate by some native who has had a better chance than they". Native Commissioner, Umtali, to Chief Native Commissioner, 6 October 1909, File NUA 2/1/8, National Archives, Harare. Another official noted that many Africans gathered together "a few of their compatriots" to regularly "instruct them in the rudiments of reading" entirely on their own initiative and without any mission backing. Superintendent of Natives, Umtali, to Chief Native Commissioner, 8 May 1912, File NUA 2/1/10, N.A., Harare.

69. The Report of Nehemiw Machayire [Nehemiah Machakare], 1908, green file, Early District Conferences, AMEC Archives, Old Umtali.

70. Rhodesia District, *Official Record* 1909, 34.

71. In 1916 one of the Muziti Christians told Howard about his conversion: "I was live at Muziti kraal but was do many heathen things. ... Nehemiah he did come to Muziti kraal. ... I did saw Nehemiah. ... This time I did repent. Nehemiah he was a great preacher". Testimony of Paul C. collected by H. N. Howard in 1916, AMEC Archives, Old Umtali.

72. E. L. Sells, The Disintegration of the African Village in Southern Rhodesia, n.d., AMEC Archives, Old Umtali.

73. Muziti made a sworn statement in May 1908 complaining that "the Native Missionary in charge of operations has taken my people both boys and girls to assist in the building of the Church. He has never asked my consent to take these people and they have been taken from their regular work in the gardens". Sworn statement, 19 May 1908, File NUA 3/1/1, National Archives, Harare.

74. Report of John M. Springer, *Official Journal* 1923, 41–42. A very similar development took place in Chief Mutambara's country. He had offered the AMEC a site at the center of his territory. In 1945 G. A. Roberts described Mutambara Mission as "the hub of a great wheel radiating power and light to the surrounding districts. The twelve village schools receive aspiration and new ideas from the Center". Report of Mutambara District, *Official Journal* 1945, 100.

75. Ibid.

76. The printed records of the AMEC give the missionary account. The missionary visit to Gandanzara's was in June 1905 when John Springer took ten trainee teachers there, holding "continuous services all day that Sunday, large numbers of both men and women attending eagerly". By 1909 Gandanzara was "a transformed village. We can safely say a Christian village". The headman placed his village, then on white-owned land, under the patronage of the AMEC, asking in 1910 that the mission buy land—"they will furnish the cash, but want the land bought as mission property, we holding the title but permitting them to occupy it so they can live and learn undisturbed". In the event, the people moved into the eastern part of Makoni Reserve, where they proclaimed their Christian commitment by erecting a brick church in 1917.

77. Letter from Daniel Chipenderu, 7 January 1923. Printed in Shona in *Umbowo* but translated into English by a Native Department employee and now in the Chief Native Commissioner's file, NUA 3/1/1, National Archives, Harare.

78. Amosi H. Karumbidza, Gandanzara Mission Station, AMEC Archives, Old Umtali.

79. Rukwadzano Southern Section Report, *Journal of the Rhodesia Annual Conference* 1951, 365.

80. Rukwadzano, Reports from the Branches, Gandanzara *Journal* 1954, 265.

81. T. Gwatidzo to District Commissioner, Rusape, 10 August 1975, File "Headman Gandanzara", District Commissioner's Office, Rusape.

82. Rukwadzano, Gandanzara to District Commissioner, 14 August 1975, ibid.

83. Old Umtali and Makomwe Circuit, *Official Journal* 1917, 75.

84. Report of the Nyadiri and Mtoko Districts, *Official Journal* 1929, 31–32.

85. Report of Nyadiri District, *Official Journal* 1937, 131–132.

86. When Savage Africa Goes on Evangelistic Trail, green file, Sells's letters.

87. Abraham Kawadza, Machuma Files, AMEC Archives, Old Umtali.

88. Report of G. A. Roberts, *Official Journal* 1933, 101.

89. The African Tribute to the Rev. H. I. James, *Official Journal* 1940, 68.

90. Report of G. A. Roberts, *Minutes of the Eighth Session* 1924, 36–37.

91. Report of Rhodesia Mission Press, ibid., 43.

92. Report of Rush Wagner, *Minutes of the Ninth Session* 1925, 41.

93. The convert cited here is Gibson Chikungwu.

94. A Report of the Inhambane District, *Minutes of the First Session* 1901, 25–27.

95. E. L. Sechrist to Native Commissioner, Umtali, 30 April 1909, File NUA 3/1/1, National Archives, Harare. The Native Commissioner, somewhat disconcerted, replied that "the military salute would be out of place".

96. Pastor-Teacher James Chikuse and His Parables, *African Advance* 1(2) (October 1916).

97. Two sermons by Moses Chisamba and one by an unknown, Capital File, Miscellaneous Correspondence, AMEC Archives, Old Umtali. The anonymous sermon runs:

> God has great power. His spirit is like the mountain. It is great, it is strong. It is always the same. But God can throw it down, with his one finger he will throw it. The people who refuse him he has only to flip as we do a fly and he will die. God has full power. He makes the river to flow. ... If a man would pour water on the ground all day yet in the morning would it be dry.

98. For a much fuller discussion of the creation and use of mission Chimanyika, see Ranger 1989.

99. Report of E. H. Greeley, *Minutes of the Eighth Session* 1924, 35.

100. Have Faith in God or Witch-Doctor versus Wonderful Counsellor. *African Advance* 1(2) (October 1916):8–9.

101. Report of Benjamin Katsidzira, *Minutes of the Twelfth Session* 1926, 55.

102. The 1918 Revival by Josiah Chimbadzwa, Machuma Files, Revival.

103. 1918 Revival and Chibvuwi, ibid.

104. Mtasa, ibid.

105. Foot-lights on Dark Pathways, *African Advance* 2(1) (April/June 1918).

106. Native Commissioner, Rusape, to Superintendent of Natives, Umtali, 6 August 1918, File NUA 3/1/3, National Archives, Harare.

107. Life History of Reverened Silas Pambayi Kasambira, Machuma Files.

108. Cited in Terence Ranger, Women in the Politics of Makoni District, Zimbabwe, 1890–1980, unpublished paper, 1982, in which the whole question is treated much more fully.

109. Report of J. R. Gates, *Official Journal* 1928, 37.

110. Herbert Carter to Moses Mfazi, 23 December 1927, Box 828, Wesleyan Methodist Mission Archives, London School of Oriental and African Studies.

111. How Rukwadzano Began, Mai W. Mandisodza, Machuma Files.

112. Rukwadzano as told by Mrs. Cheke, ibid.

113. Committee on the State of the Church, *Official Journal* 1938, 245–246.

114. *Official Journal* 1941, 126, 129, 160.

115. *Official Journal* 1941.

116. *Official Journal* 1944, 164–165.

117. Muzorewa's autobiography is not very illuminating for his later political role but its early pages splendidly reflect the atmosphere of popular Methodism in eastern Zimbabwe.

118. *Official Journal* 1949, 203–204.

119. Rukwadzano: Southern Section, *Official Journal* 1948, 92.

120. Fr. L. S. Machika to Fr. Smith, 11 February 1948, File ANG 16/1/11, National Archives, Harare.

121. E. H. Greeley, report in *Minutes of the Ninth Session* 1925, 45.

Plate 16–1. An old Rastafari man in Jamaica, 1983. Typically, he wears clothes in the colors of the Ethiopian flag: red, yellow, and green.

16

Prophetism, Democharisma, & Social Change

Asmarom Legesse

THIS CHAPTER EXPLORES THREE KEY concepts that have contributed to our understanding of prophetic or charismatic social change: the concepts of alienation, communitas, and charisma.[1] Liminality will also be discussed as a subspecies of communitas. We will examine these concepts as we apply them to the Rastafari movement. In particular, the concept of charisma needs basic rethinking because, so far, it has not adequately represented the type of charismatic community that is without a prophet, a community in which each individual assumes a decidedly charismatic posture. It is this latter phenomenon that I have labelled "democharisma".

CHARISMA AND REVITALIZATION: WEBER, SHILS, AND WALLACE

To date, sociology and anthropology have paid great attention to prophetic, messianic, or charismatic individuals: how they get their inspiration or vision, how they communicate their message to others, how their charismatic authority is authenticated, how they build up a following, what kind of crises develop as the followers evolve into an organized community whose values are codified and whose way of life is institutionalized. In all these areas, Max Weber, Edward Shils, and Anthony Wallace have given us a wealth of ideas and analytical concepts that help us to understand these phenomena. Weber's discussion of the charismatic personality and his narrower concept of the prophetic individual are seminal concepts.

For Max Weber, a prophet is the "bearer of charisma, who by virtue of his mission proclaims a religious doctrine or divine commandment" (Weber 1968a [1922]:253). The prophet is engaged in the business of rethinking society and producing a vision for a new social order. He offers "a unified view of the world derived from a consciously integrated and meaningful attitude toward life" (Weber 1968a [1922]:266). At the beginning or perhaps in the early stages of his career, the prophet does not depend on his followers to assume the prophetic role.

"It is characteristic of prophets that they do not receive their mission from any human agency, but seize it, as it were" (Weber 1968a [1922]:258). "Charisma knows only inner determination and inner restraint. The holder of charisma seizes the task that is adequate for him and demands obedience and a following by virtue of his mission" (Weber 1968a [1947]:20). Later, as the prophet actively begins to build up a following, it becomes necessary for him to validate his calling, his claim, or his special powers by performing various feats of magic or healing. "It is recognition on the part of those subject to authority which is decisive for the validity of charisma. ... If proof of his charismatic qualification fails him for long, the leader endowed with charisma tends to think his god and his magical or heroic powers have deserted him" (Weber 1968a [1947]:49). "It is only under very unusual circumstances that a prophet succeeded in establishing his authority without charismatic authentication, which in practice meant magic" (Weber 1968a [1922]:254). However critical the element of recognition may be for the continued validation of charisma, the prophet at all times denies his dependence upon his followers. "No prophet has ever regarded his quality as dependent on the attitudes of the masses toward him" (Weber 1968a [1947]:49).[2]

The prophet's leadership endures as long as he continues to command the "*complete personal devotion* of his followers" (Weber 1968a [1947]:49). The disciples of the prophet also tend to be charismatics. "The administrative staff of a charismatic leader does not consist of 'officials'; at least its members are not technically trained. It is not chosen on the basis of social privilege nor from the point of view of domestic or personal dependency. It is rather chosen in terms of the charismatic qualities of its members" (Weber 1968a [1947]:50).

In the works by Weber cited here, which are the essays that specifically deal with prophetism and charisma, he has nothing to say about the quality of the mass following of the prophet (Weber 1968a [1922, 1946, 1947]). His analysis is almost entirely focused on the top echelons of the charismatic hierarchy: on the prophet and on his immediate successors.

Weber sees prophets as impractical leaders who depend on gifts for economic support or have difficulty systematizing the economic affairs of their followers. Another dimension of their impracticality is their reluctance to give their followers a body of laws by which they can live. The prophets present their vision of the new social order in vague metaphoric language, not in the language of laws and institutions. Mohammed, who came from a family of merchants and whose religion is highly political in character, is seen as an exception in both these respects (Weber 1968a [1922]:259).

Charisma is an inherently unstable phenomenon. "In its pure form, it can exist only in the process of originating". If the community that has formed around the prophet is therefore to endure, "the character of charismatic authority must be radically changed" (Weber 1968a [1947]:54). The "administrative staff" must become officeholders whose conduct is governed by a body of laws and whose recruitment is based on "rational" or "traditional" procedures. In this process of routinization, there is always the possibility of a crisis developing over the problem of succession (Weber 1968 [1947]:55). Even after the succession is routinized, however, a residual type of charisma may endure. Weber refers to this as the "charisma of office". Similarly, in the economic sphere, the group must also undergo routinization as it abandons its dependence on gifts or booty and adopts conventional methods of "making a living" (Weber 1968a [1946]:21–22).

Anthony F. C. Wallace's attempt to examine the revitalization process draws on Weberian concepts but also expands the model in three important ways. He considers the conditions under which the prophet is most likely to arise (i.e., the conditions of "cultural distortion"), and he examines the specific psychological conditions that lead to the visionary experience. He also attempts to codify the stages of the revitalization process, a process he sees as beginning and ending in a steady state. At the center of this process is a phenomenon of cognitive transformation he calls "mazeway resynthesis". The prophet offers his followers a new and totally meaningful cognitive model that seeks to render the universe intelligible. In short, he offers a new cosmology (Wallace 1956).

Edward Shils has expanded the Weberian model in another direction. He examines what he calls "distributed charisma". This concept refers to the process by which charismatic authority is perpetuated after routinization. On the surface this sounds like a contradiction in terms. However, it makes sense if we think of it as a type of "borrowed" charismatic authority deriving from the transfer or inheritance of charismatic authority from the prophet to the successors or heirs. The phenomenon is, in some respects, comparable to what Weber called the "charisma of office" or the "charisma of kinship". However, Shils goes beyond that to say that the distribution of charisma may also be relevant not only to officeholders but also to "citizens". In this tangential manner, Shils does recognize the ordinary member of a charismatic community as a potential bearer of charisma (Shils 1958).

LIMINALITY AND COMMUNITAS: VICTOR TURNER

Since Weber, Wallace, and Shils, one other major thinker—Victor Turner—has come forth with a model for the study of revitalization and charismatic social change, a model that is quite novel and has its origins in an entirely different area of social anthropology: the study of the human life course. How studies of the life course came to contribute to our understanding of the revitalization process is itself a historic question of considerable significance that we shall not examine in depth here. We mention it here as background to the phenomenon of prophetism.

Turner was, for a major part of his career, immersed in the study of Ndembu ritual in Zambia. He produced masterful exegeses of ritual symbolism and delved deeply into the meaning of rituals of transition. In these studies, he discovered that the transitional period itself has special meaning in human thought and may shed some light on those phenomena we consider sacred. Turner draws on the ideas of Arnold Van Gennep to develop his concept of liminality. To Van Gennep, all rites of passage have a triadic structure consisting of the first stage of separation of the initiate from society, the second stage called the liminal stage (from the Latin *limen* or "threshold"), and the third stage of reaggregation in which the individual reenters the structured society, equipped with a new set of social roles (Van Gennep 1922).

Turner is struck by the qualities of the threshold phase. In that phase, there is symbolic profusion, instability, and a certain measure of calculated chaos. The group of initiates who are in that phase have a modestly anti-structural character. They exist not only outside the framework of organized society but in opposition to it, often violating norms that are firmly held by the wider society. The novel question that Turner raises is this: Are liminal phenomena, liminal symbols, and liminal personalities involved in the development of the revitalization process? Or do they merely stand in static opposition to established society offering a reversed or mirror image of it—an image that helps only to reinforce the social order rather than destabilizing it? How we answer these two questions makes a critical difference. Turner himself does not give a clear answer to these questions. He raises both possibilities but his ultimate leaning is toward the classic structural-functionalist position in which all destabilizing forces are seen as *transitory* or as *components of the larger structural system.* In other words, liminality, as he views it, does not help us to understand the process of social transformation (Turner 1969).

The treatment of destabilizing forces as transitory is not problematic because much social change has a cyclical, or recurrent, character and the structured society sustains itself by allowing a known quantity of chaos for limited periods of time and at predictable stages in the life of a community or an individual. But the second aspect of Turner's thesis is not so innocuous. It denies the possibility of fundamental change because it reduces all liminal figures into new types of players who merely broaden the game of life but leave the fundamental game plan intact. In short, liminality as conceived by Turner cannot lead to the significant transformation of human society.

In view of the fact that some prophetic individuals, such as Gandhi, have decidedly liminal properties, have a vision of a new society, and have successfully brought about meaningful and enduring social change, it is necessary to rethink Turner's model and use it to explore possibilities Turner himself did not explore. Turner does, in fact, devote one page to Gandhi merely to draw parallels between Gandhi's ideas of the virtues of poverty and those of St. Francis (Turner 1969:197–198). Granted, Gandhi was a liminal figure who resembles many other saintly hermits and monks. The fact is, however, that he used this strange liminal position to launch a campaign that had the most far-reaching consequences in the Third World. He initiated a process and nurtured a movement that ultimately brought down the British Empire. Gandhi's life, more than any other, suggests to us that liminality may be directly connected with some of the major upheavals in human society.

Communitas is another idea in Turner's model which promises to be a useful analytical tool. Communitas is the social dimension of liminality. Turner considers communitas to be a collection of individuals who are held together by deep and total bonds and refuse to relate to each other in the segmental, functionally differentiated pattern of role relationships characteristic of normal social life.

Communitas is a group without social structure that is powerfully held together by factors other than kinship and the division of labor. Communitas may be a gathering of individuals around a charismatic figure or it may consist of liminal persons drawn to each other by their deeply anti-structural proclivities and a yearning for an altered state. They need not have a vision, a program, or a positive goal. Their rejection of the existing order is enough to bring about the formation of communitas and experimentation with altered states. One of the strangest features of this process is that *the totally negative stance of such a group of individuals can have positive consequences: they sometimes invent new social structures without ever intending to do so.* This is a noncharismatic course of development that is hinted at in Turner's writings but is not fully developed. It is, however, one of the most important leads that we need to explore.

ALIENATION: KARL MARX AND KENNETH KENISTON

Before communitas happens and the charismatic process gets under way, there is, I believe, an antecedent process Weber largely ignores and Wallace and Turner barely touch upon. This is the period of alienation. Of course, Wallace's model does include a period of "cultural distortion" in which individuals are estranged from their culture, and that estrangement exhibits itself in alcoholism, drug addiction, and other behavior disorders. However, this portrait of the culturally estranged seems excessively clinical and narrow compared with the wealth of data presented by the students of alienation such as Karl Marx (1971a, 1971b) and Kenneth Keniston (1965).

Marx's thoughts about alienation are relevant to any sociological model that seeks to explain the genesis of social change, not merely those models that are concerned with the particular type of industrial alienation that he focused on. The core of his early thesis was that the deepest identity of human beings is their creative labor and that the modern industrial world has deprived them of that identity by reducing them into commodities and by divorcing them from the means of production and the fruits of their labor. This deprivation is seen as dehumanizing and a source of the most basic forms of human discontent (Marx 1971a:134ff.; 1971b:100). I believe that such alienation occurs not only in a capitalist industrial environment but in any situation in which humans are rendered incapable of engaging in creative labor. As such, it has great diagnostic value that can help the social scientist to understand the earliest stages of social change and to anticipate social upheavals before they have become full-blown revolutions.

Among the many contemporary writers who have examined the phenomenon of alienation, Kenneth Keniston stands out as one of the more astute observers. He studied the problem empirically and in great depth. He was able to shed light on the social psychological bases of change by conducting a series of in-depth life histories of a group of Harvard undergraduates in 1957. In his magnificent work, *The Uncommitted*, he manages to present a social psychological profile that, as it turned out, anticipated many aspects of the revolution of the 1960s. At the time he wrote the book, however, he was not aware that his analysis would anticipate these larger changes.

To Keniston, the alienated are not merely drug addicts, dropouts, and delinquents. They are rebels without a cause, deeply disaffected with society in general, estranged from their families, their peers, and their culture. In their view, all the rewards offered by higher education or by the affluent society are counterfeit. They state that "the thought of adjusting to society as presently constituted fills me with disgust" (Keniston 1965:25). "Life is a temporary sojourn on earth, with an inscrutable void before and after" and the universe is "random, chaotic, and stupid" (Keniston 1965:61). Since life has no purpose, the best way to spend it is by going after all the sensate experiences that one can have (Keniston 1965:68–70). In the 1960s this philosophy turned into a new way of life as drugs, rock music, and sex became instruments for the realization of that sensate world.

There are two questions we need to raise about Keniston's study. The first is whether or not alienation is a stage in the development of communitas. On the whole, Keniston regards the alienated as the product of social and technological change, *not as the beginning of social transformation*. Hence, the true diagnostic value of alienation is not fully realized. Secondly, Keniston's image of the alienated is so deeply and pervasively negative that it seems impossible for them to serve as the instrument of social transformation. Between the hopelessness and the deep existential pessimism of the alienated and the search for a better world that is the basis of the charismatic process, there is, it seems, an unbridgeable gap. That, in any case, is the impression one gets from Keniston's analysis (Keniston 1965). To my knowledge, he did not do a follow-up study to see if in fact the uncommitted youth of the late 1950s did not become the committed seekers and visionaries of the 1960s and early 1970s, or if their perspectives were transmitted to those who did.

It seems, however, that these phenomena are directly linked: *between alienation and communitas, and between communitas and revitalization, there is a probable causal chain*. This is an important aspect of the thesis presented in this chapter. The psychic void experienced by the alienated makes them eminently suitable material for salvation. In the language of Elijah Mohammad, leader of the Black Muslim movement, the alienated are "dead" and the job of the prophet is to go "fishing for the dead" and to bring them back to life (Charles Eric Lincoln 1961:115). To assume that the alienated are so dead that they cannot be brought back to life is to underestimate the power of revitalization.

Karl Marx, in the earliest stages of his career, saw alienation as a stage in the genesis of social transformation and as a potentially generative phenomenon. That perspective is perhaps closer to the mark than the curiously sterile conclusion Keniston comes to. The negativism of Keniston's subjects is, in fact, coupled with extraordinary creative language, boundless critical faculties, and undisciplined erratic intelligence. In short, they possess the type of diffuse spiritual and intellectual power that, if harnessed by a vision or a visionary, can produce significant results.

What about the question of social bonding among the alienated? Are they so asocial, so incapable of commitment to each other that they cannot form any kind of society? That is what some of Keniston's data indicate. Yet, his rich data also contain bits of evidence that suggest a different interpretation. Inburn, the star performer among Keniston's informants, states in his brilliant ramblings that he had a powerful hankering to drop out of Harvard, sever his family ties, and follow a friend called Hal to whom he was deeply attracted. That friend had become a true seeker and a wanderer, irrepressible and "utterly dissolute". So long as Inburn remained in college, he felt that he was not true to his calling and that his life was a sham. Clearly we must follow Inburn's subsequent career to see if his alienation does lead to communitas and commitment; to see if in fact he is not one of the young men and women who, in the 1960s, became the activist generation that had a far-reaching impact on American attitudes toward war and peace, sexuality and sex roles, sensuality and hedonism, asceticism and achievement (Keniston 1965:23–55).

COMMUNITAS AS DESTABILIZING OR REVOLUTIONARY FORCE

Why bring the concept of communitas into this discussion? Is communitas in any basic sense related to alienation, prophetism, and charisma? The relationship is not immediately self-evident and must be brought out in modest steps. To begin with, the most important factor in communitas appears to be psychological. By joining communitas, people are mentally liberated from their cultural and social milieu. Living in an unstructured environment, they become much more prone to experiment with new social forms than they would if they continued to live in an established social system. Rebellion from within social structure has an entirely different effect: the rebel's opposition to structure often has the potential of producing another type of structure. Furthermore, the rebel aims his criticism at specific aspects of structure, while communitas casts doubt on all types of structure. The one fact that keeps communitas alive is the fact that it stands *outside of structure*, both internally and in its relation to society. It is difficult for the group to maintain this state because of the perpetual tendency to rigidify and institutionalize their minor innovations. *The longer the group remains unstructured, the more likely they are to come up with fundamental innovations and to pass on those innovations to others.* Communitas not only lacks internal structure, it also has no boundaries and its open morality is the factor that gives it an expansive, universalistic quality.

Social science has yet to examine in depth the possible connection between communitas on the one hand and alienation, prophetism, and charisma on the other. The links as they appear at this stage can be briefly stated as follows:

1. Charismatic figures make use of communitas as a laboratory within which they hone their ideas, fashioning new ways of relating to their followers as well as to the rest of humankind. This is illustrated in Gandhi's life and the way he used the *ashrams* (communes) as crucibles for his own brand of socio-political alchemy.

2. Whether or not there is a charismatic figure present in communitas, the group serves as a niche that collects dropouts—people who are estranged from their cultural milieu and who come together in a freer association with each other than is possible in conventional society. The vast array of acephalous communes that mushroomed in the United States in the 1960s (Veysey 1978) and the many Rastafarian groups that have been observed in Jamaica and elsewhere during the

last four decades (Simpson 1955; Chavannes 1978) amply illustrate the character of this type of communitas.

In these instances it is clear that there is a connection between the alienated individuals and the agglomeration of people that makes up communitas; charismatic leadership is an optional feature that may or may not be present, but charismatic processes seem to be always at work.

Turner's interest is not to show how communitas brings about social change. His principal approach is to treat communitas as an enduring anti-structural element within the framework of an enduring social system. He deviates from this position hesitantly when he considers two religious innovators: Saint Francis of Assisi and Caitanya, the leader of the Hindu Vaisnava movement. In both cases, Turner analyzes the evolution of anti-structural human groups under the leadership of liminal-charismatic figures, who, by their exemplary conduct and by offering vague symbolic guidelines as to how the new life is to be achieved, transform their followers into a small group of undifferentiated individuals powerfully held together by the prophet's vision and by their personal attraction to him. The group's message is for humankind as a whole. They recognize no cognitive, social, or territorial boundaries. There is no question that these groups are innovative, because they lead deeply altered lives and have new patterns of social relationships among themselves. However, the movements do not continue as boundless, expansive communitas for long but are transformed into bounded, somewhat defensive communities, acknowledged by the wider society and thereby co-opted and rendered harmless. That is Turner's conclusion (Turner 1969:131–165).

I believe that this conclusion cuts a brilliant line of inquiry short and fails to assess the real historical consequences of the movements. Even the cases that he considers suggest a different interpretation. In my view, Saint Francis had a significant impact on the Catholic church. By forming a monastic order that is organized along fundamentally egalitarian lines, quite different from the structure of the hierarchical religious community, Saint Francis and his followers have introduced a major innovation into the church. New roles have been created. Future individuals who might embark on the dangerous career of closely emulating the life of Christ can be allowed to follow their career without threatening to upset entirely the clerical establishment. A source of perpetual instability has been institutionalized, whereby the religious community can continually renew itself and can reexamine the inequalities that it has come to tolerate in its ranks. By so doing, the church limits the revolutionary potential of the visionaries, but, at the same time, it expands its structural and philosophical base and becomes a more complex and more flexible institution than it was prior to the movement. The relationship is clearly reciprocal. It is not only the church that has co-opted St. Francis. It is also St. Francis who has co-opted the church by creating a permanent liminal place for himself and his followers within the hierarchical structure that was so alien to him.

This mutual co-opting is a type of social change that is of great interest to the social scientist. The revitalization process may not transform society as a whole, although in the early stages it may aspire to do just that. Instead it strikes a series of compromises that are themselves an integral part of the process by which change is incorporated into the social order. Communitas becomes community. A boundless agglomeration of human beings becomes a bounded group. Sharp distinctions are drawn between believers and nonbelievers. In due course, the proselytizing impulse declines or is abandoned altogether. When that point is reached, historians are liable to conclude that the society has triumphed over its detractors, and the social movement has "failed". This view misses an important point: *communitas creates new social forms even as it dies.*

As open communitas evolves into a closed community, a number of things happen that are of interest to students of social change. First, the social order is altered because a new type of community has come into being that can serve as a model for other such communities: a precedent has been established that legitimizes further experimentation. The hostility directed against them by the society is mitigated. The deviant role becomes part of the sociological landscape, no longer surprising or offensive. Long hair and dreadlocks, which were once the insignias of rebellion, may even become fashionable.

Secondly, those members of the movement who are absorbed by the established society take with them some of the values acquired while participating in the movement. I do not mean to suggest "once a seeker, always a seeker". However, it is important to reexamine the visionaries turned into doctors, lawyers, and stockbrokers and ask whether they help to raise the ethical standards of their profession or whether they become garden variety professionals indistinguishable from their more conventional colleagues. Too often we use the seekers turned into stockbrokers as a hasty measure of the failure of social movements. As communitas is routinized, it brings in a whole array of new values that society adopts without acknowledging their source.

PROPHETISM WITHOUT PROPHETS

Up to this point our discussion has dwelt on existing theories about revitalization and has raised questions about how these theories might be synthesized into a larger model. Before completing this exercise, however, we need to examine the *social* dimension of the charismatic personality and the charismatic process.

As I suggested at the beginning of this chapter, much sociological thought has dwelt on the prophetic or charismatic individuals, how they get their inspiration or vision, how they communicate their message to others, how their charismatic authority is authenticated through miracles, magical feats, and healing, and the kinds of crises that develop between leader and followers or between factions within the movement as the followers evolve into an organized community, their values are codified, and their way of life is institutionalized. In all this scholarship, the focus is on the impact of the charismatic figure on his or her followers. There is a great paucity of thought concerning the other side of that equation: how the "followers" induct their "leader" into a prophetic career and train him or her to think and behave like a prophet.

The question, framed in its most extreme form, is simply this: Is it possible for prophetic movements to come into being and to thrive without prophets? Is it possible for messianism to evolve without the physical presence of a messiah? Is it possible for charisma to be widely distributed in the liminal community without converging on a single individual? Is it possible for communitas to invent its prophets and attribute to them qualities they do not possess? In short, is the prophet sometimes created in the image of the liminal community? When the community genuflects before its invented image, is it correct for us to search in the life history of the "charismatic figure" to identify experiences that are said to have precipitated the visionary experience, the prophetic career, and the resulting revitalization process?

Stated differently, prophets may be nonexistent, absent, dead, or expected; and that fact does not seem to make a significant difference to prophetic movements. If anything, many revitalization movements seem to thrive after the death or removal of the prophet because they begin to organize themselves into viable communities, unencumbered by the destabilizing influences of the charismatic personality on whom they may have depended in the early stages of their history. They can also continue the prophetic career by attributing ideas and prophecies to the dead, absent, or nonexistent prophet. When they do, however, the process is decidedly social in character and we must look for an understanding of the resulting charismatic process in the social dynamic itself, not in the personality, dreams or visionary experiences of the charismatic figure.

THE RASTAFARIANS: HISTORICAL BACKGROUND

This idea of the prophetic movement without a prophet was powerfully suggested to me by Leonard Barrett's rich study of the Rastafarians of Jamaica (Barrett 1977). Rastafarianism is a revitalization movement that views Haile Sellassie I, the last Emperor of Ethiopia, as its prophet or its redeemer. Before his coronation in 1930, the emperor's name was Ras Tafari, and as such he was one of the numerous "dukes" in the empire bearing the title of Ras. That name, "Ras Tafari", and not the throne name of the emperor, Haile Sellassie, is what the movement adopted as the appellation of their redeemer. They often prefix the name with the title "Jah", which stands for the godhead.

During the first quarter of the twentieth century, at a time when nearly all of Africa had fallen prey to colonialism, Ethiopia remained independent and defiant. She had defeated the Italians at the battle of Adwa (1896) and was forever vigilant about further European attempts to colonize her. As such, Ethiopia was the bastion of African freedom and was so symbolized throughout the African Diaspora. Ethiopianism mushroomed in colonial Africa and the new world (Sundkler 1961). It represented African freedom and sometimes crystalized in the form of religious independency and separatist or revivalist African churches, often borrowing some symbols and some elements of ritual from the Ethiopian Orthodox Church. This Ethiopian church had its origins in the third century A.D. and is as venerable as any other branch of Christendom (Barrett 1968).

Against this historical background the coronation of Emperor Haile Sellassie, a grand and ancient ritual attended by representatives of monarchies from around the world, had a far-reaching impact in the African Diaspora. Ras Tafari's throne name was Haile Sellassie, "the Power of Trinity", and his titles were King of Kings, Elect of God, Conquering Lion of the Tribe of Judah. He belonged to a dynasty that was more or less in continuous control of the empire since the thirteenth century. He was "King of Kings" by virtue of the fact that he reigned over several large kingdoms and republics, each larger than some of the modern African states of today. He was "Conquering Lion of the Tribe of Judah" because his dynasty—the Solomonid dynasty—claimed direct descent from King Solomon and invoked three millennia of recorded history to validate the claim. He was "Elect of God" and that was not subject to debate. These were impressive credentials.

One community that was deeply affected by the coronation was a poverty-stricken black community in Jamaica that was estranged from the mulatto and multiethnic social class that dominated their land and their political and economic life. The destitute blacks claimed Ras Tafari as their prophet and developed an elaborate charismatic vision around that idea. They declared him to be "the living God", the redeemer who would some day take them to Ethiopia, the promised land.

Needless to say, Ethiopia was not the promised land but one of the poorest nations in Africa and the emperor was not the living God but a monarch who ruled a country struggling to maintain its autonomy in the hostile environment of European colonizers. Furthermore, Ethiopia was a colonial empire that dominated many peoples who were brought to their knees by force of arms. Indeed, Ethiopia was often on the defensive because she was accused by Western nations of practicing slavery. As such, Ethiopia was hardly the promised land destined to set poor black men and women free.

More importantly, the emperor was the supreme ruler of Ethiopia only in matters temporal; it was always understood that he had to submit to the authority of the archbishop of Ethiopia in matters spiritual. It would be blasphemy to suggest that he was, in any sense, divine. From the perspective of the Ethiopian Orthodox Church, he was not the living God, but a mere mortal elevated to high office by the grace of God and the consent of the church. The emperor was something of an upstart who came to power after the church had condemned Lij Iyasu for the close ties he maintained with the Muslim community of Ethiopia. The latter was the grandson of Emperor Menelik and a more direct heir to the Shoan Amhara throne. Haile Sellassie overthrew the heir by pointing to his Muslim connections and challenging his loyalty to the Ethiopian Orthodox Church. It is important to note, however, that the same power which the Church exercised to bring Haile Sellassie to the throne could also have been exercised to terminate his own royal career were he to have acknowledged or in any way encouraged the Rastafarians in their mistaken belief that he is God.

As a result, throughout the early history of the movement, the emperor studiously avoided contact with the Rastafarians. However, he did nothing explicitly to discourage the movement or dispel their erroneous belief in his divinity. This strange relationship between Rastafarians and the emperor turns out to be of considerable theoretical interest to social anthropology. From this case, we learn that a movement can attribute to an individual prophetic or charismatic properties he does not possess and that, furthermore, the reality of his personality or of his office may not be sufficient to significantly constrain that creative process.

In keeping with biblical tradition, the coming of the Redeemer was foretold by a charismatic figure of another era. It is said that Marcus Garvey, the Jamaican leader who headed a huge mass movement among black Americans in the 1920s, prophesied that a black king would be enthroned and that he would be the Redeemer. No hard evidence suggests that Garvey ever made this prophecy, but for our purposes, that is immaterial. Furthermore, whether the prophecy was made before or after the fact does not seem to matter. If the believers are convinced that it was a genuine prophecy, the outcome is the same.

So long as the Emperor of Ethiopia was a distant figure who could not come into contact with his followers, the Rastafarians were able to advance their cause undeterred by the realities of Ethiopia. Some evidence suggests that the movement was set back on the two occasions when they made actual contact with the emperor and with the Ethiopian Orthodox Church. In 1960, when the Rastafarian movement was at its peak, the University of the West Indies sent out a group of professors to the Rasta ghettoes in Jamaica to conduct an inquiry into the nature of the movement. Their report turned out to be very sympathetic and made a number of recommendations that brought the Rastas close to their promised land and face to face with their redeemer (Barrett 1977:99, 108). Partly because of the support they received from the academic community, they began to achieve a measure of legitimacy that culminated with the emperor's visit to Jamaica in 1966. By all accounts, this was a momentous event. One hundred thousand people, including some ten thousand Rastas, turned out to greet him. Judging from the records of Rasta expansion at that stage, it would seem that nearly all the members of the movement were at the airport on that day.

Rastafarians were overjoyed by the visit, but they were also disheartened by the emperor's failure to acknowledge the divine role they had thrust upon him (Barrett 1977:108). Similarly, when the Ethiopian Orthodox Church was established in Jamaica, the Rasta halfheartedly took part in the services only to find that the music, the rituals, and the structure of the church were completely strange to them. Between the haunting melodies of Reggae music and the extraordinarily discordant chanting of the Ethiopian Orthodox Church, there is a huge cultural chasm. Rasta communities are generally egalitarian, particularly among adult males in the community, whereas the Ethiopian Orthodox Church is rigidly hierarchical. Rastafarian music, poetry, and prose speak with disarming directness that is readily accessible to believers and, with some effort, to nonbelievers as well. The Orthodox church speaks in Ge'ez, the dead language of medieval Ethiopia, inaccessible to all but Ethiopic scholars and *some* of the more literate priests. So too are the rigid doctrinal positions of the Orthodox church and their complex system of taboos and prohibitions quite alien to the revivalist and proto-revolutionary philosophy of the Rastas.[3]

The movement has survived these crises and has expanded throughout the Caribbean and beyond. They have maintained their anti-structural position to this day and, with the aid of their extraordinary music, they have gained greater outreach in the world now than at any time of their history. Their narrow loyalty to Ethiopia and to Jah Ras Tafari has tended to give way to a more Pan-African orientation, particularly since the dethronement and the death of the emperor at the hands of the Ethiopian military. When they heard the news about the death of the emperor, their response was calm and defiant: they announced to the world that "Jah Lives!" and that "Rastas never die". These seemingly irrational statements make ample sense when viewed in the context of their belief system. If Jah (God) is in Ras Tafari and if Ras Tafari is in every Rastaman then Jah does indeed live and will continue to do so as long as the Rasta community endures.

THE RASTAFARIAN EVIDENCE
IN THEORETICAL CONTEXT

The case of the Rastafarians suggests that it is quite possible for a community to go through all the stages of charismatic transformation without becoming dependent on any one dominant figure. Instead, the community forms itself around a *charismatic idea* and exhibits essentially the same qualities as one that is under the direct guidance of a prophet. In this pattern of social transformation, the creative impulse continues to be an aspect of the social dynamic itself, not a personal vision quest of a dominant figure that is then transmitted to the followers.

RASTA ALIENATION

Before we begin to explore the character of the Rasta movement, we must examine the prior condition that led to that process of transformation. The prior condition is the deep estrangement of the destitute Jamaicans from the British colonial establishment and later from the Jamaican, predominantly mulatto, elite who inherited power from their colonial predecessors. The people who embraced Rastafarianism are "Jamaicans of unmistakenly African descent [who were] decidedly relegated to the base of society" (Owens 1976:VIII). Rastafarians live in a state of extreme poverty. They are most often unemployed, and if they are employed, they receive very low pay. Their housing is desperately poor and they have no political rights (Campbell 1987:69). Their communities on the outskirts of Kingston, Jamaica, are swamps that have been reclaimed by dumping mountains of urban waste into them. Their communities have names like Swine Lake in Montego Bay or Dungle, that is, Dung Hill, in Kingston.

The history of the movement contains much poignant testimony to the persecution of the Rasta by the colonial and neocolonial establishments. Their extraordinary attire, their outlandish hairstyle, and their bold manners were so offensive to the Jamaican elite that they were subjected to much derision and scorn (Waters 1989:70). Their communities were sometimes bulldozed and set on fire in violent "clean up" campaigns by the city governments (Barrett 1977:156). In the early stages of their history they sometimes lived like hermits, away from the cities, in rural enclaves. When they visited the city, they had to disguise their identity by shaving their beards and wearing a tam over their dreadlocks. In the words of one member of the Rasta community, "I know brethren who live in the hills ... for years ... like hermit. And police take helicopter and go in the hills and dig out those brethren and half kill them" (Owens 1976:1).

Rastas respond to the contempt and persecution that is directed at them by rejecting Jamaican society, its inherited neocolonial institutions, and its "received English" (Kitzinger 1969:241–242). They consider the goals of the society worthless, its legitimizing myths counterfeit, and its identity false. Even the services that state institutions offer such as welfare, schools, clinics, and hospitals are rejected. "They distrust all social workers, ministers of religion, and others who symbolize for them middle-class affluence, deceit, and the assumption of innate superiority. They join no Jamaican associations—and this includes trade unions" (Kitzinger 1969:34). They refuse to join political parties or to vote; they are reluctant to seek employment in establishment businesses and do not send their children to government schools (Owens 1976:241).

Rastas view themselves as "strangers in a strange land", as Africans exiled to a godforsaken world, which they call Babylon (Waters 1989:105). In their cosmology, Babylon is a complex and fully elaborated concept we cannot examine here in any great depth. We mention it merely to illustrate the depth of alienation of the Rasta from wider society. Babylon in this construction is the Western World: it includes the colonial and neocolonial states and the organized Christian church. "Ministers are Antichrists and preach Antichrist. They are the agents for the mental enslavement of the black man. Their most vicious representatives are black priests, the oppressive allies of the white man. Both the white and the black oppressors shall suffer the same fate" (Smith, Augier, and Nettleford 1960:20). Both the church and state structures of Babylon will be destroyed in the impending "eschatological battle of Armageddon" (Owens 1976:69).

The Rasta experience can now be placed in the context of the models of alienation offered by Marx and Keniston. If we acknowledge that creative work is the defining characteristic of human beings, as Marx argues, then alienation must be endemic in societies that have some segment of their population more or less permanently relegated to the "jobless" bin. Unemployment was the norm in the Rasta community. Some of them were in the "job market" going from one temporary job to the next. Many had abandoned the quest and had become self-employed craftsmen. Before their conversion, the majority of Rastas were permanently jobless and perpetually dispossessed with no hope of ever playing a meaningful role in the neocolonial economy. These men and women were, therefore, alienated in the broader sense in which we employ the Marxian concept.

We cannot be entirely sure that the prospective Rastas were also alienated in the Kenistonian sense of the word. There are no in-depth psychological-biographic studies of Rastas *before their conversion*. If we keep in mind that conversion has a healing effect, then the description of the committed, proud, and morally ascendant Rastas cannot reveal the depth of their alienation and despair before they joined the movement.

The point has general significance in studies of alienation and revitalization. In the American Black Muslim movement, the autobiography of one of its most articulate members suggests that this before-and-after factor is critical. Malcolm Little, the dope pusher and pimp who became Malcolm X, the outspoken minister of Islam, are two different persons. It is Malcolm Little that we must try to understand if we are to evaluate the role of alienation in the revitalization process. Nothing short of a time-depth study of individual Rastas before and after their conversion experience is needed to determine the nature of the condition that gave rise to the movement. As yet, no such data have surfaced in the extensive literature on the Rastafarians or in the smaller corpus of writings by the Rastas themselves.

There are a few autobiographical reminiscenses of Rastas about their earlier lives that suggest that they were alienated from their African heritage, from Jamaican society, from all its institutions, and from its cultural and moral foundations. After their conversion, their attitude toward Africa and toward that which is African in them changes dramatically, but Jamaican society and its institutions remain an object of scorn.

In the final analysis, however, the most crippling aspect of alienation is alienation from self. This too is present in Rasta autobiographical passages in the works of Joseph Owens (1976) and in the Rasta's own written testimony (Tesfa 1980). They describe themselves as wholly lacking in self-worth. The most important aspect of Rasta spiritual life is directed at this problem: learning to fend off the scorn of the Jamaican bourgeoisie and helping the believer to develop a sense of personal autonomy and pride.

RASTA COMMUNITAS:
THE EARLY COMMUNES AND ANTI-STRUCTURE

One of the earliest Rasta communes, established in 1940 by Leonard P. Howell, had the character of a community removed from society. This act of withdrawal was necessary in part because of police harassment but more fundamentally because of the deep estrangement between themselves and the rest of the society. Howell was jailed at the start of his career as a Rasta preacher, and when he was released and returned to his commune, he and his followers led a "secluded existence" (Owens 1976:19).

In the 1950s there was great proliferation of small informal groups of Rastas calling themselves by such names as the "Ethiopian Coptic Church", "The United Ethiopian Body", and the "United Afro West Indian Brotherhood". "In 1953 Simpson estimated that there were twelve groups of Ras Tafari brethren in Kingston, having memberships between 20 and 150" (Smith, Augier, and Nettleford 1960:10, 11). They operated independently of each other and attracted little public notice (Simpson 1955:167).

There was little massing effect in this process of social formation. Each small group was on its own tangent, under its own shifting leadership. The groups were antistructural in the sense that Turner defined that concept:

1. They were egalitarian and rejected rank and status distinction among themselves;
2. They had little internal organization;
3. They were reluctant to join with other groups of Ras Tafarians (Lee 1981:54; Barbara Makeda Smith 1960:18).

There was no tendency to accept organizational leadership of any kind. "Structurally, the movement remains … acephalous. No leader has arisen to unite the separate branches of the movement and there is no desire to do so" (Barrett 1977:172).

Various leaders have arisen in the Rasta community who had the potential of becoming prophets of Rastafarianism, but none of them achieved the stature that would have enabled them to lead the Rastafarian movement as a whole. Among these should be mentioned Hibbert (who was reputed to have occult powers), Dunkley, Robert Hinds (head of the King of Kings Mission), Claudius Henry, and Prince Emmanuel. That these leaders were sometimes referred to as "prophets" and sometimes divinized is well documented. Among them only Prince Emmanuel, the leader of the Bobo (Ethiopian International Congress) attempted to bring together an island-wide meeting of the faithful. In time, his movement too became a small faction. "Prince's followers became more sectarian. They began to attribute divinity to him, and separating themselves from other Rastafarians" (Chavannes 1978:197).[4]

Some significant exceptions to this anti-structural pattern in the history of the movement exist. On occasion we find that a Rasta group adopts pragmatic objectives and devises an organization to achieve them. The rise of the Ethiopian World Federation in New York City is a case in point. This federation was highly organized and regimented and was committed to the program of repatriation. The emergence of the Ethiopian Zion Coptic Church also offers a more recent example of a thoroughly organized Rasta group. This church has acquired considerable capital from the ganja or marijuana trade and uses its capital to buy up property. The authors who describe these groups, however, doubt their authenticity as Rastafarian bodies and consider them either deviants or schismatics (Owens 1976:241; Lee 1981:56; Campbell 1987:115).

RASTA "LEADERSHIP" IN AN ANTI-STRUCTURAL MILIEU

The leaders that have emerged from time to time in the history of the movement also exhibit a type of relationship with each other and with their followers that suggests they are more like the eye of a storm than the apex of a pyramid. From the very beginning it appears that there was a plurality of proto-prophetic characters who proclaimed the divinity of Ras Tafari. This happened soon after the coronation of the emperor in November 1930. Surprisingly, these men were not members of an organized or even an informal group. They began to preach that the emperor was the returned Messiah and they did so "*independently of one another*" (Owens 1976:18; emphasis added).

It is not merely at its inception that the Rasta movement exhibits these anti-structural qualities. Throughout its history the movement has not produced an overall leader, a unique individual who could actively guide the movement. The closest they came to recognizing such an individual is when they attributed the role of "forerunner" to Marcus Garvey. He was the proto-prophetic figure who antici-pated the coming of the Redeemer, but he was not himself seen as the Redeemer. His ideas have played an important role in the birth of the movement. In some branches of the movement today, Garvey can be said to have replaced Haile Sellassie as the principal charismatic authority. This happens especially with groups who have adopted a more conventional Black Nationalist ideology along with a whole firmament of Black Nationalist icons.

Garvey's relationship with the orthodox Rastafarians has always been somewhat problematic. He does not qualify as the prophetic figure because (1) he is seen as the precursor to the prophet, not as the principal Messiah; (2) he is the head of an entirely different organization (UNIA), which the Rastas did not join in any significant numbers; (3) Rasta groups were too volatile and individualistic to fit in the Garveyite mold.

The most important factor that stands in the way of Rasta-Garvey rapprochement is Garvey's hostility toward Haile Sellassie. Although Garvey is said to have prophesied the coming of Ras Tafari, the severity of his criticism of Haile Sellassie, especially after the emperor went into exile, casts some doubt upon his "forerunner" role (Campbell 1987:75). This is the reality that gets in the way of Rastas' elevating Garvey into the prophetic role.

Regardless of the position that is finally accorded to Garvey in Rasta messianic thought, it is true that the movement has remained deeply anti-structural throughout its history and, on the whole, continues in that mode today. As such, it exhibits many of the characteristics of communitas and has had a significant destabilizing effect on the wider society in Jamaica and elsewhere in the African Diaspora.

Students of Rastafari and scholars who are steeped in the history of the movement are likely to argue that the movement has had several prophets and that this study does not pay enough attention to them. The issue, however, is not that there are "several" prophets that we have neglected, but that there are thousands that we have taken into consideration. For the central thesis of this chapter still stands as long as (1) most Rastafarians believe that they are individually inspired and possess the kind of charismatic authority that empowers them to communicate directly with God, to discover the divine mission of Rastafari through personal contemplation, and to interpret the scriptures independently of any living teachers; (2) the vast majority of the faithful do not submit obsequiously to the authority of any one of the lesser prophets who have from time to time emerged in their midst; and (3) the faithful place Ras Tafari at the center of their charismatic community as a prophet who has, however, never communicated with them in that capacity. The thesis does not depend on the premise that the lesser prophets do not have charisma, but that charismatic authority is dispersed across the entire community.

INDIVIDUAL CHARISMA AND SELF-EMPOWERMENT

Rastafarians emerged from their deeply alienated condition by inventing a savior for themselves. In our effort to understand the role that this *idea of a messiah* plays in Rasta resurgence, it is important to stress the distributed quality of charismatic authority in the Rasta communitas. Although they believe that Ras Tafari (Haile Sellassie) is the living God, it is equally true that *every Rastaman is also Ras Tafari*. This is the strange and paradoxical concept that lies at the heart of their cosmology. "Any Rastafarian will tell you that ... Rastafari is in every black man and all that he has to do is to recognize it" (Owens 1976:2). "We get our spiritual communication daily from our Imperial Majesty, the Emperor Haile Sellassie. We don't have to read the bible to know that he is God. … We know he is God through *inborn conception"* (Kitzinger 1969:248). In other words the charismatic authority is present in every individual Rasta and does not depend on an external source to activate it or to keep it alive. The daily "message" from the emperor is, in fact, a message from within, an inner voice.

A Rastaman is a seeker and the experience by which he discovers the divinity of Ras Tafari and hence the divine powers within himself is vividly described in Rasta autobiographic accounts (Owens 1976:92ff.). The essence of these experiences is that the individual goes through a thought-filled search, reexamining the scriptures to gain a fresh understanding, checking his intuitions against biblical passages, and constructing a step by step personal exegesis leading toward the discovery of the divinity of Ras Tafari. This often results in a "conversion" experience for the Rasta that "involves a radical re-structuring of his world-view and his priorities" (Owens 1976:95).

It is not only individuals' lives that are restructured in the process but also their language undergoes a metamorphosis. The use of "me" as a subject, which is common in the Jamaican dialect of English, has been virtually eliminated. "Me go to town" is considered an obsequious manner of speech. Indeed, "me" has been eliminated entirely and has been replaced by "I". In the words of a Rasta writer, "The concept of I is that of One Universal Creator, whose spirit so flows Life's own creativity. 'I am that I am' … boundless in degrees of a single manifestation". "I art my brother's keeper, and he I; for I am in him, him in I, together the reflections of a single one, I-man" (Tesfa 1980:43).

The philosophy that this language represents is the philosophy of communitas— an agglomeration of individuals whose personality is not diminished by the homogenizing effect of communalism. The Rasta communitas recognizes no "We" that stands above the individual. "We" is another pronoun that has become extinct in Rasta speech and replaced by "I-and-I", reflecting the deep sense of personal autonomy that is so central to the Rasta view of the individual-in-communitas.

The most important political and economic consequence of this transformation is the self-empowerment of the disenfranchised and the construction of a self-reliant economy among the dispossessed. In Rasta writings, such as those of Ras J. Tesfa, this redemptive power of individualized charisma is clearly stated. In his essay Tesfa declares that redemption comes in the form of self-reliance, self-help, work, thrift, and investment.

> Buy a handful of newspapers and sell them, buy a few heads of cabbages and start to become a merchant, buy a few oranges from the dollar and later on you will be buying barrels. Why! take a dollar and invest in bananas and sell them at a profit. Do not eat up all your capital and profit on the first day. Keep your capital and live only on the fifty percent of your profit. You will have a bigger capital the next day. Let every day be like the day before, and then you will find how quickly you are ascending the ladder of commerce, to be probably one of its captains. This is only a small indication of what you can do before you remain idle and say you cannot find anything to do. (Tesfa 1980:8–9)

These words that inspire the Rasta to become self-reliant are the words of Marcus Garvey, not Haile Sellassie. In a strange and fascinating way it appears that the Rastafarian is using two dead prophets at different stages of the evolution of the movement. In the early stages of anti-structure, Haile Sellassie is the appropriate figure. He has legitimacy, sanctity, distance, and he serves eminently to elevate the African identity in the hostile and scornful world of the Black Diaspora. As the movement begins to routinize, they reach back to the pragmatism and organizational skills of Marcus Garvey, whose prescriptions sometimes sound like those of a devout entrepreneur.

In any case, it is clear that neither Garvey nor Haile Sellassie can be credited with having initiated or in any significant sense helped to sustain the Rastafarian movement. Both are nothing more than *charismatic ideas* that the Rasta has used most effectively to restructure his or her own world, to mobilize his or her community, and to construct a vision of a better world. In the final analysis, the vision is primarily theirs, not Garvey's and not Haile Sellassie's. The few passages from Haile Sellassie's and Garvey's speeches that the Rasta have incorporated into their oral and written literature do seem to play an appreciable role in their lives. However, they deal with these texts as creatively as they do with the Bible and subject them to the most thorough rethinking and reinterpretation.

In the political sphere, Rastafarians emerge from their original position as outcasts to become the most effective advocates of the pro-African resurgence that developed and is still developing, by fits and starts, in Jamaica. From time to time, leading politicians in Jamaica have sought to associate themselves with the Reggae stars, hoping that some of the glory might rub off on them. The bourgeois also seek to extend their political outreach and to buttress their weak African roots by making overtures to the Rasta.

EXISTING THEORY AND ITS RELEVANCE TO THE RASTA

In the present study I am raising one key question with regard to the concept of charisma that neither Weber nor Shils has dealt with adequately: To what extent can charisma be dispersed such that many, if not all, members of a movement will exhibit charismatic qualities and, therefore, need not rely on a single individual as the source of charismatic authority? So far, this issue has not received much attention in sociology or anthropology, but I will review the little that is written on the subject.

Two writers who address these questions are Douglas Masden and Peter G. Snow (1983, 1987). They start their discussion with Shils's definition of the "dispersion of charisma" and the "attenuation of charisma" during the routinization process. They acknowledge that Weber did examine the routinization process, but they say that he did not specify the stages and patterns of differentiation and the feedback processes that are exhibited as the "dispersion of charisma" goes into effect. They identify two stages in the routinization process:

> The first would involve mediation of leader-to-mass flow of communications and benefits as a result of the interposition of lieutenants and high-priests—in short, the development of structure. The second will involve the emergence of intermediaries in the flow going the other way—that is, the stream of emotional responses running from mass to leader. (Masden and Snow 1987:339)

The dispersion of charisma also has the potential of fragmenting the movement as each charismatic figure embarks on his or her own sub-prophetic career. The lieutenants go in their respective ways and develop a following that might eventually exclude the leader. Such a transfer of charismatic authority from the prophet to the disciples or lieutenants might follow the death of the prophet or it might happen during the lifetime of the prophet (Masden and Snow 1987:340). This process of dispersion of charisma comes about partly because

> the charismatic leader eventually must incorporate some intermediaries into structural locations that might lie between his following and himself. This is a critical development, for with these intermediaries, sooner or later, must come dilution, erosion, and even deliberate distortion of the leader's mission as these secondary figures move, consciously or unconsciously, to put their own stamp on the movement. ...
>
> The successful charismatic leader faces two possibilities: he can institutionalize the movement, thus preparing the way for dispersion of charisma, or he can fail to initiate structure and thereby promote the disintegration of the mass following. (Masden and Snow 1987:358)

The authors use empirical data on Peronism and the evolution of the movement after the death of Peron to test out these theories.

To sum up, the Shils thesis, as interpreted and expanded by Masden and Snow, goes a long way toward explaining how charisma passes from a leader to his or her disciples, and because the process is clearly described as an interactive process it has considerable relevance to our thesis. In the final analysis, however, even this expanded interpretation of Weber and Shils fails to answer the critical questions that are raised by the Rastafarian data.

The thesis that comes closest to the model presented in this paper is contained in a study by Roy Wallis (1982) titled "The Social Construction of Charisma". In this analysis, the charismatic feedback is not an outcome of the routinization and dispersion processes. *Feedback is present at the very inception of the prophetic career*. It is not something that happens at the end of that career.

The main position of Wallis can be stated in the following terms. "Charisma is essentially a relationship born out of the interaction between a leader and his followers ... the emergence, recognition and maintenance of charisma [being] an interactional process, in which each party secures status in exchange of recognition, affection and reinforcement of worth" (Wallis 1982:26). The case material on which the authors build their theory is the story of a prophetic figure, named David Birg, who came from a family of evangelists and whose mother had mysterious, miraculous healing powers. She also had the gift of prophecy in her preaching. Her son was a frail, shy, and reticent individual who compensated for his physical inferiority by cultivating a sense of supernatural power. However, he considered himself a complete failure as an evangelist. His wife also had a similar opinion of him. Both his own self-effacing attitude and his wife's low regard for him combined to make a prophetic career unlikely.

Radical transformation of his personality occurred when he met a woman named Maria. She is described as a woman with a homely appearance, a minister's daughter who had, up to that point, led a sheltered life. She fell in love with him and began to encourage him to think of himself as a spiritual leader. David Birg says about his mistress:

> I think I've really given up on myself ... and it almost looked like God had given up on me because I wasn't seeming to accomplish anything ... then Maria came along and all of a sudden I found somebody who believed in me! ... She just trusted and believed and I didn't dare fail her. I mean God put her where I had to deliver. So I stepped out by faith and depended on the Lord and I delivered. (Wallis 1982:31)

Birg's relationship with Maria was adulterous and they had to deal with that problem if he was to become an effective spiritual leader. They dealt with it by construing this relationship as a special type of relationship, a divine relationship, "one which represented the new relationship as a type of God's relationship with the Church. ... To illustrate how God was choosing a new church to replace the old, the Lord had given David a new love" (Wallis 1982:31). This illicit but divine sexual relationship was then generalized to become the moral basis of the entire community. The disciples developed a type of loose marital union with each other and engaged in free sex as a form of communion.

The interaction between leader and follower is fully described in Wallis's ethnography of this movement.

> Birg achieved this continual recognition in the same way he generated it originally, that is, through a system of exchanges. Birg would single people out for special attention, affection and praise. ... Flattered that they should receive so much attention and concern from God's prophet, they in turn were only too willing to accept the status accorded them and thereby confirm the status of Maw [Birg], as God's oracle, to reaffirm his conception of himself, to support his aspirations, and to encourage him at any point at which he felt disheartened, unsuccessful, or when the possibility arose in his mind that things were not as he thought—that he was not doing God's will in all this. Like Maria earlier, they too encouraged him to take himself absolutely seriously; and by their constant attention to every utterance and act, encouraged him to take seriously every whim, fancy or performance: to see this as something more than merely the passing whimsical thought or action of an individual, but indeed as a divinely ordained revelation from God. (Wallis 1982:35)

That, in Wallis's view, is how the Gemeinde, or charismatic community, comes into being.

The Gemeinde must not only help to create the prophet, it must also protect the prophet from nonbelievers who would be only too eager to tear the social construction apart.

> Considerable care must therefore be taken over the selection of those permitted access to the leader. If his standing is upset or denied, not only is the leader's self-conception jeopardized, but also that of everyone around him. Thus, the elite, the "charismatic authority", in the Gemeinde have a substantial incentive to protect his environment. They will seek to exclude from interaction with the prophet all who might see him in terms of some earlier identity,

or who—by nature of their interaction with him—undermine or discredit his identity as a prophet. (Wallis 1982:37)

An interesting phenomenon about Birg which parallels the development of charismatic movements after the death or removal of the prophet is that Birg deliberately isolated himself from his followers, and at a certain point in his career, he actually communicated with them by letter. This distancing was a way of protecting his identity and making himself mysterious. Wallis's conclusion follows:

> Charisma is constructed in the process of social interaction. It emerges out of a particular structure of social relationship in which an exchange takes place of mutual attribution of status and worth. The putative charismatic leader, emboldened by this flattering recognition of the status and identity to which he aspires, then seeks to realize in his behavior the powers and status with which he has been credited, to live up to the image with which he has been endowed. In the process others are elevated as intimates or lieutenants. This significance derives from his having been raised up, and recognized as special by him, they add to the recognition of the leader, endowing him with still further significance as author of the movement and their own fortunate condition, leading him to take ever more seriously the conception of himself as someone out-of-the-ordinary. (Wallis 1982:38)

THEORETICAL CONCLUSIONS: DEMOCHARISMA

The progression of ideas that we have gleaned from the theorists as we go from Weber, to Shils, to Masden and Snow, and finally to Wallis has taken us to the brink of heresy. We take this progression of ideas to its logical conclusion on the basis of the rich data on the Rastafarian movement. These data reveal that a charismatic community can come into being, function, thrive, evolve, and routinize without ever submitting to the authority of a prophetic figure. Nevertheless, such a community surprisingly reveals most of the qualities of a revitalization movement that is under the direct influence of a living prophet. The question of feedback and interaction between leader and follower therefore becomes largely irrelevant. The key question becomes how a community constructs and maintains its idea of the savior. Nothing demonstrates the social dimension of charismatic authority more vividly than the Rasta situation in which the prophet is almost entirely absent. Indeed the spiritual, visionary, divine African Messiah that the Rasta envisioned in their creative thinking does not even exist. What they imagine and what exists in reality are two fundamentally different persons.

If we assume that charismatic authority is specifically supernatural in origin, as Weber does, the assumption inhibits sociological explanation of the genesis of that authority. Of course the charismatic community itself—the prophet and his followers—do attach critical importance to the role that God plays in launching the prophetic career. They must, if they are to legitimize themselves as founders of a new religion and a new society. Otherwise, the desire of a handful of people to reinvent society and morality appears preposterous and presumptuous. On the other hand, we, as students of human society, must focus on the role that society plays in that process. Prophets and their followers have to build their design of the new society on the foundation of "divine inspiration". It is disastrous if sociology begins its analyses with the same premise by making the supernatural force part of the definition of prophetism. The model assumes that which must be explained.

Weber, and others who follow in his footsteps, do of course bring society back into the model in the validation (and routinization) stages: that is, when the prophet begins his career as a leader, a teacher, a propagator of the faith and when he uses miracles and other extraordinary powers to impress upon his followers that his powers are divinely ordained. It is generally assumed that before that process of validation begins, the prophetic career was a lonely quest, a dialogue between the prophet and God. Recall Weber's statement that charisma is internally defined and that the prophet does not receive his mission from any human agency. Even when Wallace gives this model a psychoanalytic twist, it still remains a lonely quest in which the prophet develops his vision on the basis of his private dreams.

This privatization of the genesis of the prophetic career that occurs in sociology is part of the same patriarchal tradition that lies at the root of the particular brand of prophetism that evolved in the Middle East and in the Western World. The prophet in both these views is an authoritative, usually masculine, often bearded, visionary who, like Moses, descends from the mountains with a fully developed blueprint of the new social and moral order.

It is therefore highly instructive that a group of exiled Africans, such as the Rastafarians, who do not share that particular brand of patriarchalism should reinvent the charismatic community as a purely sociological phenomenon—a variety of prophetism without prophets. Neither Garvey, nor any of the founding fathers of the Rastafarian movement, such as Hibbert, Dunkley, and Howell, is a true prophet in the Rasta scheme of things. Only Haile Sellassie holds that exalted position. Hence, the "prophet" at the center of their movement turns out to be nothing more than a socially constructed metaphor, an idea far removed from the living African monarch whom they chose to divinize. Superficially, this looks like another case of male-centered prophetism in which a desperate people drew hope and inspiration from a patriarchal visionary whom they chose to follow. In fact it is a thoroughly democratic type of self-empowerment, an auto-redemptive activity by individuals. The Rasta commune is a "community" of equals who individually define and redefine their prophet with little or no input from the "prophet" himself.

DEMOCHARISMA DEFINED

Simply stated, democharisma refers to a situation in which the bearer of charisma is not the prophet but the "ordinary" member of a charismatic community. The usefulness of the concept will, in the end, rest on the degree to which all or most of the defining qualities of charisma are present when charisma is distributed throughout most of the membership of a movement. The term *demo-charisma* derives from two Greek words meaning "people" and "grace or gift". This neologism is, I believe, justified because it represents a type of phenomenon that is not adequately analyzed in sociological theory. The concept differs from Shils's "distributed charisma", or Weber's and Wallis's idea of the "socially constructed charisma". Shils's concept includes the charisma of office, whereas democharisma excludes this variety of charismatic leadership. Wallis's concept is of course very useful in helping us to understand how the social dynamic operates in charismatic communities and how the "demos" is present and plays a determinative role at all stages of the prophetic career. It is a symbolic interactionist concept that focuses on the dialogue between the prospective prophet and the emergent charismatic community, between leader and followers: each helps to legitimize the other.

I have argued that the Rastafarian case goes beyond what is envisioned by Shils, Weber, and Wallis: it is a charismatic community without a prophet. We must therefore find the formative process not in the interaction between leader and followers but in the daily interaction between individual members of the acephalous charismatic community, between I-and-I.

There is no doubt whatever that the individual Rasta claims to have supernatural powers. This is most clearly illustrated in such beliefs as their immortality—"a Rasta never dies". This idea derives directly from the premise that every *Rastaman is Ras Tafari*, every black man is a fragment of the godhead. They all have the "gift of grace" and the authority to read and interpret the scriptures and, in the process, they discover their personal bonds with the godhead. They are collectively under the spell of a prophetic idea they themselves created and elaborated. They are led by a "prophet" of their own making.

The gnostic process of searching for self-knowledge and for esoteric spiritual understanding is central to Rasta religious thought. It has the effect of empowering individuals, transforming their identity, and making them willful members of a purposive community that feels free to rethink its social and moral foundations.

The sum total of all the qualities of the Rastaman that we have examined so far is that the believer is (1) immortal; (2) akin to God and a fragment of the godhead; (3) has special spiritual powers that enable him or her to gain a personal understanding of the great mysteries. He or she develops these powers (1–3): (4) by searching for self-knowledge; (5) by constructing a meaningful concept of self, society, and God; (6) by a radical restructuring of his or her worldview and priorities; (7) by believing that he or she was chosen to become a seeker and having discovered the great mysteries to share that knowledge with others. Any prophet who claimed to have such powers would undoubtedly be described as having charismatic qualities. These findings suggest that the Rasta is doing for himself or herself what prophets would normally do for their followers.

This profile does, in fact, have many points in common with what Weber called *genuine charisma* in contrast to the *charisma of office* [*amtscharisma*] or *charisma of kinship* [*genscharisma*]. It is also partially comparable to Shils's concept of *distributed charisma*. Unlike these four types, however, democharisma is permanently lodged in the lives of individual believers and is not derived from interaction with a real prophet (Weber-Wallis) or from the distributive process that follows the routinization of a prophetic career (Weber-Shils). That is why the concept of democharisma was developed: to account for the distinctively charismatic experience that Rastafarians have that is quite different from the other types of charisma so far described.

Parenthetically, the Rastafarian experience further suggests that there may be a special connection between the democharismatic process and that aspect of gnosis which deals particularly with self-knowledge.[5] Such knowledge has a self-empowering quality and is therefore liable to be especially relevant to the issues under discussion. The more general significance of this connection is yet to be explored.

A key question we need to consider now is whether the democharismatic alternative is peculiar to the Rasta or whether it occurs in other situations as well. I believe that democharisma is in fact present in most prophetic movements. However, there are powerful reasons why we cannot readily observe the role of such charisma when a dominant prophetic figure is present: the vision, aspirations, and innovative thought of the individual believer have a tendency to be taken over by or attributed to the prophet. As a result, the creativity of the ordinary believer is no longer within our purview. This is a type of divine plagiarism that is necessary if the community is to maintain the illusion that it has one, and only one, fountain of creativity, knowledge, and inspiration. Living under the aura of a dominant charismatic leader necessitates a self-effacing attitude on the part of the followers. It necessitates also that the followers view their own creative powers as being largely derived from the leader's. In this regard the consequences of charisma and democharisma for individuals are vastly different.

Although the presence of a strong charismatic figure in a movement tends to obscure the phenomenon of democharisma, it is not nearly as obscure when the prophet is dead, absent, or anticipated. Each of these types can be associated with successors or precursors who are themselves prophetic in character. Thus the prophets who predict the coming of the Messiah may play a charismatic role themselves. So also may the dead or absent prophets leave behind successors who emulate their lives and behavior. These types of phenomena can be adequately analyzed within the framework of the Weberian model. Conversely, it is also possible for an entire society to democratically evolve a messianic vision in precisely the same fashion that a people might develop their myths. Neither is likely to be the work of extraordinary individuals. Prophets may also die without successors, but the community as a whole may continue to draw inspiration and power from their example. In these instances, the model of democharisma is the only model that makes sense.

INVENTED VERSUS REAL PROPHETS

There are some significant differences between real prophets and invented prophets that we need to consider here. Real prophets are a continual source of instability because they loathe to codify their relationship with their followers. Prophets cannot be readily constrained by laws. There is a dimension of their personality that is quite antithetical to formalization. Living prophets are, in short, uncontrolled factors that the followers must learn to live with. Sometimes they are veritable loose cannons. By contrast, the invented prophet is more manageable. He or she "produces" only such innovation as the community can absorb and when the community is ready to embark on a program of routinization, his or her unstable, elusive, vague, and metaphoric pattern of thought does not stand in the way of the organizers. Nor are the disciples in mortal danger of being disowned by the prophet if they suggest procedures by which his or her charismatic leadership can be replaced by officeholders or if they attempt to elevate the prophet to the position of a figurehead who could be persuaded to step aside while the organization men take over. All that can often be accomplished without the threat of schismatic eruptions if the prophet is fictitious, absent, or dead.

CONCLUDING NOTE

The present discussion is purely exploratory. It would therefore be premature to draw any formal conclusions from the above analysis. The ideas presented by Weber, Wallace, Keniston, and Turner give us some analytical concepts we need in order to fashion an interpretative model for the particular type of social change we are considering here. The main elements of the model are alienation, charisma, liminality, communitas, and routinization. These elements are causally linked, but they do not necessarily occur in a sequential order. Alienation is clearly antecedent and routinization is clearly consequent. Charisma, liminality, and communitas, on the other hand, can coexist. If we attempt to reduce the whole process to a linear scheme, such as Wallace's, it becomes less useful as a model. Whether or not a linear progression is appropriate, however, it is clear that all the five phenomena analyzed here are part of one and the same process.

With regard to charisma, the Weber-Shils-Wallis model must also be extended somewhat to accommodate the social dynamic within which the charismatic process develops and, more specifically, the way a community goes about inducting its prophets, attributing to them properties they may not possess or training them to develop such properties. Our model distinguishes between the role of charismatic individuals who lead social movements and the social dynamic that can, just as effectively, produce the same results without relying on a single charismatic figure.

Many social movements fall apart after the death of the prophet; many do not. The former suggest that we must continue to give the life and thoughts of the prophet a central role in the analysis of the movement. The latter suggest that there are equally significant charismatic processes that inhere in the community at large and are fundamentally "social" in character. Our model must build on both these perspectives if we are to fully understand these processes and their impact on human religion and society.

NOTES

1. I use the term *prophet* in a very broad sense to include any individual, real or imaginary, past, present, or anticipated, who is believed to be a redeemer who would or does lead a people to the promised land. More realistically, he or she is a visionary with a blueprint for a new social system and is able to mobilize a following to try to realize that vision.

2. I believe I am right in assuming that Weber recognizes two phases in the development of the prophetic career. The first is the phase of *internal determination* in which the prophet receives his *calling*. At this stage Weber does not consider social processes. The second phase begins when the prophet actively tries to build up a following. To do that, he must *validate* his claim and win the *recognition* of his followers. That stage is decidedly social in character.

3. I am indebted to Frank Jan van Dijk , who has commented on this chapter on the basis of his research on the Rastafarian community. He believes that the gulf that separates

Rastafarians from the Ethiopian Orthodox Church is more a result of the differences in social structure, particularly the hierarchical organization of the church, than the cultural and more specifically musical differences discussed here (van Dijk, *Comments on Prophetism and Social Change*, 7 August 1992).

4. Frank Jan van Dijk has commented on the character of the early leaders of the Rasta community as it relates to the central thesis of this chapter. He considers some of these leaders to be "prophets" of Rastafarianism as a whole (van Dijk, 1992). The evidence and analysis presented by Simpson (1955), Barbara Makeda Smith (1960), Owens (1976), Barrett (1977), and Chevannes (1978), however, suggest otherwise. All this evidence indicates that the movement has no one leader, but only minor figures who emerge from time to time as leaders of very small groups of believers. I have no access to van Dijk's own data on Vernon Carrington, called "the prophet Gad" and head of the movement called "The Twelve Tribes of Israel", and cannot, therefore, determine whether his data do or do not support the thesis presented here (van Dijk 1988).

5. On the whole, there seems to be no connection between the ancient Christian gnostics and the variety of gnosticism that has arisen among the Rastafarians. Occasionally, however, Rastafarian scholars become fully aware of the gnostic texts discovered near Nag Hammadi, Egypt, in 1945 and make direct parallels between this religious tradition and their own. The fact that these texts were discovered on African soil and that the authors were treated as heretics by the church of Rome gives the Rasta thinker an added reason for claiming special kinship with the ancient gnostics (Forsythe 1983:14–17).

Plate 17–1. "The Chief's Wife", Gola peoples, Lofa-Gola Chiefdom, Liberia, 1957. Artist, anon.; wood, palm oil, and black boot polish; H. 18 1/2"; sculpted portrait in highly innovative style of a chief's admired headwife renowned for her extraordinary beauty, hauteur, and suspected occult powers. The young carver, claiming to be infatuated and fearing the chief's wife's displeasure more than that of her jealous husband, gave the piece away to a foreign friend with the proviso of anonymity. "Such women are dangerous", he explained, "and men cannot play with them. Perhaps she will see my work in a dream and know secretly of my love. But if I speak it out like a fool, my life is in jeopardy".

17

Gola Womanhood & the Limits of Masculine Omnipotence

Warren L. d'Azevedo

"SECRET SOCIETIES" AND THE LURE OF ARCANA

SINCE THE EARLIEST COMMENTARY by Europeans about the portion of the West African coast now comprising Liberia and Sierra Leone, a major focus of interest has been the manifestation throughout the region of a mysterious "secret society" referred to as "the Poro" and, secondarily, its ostensible counterpart for women, the Sande or Bundu.[1] Each required universal membership of either males or females and exercised what seemed to be a degree of authority more compelling than that of local political leadership, thus suggesting to many observers the existence of an extensive, largely covert, ecclesiastical organization uniting in its powerful web the many disparate political and ethnic units. In the older literature, the Poro phenomenon attracted most attention not only because of its apparently ubiquitous presence along the coast and in the interior, but also because of the apprehensive curiosity evoked by its extreme secrecy and the unquestioned obedience given to its dictates that raised the specter of an inscrutable challenge to European commercial competition and eventual control. Thus the urge to penetrate its "mysteries" was a corollary of the drive to penetrate the African interior and to diminish the hegemonic position held by the indigenous polities in trade and access to resources.

In this process the notion of "secret societies" came to permeate all descriptions of political relations, social organization, economy, warfare, the arts, and cosmologies of the peoples of the region. In fact, "secret societies" were viewed as tantamount to a hidden government exercising authority by supernatural sanction and constituting the organized expression of local "religion". Scarcely forty-five years ago, George Schwab quoted with approval the missionary-ethnologist Diedrich Westermann, who, in 1921, observed among the Kpelle of Liberia that "the religious practices of the tribesmen are entirely cult rites". Schwab then prefaced his extensive discussion of the Poro and Sande with the statement "we shall deal first with the cults, since it is in these that the religious life of the tribesmen centers, is fostered and developed, and given opportunity for fullest expression" (Schwab 1947:266–267). It is here also that further currency was given to the tenacious lore of the urban Liberian settler class that Poro and "Masonry" were parallel organizations (a view derided by Poro officials) and that membership in one provided knowledge of the structure and rites of the other. Two decades later Kenneth Little (1965, 1966) presented a landmark analysis of the political functions of the Poro, including a valuable resume of eighteenth-and-nineteenth century European impressions of the organization that reveal the ambivalent preoccupation with which Poro was perceived (Little 1965:349–356). Little disclaims one earlier notion that the "civil" and "religious" functions of the Poro were separate, concluding that these were merely aspects of the same unitary organization that "make the Poro the main arbiter in the indigenous culture, and, in effect, enable it to perform a role analogous to that of the medieval church in Europe". Nevertheless, much to his credit, Little does express doubts about the notion (attributed to Migeod and Harley, among others) that the Poro constituted a region-wide secret government controlled by a centralized hierarchy of officialdom: "When a European outsider is confronted by such widespread and coordinated activity as the Poro was undoubtedly able to organize, it is tempting to explain it in terms of a culturally familiar model" (Little 1965:361–362).

Perhaps even more to the point is M. C. Jedrej's reminder of E. E. Evans-Pritchard's suggestion that Azande "secret societies" were the creation of Europeans who, in proscribing certain ritual activities, helped to induce their transformation into the very forms anticipated by the stereotypes of native life they had brought with them (Jedrej 1976: 234–235). Jedrej proposes that this process also impeded the comprehension of West African "secret societies" and further compounded the problems of ethnography with the conflicting claims of authoritative writers. "The simplest solution", he writes, "was to shift the bewilderment onto the African where it became a cultural trait of whole peoples instead of the mental state of a few observers. Thus we read that 'mystery permeates the whole of the African's life day by day and night' (Butt-Thompson 1929:55)".

This cogent insight underscores a central argument of the present chapter, which is essentially that the lure of "secret societies", and the desire to penetrate the "secrets" of the most sacred rites and symbols of these organizations, is not a thing of the past but continues as a latent and unrecognized incentive in much of the ethnographic literature of the region. Over the last two decades, however, there has been an important shift in concerns from an emphasis on the role of Poro in the male-dominated political and ritual structure of local polities to an intensive examination and reassessment of the Sande association as more than the feminine counterpart (or appendage) of male Poro to which it had been relegated in the earlier literature. Significantly, much of this recent work has been carried out by women researchers whose access to information hitherto restricted from and neglected by male investigators has brought to the fore a wealth of new material and an entirely new perspective with regard to the distinctive orientation and status of women in these societies.[2] Issues of gender relations and the instruments of female empowerment have become major themes, and the Sande association has emerged as a prime example in West Africa of a widespread women's organization that provides a vehicle for female influence in the political arena and in the maturation of female youth as well as female eminence in the spheres of ritual and cosmology. The tendency has been to seek equivalence or a kind of balanced symbiosis between Poro and Sande as two cooperating gender-specific institutions in which the presumably high relative status of women is demonstrated and defended by the predicated role of Sande. Caroline Bledsoe refers to this view as representing a "female solidarity model" which posits "that by socially and ritually separating themselves on occasions, Sande women attempt to widen the gap between themselves and men and to promote female cohesiveness" (Bledsoe 1984:455).

The problem with this model, as Bledsoe goes on to indicate, is that independent female solidarity is ultimately constrained by the social status differences among women themselves and an alliance of dependency on the part of the leaders of Sande in their relations with the elite of Poro. The position of women remains subordinate to that of men, and Sande may be viewed as an instrument of male control of women in which the high-ranking leaders of Sande engage in an ancient conspiracy with their dominant male lineage-mates to sustain the principles of patrimony. As I will suggest below, this state of affairs is not one in which women can be expected to achieve equivalent empowerment—any more than what might be expected in any society of male political dominance. On the other hand, in such a situation women can be expected to utilize strategies of personal emancipation outside the realm of social legitimacy prescribed by myth and masculine privilege. "Women do not play fair" is a lament heard not only among the Gola but most likely in any society where the power of maleness is subject to constant challenge from the spiritually insubordinate guiles of dissident women and social outcasts. Thus Gola men ask: Isn't it true that most witches are women? And why should this be so when women are also compliant lovers, bearers of children, and nurturing mothers?

Such questions are seldom raised as substantive issues in the recent literature on Sande in which the association has been defined as the sacred custodian of female powers and the expression of ideal femininity. The work of many of the art historians and anthropologists recently attracted to study in the area shows a decisive shift from functionalist strategies of research to intensive semantic or semiotic analyses in a structuralist mode.[3] The result has been to enrich our comprehension of the dynamic agency of symbolism in the cultures of this region and to illuminate meanings and intellectual processes previously unperceived. At the same time, the refinements in probing the intricacies of female consciousness as exemplified by Sande symbolism have not been balanced by equivalent analyses of symbols of male power generated through Poro or of the dynamic interaction between these systems of symbolic meanings as expressed in general social relations. Thus in some of the writings on peoples such as the Mende, for example, one might be led to conclude that the whole of the social organization and cosmological knowledge of their patrilineal and largely patriarchal unit societies is a virtual embodiment of a feminine mystique engendered and monitored by the priestesses of Sande. Over-parochial analysis of discrete symbols and their expressions in speech or other events also leads to the production of a spate of highly speculative and often contradictory explanations of meaning that are largely unverifiable ethnographically and serve only to divert inquiry into cul-de-sacs of compulsive and pointless disputation.[4]

At the risk of embarking on such a course myself, in this chapter I will examine and reflect upon interpretations that have been offered about a specific object of symbolization in a crucial Sande rite. It is a rite that continues to puzzle observers attempting to decode its deeper significance as a likely pivotal emblem in the assertion of female identity and power. My approach will be frankly ethnographic, with interpretations limited as much as possible to the direct observations of my own fieldwork and the implications I have derived from them. Therefore, I shall begin with the description of an encounter I had with a group of Gola men that I feel provides diagnostic markers for approaching the problem under discussion.

TANGENTIAL CLUES FROM A FORTUITOUS ENCOUNTER

In the spring of 1985, I heard an anecdote in Monrovia, Liberia, that apparently had been circulating among some urban Liberians as well as members of the foreign community. It was told with suppressed hilarity because of its ostensibly obscene subject matter and insolent political implications. One version I heard from a resident American woman provided the following account: Two young and well-to-do Liberian women from Monrovia made frequent trips by automobile up the Bomi Road to Tubmanburg in the northwestern interior of Liberia for the purpose of visiting friends. Each time they went they were harassed by Kran soldiers placed by the military government at checkpoints along the way. They were forced to endure humiliating remarks and to open the trunk of the car for search until they gave money for passage. In fury, they contrived a scheme. Knowing that Kran men are said to have one particular and overwhelming aversion, they set out once more up the road. At the first checkpoint they were stopped as usual and the soldiers insulted them and demanded to inspect their car. "There is nothing there to interest you", the women said. But the soldiers persisted and the trunk was opened. "What are you carrying in those bags?" they shouted. "See for yourself", the women answered. But when a soldier opened the finest bag, he and his fellows stumbled back in horror, covering their faces as though burned. The women drove on and the scene was repeated at each checkpoint along the way. On their return, and thereafter, they were not bothered again by the soldiers. The bag in the trunk of the car had contained used menstrual napkins.

Now the impact of this story would be obvious to anyone who had lived in Liberia during the period of increasing government suppression after the military coup of 1980. The revolutionary fervor and anticipation of reforms soon gave way to disillusionment and cynicism. Many saw the new government as more corrupt and ruthless than any that had gone before. Moreover, most Liberians feared the emergence of despotic tribalism in an army and government dominated by a nepotistic core of members of the Kran ethnic group noted in coastal lore for its mysterious isolation in the eastern interior and its "uncivilized" ways. Thus, the tale of two young "civilized" women putting the soldiers to rout was bound to strike a resonant chord in many listeners.

The reaction of certain of my Gola friends in Monrovia, however, was somewhat more complex. A few were lower echelon government officials; others were students, small business employees, or laborers in the city. All had close family connections in the villages of Bomi County to the north of Monrovia, where the Gola population predominated and which was reached by the Bomi Road, the only direct access to that section of the Liberian interior. Though the incident was well known among them, I never heard the story as a narrative from any of the urban or rural Gola men I knew and my informed judgment assured me that I would not hear of it from Gola women. It was referred to by allusion and innuendo in casual conversation, always accompanied by extravagant expressions of male jocularity. On one occasion I made the mistake of reviewing the story to a small group of acquaintances with the questionable objective of confirming its validity: were the women Gola, did anyone know who they were, and did they have relatives up country? I was immediately aware that something had gone wrong. The mood of easy good humor changed abruptly to one of embarrassment and personal conster- nation. I had been guilty of a most serious breach of form and it was only out of deference to me that conversation continued at all or that concerted effort had not been made to shame me as a knave or a fool.

The subsequent responses to my blunder were, nevertheless, instructive. Gola men, I was informed, do not talk about such matters, even with their very close male friends or relatives. And, certainly, women do not talk about it. Even if you know something, you do not speak it out, though you may make "signs" (allusions) or jokes so that no one can say exactly what you mean. What happened there was "women's business". Those Kran soldiers deserved to learn a lesson. Their guns and big talk were useless to them. They were helpless. Women are strong. You must not push them too far. They will do anything when they are vexed. No, it could not have been real Gola women who did that. They are well trained and would be too ashamed. It was some kind of "civilized" [*kwi*] women who did that, or some kind of mixed tribe women in the city who care for nothing. Maybe Kru or Grebo women would do that, but not Gola. In Gola country it is the women's secret association, Sande, that takes care of all that. In Bon, the men's Poro association, men learn never to think of such things. Women have strong medicines in Sande and men are respectful. What those two women did on the road was too terrible to think of. A Gola man would be ready to die if it happened to him. It is more terrible than the *kínú*, for the Sande controls all that.

Though I was already well aware of the profound separation the Gola perceive between male and female natures, and the wariness Gola men exhibit with regard to female genitalia, menstruation, and childbirth, the magnitude of feeling that was evoked by this incident surprised me. Most of the men present had spent much of their adult lives in an urban environment and their ties to village culture, though continuing, were somewhat attenuated. Under these conditions discourse is often more frank and less concerned about the strictures imposed by a rural community. It was possible, of course, that my presence as an informed outsider exacerbated the sense of being observed or critically appraised by someone who knew and worked with their conservative elders. Whatever the reason, my impropriety had triggered a rare moment of ambivalent male expressive behavior about an aspect of female nature that is deemed an ultimate mystery and potentially perilous to men. Their tone of admonition was reminiscent of those many times during my field work that I have been brought to task by an irritated elder respondent for delving too insistently into matters of sacred ritual or cosmogony. As a proven friend, I should be properly advised. Otherwise, I might deserve the fate of the Kran soldiers.

The most significant detail, however, was the mention of the *kínú* in this context. This is the special object of the *egbíya*, a ceremony that occurs at the termination of the Sande initiation session in the major groves of the Gola chiefdoms.[5] In recent times it is not always performed, and most persons are extremely reluctant to talk about it except in general public terms. The mention of it in the context of the above incident inadvertently provided one of the few clues I had to its symbolism. Apparently, the use of menstrual blood by the two women was considered to be analogous in some way to what takes place in the Gola women's *egbíya* rites, yet it was deemed even more alarming because it was an independent action outside of the traditional auspices of the Sande, whose protective monitoring of female sexuality defends the community (and particularly males) from a potentially dangerous intrusion.

SACRED RITES AND THE ELUSIVE *KÍNÚ*

During the three-year period when Sande is said to "rule the country", no rites or emblems of the male association, Bon, are allowed except by permission of the sacred female elders of Sande, the Mazonya. The women are governed by representatives of the powerful mountain spirits and ancestors, the Zogbénya, who make their appearance at the beginning of the Sande session to take the country over from the men's Bon association, which has "ruled the country" for the previous four years and initiated the eligible male youth. The Zogbénya, in the form of masked spirit impersonators, declare that they have come as "the true husbands" of all the women of the community to claim their "wives" and to preside over the initiation of young girls into proper female adulthood. Their manner is imperious, and recalcitrant men are warned of the strong medicine of Sande and the power of their wands that can strike a man impotent. At the end of the Sande session when the cycle of Sande rites is near completion and the initiates are ready to be returned to their families, the Zogbénya withdraw. On the third day of the final festivities, when the girls are about to be "washed" and released, the much anticipated *egbíya* rite takes place.

This rite does not take place regularly or in all groves. I had not witnessed it personally, for it seemed that something had always intervened to prevent me from seeing it at villages where it had been scheduled in the past, or I would learn that it would be held in a different village than the one I had been directed to, or at a different time, or had been called off because of some palaver or some whim of the women involved. During the spring of 1985, about the time of my encounter with the group of Gola men described above, I heard reports of performances in some widely scattered Gola villages with Sande groves, but always after the fact. However, two of the young men in the group had informed me that *kínú* was about to occur in a small Gola-Dei village near Monrovia on a certain day and invited me to go there with them. They had relatives there and I would be welcome. These plans undoubtedly accounted for the fact that the *kínú* had been mentioned during the discussion. We did go to the village on the appointed day and waited with a small crowd of locals for hours, only to be told that the rite had been called off. My companions were irritated on my behalf and attributed the situation to "those old women who cannot be satisfied with anything". One had learned that there had been objections about too many "civilized people" and unknown strangers in town: "They say *kínú* is easily spoiled by outsiders". Another report was that a leading woman was ill. Nonetheless, once again I was to miss observing the rite firsthand. So, what follows has been gleaned from accounts given me by Gola friends—all men, though a few women have offered confirming comments.

On the afternoon of the last day of the Sande session, all the people of the town and those of surrounding villages who have had girls in the bush for training assemble near the road to the Sande grove. The Mazo and other leading women of the Sande cluster near the entrance to the grove. The excitement is intense but suppressed, and all eyes are on the grove. Then the sound of a special song is heard as four women, naked except for thongs about their groins, move from the forest toward the town, bearing a large bundle on a pallet covered with a red throw cloth. The women stagger under the burden as though dazed and unable to control it. The crowd gasps and people wave palm fronds at the object, begging it to go away. The men shout Bon (Poro) signs and some fire guns to turn back the dreaded *kínú*. Three times it attempts to come into the town, and on the third time it finally withdraws. The powerful Zogbé masked figures are not to be seen, for they too fear the *kínú*. When it returns to the forest grove, there is a great cry of victory from the crowd. The Zogbénya appear again, and the town is saved. If the *kínú* had actually been able to come into town everything would have been destroyed by fire and pestilence. Now that it is gone it will not be seen again for years, until the end of the next Sande session. The initiated girls are then given their final "washing", dressed in finery and brought into town to their waiting families.

The *kínú* is referred to euphemistically as *negbé Sande* (the "big thing of Sande"). Men speak of it as "the most terrible medicine of the women". Its power is as great as any owned by men, even as much as the frightful spirit of Bon, the Dadévè, which presides over the male initiation rites. Women will seldom speak of it at all except perhaps to describe the public rite in a tone of joyful bravado and say "the *negbé Sande* is a special thing women have, the most powerful medicine, and men must respect it". To ask a question about the contents of the burden carried by the women is an outrage so serious that children are harshly punished for it, and men are threatened with disease or death, fined by the Sande or Bon Poro and, formerly, even banished for showing such disrespect.

This may account in part for the paucity of any mention of the *kínú* in the recent literature on the region. Svend Holsoe provides a brief description of the "*je tiye* ceremony" among the Vai in which the "*kindu*" is considered to be "the main spirit or soul" of the Sande and has a role in the public performance similar to what I have indicated for the Gola (Holsoe 1980:102). He notes, moreover, additional interesting material about a secret rite in the Sande bush where certain girls are forced to leap over the dreadful object in order to earn second degree status. Jedrej also mentions the "bier-like construction called *kendue*" that appears in the final rites of the Sande among the Mende of Sierra Leone (Jedrej 1980:138–139). He states, however, that the object "is carried through the village" (something quite antithetic to the Gola and Vai cases) and that the Sande masked spirits (corresponding to the Gola Zogbénya) run ahead of it in an agitated fashion "as if repelled by it". Then Jedrej speculates that "this behavior suggests that the *sande* spirits and the bier are two antithetical representations as would be the case if the *kendue* included the 'corpse' of the male genital residue, and *sande yafe* (the masked performer) were a spirit of feminine beauty".[6] Parenthetically, it may be noted Harry A. Sawyerr mentions that "Mende women are seen to carry a large package which rests unsteadily on the head of the bearer", but that this package is said to contain a python (Sawyerr 1970:75, quoted in Lamp 1985:38).

Two observations of refreshing simplicity and directness should be mentioned here, the one from the turn of the century and the other from the 1980s. While traveling in "Mendi country" Thomas J. Alldridge reports witnessing the following:

> About five o'clock, the town was entered by four sowehs carrying a mysterious "something" that was covered by a white country-cloth over some coloured ones. This mysterious something was the great fetish medicine called the "Kendu", which forms the essential part of the Bundu order. ... No Bundu devils [the masked spirit impersonators] were present, as it is contrary to the laws of the society that they should be present at the parade of this fetish medicine. (Alldridge 1910:225–226)

I cannot help but reflect on how pleased my elder Gola mentors, both male and female, would have been had I never referred to the *kínú* as other than that "mysterious something" and promised never to speculate further, in spoken or written word. The second remarkable observation was made by Ariane Deluz who was initiated into the Knɛ society of the Guro of the Ivory Coast and observed that the material aspects of the Knɛ were "a stick covered in feathers which all may see but not touch, and a bunch of white 'pagnes' which surround and hide the sacred 'thing', a half-gourd ..." (Deluz 1987:114–115, 122).[7] She actually *saw* the "something"!

What I find intriguing about these brief reports is, of course, the fact that something like the *kínú* of Gola Sande appears in similar public rites among other related peoples of the region. Equally intriguing is the apparent meagerness of any direct knowledge of the object itself, its contents (except for Deluz), or symbolic meaning, a circumstance that might be attributed in all humility to the limits of the ethnographer's privilege. There is no good reason why the alien observer of another culture (and, in this instance, alien males) should expect to learn what children, uninitiated females, and males in general must not know or even reveal curiosity about. Yet we continue to try, for that is our calling and, if all else fails, we extrapolate from any seeming relevant sources of data, ferret out symbolic congruences, construct models for guidance or assurance, and sometimes second guess our beleaguered respondents in the field to our ultimate peril.[8]

It is in context of these concerns that I find Jedrej's speculations about the meaning of the *kendue* in Mende Sande especially relevant. He writes that the intricately carved black helmet mask worn by the female impersonators of Sande spirits (a phenomenon found widely in the region in Sande ritual) "is said to represent feminine beauty". This view of the gender of the masked and costumed spirit impersonations, and the ideal of womanhood they are said to represent, has been widely reported by recent students of the Mende Sande association. Though the masks, paraphernalia, and ritual role of these figures are almost identical to those of the Vai, Gola, and Dei to the south, among the latter peoples they are perceived and referred to as male spirits sent by the mysterious autochthonous ancestors to be the guardians and advisors of women during the periodic Sande sessions. The consequences of these differences are considerable for the understanding of the cosmogony of the respective cultures and the interpretation of ritual and its symbolism. If, as Jedrej surmises, the gender of the masked figures of Sande ritual is archetypically feminine, then it might logically follow that the *kendue* is an antipodal and irreconcilable element as witnessed by their public behavior with regard to it. This would be the case "if the *kendue* included the 'corpse' of male genital residue" derived from male circumcision rites. Thus, if we can suppose that the *kendue* bundle contains prepuces, or an amalgam of male and female genital residue, we have solved the riddle by a logical tour de force. But *is* this the case? Can we know?

QUANDARIES OF ANDROGYNY: PRESENTATIONS AND PERCEPTIONS OF SPIRIT PERSONAGES

I have no quarrel with Jedrej's model of male/female opposition or with his thoughtful interpretation of the Mende material at his disposal, though I would have been more comfortable with at least a minimum of direct confirmation from the Mende themselves about the meaning and contents of the *kendue*. I do believe that gender opposition is fundamental, not only to our understanding of Poro and Sande ritual, but also as a ubiquitous principle manifested in the social relations and cultural formations of this region (and, perhaps, even universally). Nor do I have a serious problem about his frank speculations. I intend, momentarily, to do a bit of speculation myself, for my direct data concerning the Gola *kínú* seems to me all but as sparse as that reported by the authors cited above. Nevertheless, one important difference between the Gola case and that of the Mende as discussed by Jedrej and others is that the gender identities of the sacred objects appear to be reversed. The Gola Zogbé (corresponding to the *sande yafe* or *sowei* of the Mende) is presented and perceived in its public form as a masculine personification. I say "presented and perceived" because the fragmentary Gola exegesis concerning the origin or cosmological placement of the Zogbénya is more complex and ambiguous than can be adequately presented here. Essentially, they are said to be emissaries "sent by" the mysterious *a netónya* (sing. *o netó*) nature spirits of the forests and mountains or waters who are in some way associated with the most ancient ancestors. The sexuality of the *netónya* is unknown, but the Zogbénya appear in the form of male spirits "because that is the way women see them ... as powerful men

... for men are above women".[9] I would, therefore, accept Frederick Lamp's caution concerning the intricate symbolic manipulation of gender transformations in these cultures (Lamp 1985:31), yet I must be guided primarily by the public expression of Gola ritual behavior as it has been most concretely accessible to me before engaging in any interpretive exercise.

The deferential reference to the Zogbénya as male [o fela] is consistently and emphatically affirmed in Gola public discourse. They are spoken of as the "husbands", "lovers", or "leaders" of women during the Sande session.[10] When they make their first appearance during the opening rites, the matrons of the community announce that there will be little time to attend to their human husbands either sexually or in domestic chores. Though much of this constitutes mutual joking and banter, it is actualized to the extent that many of the women are busy with Sande activities and many others utilize the lifting of normal role requirements as an opportunity for engaging in the festivities, visiting friends and relatives, or having sexual adventures. Men must neither complain nor punish their wives during this period under threat of severe sanction from the Sande and the Zogbénya spirit guardians. No one should even allude to the generally known fact that the maskers are local females impersonating the Sande spirits, and children are severely reprimanded for the slightest display of curiosity or lack of respectful diffidence with regard to them. The sacredness of the Zogbénya does not reside in the masked and costumed performer but in the spiritual forces and entities it represents.[11]

The Zogbénya preside over all Sande activities from the very first day—when they lead throngs of joyous women through the villages announcing that they are "taking the country from the men"—to the end of the session some three years later when the female initiates are returned to their families as properly trained and marriageable. Only then do they withdraw from human company, "leaving the land to rest" before the Dadévè, the great spirit of Bon, returns once again to reinstate the dominion of men and commence the initiation of male youth over the following four or more years. The Zogbénya of Sande and the Dadévè of Bon are never "in the country" other than during the session over which each presides. All emblems and activities of Bon are prohibited during the Sande session, as are those of Sande during the Bon session. The only exception to this rigidly enforced jurisdictional division is on those occasions when, during the phase of Sande jurisdiction, men might petition the women to bring out their own nonsacred masked performers to entertain an especially important notable.

There is one other exception, the execution of which is so rare that only two or three instances can be recalled by elders since the turn of the century. It is, nevertheless, frequently referred to by men as a latent privilege of Bon that supersedes any held by Sande. This is the right of Bon to reconvene at any time of dire emergency, such as war, rebellion, pestilence, epidemic witchcraft, natural catastrophe, or an extreme violation of sacred proscriptions. The leader of Bon, the Dazo, returns in full regalia to the men's grove in the company of the great unseen spirit of Bon, the Dadévè, proclaiming the dissolution of the Sande session and demanding the complete submission of women. Thus, the orderly cycle of Sande and Bon sessions has been disrupted and a sense of ultimate crisis pervades the land. The right of Bon to exercise such unilateral power is legitimized by myth which holds that women once were dominant and Sande was the only sacred institution (d'Azevedo 1973).[12] But when war and political strife began to trouble their ancient chiefdoms, they were unable to maintain order. It was then that men sought and found the Dadévè spirit in the forest, a being so mysterious and terrifying that women were subdued by it. With the aid of this power they instituted their own association, the Bon, demanded the removal of male youth for initiation and training into proper manhood, and usurped political authority. But this transition was not made easily, for the power of Sande was great. With the intervention of the ancestors and their nature spirit colleagues, an agreement was reached by which Sande would preside over the country for three years in order to train female youth and to "cleanse the land" through rites that would return it to the pristine condition it enjoyed prior to male dominion. Following the Sande session, Bon would take the country for four years to prepare male youth for adult life and to affirm male principles of social governance. Ultimate male authority was preserved by the license of Bon to assert sovereignty at any time.

Now, since the public image of the Gola Zogbé masker is perceived as masculine, it would seem that the source of the "antithesis" Jedrej suggests between the Sande spirits and the bundle carried by the women in the closing rite of Sande among the Mende might not be the same in the Gola case. As with the Mende spirits, the Gola Zogbénya are repelled by the object; they are said to fear it and, in fact, the *kínú* is the one Sande rite at which their incompatibility with the proceedings is publicly dramatized and commented upon. They withdraw because "the *kínú* is a special thing of women that is dangerous to all men; you can see it, but that is all" Consequently, the content of the object is not something I would normally have asked about or expected to have been divulged to me. The possibility that it contains the residue of either clitoridectomy or circumcision, an amalgam of both, or even a snake is a matter about which I have no actual data. But what is most clear and obvious to me is that the *kínú* represents something extraordinarily potent and hazardous among the "medicines" owned by the women of Sande. It commands a greater apprehensiveness and wonderment than any symbolic device of the Bon association excepting, perhaps, the dreaded unseen but audible Dadévè spirit that periodically inhabits the men's grove and roams the countryside ravenously "eating" prospective male initiates.

THE ARDUOUS MANAGEMENT OF FEMALE NATURE

If I were to venture a speculation in this regard, it would derive from the clue intimated by my discussion with the group of young men described above suggesting a possible relation between the meaning of *kínú* and the male aversion to menstrual blood. From this perspective the object of the rite may be taken to symbolize the unique biological attributes of the female body and their attendant powers that men neither possess nor can control. These attributes are associated specifically with female genitalia, the womb, gestation, and childbirth—female organs and functions about which male discourse is constrained to the extreme and relegated to the category of "women's business". Menstruation is a profounder mystery, the noxious flow of a substance so potent that contamination can diminish the fertility of the land, confound male virility, and interfere with the successful pursuit of goals in war, hunting, litigation, or other crucial tasks. Yet it is this substance that is the vital force of life, that ceases to flow when a child begins to form in the womb, and that mixes with the semen supplied by the father from which the child acquires its actual personhood. The enigma of menses [e wáá, literally "pertaining to the moon"] is deemed so esoteric, and its periodicity so aligned to the seasonal pulse of nature itself, that its monopoly by women constitutes a potential threat to those principles of civil order which men have devised and by which they dominate.[13]

Aside from the act of copulation and the legal ownership of a woman's reproductive capabilities legitimized by marriage, Gola men have little involvement in or knowledge of the procreative process. Women are said to be so reticent about their genitals that most men, even their husbands, have not seen the vagina. Evidence of menses is rigorously concealed (a matter supposedly dealt with in Sande training), and sexual activity is avoided by the excuse of illness or visiting away from home. A menstruating woman must not go to the farm, cook for any man, or handle the implements of males. A man should avoid sex prior to any important endeavor, for he will risk contamination and loss of strength.

Both men and women are bound by numerous proscriptions during the period of pregnancy, but the restrictions placed upon a woman are more serious and extensive than those of a man, and it is she who has the major responsibility for successful completion of the process. She is to have no sexual intercourse other than with her husband, for the "mixing" of semen may result in a sickly or deformed child and a difficult delivery. Males are entirely excluded from the event of childbirth and the husband must remove to a distant part of the village or elsewhere so that he does not hear cries of pain or see the activities of the attendant women.

If the woman dies in childbirth, the delivery is unusually protracted, or the child malformed, the onus lies primarily with the woman. She is forced to confess whether she had a lover, has broken food taboos, let her eyes dwell upon some hideous object, is a witch, or whether she exposed her genitals while bathing in a stream or defecating in the forest where lurking spirits might seize the opportunity for sex and thus "spoil" her womb. When a woman dies in childbirth she is buried immediately in a swampy area with no ceremony. Her body is a danger to the community: she is a casualty of a "war" with evil spirits. Should the child live, it is given away to strangers, for no local family will have it.

There also is a postnatal proscription against sexual relations until after the child is weaned, though a husband and wife may purchase certain amulets or medicines from a practitioner to protect the child and the parents from the harmful effects. Men usually turn to other wives or lovers during the postnatal period which may last for two or three years. For women this often is a source of bitterness and depression. It is a time when many will seek medicines to hold their husband's affections or give their child over to another for early weaning.

Though males and their patrilineages are the ultimate beneficiaries of female reproductive faculties, there is a deep ambivalence about the female body and its powers males cannot fully comprehend or control. And though male and female natures are considered to be necessarily complimentary, that of the female is felt to be more elemental and susceptible to the influence of errant forces in the world. Males, on the other hand, are the creators of civil institutions women are incapable of managing. Thus, the relations between them also are seen as fundamentally antagonistic. Without male dominion there would be no society, no tradition, no future. The body of a woman is "the pot" [*ekpo*] within which a man forms his descendants by infusion of semen. The blood of the womb is transformed by semen into a human image, a creation that the man owns through the right of patriliny. Yet subordination of females by men is never total, for women actually possess their own bodies and their ways are secretive and secluded. Moreover, they are coveted by other men as well as by numerous wild spirits of the forests and waters who desire their love and fruitfulness.

This obliquity in gender attributions is an underlying theme of public discourse concerning the female character and is shared by both men and women in conformance with the dominant cultural ideology. Women are not to be trusted. They use their bodies to subvert the socially indispensable endeavors of men. They are jealous of other women who are more successful with men, especially co-wives who have many children or who are favorites of the husband. When women are angry, they will do anything. They are potential betrayers of their husband's family and will expose its secrets to its enemies. Mothers are frequently more attached to their own natal family than to that of their husband and may try to instill disloyalty in their children. Women have been the main cause of wars and social disorder. Men must maintain constant vigilance against the powerful medicines of women, their knowledge of leaves (learned from their mothers or in Sande) and, most appalling of all, their concealed deployment of menstrual blood. Moreover, women are far more prone to consort with evil spirits than are men. Thus women have the power to deprive men of offspring. All of these factors, it is said, explain why vastly more women than men become witches, for a witch has the most terrible power to destroy.

Such testament of the negative proclivity of womanhood is customary in male discourse and is quietly acquiesced to by most women as a social image from which they must extricate themselves by proper Sande training and deportment. Just as clitoridectomy is said to be an essential genital alteration to reduce female aggressiveness in sexual relations, Sande initiation and training directs women's powers to the socially crucial tasks of marriage and childbearing. It seems especially significant here that the appearance of the *kínú* in the final rite of the Sande session, and its rout by the ritually alarmed community, is spoken of as evidence of the most potent of the secret medicines owned by the women's organization. Immediately following the rite, the initiates are "washed" of all the most sinister and socially intractable inclinations of their sex and returned to their families. It may be suggested that the *kínú* symbolizes the epitome of those primordial forces that the Sande is charged with restraining. The spheres of power of the human sexes must be maintained as separate and distinct in contrast to the apparent androgyny of much of nature and the spirit world. Clitoridectomy is said not only to reduce the sexual aggressiveness of women (thus promoting the interests of polygyny) but also to remove those parts that "make women like men". Circumcision, on the other hand, is said to increase virility and remove the "filth" of childhood for male initiates.

Menstruation, the most enigmatic marvel of the female body, presents a particularly ominous challenge to male power and to the success of male endeavors. The processes of gestation and childbirth also are exclusively female preoccupations that require of Sande the utmost vigilance in preventing unauthorized contact between the sexes. Sexual relations with an immature girl or with a Sande initiate who has not been "washed" is a crime of immense proportions, for it is the task of Sande to present the young women in their charge to the community as "virgins" ready for marriage and reproduction. Any sign of prior sexual contact with men or spirits must be obliterated, especially the aborted fetuses from new initiates guilty of such encounters. The *kínú*, therefore, may well represent all or any of these elements of proscription and eradication, the symbol of Sande service to the community, the crucial monitoring of separation, distinction, and the eventual sanctioning of legitimate sexual relations.

Thus Sande, as a partner in the combined sacred institution known as the Bemba, cooperates with the men of Bon to prepare women for their subordinate position in society as depicted in ritual and legitimized by myth. This does not mean that there is not an exclusively female model of gender relations expressed among Gola women, such as that which Ladislav Holy describes for the Berti of the Sudan (Holy 1985:182–189). For when speaking among themselves, or in banter with men, they frequently allude to the "deep secrets" owned by women (e.g., "the *kínú* which you fear"); to male dependency on mothers, wives, and lovers; to male helplessness in domestic matters; to their envy of the womb; or to their lack of subtlety and their blundering self-importance. Yet women publicly accept the culturally sanctioned dominant ideology of male eminence as validated by a tradition that deems it necessary and irrevocable.[14]

There are women, however, whose "perverse natures" cause them to dissent from socially approved norms of behavior. They are said to be continually dissatisfied with their condition. They are jealous of the good fortune of others and competitively seek to emulate or acquire the prerogatives of men. Their quarreling with co-wives or their husband's lovers creates serious discord within the family. Such women are a potential danger to the community, for in their bitterness they strive to frustrate the ambitions of others by invoking malevolent antisocial forces. The inability or the refusal to bear children, abortion or promiscuity, too frequent death or illness in the family, overly aggressive behavior, fits of destructive anger, laziness and unproductive farming, the yearning for independence from husband or kin are all signs of aberrant female character. The Gola say that many women of this kind make private alliances with nature spirits [*a jinanya*] to whom they give sexual favors and their unborn children in exchange for wealth, beauty, and independence. Their human husbands or lovers are enthralled by them, but unable to control them.

Some women simply run away to distant towns seeking men who will provide them what they want. Still others turn to witchcraft [*kèsɛ̃*] by welcoming the invasion of a witch spirit [*osɛ̃*] into their bodies or, as is often the case, discover that they were born as witches and can solicit the services of other witches. They become the most frightful and evil of persons whose main occupation is to eat babies, suck the souls from men, bring death and pestilence, and recruit others to their ways. Neither Sande nor Bon can exert sufficient authority to quell the insidious pervasiveness of this deviant behavior. Because women are more prone to become witches as well as to the illicit manipulation of female powers, it is said that the major responsibility rests with Sande to see to the discipline of women and suppression of their erratic nature. Deviant behavior is one of the bases upon which male privilege is rationalized and the necessity of ultimate jurisdictional authority of Bon over Sande is substantiated.

BON AND SANDE: SACRED COLLUSION FOR ETERNAL MAINTENANCE OF THE PATRIARCHAL ORDER

The asymmetry between Sande and Bon jurisdictions brings to mind Simon Ottenberg's cogent remark that gender exclusive secret associations are often "a metaphor for sex" (Ottenberg 1989a:54–55). They reflect in their structures and distinctive mandates the culturally defined significance of gender opposition and accommodation, the mystery of sexual dimorphism, and the exigency of procreation. There has been a convention in the literature concerning the Sande and "Poro" associations of this general region to cast them as counterparts of one another, as juxtaposed oppositions in dynamic equilibrium, each promoting either female or male solidarity and interests. Sande is depicted as the institutionalization of female rights, as the protector of women against male exploitation and suppression. Though it is quite obvious that the indigenous women's associations in these cultures provide women with instruments of social power somewhat more effective than in many other societies, the status of women is nevertheless subsidiary and auxiliary to that of the politically omnipotent organization of men. The ideology of male superiority pervades the cultures and their social arrangements.[15]

Bledsoe has suggested that a "stratification model" offers an important corrective to the assumption that social solidarity or the striving for balance in jurisdiction and authority are fundamental factors in the relations between the two gender-specific associations (Bledsoe 1984:459–462). She points out that within the Sande of the Mende, status differentials between the initiates, the female members in the community, and the leaders are rigorously hierarchical and based upon lineage rank, status of husbands or other male relatives, and the ultimate acceptance of male authority as the requisite of social order. The female leaders of Sande, though having significant social influence, are nonetheless in league with the high-ranking males of Poro to whom they defer in all important matters and with whom they share the emoluments of office. This also is the case for the Gola: the most sacred elders or leaders of Sande and Bon are close lineage mates in the core patrilineage of the chiefdom and meet together in the supreme councils of the Bemba where the Mazo of the Sande and her most important assistants are instructed by their "brothers" and "fathers" of Bon regarding female compliance and male responsibility for the maintenance of social cohesion.

In male-dominated Gola society the ideology of political power derives its essential cogency from ancestral dicta that prescribe the patriarchal order and the integrity of ruling patrilineages. All symbols of authority, whether in the secular or sacred spheres of action, underscore the privileged status of males and the adjunctive idealized statuses of women as wives, childbearers, nurturers or, in their semiclandestine romantic role, as "lovers". Women as well as men share a common public disparagement of women who exhibit aggressive or competitive behavior, who are promiscuous, who object to co-wives, who avoid having children, who achieve a degree of economic independence from husbands and fathers, or who occasionally rise to positions of leadership in secular society.[16]

This ideology is legitimized by the core rituals of Bon and Sande in which the gender ambiguity of the presiding spirit of Bon dramatizes the male appropriation of female reproductive powers in the initiation of boys,[17] while the sacred masked performers of Sande represent ostensible male autochthons who appear at intervals among humans to monitor the prescribed relations between the sexes and to reiterate the doctrine of ideal masculinity and femininity. Though myth affirms the original preeminence of women as founders of a primeval matriarchy, it also reveals how historical necessity compelled men to usurp the authority of women and subordinate them to principles of male dominion. Thus Sande, though the most ancient and sacred of the associations, must defer to Bon, whose charge is the governance of secular society on behalf of the leadership and power of the land-owning patrilineages.

Yet this patriarchal omnipresence in Gola culture is perceived by men as a precarious state under continual siege by an intrinsic female power that defies normal proscription. A customary expression of the female proclivity to unruly assertiveness is contained in a phase of Sande ritual when women, under the protection of their secret medicines and masked spirit "husbands", pronounce their temporary liberation from human spouses, from domestic chores and this-worldly obligations. Also, there is the moment when the kínú appears, perhaps to remind the community of those profoundly disquieting attributes of female nature that Sande has attempted to suppress. But these symbolic acts consecrated by ritual are a mere harbinger of what men perceive to be an innate and intractable propensity of women to resist their natural condition of subordination. The all too frequent incidence of unsanctioned abandonment of husbands and children, of shameless promiscuity, of willful barrenness—often justified as the requirement of a private alliance with a spirit tutelary—or, most ominous, the generally recognized prevalence of female witchcraft, reinforces the conviction that only vigilant masculinity and the exclusive guardianship of the terrifying mysteries of Bon can protect society from the threat of primordial apostasy. Though Sande institutionalizes the communal powers of women and their control of reproduction, it is, nevertheless, subject to the patriarchal supervision of the ancestors, thus insuring the hierarchial structure of male dominion and the suppression of the latent striving for equity of females and other subordinates.

Therefore, the alternative means for the exercise of personal autonomy for many Gola women lie outside the sphere of privileged public polity and ideology. These instruments are negations of the existing order—resistance to childbearing, sexual independence, the assumption of male prerogatives in public achievement, privatized consort with errant spirits, the threat of willful menstrual contamination, and, finally, the ultimate retaliation of witchcraft or the threat of it.

NOTES

1. An early version of this chapter was read at the annual meeting of the African Studies Association in Denver, Colorado, November 1987. The simplified orthography employed here for Gola terms utilizes the acute and grave accents for high and low vowel tones, respectively, and the tilde for nasalization. Titles or names of Gola sacred personages and institutions are given as proper nouns in roman type.

2. It is noteworthy that much of this new work has been based upon research by women among the Mende of Sierra Leone. Examples of different approaches to the analysis of the role of women and the Sande may be found in the writings of Carol P. (Hoffer) MacCormack (1979) and Caroline Bledsoe (1980, 1984). A recent and remarkably intimate study of Mende women (Boone 1986) attributes the "essence of Sande" to the phenomenon of "women in fellowship" with scarcely any indication of the roles of men or of patrimonial dominance in Mende society.

3. In this vein, Tonkin faults "functionalist explanations" of "secret societies" and their masking phenomenon as operationally weak and lacking in the sophistication necessary for analyses of indigenous philosophies free of Western categories (Tonkin 1979:273, 244–245). Similarly, Jedrej observes that "secret societies in West Africa have largely been considered from the point of view of their social functions" rather than the analysis of "the relevant collective representations from a structural standpoint" (Jedrej 1976:234, 1980:133).

4. This brings to mind Bledsoe's cogent comment: "My criticism of analyses of the symbolism of femaleness is that they tend to take the symbols at face value and fail to situate them in the wider political economy" (Bledsoe 1984:462–463). One might add that there is often also a failure to situate symbolic analyses in the context of normative social interactions and popular attitudes. Frequently, the refinements of interpretive strategies produce designs of cultural inference that have a life of their own unencumbered by the turbulent reality of on-going, historically derived societies of human beings. Though Valerie cautions that "the risks of 'overinterpretation' or 'misinterpretation' inherent in the hermeneutic approach" should not justify the view that "the less interpretation, the greater the truth of ethnographic accounts", those risks are, nevertheless, real (Valerie and Keesing 1987:356). Keesing's response to Valerie is that the argument is

> not against cultural interpretation but against a seductive view that sees anthropology's task as quintessentially interpretive (rather than sociological and historical as well). ... An "interpretive system" or universe of discourse cannot "cause" anything, cannot "do" anything: it is a system humans do things with—an analytic abstraction that too easily metamorphoses, in our analyses, into an agent or an explanatory force. ... We are led, then, not only to take its most elaborated and coherent versions as quintessential but (where the experts are not expert enough) to supply our own connections between fragments of what our subjects do and say on the basis of the "immanent logic" which ... they seem to imply. (Valerie and Keesing 1987:356–357)

5. The term *kínú* is general colloquial usage, but the formal reference to the rite is *ó kendua* as it appears in the *egbíya* phase of Sande. In Gola society the universal and gender-specific Sande and Poro (Bon) associations are referred to collectively as the

Bemba, the sacred authority prescribed by myth and actualized in the cycles of ritual dominance. Each of the associations in turn are charged with the tasks of initiating female and male youth into adulthood in accordance with principles passed down by the ancestors (cf. d'Azevedo 1973, 1980).

6. In the earlier version of his article this sentence reads: "this behavior suggests that the *sande* spirits and the bier are two antithetical representations as would be the case if the *kendue* was the 'corpse' of the excised clitorises, the male genital residue" (Jedrej 1976:241). Thus, in the earlier version, it would seem that it is the "refuse" of clitoridectomy (rather than the prepuces of male circumcision!) that provides the symbolic male opposition to the masked *sande yafe* who represent "the spirit of feminine beauty". The Sande masked performers are repelled by it as the antithesis of femininity. Among the Gola, adjacent to the Mende south of the Mano River, the Zogbénya, like their *sande yafe* counterparts, are also repelled by the *kínú* and, moreover, are notably absent during the rite. In that they are publicly perceived as male spirits, it would seem to follow that the *kínú* contains something other than "male genital residue" in order to complete the symbolic opposition. If we are to continue in this speculative mode, it would seem to me that a most promising candidate for what Alldridge in 1910 referred to as that "mysterious something" might be menstrual blood (as strongly implied in my encounter with the group of Gola men as reported earlier). There is remarkably little mention of the menstrual element in the recent literature of Sande and Poro symbolism, a not surprising fact in view of the extreme secrecy and reticence surrounding it. (See, however, the singular and provocative conjectures offered by Frederick Lamp concerning ethnoastronomy, menstrual synchrony, and Sande/Bondo autonomy among the Mende, in Buckley and Gottlieb 1988.) In her valuable discussion of Sande ideology, Bledsoe includes a critical review of the various elements of sexual symbolism indicated in previous ethnographic reports (Bledsoe 1984:463–464). I found the most striking material to be from H.V. Hall's unpublished Sierra Leone fieldnotes of 1937 in which he describes menstrual napkins and blood as "the heart of the Bundu [Sande] medicine" (quoted in Bledsoe 1984:464).

7. I am grateful to Ariane Deluz for sending me the article in which this observation appears, along with an accompanying note confirming that it had happened in 1982. For it was in 1987, during a passionately speculative discussion that had followed my reading of an earlier version of the present paper (in which I had challenged my colleagues to provide direct evidence about the contents of the bundle, or else desist from hazardous guesses) that Deluz brought the proceedings to abrupt and remedial closure by rising to announce that she had seen the sacred object, at least as it was manifested among the Guro—a simple half-gourd, seemingly, but not necessarily, empty. So, back to the drawing boards!

8. In that I never found it possible to discuss with any Gola person (and certainly no Gola woman) the physiology of female sex organs and menstruation, or about their symbolic representations in art or ritual, I, like many of my male colleagues, am relatively unencumbered by detailed exegesis about such matters directly from members of the cultures we have studied in the region. The opportunity to exercise interpretive license is a compelling one, particularly with regard to sexual symbolism in those ambiguous domains of "religion", "art", and "ritual". A singular event, an object, an illusive metaphor can become the linchpin of intricate constructions purporting to model fundamental cultural structures or meanings. Driven by inherent professional inquisitiveness, we seek to penetrate "mystery" after mystery, "secret" after secret in worlds other than our own, often to discover only that *we* are the mystery, the secret stranger. Meanwhile, back on the ground, people do their best from day to day with the materials at hand—in ordinary rather than virtual reality—much like their counterparts in our own society.

9. This statement was made by the presiding Mazo of Sande in the Gola village of Gbelasua, an elder relative of one of my close associates. It is one of the rare comments about Sande matters I ever heard from a respected Gola woman. Another came from the mother

of a friend who, irritated by questions from me and her urban-educated daughter, blurted out, "Do you want me to die by speaking of this? The Zogbénya are neither men nor women. They are *netónya* [spirits]. But they are men to women. No matter who sees it otherwise, women see Zogbé as *fela* [man]". For Gola, gender ambiguity and androgyny are potential qualities of all living things as well as of spirit entities. Cross-sex impersonations and role exchanges occur in a number of Gola rites, and gender transformation or ambisexuality is a facility of wild animals of the bush and of all nature spirits. In fact, all nature is capable of assuming different forms for different purposes. It is important to know when something is "in its form"—that is, accoutered for a special role or task. Thus a funny old man, the butt of jokes in the village, suddenly makes an impressive appearance at a solemn rite dressed in the vestments ("in the form") of a sacred Dazo of Poro. And thus, the obdurate Zogbénya, whatever may be their forms in the mysterious spirit realm, appear among humans "in the form" of the male spiritual guardians of Gola women and ancestral dicta.

10. Such allusions become commonplace in female discourse during the phase of Sande dominance but, in public display in the presence of men, groups of women may indulge in a tone of heightened jocularity laced with extravagant romantic metaphor obviously intended to exert a competitive female prerogative and "to make men small".

11. The black raffia raiment of the Zogbénya is unique among the masked spirit performers associated with Gola Sande and Poro (Bon). It is said to represent creatures of the deep waters, whereas the natural raffia of masked performers in the male association is said to represent spirits of the mountains and forests.

12. Similar myths of the origin of society and of the secret associations occur throughout the region. Among the Senufo, for example, the Poro is said to have first belonged to women, while men were excluded and relegated to domestic chores until the Creator became dismayed by the wickedness of women and gave Poro to men (Glaze 1981:91–93). As Horton points out, the theme of women creating male institutions is widespread in Africa, including "a recurrent mythical pattern in which men assume control of what women originate" (Horton 1963:94–95).

13. It may be noted here that only after a woman has entered menopause is she considered sufficiently beyond reproach for appointment to the highest Sande office or for mingling with Poro elders in ritual matters. A daringly improper allusion to a sacred Mazo by a man among his cronies might be "she cannot stink". Conversely, there is no greater insult than to accuse a woman or another man's mother of smelling bad. It is a common epithet among children, but subject to severe punishment if overheard by adults.

14. Commenting on the comparative implication of this phenomenon, Valerie and Keesing concur that "subaltern classes" often contribute to and participate in the ideologies that sustain their subjugation: "In the case of pollution rules ... women as well as men have participated in their creation and perpetuation" (Valerie and Keesing 1987:355, 357). Considerable insight into this process is provided by Messick's 1987 analysis of a "subordinate discourse" among Muslim women domestic weavers of the Moroccan town of Azrou. It is suggested that such a discourse "in communicative worlds jammed with patriarchal culture constructs, a distinctively female perspective is to be found not so much in what women say as in what they do". These comments are most relevant to the predicament of Gola women, but what is not adequately addressed is the extent to which women may manipulate the dominant ideology to counter patriarchal control.

15. There has been a tendency to invoke the institution of Sande to explain the ostensibly high status of women in the ritual and general social spheres in this region. Though this may be the case relative to other regions, the Sande is actually a reflection of the profound asymmetry in male-female empowerment. Sexual separation and female solidarity are ultimately instruments of patriarchal control of female reproductive capacities and the preparation of women for exchange in marriage (cf. Bledsoe 1984).

16. It should be noted here that there were frequent instances in the past of honored women presiding as chiefs or family heads, usually in the absence of eligible male lineage mates and always under the protection of elder agnates. Should such a woman acquire too much independent power, she was conspired against as a usurper, was deposed in rebellion or war, and subjected to Poro sanctions. This does not mean that individual women with admired personal abilities could not wield considerable influence in Gola society, either through the auspices of Sande or their status in important lineages. They did and do, so long as their conduct can be perceived as legitimized by the partriarchy.

17. Though the Dadévè is perceived as a masculine being, one of its mysteries is the act of giving "rebirth" to the initiated boys at the conclusion of the Poro (Bon) session. One can hear its moans of pain and lamentation from the bush during the rites of parturition as the graduates appear to the community in their "new form". In some Gola areas, however, Dadévè is said to have a wife who performs the maternal function and whose high melodic voice can be heard along with the solemn tones of her husband.

18

Male & Female Secret Societies

Among the Bafodea Limba of Northern Sierra Leone

Simon Ottenberg

INTRODUCTION

IN THIS CHAPTER,[1] I lay out basic details of the village men's and women's secret societies of one Limba chiefdom, Wara Wara Bafodea. Within this framework, I focus on the similarities and differences between the organization and rites of the male and female societies. It is my contention that (1) the male society, Gbangbani, is older, and (2) when the female society, Bondo, came to Bafodea, it emulated the social framework of the male group, as well as drawing from the more southern Sierra Leone women's societies. The similarities between the two societies vastly outweigh the differences. When differences occur, they largely reflect the dominant political position of men in the chiefdom, the general distinctiveness of sex roles, and existing traditions of craft specialization by gender (Ottenberg 1983).

Wara Wara Bafodea is the most northern and isolated of all the Limba chiefdoms in Sierra Leone, a modern amalgam of an older chiefdom of the same name and of Kamuke chiefdom to its north; the northernmost villages of the latter now lie within Guinea (Finnegan 1965:10, 13, foldout). When I refer to Bafodea or the chiefdom, I mean both groups in Sierra Leone.

Located in a transitional zone between tropical forest and savanna, the people of Bafodea variously produce rice, cassava, groundnuts, millet, palm oil, and palm wine. The grassland areas are partly occupied by cattle-herding Fulani. The chiefdom capital, Bafodea Town, the largest settlement, is in the south and comprises perhaps 1,800 persons; the chiefdom as a whole has approximately 15,000 members. Among Limba chiefdoms, Bafodea has been the most isolated from Temne, Mende, and Lokko influences to the south and from modern urban cultural developments; most of the Bafodea communities until the 1950s were located in hilly fortified sites. Bafodea is predominantly indigenous in religious outlook, although Muslim influences from Fulani, Mandingo, and other neighboring peoples are increasing, and Christian features have existed in the south since the

1950s (Ottenberg 1986, 1988b). At this point in time, the chiefdom is quite unified in the nature of its secret society organizations, even though Bafodea is both at the edge of the forest area and at the edge of the so-called Poro secret society region (see Adams 1980:2 [map]). To the north are found Susu, Mandingo, and Fulani communities, which either do not do initiations or have initiations with very truncated secret society organizations. The neighboring chiefdom of Wara Wara Yagala to the southeast of Bafodea appears to have similar cultural features to the Bafodea, although in recent years the Wara Wara Yagala have been heavily influenced by the ethnically mixed town of Kabala on their border. Kasonko and Biriwa Limba chiefdoms to Bafodea's south have somewhat similar features as well (Finnegan 1965:77–79), while the Western Limba differ in many details (Banton 1955:245– 249).

History

The men's secret society, Gbangbani,[2] is ancient, although I was unable to obtain an origin myth or much other information about its origin. People at Bafodea simply say that "We met it". Bafodeans see Gbangbani as differing from male secret societies among the Mende and Temne while being common in name and rites to all Limba peoples, and thus acting as an ethnic identifier. This is not to say that Gbangbani does not have features in common with the male societies in these other cultural groups or that there have not been changes in Gbangbani at Bafodea. About twenty-five years ago the dancing of the initiands, as I call those being initiated, at the important preinitiation dance changed from a rapidly twirling style to an acrobatic form, and earlier the dancers had replaced iron rattles with European whistles to indicate the desired beat to the musicians. New songs have appeared. In recent years some of the southern Bafodea villages have adapted a more elaborate form of initiation, and new musical instruments have been employed in preinitiation dances. All these changes emanate from the Limba chiefdom of Kasonko, south of Bafodea, actually an amalgamation of a number of chiefdoms (Finnegan 1965:11). Bafodea Limba Muslims may allow their sons to participate only in the circumcision part of the initiation, and Christians may have their boys circumcised by the dispensary at Bafodea or at a hospital elsewhere and do little or nothing further. Thus there are a variety of interpretations of the value and use of the men's society activities, despite the antiquity of the organization and its rites.

The female secret society is of more recent origin at Bafodea. Clitoridectomy seems to have come into the chiefdom in the early part of this century, during the reign of Chief Alymamy Fana, and began in Bafodea Town, the chiefdom center. At first there was secret clitoridectomy in the bush without any of the impressive preinitiation dancing of today and no calling in of large numbers of relatives. Gradually these features were added and the Bondo society evolved, spreading to all the villages in Bafodea and causing changes in female leadership as different women came into prominence along with the society. Bafodea Town people mocked uncircumcised women and captured them and operated on them if they came to town, whether married or not, apparently with the chief's acquiescence. The idea of initiation and the society came from the Kasonko Limba area. Even today, influences still emanate from there: currently spreading to the southern Bafodea villages is an additional initiation rite involving women dancing with a stretcher-like apparatus called *kampa*. Other changes are internal, such as in the south of Bafodea where male and female musicians no longer play together in the society's rites; the females play alone.

Bondo (the term *Sande* is not used) supplements two earlier forms of women's societies that have initiations but no clitoridectomy; Gboki and Kulongpon still exist today, and both have secret elements. In the south of the chiefdom, Gboki is a voluntary society open to any female who has gone through Bondo initiation, while in the north only middle-aged and older women belong. In the north, the town is "closed" when the Gboki society is active, nonmembers having to stay in their closed-up houses regardless of sex or age; but in the south, Gboki plays inside a closed house and the town is open. In both areas the musicians are male. The society plays at funerals of members. It plays to cure illness, both of members and others, including males. Once, for example, while I was conducting research, the society performed at Bafodea Town for a man with swollen feet believed to be caused by witches, and once in Mandia, a northwestern town, it performed to ensure that a new market would be located there and not elsewhere, in an intervillage market-site dispute. In any case, there is dancing and singing but no masking. Different villages have their own separate societies.

Kulongpon is the name of a society of elderly women organized separately in some southern Bafodea villages (which suggests ultimate Kasonko area origin). It is mainly a funeral society, playing at the death of a member and employing male musicians. Some of its activities are secret, taking place in the bush outside the settlement, but parts of the funeral are public, and here very old women dance most of the night, variously holding swords or iron rattles, the leaders in headdresses with bird's feathers and large bird beaks. It is a very impressive sight.

Since members of Gboki and Kulongpon are also members of Bondo, it might be thought that these are simply segments of Bondo, but they appear to be distinct organizations with earlier origins than Bondo.

ORGANIZATION

Both Bondo and Gbangbani operate autonomously of one another and to a certain extent of male political authority, having their own leadership in each town and village. Nevertheless, the heads of Bondo are often middle-aged to older women who are married to, or related by descent to, the Bafodea Paramount Chief, the head of the local community or other political leaders where the society is found. Though female leadership is directly connected with political leadership and high status, this does not mean that the male relatives direct Bondo. These female leaders often are also the circumcisers; younger females in Bondo seem to play a relatively passive role compared with the active young males in Gbangbani. A local Bondo society often includes one medicine man as a member, and he is said not to take part in the male society's activities. In the north, males play the small skin *samburi* drums of the Bondo society; in the south, women play these drums. In the southern villages away from Bafodea Town and its chief, men also play hollowed-out wood gongs, although these were banned by the chief after a dispute. So there is a male presence in the female society, although females clearly lead it. Bondo heads normally do obtain permission of the chief in Bafodea Town, or elsewhere from the settlement head, to "close" the community for a rite and to hold their initiation. Today, there is an official female secular leader, called Mamy Queen, in most communities, but she is not necessarily an influential Bondo leader. There are no female village heads, nor has there been a female Paramount Chief at Bafodea.

The Bondo societies in various communities may cooperate by joining to "close" a settlement if there is a special rite or a violation of Bondo rulings, especially by a nonmember. The leaders of a society in one settlement may at times play important roles in rites in other communities, which is not surprising, since women often change their community residence because of marriage and divorce, remarriage, or the death of the husband. However, no organized pan-Bondo society exists, nor is there any history of all Bondo groups joining together over an issue.

The Gbangbani men's societies similarly operate independently at the settlement level and cooperate with one another. They are led by middle-aged men (rarely older men) who are generally blacksmiths and hunters, although not all men with these occupations are leaders. Blacksmiths and hunters do not come from any single one of the three major patrilineal clans in the chiefdom and these occupations are not restricted hereditarily. But the dominant and ruling clan in the community will have persons among the leaders in the local society. In any case, the Gbangbani societies are much controlled by young men, aged twenty to thirty, who have the enthusiasm to be active and are often the purest upholders of its rules, the most sensitive to violations of its regulations, the most eager for punishment for violators, and the hardest for the leaders to control. There are no female members.

The chief and/or village heads (depending on the locality) give permission for Gbangbani to hold rites and to "close" the town to nonmembers, and may be involved in settling cases growing out of secret society violations, but they do not formally lead the society. Indeed, Paramount Chief Alymamy Salifu, who was in office when I carried out this research, was a Muslim who was not an active leader in the Gbangbani societies of his chiefdom, though he played important roles. As in the female society, each male Gbangbani has a designated head but is in fact ruled by a number of cooperating leaders. The male society's leaders may later become "big men" politicians in the chiefdom; it is not a necessary stepping-stone, and especially nowadays Muslim big men do not go this route.

Neither Bondo or Gbangbani appear to be involved in everyday political affairs in the chiefdom (Finnegan 1965:77–78), such as the allocation of Sierra Leone government resources and chiefdom taxes, the settling of the endemic disputes about Limba crop damage from Fulani cows, land ownership cases, and divorce matters, or in theft cases, except when men's secret society protective charms have been established (which is not a frequent matter). Rather, both male and female secret societies are primarily concerned with the proper initiation of the young; the ritual curing of disease (especially disease caused by witchcraft); the catching of witches, witch beliefs being endemic in the chiefdom; the burial and the later second funeral of members; the prosecution of those who violate taboos of the societies; and the enjoyment of the music, song, dance, and dress associated with particular rites. I do not have any evidence (though this may be a closely guarded secret) that political leaders use the support of a secret society to maintain or increase their power, or that the societies take part in succession disputes to political office (which have kinship and descent aspects), or that the societies have tried to overthrow political leaders. Nor is there much evidence that in earlier more militaristic times and during the conflicts in the late nineteenth century over the Falaba-Freetown trade route, which passed through Bafodea (Fyle 1979), that the secret societies played much of a political or military role. The autonomy of the societies at the village level, yet their interrelationship with leadership, fits well with the considerable autonomy of Bafodea's communities within the framework of a chiefdom with a central leading figure, the Paramount Chief and his aides. A cooperative rather than competitive air exists between political leadership and the leaders of the societies. In both Gbangbani and Bondo, the political leaders employ their kinship links with some of the societies' leaders to maintain a spirit of mutual assistance.

The male and female societies in a community do not seem to cooperate in rites or activities beyond ensuring, often through the local political head, that they are not both active at the same time. For both sexes, membership is essential for persons to have status in the community, and membership is demanded of those born Limba in the chiefdom, but not of Fulani, Mandingo, or others. Both Limba males and females may be initiated in a community other than where they were born, if they live with a divorced parent or with stepparents, or if there is a reason to rush the initiation and the rite is not being conducted in the village of residence at that time. Some Fula girls and boys also join the respective societies. However, beyond initiation, taking part in activities as an adult is largely voluntary, and there are not only Muslim and Christian Limba who do not participate but also even some practitioners of indigenous religion who are not particularly interested; thus the societies have both a voluntary and a compulsory quality.

INITIATION

The basic initiation is called *bure* for boys entering the Gbangbani society and *bondo* for girls entering the Bondo society. Each initiation has five phases.

PHASE I: PRELIMINARY ACTIVITIES

The initiation takes place in the dry season, when food is most plentiful and there is free time. Bondo rites generally occur in January and February, while the male rites occur in April, May, and June; the times accord with farm-work schedules for each gender. In each case the parents must decide if they have sufficient resources to initiate a child in a particular year or if they will postpone it. Children often voice their view as well, for they may wish to be initiated with age mates and pressure their parents not to delay. For girls, marriage considerations may also be involved, as they may wed in the next several years after initiation, while boys may not marry for ten or fifteen years or more after initiation. The initiands range in age from about eight to eighteen, whether boys or girls. If a boy or girl is from a poor family or does not know how to do the preinitiation dance—sometimes true of children who have lived away from the chiefdom—the child will not do the major preinitiation events and the parents will not invite relatives and friends to the initiation but will simply send the youngster to the bush when the others go in. Otherwise, there is no difference in the initiation of a child of the Paramount Chief, village head, or "big man" from that of other children.

Except in Bafodea Town, where initiations for both sexes are held annually, probably due to the substantial population size, initiations for boys and girls do not normally take place the same year. A typical pattern in a village is for the girls' initiation to occur every three years and the boys' every four or five. Since girls more quickly mature and become ready for marriage, there is a need to keep them moving through the system, and Bafodeans also seem to prefer smaller initiation groups for girls than for boys. In fact, in Bafodea Town, but not usually elsewhere, girls may enter and leave the bush individually, or in small groups, rather than all together for the year, so that the preinitiation dance and coming-out activities may be seen a number of times in one year. This is not true for boys, who do their dancing and coming-out all together.

There is no system, as among the Gola of Liberia (d'Azevedo 1980 and Chapter 17, this volume), of females being in ritual charge of the settlement for a certain number of years, in an alternating pattern with males, and there is little regularity to the dates of initiation by years; the prime factors are the availability of candidates and the ability to provide food for the many visitors who are invited to the rites. In 1979 there were few Gbangbani society initiations in the chiefdom; in 1980 many villages held them.

In both the girls' and the boys' initiation in Bafodea Town, the parents of prospective initiands join with the Paramount Chief and leaders of the society to arrange the date. In the southern villages, the village head and Paramount Chief choose the date together; in the north, the society and village head decide, and the Paramount Chief is merely notified of the date. In some communities there is a rite of the boy initiands presenting palm wine that they have collected to the village head to inform him of their intentions, and in all villages there is the ceremony of measuring the cloth to be used by the boys in the bush: bands of native cloth are measured out in front of the settlement head for each boy who is to be initiated.

PHASE II: PREPARATIONS

After the consultation with the political leader involved (and often other settlement leaders), or at the cloth-measuring event for boys, the date of going to the bush is announced. Boys dance on Friday, and go into the bush the next day, while girls dance any day that is set and also go in the following day. The boys' case does not indicate Muslim influence; it is pre-Muslim, fitting into the seven-day Limba week.

During the two to four weeks between the time of the announcement and the beginning of the initiation, the initiands do not work, they are treated with respect by others, and people avoid disputing with them (a dispute would invoke the concerned society): the initiands are in a period of grace. The boys dress up as females, wearing blouses, a wrap-around waist cloth, a female beaded headband (Ottenberg 1992), head-ties as headpieces (but shaped in a special style), and other head-ties as shoulder cloths (Plate 18–1). They borrow these things from mothers or sisters, and a female relative plaits their hair in a special design or in female style; this is the only time that males have their hair so fixed. People say they dress this way just to look different and think this obvious sex reversal is enjoyable. Girl initiands do not dress as boys but wear fancy European cloths and the beaded headband on the forehead.

In both cases, the initiands are given kola nuts by their parents, or coins as a substitute, and are instructed to go to designated relatives and friends with these gifts to inform them of the coming event and invite them to attend. The children not only do this in their own community but also go to many other villages and towns, often in groups. This is an enjoyable experience for them, as they are well received and fed wherever they travel. Those invited know they must come to the initiation with gifts and often plan to stay for several days. The villages involved are jammed with persons at the initiations.

In this preparatory phase the initiands practice their preinitiation dance in the evenings and at night, getting local musicians or young people at home or where they visit to play for them. The girls and boys each practice before crowds, and women especially come out to sing and dance. Children start to learn their preinitiation dances when they are five or six years old and are often quite proficient by initiation time.

Plate 18–1. Five Limba boys, shortly to be initiated, in their preliminary dress, Kpongkpon village, Wara Wara Bafodea Chiefdom, Sierra Leone, 1979.

During this phase parents consult diviners to see what needs to be done to protect their initiating child against sickness or death while in the bush. Sickness or death is generally not attributed to malevolent bush spirits but to witches, and an initiand may wear a small ceremonial knife or other charm tied to one wrist, or a native cloth band around the neck with a piece of kola or other object attached to it, as a protective charm. If the child is a twin, the parents, especially the mother, have to perform special rites that depend on whether the other twin is living or not and whether or not the twins are of the same sex. Same sex twins are expected to be initiated together. Limba say that twins are easily made jealous of one another and can become mystically dangerous, whether dead or alive, so these precautionary rites must be done.

Also at this time the initiands, whether girls or boys, arrange for skilled musicians to play for them the night before they go into the bush. The parents pay for these professionals, who may come from afar, even from the Kasonko chiefdom to the south; rarely do the Limba believe that the best musicians are local persons. A single initiand may have his or her own musicians, while at other times two or three initiands who are friends or relatives join together to hire one group. When musicians play, there may be as many as ten or more groups going at once in a community, and there is a competitive air over securing the best musicians and fostering the best dancing skills by the initiands.

During this period the members of the Bondo or Gbangbani society prepare the bush area to be used during the rites, the younger members of the society building simple structures there. The bush areas are generally just outside the community, in a place with some trees or brush, with each gender having its own place.

During this time too, a guide, called *soma*, is chosen for each initiand in the bush by the parent of the same sex as the child. In the case of boys, the *soma* is often middle aged or an elder and he guides one boy alone, or perhaps one or two others. In the case of girls, the *soma* is also middle aged or older, but she may guide a larger number of initiands. The *soma* is generously paid by the parents. The male *soma* is responsible for seeing that the cloth for the boy's bush dress is prepared through sewing and dying—in some villages this is done secretly, while in others it is prepared in public. In the case of girls, the future husband in an arranged marriage provides part of the blue poplin cloth for the girl in the bush, and the parents provide the rest (Ottenberg 1989b:59). This "husband" is invited by the girl's parents and brings other presents for her as well. In the case of a boy initiand, a wife-to-be does not bring presents.

Also in this phase, the circumcisers are chosen, as will be discussed below.

PHASE III: THE PREINITIATION DANCE

On the day of the preinitiation dance, or the day before, the musicians and guests arrive and are housed under the direction of the family concerned or by the village head. Traders come and lay out their small goods for sale—from toothpaste to head-ties to aspirin. Uninvited musical groups, sometimes including Fulani and Mandingo ensembles (Ottenberg 1988b), also come playing different music and often playing instruments unlike those of the initiation musicians. They play for pleasure until the children go into the bush but are careful not to interfere seriously with the musicians hired for the preinitiation dancing. All of this lends the settlement a very joyous and varied musical air. Again during this time, parents may carry out special rites to protect an initiand boy or girl from harm in the bush. The performance of such rites is often indicated by a small European black iron pot filled with water on the ground outside the house, containing kola, pieces of iron, and bits of rice. Another indication is the presence of an old sword stuck vertically into the earth nearby. One or both parents may put on charms to protect themselves. The social transition of initiation for both sexes is clearly seen as dangerous.

Girls have their hair plaited in the afternoon in a special style by a female relative, who is given food (uncooked beans, rice, kola) by friends and relatives of the girl. The plaiting is done on the porch of the girl's home, in public, with other girls and women around her, some of whom do each other's hair at this time, too.

On this day the arriving guests bring presents to the initiand and his or her parents, and these may be given publicly at a gathering. As one might expect, gift-giving is very important, and when the initiand dances he or she continually receives small presents of money, sometimes so frequently that the performance is interrupted, especially if the giver also wishes to make a speech. Even on the final morning of the dance, just before the initiands go into the bush, there is an almost desperate moving about the community of the initiand and his or her following to get the last monies.

In the case of boys, other boys who are friends of the initiand build a small cloth-covered resting-place outside the initiand's house, where he will lie at rest between

Plate 18–2. Limba girl dancing to the beat of women drummers just previous to going into the bush for her initiation, Kakpongkpon village, 1979.

dances at night, surrounded by his girlfriends, who fan him and talk to him sweetly! No such arrangement exists for female initiands, who may rest in their homes from the dancing for short periods at night.

Although many relatives, heads of surrounding villages, the Paramount Chief, and other persons may be invited to attend the rite, they do not engage in the settling of disputes and other cases at this time, but they sometimes do so the following day, shortly after the initiands go into the bush, when the community is quiet.

The girl initiands dress in fine clothes and beads and jewelry in their homes after their hair is plaited, and then they gradually appear to commence dancing in the evening, with their musicians—generally two or more women playing small skin drums. In some villages men also play hollow gongs; in the north all musicians are male. The initiating girls do not have a collective dance but perform singly with their musicians and followers in front of their homes and then move about town to other homes, then back home again, repeating this cycle again and again (Plate 18–2).

The initiating boys dance at their own homes and at other homes too, but toward evening they converge on the home of the Paramount Chief in Bafodea Town—or at the community head's house in the villages—with their *soma* guides, their male and female relatives, and friends, to dance competitively before the political leaders. Then the boys go together to a bush area outside the settlement (not the same as their initiation site) with their male followers, while female relatives and friends remain at the edge of the settlement, some singing special songs. In the bush the initiands' head hair is shaved off, and they are dressed with the help of their *soma* and his helpers in an elaborate costume of bunches of bright wool thread hangings or bundles of rolled cloth, in either case tied from the shoulders. They wear a native cloth cap and leggings, colored beaded bands attached to their front, colored cloths, and in the north of the chiefdom a cowrie-shell eye-frame piece (Plate 18–3). They are no longer dressed as females, but in a style considered quite male. Then all return as a group, the boy initiands on the shoulders of their followers, joined by the females, who have been waiting for them, and appear again briefly before the political leaders before dispersing to their home areas with their *soma* guides, musicians, and followers, for a night of dancing.

In several southern villages during the last day or two of the preinitiation period for boys, as visitors and musicians arrive and the dancing occurs, a fiber mask [*batoro*] is seen. It has large open eye spaces and a peaked top with black feathers on it. The mask is worn by a messenger of the men's secret society, who appears publicly with it over his face and then lifts it up to make announcements, so that his face is visible when saying, for example, that the society members should meet at such-and-such a place or that girls should now carry water to the bush (to the edge of where the initiands will live) for initiands' use. The masker then covers his face and moves on and is only occasionally seen; he does not dance. In several other southern villages the mask is of wood and is called *kuboli* (compare with Hart 1989:53, figs. 13–14). Here, it is black and long faced with a bottom peg to hold it vertically. The *kuboli* user, again a men's society messenger, makes announcements or welcomes "big men" as they arrive, talking while holding the mask to his

Plate 18–3. Boy performing initiation dance. Kamabonsi village, 1979. He is wearing the cowry face decorated piece commonly used in the north of the chiefdom, but not in the south.

face; otherwise he holds it in his hand or lays it down. On one occasion just before the final dance of the initiands, the mask was decorated with red and white spots of European paint.

The *batoro-* and *kuboli*-masked men are secret society officials helping to direct the rite, but they do not represent spirits; the masks call attention to the speaker at a time when there is a lot of talk going on, and the masks are used in a like manner in the bush. There are no equivalent masks for the girls' initiation.

For both boy and girl initiands, the pattern for the preinitiation night is similar. The initiands dance intermittently all night with the accompanying musicians and a crowd of followers. For the boys, long skin drums and hollow wood gongs are played by male musicians, and the dancing involves cartwheels, backflips, side flips, and other feats of physical skill. For girls, the dancing is intensive in front of the drummers, but not acrobatic. Music and dance clearly differ for each sex, though the content of many of the songs is similar and in both cases sung mainly by women. These songs refer to the fact that the initiands will be going away on the morrow. "Who will wash and launder for me now?" the women sing of a girl initiand, or "Dance, for tomorrow you go to the bush", for initiands of either sex. The words generally refer to departure, loss, and change, but not to any dangers of the bush. The *soma* guides are in charge of the dancing, but older boys and young men actually run it most of the time for the male initiands, and interested women and female relatives, such as a sister, do so for the girl.

For boy initiands, other boys also dance in the same style, especially noninitiates (initiated boys are not supposed to dance here but they sometimes do). For girls, both other girls and older women dance, but the initiated ones dance in a different style. For each gender, the initiand dance differs from other dances done at other times in Bafodea, clearly marking this unique event. As the initiand and his or her followers and musicians move about town, stopping to perform here and there, they receive "dashes" from relatives and friends, and everyone stops at the house of a "big man". Before the dancing starts in the evening, a medicine man or diviner often performs a blessing for the initiand in a public or a secret way, again to protect him or her from evil, especially witches. There is much drinking of palm wine and native gin, in which the initiands also participate, and heavy eating by guests. The long night of dancing and festivity begins to quiet down toward the early morning. There is usually another competition by male initiands in front of the political leader's home at daybreak, with all their musicians playing together, and the best dancer is chosen, more by common agreement than through any formal decision. The girl initiands do not have a similar competition, although the individual dancing groups appear before the leaders' homes at night and the next morning, and spectators certainly judge the girls' skills privately.

A few hours into the morning, there is, for both Bondo and Gbangbani, a final moving around town for "dashes". The final protective rituals may be done by medicine men or diviners, and the initiands move off into the bush, with many initiated persons of the initiands' sex going to watch the physical operation, which occurs right after entering the bush. The initiand, or one of his or her helpers, often carries a small white chicken to the bush; this white chicken lives with the initiand as a magical protection and is generally eaten at the end of the initiation by the society members.

PHASE IV: INITIATION

The initiands are often exhausted from the night of dancing. This exhaustion is perhaps a desirable state for the operation, which is a key part of the initiation. When persons refer to "initiation", they mean the excision; it is the minimum action to be taken with both boys and girls. The operation is not performed where the initiands will stay, but nearby, where the initiands remove their dancing clothes. Following the operation, the initiands put on their bush clothes. In Gbangbani, older boys run back through town carrying branches and waving them and singing to indicate that the operation is finished, while in Bondo older girls do this, but using a different song and without carrying anything. In both cases others who came to watch gradually drift back to the settlement.

For boys, the circumcisers have been chosen earlier by the Gbangbani society's leaders, although sometimes a father may choose, and at other times one of these professionals may simply show up and demand work. They are often from other settlements in the chiefdom, are not usually leaders in the men's society, and are paid by the parents of the initiands. For girls, the circumcisers are generally middle-aged or older leaders of Bondo. For both sexes, there is a chiefdom circumcision fee (one Leone in 1980) and the year after initiation the boys start paying the annual chiefdom tax (about 4.50 Leones in 1980) whether they are twenty-one or not, for they are considered adults for tax purposes.

Boys and girls I talked to looked forward to the operation as a necessary, if painful, part of growing up, something to be done with friends and age-mates. It is believed that the clitoridectomy makes a female grow quickly; I did not hear this of male circumcision.

The boys remain in the bush about three to five weeks, while the girls stay for two to three weeks. In fact, the girls sleep in houses at the edge of the settlement at night, entering after dark and leaving in the early morning for the bush so that they will not be seen. In both cases, the initiands generally stay until the wound has healed. They are under the immediate care of their *soma,* who maintains contact with the children's parents: a *soma* can move in and out of the bush at will and collects fees from the parents for fines levied against the child for breaking taboos or for special rites. The parent of the same sex as the child may witness his or her operation, although this does not seem to be common, and they may visit the initiand in the bush. A *soma* is responsible for the health of the initiand; they dress the wound and may call in medical specialists to assist them.

I will not go into the details of bush life, for I have limited knowledge of these activities, but both boys and girls learn songs, are subject to physical trials and tests, and hold to numerous troublesome taboos. I do not think that the girls are taught about carvings or masks; there are no masquerades associated with Bondo.

The boys learn to play two kinds of wood gongs associated with Gbangbani. One is a wood slit gong, approximately four feet in length, usually played with a simple stick (Hart 1989:51, figs. 8–9). Often at its upper end is a rounded element, which is sometimes undecorated but at other times is in the shape of a crudely carved male head, similar to carvings of faces on statues made by boys to amuse themselves. This head is carved entirely or almost completely with an adze. There is also a smaller wood gong without a decorated end. While in the bush the *soma*, or his initiand, makes one of these smaller gongs and puts incised geometrical designs on it with a hot blade; the initiand plays this instrument the day he comes from the bush. Some smaller gongs are undecorated, but I also have seen one with a full-body carving of a female forming its core. The initiands also hear the sound of the sacred wood horn of Gbangbani, which generally has a simple carving of a female encompassing the entire body of the instrument (Hart 1989:50–51, figs. 6–7), but they are not yet permitted to see it, nor do they yet see the fiber-masked and body-draped figure of the Gbangbani "devil" at this time. The wood horn and this masked "devil" figure are the two core elements of the Gbangbani society.

Should an initiand of either sex die in the bush, he or she would be buried there and the parents would not be told, so they would still send food. After the youngsters come out of the bush, the deceased child's clothes would be placed on the porch of the parents' home as a sign. I believe that death in the bush is rare: I never heard of a case and was told it would not be kept secret after the initiation.

I do not believe that in either initiation the initiands are taught much of the history and indigenous everyday customs and practices of the chiefdom, although they do learn their initiating society's rules. They learn secret songs and practices, which they will either use later as full secret society members or will never employ again after the initiation. They will, however, teach them to other initiands in subsequent years, for it is the older youths who, under the direction of the *soma* guides and society leaders, are the most enthusiastic teachers in the bush. I am not surprised at the lack of learning of history and myth here, for Bafodea as a whole is not particularly historically minded, nor does it dwell much on myths of origin or other like material. Rather its people are practical and present-day oriented.

At the end of their bush period, the male initiands come out to their community in single file, wearing their brown native sacklike cloths and a native cloth cap or a wool crocheted head piece, followed by each *soma* and other society members. Each boy carries from his shoulder the small decorated wood slit gong prepared in the bush, which he hits with a stick in a rhythm particular to this event (Plate 18–4). These boys come out and play before the political head of the settlement—in Bafodea Town before the Paramount Chief—and perhaps in front of the homes of one or two other leaders, and they sing, with some bowing down. This performance contrasts with their performance before they went into the bush. Here after initiation they sing and play and move in calm unison and in deference to older men, and they do so briefly and quietly, while before entering the bush their dancing was individualistic, assertive, and competitive with other boys with a visible sense of excitement. It is as if they have been trained and controlled by their bush experience, and of course they have.

On the house porch of the settlement head, or another "big man", the initiands eat food contributed by their families. Then they are free to go home, where they

Plate 18–4. Initiated boys just out of the bush, Bafodea Town, 1979. They wear wool crocheted hats and also wool gowns that they wore during the initiation. The Wesleyan Methodist church is in the background.

receive presents of money and other things from their parents, relatives, and friends. There is no large group of visitors from other settlements for this coming out; it has a quiet, toned-down quality. The next couple of days the initiands, wearing their bush dress, go around their own and other settlements in small groups, or individually, and receive "dashes" wherever they move. The wood gongs belong to the *soma* guides and disappear from public view, going back to the society, or occasionally appearing as a protective charm against thieves on the farms, particularly where cassava is planted beside the paths, so that females, who are said to fear the gong, will not steal any of the food.

The girls come out in similar fashion, accompanied by Bondo society women, some of whom play small drums or a gourd rattle, and they too go to the political leader's house, but only rarely to that of the Mamy Queen. The girls are in blue poplin dresses that they wore in the bush, with a blue cloth band around the forehead and a band of white locally woven cloth around the waist; their bodies are covered with white chalk or mud. They too move in a bowing, controlled fashion, in line, showing obeisance to their Bondo leaders in movement and song (Plate 18–5): again it is a brief performance without much of a crowd. The songs they sing differ from those of the boys. Again there is the eating, the breaking-up of the group, the receiving of presents, and the visiting about for a few days. For both sexes, the music and dance when they leave the bush are quite different from when they enter, and for both sexes they have about a two-week period of freedom after the initiation when they often visit other communities in groups with their friends. Some girls, the day they come from the bush and perhaps the next day or two, put white mud or chalk geometric designs on their upper bodies; they claim these have no mystical purposes but are simply to make themselves look fine.

During this immediate post-bush period both boys and girls transform into their individualistic and often competitive selves again.

PHASE V: FINAL PERIOD

About a week or two after the boys leave the bush, the town is closed for one night by the male society. The initiands return to Gbangbani to learn the secret of its mystic wooden horn, which they see for the first time, and of the fiber-covered masked figure, which dances to the music of the wood gongs of the society. This rite is not compulsory, but it is necessary in order for males to take part as society members in most of its activities. Most boys do participate, usually in the community where they went through the earlier rite. The next morning they are free; there is no big feast. In the very southern area of the chiefdom, but not in Bafodea Town, there is a more complex final phase, which came in from Kasonko chiefdom and is now spreading among the villages; boys from other communities sometimes go to these villages in the same year or in another year to do this additional complex rite as well.

Girls, after the time in the bush and a period of rest, go back to helping their parents with work, although they also play particular roles in the marriage rites of girlfriends and relatives (Ottenberg 1988b, 1989b). Their final initiation phase, called "washing hands" or "turning" [*kakunutu*], may occur several months later,

Plate 18–5. Girls just back from the bush, finishing the first part of their initiation, Seredugu village, 1978. Bondo society leaders are in the foreground and background.

or the next year in about April or May, or even two or three years later—whenever their parents and their community head determine it should be done for them as a group. The time depends upon the availability of food supplies for this final female rite, because another big invited feast is involved, unlike the case of boys. The time of this event may also depend on pressures to marry, for most of the girls have been long betrothed, and marriage should not occur (though exceptions exist) until after this final event. The rite is compulsory for girls, but they do not have to do it in the community where they went through the earlier initiation. Until this rite is completed, they continue to wear their blue poplin clothes and cloth bands, except if they go to the Bafodea Primary School, where they dress in school uniforms while in class. But in any case, the white mud or chalk is no longer employed. The yet "unwashed" girls are often seen at settlements other than their own in their special dress, at boys' or girls' preinitiation rites, and at marriage ceremonies. As are the boys before their final rite, these girls are in a special status, a suspended state. They have had their excision but are not yet full secret society members.

For the girls' final rite there is again the plaiting of hair by other females on the porches, and each initiand's head is then covered with cloth. Many relatives are invited for the feast. The husband-to-be again gives presents to the girl. The settlement is full of adult females, including Bondo leaders from other Bafodea villages; women dance publicly, and some play drums. In the evening, the Bondo closes the town to nonmembers and the men and children go inside houses and close them up. The women sing and dance with the girl initiands on the streets and then lead them into one or two fenced-off houses where they spend the night singing and dancing some more, although the settlement is no longer "closed", and they can be heard from outside. They remain there the next day and night, and then in the early morning of the following day the town is again "closed" while the girls are led by the women to a stream. At the edge of the stream they wash and are elaborately dressed in brightly colored cloths and bands of beads. Their bodies are covered with heavy oil, and their fancy hairdos are prepared. They then return to the village for a brief, final, very controlled dance (Plate 18–6). Bondo elders also dance and some of them carry on their heads boxes containing sacred objects of the society. The girls receive presents from parents, other relatives, and friends and are then free, keeping their fancy dress for a few days to visit other settlements. During this last rite the girls learn certain secrets of their society, but there appears to be no secret musical instrument as in the men's organization.

After this rite, for the first time since entering the bush, the girls wear ordinary clothes and many put on bright new ones (Plate 18–7, p. 383), preferring them to the drab blue they have been wearing. The clothes the boys and girls bring out of the bush from their initial initiation period are not sacred; they can be worn as ordinary dress—in the case of boys redone into normal clothes from their sacklike shape.

Neither the female nor the male initiation is unusual in terms of its role in status change, the symbolic death and rebirth of the youngsters, in its sex role emphasis, and in its being preparatory to marriage. It is a happy time for the

Plate 18–6. Girls finishing the washing rite, Bafodea Town, 1979. They have just returned from the bush.

parents, if not always for the initiands in the bush. The rites also make an implicit statement of joy that the children have survived illness, death, witches, and uncooperative ancestors (in a world where many children die young) as well as happiness over survival to nearly adult age, so that the children can marry and raise a family.

OTHER ACTIVITIES

During the dry season the men's Gbangbani society closes the town as many as two or three nights a week, for all or part of the night. All members of the opposite sex and noninitiates of the same sex must remain in their closed houses. The women's Bondo society closes the town much less often, but it also frequently holds events in a house of one of its leaders, without closing the town. These women's society events also occur in the evening or at night, and the men are excluded. The reasons for these activities are various, but in both men's and women's events singing, dancing, and playing the society's musical instruments are inevitably involved; while the rituals often have serious purposes, the element of pleasure is important. The men's and women's societies in a community never perform at the same time; they coordinate their activities, often through the settlement head, and when either is playing, other musical activities are forbidden.

Each society frequently performs for sick persons: the individual does not have to be a society member and can be of either gender. This performance is generally done to drive away or kill witches believed to be the cause of the affliction; most serious illnesses at Bafodea are explained in this way, witches being either close relations of the ill person or spirits manipulated by close relatives. These rites may even occur in the rainy season, although at these times many people are dispersed at farm villages.

At the time of the death of a member, his or her society performs, again Gbangbani closing the town, Bondo without doing so, and burial rites are held by the society. If the deceased was a Muslim or a Christian, other rites are held instead. For a secret society member, at seven and at forty days after death the society may perform again, and then again at a massive second funeral a year or more later, when many relatives and friends are invited, and where feasting and drinking and the killing of cows occur, and a variety of musical groups appear publicly. At the second funeral there is little mourning, unlike the burial; it is a joyous occasion to honor the dead, and also honors the living who give the event. For both sickness and death, when the Gbangbani plays and the town is closed, the sacred horn is heard and I believe the masquerade figure appears.

Either society may also close the town and perform in case of a violation of its rules by a member or nonmember. Once a girl came out when the Gbangbani was performing, unaware of its presence, and the society closed the town for a number of days until the girl's parents paid a fine. Usually a purification ceremony is performed in such a case as well. For another example: a woman, angry at a man, may make a reference to his circumcision—in one particular case a woman screamed at a man that she would take him to the bush and circumcise him again. In such an instance, the Gbangbani appears until the person pays for the indiscretion. If a man violates the rules of Bondo by a similar reference to females, the Bondo society will perform until he pays a fine. The secret society involved generally gets permission from the community head to perform, or in Bafodea Town from the Paramount Chief; and the political leader and other elders, along with the secret society leaders, take part in reaching a settlement with the person involved and his or her relatives. Closing the town to

Plate 18–7. Girl who recently finished her washing rite and will soon marry. She wears appropriate dress for this transitional period. Kasonko village, 1978.

nonmembers by either society obviously puts pressure on those involved and their relatives to settle the case, to arrive at a suitable punishment, and to open up the community, so that persons can go about their business. In cases of rule violation, as well as death and even occasionally illness, the Bondo or Gbangbani societies from other settlements connected with the persons involved may come and join the playing. Secret societies, out of instant reaction to a situation or in opposition to political leaders, occasionally close a community without permission, thus forcing the involvement of its political head and the elders whether they wish to be involved or not.

The men's and women's societies play their music on other occasions as well, again closing the community. The Gbangbani is heard when the men rebuild the society's hut on the edge of town, where its members meet and its musical instruments are kept; the music is played so nonmembers will stay away and will not see the work done. The Gbangbani played once in Bafodea Town when men carried in the thrashed rice of the Paramount Chief from the farms to his home. Normally, a man's wives and other female relatives do this, but they are said to steal so much of the crop on the way that the chief employed the men's society instead. The society can play for a prominent visitor who is a member, such as a politician. In one case they played for a Catholic priest who belonged to the society in another Limba chiefdom. While I was doing research, the society, in agreement with the chief, placed one of its long wood gongs with a carved head at a site near Bafodea Town to prevent women from dumping their garbage there. These gongs are also sometimes visible at the men's society hut, which may be located near a major path going out of the settlement, or they may be seen lying at a blacksmith's shed. Females can see them but are not supposed to touch them or to know how they are used—but they certainly are aware that they are associated with the Gbangbani society.

Bondo may come out and perform for women in public at a rite for a family's ancestors when there is "confusion" in the house—when wives quarrel and do not bear children, or there is no food, or family members are frequently ill and this is attributed to female ancestors by a diviner. Then sacrifices are offered, Bondo performs in public at the house concerned, and there is feasting for three days to appease the ancestors. At a small rite to appease the ancestors held as a temporary substitute (for that year) for a second funeral for a dead woman, Bondo women perform publicly. Public Bondo performances do not have quite the spiritual force as the more secret ones in a house, where the gourd rattles are heard as well as drums; even I as a foreign, noninitiated outsider could hire Bondo players to perform public Bondo-type music with preinitiation songs. In the case of male ancestors, feasting and sacrifice also occur, nonsociety musical groups play publicly, and the Gbangbani may close the town late at night to play. It is clear that both societies are concerned with the control of ancestors as well as witches, ancestors being the second most common cause of illness and trouble in Bafodea communities, next to witches. But these societies do not seem to be associated with the Limba High God [Kanu or Masala], who is, characteristically, as in much of West Africa, a distant, withdrawn spirit.

CONCLUSIONS[3]

Overall, I am impressed by how *similar* the organization of Gbangbani and Bondo is, including the pattern of their initiation rites and other activities. In a sense, the common elements of the two societies make a statement that members of both sexes are one, as both go through maturation, leave childhood, and prepare for marriage. At the same time, the differences between the societies affirm by contrast that each sex differs. Since the male society is older, I have to assume that the female society developed not only through diffusion from other Limba areas to the south (and probably ultimately from the Temme or Lokko) but also through emulation of the male society pattern, whose general outlines are clear to everyone at Bafodea, even if the details are not. The many commonalities between the male and female societies indicate strong pressure for cultural uniformity, which is not surprising since Limba is probably one of the oldest cultural groups in Sierra Leone and Bafodea is its most isolated chiefdom. The similarities do, however, raise the question of whether the male and female societies in the more central so-called Poro areas share such likenesses as well. My impression is that there is greater differentiation (Adams 1980).

Many of the features that differentiate Gbangbani and Bondo can be attributed to gender differences in political roles, social roles, and craft specializations at Bafodea (Ottenberg 1983). It is not surprising, for example, that the men frequently "close" the town for ritual purposes, while the women do so less often (men sometimes grumble over being closed in their houses for even a few hours by women), for this reflects the political conditions in which males dominate the political process of resource allocation and the settlement of serious disputes. Yet in areas in which women have primary responsibility, women have great freedom, which is reflected in the independence of the women's society from the men's. The women's secret society does not submit to the men's society but acts as a separate agent under the same secular male leadership of the community and chiefdom as does the male secret society.

That women cook for initiands of both sexes reflects the female domestic role. That female initiands do not spend nights in the initiation bush, while males do, and that the female initiation period is shorter than the male one, all reflect a more protective attitude toward females and a more assertive stance toward males. That men carve and use carved musical instruments in the bush but women do not reflects the fact that woodworking is blacksmith's work, done by males. The female Bondo musical gourd—a whole gourd with a net around it with beads—reflects the female preparation and use of beaded objects in dress and women's use of gourds in food preparation. Other examples to explain differences between the two societies can be given. But to me, the range of unities of these two organizations is impressive, even though both are undergoing changes today that come from other traditional Sierra Leone areas and from modern influences.

I am also impressed with the *flexibility* within the tight regulation in both Bondo and Gbangbani. Children do not have to be initiated at a specific age, they can be initiated away from home, and the initiand can skip the preinitiaton dance phase. I have even seen a boy doing the preinitiation dance with Fulani musicians and dancing Fulani music—a boy who had been studying the Koran with a Fulani *karemoko* outside of the chiefdom—and this was acceptable. Boys also can be circumcised at a dispensary or a hospital (girls have their operation only within the bush in a traditional way). This quality of flexibility in the men's and women's societies counterpoint the rigor of the initiation and the severity of punishment for violating rules.

As to whether Bafodea should be included in a Poro area or not, I leave this to the experts in that subject (d'Azevedo 1980; Adams 1980). There are some obvious differences. The Bafodea men's and women's societies do not play important political roles—they do not seem to put a check on the power of the chief or on village heads, as in some Poro areas. There is very little in the way of public appearance for the male society in particular, or for the female society either; even in the extensive preinitiation dances, the societies do not appear as such, but as individual members. Public performance in some Poro areas in Sierra Leone and Liberia seems more common for men's and women's societies. At Bafodea there is no masking in the female societies. For Limba males, there is one important secret masked figure that. as in other Poro areas (Siegmann and Perani 1980), is not made of wood. There are also the nonsecret messenger masks of some of the southern Bafodea villages, either of raffia or wood, and carved heads on the men's society's large gongs, incised designs on small gongs, the carved wood horn, and an occasional figure encompassing a small wood gong. There are apparently no secret society wooden statues. There is less emphasis on masking, carving, and visual aesthetics in the Bafodean secret societies than in those in the more central Poro area, although dress does remain important . There is no other masking at Bafodea except for the *talabi* [devil] figure, which plays at Christmas in Bafodea Town in a secular performance deriving from Freetown.

There also seems to be less of a mythic element to the men's and women's societies at Bafodea than in the more central Poro areas and, perhaps because of this lesser elaboration of art and masquerading, less of a symbolic content. Yet, I am not certain these impressions are accurate; it may be a function of only one two-year research trip to the area, though I suspect that I am correct.

Nevertheless, the Bafodea secret societies appear to be just as strong as those in the main Poro area in controlling individual behavior, just as important in the incision ceremony and initiation, just as autonomous and cooperative with each other. They prominently feature song, the playing of musical instruments, dance, and dress, which are richly aesthetic. They are powerful and compelling organizations in people's lives. If the Bafodea secret societies for men and for women are peripheral to the main Poro area, they are not peripheral in the social life of Bafodea chiefdom, but in fact are very central to it.

It may be that Gbangbani and the two historically earlier female societies, Gboki and Kulongpon, represent earlier versions of ancient secret societies in the main Poro area, in Sierra Leone and Liberia. Later changes in that area brought in female circumcision, the growth of more extensive wood masking for both sexes and the use of statues, the development of political power through the secret organizations, the growth of more elaborate public performances, and the development of a greater mythological elaboration—changes that did not occur in Limba country. Such changes would have involved a greater emphasis on visual aesthetics than in the past and emphasis on the role of nonverbal communication in masking (Ottenberg 1982b). Since the Limba are old to the area, more so than some groups in the more central Poro area, perhaps Gbangbani, Gboki, and Kulongpon represent earlier stages in the growth of Poro-like societies. I offer this hypothesis to other scholars.

NOTES

1. This is a revised version of a paper presented at the panel "Art of the Poro Area" at the annual meeting of the African Studies Association, Bloomington, Indiana, 24 October 1981. Field research between 1978 and 1980 was carried out with the aid of a National Endowment for the Humanities fellowship and sabbatical leave from the University of Washington.

2. Although I was able to observe the preliminary male secret society initiation rites, this chapter focuses on the more public activities of both men's and the women's secret organizations, not on the more private aspects beyond that which is public knowledge. I believe, however, that the contrastive comments about the men's and women's groupings probably hold for the more secret materials as well, which in this chiefdom are very secret indeed.

3. I have elsewhere given a more ecological and psychological interpretation of the Bafodea men's secret society and compared it with the men's secret society of Afikpo Village Group, a collectivity of settlements in Igbo country, southeast Nigeria (Ottenberg 1990).

Plate 19–1. Male dancer at an entertainment event, Massaquoitaa, Liberia. One of the drummers is playing a cylindrical drum [*gbùng-gbùng*] with sticks, supporting the lead goblet drum [*f̣eli*] behind the dancer.

19

Bringing the Extraordinary into the Ordinary:

Music Performance among the Kpelle of Liberia

Ruth M. Stone

T HE KPELLE PEOPLE, slash-and-burn rice farmers of the Pepper Coast in West Africa, perform a variety of music in ritual settings. They sing, dance, play instruments, wear costumes, speak, and act for events of the men's Poro and women's Sande secret societies as well as a host of specialized religious groups organized around supernatural powers. The Kpelle communicate through the intermediate spirits associated with these organizations, spirits who stand between humans and the high god, Yala (Gibbs 1960; Harley 1970b [1941]; Mengrelis 1963). Life cycle rituals, particularly those associated with initiation at social puberty and those accompanying death, as well as year cycle rituals call for a variety of musical activity.

Aside from these ritual and religious events, which have attracted particular attention of outside observers (Murphy 1980; Bellman 1984), the Kpelle also enjoy an array of entertainment genres that exude a sense of the religious in their execution. In this chapter, I will examine some of the religious processes and show how they are placed and meshed into entertainment musical performance. By including a religious accent in the ordinary, the Kpelle permeate aesthetic expression with the awareness of the supernatural and integrate the most mundane acts with the extraordinary.

The Kpelle live in the central region of Liberia, stretching across the border into Guinea; they number roughly 300,000.[1] In recent years a number of Kpelle men have moved to work in nearby rubber and iron ore concessions. Some women have become entrepreneurs, earning cash in developing local produce markets. Rice farming, however, remains the basic form of subsistence.

After a day at their rice farms, the Kpelle people of Gbeyilataa and other towns return to the village for the evening meal of rice and stew. Later a variety of entertainments with music making may follow. The names for the entertainments all include the term *pele*, borrowed from the English word "play": renditions of

Plate 19–2. Kulung, epic performer, enlivening his narration and singing with mime and gesture.

folktales with a choral background [*mɛni-pele*]; a full-blown performance of epic with singers, instrumentalists, and a professional teller [*Wɔi-mɛni-pele*]; singing and dancing to the drumming of goblet drums [*fɛli*] and cylindrical shaped drums [*gbùng-gbùng*, the whole performance is *fɛli-pele*]; singing and dancing with the accoutrements of the chief of the witches [*Kɔli-gong-song-pele*]; or any other of a host of choices.[2]

Musical events for the Kpelle need to be studied as processual occasions— flowing, moving, and changing. Music sound cannot be simply a thing or object plucked from its environment. Rather, music is created in a constellation of action that is multiple in nature.[3] Often music, dance, and speech are so intimately bound together that it is hard to separate them (Stone 1988a). Religious aspects are fundamental to the very being of many musical acts and cannot be stripped from the performance. Thus, it is only for analytical ends that we can, to any extent, pull the religious from the performance bundle for temporary scrutiny.

In order to present conclusions that both reflect and are compatible with the way many Kpelle view life, I consider the ideas of the Kpelle people about the nature of performance to be critical to a full ethnographic picture. In the field, I showed videotapes of events to Kpelle performers and audience members for their comments, which were then transcribed and translated as data (Stone and Stone 1981). I worked and interviewed through the medium of the Kpelle language to best obtain the Kpelle consultants' points of view and to better understand the nuances in the delicate web of performance.

SETTING THE STAGE

Entertainment events for the Kpelle begin with careful attention to religious aspects. An ensemble approaching a neighboring village proceeds grandly around the edge of town, playing their instruments, singing their songs, and attracting the attention of the villagers. Children gather in the wake of the procession as it moves. More important to the success of the upcoming performance than the procession, however, is the sound, which the musicians use to separate lingering unfriendly spirits from the village center and to move them away. Space is marked for performance and an invisible boundary is made. Symbolically the performance arena is set aside as special and bounded for the occasion.

Taking no chances with unwelcome spirits who might linger, dancers customarily begin their solo exhibitions in *pele* by circumscribing the dance arena in a counterclockwise direction, moving in slow, nondance steps to the music sound. Their individual processions clear out the dance circle in much the same way that the village was cleared out earlier, but with a smaller unit of space. At various points throughout the performance, dancers clear out the space again.

ELUSIVE PLAYERS

Along with the various types of dancers, the players in a performance include drummers, gourd players, singers, a zither player, a master of ceremonies, and certain welcome spirits. Tutelary spirits become, for the duration of the performance, what Alfred Schutz calls "consociate" and share both time and space (Schutz 1962:17–18).

These beings may be witnessed only by the player who has a special relationship with them and by a few select others. Animal or human in nature, they first reveal themselves in dreams [*nyii-pere*, lit. sleep-road] and make high demands upon their human clients. In exchange for making the music extraordinarily sweet, the spirits may bring about insanity or even the loss of life itself.[4]

Among the musicians with whom I studied, several provided indications of their tutelary spirits, albeit in indirect ways. Kulung, an epic "pourer", called on his tutelary throughout the evenings when the townspeople of Gbeyilataa gathered around him to hear of the exploits that recalled the mythic Kpelle hero Wǫi. Calling his beloved *Maa-laa-ke-ma,* he sang, "*Ee Maa-laa* doesn't fool around *Zoo-lang-kee*", or "*Oh Maa-laa* bring my voice, oh my people", or "Oh, what does *Maa-laa* say?"

A flamboyant sanza player, Kekula, possessed a tutelary who was not only a predecessor but also had been a well-known performer before moving to ancestor status. As he plucked his instrument, Kekula called out, "*Gbono-kpate, wee!*" Shortly thereafter he answered in a high-pitched voice, "*Oo*". Gbono-kpate was now present and speaking through the voice of Kekula (cf. Dan Ben-Amos 1972:177–184).

A quality performance, said a number of Kpelle people, depends upon the aid of the supernatural. Really good singers, dancers, or instrumentalists could not operate at such a level unaided. Normal human performance was simply much more ordinary. As I apprenticed myself to learn to play the *kǫning*, a triangular frame zither, I learned firsthand about this. At my third lesson when I was still playing rather crudely, Bena, my tutor and an expert *kǫning* player, said, "You need to know about the spirit. As soon as you start playing fine, it will not be you who is playing but the thing that is behind you [spirit]". And so I learned concretely of the supernatural part in all excellent music even as I was warned to store my instrument carefully so that it might not be misused, for it also possessed certain power from the spirit.

The finer a performance, the more likely that spirits are part of the execution. Even ordinary entertainment calls for spirits to attend and participate. With this participation comes the possibility of the manipulation of power by people as well as spirits. Secrecy is, therefore, required to protect the musicians in their very delicate relationships.

The spirits, controlling musicians, create sounds and movements within a shadowy world, very partially shared and known only in bare outline to the audience. Yet such power is the necessary ingredient that turns a pedestrian event into one of aesthetic force. Only when people are emotionally moved to do things they would not otherwise do is an event judged outstanding. Only with the aid of the supernatural can such depth of artistry emerge.

The characters portrayed and given life in a musical event such as the epic are not simple spirits. They may possess the ability to transform themselves to human and even animal form and back to spirit guise again. One of the most wily of these is *Męni-maa-fa*. In the Wǫi epic *Męni-maa-fa* is human as he courts and marries the hero's sister. Later he transforms himself into a supernatural lizard who slaps a severed tree with his head and restores the tree in time for it to block the forward movement of Wǫi (Stone 1988a).

The participants and characters in Kpelle entertainment music performance are, therefore, spirit as well as human, substantial as well as ethereal, real as well as invisible. To maintain otherwise is to deny the religious core that permeates the everyday and the ordinary for the Kpelle.

VOICES OF SPECIAL POWER

Kpelle musicians admire the human voice. They call the sounds of instruments "voices". They speak of the "voice of the mother", "voice of the child", or "voice of the chief" in naming the strings of the frame-zither [koning]. They say that voices can also possess certain magical or superhuman capabilities. One *chante-fable* [meni-pele] relates the story of an orphan with the special gift to kill animals by singing a magical song. And the enactment of this *meni-pele* includes the repeated

Plate 19–3. Bena Kolo-Kuū, expert *koning* player. The higher-pitch strings closer to the player are "voices of the children". The lower-pitch strings farther away are "voice of the mother" and "voice of the chief".

demonstrations of the voice singing the song that kills different animals: bush cow, deer, and finally the forbidden wild boar (Stone 1972).

The Wǫi epic features, in one episode, a jealous wife who is banished to the edge of town for her poor relations with her co-wives. There she makes a living by carving shiny, black, thin-walled wooden bowls with her magical voice. She displays her special power by the varied sounds of carving that we hear: *bongkai* [large inside], *mǫnǫ-mǫnǫ* [shiny blackness], *koro-koro* [small adze strokes]. Here the subtleties of voice timbre are not only beautiful as music sound, but they are translated into an artistic object in the medium of wood. Through music a plastic and visual art is created. The dominant voice makes not only beautiful sounds but also beautiful bowls (Stone 1988b).

SHADOWY SOUNDS

If spirits performing along with human counterparts or magical voices are wispy concepts, the religious implications of certain tone colors or timbres of sound may be even more subtle. Ordinary song can, for brief periods, indicate excursions into the religious. The singer sings not only explicit text that may allude to the Poro or Sande or other society and associated deities. More elusively, the singer reveals this allusion with the changing of her or his voice color. The quality of sound may shift from the ideal penetrating, driving, "clear" sound to a hollow, muffled, nasal, and murky tone. Attuned as the Kpelle are to tone colors, this shift is unmistakable and noticed.

Kulung switches to the hollow sound immediately after he sings, in the Wǫi epic, "Blackbird come and see me, see me, see me". In his new timbre he sings, "The Poro is on a person, the matter angers him. Night falls on him, the daylight bewitches him". His tone clearly communicates that he is singing of the supernatural. With the next line, his voice reverts to the normal tone, "The large, large rooster, the hen's voice is sweet". His timbral switch has helped the audience locate themselves for a brief phrase in matters associated with the Poro.

CREATING A FENCE

Underlying the presence of spirits, voices of supernatural power, and the murky tone colors that symbolize the religious are structural patterns of sound through time. Certain formal features signal to the audience the accent of the religious in everyday entertainment. Basic to Kpelle religious cosmology is the sense of the eternal and unchanging. This concept is graphically represented by the symbol of a fence, the kind that encircles the odd-shaped farms and bounds them from encroaching cattle and rodents. The word for "fence", *korang*, happens also to be the word for "ritual" and for "year". Thus ritual can be understood as that which encloses acts valuable to the Kpelle as a fence protects the rice crop. To speak ritual, the Kpelle say, is to *korang bo* [open the fence]. The young initiates in Poro and Sande live apart from the village in an enclosure that contains them like a fence encloses a rice field. Thus whether spoken or acted, ritual conserves Kpelle culture.

Everyday entertainment music ordinarily emphasizes a highly segmented form. Singers sing short phrases, dancers dance for brief sequences, and six horn players in a chief's ensemble may each play only one or two notes in their portion of a deftly dovetailed larger whole. Elaborate cues exaggerate the "edge cutting" and point up the fragments that are ultimately joined in the event.

The religious tone emerges when players mute these parts and stress connectedness and continuity as symbolized in the ritual fence. In epic, for example, the segmentation between episodes is avoided by foreshadowing the upcoming episode before the present one is ended. Threads of the new episode are firmly in place before the old episode concludes. The foreshadowing may occur in musical sound as well as in the text. Furthermore, a fine epic singer should not sing all the episodes he knows at any one performance since his repertoire is ideally infinite rather than finite. These religious undercurrents run throughout a Wọi epic performance, which the untutored ear might often mistake for an evening of secular entertainment. All Kpelle are believed to have come from Wọi, and this epic in all its rich layers of significance contains the core of what it means to be Kpelle.

The Kpelle build religious accent into very new types of events as well as the traditional epic. I was fortunate to watch the creation of one such event over fourteen months during my fieldwork from 1975 to 1976. *Kọli-gong-song(-pele)* (the name of both the event and the chief of the witches) was the performance created by the young men, and later young women, of Gbeyilataa in central Bong county. Performed by both the permanent residents and the wage laborers who returned on weekends from nearby concessions or the more distant capital city of Monrovia, it contained enactment and voicing of concerns of the young, particularly as they faced changes in the modern world: separation from families and lovers as they traveled to earn money; anxiety in modern transactions, like writing checks; treachery in the cities; and lonely hours in the rubber plantations.

A distinctive feature of *Kọli-gong-song-pele* was the absence of edge-cutting. Young dancers, for example, did not end their dances with the flourishes so important in entertainment. Rather they simply stopped and walked out of the dance arena. For the people of Gbeyilataa who spoke to me about this event, this avoidance stressed continuity and the eternal nature of the religious and thus added an important religious flavor to this community-affirming event involving young people who for much of the week were separated from one another and their home traditions.

One formal part of religious ritual that we might expect to see added to ordinary performance is the special association of certain numbers with men and other numbers with women in ritual contexts. For Kpelle the number four is tied to males and the number three to females throughout their lives, starting in the period immediately following birth. A baby boy emerges from seclusion four days after birth, a girl three days after birth. The session for the Poro lasts four years for men while the Sande convenes for three years. After death and burial, the death feast takes place on the fourth day for a man and on the third day for a woman.

In all the everyday musical performance that I have studied, however, I have not discovered a similar association of numbers. The Kpelle do not seem to strive for three or four repetitions of a phrase, for example. Thus it appears that only certain of the religious characteristics are adopted in everyday music, and special quantitative associations are not among them.

THE INFLUENCE OF RELIGIOUS PROCESSES

We find that spirits attend and participate in performance even if the knowledge of their presence may be only partially shared among the other participants. The spirits bring with them both danger and power, necessary components in the daring enterprise of making good music. The knowledge of these spirits is limited to a special few in any event and that knowledge in itself is a form of power for those who possess it. Spirits enter events as they are summoned by singers and players carrying responsibility for quality. They also come as characters in musical dramatizations such as those of the epic. They are often beings who are not necessarily permanent spirits but creatures who move easily from human to spirit and even to the animal world. Thus the universe of everyday Kpelle performers includes participants who transform themselves quite easily, not unlike the shape shifting reported by Michael Jackson among the Kuranko (1989:102–118).

The assistance of tutelary spirits is also helped by the magical voice powers that some singers have, the powers that allow them to carve bowls or kill animals with sound, tasks ordinarily performed through other media. Even at moments when the voice is not used for anything as spectacular as hunting, it can communicate excursions into the religious. As the vocal timbre changes to a cloudy sound, audience members know that things religious are being addressed in the music. Even the skeleton of the performance, the way the pieces are put together, represents the religious and ritual side of Kpelle life. As everyday performance

Plate 19–4. Performance of *Kǫli-gong-song-pele* in Gbeyilataa as dancer moves on hands and feet simultaneously.

hides segments and attempts to point out continuity, this religious accent on the eternal comes forth. Everyday Kpelle performance is fascinating in its intricate joining of religious and secular, for its playing with ideas from both realms without strictly segregating one from the other.

Basic Kpelle beliefs indicate that true excellence in the arts derives from the supernatural realm. No really fine singer or drummer or dancer is outstanding simply by relying on his or her own efforts. Each of these masters engages in a relationship with a tutelary spirit in order to attain excellence. Thus the very foundation of artistic performance rests on a religious basis. This religious basis, however, though implicitly understood is not openly or easily discussed. The nature of any musician's precise relationship to the supernatural is kept quite hidden and is revealed only in indirect ways.

Religious processes further provide an accent for events that appear to be predominantly entertainment and recreation. When an event is structured without the usual segmentation, as in the case of *Kɔli-gong-song-pele*, the continuity communicates aspects of ritual and its emphasis on eternity. Structural features communicate these religious processes and can subtly nuance a particular performance that in many other respects is purely entertainment.

When Kpelle events are considered in this way, the religious processes provide certain of the voices to be heard and the secular processes provide some of the other voices to be heard. The events are multivocal in a Bakhtinian sense (1981) and a ritual accent does not negate the entertainment value nor does the entertainment accent negate the ritual value. In sum, religious performance permeates a wide range of events in ways that Kpelle people consider quite natural and usual. The interpenetration of the extraordinary into the ordinary provides a linking of the realms in intricate fashion.

NOTES

1. Recent census figures have not been released and the *1974 Census of Population and Housing* lists no ethnic breakdown, though we can assume that a large proportion of the 194,186 population of Bong County are Kpelle. For Guinea figures, see Picot (1958: 273–286).

2. *Pele* in its unmodified form also refers to children's games.

3. For a detailed discussion of Kpelle performance events studied from the perspective of phenomenology and symbolic interactionism, see Stone 1982.

4. Warren d'Azevedo describes a similar situation for the neighboring Gola people (1966:16–26).

Plate 20–1. Headman Lwámbá Múkálámúsí pours palm wine for the ancestors as he eloquently requests their positive intervention to ensure health, peace, fertility, fecundity, and freedom from "witchcraft" for the residents of M.K.I. village in eastern Zaïre. 30 April 1978, 10:30 a.m., courtyard of headman Kíndéngá Kángélá.

20

Ancestors, "Witchcraft", & Foregrounding the Poetic:

Men's Oratory & Women's Song-Dance in Hêmbá Funerary Performance

Pamela A. R. Blakely &
Thomas D. Blakely

A WISE ELDER, Lwámbá Múkálámúsí, the Yílúngá Mwéngé titleholder for many years and one of the most talented orators of his generation, remained sitting in what was left of the circle of men, his closest relatives, who had met in the coolness of the early morning to resolve a pressing dispute between two village residents. That urgent business now done and several men having departed to their farms, the headman quietly and carefully was considering how to address another important concern.

Why, he was asked, had he not flown into a rage and disciplined his patrilineal "sons" and "grandsons". They had been burning off the sword-grass that was choking their soccer field but had let the fire get out of control, destroying a small pathside shrine. He had lovingly been tending this shrine in honor of a recently deceased patrilineage "father".

YílúngáMwéngé spoke obliquely, saying with a slight smile as if nothing were dangerous or wrong, *"Gwayísumbúlé hégúlú nzogolo...?"* ["Should one throw (his) chicken upwards toward the sky ...?"].

To a quizzical face, he leaned slightly forward and softly mouthed the whisper, *"...'áyûndú"* ["wild cat-of-the-bush"].

As in, ... so a wild cat-of-the-bush will notice the squawking?

We all silently completed the second half of the (old? new?) proverb and sat thinking for a while.

And then we all seemed to change the subject. ...

RELIGIOUS DIVERSITY IN EASTERN ZAÏRE

The Republic of Zaïre, a country of about 30 million inhabitants with a land area as large as the United States east of the Mississippi, might be called one of the most

Catholic countries in Africa. It might also be called one of the most Christian countries in Africa, with over seventy Protestant denominations plus millions of members in the Kimbanguist church and other African Christian churches. In eastern Zaïre, in northern Shaba and southern Kivu regions, where we focus our attention in this chapter, a few Muslims are well installed after a century-and-a-half tradition of Arab and Ismaili Pakistani trading.[1] But much more prominent even in this remote part of Zaïre are the many Christians, whether in the 20,000 person multiethnic town of Kongolo or throughout the rural areas of northeastern Kongolo Zone, the ancestral home for 400,000 Báhêmbá people. Large numbers of Báhêmbá engage in indigenous forms of religious expression; some of these Báhêmbá have little to do with Christianity, while others prefer to include one or another form of Christianity among the several kinds of belief and practice they utilize alternately or concurrently.

Half of the Báhêmbá live in rural Hembaland [Búhêmbá] and farm the fertile volcanic soil, where fifty-five inches of rain per year and an eight-month growing season permit them to harvest two maize crops and a cornucopia of other agricultural products. They live in single-line villages, long double-line villages, and grid-pattern villages averaging around 300 people each, with the smallest having ten inhabitants and the largest about 4,000. They usually practice virilocal residence, with the wife almost always moving from her childhood village to live with her husband in his village with his patrilineal relatives. The localized patrilineages are complemented by socially salient matrilineages, making the inhabitants of this area part of a small percentage of rural Africans who practice double unilineal descent (Blakely and Blakely 1979)—a social structural arrangement with implications for indigenous Hêmbá religious practices, since the lines of descent both through women and through men are here crucial in the ritual and everyday matters of life, and also in the questions surrounding death.[2]

The other 200,000 Báhêmbá, who live in the towns of northern Shaba, the copper-mining cities of southern Shaba, and elsewhere in urban Zaïre similarly are members of Catholic or Protestant churches or are practitioners—simultaneous with a Christian faith, or not—of more straightforwardly indigenous kinds of religion. Some of the Catholics are members of the Jamaa movement that Johannes Fabian has studied for many years (Fabian 1969, 1971, 1979a, 1979b, 1979d, 1985) and discusses in chapter 14 in this book. A few Báhêmbá are Kimbanguists, an independent African Christian religion (MacGaffey 1977, 1983, 1986, and chapter 13 of this book). And some are Methodists, a Protestant denomination whose missionary work in Zimbabwe is the subject of chapter 15 by Terence Ranger. These urban Báhêmbá are very interesting in their own right, but they will not be our subject here. Certainly the diversity of religious expression present in rural Hembaland is also present among the urban Báhêmbá. Báhêmbá relatives and friends along a rural-urban continuum constantly exchange, adopt, and modify each other's beliefs and rituals as they travel and migrate back and forth. Nonetheless, to adequately discuss the religious practices of Báhêmbá in the cities would unduly complicate and lengthen this chapter.

Our focus is the rural homeland of the Báhêmbá, especially Collectivité Nyembo of Kongolo Zone. In Collectivité Nyembo, as elsewhere in this general area, missionary-inspired churches and African Christian gatherings are very much in evidence, as well as a wide variety of forms of indigenous religious expression.

Active and nominal members of the Catholic church are numerous in Hembaland, their conversion having originally been fueled, beginning in the early 1900s, by the presence of two European-based missionary congregations: the White Fathers [*Pères Blancs*] on the east bank of the Lualaba River and the Holy Ghost Fathers [*Pères du Saint Esprit*] on the west bank. In Kongolo town, on the west bank, are the administrative offices of the reorganized diocese spanning large parts of both of these formerly distinct missionary concessions. The earliest Catholic missionaries studied Kíhêmbá but soon turned to Kiswahili as the language of instruction in the schools and the medium of communication with Báhêmbá generally.[3] Since Vatican II, Kiswahili also has become the liturgical language. Local drums, rattles, rhythms, melodies, ululation, metaphors, and verbal art (especially proverbs) also are integrated into the Mass and other ritual. During the last twenty years, a small handful of Belgians, French, Spaniards, and French Canadians have served in support positions, but the Catholic bishop and most of the priests and nuns are Zaïreans, including those based in Mbúlúlá and in 'Áyânzá, the two largest settlements in Collectivité Nyembo. In Nyembo, as in the rest of Hembaland, some of the Catholic parishioners are simultaneously members of what is referred to in local Kiswahili as the "*Bababa na Bamama*", the Jamaa movement.

The largest Protestant mission presence in Collectivité Nyembo is the Seventh-Day Adventist church, now completely run by Zaïreans. The last American missionaries left during the Independence era strife of the early 1960s. From the beginning, Seventh-Day Adventists in this area have conducted their church services in Kíhêmbá.[4] A few Jehovah's Witnesses [Bákítábálá] struggle to keep alive a remnant of a faith community that, as a vibrant "Kitawala" movement in the 1920s, attracted fearful and punitive attention from Belgian Congo government officials, who saw in the religious fervor a serious political threat. In Nyembo today there also are "Pentecostals" [Bápéntékóst], who more readily incorporate whole polygynous families than do the other Christian churches. During the last fifteen years an increasing number of newly emerging Christian-related groups have come on the scene, their appearance roughly corresponding with the arrival of a large Zaïrean-American agricultural development project and the beginnings of a hoped-for economic renaissance in this area that had been largely forgotten by the central government since Independence.

MULTIPLE MEMBERSHIPS IN SEMISECRET SOCIETIES AND HEALING ASSOCIATIONS

Variety in the choice of religious beliefs and practices is not new to Hembaland, known to its neighbors as a spawning ground for semisecret societies and healing associations as far back as written or oral historical knowledge goes.[5] Some of these experiments have remained local, while others have spread rapidly to nearby areas.[6] Some have come to Báhêmbá from their ethnic neighbors. Over a century ago, for example, the Bámbúlǐ semisecret society was adopted from the more hierarchical Bálúbǎ and their empire to the south and southwest. Bámbúlǐ beliefs and practices, however, have been altered to fit in with the more egalitarian and acephalous Hêmbá sociopolitical organization, rather than counterpointing *vidje* priesthood and political hierarchy.[7] Among the Báhêmbá, membership in this semisecret society serves as a means of providing friendly and supportive relationships that crosscut and counterbalance patrilineage and matrilineage affiliations. And Bámbúlĭ healers help diagnose and provide therapies for the kinds of illness and death that arise out of hostilities among individuals, whatever their lineage affiliations: from problems between people in separate villages to tensions among agnates living closely together (whose wives are from other lineages). The Bámbúlĭ use the large slit-gong talking drum [mûlíímbá] less as a prerogative of high office among the Báhêmbá than for funerary announcements of deceased initiates and for the ritual dances of costumed members possessed by ancestor spirits, variegatedly attired in pelts, feathers of the bush and village, raphia cloth, trade beads, and small items of recent industrial manufacture (Plate 20–2).

Two other semisecret societies (said to be of strictly Hêmbá origin) enjoy a kind of kinship with the Bámbúlĭ. The Bálúbwĭló society is known for prodigious feats of wonder, some asceticism, highly athletic dancing, a distinctive nasal singing style, and the ability to cure very poisonous snakebite and to heal multiple other ills, including the sociosomatic ones the Bámbúlĭ cure. Members of the Bámúkótá semisecret society are especially skilled in praise poetry, though not here in the service of royalty or lordship as in some other places in Africa, and they too are healers. A Múhêmbá can be a member of only one of these three groups, jointly referred to as bísélá (s. 'ísélá), but each group is on very friendly terms with the other two.

A Múhêmbá may also be a member of the Bágábó, the most ancient of the semisecret societies still extant and the one not only concerned with profound

Plate 20–2. Participating audience at a Bámbúlĭ semisecret society ritual performance. Women from the "audience" dance into the center of the circle to praise and encourage the talented dancing of the ngángá ya Sulabíkă Múyûmbá, a healer possessed by an ancestor spirit. Dancing, singing, and slit-gong drumming celebrate the return to the village of new inductees from the society's bush camp. Funeral of Kílátú, a senior Múmbúlĭ, 15 July 1978, 2:30 p.m., Lúhóngá village.

fundamentals of health and illness, but also most closely associated with one's immediate family and lineage-segment ancestors and with procedures surrounding birth and fertility. The Bágábó do both diagnosis (divination) and healing, though they are sometimes consulted only for diagnosis, with the therapeutic procedures provided by specialists from other semisecret societies or healing associations. Another group with origins long before colonial times is the Básó'ó, closely concerned with problems of fertility and fecundity of people and of crops, and the only Hêmbá society to use carved, spirit-invested wooden masks (Blakely and Blakely 1987). A Múhêmbá male may also join the Báliingii hunting society. On a continuum—from the more indigenous to a greater incorporation of activities, ideas, and things from the Western world—the Bágábó, the Básó'ó, and the hunting society are currently the farthest toward the indigenous side, though certainly processes of change and positive "syncretism" are implicated in members' continual re-creation and construction of the beliefs and practices of each Hêmbá group, no matter how supposedly "indigenous" or "subject to 'outside' influences".

In addition to membership in one of the three *bísélá* semisecret societies, plus possible membership in the Bágábó or the Básó'ó, a male or female Múhêmbá may become a member of one or more of the healing associations. The Báléká healing association originated in the 1920s, though people give accounts of healing associations with earlier origins whose members are no longer alive or no longer active. Most current healing associations have a much more recent origin. All these healing associations link divination and healing quite closely and involve being possessed with one or another kind of ancestral spirit—ranging from foreign ancestors, such as those of the neighboring Basongye or the Bátembó [pygmies] or Europeans, to ancestors of more local origin. The pattern of being cured from a serious illness, being initiated into the "cult", and then optionally practicing as a healer is the widespread one that John Janzen is studying, under the heuristic label "drums of affliction", except that in Kíhêmbá there does not seem to be an overarching named category such as *ngoma* or *n'kisi*, as has been reported elsewhere in Central, Southern, and East Africa. For some of the healing associations, the variations of singing, dancing, and drumming with wooden single-membrane drums are similar to those noted by Janzen in chapter 9, as are the psychotherapeutic and conversion-like qualities and the ongoing definitions and redefinitions of experience by participating healing association members.[8]

Choices and Alternatives for Crisis Resolution, Problem Solving, and Healing

Multiple memberships in the various indigenous forms of religious expression allow for great individual choice in the means of recourse and remedy for crisis situations. With long-standing, chronic problems, one sees several strategies used, alternating back and forth or concurrently. Consequently, Báhêmbá sometimes incorporate the strengths of outside religious influences in much the same multiple membership, polychronic manner—doing and believing more than one thing at a time. They may in fact be quite practical about it, rather than being doctrinaire or exclusionistically sectarian, utilizing what seems to work in particular cases.

Plate 20–3. Dancers, singers, and percussionists transform everyday family courtyard space into a ritual area for a Bátámbwé Súkú healing ceremony. Healers and residents surround the patient, seated on a mat (bottom, third from right). 20 March 1977, 3:30 p.m., M.K.I. village. This healing association uses the *ngómá* membranophone drum and has other traits of "drums of affliction" groups discussed in chapter 9.

For some of the healing associations (as for forms of missionary and African Christianity), there can be a fairly rapid change in fashion—membership burgeons for some months or years and then slackens as a new association gains in popularity and perceived efficacy or an older one enjoys a revival of interest. These groups simultaneously harness potential both for maintenance of basic social structural arrangements and for gradual shifts in this basic alignment, as well as occasionally the potential for more radical social change (see Asmarom Legesse's discussion in chapter 16 of this book; also Turner 1986:24).

All these Báhêmbá semisecret societies and healing associations seek to remedy what, in Western-world categories, at first seems a strange combination of medical, social relationship, and community ills, including defenses against human out-of-control interpersonal hostility (known to Báhêmbá as *bútĭ*), which sometimes gets inadequately glossed as "witchcraft" and "sorcery". These groups share a basic belief in much less separation between the living and the dead than is generally found in European and Euro-American cultures. The dead [*báfú*, s. *múfú*] can affect the health of the living. The living can communicate quite directly with the dead and develop procedures in relation to the dead that reduce risk and promote healing in a broad sense—healing psychological, sociological, and political ills implicated in somatic ailments. The creator god ['Ábezhá Mbungú], in this view, remains quite distant and uninvolved, with little about the creator god thought to be relevant to contemporary human problems.

These beliefs may not be fundamentally irreconcilable with some forms of Christianity, though incoming missionary societies did (partly based on superficial knowledge) originally take adversarial views of these beliefs and most of the related ritual, art, dance, and music. Nevertheless, many Báhêmbá have come to perceive missionary and African Christian religion as closely implicated in diagnosis and healing and thus as providing additional options and resources for constructing efficacious approaches to a variety of ills, problems, and crises.

With this background of religious diversity and religiously linked healing in Hembaland, we now turn more specifically to Hêmbá funerals. Men's and women's artful performances in formal discussion oratory and mourning song-dances are used in distinctive yet complementary ways for conflict resolution, cleansing, and healing in Hêmbá funerary observances. These genres of expressive culture (and the way their creators and users interpret and modify them) provide productive means for understanding the relationship between the living and the dead, the nature of Hêmba *bútĭ*, and other aspects of indigenous belief and ritual in this Bantu-speaking part of Africa.

HÊMBÁ FUNERALS: CLEANSING, HEALING, AND ANCESTORS

A funeral [*málíló*] is a complex and centrally important series of events in the ritual life of Báhêmbá, as it is for many African peoples (G. Wilson 1939; Goody 1962; Devisch and de Mahieu 1979; Glaze 1981; Eschilmann 1985; Smith 1987). Though Hêmbá funerals differ in size and complexity depending on the circumstances of death and the age, gender, social position, semisecret society, healing association, and other formal religious affiliations of the deceased, Hêmbá funerals are all highly elaborated rites of passage, often involving the entire village community and residents of other villages who have particular kinds of relationships to the deceased. The duration of a Hêmbá funeral varies from one week for a small child, to several months or longer for an elder. In the latter case, the funeral events occur intermittently, culminating in a cleansing requiem festival, a *músúúsa* song-dance, and formal discussions and oratory, marking the end of mourning and the resumption of normal social life for the bereaved. The sequence of funeral events is intended to honor the dead and to be a healing process for the living descendants and other relatives plus several kinds of neighbors, friends, and associates. Through these ritual activities, Báhêmbá seek to facilitate a peaceful journey for the deceased's spirit to the spirit world [*kúkesí*], to cleanse the village(s), and to bring "coolness" and tranquility to everyone involved, living and dead.

Every week or two in each local area, some major funeral event will be held that involves large numbers of people from nearby villages. Funeral events do not occur only when people have recently died: some important events in a funerary sequence

Plate 20–4. Near the end of a Hêmbá funeral festival, members of the Bámbúlĭ semisecret society honor the deceased Sungúlă 'Áhyá—the Simágángá title holder, a great orator, and fellow Bámbúlĭ member. The *ngángá ya Mokéé*, a prominent and highly respected Múmbúlĭ, lies on the ground, playing the large trapezoid slit-gong drum [*múlíímbá*] on his chest in a dramatic tour de force. 27 December 1976, 4:00 p.m., M.K.I. village.[9]

may be scheduled weeks, months, even years after the burial. If no funeral activity is being held nearby or for a close relative, Báhêmbá may activate more distant relationship ties to attend a funeral.

In the earliest conceptualizations of our research, we had planned to study language, speech, and verbal art, as well as visual signification and communication of many kinds, but we had no special interest in funerals. The central importance of funerals to Báhêmbá, however, became evident to us within the first few days of field research in the summer of 1974. On a short walk from the Catholic mission church at Sola, we found ourselves at the edge of a boisterous crowd of people participating in an end-of-mourning festival. We were struck by the energy and enthusiasm of the participants as they danced, drank, talked, and sang, and we remarked on what a short distance we were from the Sola mission, then a nearly seventy years' presence in the village.

During our first months of field research, we encountered many funeral festivals and other funeral events, but practically no other large-group events in Hêmbá villages—so much so we began to wonder, "Why is the *málíló* [funeral] so conspicuous an institution among the Báhêmbá?" Indeed, though *Bonne Année* [New Year] inspires joyful village dancing and special family meals of duck and chicken once a year (in good years), funeral events stand out as the major community and intervillage gatherings. One important reason, we came to understand, is that Báhêmbá ancestors play a large part in the lives of the living—the importance of funerals relates directly to the importance of ancestors in Hêmbá life and death.

Báhêmbá are involved with their ancestors in a wide variety of ways extending well beyond the funeral activities we are considering here. As a polite act, a bit of palm wine is regularly poured on the ground "for the ancestors" before someone drinks. Sharing palm wine with one's ancestors is also a component of prayerful supplication [*úlómbá*]—for health and bounty generally as well as for specific requests such as seeking victory in an intense land dispute—whether or not the supplicants gather around the hearth or near a shrine inside a house, near an oil palm in a current headman's compound (Plate 20–1, p. 398), or out in the bush at a sycamore tree marking an earlier village long abandoned and overgrown, where people who are now ancestors once lived. A Hêmbá ancestor statue [*lúsíngití*] kept mostly in the house, a group of rocks in the courtyard brought from earlier settlements, and the janus-headed, simply carved post [*lágálá*] in a headman's compound are all spirit-invested objects [*miisí*] providing a link between ancestors and their living descendants. These particular *miisí* can be touched, even held, by children with the playful attitude one might have relating to an aged grandfather or grandmother—a sharp distinction from the more dangerous *miisí* such as the janiform *'ábezhá 'a mákúwá*, a smaller statue for which strict prohibitions apply.[10]

The importance of funerals lies not only in this fundamental relationship to ancestors, however, but also in the funeral's bearing on relations among the living. The many events of the funeral provide occasions for family reunion, therapeutic expression of anger and grief, mutual consolation, healing of strained relationships, courtship, sociopolitical succession, transmission and creation of knowledge, historical commentary, and performances of verbal and gestural art, music, and dance.

All the religious groups mentioned earlier in this chapter are involved in the funerals of their members, sometimes even of members who have not been very active. Along a continuum, the further the group is toward indigenous kinds of religious expression, the more likely special funeral events and additional activities within other events will be added to the weeks- or months-long funerary sequence. This sequence includes gatherings of current members and initiation of new members into the deceased's semisecret society, especially adults or children who are the deceased's close relatives (plates 20–2 and 20–4). For the healing

Plate 20–5: A carved wood *lúsíngití* statue of the founding ancestor of a patrilineage segment [*'íbeló ya músu'ú*] can serve as a spirit-invested object linking Báhêmbá ancestors with their living descendants. Báhêmbá find their direct lineal ancestors to be mostly benevolent unless unduly provoked. Problems caused by the ancestors of *others*, or the dead of unidentified lineage, can necessitate protective and remedial help from friendly ancestors in one's patrilineage or matrilineage or ancestors involved with one's semisecret societies or healing associations. H. 26 in. (66 cm.), wood. National Museum of African Art, Eliot Elisofon Archives, Smithsonian Institution.

associations, someone may agree to make the requisite sacrifices and payments to take over the deceased's healing substances and powers [*búgángá*]. If not, these substances and powers are disposed of through a ritual process that includes minor sacrifices and payments by the deceased's relatives under the supervision of at least one of the healing association's active members. In any case, the relevant ancestors must be satisfied in order to avoid illness and misfortune among the village's residents and other close relatives of the deceased and, indeed, to lay the groundwork for later enlisting ancestors' aid in fighting against illness and misfortune. These procedures are often rigorously followed by prudent relatives even when the deceased has said he or she does not want it done, or when his or her Christian or Muslim beliefs forbid it. It is better to be safe than sorry, funeral participants seem to say.

Up to this point we have been speaking of Hêmbá funerary observances as we came to know them in the period 1974–1985. One view of these observances was expressed by Nyémbó 'Íhúyá (later Kíndéngá headman) during a mourning dance: "*Ga málíló úlílagííbwá wa goógó mútindí ni gó gwa kúnwĕ wêtu"* ["This kind of funeral, to be so lengthily and repeatedly mourned and wailed over this way is the authentic way we do it"]. This oft-heard Hêmbá perspective emphasizes rootedness in the past and the "maintenance of tradition", or at least a synchronic, "timeless" orientation.

In short, evoking the authority of the past gives bedrock support to current ritual action. Further noting that "this is the way our ancestors did (or said) it, though of course we are not as competent", provides a favored legitimizing frame for contemporary Hêmbá funerary ritual as well as an appropriately humble disclaimer of individual performance excellence. Though some things stay the same and some things change, Báhêmbá profess a metaphor of cultural continuity, in contrast to places in the world where many things are legitimized with metaphors of change, "progress", the new, and the "improved".

Many Báhêmbá, including Nyémbó 'Íhúyá, nevertheless readily describe major changes in funerary practices in their lifetimes. In our short diachronic perspective of twelve years, we witnessed the introduction and routinization of a significant new category of participants: important "friends" [*balafíkĭ*] of the deceased or of the funeral organizers who would otherwise have no close affiliation at the funeral. *Balafíkĭ*, who formerly might have been included only marginally in some other social category, if at all, are now sent invitations and afforded special group status at the funeral festival. They are given their own designated drink, food, and sheltered seating space, set apart in ways similar to those in the already established categories of "elders from surrounding villages" [*háándú bálágálá*], the deceased's patrilineage members and their relatives [*bámúsu'ú*], the deceased's matrilineage members and their relatives [*bá'ílóóngó*], the lineages' sons-in-law [*bábúŏ*], fathers-in-law [*básheetú mwénú*], mothers-in-law [*bányízheetú mwénú*], mother's-brothers-in-law [*bámwetú gwa búŏ*], and the invited musicians and dancers [*bámútálwá*].

Burial practices have also been modified within living memory: graves are now dug differently than they used to be. Formerly the hole was dug down three to four meters and then a chamber cut into the side wall near the bottom. This technique required considerable expertise to prevent the chamber from collapsing. Now, though the short-handled hoe is still the primary tool for digging, most graves are dug without a side chamber, but with ten centimeter ledges cut on opposite sides above the floor where the corpse will rest in its carpentered wood coffin or wrapped in a woven mat. Lengths of stout branches, cut to fit, will be lowered into place: one end on one ledge and the other fitting snuggly on the other side, forming a shelf above the corpse. As the corpse is being lowered—and as grave goods such as dress clothes, shoes, cloth wraps, mats, metal pans and basins, and "iron objects" are being put into the grave—close relatives of the deceased wail, exclaim, and direct their talk toward the corpse, addressing the dead person's lingering spirit [*chuulí*; a corpse is a *lúfú* while the *chuulí* remains, an *'ítímbílí* after the *chuulí* departs]. Some even try to climb into the grave with the corpse, but are restrained by others nearby. With everything in place, two or three men start filling the grave with earth. Men from the host patrilineage (plus sisters' sons and sometimes a son-in-law) remain at the cemetery while the other mourners walk back to the village, alternately wailing and talking. When the grave is filled and dirt mounded on top, one of the senior men gives a farewell speech, urging the deceased to avenge his or her death. At the end, the group makes a unison vocal response while each man slaps the upturned end of his left fist with sharply descending right hand [*lútumbá*] and lets a leaf (smashed on the end of the fist) fall to the ground. Meanwhile, in the village, some of the women relatives may start a *músúúsá* song-dance, circling around the family compounds in grieving honor for the deceased.

What significance one can find in the burial modifications is not immediately evident, beyond Hêmbá willingness to alter their ritual practices. Or perhaps there is an ecological dimension, since with the advent of ever-larger farms and a growing population, only a small number of overhunted wild pigs remains in the forest and thus poses less threat to dig up a corpse than did the larger number of pigs some years ago.

Other changes in funeral practices, however, do point to a significant shift in the tenor of the funeral. Funerals are longer today and incorporate more celebration and energetic affirmation of life than they did some years past (as we discuss in the section "*Músúúsá*: Women's Ritual Song-Dance"). When a patrilineage segment headman—

Plate 20–6. Women relatives wail and talk to Télésá, who tragically died in late pregnancy, as they place grave goods with her corpse. The hands-on-the-head body posture (upper right) is emblematic of sorrow. For the women vocalizing into the grave, open-faced gazes denote direct address. In any Hêmbá speech event, the "audience" or "addressees" may include the dead, and never more so than during funerary activities in a cemetery. 31 July 1978, 12:09 p.m., near M.K.I. village.

the father of our teacher Kíndéngá Málází—died approximately fifty years ago, the main events of the funeral lasted only one week. There was no end-of-mourning festival, and only a small group of close relatives were in attendance. Now the first funeral events involve greater numbers of people (plus greater expenses for food, palm wine, and musicians) and the large end-of-mourning festival requires even more time and effort to finance and organize, so the full sequence of funeral events lasts much longer for someone of comparable social status.

Seen over an even longer time perspective, prominent elements of Hêmbá funerals have both waxed *and* waned. From 1908 to 1960, Belgian Congo administrators, merchants, and clergy increasingly discouraged and even legally proscribed activities that have again flourished after Independence. Those that contribute to today's longer funeral event sequence include palm wine drinking and palm wine harvesting (crucial for hosting Báhêmbá funeral guests), large group gatherings, employee time-off for funerals of kin beyond immediate family, and energetically demonstrative funeral wakes and other celebrations.

RESEARCH METHODS IN ETHNOGRAPHY OF SPEAKING, COMMUNICATION, AND PERFORMANCE

Some of the most useful sources of information concerning beliefs about the relationship of ancestors to living Báhêmbá and about the nature of "witchcraft" are the various kinds of verbal and kinesthetic art performed by men and women in separate but related funeral events. We will first turn to proverbs, oratory, and associated artful speech and gesture in the ubiquitous formal discussion [*mwândá*] in which performances by men predominate, and then we will focus on the centrally important women's song-dance performance [*músúúsá*] From the beginning, we conducted our research as a male/female team and were thus able to build upon our differential access to men's and women's spheres of activity. Similarly, Richard Katz and Megan Biesele have been co-investigators of sex roles in !Kung healing practices and have pointed out that their work is motivated by "a call for information on sexually differentiated religious activities to be provided by male and female researchers working in collaboration" (Katz and Biesele 1986:196).

Báhêmbá men and women utilize a variety of words and phrases to label, delimit, describe, and make evaluations of situated speech and movement, or what we sometimes call in outsider analytic terms "speech acts" and "speech events". During our field research, we discovered, discussed, and confirmed these categories and critiques in a number of ways while living and working with Báhêmbá over the years. We early and continually listened quietly and nondirectively for the category labels and attributes, partial definitions, semantic linkages, and expressions of deprecation or praise in the flow of "naturally occurring" discourse, while doing participant observation or otherwise participating in village and family compound activities (Bowen 1954; Geertz 1973; Spradley 1980; Golde 1986; Jackson 1989). We also searched for similar information about speech and movement categories—plus paralinguistic, proxemic, and other signs, whether lexicalized or not (some are not)—in our field audiotape recordings that we were transcribing but that were nominally about other subjects, in our sequences of photographs of face-to-face interaction, and later in our super-8 film and videotape of speech, communication, and performance events in Hêmbá ritual and everyday life (Bateson and Mead 1942; Hall 1974; Collier and Collier 1986; T. Blakely forthcoming). More active yet still fairly unobtrusive inquiries included inserting a simple question into an ongoing conversation or quietly asking a fellow participant more about an activity we had just taken part in or that was going on nearby. Informal and formal interviewing with local community members spanned the range from open-ended questioning—in which interlocutors discussed their cultural knowledge fairly uninterruptedly—to the systematic elicitation of lexical/ semantic fields and specification of Hêmba aesthetic criteria (Conklin 1955; Frake 1964; Sturtevant 1968; Spradley 1979; Werner and Schoepfle 1987).

Each of these ways of working was frequently also used to inform and cross-check the others. Leads that developed during participation in community events and unobtrusive kinds of participant observation, for example, were later followed up through informal questions and systematic interviewing. Conversely, insights articulated during the interviewing proved very useful in learning to touch, move around in, smell, taste, hear, and see the Hêmbá world around us from more Hêmbá-centered perspectives and guided us in more knowledgeably interpreting and participating in Hêmba communication and performance (Stoller 1989). We thus were able to increase our understanding of the background knowledge Báhêmbá bring to particular events, in order to illuminate the creativity involved in the process of speaking and moving in ordinary and artful ways.

We were also able to complement this field research with extensive interviews with Faílǎ Mwa'á, the talented and articulate Múhêmbá verbal artist who came to live with us in the United States for two-and-a-half years while recovering from a life-threatening illness. She helped us enormously with the microanalysis and interpretation of our field photographs, audiotape, videotape, and written notes, greatly furthering our work on Hêmbá religion and ritual, aesthetics, performance, language, and many other topics. Particularly enlightening was working with her on the audiotapes and videotapes of men's-group discourse (including formal discussion), women's *músúúsá* song-dance, and other funeral activities. She was able to help us see and hear how Báhêmbá utilize their background knowledge during conversation and performance as resources for negotiating understandings, creating knowledge, engaging in social action, and producing social organization and even social structure (Moerman 1988; C. Goodwin and Heritage 1990; Pomerantz 1990–91; M. Goodwin 1990).

An ethnography of speaking framework—or, more broadly, ethnography of communication—has been particularly useful in helping us more accurately specify and meaningfully comprehend how Báhêmbá think about their kinesthetic and verbal art in relation to other forms of communication and speech. The terms "ethnography of speaking" and "ethnography of communication" were coined by Dell Hymes, who set forth a research agenda calling for studies of the patterning of language use in social life (Hymes 1962, 1964, 1967, 1974).[11] This patterning includes—among many other things—the "communicative competence" and strategies that are utilized, made available to, and created by people who share, mutually understand, or negotiate ground rules for the production and interpretation of speech and other modes of communication. Among rural Báhêmbá in this instance, who can say or otherwise communicate what, to whom, in what manner? And when *can* they say or do it, in what settings, using what means, and for what purposes? Or, who *cannot* say or communicate what, to whom ... for what purposes? For example, not just any Múhêmbá can use or create proverbs in any situation; only certain senior men regularly perform proverbs, and they do so especially in formal discussions punctuated and enlivened by artfully expressive gestures. Other men use proverbs when constrained to do so by the occasion and their role in it. Women, younger men, and even children know the formal discussion polygenre, but perform it infrequently, except that boys and younger men will use proverbs around each other when no senior men are present. Báhêmbá women, on the other hand, are expert at veiled insult [*ngîndí*], a way of speaking used both in informal situations and in ritual song-dance performance in funerals.

Further, what communicative resources do Báhêmbá bring more or less *ready-made* for use in particular speech events, for certain purposes, in the presence of various kinds of people? And what communicative resources are more *emergent* in the event, improvised for particular purposes of mutually negotiated verbal (and other) interaction, discourse, and performance with certain people? (Voloshinov 1973 [1929]:48, 57, 77–98; Bauman and Sherzer 1989 [1974]:xix). Questions such as these bring into focus interesting issues concerning tradition and creativity. For example, Báhêmbá do include in their conception of "proverb" [*múgélě*; pl. *mígélě*] the kind of old-chestnut proverbs that are widely known and handed down from times past, but also "new chestnuts" whose provenance is less ancient or only locally familiar, and indeed some recent and even idiosyncratic inventions in the same pithy poetic mode. The full range of what is considered a proverb, a morphological or syntactic and also a semantic issue (Peirce 1931–1958; Morris 1938), remains at least partially inaccessible without a thorough comprehension of proverb *pragmatics*, including a lively concern for how these forms are used, interpreted, and created in "naturally occurring" performance context.

Particularly talented speakers, especially if they are senior men, use proverbs liberally in oratory during formal discussions. They also weave in lively parables, entertaining stories, succinct expressions, pithy examples, and other artfully veiled and witty speech—all of which, in Kíhêmbá, are other senses of the term *múgélě* in a broader part of its semantic range. Certain topics, including issues that arise in major funerary disputes and negotiations, are so emotionally charged and have such important implications as to almost assure virtuoso performances, including the use of numerous proverbs and related forms, as each senior speaker with even a modicum of talent rises to the occasion.

Interestingly for genre theory, as elaborated by folklorists and other scholars concerned with the comparative study of oral literature (Dan Ben-Amos 1969; Finnegan 1970; Ben-Amos and Goldstein 1975), these Central Africans define proverbs partly morphologically, yet also partly situationally. The "same text" can be classed differently depending on the setting, the purpose, and the participants. If a pithy wise saying is used pedagogically with children, it is called a *lúgónó* (pl. *ngónó*). If a *lúgónó*-like text is used between adults in spite, to wound and tease, ideally with its most personal implication hidden from the intended victim, it is termed an *ngîndí* [veiled insult]—whether said in conversation; sung while pounding flour

Plate 20–7. Interest and excitement run high at a funeral inquest into how Lıkopá died from a human-induced lightning bolt. Momentary disorder prompts an elder to enter the center of the men's formal discussion circle, clapping and here spreading his hands in dramatic gestures as he calls "*bákáléngé!*", in hopes of refocusing everyone's attention. Many give him a listening gaze, but others point at him [*tásungá múnwé*], urging him to sit down. 29 February 1976, 2:04 p.m, Mázhyóómbó village.

with mortar and pestle; or said, shouted, and sung during *músúúsá* funerary song-dance performance. If, on the other hand, an *ngónó*-like or *ngîndí*-like text is performed during a formal discussion, such as a men's formal discussion of death payments between lineages, for example, it will be labeled a *múgélĕ* [proverb]. A *múgélĕ* can be so poetically terse that some of the participants will likely not understand it at first encounter, but it eventually will be explicated for all to understand (all, anyway, as Báhêmbá say it, who have a reasonably mature intelligence). In contrast, the artfully veiled insult most typically remains unexplained for its victim and leaves significant implications plausibly deniable.

VERBAL ART AND ARTFUL GESTURE IN FUNERARY "FORMAL DISCUSSION"

Báhêmbá men employ a wide range of linguistic and interactional resources for agonistic interchange and for interpersonal or intergroup conflict resolution. But the artfully demonstrative use of proverbs and other verbal and visual means of foregrounding the poetic are especially highly valued in negotiation, dispute settlement, ritual, and other occasions for "formal discussion" [*mwândá*] associated with important funeral events, other times when ancestors are the most likely to listen, times when "witchcraft" is prominently implicated, and other especially salient situations in Hêmbá society. Complexly subtle proverbs and other verbal art, combined with proxemically appropriate and vigorously expert gestural performance, can connote superior insight and wise tactfulness, carrying greater weight in some kinds of dialogue and decision making than straight-line logic, plain talk, or a quietly unadorned and unpunctuated manner of speaking.

The term *mwândá* refers both to the kind of speech event that is an essential part of many funeral gatherings and to the (poly)genre that occurs prominently in this event and gives the event its name. In the *mwândá* event, other activities such as palm wine drinking, mat weaving, and social interactions surrounding tobacco smoking might or might not require audible speech, but only at certain times require formal discussion, if at all. Embedded in the *mwândá* polygenre are proverbs and other genres such as genealogical legend and historical narrative [*mwândá gwa úbangúlá*], praise formula [*ngúmbú*], phatic gesture [*'íbágí*], song [*'ísimó*], drum poetry [*'ísímă*], and the longer *múgélĕ* that we might alternately gloss as "parable", "story", and "folktale".

Though Ruth Finnegan (1970) uses the term "formal speaking" for a similar speech genre elsewhere in Africa, for Báhêmbá the term *mwândá* goes beyond the focus on an individual speaker, encompassing minimally a triad of individual or group interests. At least three participants are typically present for an event to be considered a formal discussion, and usually many more: in addition to antagonists and protagonists, essential in Hêmbá formal discussions are one or more mediators, go-betweens, or middlemen [*bátá hábwatabwátá*]. A formal discussion always involves a dialogue among speakers, or among lead speakers and one or more responding groups, and is also "dialogic" in the Bakhtinian sense of "a constant interaction [among] meanings" (Bakhtin/Holquist 1981:426–430). A formal discussion is visibly and audibly punctuated by call-response sequences of special claps, associated elegant gestures, and verbal calls from the speaker, followed by unison verbal (and sometimes gestural) responses from the other participants. The importance of taking account of this actively participating audience comes not just from Hymes's insistence on studying all participants as a central "component" of speech events (1974), Bauman's parallel stress on the audience as an essential part of any performance event (1986), or Voloshinov's earlier assurance that the addressee is indispensable to understanding the utterance (1973 [1929]), but indeed in the emphasis Báhêmbá themselves place on these matters. All participants, audience, and addressees—including both the living and the ancestors—are integral to any Hêmbá formal discussion and crucial to a full understanding of it (see also Dan Ben-Amos 1972a; Pamela Blakely 1992:80–99).

An indubitable *key* to the formal discussion performance frame is the series of claps [*ngwásó*] and other associated gestures that mark the beginning and ending of turns at talk in formal discussion, punctuate every minute of continuing formal discussion,

Plate 20–8. Just minutes after Kítófú, the talented go-between from Lúgábá village, has made a somber disclaimer (and keying) of performance, denying he came to do expert speechmaking [*búndendagámbó*], he uses rhetorical flair to try to resolve a grim, deadlocked debate about the death of his niece, 'Ánásá. " *'Aa Tomá, ... góvwá 'áyî?*" ["Hey Tomá, what do you come for?"], exclaims Kítófú, miming and quoting speech from happier times at the betrothal ceremony for 'Ánásá and her husband Máyâní. Kítófú hopes that by vividly evoking that day's successful bridewealth negotiations he will encourage agreement on today's wrongful death payments. But to accomplish this, he knows that the *way* he speaks must be interesting enough to also divert some attention away from the divisive accusations of mother-in-law and co-wife *bútĭ* ["witchcraft"] implicated in the young mother's lingeringly slow death. 28 November 1982, 9:30 a.m., M.K.I. village.

and aid in orchestrating the call-response sequences so essential for the active participation of the "audience". Báhêmbá call these dramatic claps and other gestures *bíbágí*, [s., *íbágí*] which literally means "posts", the same word as for the stout wooden posts that hold up a Hêmbá house. Here these *bíbágí* provide analogously crucial phatic support for the ongoing formal discussion (Malinowski 1923; Jakobson 1960). A Hêmbá formal discussion does not take place without *bíbágí*, which openly and metacommunicatively mark the speech as subject for evaluation not only for its referential content but also for the proficiency with which it is done, very visibly and audibly calling attention to the speaker as accountable for how well or how poorly he speaks.

Typically the speaker bends forward while extending his arms outward and downward toward the ground, claps his hands at least three times (to start to talk; sometimes less to punctuate continuing talk), reaches down and touches the ground with his right

Plate 20–9. Members of the husband's Bágá' ítûngwá patrilineage and Bakwámwéngé matrilineage sit across the discussion arena facing Kítófú (Plate 20–8). Tomá, the other go-between (center, hands clasped, wearing a hat), grimaces and prepares an artfully diplomatic response, but Kíndéngá Málází (far left)—the principal "father" of the bereaved husband—does a disgusted gaze cut off, refusing to even look at the representatives of the opposing side's Bálúgábá patrilineage and Bágwéyé matrilineage. The intractability of the discussion finds spatial expression in not rounding out the usual friendly circle; instead, the two sides confront each other in separate, opposing groups. Fierce contentiousness in a three-year dispute over how 'Ánásá died has adversely affected the lives and health of people from the two villages. 28 November 1982, 9:32 a.m., M.K.I. village. Plate 20–16 (p. 433) shows the *músúúsá* funerary song-dance that alternated with this formal discussion.

hand just as he starts to utter a vocal salute such as *"báfumú!"*["leaders/headmen!"].
In the brief time this call is being uttered, the speaker starts to straighten up and slightly
rock back, simultaneously bringing his hand up toward his chest, touching the chest
just as the call is ending or a short beat after the sound of the call ends. The chest touch
is standard, but not always fully completed or even started. Emphatically thrusting the
hand to the ground and leaving it there for more than the usual brief ground touch—
perhaps for a second or two—adds flourish to a performance, pumps enthusiasm and
energy into the event, and almost always is reciprocated in the vocal and gestural
response from the intently gazing circle of formal discussion interlocutors.

In his discussion of "The Keying of Performance" in *Verbal Art As Performance*,
Bauman credits Erving Goffman for naming "the process by which frames are invoked
and shifted, how the performance is *keyed* " (Goffman 1974) and also builds from
Gregory Bateson's "powerful insight" that

> it is characteristic of communicative interaction that it include a range of explicit
> or implicit messages which carry instructions on how to interpret the other mes-
> sage(s) being communicated. This communication about communication Bateson
> termed metacommunication (Ruesch and Bateson 1968:209). In Bateson's terms,
> "a frame is metacommunicative. Any message, which either explicitly or implic-
> itly defines a frame, *ipso facto* gives the receiver instructions or aids in his attempt
> to understand the messages included with the frame" (Bateson 1972 [1955]:188).
> ... [And, further,] each speech community will make use of a structured set of
> distinctive communicative means from among its resources in culturally conven-
> tionalized and culture-specific ways to key the performance frame. (Bauman
> 1977:15–16)

Bauman gives a list of "communicative means that have been widely documented
in various cultures as serving to key performance", including "special paralinguistic
features" (Bauman 1977:15–16, 18–19).[12] He does not mention gestural or other
kinesthetic-visual means of keying, though he does note that the list is open-ended. The
use of *ngwásó* claps and associated gestures as a key to the performance of Hêmbá
formal discussion [*mwândá*] provides a substantive example—among surely other
examples in other cultures—that helps expand the list of communicative means that
key a performance frame.

Other gestures are used to synchronize both verbal and visual aspects of the many
call-response sequences in Hêmbá formal discussion. For example, in a movement
like a classical music conductor's upbeat and downbeat—moving one hand sharply
up in a slight curve out, forearm slightly extended, elbow bent about 90 degrees—then
immediately bringing the hand-arm straight down to an abrupt stop (a little farther
than where it started) orchestrates the joint uttering of *"na ééééé ... pa!"* in which
the speaker starts the lower-pitched *na* and the "audience" may join the higher
pitched *ééééé* as the hand swings up. Most certainly the audience exclaims *pa!* in
unison as the hand hits the bottom of the downbeat. In fact, the speaker may say only
the *"na",* or say nothing and silently do the gestures at the apt juncture in his speaking,
letting the other participants complete the utterance. Similar gestures and gesturally

orchestrated call-responses proliferate in formal discussions, particularly the formal discussions most expertly and artfully done.

FOREGROUNDING THE POETIC IN BÁHÊMBÁ MEN'S ORATORY

A formal discussion does not necessarily include proverbs and expertly performed gestures enlivening the basic call-response sequences and interactive talk, though Báhêmbá point out that the most interesting and aesthetically pleasing ones do. Some formal discussions about mundane matters are done with little energy, spoken in an uninspired, unanimated, or even boring manner, as if those present can hardly wait to go to their farms or for the morning's palm wine harvest to arrive in the village.

While proverbs do not accompany all formal discussions, they are seen as crucial for the highly valued eloquence that we would gloss in English as "oratory". (Oratory is also called *mwândá*, but at another level in a semantic taxonomy of Kíhêmbá speech categories.) Some formal discussions contain one oration after another in expertly rapid succession, the skill and wit building with each rejoinder, delighting and exciting the audience to appreciative attention and response. Other formal discussions involve little of what Báhêmbá call oratory, so the animation of the listening and participating group suffers accordingly and so does the persuasive effectiveness of the speakers' rhetoric. To highlight this connection between oratory and proverb, wizened Báhêmbá orators use the metaproverb

Mwândá guli múgélĕ;	Oratory it is [requires] proverb;
Gusi múgélĕ guli ngélá.	Without proverb it is naked.

Or, in a broader sense of *múgélĕ* and with further interpretation of the polysemic metaphor *ngélá* :

Oratory is proverb-filled poetic speech;
Without proverb filled poetic speech, it is not fit
for performance in front of people.

This metaproverb cogently states the Hêmbá preference for foregrounding the poetic function of speech (Jakobson 1960) when discussing the most important issues of life and of death. Artfully indirect speech that tactfully foregrounds message *form* and the *way* something is said—and thus takes the prime focus away from referential content—is seen as a wisely calming alternative to the often embarrassing and potentially inflammatory "naked truth" of straight-line logic. Appealing to aesthetic sensibilities tactfully diverts attention from the most disputed points, helps make one's perspectives more palatable, and provides common ground for a more enjoyable and productive discussion.

In addition to metaproverbial comment on the verbal aspects of performance poetics, talented Báhêmbá speechmakers further note that

Tóni mutááti bá:	Birds filling a tree:
'ámônga mulómó nga'ulú	little red beak is the elder.

Or, no matter who is vocalizing, "flapping around", or otherwise holding forth, there are senior people who sometimes make a very unobtrusive presence yet who carry great weight in the debate. The "red beak" is a veiled reference to the red feather of an Ndúbá bird, worn ceremonially on the head of a *mânzí*—a person who has killed another person in battle or with poison and is knowlegeable about potentially lethal *bútǐ* "witchcraft" and defenses against it. Not unrelatedly, a red Ndúbá feather may be worn or carried by a very senior member of the Bámbúlǐ semisecret society who has the power to kill, but especially the power to protect people from being killed and to heal them from attacks involving the out-of-control hostility of other people. Similarly, with Básó'ó healers, some of the frighteningly anomalous masked figures wear a smaller version of this feathered visual sign to mark seniority, power, and healing competence (Blakely and Blakely 1987).[13]

Expert speechmakers [*bándendagámbó*] use this proverb to underscore their great appreciation for the knowledgeable interpretation of subtle social, cultural, and situational cues, especially the numerous visual signs that play a crucial role in Hêmbá oratory. No considered elucidation of what the speakers and audiences intended is made without recourse to the multiplicity of spatial, material, postural, gestural, facial, and colorful signs that perfuse Hêmbá performance.[14]

Báhêmbá choose to sit in a circle [*'ítangó*] during oratory and formal discussion. In this configuration, they are able "to look each other in the face" [*wílóléná 'u ngébó*], not "in the back of the head" [*'u ngómó yá*], or "only in the ear" [*mu chwǐ yá*], spatially stating a fundamental preference for egalitarian social organization. This preference for the egalitarian circle finds expression in other Hêmbá events, too, especially in some kinds of palm wine drinking and in the *músúúsá* funerary song-dance. Orators and other speakers in Hêmbá formal discussion mostly remain seated, speaking from where they are sitting in the circle of participants. So, a speaker injects great emphasis and emotion into the discussion—and opens himself to even more stringent evaluation of his performance—by standing up and stepping into the center of the circle to do an energetic version of his *ngwásó* claps and ground-touch sequence, or to display his verbal and gestural talent during a peak moment of the discourse, or to delight his interlocutors with a vivid quotation of Bálúbwíló singing and dancing.

Several important events in the sequence of funerary observances produce high densities of proverb- and gesture-filled oratory, most especially in an inquest exploring the manner of a person's recent death, during which blame for the death is at least tacitly a subject under discussion (plates 20–7 and 20–10). Báhêmbá similarly foreground the poetic in the formal discussion held parallel to a cleansing *músúúsá* song-dance (plates 20–8, 20–9, and 20–16), diplomatically masking subtle accusations of complicity in the death, tactfully denying such complicity, attempting to assign or accept some collective blame for the death, negotiating death payments, and resolving conflict among the individuals and lineage segments involved. Figuring out the human causes of particular deaths is a most crucial issue in this very humanized Bantu universe. Regardless of proximate cause, death is ultimately a result of intervention by living or dead people.

Another funeral event with many formal discussions and opportunities for scintillating oratory is the large and complex requiem festival [*úbǔzhá málíló*] that marks the formal end of the mourning period: skillful speaking here can have significant implications for the reinforcement, manipulation, or rearrangement of lineage segment alliances and leadership. Also important is the inheritance formal discussion, sometimes held at the end of the requiem festival, sometimes on a separate occasion. During this formal discussion, it is decided who will receive which of the material goods of the deceased, who will take care of the children, who will accept the responsibilities of any titles the deceased may have had, and who—if the deceased was male—will be accepted as new husband by the deceased's wives (each wife may choose the same new husband as the other wives or a different one). The initiations of new semisecret society members and the transference or neutralization of healing association powers are also times during the funerary event sequence for the skilled

Plate 20–10. For a raptly attentive audience at a funeral gathering marking the "end of sleeping outside", one week following the burial of Hamúnǎ, her father Byaaná delivers a greatly anticipated oration on how his young married daughter died suddenly while in his care. Though Byaaná is renowned for curing mental illness, which Hamúnǎ was said to have had, rumors of malpractice (and worse)—fueled by the ever-present Hêmbá concerns about whose out-of-control hostility might be implicated in a death—have increased the already avid interest in the account of her dying last days. Here his backward gaze and sweeping straight-arm gesture give the time of day when her condition worsened, indices of sun position that visually complete the utterance more memorably than words. 10 August 1985, 12:30 p.m., 'Áyânzá village.

use of gestures, proverbs, oratory, and other artful forms, with the additional communicative resources of special lore, music, costume, and situational frame appropriate to the particular group involved.

ANCESTORS AND "WITCHCRAFT": JOKING AND ARTFULLY INDIRECT SPEECH

While these various funeral events may have great impact on the social and material lives of living people [*báándú,* or *básigé,* lit. "people left behind"] in very direct ways, they also are designed to communicate with the dead [*báfú*], particularly ancestors [*báfú bêtú,* lit. "our dead"; or *bá'ulú ba kálá,* "elders of long ago"], to let them know that they are not forgotten and are still appreciated. The living are also trying to demonstrate that they are cleansing and healing the world sufficiently so that the ancestors need not get involved in any punitive way and can instead be available to be called upon to help their living descendants in positive, nurturing ways.

Especially interesting is the frequent lack of somber demeanor in word, gesture, and facial expression when Báhêmbá directly talk to their ancestors during rituals. Mirthful joking, smilingly witty remarks, intimate (rather than formal) ritual requests, and

Plate 20–11. Headman and expert speechmaker Simágángá Sungúlǎ 'Áhyá (right) makes a point during a midweek formal discussion at the funeral of Bembalézhá, a young girl in the Símágángá patrilineage segment. His riveting manner of speaking— rich in energetic gestures [*bíbágí*], old and new proverbs, and artfully indirect and witty speech—intrigues and gives aesthetic pleasure to two main audiences: ancestors (who are especially attentive during funeral events) and the girl's close living relatives assembled here. Such a "breakthrough into performance" increases the positive, healing "heat" of the discussion and helps mourners interactively work through their grief while passing the long days together between the burial and the "end of sleeping outside". 27 February 1976, 12:05 p.m., M.K.I. village.

relaxed body motion imbued with a tactile kind of friendliness often characterize the performance style of these conversations between the living and the dead. Similar audial, visual, kinesthetic, and tactile nuances proliferate in the *joking relationship* everyone has with the grandparent generation (and up) in Hêmbá society. The way one acts in the presence of dead Grandfather or Grandmother vividly recalls how one related to Grandfather and Grandmother when they were alive, with heavy emphasis on one's repertoire of artful joking. Veiled, indirect, and elaborately intertwined discourse also is especially pleasing and persuasive when the ancestors are concerned, similar to when one wishes to convince senior living elders of the worthiness of one's views, except that even more proverbs surface here since the speakers are now of more senior earthly status than when their ancestors were alive.

More generally, in formal discussions of the legal matters involved with funerals, Báhêmbá do not highly value the kind of precise language that is favored in the Anglo-American system of jurisprudence. Straight-line logic is definitely not excluded from the determination of the proximate causes of death, general assignment of blame, inheritance discussions, official resolution of semisecret society and healing association matters, litigation concerning outstanding debts, child custody disputes, and other legal issues implicated in funerals, but it is considered markedly inferior in persuasive power. Comparing considerably more favorably are the poetically condensed witticisms of proverb, metaphor, aptly evocative gesture, proxemic allusion, and other interesting verbal and visual signs—even more so when the issue under discussion is serious and difficult, when one is facing worthy opponents, or when the shadowy interlocutors are even more senior and much less predictable than one's living adversaries. Moreover, Báhêmbá do not feel that it is appropriate or wise to refer too directly to the *bútí* out-of-control interpersonal hostility that is potentially present in anyone. These are matters of extreme delicacy and one does not at all wish to exacerbate a situation by discussing them indiscretely.

Oratorical gesture and proverb-laced speech invoke the aesthetic sense, a more complete range of emotions, amused admiration for the humanly sensitive subtlety and socially mature intelligence [*luéní*] of the speaker, and greater respect for the points he and his interlocutors wish to make to each other. These points are more effective precisely because they have *not* been stripped of all mention of domains of knowledge and experience *shared* by the litigants or the opposing sides in a negotiation, rather than focusing solely on the contentious issues. Straightforward explication of deeply felt concerns can easily polarize and harden opposing opinions in Hêmbá formal discussions, whereas witty, polysemic, and wispily elusive nuggets of verbal and gestural art serve to divert everyone's attention to pleasurable literary puzzles and aesthetic insights, to simultaneously diffuse confrontation and soften the hearts of the combatants, and to suggest common grounds for mutual understanding and problem resolution. Not only that, but negotiations have been successfully concluded and disputes settled in the distinct favor of someone whose artful *performance* was superior, even though the content of his case may have been otherwise weak. At times there is such a focus on the way things are said that poetic criteria completely override other means of rhetorical evaluation of the utterance, including the referential appropriateness of what is said or the straight-line logic of the argument.

MÚSÚÚSÁ : WOMEN'S RITUAL SONG-DANCE

To see the limitations of exclusively looking at men's domains of verbal and kinesthetic art is also crucial when seeking to understand what is going on in Hêmbá funerals. Particularly, men must be even more veiled and elusive than they might wish when inquiring into the active human agents, whether alive or ancestral, involved in the death of a human being. Few deaths are thought of as "accidental" or as exclusively resulting from "natural causes". Yes, Báhêmbá agree, the lion may have eaten the man, or the woman may have died of cholera or in an auto crash. But, Báhêmbá will ask, why did it happen to that person on that day and not to someone else? They are somewhat interested in these kinds of causes but always resolutely go beyond them to a questioning of the more ultimate cause of someone's death. They are like readers of Agatha Christie books who want to know "who done it?". Moreover, they want to expose the perpetrator to the living and to the ancestors in order to combat the death and to foster social healing.

The problem is that Báhêmbá men are severely constrained in their deliberations by indigenous legal practice as well as by national law. In former times, if someone openly accused another of unconscious "witchcraft" or conscious poisoning or "sorcery" (all called *bútĭ* in Kíhêmbá)[15], that person had to prove his or her case or suffer the same punishment—including death—that the accused would have undergone had that person been proven guilty. Moreover, it is now against the law even to make the *accusation*, so that the offended person has only to prove the fact of accusation, regardless of innocence or guilt. Men in their formal discussion circles thus restrict themselves, in their overt content and to a large extent in their indirect speech, to decrying interpersonal conflict and hostility in general and discussing formulaic responses to the situation. They devote eloquent words and gestures to the assignment of collective responsibility for the death and attendant recompensatory payment by social groups, such as the father-in-law's patrilineage and mother-in-law's matrilineage. But they do not directly say much about potentially implicated individuals.

Where, then, do these issues of ultimate cause-of-death get discussed more fully, if at all? Are they just socially submerged and reserved for private speculation or fragmentary allusion? In this instance, Báhêmbá women examine these central issues in their performances of dance, song, dirge, veiled insult, and harangue: a polygenre called *músúúsá*.

Unlike any other time in Hêmbá life, performance of the *músúúsá* polygenre fosters a license to sing, dance, wail, and comment a bit more about the usually unspeakable human reasons behind the death. To be sure, this open expression of outrage still requires circumspection, given the dangerous forces involved, so the Hêmbá talents for emphasizing the poetic in the most difficult moments here come to the fore with artfully composed tropes and clever indirection. The *músúúsá* performance frame also provides a cover for somewhat more direct side-comments, interjections, and occasional harangue. The *músúúsá* thus creates a liminal period of time-out-of-time when female relatives of the deceased make veiled references to those responsible for the death, coming to voice with the concerns that are widely shared but which others feel severely constrained not to address as fully in any other Hêmbá speech event.

Since a married woman usually lives with her husband in his patrilineage seg-ment's village, when she dies, an emotionally charged *músúúsá* performance is often done in this village where the majority of prime suspects live. Female relatives from the deceased's patrilineage, her matrilineage, her mother's patrilineage, and her father's matrilineage, as well as various affinal relatives, are prominent in the *músúúsá*. Adorned with vine garlands and palm fronds gathered in the bush, the women make a forceful, energetic entrance as their path-travelers' single file coalesces into a closely bunched phalanx dancing resolutely forward into the village, footsteps beating rhythm for the *músúúsá* arrival song. They pause several times to circle counterclockwise in family compounds, singing in full voices and dancing animatedly, before finally locating their performance near the house in which the person died or upon which the funeral is focusing. As they arrive through the village (and later when they circle-dance in more family compounds), the women not only announce their presence and their concerns to a wider community, they also gather up the deceased's spirit and focus it at the funeral house.[16]

The *músúúsá* can occur at several points in the funeral: on the burial day after returning from the cemetery; again or for the first time days, weeks, or even years later during purification ceremonies; and during the festival that closes the mourning period. Báhêmbá expect this cleansing performance in sound and

Plate 20–12. Women mourners perform a *músúúsá* song-dance, moving counter-clockwise in a large, open-circle formation, helping to focus the deceased's spirit at her house. This *músúúsá* expresses respect for recently deceased Faílá Mámbá and aids her transition to the spirit world. The ritual also comforts her bereaved relatives and promotes "coolness" and healing in the village. 3 September 1982, 11:08 a.m., M.K.I. village.

movement to take place in the current marriage-home village of the deceased and in his or her patrilineage segment's village if he or she is buried there (which may be the same village for men), plus other funeral locations, such as another village where the person was living or in which he or she died. But wherever or whenever else it is also held, a *músúúsá* must precede or accompany a negotiation of death payments and is by far the most important requisite for successfully completing this formal discussion. So, the male funeral participants sit in a formal discussion circle near the deceased's house [*ngíngó*], or host's house, listening to the women's "accusations surrounding the death" [*bigeléó bya lílô*] in shifting song lyrics and grief-filled dirge. The men mutely consider the implications of the artfully veiled assertions—and occasional more-direct words and phrases that at any other time might be considered verbal assaults—that they themselves cannot address, for fear of conscious or unconscious retribution from those responsible for the death or from others similarly inclined.

The *músúúsá* as a performance polygenre—with special songs and unique circle dancing, plus incorporation of other genres that can also stand alone—is not more than a few decades old. The *músúúsá* as we now know it emerged from the "crying without tears" dirge [*'ábembegélé*], a more ancient women's performance genre in Búhêmbá. This dirge still is used in funerals both separately from the *músúúsá* and incorporated in it. The dirge singer will often lean on a cane—one kinesthetic-visual key to performance of the *'ábembegélé* genre—and wail her plaintive phrases solo, in counterpoint to the call-and-response singing and counterclockwise dancing of the larger group. Sometimes she will stay in the dance circle, moving up and down with her cane; often she will move out apart from the group as she wails. Occasionally at a funeral an *'ábembegélé* mourner dresses in a cloth wrapped between her legs, in what Báhêmbá consider an otherwise very degrading style, to express the depth of her anguish. The *'ábembegélé* is an impassioned, somber expression of a deeply grief-stricken relative, in contrast to the livelier *músúúsá* song-dance of other mourning relatives and supportive village helpers.

When the *ábembegélé* is done with skill and energy, overwhelming feelings of grief well up in everyone within earshot. It puts people in touch with all their grief for loved persons lost to death—recent grief as well as long-standing grief that one never really gets over but learns instead to live with and to endure. A skillful *'ábembegélé* performance is so moving that our teacher Faílă Mwa'á found it difficult to listen to a tape-recorded version, even when she was no relation of the deceased for whom the dirge was originally sung.

Formerly the *músúúsá* was sung by fewer women than today and with a much more somber attitude, more like the dirge from which it developed. In the last forty years or so, the women in Collectivité Nyembo have had greater interest in incorporating songs from the neighboring Collectivité Mambwe, where a slightly different dialect of Kíhêmbá is spoken. These songs are livelier still and have shifted the emphasis of *músúúsá* performance in Nyémbó somewhat away from the grim expression of grief and anger, to a more enthusiastic and animated consoling of the bereaved. Local people draw the contrast between the earlier *músúúsá* of sadness and the *músúúsá* of today in which one wears bright, colorful clothes.

Looking at the wider social and religious context for the *músúúsá* in this time period suggests an explanation for the shift in emotional tone. Catholic parishioners and other local residents report that Catholic church leaders in the area have opposed performance of the *músúúsá* because they see it as an overly distraught and fearful response to death. Catholic leaders in the town of Mbúlúlá where the Catholic church is prominent have eroded support for the funeral *músúúsá* and have appropriated the song-dance genre for Catholic wedding celebrations (though non-Catholics do not concur with this usage). Local Catholic leaders' disapproval of this Hêmbá funerary ritual may have contributed to the development of the lively, more upbeat style.

Plate 20–13: During the Faílă Mámbá *músúúsá* event, 'Apendáké sorrowfully intones praises of the deceased and laments her loss with an *'ábembegélé* [crying without tears] dirge. Máhalákĭ and other male relatives offer contrapuntal testimonials about the deceased. A woman (right) ululates enthusiastically about the eloquence of 'Apendáké, imbuing "heat" in the performance. 3 September 1982, 3:42 p.m., M.K.I village.

Ironically, this transformation serves well indigenous aesthetic priorities, taking account of the Catholic critique without modifying underlying concerns and understandings about death, ancestors, and "witchcraft".

IMBUING "HEAT" IN PERFORMANCE

A *músúúsá* performance is the emergent accomplishment of individual performers interacting with other performers in the dance circle. Informal practice singing occurs as the women travel together on roads and paths toward the town or village where the *músúúsá* will be held. Some of these women also share the experience of singing with male mourners carrying the body for burial. Though these events help prepare the women, the actual songs sung in a *músúúsá* are selected at the moment of performance. Near the end of a song or in the intervals between songs, performers attempt to initiate new songs, drawing on their knowledge of songs from funerals and other performance situations, adapting lyrics to fit the funeral at hand, and even composing entirely new songs that address immediate concerns surrounding the death. All these various kinds of creativity in composition, termed *úwangányá* [improvising], are said to add "heat" to the performance.

Úchwězhá yûhyá [imbuing heat] is a core aesthetic criterion Báhêmbá use in evaluating *músúúsá* performance. In addition to creativity in song competition, "heat" is also imbued by ululating, singing praise names, improvising new movements, and accentuating dance steps. All these actions intensify the performance and make it better and more efficacious—embellishing and augmenting a standard rendition and inspiring the other performers to greater investment of themselves in the performance.

Plate 20–14. An energetic lead singer (patrilineal "younger sister" of deceased Faílă Mámbá) bursts into the dance circle. Carrying palm fronds and wearing *mwândúlá* vine garlands, she "imbues heat" with her display of skill and personal effort, intensifying the performance and increasing its efficacy. Our teacher, FaílăMwa'á, is at far right (wearing striped jersey). 3 September 1982, 11:43 a.m., M.K.I. village.

When a woman ululates, she is simultaneuously praising the performance of another, augmenting the performance by her effort, and encouraging others to do likewise. Energy and enthusiasm that are effectively coordinated with the group are valued and praised audibly and visibly in performance. Uninspired, lackadasical singing and dancing are severely critiqued. Such critique occurs within the performance as lead performers admonish others to keep the circle open, stay out of the weeds, substitute a singer who can stay on key, and so forth. This Hêmbá aesthetic of heat can be seen as closely related to the "intensification factor" that J. A. Kwabene Nketia has identified as a widespread value in African performance (1988:84–85).

In the *músúúsá* song-dance, the aesthetics of ritual performance and the efficacy of ritual action as interpreted by the participants are strongly interrelated. A heat-filled performance is important for consoling the closest relatives of the deceased. The singers, who are relatives and friends of the primary mourners, want to help the mourners direct their attention outward toward living people and not to become completely overwhelmed by their grief or overly oriented toward the dead and longings for the afterworld.[17] The singer-dancers want the performance to be skillfully performed, with enthusiasm, so that all the mourners will be comforted.

A well-executed, energetic performance demonstrates that the person who died was held in high esteem. The performers cared enough about the deceased to come and invest themselves to achieve a respectable performance. The *músúúsá* is seen as a proclamation that their relative has died. The women want others to take note of the one who has died and to recognize the singer-dancers' and other mourners' efforts and concern in behalf of the deceased. The women in the *músúúsá* feel that if their performance is mediocre people not directly involved in the funeral will be indifferent.

Moreover, the women are concerned with the deceased's evaluation of their performance and they want to communciate effectively with him or her during the performance. Heated, artful performance is thought to engage the attention of the deceased and other ancestors, a practical reason for foregrounding the poetic in sound and movement during the *músúúsá*. The performers sing about doing what a polite Múhêmbá host does for a well-liked guest who is now leaving to return home: they work to "escort [the deceased] to the beginning of the path" [*úsiindílá*]— the path toward the deceased's new home among the other ancestors, *kúkesí*.

Thermal analogies for good and bad performance relate directly to the fundamental concern Báhêmbá have with social health.[18] Imbuing "heat" in the *músúúsá* is seen as helping to promote harmonious "coolness" in social relations. For Báhêmbá both "heat" and "cold" have positive and negative aspects. Such phenomena as illness, death, and out-of-control interpersonal hostility are associated with negative heat [*yûhyá*]. Competence, vigor, and energy are associated with positive heat [*yûhyá*]. Negative "cold" [*'ínyôngá*] pervades such undesirable states as fatigue, incompetence, and despair. Positive "coolness" [*'ínyôngá*] associates with self-control, social harmony, and health. Thus, from a Hêmbá view, when women infuse the healing, cleansing, positive heat of competence and skill in the *músúúsá* song-dance, they seek to counter the negative heat of death, illness, and dangerous human hostility. Positively heated performance, the investment of human effort and talent, facilitates the restoration of harmonious social relations, or "coolness".[19]

MAKING VEILED "WITCHCRAFT" ACCUSATIONS

Through *músúúsá* song-dance performance, women combat out-of-control interpersonal hostility [*bútí*, "witchcraft"]—the very root cause of serious illness, death, and social disorder. What might be at first mistakenly interpreted as peripheral, relatively unimportant singing and dancing is, in fact, a powerful forum for making accusations, ascribing blame for the death, and calling on the deceased to avenge his or her death. Let us underscore the crucial point here that hostile human agency— including action by either the living or ancestors—is present in some way in almost every person's death. Women performers do not remain complacent in the face of this lethal hostility but actively seek to expose the perpetrators and their grievous actions, using means that are effective yet substantially veiled so as to be relatively safe.

Women performers raise poignant issues related to the cause of death through their skillful use of verbal art and through their choice of location for their artful movement within the *músúúsá* performance. They use a variety of rhetorical strategies including understatement, indirection, asserting the opposite, and euphemisms to refer to the accused and his or her actions, or to refer to a person or group in order to implicate another person or group indirectly. Even when occasional asides and shouted interjections are more incautiously direct, by embedding all these forms of "dangerous thoughts" [*bigeléó bya lîló*] within the *músúúsá* performance frame, women are able to make their accusations without recrimination and without leading to the open hostilities and retaliation such socially inflammatory remarks would otherwise trigger.

Plate 20–15: Women mourners bring their grief and accusations to the marriage village of their deceased relative, Télésá (Plate 20–6 shows the burial near her natal village). Her grandmother counterpoints the women's song-dance with anguished, angry cries as part of an *'ábembegélé*. She brandishes a pole, accentuating and punctuating her movement and speech. 3 August 1978, 11:50 a.m., Lúlíyá village.

Keys to the *músúúsá* performance frame include the counterclockwise circle dance (a configuration utilized for no other kind of Hêmbá dance), the intermittent use of special funerary lyrics (not sung in any other kind of singing) alternating with lyrics borrowed from other kinds of songs, and the choice of certain melodies reserved only for these events (and not used on any other occasion). In fact, these keys to the *músúúsá* performance are not performed at any other time for "fear of creating conditions for another death" [*móyó ya úbŭlá lúfú*].[20]

In the *músúúsá* performance event, women employ contrasting and complementary genres—song-dance, dirge, praise name, veiled insult, and harangue—to communicate directly and indirectly with different groups of addressees. Ambiguities about exactly who is being accused, and who is being told about it, serve as protective devices for those voicing the accusations. As part of the performance frame and the rules for speaking and communicating in it, moreover, the people who think they are implicated are expected to control their anger and not respond to the accusations. Artless, angry responses may be viewed as indications of guilt and, at the very least, are considered poor form. Most importantly, angry responses endanger the success of this cleansing ritual. The roles here are deliberately asymmetrical: the *performers* have license to make accusations, preferably in artful and veiled ways; their *hosts* must remain calm and not retaliate if the ritual is to achieve its healing success.

A performer must be careful in ascribing blame since the living or dead person who had the power to kill your relative could consciously or unconsciously turn his or her hostility on you as well. This concern is expressed directly by one of the *músúúsá* performers as a "dangerous thought", when in performance she cautions a fellow performer about her verbal harangue:

Bé limulún[ga] gúla gúla,	You who will critique on and on,
gúmwacháá wênu 'ú Mômbwé,	you will dwell at your home in Mômbwé,
nákwaandíí.	so it is.

That is, if you are not circumspect, you will meet the same fate of being buried at your home village cemetery. Responding in unison, the other women agree.

Song Interpretation

When Báhêmbá women are asked to interpret *músúúsá* song lyrics, many women dissimulate with responses such as, "Oh, these are just songs we sing for the *músúúsá*", or "We just sing songs, semisecret society songs, youth performance group songs, whatever". This type of response illustrates the difficulty of interviewing with Báhêmbá on this sensitive topic.

Since we had developed a long-term relationship with a particularly insightful and articulate senior woman—Faílǎ Mwa'á, the verbal artist who became our teacher—we were able to discuss with her the interpretation of song-dances we had recorded, deepening and expanding understandings we gained in talking with other Báhêmbá. She had been an active participant in performances we studied and was acquainted with the other participants and the accusations associated with each death, yet she was related to each deceased person only distantly through marriage so the issues were not personally troubling or difficult for her to consider.

It became evident during the course of our work that some songs deserve more in-depth interpretation than do others. Songs composed for the occasion or adapted to it were intended to be especially meaningful in the particular funeral under consideration. Faílǎ Mwa'á came to speak of these songs as having an *'ísímǎ yátábéyá* [major significance]. A song with an *'ísímǎ yátábéyá* makes an important statement about who was responsible for causing the death. Other *músúúsá* songs were considered simply "appropriate" but did not address profound issues associated with the particular death. Songs borrowed from children's games and other performance frames also often fell in this latter category, having less immediate relevance. These songs added variety to the repertoire and enlivened the performance. They were reinterpreted for this funeral situation, related to the funeral issues in a general way. So, some songs are sung just because they are *músúúsá* songs or are songs people like to sing, as women casually reported. Others have greater import.

Músúúsá songs can be seen to permit at least three levels of interpretation. First, the song lyrics themselves have intrinsic funerary and "witchcraft" meaning independent of the particular funeral situation to which they are applied. The song *'Alínga 'ámwáálá* [Spying mongoose], for example, accuses someone close to the deceased of responsibility for the death. It may be sung at a funeral where this accusation is not relevant, in which case it would be seen simply as a *músúúsá* song, without strong import for the situation at hand.

A second level involves interpretation of the song as it bears on the issues related to the death of a particular individual. Occasionally a song will have specific relevance to the funeral at hand, yet not have major significance. A good example is when performers sang songs usually sung to celebrate the birth of twins at the funeral of a woman with one sister. The woman's death was like the loss of a fellow twin for her sister. This idea fits the kinship link, by analogy, but makes no reference to possible causes of death and is not considered to have weighty import.

A third level of interpretation emerges within the performance event itself. (To a certain extent, the second level is also event based, as themes and concerns are developed and clarified in the performance.) For some songs it is even crucial to know the immediate concerns of the singers to understand the song's central significance. *Mwiúmbugúlé bwa mbógǒ* [Lumbering around of the buffalo], sung after the women finish drinking palm wine, for example, is a critique of their own dancing. Other songs have their meaning enhanced through their enactment at a particular time in the *músúúsá*. Ruth Finnegan has elaborated on the importance of the time dimension in oral literature—in contrast to the space dimension of written text (Finnegan 1981). For example, *"Yubá líílii"* [This day] is a powerful song of introduction, setting the stage for what is to come.

Associations beyond the immediate performance context may enhance the significance and relevance of a song performance. One poignant example is a song about the soccer ball entering the goal, a soccer victory song. In general this song occurring in a *músúúsá* would refer to the theme of danger entering the deceased's house and also to the aggressive success of the killer who "scored"—

basic notions applicable to any death in Hembaland. When the song was sung during the *músúúsá* for Faílă Mámbá—who had died soon after she and her relatives had won a fiercely contested land dispute—its import could be fully appreciated only by recognizing that the same song had been sung a few weeks earlier as a song of victory in the decades-long dispute. The implication here was that Faílă Mámbá died as a consequence of specific out-of-control interpersonal hostilities provoked during her involvement in the legal battles over lineage land rights.

This same *músúúsá* performance also provides an excellent illustration of how performers themselves are continually involved in this interpretive process during the performance itself, as they consider the appropriateness of their songs and adjust song lyrics to better fit the circumstances and implications surrounding a particular death. The group took up a funeral song about a pig rooting around in a garden, which implies personal gain through another's demise. After twenty repetitions of the basic phrase *Ngulúbe gwitúlúgúlé* [Pig roots around everywhere], a singer replaced the name "Pig" with the deceased's name, a common technique

Plate 20–16. During the cleansing ritual more than three years after the death of 'Ánásá, sisters and other relatives embed artful accusations about the cause of her death in graceful *músúúsá* performance. White headscarves indicate that three of these women are members of the Bápéntákóst church. Nyémbó 'Íhúyá (2nd from right) and Nyémbó Mátésó—a host-village father-in-law and mother's-brother-in-law of the deceased—join one of her fathers in momentarily giving support and enthusiasm to the women's performance. 28 November 1982, 1:30 p.m., M.K.I. village. Plates 20–8 and 20–9 show the formal discussion part of this ritual.

making ephemeral accusations. Initially the women may have thought the song would be appropriate, since rooting around in a garden readily associates to palm and farmland rights, but after inserting the deceased's name, they found their adaptation of the lyrics to be inappropriate because the deceased did not profit by her own death. So, after a few minutes, one of the lead singers substituted the phrase *Mámbá gwigóbógólé* [Mámbá keep quiet], a phrase with comparable tonal pattern, syllable length, and initial sound, which advises the deceased, post hoc, not to get involved in the land dispute.

Examining song lyrics has provided special access to certain Hêmbá concepts not easily obtained through nondirective participant observation or even direct interviewing. For example, a particularly rich and interesting song phrase—recorded in a funeral song being sung by men and women carrying a corpse for burial—led to a discovery of what had never been said in hundreds of hours of interviews with numerous Báhêmbá: the phrase *mágóndé ga mêbá* [literally, thorny plantains or thorny plantain plants], a metaphor for *kúkesí*, the afterworld. We had never heard this trope mentioned in direct questions about the afterworld, much less at any other time. Through direct questioning we had repeatedly been told that no one really knows what the afterworld is like but that it is probably a lot like here. Senior headman Kíndéngá Kángélá once told us that after you die you wait three days in an intermediary zone and then someone takes you to your relatives, but he hastened to qualify it by saying he did not know for sure. The use of the phrase *mágóndé ga mêbá* in lyrics reserved especially for a funeral song, in contrast, evokes visual and tactile images of differences between existence among the living and existence among the dead. The rhetorical response of Faílǎ Mwa'á to our questions was, "Have you ever seen thorny plantains?" Of course we have not—they are something of that other world. This imagery is more vividly meaningful to rural Báhêmbá than for most urban (or suburban) dwellers or even farmers who work in leather gloves and sturdy boots. Thorns [*mêbá*] are anathema to barefooted Central African farmers. Thorns can cause disabling injuries that can lead to lingering illness, inadequate farm production, hunger, hardship, and even death. The thorny plantains anomaly has rhetorical value when one is trying lyrically to convince a severely grieving living person not to dwell on how nice it would be to join his or her recently deceased close relatives, but instead to hear and see the aesthetically pleasing funeral song-dance performance and think about the attractive things and people in this world of the living.

"WITCHCRAFT", ALLUSIVE REFERENCE, AND LONG-TERM FIELD RESEARCH

As our field research progressed, we increasingly realized the potential of proverb and oratory, gesture, song-dance, veiled insult, and dirge in Hêmbá funerals as sources of information on the hidden matters of relations with ancestors, the dead, and what Báhêmbá see as the endemic human potential for "witchcraft". The more we found out from the transcription and explication of artful performance, the more deeply we became aware of the multiplicity of fragmentary and indirect references to *bútĭ* in everyday Kíhêmbá speech. In retrospect, this increase in awareness appears to have developed in occasional big jumps rather than gradually and incrementally, until after several years it was hard not to hear these snippets almost everywhere. Doing interviews on the subject of *bútǐ* remains difficult, however, and in most cases probably ethically inadvisable. People do not want to directly speak of *bútǐ* and risk bringing down retribution consciously or unconsciously upon themselves from other humans, living or dead. Thus allusions to *bútǐ* are made everywhere, but nowhere with much length or directness. Comments on *bútǐ* initially passed us by, unnoticed for a very long time until we developed the ears to hear and the eyes to see it all around us in verbal art and artful movement—and eventually as a worldview unobtrusively and subtlely present even in seemingly mundane conversation, though in much less concentrated form.

Raoll Naroll, an expert in cross-cultural research methodologies using the Human Relations Area Files, in the early 1960s did an extensive "fishing expedition" search, focusing on witchcraft, attempting to find a cross-cultural correlation of witchcraft to the presence of anything else in human culture and society. He tested a large number of variables but found that not patrilineal descent, patrilocal residence, incidence of infidelity or divorce, child-rearing practices, ecological adaptations, or any other variable correlated positively, except one: ethnographic reports of witchcraft correlate very strongly with the *length of stay in the field by the ethnographer!* This strong statistical correlation is even more remarkable since the HRAF ethnological sample obviously includes reports from some ethnographers who searched for witchcraft assiduously as a primary focus and were highly motivated to find it early in their stay in the field, whereas hardly anyone was motivated *not* to find it. During Naroll's other cross-cultural work at this time, he found that many kinds of ethnographic account were strengthened by longer periods of fieldwork, mostly along a continuum of evolving competence. But witchcraft reports were more digital—either witchcraft was reported or it was not, and the only strong correlation over a large number of studies was to the length of time of the ethnographer's fieldwork.[1]

In other words, while most agree that longer periods of fieldwork tend to produce more and better ethnographic knowledge, at least up to a point, *long-term ethnographic field research*—informed by the closely experienced sensations and subtleties of interactive participation in and discourse about everyday and ritual life—may provide a *primary* way to learn about some aspects of religion in Africa.

HÊMBÁ ARTISTIC PERFORMANCE: REFLECTING AND CONSTRUCTING RELIGIOUS BELIEF AND PRACTICE

During the performance of men's oratory and women's song-dance in a variety of funeral events—as well as during the rituals and other performances of semisecret societies and healing associations such as Bámbúlǐ and Bátámbwé Súkú—Báhêmbá creatively dialogue with their ancestors and with each other in ways that both reflect and construct their fundamental perspectives on matters of religion, including associated concepts of illness and health.

On the one hand, Hêmbá artistic performance reflects—similar to the way language does—its embeddedness in other domains of Hêmbá culture and society. Religion, social organization, politics, economics, and other salient concerns guide, impinge upon, encourage, and constrain artistic performance. So, the study of Hêmbá artistic performances provides us with a wealth of information and a "royal road" to understanding other salient aspects of Hêmbá life, including issues of life and death, morality and ethics, and bedrock perspectives on human nature and on the nature of the universe and human beings' place in it.

With patient attention to allusive references, veiled signs, the tactics of indirection, and the foregrounding of the poetic in the performance of verbal art and artful movement, one can come to glimpse basic Hêmbá religious concepts (and the manner in which they are very warily and obliquely discussed) in some ways more profoundly than from any didactic statement by Báhêmbá or from focused interviews on the subject. Báhêmbá themselves learn about these matters largely in this same indirect, fragmentary way.

The very essence of core Hêmbá beliefs about *bútǐ* ["witchcraft"]—as partly unconscious out-of-control interpersonal hostility that anyone has the potential of generating—precludes people from directly discussing the dangerous aspects of these beliefs. People are also circumspect about *báfú* [the dead, including one's ancestors], who are potentially present to the living at any time, can make mischief or even cause trouble if bothered, and so are best not disturbed until their assistance is truly needed. Báhêmbá instead follow a cautious strategy so as not to incur the risk of negative consequences, sort of a combination of "let sleeping dogs lie" and "loose lips sink ships" approach.

Indeed, would a thoughtfully prudent person "throw his chicken upwards toward the sky"—a chicken he had carefully raised from when it was a tiny chick—since a carnivorous "wild cat-of-the-bush" might then spy it more easily and plan to come and eat it during the night? This was what the wise elder asked the ethnographer in the episode recounted at the beginning of this chapter. In the nature of life and death, predators abound. But why call their attention to something that might endanger someone you do not want to die? Parenthetically, not only is the *'áyûndú* a vexing nighttime chicken thief: when this mostly silent "wild cat-of-the-bush" cries out near the village, it brings news of *bútǐ*-generated death. No wonder Lwámbá Múkálámúsí, who in many other matters would not hesitate to upbraid his sons and grandsons, said nothing straightforwardly direct about the destruction of the ancestor shrine.

When confronting weighty issues, Báhêmbá men and women wax poetic in sound and movement. Báhêmbá consider bluntness to be a very naked kind of truth for dealing with the most salient concerns—a strategy more suited for angry outburst, bullying, or inflammatory provocation than for calming indirection, wise deliberation, collaborative decision making, efficacious ritual song, or healing discourse. Well-timed verbal art and artful movement appropriate to the question at hand and the personalities involved are really a more direct route to consensus, "coolness", and health in Hêmbá society. Only within very special performance frames, such as the *músúúsá* event, are a modicum of directly expressed anger, insults, and accusatory remarks seen as making contributions toward cleansing, reconciliation, and healing.

Also important to consider is that Hêmbá religious knowledge is characteristically noncentralized—as is the related Hêmbá ethnomedical knowledge—such that no one person or even one group of people is widely considered the final repository of definitive opinions on key questions, much less privileged cosmological systematizations. The checks and balances of the Hêmbá double segmentary lineage system, linked to local ancestors, help guard against and express distaste for overcentralization. So do the crosscutting allegiances of multiple memberships in semisecret societies, healing associations, and churches, plus the resulting rich and changeable range of choices for crisis resolution, problem solving, and healing. Báhêmbá also point out that the egalitarian circle formations of the men's formal discussions and women's song-dances spatially enact and emphasize the Hêmbá penchant for noncentralization. Hêmbá distrust of sociopolitical hierarchy or any other kind of overarching elite-formation mechanism here also comes into play. More generally, the "proliferation of religious groups" historically and currently in the Búhêmbá home area in northern Shaba may have some connection to what Fabian in chapter 14 (pp. 271–272) calls "a particular cultural notion of power"—that is, "a cultural preference for a kind of anarchy, be it in religion, economics, or politics" in this part of Central Africa.

In any case, the Hêmbá noncentralization of knowledge extends also to gender in matters of religious expression. Funeral-related men's oratory and women's ritual song-dance deftly interweave artful movement with verbal art to express and work through concerns about "witchcraft" and the role of ancestors in Hêmbá life and death. Working collaboratively, we have been able to explore these gender-specific performance genres and eventually also to see their commonalities, their distinctiveness, and their interdependence. The men's formal funeral discussions greatly depend on what takes place in the women's mourning song-dances and vice versa. Resolving important issues during formal discussion is contingent on the expression by the women performers of otherwise socially unacceptable thoughts and feelings and the concomitant ritual "cooling" of the village in the song-dance performance. The *músúúsá* song-dance does not successfully end, nor are related funerary matters properly settled in a way that leads to health and prosperity, without artful oratory in the service of negotiation and dispute settlement in the *mwândá* formal discussion. Thus, for us as researchers, trying to more fully understand basic Hêmbá religious orientations, studying performances of both women's and men's genres—and women's and men's performances of genres that are not so gender specific—has been essential.[22]

In other societies, women's and men's ways of speaking have sometimes been characterized as opposites, with men's direct speech in public arenas contrasted with women's indirect speech in domestic spheres.[23] In Burundi and Madagascar, on the other hand, allusive, metaphoric speech is reported to be highly valued and reserved for men.[24] In Hêmbá funerals, in contrast to these polarities, even when genres are strongly gender linked, both men and women use artfully veiled speech in large events in public arenas. On some occasions, women's speech is more direct and men's is much less so; at other times women speak less directly than men do. Women go further in making direct cause-of-death accusations within the *músúúsá* performance frame, while men resort to cautious indirectness about these matters in their oratory and formal discussion. Men's proverbs, however, are more directly explicated for listener-viewers than are women's veiled insults. Such nuances in situated men's and women's speech caution against premature cross-cultural generalization, while recommending more research on these issues throughout the full range of human cultures and social situations.[25]

Hêmbá verbal, visual, musical, and kinesthetic art, moreover, are not only a *reflection* of religious, social organizational, and other domains of Hêmbá culture and society, but are also powerful means for *constituting* and *constructing* important aspects of and insights about such domains. In their performances, Báhêmbá engage in multimodal discourse with each other (and with the dead) about ancient, new, and evolving perceptions and interpretations of the human world. These artistic talents can, when skillfully employed, be used to make modifications and induce change not only in individuals' viewpoints, but also in social and cultural forms, and are not merely instruments with which to play out a predetermined score.

So, Hêmbá artistic performance can serve as an index to Hêmbá thought and belief—providing evidence of rather stable and unchanging (or very slowly changing) views Báhêmbá share about ancestors, "witchcraft", the afterlife, and other central matters of life and death. But also through the study of artistic performance come glimpses of the emergent nature of these views, as Báhêmbá interactively explore religious mysteries about which they feel no one has much more knowledge than does anyone else.

Notes

1. Azim Nanji writes about this Islamic tradition in East Africa (1974, 1986, chapter 2—this volume).

2. For more on Hêmbá social structure, residence patterns, and agriculture, see Sweet, T. Blakely, P. Blakely, and Roth 1977; and T. Blakely forthcoming.

We did the field research on which this chapter is based from 1974 to 1979, during 1982, and in the dry season of 1985 in rural and urban Zaïre. When we were in Zaïrean cities and towns—Kinshasa, Lubumbashi, Kongolo, Kindu, Kisangani, Bukavu, Kalemie—we stayed mostly in the homes of generous and hospitable families or in various organizations' guest rooms, and three or four times in modest hotels. In rural Hembaland, for nine months near the beginning of our research we lived in the large grid-pattern village of Mbúlúlá in the family compound of Túbazalíé Mwa'á and Nzaínǎ Nzugú and their husband Mámbá Némbá (one of Tom's "mother's brothers" in fictive kinship). We eventually moved into our own adobe brick, thatched-roof house in a two-line village of the Bágá'ítûngwá patrilineage (the patrilineage that adopted Tom), a two hours' walk north of Mbúlúlá. The name of this village still is under fierce debate—one aspect of a long-running political dispute—so when we refer to it in writing we call it "M.K.I.", from the first initials of several of the preferred names. We soon learned to enjoy the local foods, farmed gardens with a short hoe, traveled between villages mostly on foot and occasionally by bicycle, and willingly acquired the Hêmbá penchant for becoming well acquainted by *wíizhá na báándú*—sitting down, relaxing, and talking with people for hours on end.

For Kíhêmbá: á=high tone; a=low tone; â=falling tone; ǎ=rising tone.

3. In the second decade of the twentieth century, Joseph Vandermeiren wrote a catechism in the Kínyánkuvú dialect of Kíhêmbá while at the Bruges-St. Donat (Sola) Mission of the Pères Blancs, but copies of the catechism are now extremely rare in Hembaland.

4. Copies of a Seventh-Day Adventist publication, *Agole Atabeya a Vidye* [God's Great News], are still kept and used by local church members. Nyembo Kilongozi, a Seventh-Day

Adventist pastor who formerly worked for the Adventist radio station and publications center in Lubumbashi and who at last report was based in Kamina, has been working on a dictionary project for more than twenty-five years, the first volume of which is entitled *Vocabulaire ou Dictionnaire Français-Kihemba.*

Other Báhêmbá refer to Seventh-Day Adventists as "Báávántíst" or, more usually, "Básábátó"—referring to the members' relatively rigorous observance of the sabbath [*sábátó*] on the day prior to other Christians' *siku ya Mungu* [in Kiswahili, literally "God's day"], also called *sábátó* in religious contexts.

5. Colonial territorial administrators took a great interest in these matters, worried that such organizations might be involved in antigovernment activities. One of the most energetic of these administrators, René Wauthion, served three separate periods in Kongolo, wrote administrative reports about local "secret societies", and even published on this subject (Wauthion 1940).

6. Allen Roberts and Christopher Davis-Roberts noted during their fieldwork and archival research in the 1970s on the Batabwa (along Lake Tanganyika, neighbors-of-neighbors southeast of the Báhêmbá) that the people living in the area of what is now northeastern Kongolo Zone (Hembaland) have long been considered prolific generators of healing associations that find their way, one way or another, to surrounding peoples (A. Roberts, personal communication, 1976, Lubumbashi).

7. For the Bambudye among the Baluba, see Reefe 1981. From a Hêmbá perspective, Lúbă sociopolitical organization historically was more hierarchical than Hêmbá sociopolitical organization, even at the village level, and was more centralized both locally and over large areas. Compared to the hierarchical centralization of the Belgian Congo administration, the Roman Catholic church, or a large mining company, however, the Lúbă and Lunda empires were relatively noncentralized, with villages and segmentary kinship units the focus of most activities (see Fabian 1970:13–14).

8. With the contrast between "semisecret society" and "healing association", we have tried to maintain the Kíhêmbá semantic and pragmatic distinction between the long-established groups (Bágábó, Bámbúlĭ, Bálúbwílŏ, Bámúkótá) and the groups of more recent origin whose new initiates are primarily persons healed by the group's therapeutic procedures.

Much knowledge about the Bágábó and the three *bisélá* is widespread among Báhêmbá nonmembers, such that "semisecret society" is more appropriate than "secret society" (see also Biebuyck 1973). Initiation into a semisecret society usually does not stem from the initiate's being cured of an illness or solving a major life problem. Instead, the prototypical new initiates are descendants of a recently deceased society member (who ceases to be a member, but whose possessing ancestor now becomes associated with these new initiates). Other new initiates are close lineal relatives or friends of current (living) members or are chosen because of an aptitude or affinity for the activities of the particular semisecret society. An initiation of Bámbúlĭ, Bálúbwílŏ, or Bámúkótá is a major milestone in a senior member's funeral event sequence, culminating in much-anticipated celebratory performances by new initiates and the society's adepts (plates 20–2 and 20–4).

The term "healing association" is meant to emphasize the positive social and medical aspects of the Báhêmbá medico-religious groups of more recent origin. Members of healing associations have expertise in the diagnosis, treatment, and healing of sociosomatic causes of illness, not excluding synergistic linkages with more straightforwardly ethnopharmacological remedies. Healing associations and semisecret societies exhibit similar fundamental perspectives on ancestors, the possibilities of communication between the living and the dead, *bútĭ*, and human nature in general, but differ on the specifics of problem targets, solutions, ancestral and living human resources brought to bear, and varieties of therapeutic performance.

In earlier versions of this chapter, we used the term "healing cult" for these groups since "cult" has been commonly used in the scholarly literature on Central Africa. Appropriate to the Hêmbá situation, "cult" denotes religious belief and activity while implying a shallower time depth for the religious system or community than the term "religion" or even the Africanist term "(semi)secret society". "Healing cult" adds the positive central focus on *healing* for Báhêmbá in these groups, rather than the emphasis on affliction in the term "cults of affliction" used by Turner, Janzen, and others (chapter 9). "Drums of affliction" does not seem appropriate as a general term for these Hêmbá groups, though the beliefs and activities Turner and Janzen chronicle have many Hêmbá parallels. In the Kíhêmbá language, the word *ngómá* does not mean "drum" in general but refers only to some kinds of membranophone drums and definitely not slit-gong drums. Some Hêmbá semisecret societies and healing associations never use drums at all. Indeed, various kinds of rattles are the omnipresent musical instruments in many groups. Most importantly, in Kíhêmbá the term *ngómá* does not also mean "dance", "curing ceremony", or the event more broadly, as it does in some other Bantu languages.

The term "healing cult" thus has some advantages. But it also carries unfortunate semantic baggage, since "cult" involves inaccurate connotations (for Hêmbá belief and ritual) such as "focusing upon a single deity or spirit" and derogatory overtones such as "obsessive devotion or veneration" [*American Heritage Dictionary*]. In everyday English usage as well as in broadcast and print journalism, cults are contrasted very negatively to longer-established religions, with some senses of "cult" being directly pejorative, and cults being considered undesirable or even despicable, crazed, illegal, or dangerous. Further, "cult" denotes "worship" in both French and English, but "worship" does not at all accurately describe what happens in these Hêmbá groups.

In this dichotomous classification of medico-religious groups as semisecret societies or healing associations, the Básó'ó—and the Bálúngú to a degree—seem to be anomalous. As with the Bágábó, both groups address human fertility problems. As with all the semisecret societies, they date from long ago and men do all or nearly all of the healing ritual and related performances, unlike the extant healing associations in which women undertake some or all of the leading diagnostic and therapeutic roles (Plate 20–3). However, initiations of the Básó'ó (and to a lesser extent, the Bálúngú) are associated with attempts to cure the entering initiate's illness or other misfortune—crop failure or unsuccessful hunts—similar to healing associations and attesting to a long time-depth for these kinds of ritual process among Bahêmbá. Básó'ó and Bálúngú group longevity may partly come from their close identification with the basic rural subsistence activities of farming and hunting.

9. Singular, *ngángá*; plural, *bángángá*. Báhêmbá primarily use the terms *ngángá* and *bángángá* in reference to spirit-possessed members of the Bámbúlĭ, Bálúbwíló, or Bámúkótá semisecret societies, as in "*bángángá bamúvwǎ bútufú*" ["semisecret society healers will come tonight"].

Interestingly, in Kíhêmba the terms *múngángá* [medical doctor; pl. *bámúngángá*] and *míngángá* [clinic nurse; pl., *bámíngángá*] also incorporate the -*gángá* root and a core part of its semantic range [healer, healing]. The term *búgángá* encompasses the healing substances, healing procedures, and healing powers of the *ngángá*, the *múngángá*, the *míngángá*, and all other kinds of healer. Similar to how a curative dose of some pharmaceuticals is not far from a toxic dose—and a medicine at one dosage can be a poison at another—*búgángá* knowledge and materials can be used to harm as well as to help (see e.n. 15).

10. For photographs as well as morphological and stylistic analyses of these kinds of Hêmbá sculpture and formerly spirit-invested objects, see Neyt and de Struyker 1975, 1979; Neyt 1977. Only some of Neyt and de Struyker's seemingly ethnographic information is accurate, however, concerning the uses of these objects and their significance in Hêmbá culture, not to mention the explicit and implicit suppositions about Hêmbá social and political structure. Unfortunately, their "facts" and subsequent interpretations are too frequently misleading, inaccurate, definitely wrong, or unverified from solidly grounded Hêmbá perspectives. For a study of another type of Hêmbá spirit-invested object in its sociocultural, linguistic, and performance context, see Blakely and Blakely 1987.

11. Pioneering substantive studies (e.g., Albert 1964; Frake 1964; Abrahams 1967, 1972a, 1972b; Basso 1970; Bauman 1972; Dan Ben-Amos 1972a, 1972b, 1975; Mitchell-Kernan 1972; Rosaldo 1973, Gossen 1974) and collections of such studies (Gumperz and Hymes 1964, 1972; Bauman and Sherzer 1989 [1974]; Ben-Amos and Goldstein 1975), as well as a review essay summarizing the first decade of research (Bauman and Sherzer 1975) and a critical appraisal pointing ahead to new directions (Sherzer 1977), have now been joined by a sizeable number of works in the ethnography of speaking and communication. Philipsen and Carbaugh's 1986 bibliographic essay cites over two hundred very strictly selected titles in the ethnography of communication, most of which deal primarily with speech in the more narrow sense. The bibliography of Bauman and Sherzer's second edition of *Explorations in the Ethnography of Speaking* (1989) lists additional works, though still reflecting a dearth of studies focused much beyond the aural-audial communication channel (or written language, e.g., Heath 1983), with the partial exception of ethnomusicology in which various audial channels remain the central focus while some attention is paid to visual aspects of music performance.

12. All the "communicative means" Bauman lists as being well documented for "serving to key performance" (1977:15) are present in Hêmbá proverb performance: "special codes", including archaic words and meanings; a prominent emphasis on "figurative language"; "parallelism" as in *Mwândá guli múgélĕ; Gusi múgélĕ guli ngélá*. [Oratory it is proverb-filled poetic speech; (if) it is not proverb-filled poetic speech it is naked]; "special paralinguistic features", for example the occasional pause after the first half of a proverb to allow one's fellow participants to dialogically complete the second half; "special formulae" and "appeal to tradition" such as *Bá'ulú ba kálá benábéló* ... [According to the elders of former times ...]; and "disclaimer of performance" such as when Bûhêmbá key proverb performance by saying "I am but a youngster compared to the talented elders who have gone [to the afterworld, to the farms for the day, on a trip elsewhere], but there is no one else to speak for us, so ..."

13. In Blakely and Blakely 1987, the photographs on pages 31 and 33 show a small red Ndúbá feather at the top of the *só'ó* mask worn by a "chimpanzee-human" masquerade figure—a tiny but telling visual sign indicating this *só'ó* figure is senior, powerful, and an efficacious healer.

14. While scholars have made claims, pro and con, tacitly and explicitly, concerning the importance of "nonverbal" aspects of performance, more systematic *ethnographic* attention in published works in folklore, anthropology, linguistics, and related fields until now has been given to the "language" or "speech" aspects of performance in the more restricted sense of these terms, except for music performance (Stone 1982; Feld 1982; E. Basso 1985) and some semiotic studies (e.g., Stoeltje 1985). The works of Gregory Bateson, Ray L. Birdwhistell, Edward T. Hall, and many others have established the salience of "nonverbal" communication in face-to-face interaction (see bibliographies in Key 1975, 1977; Kendon 1981; Blakely and Blakely 1989). Conversation Analysis "integrates body movement into the analysis of talk and action" and investigates "how body movement and speech are coordinated during conversation", including the implications of gaze and gaze-avoidance (Goodwin and Heritage 1990:292–293). Adam Kendon has shown that gesticulation, moreover, can very much be part of an utterance (as in Plate 20–10, p. 421) and has found gestural sign languages and other gestural systems to have decidedly verbal qualities, calling into question the traditionally accepted and largely unexamined boundaries of the " verbal" (Kendon 1980, 1988). Researchers such as Roger Abrahams, Richard Bauman, Dan Ben-Amos, Henry Glassie, Kenneth Goldstein, Joel Sherzer, and Beverly Stoeltje who contribute to the growing scholarly literature on performance do assert the importance of ethnographically studying the full variety of communicative modes in performance events (see also Turner 1986; Conquergood 1991:187–191; and Margaret Drewal's 1991 review of performance studies in Africa). But much more ethnographic research is needed on the complexities of how artful speech and visual signs are

interrelated—and the ways in which audible and visible (and other) communicative forms do, or do not, illustrate, qualify, elaborate, contradict, reinforce, amplify, or take precedence over one another during performance.

15. *Bútǐ* has the same root [*-tǐ*] as does *mútǐ* [tree, wood, medicinal plant; pl. *mítǐ*]. Expert ethnopharmaceutical knowledge of medicinal plants is an important part of *búgángá* in both its positive and negative aspects: as medicine for healing or preventing illness, misfortune, or death; and as poisonous concoction intended to *cause* such calamities. This latter, negative usage of *búgángá* is called *bútǐ bwa bánabálumé* [men's *bútǐ*], although both women and men can voluntarily acquire and utilize such knowledge. *Bútǐ bwa bánábaazí* [so-called "women's *bútǐ*"]—said to involve flying through the night, nibbling on victim's souls, and other relatively intangible acts of out-of-control interpersonal hostility—also is done by both men and women: consciously and voluntarily by some individuals but quite unconsciously and involuntarily by others. Awareness of the potential in every human being for generating both kinds of *bútǐ* encourages Báhêmbá to develop positive human relationships, to work hard to avoid actions that cause jealousy (seen as leading all too directly to *bútǐ*), and to practice medico-religious group therapies that seek to reduce sociosomatic causes and accelerators of dis-ease and death.

16. As an interesting comparison: Ruth Stone (1982:100) found that Kpelle musicians she studied in Liberia first made a counterclockwise sweep of the outer perimeter of a town other than their own, to clear the performance arena of *malevolent* spirits.

17. This same concern comes forth when a group of women relatives sleep together in the same room of the funeral house with a woman who has recently lost a close family member, or when a group of men relatives and neighbors sleep shivering together outdoors in a palm frond-covered funeral shelter [*úmbí lya málíló*], until at the end of one to two weeks they hold a preliminary funeral festival marking the "end of sleeping outside" [*úangázhá báándú hânzá*; literally, putting people (in their regular houses) from outside (them)"]. They say that during this critical time they are helping the most greatly bereaved not to listen too much to their recently departed loved one or to be seduced into joining them in the afterworld.

18. For thermal concepts in other African cultures, see Turner 1969; Thompson 1973; de Heusch 1980; Davis-Roberts 1980, 1981; and Jacobson-Widding 1987.

19. Some women say they literally sweep the village clean at a later point in the funeral using the *mwândúlá* vine garlands and palm fronds worn to perform the *músúúsá*, though we have never witnessed it and believe it is infrequently done.

20. Note that a kinesthetic-visual key to Hêmbá performance (the distinctive *músúúsá* circle dance) and an aural-audial musical key to Hêmbá performance (the special *músúúsá* melodies) also augment Bauman's provisional list (1977:15).

21. Ronald Cohen, personal communications: Winter 1972, Northwestern University, Evanston, Illinois; reconfirmed, November 1990, American Anthropological Association annual meetings, New Orleans.

22. Genres performed during Bátámbwé Súkú healing ritual (Plate 20–3), for example, include song ['*ísimó*] by women and men here and in many other kinds of performance; dance [*mázhá*] only by women here but also by men in other kinds of performance; drumming the *ngómá* membranophone drum by men only; and performing with various rattles and percussion sticks [several terms] by women and men, here and elsewhere.

23. For example, women's veiled speech and song circumspectly protest gender subordination in Bedouin society in Egypt (Abu-Lughod 1986). Similarly, allusive references in *utenzi* poetry protest other forms of sociopolitical subordination on the East African coast (Knappert 1967).

24. Studies by Ethel M. Albert (1964) and Elinor Ochs Keenan (1973, 1974).

25. See also Sherzer 1987; Borker and Maltz 1989; Gal 1991.

Bibliography

Abímbọlá, Wándé (n.d.). *Àwọn Ọmọ Odù, Àpólà Ogbẹ.* Manuscript in author's possession.

_____ (1968). *Ìjìnlẹ Ohùn Ẹnu Ifá, Apá Kìíní.* Glasgow: Collins.

_____ (1975a). Ìwàpẹlẹ: The Concept of Good Character in Ifá Literary Corpus. In *Yoruba Oral Tradition*, 389–420. Ilé–Ifẹ̀: University of Ifẹ

_____ (1975b). *Sixteen Great Poems of Ifá.* Niamey: UNESCO.

_____ (1976a). *Ifá: An Exposition of Ifá Literary Corpus.* Ibadan: Oxford University Press.

_____ (1976b). *Yoruba Religion in Brazil: Problems and Prospects.* Field Report. Ilé–Ifẹ̀: University of Ifẹ.

_____ (1977). *Ifá Divination Poetry.* New York: NOK Publishers.

Abrahams, Roger D. (1967). The Shaping of Folkloric Traditions in the British West Indies. *Journal of Interamerican Studies* 9:456–480.

_____ (1972a). Joking: The Training of the Man of Words in Talking Broad. In *Rappin' and Stylin' Out: Communication in Urban Black America*, 215–240. Thomas Kochman, ed. Urbana: University of Illinois Press.

_____ (1972b). The Training of the Man of Words in Talking Sweet. *Language in Society* 1:15–29.

_____ (1983). *The Man-of-Words in the West Indies.* Baltimore: Johns Hopkins University Press.

_____ (1992). Insult. In *Folklore, Cultural Performances, and Popular Entertainments*, 145–149. Richard Bauman, ed. New York: Oxford University Press.

Abu-Lughod, Lila (1986). *Veiled Sentiments.* Berkeley: University of California Press.

_____ (1993). *Writing Women's Worlds: Bedouin Stories.* Berkeley: University of California Press.

Abun-Nasr, Jamil M. (1987). *A History of the Maghrib in the Islamic Period.* 3rd ed. New York: Cambridge University Press.

Adams, Marie J., ed. (1980). *Ethnologische Zeitschrift Zürich* 1 [Special issue on secret societies in Sierra Leone and Liberia.]

Adams, William Yewdale (1977). *Nubia: Corridor to Africa.* London: Allen Lane.

Adejunmobi, T. A. (1963). Polygamy. In *African Independent Church Movements*, 52–59. Victor E. W. Hayward, ed. Edinburgh: Edinburgh House Press.

AFER: African Ecclesiastical Review. (1959–). Eldoret, Kenya: AME-CEA Pastoral Institute.

Agbeti, J. Kofi (1986). *West African Church History: Christian Missions and Church Foundations.* Leiden: E. J. Brill.

Ahanotu, Austin Metumara, ed. (1992). *Religion, State, and Society in Contemporary Africa: Nigeria, Sudan, South Africa, Zaïre, and Mozambique.* New York: Peter Lang.

Ajayi, Jacob F. A. (1969). *Christian Missions in Nigeria, 1841–1891: The Making of a New Elite.* Evanston, Illinois: Northwestern University Press.

Ajayi, Jacob F. A., and Emmanuel A. Ayandele, eds. (1974). Emerging Themes in Nigerian and West African Religious History. *Journal of African Studies* 1(1):1–39.

Albert, Ethel M. (1964). "Rhetoric", "Logic", and "Poetics" in Burundi. In *The Ethnography of Communication.* John Gumperz and Dell Hymes, eds. Special issue. *American Anthropologist* 66(6, pt. 2):35–64.

Alimasi, Babwile C., and Kasongo N'konko P. (1985). *Kristu jana na leo na milele.* Lubumbashi. Mimeographed.

Alldridge, Thomas J. (1910). *A Transformed Colony, Sierra Leone As It Was and As It Is, Its Progress, Peoples, Native Customs and Undeveloped Wealth.* London: Seeley and Co.

Amistad Research Center (1970). *Author and Added Entry Catalog of the American Missionary Association Archives.* Westport, Connecticut: Greenwood.

Anderson, James Norman Dalrymple (1970). *Islamic Law in Africa.* London: Frank Cass.

Anderson, Lisa (1991). Obligation and Accountability: Islamic Politics in North Africa. *Daedalus* 120(3):93–112.

Andersson, Efraim (1958). *Messianic Popular Movements in the Lower Congo.* Studia Ethnographica Upsaliensia 14. Uppsala: Almqvist and Wiksells.

_____ (1968). *Churches at the Grass-Roots.* London: Lutterworth.

Andrews, Carol, ed. (1985). *The Ancient Egyptian Book of the Dead.* Raymond O. Faulkner, trans. New York: Macmillan.

Appiah-Kubi, Kofi (1974). The Independent African Churches: Forerunners to Authenticity. *7AACC Bulletin* 9:31–36.

_____ (1981). *Man Cures, God Heals.* Totowa, New Jersey: Allanheld, Osmun & Co.

Appiah-Kubi, Kofi, and Sergio Torres, eds. (1979). *African Theology en Route: Papers from the Pan African Conference of Third World Theologians.* New York: Orbis.

Apter, Andrew (1992). *Black Critics and Kings: The Hermeneutics of Power in Yoruba Society.* Chicago: University of Chicago Press.

Arens, William (1979). The Divine Kingship of the Shilluk. *Ethos* 7:168–181.

Arens, William, and Ivan Karp, eds. (1989). *Creativity of Power, Cosmology, and Action in African Societies.* Washington, D.C.: Smithsonian Institution Press.

Arewa, Ojo, and Alan Dundes (1964). Proverbs and the Ethnography of Speaking Folklore. In *The Ethnography of Communciation.* John Gumperz and Dell Hymes, eds. Special issue. *American Anthropologist* 66(6, pt. 2):70–85.

Arinze, Francis A. (1970). *Sacrifice in Ibo Religion.* Ibadan: Ibadan University Press.

Asamoa, E. A. (1955). The Christian Church and African Heritage. *International Review of Missions* 44:292–301.

Asiwaju, A. I. (1976). Political Motivation and Oral Historical Traditions in Africa: The Case of Yoruba Crowns. *Africa* 46(2):113–128.

Assimeng, J. Max (1989). *Religion and Social Change in West Africa: An Introduction to the Sociology of Religion.* Accra: Ghana Universities Press.

Atherton, John (1983). Ethnoarchaeology in Africa. *African Archaeological Review* 1:75–104.

Augé, Marc (1982). *Génie du paganisme.* Paris: Gallimard.

Awolalu, J. O. (1970). The Yoruba Philosophy of Life. *Présence Africaine* 73(1):20–38.

_____ (1979). *Yoruba Beliefs and Sacrificial Rites.* London: Longman.

Axelson, Sigbert (1970). *Culture Confrontation in the Lower Congo.* Falkoping, Sweden: Gummessons.

Ayandele, Emmanuel Ayankanmi (1966). *The Missionary Impact on Modern Nigeria, 1842–1914: A Political and Social Analysis.* London: Longmans.

_____ (1970). *Holy Johnson: Pioneer of African Nationalism, 1836–1917.* New York: Humanities Press.

_____ (1971). *A Visionary of the African Church: Mojola Agbebi, 1860–1917.* Nairobi: East African Publishing House.

Babayemi, S. O. (1980). *Egungun among the Oyo Yoruba.* Ibadan: University of Ibadan.

Baeta, Christian (1962). *Prophetism in Ghana: A Study of Some "Spiritual" Churches.* London: SCM Press.

_____, ed. (1968). *Christianity in Tropical Africa.* London: Oxford University Press.

_____ (1971). Some Aspects of Religious Change in Africa. *Ghana Bulletin of Theology* 36:9–22.

Bakhtin, Mikhail M. (1981). *The Dialogic Imagination: Four Essays.* Michael Holquist, ed. Caryl Emerson and Michael Holquist, trans. Austin: University of Texas Press.

_____ (1986). *Speech Genres and Other Late Essays.* Caryl Emerson and Michael Holquist, eds. Vern W. McLee, trans. Austin: University of Texas Press.

Balandier, Georges (1955). *Sociologie actuelle de l'Afrique Noire.* Paris: Presses Universitaires de France.

Balogun, Ismāʿil A. B., ed. and trans. (1975). *The Life and Works of ʿUthmān dan Fodio.* Lagos: Islamic Publications Bureau.

Banton, Michael (1955). The Ethnography of the Protectorate: Review Article. *Sierra Leone Studies* n.s. 4:240–249.
_____ (1963). African Prophets. *Race* 5:42–55.
_____ (1966). *Anthropological Approaches to the Study of Religion.* ASA Monograph 3. London: Tavistock.
Barber, Karin (1991). Multiple Discourses in Yoruba Oral Literature. *Bulletin of the John Rylands University Library of Manchester* 73(3):11–24.
Barnes, Sandra (1980). *Ogun: An Old God for a New Age.* ISHI Occasional Papers in Social Change 3. Philadelphia: Institute for the Study of Human Issues.
_____, ed. (1989). *Africa's Ogun: Old World and New.* Bloomington: Indiana University Press.
Barrett, David B. (1968). *Schism and Renewal in Africa: An Analysis of Six Thousand Contemporary Religious Movements.* Nairobi: Oxford University Press.
_____, ed. (1971). *African Initiatives in Religion: Twenty-One Studies from Eastern and Central Africa.* Nairobi: East African Publishing House.
_____, ed. (1982). *World Christian Encyclopedia: A Comparative Survey of Churches and Religions in the Modern World, AD 1900–2000.* Oxford: Oxford University Press.
Barrett, David B. et al., eds. (1973). *Kenya Churches Handbook: The Development of Kenyan Christianity, 1498–1973.* Kisumu: Evangelical Publishing House.
Barrett, Leonard (1977). *The Rastafarians: Sounds of Cultural Dissonance.* Boston: Beacon Press.
Bartels, Francis Lodowic (1965). *The Roots of Ghana Methodism.* Cambridge: Cambridge University Press.
Bascom, William (1960). *The Yoruba of Southwestern Nigeria.* New York: Holt, Rinehart, and Winston.
_____ (1969). *Ifá Divination.* Bloomington: Indiana University Press.
_____ (1980). *Sixteen Cowries: Yoruba Divination from Africa to the New World.* Bloomington: Indiana University Press.
Basso, Ellen (1985). *A Musical View of the Universe: Kalapolo Myth and Ritual Performances.* Philadelphia: University of Pennsylvania Press.
Basso, Keith (1970). To Give Up on Words: Silence in Western Apache Culture. *Southwestern Journal of Anthropology* 26:213–230.
Bastide, Roger (1960). *Les Religions Africaines au Brésil.* Paris: Presses Universitaires de France.
_____ (1971). *African Civilizations in the New World.* Peter Green, trans. Geoffrey Parrinder, foreword. New York: Harper & Row.
_____ (1974). *La femme de couleur en Amérique Latine.* Paris: Editions Anthropos.
_____ (1978a). *The African Religions of Brazil: Toward a Sociology of the Interpenetration of Civilizations.* Helen Sebba, trans. Baltimore: Johns Hopkins University Press.
_____ (1978b). *O candomblé da Bahia (Rito Nago).* São Paulo: Companhia Editora Internacional.
Bateson, Gregory (1956). The Message "This is Play". In *Group Processes: Transactions of the Second Conference,* 145–242. Bertram Schaffner, ed. New York: Josiah Macy, Jr., Foundation.
_____ (1972). *Steps to an Ecology of Mind.* New York: Ballantine.
Bateson, Gregory, and M. C. Bateson (1987). *Angels Fear: An Investigation into the Nature and Meaning of the Sacred.* London: Rider.
Bateson, Gregory, and Margaret Mead (1942). *Balinese Character: A Photographic Analysis.* New York: New York Academy of Sciences.
Bauman, Richard (1972). The La Have Island General Store. *Journal of American Folklore* 85:330–343.
_____ (1977). *Verbal Art As Performance.* Rowley, Massachusetts: Newbury House.
_____ (1983). *Let Your Words Be Few: Symbolism of Speaking and Silence among Seventeenth-Century Quakers.* Cambridge: Cambridge University Press.

_____ (1986). *Story, Performance, and Event: Contextual Studies of Oral Narrative.* Cambridge: Cambridge University Press.

_____ (1989). Performance. In *International Encyclopedia of Communications* 3:262–266. Eric Barnouw, ed. Oxford: Oxford University Press.

Bauman, Richard, and Charles Briggs (1990). Poetics and Performance as Critical Perspectives on Language and Social Life. *Annual Review of Anthropology* 19:59–88.

Bauman, Richard, and Joel Sherzer (1975). The Ethnography of Speaking. *Annual Review of Anthropology* 4:95–119.

_____, eds. (1989 [1974]). *Explorations in the Ethnography of Speaking.* 2nd ed. Cambridge: Cambridge University Press.

Beattie, John, and John Middleton, eds. (1969). *Spirit Mediumship and Society in Africa.* London: Routledge & Kegan Paul.

Becken, Hans–Jungen (1975). The Experience of Healing in the Church in Africa. *Contact* (October):7–11.

Beidelman, Thomas O. (1982). *Colonial Evangelism: A Socio-Historical Study of an East African Mission at the Grassroots.* Bloomington: Indiana University Press.

Beier, Ulli, ed. (1966). *The Origin of Life and Death: African Creation Myths.* London: Heinemann.

_____, comp. (1980). *Yoruba Myths.* Cambridge: Cambridge University Press.

Bellah, Robert (1985). *Habits of the Heart.* Berkeley: University of California Press.

Bellman, Beryl L. (1984). *The Language of Secrecy: Symbols and Metaphors in Poro Ritual.* New Brunswick, New Jersey: Rutgers University Press.

Ben-Amos, Dan, ed. (1969). Analytic Categories and Ethnic Genres. *Genre* 2:275–301.

_____ (1972a). The Elusive Audience of Benin Narrators. *Journal of the Folklore Institute* 9:177–184.

_____ (1972b). *Toward a Definition of Folklore in Context.* In *New Perspectives in Folklore.* Américo Paredes and Richard Bauman, eds. Austin: University of Texas Press.

_____ (1975). *Sweet Words: Storytelling Events in Benin.* Philadelphia: Institute for the Study of Human Issues.

_____, ed. (1976). *Folklore Genres.* Austin: University of Texas Press.

Ben-Amos, Dan, and Kenneth Goldstein, eds. (1975). *Folklore: Communication and Performance.* The Hague: Mouton.

Ben-Amos, Paula Girshick (1969). Ekpo Ritual in Avbiama Village. *African Arts* 2(4):8–13, 79.

_____ (1973). Symbolism in Olokun Mud Art. *African Arts* 6(4):28–31.

_____ (1980). *The Art of Benin.* London: Thames and Hudson.

_____ (1986). Artistic Creativity in [the] Benin Kingdom. *African Arts* 19(3):60–63.

_____ (1989). African Visual Arts from a Social Perspective. *African Studies Review* 32(2):1–53.

Ben-Amos, Paula Girshick, and Arnold Rubin, eds. (1983). *The Art of Power: The Power of Art. Studies in Benin Iconography.* Los Angeles: Museum of Culture History.

Bendix, Reinhard (1980). Reflection in Charismatic Leadership. In *Charisma, History and Social Structure,* 17–25. R. Glassman and W. H. Swatos, eds. New York: Greenwood.

Berger, Iris (1976). Rebels or Status Seekers? Women As Spirit Mediums in East Africa. In *Women in Africa: Studies in Social and Economic Change,* 157–182. Nancy J. Hafkin and Edna G. Bay, eds. Stanford: Stanford University Press.

_____ (1981). *Religion and Resistance: East African Kingdoms in the Precolonial Period.* Annales 105. Tervuren: Museé Royal de l' Afrique Centrale.

Berger, Peter (1967). *The Sacred Canopy: Elements of a Sociological Theory of Religion.* New York: Doubleday.

Bernardi, Bernardo (1959). *The Mugwe: A Failing Prophet. A Study of a Religious and Public Dignitary of the Meru of Kenya.* London: Oxford University Press.

Berque, Jacques (1978). *L'intérieur du Maghreb: XVe–XIXe siècle.* Paris: Gallimard.

Bibeau, Gilles et al., eds. (1979). *La médecine traditionnelle au Zaïre*. Ottawa: Centre de Recherches pour le Développement International.

Biebuyck, Daniel (1973). *Lega Culture: Art, Initiation, and Moral Philosophy among a Central African People*. Berkeley: University of California Press.

_____ (1981). *Statuary from the pre-Bembe Hunters: Issues in the Interpretation of Ancestral Figurines*. Tervuren: Musée Royal de l'Afrique Centrale.

_____ (1987). *The Arts of Central Africa: An Annotated Bibliography*. Boston: G. K. Hall.

Bimwenyi, Kweshi O. (1981). Inculturation en Afrique et attitudes des agents de l'évangélisation. Aspects du Catholicisme au Zaïre. Special issue. *Cahiers des Religions Africaines* 14(27–28):49ff.

Birdwhistell, Ray L. (1970). *Kinesics and Context: Essays on Body Motion Communication*. Philadelphia: University of Pennsylvania Press.

Bitek, Okot (1970). *African Religions in Western Scholarship*. Kampala: East African Literature Bureau.

_____ (1971). *Religion of the Central Luo*. Nairobi: East African Literature Bureau.

Bittremieux, Leo (1936). *La société secrète des Bakhimba au Mayombe*. Brussels: Institut Royal Colonial Belge.

Blackman, Aylward M. (1992). *Gods, Priests, and Men: Studies in the Religion of Pharaonic Egypt*. Alan B. Lloyd, comp. and ed. London: Kegan Paul International.

Black Star Line (1980). *Rasta: Emperor Haile Selassie and the Rastafarians*. Port of Africa, Trinidad: Black Star Line.

Blakely, Pamela A. R. (1992). Performing Dangerous Thoughts: Women's Song-Dance Performance Events in a Hêmbá Funeral Ritual (Zaïre). Ph.D. dissertation, Folklore Institute, Indiana University, Bloomington.

Blakely, Pamela A. R., and Thomas D. Blakely (1979). *Working Toward Self-Sustaining Increases in Small Farmer Maize Production and Real Income: Case Studies of Selected North Shaba Project Farmers' Centers*. Kinshasa: Development Alternatives and U.S.A.I.D.–Zaïre.

_____ (1992). Review of *Becoming a Woman in Okrika* [video], by Judith Gleason and Elisa Mereghetti. *American Anthropologist* 94(4):1022–1024.

Blakely, Thomas D. (1983). To Gaze or Not to Gaze. In *Case Studies in the Ethnography of Speaking*, 234–248. Richard Bauman and Joel Sherzer, eds. Austin, Texas: Southwest Educational Development Laboratory.

_____ (forthcoming). *Hêmbá Visual Communication and Space*. Lanham, Maryland: University Press of America.

Blakely, Thomas D., and Pamela A. R. Blakely (1987). Só'ó Masks and Hêmbá Funerary Festival. *African Arts* 21(1):30–37, 84–86.

_____ (1989). *Directory of Visual Anthropology*. Washington, D.C.: American Anthropological Association.

_____ (forthcoming). Performance Processes in Hêmbá Music. In *Garland Encyclopedia of World Music. Volume 2. Africa*. Ruth M. Stone, ed. New York: Garland.

Blakely, Thomas D., and Eliot Elisofon (1974). *African Carving: A Dogon Kanaga Mask* [film]. Cambridge: Harvard Film Study Center; New York: Phoenix Films.

Blakely, Thomas D., and Adam Kendon, eds. (1986). *Approaches to Gesture*. Special issue. *Semiotica* 62(1–2).

Bledsoe, Caroline (1980). Stratification and Sande Politics. Marie J. Adams, ed. Special issue. *Ethnologische Zeitschrift Zürich* 1:143–149.

_____ (1984). The Political Use of Sande Ideology and Symbolism. *American Anthropologist* 11(3):455–472.

Bloch, Maurice, ed. (1975). *Political Language and Oratory in Traditional Society*. London: Academic Press.

Bloomberg, Charles (1990). *Christian Nationalism and the Rise of the Afrikaner Broederbond in South Africa, 1918–48*. Saul Dubow, ed. London: Macmillan.

Blyden, Edward Wilmot (1908). *African Life and Customs*. London: C. H. Phillips.
_____ (1967 [1887]). *Christianity, Islam, and the Negro Race*. Edinburgh: Edinburgh University Press.
Boddy, Janice (1989). *Wombs and Alien Spirits: Women, Men, and the Zar Cult in Northern Sudan*. Madison: University of Wisconsin Press.
Boelaert, Edmond (1934). Nsong'a Lianja. Het groote epos der Nkundo-Mongo. *Congo* 1(1):49–70; 1(2):197–215.
_____ (1949). *Nsong'a Lianja: L'épopée nationale des Nkundo*. Antwerp: de Sikkel.
_____ (1962). La procession de Lianja. *Aequatoria* 25:1–9.
Bohannan, Paul, and Laura Bohannan (1969). *A Source Notebook on Tiv Religion*. New Haven: Human Relations Area Files.
Bond, George, Walton Johnson, and Sheila S. Walker, eds. (1979). *African Christianity: Patterns of Religious Continuity*. New York: Academic Press.
Book of Mormon (1981 [1830]). Salt Lake City: Church of Jesus Christ of Latter-day Saints.
Boone, Sylvia Ardyn (1986). *Radiance from the Waters: Ideals of Feminine Beauty in Mende Art*. New Haven: Yale University Press.
Borker, Ruth A., and Daniel N. Maltz (1989). Anthropological Perspectives on Gender and Language. In *Gender and Anthropology: Critical Reviews for Research and Teaching*, 411–437. Sandra Morgen, ed. Washington, D.C.: American Anthropological Association.
Bottingnole, S. (1984). *Kikuyu Traditional Culture and Christianity*. Nairobi: Heinemann.
Bourdieu, Pierre (1979). Symbolic Power. *Critique of Anthropology* 4(13–14):77–85.
Bourdillon, M. F. C., ed. (1980). *Sacrifice*. London: Academic Press.
Bowen, Elenore Smith [Laura Bohannan] (1954). *Return to Laughter*. New York: Doubleday.
Bradbury, R. E. (1969). *Benin Studies*. London: Longmans.
Brain, J. B. (1983). *Christian Indians in Natal, 1860–1911: An Historical and Statistical Study*. Cape Town: Oxford University Press.
Brandon, George (1993). *Santeria from Africa to the New World: The Dead Sell Memories*. Bloomington: Indiana University Press.
Bravmann, René (1983). *African Islam*. Washington, D.C.: Smithsonian Institution Press.
Breasted, James Henry (1972 [1959]). *Development of Religion and Thought in Ancient Egypt*. John A. Wilson, intro. Philadelphia: University of Pennsylvania Press.
Brelvi, Mahmud (1964). *Islam in Africa*. Lahore: Institute of Islamic Culture.
Brenner, Louis (1984). *West African Sufi: The Religious Heritage and Spiritual Quest of Cerno Bokar Saalif Taal*. Berkeley: University of California Press.
Briggs, Charles L. (1988). *Competence in Performance: The Creativity of Tradition in Mexicano Verbal Art*. Philadelphia: University of Pennsylvania Press.
_____ (1992). "Since I Am a Woman, I Will Chastise My Relatives": Gender, Reported Speech, and the (Re)production of Social Relations in Warao Ritual Wailing. *American Ethnologist* 19(2):337–361.
Bruner, E. M. (1986). Experience and Its Expressions. In *The Anthropology of Experience*, 3–32. V. W. Turner and E. M. Bruner, eds. Chicago: University of Illinois Press.
Buakasa, Gérard (1968). Notes sur le kindoki chez les Kongo. *Cahiers des Religions Africaines* [Kinshasa] 2(3):153–169.
Buana Kibongi, R. (1969). Priesthood. In *Biblical Revelation and African Beliefs*, 47–56. Kwesi A. Dickson and Paul Ellingworth, eds. London: Lutterworth.
Bucher, Hubert (1980). *Spirits and Power: An Analysis of Shona Cosmology*. London: Oxford University Press.
Buckley, Thomas, and Alma Gottlieb, eds. (1988). *Blood Magic: The Anthropology of Menstruation*. Berkeley: University of California Press.
Buhrman, Vera, and J. Nqaba Gqomfa (1981–82). The Xhosa Healers of Southern Africa. *Journal of Analytical Psychology* 26:187–201, 297–312; 27:41–57, 163–173.
Bureau, Renté (1985). Un mythe gabonais. In *Violence et vérité: Autour de René Girard*, 19–34. Paul Dumouchel, ed. Paris: Bernard Grasset.

Burton, Richard F. (1864). *A Mission to Gelele, King of Dahome*. 2 vols. 3rd ed. London: Tinsley Brothers.

Butler, A. J. (1884). *The Ancient Coptic Churches of Egypt*. Oxford: Oxford University Press.

Butt-Thompson, F. W. (1929). *West African Secret Societies: Their Organizations, Officials, and Teaching*. London: H. P. and G. Witherby.

Buxton, Jean C. (1973). *Religion and Healing in Mandari*. London: Oxford University Press.

Cahiers des Réligions Africaines (1967–). Kinshasa: Université Nationale du Zaïre.

Cairncross, John (1974). *After Polygamy Was Made a Sin*. London: Routledge & Kegan Paul.

Calame-Griaule, M. (1965). *Ethnologie et langage: La parole chez les Dogon*. Paris: Gallimard.

Campbell, Horace (1987). *Rasta and Resistance: From Marcus Garvey to Walter Rodney*. Trenton, New Jersey: Africa World Press.

Campo, Juan E. (1991). *The Other Sides of Paradise: Explorations into the Religious Meaning of Domestic Space in Islam*. Columbia: University of South Carolina Press.

Canadian Journal of African Studies (1984). Special issue on Zaïre. 18:5–161.

Caraman, Philip (1985). *The Lost Empire: The Story of the Jesuits in Ethiopia, 1555-1634*. Notre Dame, Indiana: University of Notre Dame.

Carlier, Jeannie (1974). Science divine et raison humaine. In *Divination et Rationalité*. J. P. Vernant et al., eds. Paris: Seuil.

Carneiro, Edison (1948). *Candomblés da Bahia*. Desenhos de Paulo Flores, transcrições musicais de Marshall Levins. 2nd ed. Bahia: Publicações do Museu do Estado.

_____ (1981a). *Negros bantos*. 2nd ed. Rio de Janeiro. Civilização Brasileira.

_____ (1981b). *Religões negras*. 2nd ed. Rio de Janeiro: Civilização Brasileira.

Castro, Ieda Pessoa de (1976). De l'intégrations des apports africaines dans les parlers de Bahia au Brésil. Ph.D. dissertation, Université National du Zaïre, Lubumbashi.

Catholic Periodical and Literature Index. (1930–). Bimonthly.

Cavazzi da Montecuccolo, G. A. (1965). *Descriçao histórica dos tres reinos do Congo, Matamba e Angola*. Vol. 2. G. Maria de Leguzzano, trans. and annotator. Lisbon: Junta de Investigações do Ultramar.

Chakanza, Joseph (1985). Provisional Annotated Chronological List of Witch-finding Movements in Malawi, 1850–1980. *Journal of Religion in Africa* 5(3):227–243.

Chavannes, Barry (c1978) *Social Origins of the Rastafari Movement*. Kingston, Jamaica: Institute of Social and Economic Research.

Christensen, Thomas G. (1984). The Gbaya Naming of Jesus: An Inquiry into the Contextualization of Soteriological Themes among the Gbaya of Cameroon. Ph.D. dissertation, Lutheran School of Theology, Chicago.

_____ (1990). *An African Tree of Life*. Maryknoll, New York: Orbis.

Christian Periodical Index: A Selected List. (1956–). Semiannual.

Chum, Haji, and H. E. Lambert (1962). *Utenzi wa vita viya Uhud [The Epic of the Battle of Uhud]*. Dar es Salaam: East African Literature Bureau.

Claerhout, A. (1984). *Ancient Terracotta Statuary and Pottery from Djenne, Mali*. Antwerp: Dessers.

Clarke, Peter Bernard (1982). *West Africa and Islam: A Study of Religious Development from the 8th to the 20th Century*. London: Edward Arnold.

_____ (1986). *West Africa and Christianity*. London: Edward Arnold.

Clawson, Rudger (1908). *Conference Report*. The Church of Jesus Christ of Latter-day Saints. (October):74.

Clifford, James (1983). On Ethnographic Authority. *Representations* 1:118–146.

Clifford, James, and George Marcus, eds. (1986). *Writing Culture: The Poetics and Politics of Ethnography*. Berkeley: University of California Press.

Cochrane, James R. (1987). *Servants of Power: The Role of English–Speaking Churches in South Africa, 1903-1930*. Johannesburg: Ravan.

Cole, Herbert M. (1982). *Mbari: Art and Life among the Owerri Igbo*. Bloomington: Indiana University Press.

Collier, John R., Jr., and Malcolm Collier (1986). *Visual Anthropology: Photography as a Research Method*. 2nd ed. Albuquerque: University of New Mexico Press.

Collins, Robert O., and Peter Duignan (1963). *Americans in Africa: A Preliminary Guide to American Missionary Archives and Library Manuscript Collections on Africa*. Stanford: Hoover Institution on War, Revolution, and Peace.

Comaroff, Jean (1991). Missionaries and Mechanical Clocks: An Essay on Religion and History in South Africa. *Journal of Religion* 71(1):1–17.

Comaroff, Jean, and John L. Comaroff (1991). *Of Revelation and Revolution: Volume 1. Christianity, Colonialism, and Consciousness in South Africa*. Chicago: University of Chicago Press.

Comité ya Jamaa (1975). *Mafundisho ya Eklezya Katolika. Jamaa Takatifu*. Lubumbashi. Mimeographed brochure.

Cone, James H. (1979). A Black American Perspective on the Future of African Theology. In *African Theology en Route*, 176–186. Kofi Appiah-Kubi and Sergio Torres, eds. New York: Orbis.

Conklin, Harold C. (1962). Lexicographic Treatment of Folk Taxonomies. In *Problems in Lexicography*. Fred W. Householder and Sol Saporta, eds. *International Journal of American Linguistics* 18(2, pt. 4):119–141.

Conquergood, Dwight (1991). Rethinking Ethnography: Towards a Critical Cultural Politics. *Communication Monographs* 58(2):179–194.

Constantin, François (1987). *Les voies de l'Islam en Afrique orientale*. Paris: Karthala.

Constantinides, Pamela (1979). Women's Spirit Possession and Urban Adaptation in the Muslim Northern Sudan. In *Women United, Women Divided: Comparative Studies of Ten Contemporary Cultures*, 185–205. Patricia Caplan and Janet M. Bujra, eds. Bloomington: Indiana University Press.

Cooley, John K. (1965). *Baal, Christ, and Mohammed: Religion and Revolution in North Africa*. New York: Holt, Rinehart & Winston.

Corin, Ellen (1979). Possession Psychotherapy in an Urban Setting: Zebola in Kinshasa. *Social Science and Medicine* 13(4B):327–338.

Cory, Hans (1936). Ngoma ya sheitani. *Journal of the Royal Anthropological Society* 66:209–217.

_____ (1955). The Buswezi. *American Anthropologist* 57:923–952.

Cosentino, Donald (1987). Who Is That Fellow in the Many-Colored Cap? Transformations of Eshu in Old and New World Mythologies. *Journal of American Folklore* 100:261–275.

Costa Lima, Vivaldo (1967). O conçeito de naçao dos candomblés da Bahia. *Afro-Asia*.

_____ (1977). A familia-de-santo nos candomblés jeje-nagos da Bahia: Um estudo de relaçoes intra-grupais. Salvador, Bahia: Tese de mestrado em ciéncias humanae, Universidade Federal da Bahia.

Crawford, J. R. (1967). *Witchcraft and Sorcery in Rhodesia*. London: Oxford University Press for the International African Institute.

Crowley, Daniel J. (1984). *African Myth and Black Reality in Bahian Carnaval*. Los Angeles: UCLA Museum of Cultural History.

Cruise O'Brien, Donal B. (1971). *The Mourides of Senegal: The Political and Economic Organization of an Islamic Brotherhood*. Oxford: Clarendon Press.

Cruise O'Brien, Donal B., and Christian Coulon (1988). *Charisma and Brotherhood in African Islam*. Oxford: Clarendon Press.

Cuoq, Joseph (1984). *Histoire de l'islamisation de l'Afrique de l'Ouest: des origines à la fin du XVIe siècle*. Paris: Geuthner.

_____ (1986). *Islamisation de la nubie chrétienne: VIIe–XVIe siècle*. Paris: Geuthner.

Curtin, Philip D. (1984). *Cross-Cultural Trade in World History*. New York: Cambridge University Press.

Cuvelier, Jean (1953). *Relations sur le Congo du Père Laurent de Lucques (1700–1717)*. Brussels: Institut Royal Colonial Belge.

Dachs, Anthony J., and W. F. Rea (1979). *The Catholic Church and Zimbabwe, 1879–1979.* Gwelo, Zimbabwe: Mambo Press.

Daftary, Farhad (1990). *The Isma'ilis.* New York: Cambridge University Press.

Daneel, Martinus L. (1970a). *The God of the Matopo Hills: An Essay on the Mwari Cult in Rhodesia.* The Hague: Mouton.

_____ (1970b). *Zionism and Faith-Healing in Rhodesia.* The Hague: Mouton.

_____ (1971). *Old and New in Southern Shona Independent Churches. Volume 1.* The Hague: Mouton.

d'Aquili, Eugène G., C. D. Laughlin, Jr., and J. McManus (1979). *The Spectrum of Ritual.* New York: Columbia University Press.

David, A. Rosalie (1982). *The Ancient Egyptians.* London: Routledge & Kegan Paul.

David, Nicholas (1982). Tazunu: Megalithic Monuments of Central Africa. *Azania* 17:43–77.

Davidson, Basil (1985). *Africa: The History of a Continent.* London: Macmillan.

Davies, W. V., ed. (1991). *Egypt and Africa: Nubia from Prehistory to Islam.* London: British Museum Press in association with the Egypt Exploration Society.

Davis, Asa J. (1967). The Orthodoxy of the Ethiopian Church. *Tarikh* 2(1):62–69.

Davis, Gerald L. (1985) *I Got the Word in Me and I Can Sing It You Know: A Study of the Performed African-American Sermon.* Philadelphia: University of Pennsylvania Press.

Davis, Whitney (1984). Representation and Knowledge in the Prehistoric Rock Art of Africa. *African Archaeological Review* 2:7–35.

Davis-Roberts, Christopher (1981). Kutambua Ugonjwa: Concepts of Illness and Transformation among the Tabwa of Zaïre. *Social Science and Medicine* 15B(3):309–316.

d'Azevedo, Warren L. (1966). *The Artist Archetype in Gola Culture.* Reprint no. 14. Reno: Desert Research Institute, University of Nevada.

_____ (1973). Mask Makers and Myth in Western Liberia. In *Primitive Art and Society,* 126–150. Anthony Forge, ed. London: Oxford University Press.

_____ (1980). Gola Poro and Sande: Primal Tasks in Social Custodianship. Marie J. Adams, ed. Special issue. *Ethnologische Zeitschrift Zürich* 1:13–34.

_____ (1989 [1973]). *The Traditional Artist in African Society.* Bloomington: Indiana University Press.

De Craemer, Willy (1977). *The Jamaa and the Church.* Oxford: Clarendon.

De Craemer, Willy, Jan Vansina, and René Fox (1976). Religious Movements in Central Africa: A Theoretical Study. *Comparative Studies in Society and History* 18:458–475.

.De Gruchy, John W. (1979). *The Church Struggle in South Africa.* Grand Rapids, Michigan: W. B. Eerdmans Publishing Company.

De Heusch, Luc (1970). Pour une approche structuraliste de la pensé magico–religieuse bantoue. In *Mélanges offerts à Claude Lévi–Strauss,* 801–818. Jean Pouillon and Pierre Maranda, eds. The Hague: Mouton.

_____ (1971). *Pourquoi l'épouser?* Paris: Gallimard. [English edition 1981 *Why Marry Her?* Cambridge: Cambridge University Press.]

_____ (1972). *Le roi ivre ou l'origine de l'Etat.* Paris: Gallimard. [English edition 1982 The Drunken King or the Origin of the State. Bloomington: Indiana University Press.]

_____ (1980). Heat, Physiology, and Cosmogony: Rites of Passage among the Thonga. In *Explorations in African Systems of Thought,* 27–43. Ivan Karp and Charles S. Bird, eds. Bloomington: Indiana University Press.

_____ (1982). *Rois nés d'un coeur de vache.* Paris: Gallimard.

_____ (1985). *Sacrifice in Africa: A Structuralist Approach.* Bloomington: Indiana University Press.

Deluz, Ariane (1987). Social and Symbolic Values of Feminine Knε Initiation among the Guro of the Ivory Coast. In *Tranformations of African Marriage,* 113–135. David Parkins and David Nyamwaya, eds. Manchester: Manchester University Press.

De Maret, Pierre (1978). Chronologie de l'Age du Fer dans la dépression de l'Upemba en République du Zaïre. Ph.D. dissertation, Brussels Free University.

_____ (1980). Preliminary Report on 1980 Fieldwork in the Grassfields and Yaounde, Cameroon. *Nyame Akuma* 17:10–12.

_____ (1985a). *Fouilles archéologiques dans la vallée du Haut–Lualaba, Zaïre: II. Sanga et Katongo 1974.* Tervuren: Annales du Musée Royal de l'Afrique Centrale.

_____ (1985b). The Smith's Myth and the Origin of Leadership in Central Africa. In *African Iron Working Ancient and Traditional,* 73–87. Randi Haaland and Peter Shinnie, eds. Bergen: Norwegian University Press.

_____ (1986). The Ngovo Group: An Industry with Polished Stone Tools and Pottery in Lower Zaïre. *African Archaeological Review* 4:103–133.

Deng, Francis Mading (1978). *Africans of Two Worlds: The Dinka in Afro-Arab Sudan.* New Haven: Yale University Press.

_____ (1980). *Dinka Cosmology.* London: Ithaca Press.

De Rosny, E. (1986). Mallah et Marie-Lumière, guérisseurs africaines. *Etudes* 364(4): 473–488.

Deshen, Schlomo A. (1989). *The Mellah Society: Jewish Community Life in Sherifian Morocco.* Chicago: University of Chicago Press.

Desroche, H., and P. Raymaekers (1946). Départ d'un prophète, Arrivée d'une église. *Archives de Sciences Sociales des Religions* 42:117–162.

Devisch, Renaat (1975a). Authority in the Yaka Diviner's Oracle. *Bijdragen Tot di Dierkunde* 39:270–288.

_____ (1975b). Towards a Semantic Study of Divination: Trance and Initiation of the Yaka Diviner as a Basis for His Authority. *Bijdragen Tot di Dierkunde* 39:173–189.

_____ (1985). Perspectives on Divination in Contemporary Sub-Saharan Africa. In *Theoretical Explorations in African Religion.* Wim van Binsbergen and Matthew Schoffeleers, eds. London: Kegan Paul International.

Devisch, Renaat, and Wauthier de Mahieu (1979). *Mort, deuil et compensations mortuaires chez les Komo et les Yaka du nord au Zaïre.* Tervuren: Musée Royal de l'Afrique Centrale.

Dickson, Kwesi A. (1984). *Theology in Africa.* Maryknoll, New York: Orbis.

Dieterlen, Germaine (1966). Les fresques d'époque bovidienne du Tassili n'Ajjer et les traditions des Peul. *Journal de la Société des Africanistes* 36:141–157.

Dillon-Malone, Clive Mary (1978). *The Korsten Basketmakers: A Study of the Masowe Apostles, an Indigenous African Religious Movement.* Atlantic Highlands, New Jersey: Humanities Press.

_____ (1983). The "Mutumwa" Churches of Zambia: An Indigenous African Religious Healing Movement. *Journal of Religion in Africa* 14(3):204–222.

DjeDje, Jacqueline Cogdell, ed. (1989, 1992). *African Musicology: Current Trends. Festschrift Presented to J. H. Kwabena Nketia.* 2 vols. [William G. Carter, assoc. ed., Vol.1.] Los Angeles and Atlanta: Crossroads Press/African Studies Association.

Doctrine and Covenants (1981). Salt Lake City: Church of Jesus Christ of Latter-day Saints.

Dodds, Eric R. (1970). *Pagan and Christian in an Age of Anxiety.* New York: W. W. Norton.

Domowitz, Susan, and Renzo Mandirola (1984). Grave Monuments in Ivory Coast. *African Arts* 17(4):46–52, 96.

Douglas, Mary (1966). *Purity and Danger.* London: Routledge & Kegan Paul.

_____ (1973). *Natural Symbols: Explorations in Cosmology.* New York: Pantheon.

_____ (1978). *Implicit Meanings.* London: Routledge & Kegan Paul.

Doutreloux, Albert (1967). *L'ombre des fétiches.* Louvain, Belgium: Nauwelaerts.

Doxey, Roy W., comp. (1978). *Latter-day Prophets and the Doctrine and Covenants.* Vol. 4. Salt Lake City: Deseret Book.

Drewal, Henry John, and Margaret Thompson Drewal (1983). *Gèlèdè: Art and Female Power among the Yoruba.* Bloomington: Indiana University Press.

Drewal, Margaret Thompson (1986). Art and Trance among Yoruba Shango Devotees. *African Arts* 20(1):60–67, 98–99.

_____, ed. (1988). Special issue on Africa. *TDR, The Drama Review: A Journal of Performance Studies* 32(2).

_____ (1991). The State of Research on Performance in Africa. *African Studies Review* 34(3):1–64.

_____ (1992). *Yoruba Ritual: Performers, Play, Agency.* [Linked with *Yoruba Ritual: A Companion Video* (VHS).] Bloomington: Indiana University Press.

Drewal, Margaret Thompson, and Henry John Drewal (1983). An Ifá Diviner's Shrine in Ijebuland. *African Arts* 16(2):60–67, 99–100.

Dumézil, Georges (1949). *L'héritage indo-européen à Rome.* Paris: Gallimard.

Dumouchel, Paul, ed. (1985). *Violence et vérité: Autour de René Girard.* Paris: B. Grasset.

Durkheim, Emile (1947). *Elementary Forms of Religious Life.* George Simpson, trans. New York: Free Press.

Du Toit, Brian M. (1974). *People of the Valley; Life in an Isolated Afrikaner Community in South Africa.* Cape Town: A. A. Balkema.

Dvornik, Francis (1970). *Byzantine Missions among the Slavs: SS. Constantine-Cyril and Methodius.* New Brunswick, New Jersey: Rutgers University Press.

EJCSK [Eglise du Jésus Christ sur la terre par le prophète Simon Kimbangu] (n.d.). *Nsadulu ye ntwadusulu ya dibundu dia Kimbanguisme.* Privately printed.

Eibl-Eibesfelt, Irenäus (1972). Similarities and Differences between Cultures in Expressive Movement. In *Nonverbal Communication.* R. A. Hinde, ed. Cambridge: Cambridge University Press.

Eickelman, Dale F. (1976). *Moroccan Islam.* Austin: University of Texas Press.

Ekechi, Felix K. (1972). *Missionary Enterprise and Rivalry in Igboland, 1857–1914.* London: Frank Cass.

_____ (1976). African Polygamy and Western Christian Ethnocentrism. *Journal of African Studies* 3:329–350.

Ekman, Paul, and H. Oster (1979). Facial Expression of Emotion. *Annual Review of Psychology* 30:527–554.

Eliade, Mircea (1969). *The Quest: History and Meaning in Religion.* Chicago: University of Chicago Press.

_____, ed. (1987). *The Encyclopedia of Religion.* 16 vols. New York: Macmillan.

El-Shamy, Hasan (1979). *Folktales of Egypt: Translated and Edited with Middle Eastern and African Parallels.* Chicago: University of Chicago Press.

El Zein, Abdul Hamid M. (1974). *The Sacred Meadows: A Structural Analysis of Religious Symbolism in an East African Town.* Evanston: Northwestern University Press.

Engel, Lothar (1976). *Kolonialismus und Nationalismus in Deutschen Protestantismus in Namibia 1907 bis 1945.* Frankfurt. Peter Lang.

England, Frank, and Torquil Paterson (1989). *Bounty in Bondage: The Anglican Church in Southern Africa.* Johannesburg: Ravan.

Eschlimann, Jean-Paul (1985). *Les Agni devant la mort (Côte d'Ivoire).* Paris: Editions Karthala.

Etherington, Norman (1978). *Preachers, Peasants and Politics in Southeast Africa, 1835–1880: African Christian Communities in Natal, Pondoland, and Zululand.* London: Royal Historical Society.

Etuk, U. (1984). Render unto Caesar the Things Which Are Caesar's. *African Theological Journal* 13(2):83–91.

Eusebius (1984 [1965]). *History of the Church.* New York: Penguin.

Evans-Pritchard, E. E. (1937). *Witchcraft, Oracles, and Magic among the Azande.* Oxford: Clarendon.

_____ (1956). *Nuer Religion.* London: Oxford University Press.

_____ (1958). *The Divine Kingship of Shilluk of the Nilotic Sudan.* Cambridge: Cambridge University Press.

_____ (1965). *Theories of Primitive Religion.* London: Oxford University Press.

Fabian, Johannes (1969). Charisma and Cultural Change: The Case of the Jamaa Movement in Katanga. *Comparative Studies in Society and History* 11:155–173.

_____ (1971). *Jamaa: A Charismatic Movement in Katanga.* Evanston, Illinois: Northwestern University Press.

_____ (1978). Popular Culture in Africa: Findings and Conjectures. *Africa* 48:315–334.

_____ (1979a). The Anthropology of Religious Movements: From Explanation to Interpretation. *Social Research* 46(1):4–35.

_____ (1979b). Man and Woman in the Teachings of the Jamaa Movement. In *The New Religions of Africa,* 169–183. Bennetta Jules-Rosette, ed. Norwood, New Jersey: Ablex.

_____ (1979c). Rule and Process: Thoughts on Ethnography as Communication. *Philosophy of the Social Sciences* 9:1–26.

_____ (1979d). Text as Terror: Second Thoughts on Charisma. In *Beyond Charisma: Religious Movements as Discourse.* Johannes Fabian, ed. Special issue. *Social Research* 46:166–203.

_____ (1981). Six Theses Regarding the Anthropology of African Religious Movements. *Religion* 11:109–126.

_____ (1983). *Time and the Other.* New York: Columbia University Press.

_____ (1985). Religious Pluralism: An Ethnographic Approach. In *Theoretical Explorations in African Religion,* 138–163. Wim van Binsbergen and Matthew Schoffeleers, eds. London: Kegan Paul International.

_____ (1986). *Language and Colonial Power: The Appropriation of Swahili in the Former Belgian Congo, 1880–1938.* Cambridge: Cambridge University Press.

_____ (1990). *Power and Performance: Ethnographic Explorations through Proverbial Wisdom and Theater in Shaba.* Madison: University of Wisconsin Press.

_____ (1991). *Time and Work on Anthropology.* Philadelphia: Harwood.

Fagan, Brian, David Phillipson, and S. Daniels (1969). *Iron Age Cultures in Zambia. Volume 2.* London: Chatto and Windus.

Fagg, William B., and John Pemberton III (1982). *Yoruba: Sculpture of West Africa.* New York: Knopf.

Falk, Nancy Auer, ed. (1980). *Unspoken Worlds: Women's Religious Lives in Non-Western Cultures.* San Francisco: Harper & Row.

Falola, Toyin, and Biodun Adediran (1983). *Islam and Christianity in West Africa.* Ilé-Ifè: University of Ifè Press.

Fardon, Richard (1991). *Between God, the Dead, and the Wild: Chamba Interpretations of Religion and Ritual.* Washington, D.C.: Smithsonian Institution Press.

Fashole-Luke, Edward, Richard Gray, Adrian Hastings, and Godwin Tasie, eds. (1978). *Christianity in Independent Africa.* Bloomington: Indiana University Press.

Feld, Steve (1982). *Sound and Sentiment: Birds, Weeping, Poetics, and Song in Kaluli Expression.* Philadelphia: University of Pennsylvania Press.

Fernandez, James W. (1964). The Idea and Symbol of the Saviour in a Gabon Syncretistic Cult: Basic Factors in the Mythology of Messianism. *International Review of Missions* 35:281–289.

_____ (1965). Politics and Prophecy: African Religious Movements. *Practical Anthropology* 12:71–75.

_____ (1982). *Bwiti: An Ethnography of the Religious Imagination in Africa.* Renate Lellep Fernandez, illus. Princeton: Princeton University Press.

_____ (1986). *Persuasions and Performances: The Play of Tropes in Culture.* Bloomington: Indiana University Press.

Fernea, Elizabeth Warnock, and Robert A. Fernea, with Aleya Rouchdy (1991). *Nubian Ethnographies.* Prospect Heights, Illinois: Waveland Press.

Fetter, Bruce (1976). *The Creation of Elisabethville 1910–1940.* Stanford: Hoover Institution Press.

Finn, Thomas M. (1992). *Early Christian Baptism and the Catechumenate: Italy, North Africa, and Egypt.* Collegeville, Minnesota: Liturgical Press.

Finnegan, Ruth H. (1965). *Survey of the Limba People of Northern Sierra Leone.* London: H.M.S.O. Great Britain. Department of Technical Cooperation.

_____ (1967). *Limba Stories and Storytelling.* London: Oxford University Press.

_____ (1970). *Oral Literature in Africa.* London: Oxford University Press.

_____ (1977). *Oral Poetry.* Cambridge: Cambridge University Press.

_____ (1981). "Short Time To Stay": Comments on Time, Literature and Oral Performance. Twelfth Annual Hans Wolff Memorial Lecture. Bloomington: African Studies Program, Indiana University.

Fisher, Allan, and Humphrey J. Fisher (1970). *Slavery and Muslim Society in Africa.* London: C. Hurst.

Fisher, Humphery J. (1973). Conversion Reconsidered: Some Historical Aspects of Religious Conversion in Black Africa. *Africa* 43(1):27–39.

Forde, Daryll, ed. (1963). *African Worlds: Studies in the Cosmological Ideas and Social Values of African Peoples.* London: Oxford University Press.

Forsythe, Dennis (1983). *Rastafari: For the Healing of the Nation.* Kingston: Zaika Publications.

Fortes, Meyer (1983 [1953]). *Oedipus and Job in West African Religion.* Jack Goody, new intro. Robin Horton, essay. Cambridge: Cambridge University Press.

_____ (1987). *Religion, Morality, and the Person: The Essays on Tallensi Religion.* New York: Cambridge University Press.

Fortes, Meyer, and Germaine Dieterlen, eds. (1965). *African Systems of Thought.* London: Oxford University Press for the International African Institute.

Frake, Charles O. (1964). How to Ask for a Drink in Subanun. In *The Ethnography of Communication.* John Gumperz and Dell Hymes, eds. Special issue. *American Anthropologist* 66(6, pt. 2):127–132.

Frankenberg, Ronald, and Joyce Leeson (1976). Disease, Illness, and Sickness: Social Aspects of the Choice of a Healer in a Lusaka Suburb. In *Social Anthropology and Medicine,* 223–258. J. B. Loudon, ed. London: Academic Press.

Freedman, Jim (1984). *Nyabingi: The Social History of an African Divinity.* Annales, Série-in-80, Sciences humaines 115. Tervuren: Musée Royal de l'Afrique Centrale.

French, Tom, comp. and ed. (1992). *The SCOLMA Directory of Libraries and Special Collections on Africa in the United Kingdom and in Europe.* 5th ed. Oxford: Hans Zell.

Frend, W. H. C. (1984). *The Rise of Christianity.* Philadelphia: Fortress Press.

Fry, Peter (1976). *Spirits of Protest: Spirit Mediums and the Articulation of Consensus amongst the Zezuru of Southern Rhodesia.* Cambridge: Cambridge University Press.

Fūdī, ʿAbdallāh B. (1963). *Tazyīn al–Waraqāt.* Mervyn Hiskett, ed. and trans. Ibadan: Ibadan University Press.

Fyle, C. Magbaily (1979). *The Solima Yalunka Kingdom. Precolonial Politics, Economics, and Society.* Freetown: Nyakon Publishers.

Gabriel, Manuel Nunes (1979). *Angola: cinco séculos de Cristianismo.* Queluz, Portugal: Literal.

Gabrieli, Francesco (1991). *Magreb médiéval: l'apogée de la civilisation islamique dans l'Occident arabe, XIIIe–XVI siècle.* M. Pozzoli, trad. Aix-en-Provence: Edisud.

Gal, Susan (1991). Between Speech and Silence: The Problematics of Research on Language and Gender. In *Gender at the Crossroads of Knowledge: Feminist Anthropology in the Postmodern Era,* 175–203. Micaela di Leonardo, ed. Berkeley: University of California.

Garlake, Peter (1977). *Great Zimbabwe.* London: Thames and Hudson.

_____ (1978). *The Kingdoms of Africa.* Oxford: Elsevier-Phaidon.

Gbadamosi, T. G. O. (1978). *The Growth of Islam among the Yoruba, 1841–1908.* London: Longman.

Geertz, Clifford (1966). Religion as a Cultural System. In *Anthropological Approaches to the Study of Religion,* 1–46. Michael Banton, ed. London: Tavistock.

_____ (1973). *The Interpretation of Cultures.* New York: Basic Books.

_____ (1984). *Local Knowledge.* New York: Basic Books.

_____ (1986). Making Experiences, Authoring Selves. In *The Anthropology of Experience,* 373–380. Chicago: University of Illinois Press.

Gelfand, Michael (1964). *Witch Doctor: Traditional Medicine Man of Rhodesia*. London: Harvill Press.

Gerard, Albert S. (1981). *African Language Literatures*. Washington, D.C.: Three Continents Press.

Gibb, Hamilton A. R. (1974 [1963]). *Arabic Literature: An Introduction*. 2nd ed. London: Oxford University Press.

Gibbs, James L., Jr. (1965). The Kpelle of Liberia. In *Peoples of Africa*, 197–240. James L. Gibbs, Jr., ed. New York: Holt, Rinehart, and Winston.

Gifford, Paul (1990). Prosperity: A New and Foreign Element in African Christianity. *Religion* 20(4):373–388.

_____(1993). *Christianity and Politics in Doe's Liberia*. New York: Cambridge University Press.

Gillies, Eva (1976). Causal Criteria in African Classifications of Disease. In *Social Anthropology and Medicine*. Joseph B. Loudon, ed. London: Academic Press.

Girard, R. (1972). *La violence et le Sacré*. Paris: Grasset.

_____ (1982). *Le bouc émissaire*. Paris: Grasset.

Glassman, Ronald (1975). Legitimacy and Manufactured Charisma. *Social Research* 4(Winter):615–636.

Glaze, Anita J. (1981). *Art and Death in a Senufo Village*. Bloomington: Indiana University Press.

Gluckman, Max (1965). *Politics, Law, and Ritual in Tribal Society*. Oxford: Blackwell.

Goddard, Burton L., ed. (1967). *The Encyclopedia of Modern Christian Missions: The Agencies*. Camden, New Jersey: T. Nelson.

Godlewski, Wodzimierz, ed. (1990). *Coptic Studies*. Warsaw: PWN–Polish Scientific Editions.

Goff, Beatrice (1979). *Symbols of Ancient Egypt in the Late Period: The 21st Dynasty*. Religion and Society 13. The Hague: Mouton.

Goffman, Erving (1974). *Frame Analysis: An Essay on the Organization of Experience*. New York: Harper Colophon.

Goldberg, Harvey E. (1990). *Jewish Life in Muslim Libya: Rivals and Relatives*. Chicago: University of Chicago Press.

Golde, Peggy (1986 [1970]). *Women in the Field: Anthropological Experiences*. 2nd ed. Berkeley: University of California Press.

Gomez, Michael (1992). *Pragmatism in the Age of Jihad: The Precolonial State of Bundu*. New York: Cambridge University Press.

Gomm, Roger (1975). Bargaining from Weakness: Spirit Possession on the South Kenya Coast. *Man* n.s. 10(2):530–543.

González-Wippler, Migene (1982). *The Santeria Experience*. Englewood Cliffs, New Jersey: Prentice-Hall.

Goodman, Felicity D. (1988). *How about Demons? Possession and Exorcism in the Modern World*. Bloomington: Indiana University Press.

Goodwin, Charles (1981). *Conversational Organization: Interaction between Speakers and Hearers*. New York: Academic Press.

Goodwin, Charles, and Marjorie Harness Goodwin (1990). Interstitial Argument. In *Conflict Talk*, 85–117. Allen D. Grimshaw, ed. Cambridge: Cambridge University Press.

Goodwin, Charles, and John Heritage (1990). Conversation Analysis. *Annual Review of Anthropology* 19:283–307.

Goodwin, Marjorie Harness (1990). *He–Said–She–Said: Talk as Social Organization among Black Children*. Bloomington: Indiana University Press.

Goody, Jack (1962). *Death, Property, and the Ancestors. A Study of the Mortuary Customs of the Ladagaa of West Africa*. Stanford: Stanford University Press.

_____ (1977). *The Domestication of the Savage Mind*. Cambridge: Cambridge University Press.

Gossen, Gary (1974). *Chamulas in the World of the Sun: Time and Space in Maya Oral Tradition*. Cambridge: Harvard University Press.

Gottlieb, Alma (1992). *Under the Kapok Tree: Identity and Difference in Beng Thought.* Bloomington: Indiana University Press.

Graves, Robert (1955). *Greek Mythology.* 2 vols. New York: Penguin.

Gray, John (1960). *Early Portuguese Missionaries in East Africa.* London: Macmillan.

_____ , comp. (1989). *Ashe: Traditional Religion and Healing in Sub-Saharan Africa and the Diaspora. A Classified International Bibliography.* New York: Greenwood.

Gray, Richard (1990). *Black Christians and White Missionaries.* New Haven: Yale University.

Gray, Robert F. (1963). *The Sonjo of Tanganyika.* London: Oxford University Press.

_____ (1965). Some Parallels in Sonjo and Christian Mythology. In *African Systems of Thought,* 49–61. Meyer Fortes and Germaine Dieterlen, eds. London: Oxford University Press.

Greenberg, Joseph Harold (1946). *The Influence of Islam on a Sudanese Religion.* New York: J. J. Augustin.

_____ (1966). *The Languages of Africa.* Bloomington: Indiana University Press.

Greenfield, Liah (1985). Reflections on Two Charismas. *British Journal of Sociology* 36(1):117–132.

Greenwald, Anthony G., and D. L. Ronis (1978). Twenty Years of Cognitive Dissonance: Case Study of the Evolution of a Theory. *Psychological Review* 85(1):53–57.

Greindl, Léopold (1975). Notes sur les sources des missionaires d'Afrique (Pères Blancs) pour l'est du Zaïre. *Etudes d'Histoire Africaine* [Lubumbashi] 7:175–202.

Griaule, Marcel (1934). Rites relatifs aux peintures rupestres dans le Soudan français. *Comtes Rendus des Séances de la Société de Biogéographie* 95:65–68.

_____ (1938). *Masques Dogons.* Paris: Institut d'Ethnologie.

_____ (1948). *Dieu d'eau: Entretiens avec Ogotemmeli.* Paris: Edition du Chêne.

_____ (1965). *Conversations with Ogotemmeli: An Introduction to Dogon Religious Ideas.* New York: Oxford University Press for the International African Institute.

Griaule, Marcel, and Germaine, Dieterlen (1965). *Le renard pâle.* Paris: Institut d'Ethnologie.

Groves, Charles Pelham (1948–1958). *The Planting of Christianity in Africa.* 4 vols. London: Lutterworth.

Guillaume, Alfred (1962 [1956]). *Islam.* 2nd ed. New York: Penguin.

Gumperz, John, and Dell Hymes, eds. (1964). *The Ethnography of Communication.* Special issue. *American Anthropologist* 66(6, pt. 2).

_____ (1972). *Directions in Sociolinguistics: The Ethnography of Communication.* New York: Holt, Rinehart, and Winston.

Guthrie, Malcolm (1967–1971). *Comparative Bantu: An Introduction to the Comparative Linguistics and Prehistory of the Bantu Languages.* 4 vols. Westmead, England: Gregg International Publishers.

Haafkens, Johannes (1983). *Les chants musulmans en Peul.* Leiden: E. J. Brill.

Hackett, Rosalind I. J. (1987). *New Religious Movements in Nigeria.* Lewiston, New York: Edwin Mellen.

_____ (1988). *Religion in Calabar: The Religious Life and History of a Nigerian Town.* Berlin: Mouton de Gruyter.

Haliburton, Gordon Mackay (1973). *The Prophet Harris: A Study of an African Prophet and His Mass-Movement in the Ivory Coast and the Gold Coast, 1913–1915.* New York: Oxford University Press.

Hall, Edward T. (1959). *The Silent Language.* New York: Doubleday.

_____ (1966). *The Hidden Dimension.* New York: Doubleday.

_____ (1974). *Handbook for Proxemic Research.* Washington, D.C.: Society for the Anthropology of Visual Communication/American Anthropological Association.

Hallencreutz, Carl F., and Ambrose M. Moyo, eds. (1988). *Church and State in Zimbabwe.* Vol. 3 of *Christianity South of the Zambesi.* Gwelo, Zimbabwe: Mambo Press.

Hallencreutz, Carl F., and Mai Palmberg, eds. (1991). *Religion and Politics in Southern Africa.* Uppsala: Scandinavian Institute of African Studies.

Hammel, E. A., ed. (1965). *Formal Semantic Analysis*. Special Issue. *American Anthropologist* 67(5, pt. 2).

Hammoudi, Abdellah (1988). *La victime et ses masques: essai sur le sacrifice et la mascarade au Maghreb*. Paris: Editions du Seuil.

Hansen, Holger Bernt (1984). *Mission, Church, and State in a Colonial Setting: Uganda, 1890–1925*. London: Heinemann.

Harley, George W. (1970a [1941]). *Native African Medicine*. London: Frank Cass.

_____ (1970b [1941]). Notes on the Poro in Liberia. Cambridge, Massachusetts: *Papers of the Peabody Museum of American Archaeology and Ethnology* 19(2).

Harmon, Nolan B., ed. (1974). *The Encyclopedia of World Methodism*. 2 vols. Nashville, Tennessee: United Methodist Publication House.

Harris, Grace Gredys (1978). *Casting Out Anger: Religion among the Taita of Kenya*. Prospect Heights, Illinois: Waveland Press.

Harris, William Thomas, and Harry Sawyerr (1968). *The Springs of Mende Belief and Conduct: A Discussion of the Influence of the Belief in the Supernatural among the Mende*. Freetown: Sierra Leone University Press.

Harrison, Christopher (1988). *France and Islam in West Africa*. New York: Cambridge University Press.

Harrow, Kenneth W., ed. (1991). *Faces of Islam in African Literature*. Portsmouth, New Hampshire: Heinemann; London: James Currey.

Hart, W. A. (1989). Woodcarving of the Limba of Sierra Leone. *African Arts* 23(1):44–53, 103.

Hastings, Adrian (1976). *African Christianity*. New York: Chapman.

_____ (1979). *A History of African Christianity 1950–1975*. Cambridge: Cambridge University Press.

_____ (1989). *African Catholicism: Essays in Discovery*. Philadelphia: Trinity Press.

Haule, Cosmas (1969). *Bantu Witchcraft and Christian Morality*. Schoeneck-Beckenried, Switzerland: Nouvelle Revue de Science Missionaire.

Healy, Joseph (1981). *A Fifth Gospel: In Search of Black Christian Values*. New York: Orbis.

Heath, Shirley Brice (1983). *Ways with Words*. Cambridge: Cambridge University Press.

Henige, David P. (1980). *Catholic Missionary Journals Relating to Africa: A Provisional Checklist and Union List for North America*. Los Angeles: Crossroads Press.

Herskovits, Melville J. (1958a). *Dahomean Narrative*. Evanston, Illinois: Northwestern University Press.

_____ (1958b). *The Myth of the Negro Past*. Boston: Beacon Press.

_____ (1966). *The New World Negro: Selected Papers in Afro-American Studies*. Frances Herskovits, ed. Bloomington: Indiana University Press.

Heuger, Frederick J., Jr. (1988). *A Guide to Foreign Missionary Manuscripts in the Presbyterian Historical Society*. New York: Greenwood.

Hewitt, Gordon (1971). *The Problems of Success: A History of the Church Missionary Society, 1910–1942*. London: SCM Press.

Hexham, Irving (1981). *The Irony of Apartheid: The Struggle for National Independence of Afrikaner Calvinism against British Imperialism*. Lewiston, New York: Edwin Mellen.

_____, ed. (1987). *Texts on Zulu Religion: Traditional Zulu Ideas about God*. Lewiston, New York: Edwin Mellen.

Hickey, Raymond (1981). *A History of the Catholic Church in Northern Nigeria*. Jos: Augustinian Publications Nigeria.

Hiernaux, Jean, Emma Maquet, and Jos De Buyst (1972). Le cimetière protohistorique de Katoto (vallée du Lualaba). In *Sixième Congrès Panafricain de Préhistoire, Dakar 1967*, 148–158. Henri Hugot, ed. Chambéry: Les Imprimeries Réunies.

Hiskett, Mervyn (1962). An Islamic Tradition of Reform in the Western Sudan from the Sixteenth to the Eighteenth Century. *Bulletin of the School of Oriental and African Studies* 25(3):577–596.

_____, ed. and trans. (1963). *Tazyīn al–Waraqāt*. By ʿAbdallāh B. Fūdī. Ibadan: Ibadan University Press.

_____ (1973). *The Sword of Truth: The Life and Times of Shehu Usuman Dan Fodio.* New York: Oxford University Press.

_____ (1975). *A History of Hausa Islamic Verse.* London: School of Oriental and African Studies.

_____ (1984). *The Development of Islam in West Africa.* New York: Longman.

Hobsbawm, Eric, and Terence O. Ranger, eds. (1983). *The Invention of Tradition.* Cambridge: Cambridge University Press.

Hoch-Smith, Judith, and Anita Spring (1978). *Women in Ritual and Symbolic Roles.* New York: Plenum.

Hodder, Ian (1986). *Reading the Past: Current Approaches to Interpretation in Archeology.* Cambridge: Cambridge University Press.

Hodgson, Janet (1982). *The God of the Xhosa: A Study of the Origins and Development of the Traditional Concepts of the Supreme Being.* Cape Town: Oxford University Press.

Hofmeyr, J. W., and K. E. Cross, eds. (1986). *History of the Church in Southern Africa: A Select Bibliography of Published Material to 1980.* Pretoria: University of South Africa.

Hofmeyr, Jan H., and Gerhardis C. Oosthuizen (1981). *Religion in a South African Indian Community.* Durban: I. S. E. R., University of Durban-Westville.

Hollis, M., and S. Lukes, eds. (1982). *Rationality and Relativism.* London: Oxford University Press.

Holsoe, Svend (1980). Notes on the Vai Sande Society in Liberia. *Ethnologische Zeitschrift Zürich* 1:97–111.

Holy Bible. King James Version.

Holy, Ladislav (1985). Fire, Meat, and Children: The Berti Myth, Male Dominance, and Female Power. In *Reason and Morality,* 180–199. Joanna Overing, ed. London: Tavistock.

_____ (1991). *Religion and Custom in a Muslim Society: The Berti of Sudan.* New York: Cambridge University Press.

Hope, Marjorie, and James Young (1981). *The South African Churches in a Revolutionary Situation.* Maryknoll, New York: Orbis.

Horton, Mark (1987). The Swahili Corridor. *Scientific American* 257:86–88.

Horton, Robin (1963). The Kalabari Ekine Society. *Africa* 33:94–114

_____ (1967). African Traditional Thought and Western Science. *Africa* 37(1):50–71, 155–187.

_____ (1971). African Conversion. *Africa* 41(2):85–108.

_____ (1975a). On the Rationality of Conversion. Part I. *Africa* 45(3):219–235.

_____ (1975b). On the Rationality of Conversion. Part II. *Africa* 45(4):373–399.

_____ (1993). *Patterns of Thought in Africa and the West: Magic, Religion, and Science.* New York: Cambridge University Press.

Hountondji, Paulin J. (1983). *African Philosophy: Myth and Reality.* Bloomington: Indiana University Press.

Howard, H. N. (1916). The Primitive Mind and Natural World. *African Advance* 1(2).

_____ (1918). Foot-lights on Dark Pathways. *African Advance* 2(2).

Hughes, Martin (1948). *Christian Foundations.* London.

Hunwick, John (1985). *Sharīʿa in Songhay: The Replies of al–Maghīlī to the Questions of Askia al–Ḥājj Muhammad.* London: Oxford University Press.

_____, ed. (1992). *Religion and National Integration in Africa: Islam, Christianity and Politics in Sudan and Nigeria.* Evanston, Illinois: Northwestern University Press.

Hussein, Ebrahim N. (1970). *Kinjeketile.* [Swahili and English versions.] Dar es Salaam: Oxford University Press.

Hymes, Dell (1962). The Ethnography of Speaking. In *Anthropology and Human Behavior,* 13–53. Thomas Gladwin and William C. Sturtevant, eds. Washington, D.C.: Anthropological Society of Washington.

_____ (1964). Introduction: Toward Ethnographies of Communication. In *The Ethnography of Communication.* John Gumperz and Dell Hymes, eds. Special issue. *American Anthropologist* 66(6, pt.2):1–34.

_____ (1967). Models of the Interaction of Language and Social Setting. In *Problems of Bilingualism*. John Macnamara, ed. Special issue. *Journal of Social Issues* 23(2): 8–28.

_____ (1974). *Foundations in Sociolinguistics: An Ethnographic Approach*. Philadelphia: University of Pennsylvania Press.

_____ (1975). Breakthrough into Performance. In *Folklore: Communication and Performance*, 11–74. Dan Ben-Amos and Kenneth S. Goldstein, eds. The Hague: Mouton.

I.A.M.S. (1985). *Christian Mission and Human Transformation*. Special issue. *International Association for Mission Studies* 2(1).

Ìdòwú, E. Bọ́lájí (1962). *Olódùmarè: God in Yoruba Belief*. London: Longmans.

_____ (1973). *African Traditional Religion: A Definition*. London: SCM Press.

Iliffe, John (1967). The Organization of the Maji Maji Rebellion. *Journal of African History* 8(3):495–512.

_____ (1979). *A Modern History of Tanganyika*. Cambridge: Cambridge University Press.

Imperato, Pascal J. (1977). *African Folk Medicine: Practices and Beliefs of the Bambara and Other Peoples*. Baltimore: York Press.

Index Islamicus, 1665–1905 (1989). Wolfgang Behn, comp. Millersville, Pennsylvania: Adiyok.

Index Islamicus, 1905–1955 (1972 [1958]). J. D. Pearson and Julia F. Ashton, comps. [School of Oriental and African Studies, University of London]. London: Mansell.

Innes, Gordon (1974). *Sunjata: Three Mandinka Versions*. London: School of Oriental and African Studies.

Inongo, Sakombi (1973). L'authenticité à Dakar. *Cultures au Zaïre et en Afrique* [Kinshasa] 1:216.

International African Bibliography (1971–). Quarterly. Oxford: Hans Zell. [SOAS, London. Continuation of bibliography in journal *Africa*, 1929–1970.]

International Bibliography of the History of Religions (1952–1973). Leiden: E. J. Brill.

Isichei, Elizabeth, ed. (1982). *Varieties of Christian Experience in Nigeria*. London: Macmillan.

Jackson, Michael (1989). *Paths toward a Clearing: Radical Empiricism and Ethnographic Inquiry*. Bloomington: Indiana University Press.

Jackson, Samuel Macaubey, ed. (1977). *The New Schaff–Herzog Encyclopedia of Religious Knowledge*. 13 vols. Grand Rapids, Michigan: Baker.

Jacobson-Widding, Anita (1987). *Notions of Heat and Fever among the Manyika of Zimbabwe*. Working Papers in African Studies 34. Uppsala: University of Uppsala.

Jacobson-Widding, Anita, and Walter E.A. van Beek (1990). The Creative Communion. In *African Folk Models of Fertility and the Regeneration of Life*. Uppsala: Acta Universitatis Upsaliensis.

Jakobson, Roman (1960). Concluding Statement: Linguistics and Poetics. In *Style in Language*, 350–377. Thomas A. Sebeok, ed. Cambridge: MIT Press.

James, Wendy, and Douglas H. Johnson, eds. (1988). *Vernacular Christianity: Essays in the Social Anthropology of Religion*. Presented to Godfrey Lienhardt. Oxford: JASO.

James, William (1902). *Varieties of Religious Experience*. New York: Longmans.

Jan Mohamed, Abdul R. (1983). *Manichean Aesthetics*. Amherst: University of Massachusetts Press.

Janzen, John M. (1969). Vers une phénoménologie de la guérison en Afrique centrale. *Etudes Congolaises* 12(2):97–115.

_____ (1974). *An Anthology of Kongo Religion: Primary Texts from Lower Zaïre*. Lawrence: University of Kansas.

_____ (1977). The Tradition of Renewal in Kongo Religion. In *African Religions: A Symposium*, 69–114. Newell Booth, ed. New York: NOK Publications.

_____ (1978). *The Quest for Therapy in Lower Zaïre*. Berkeley: University of California Press.

_____ (1979a). Deep Thought: Structure and Intention in Kongo Prophetism, 1910–1921. In *Beyond Charisma: Religious Movements as Discourse*. Johannes Fabian, ed. Special issue. *Social Research* 46(1):106–139.

_____ (1979b). Ideologies and Institutions in the Precolonial History of Equatorial African Therapeutic Systems. *Social Science and Medicine* 13(B):317–326.

_____ (1982). *Lemba 1650–1930: A Drum of Affliction in Africa and the New World*. New York: Garland.

_____ (1983). Towards a Historical Perspective on African Medicine and Health. In *Ethnomedicine and Medical History*, 99–138. J. Sterly and F. Lichtenthaeler, eds. Berlin: Verlag Mensch u. Leben.

_____ (1987). African Cults of Affliction. In *The Encyclopedia of Religion* 1:55–59. Mircea Eliade, ed. New York: Macmillan.

_____ (1988). Health, Religion, and Medicine in Central and Southern African Traditions. In *Caring and Curing: Health and Medicine in the World's Religious Traditions*, 223–254. L. Sullivan, ed. New York: Macmillan.

_____ (1992). *Ngoma: Discourses of Healing in Central and Southern Africa*. Berkeley: University of California Press.

Janzen, John M., and Wyatt MacGaffey (1974). *An Anthology of Kongo Religion*. Lawrence: University of Kansas Press.

Jedrej, M. C. (1976). Structural Aspects of a West African Secret Society. *Journal of Anthropological Research* 32:234–245.

_____ (1980). Structural Aspects of a West African Secret Society. Marie J. Adams, ed. Special Issue. *Ethnologische Zeitschrift Zürich* 1:97–111.

Jedrej, M. C., and Rosalind Shaw, eds. (1992). *Dreaming, Religion, and Society in Africa*. Studies on Religion in Africa 7. Leiden: E. J. Brill.

Johnson, G. Wesley, ed. (1985). *Double Impact: France and Africa in the Age of Imperialism*. Westport, Connecticut: Greenwood.

Johnson, G. Wesley, and Martin A. Klein (1972). *Perspectives on the African Past*. Boston: Little, Brown.

Johnson, John William, and Fa-Digi Sisòkò (1992). *The Epic of Son-Jara: A West African Tradition*. Bloomington: Indiana University Press.

Johnson, Marian A. (forthcoming). Golden Art of the Wolof and the Toucouleur in Senegal. *African Arts* 27.

Jones, J. (1985). *Jezus Christus, bonoeman? Katechetisch Centrum Paramaribo, Surinam*. Mimeograph.

Journal of Religion in Africa/Religion en Afrique. (1967–). Leiden: E. J. Brill.

JTAF [Jamaa Takatifu mu Afrika] (1984). *Katekismu ya kanisa la Jamaa Takatifu mu Afrika*. Lubumbashi. Mimeographed brochure.

_____ (1984–85). *Mupango wa kila kazi katika kanisa letu la Jamaa Takatifu mu Afrika*. Lubumbashi. Mimeographed brochure.

Jules-Rosette, Bennetta (1975). *African Apostles: Ritual and Conversion in the Church of John Maranke*. Ithaca, New York: Cornell University Press.

_____, ed. (1979). *The New Religions of Africa: Priests and Priestesses in Contemporary Cults and Churches*. Norwood, New Jersey: Ablex.

_____ (1988). Prophetic Performances: Apostolic Prophecy As Social Drama. *Drama Review* 32(2):140–159.

Kabanga, Eugène (n.d.). *Directives pastorales aux groupes de prière du renouveau dans l'Esprit. Maongozi ya askofu kwa makundi ya sala*. Lubumbashi. Printed brochures.

Kabasele, F., J. Dore, and R. Luneau, eds. (1986). *Chemins de la Christologie africaine*. Bruges, Belgium: Desclée.

Kagabo, Jose Hamim (1988). *L'Islam et les "Swahili" au Rwanda*. Paris: Editions de l'Ecole des Hautes Etudes en Sciences Sociales.

Kaggwa, Apolo (1971). *Basekaka be Buganda* [*The Kings of Buganda*]. Nairobi: East African Publishing House.

Kalu, O. U., ed. (1980). *The History of Christianity in West Africa*. London: Longman.

Kankwatira, Exon (1975). Bwanali and the Problem of Evil. Seminar paper HB/2483/75. Department of Human Behaviour, University of Malawi.

Kapferer, Bruce (1986). Performance and the Structuring of Meaning and Experience. In *The Anthropology of Experience*, 188–206. Victor W. Turner and Edward M. Bruner, eds. Chicago: Illinois University Press.

Kaplan, Steven (1984). *The Monastic Holy Man and the Christianization of Early Solomonic Ethiopia*. Wiesbaden: F. Steiner.

Karp, Ivan (1988). Laughter at Marriage: Subversion in Performance. *Journal of Folklore Research* 25(1–2):35–52.

_____ (1990). Power and Capacity in Iteso Rituals of Possession. In *Personhood and Agency: The Experience of Self and Other in African Cultures,* 79–93. Michael Jackson and Ivan Karp, eds. Washington, D.C.: Smithsonian Institution Press.

Karp, Ivan, and Charles S. Bird (1980). *Explorations in African Systems of Thought*. Bloomington: Indiana University Press.

Karp, Ivan, and Patricia Karp (1979). Living with the Spirits of the Dead. In *African Therapeutic Systems*. Dennis M. Warren, et al., eds. Boston: Crossroads Press.

Kasozi, Abdu B. K. (1981). The Impact of Islam on Ganda Culture. *Journal of Religion in Africa* 12(1):127–135.

_____ (1986). *The Spread of Islam in Uganda*. Nairobi: Oxford University Press.

Katjavivi, Peter et al., eds. (1989). *Church and Liberation in Namibia*. London: Pluto Press.

Katz, Richard, and Megan Biesele (1986). !Kung Healing: The Symbolism of Sex Roles and Culture Change. In *The Past and Future of !Kung Ethnography,* 195–230. Megan Biesele, ed. Hamburg: Helmut Buske Verlag.

Kearney, Richard (1985). Le mythe chez Girard: Un nouveau bouc émissaire. In *Violence et vérité: Autour de René Girard,* 35–49. P. Dumouchel, ed. Paris: B. Grasset.

Keenan, Elinor Ochs (1973). A Sliding Sense of Obligatoriness: The Poly-Structure of Malagasy Oratory. *Language in Society* 2:225–243.

_____ (1974). Norm-Makers, Norm-Breakers: Uses of Speech by Men and Women in a Malagasy Community. In *Explorations of the Ethnography of Speaking,* 125–143. Richard Bauman and Joel Sherzer, eds. Cambridge University Press.

Kendon, Adam (1980). Gesticulation and Speech: Two Aspects of the Process of Utterance. In *The Relationship of Verbal and Non-Verbal Communication*, 207–227. Mary Ritchie Key, ed. The Hague: Mouton.

_____, ed. (1981). *Nonverbal Communication, Interaction, and Gesture*. The Hague: Mouton.

_____ (1988). *Sign Languages of Aboriginal Australia*. Cambridge: Cambridge University Press.

Keniston, Kenneth (1965). *The Uncommitted: Alienated Youth in American Society*. New York: Harcourt Brace and World.

Kennedy, John G. (1967). Nubian Zar Ceremonies as Psychotherapy. *Human Organization* 26(4):185–194.

_____, ed. (1978). *Nubian Ceremonial Life: Studies in Islamic Syncretism and Cultural Change*. Berkeley: University of California Press.

Keruyn, E. (1912). Les missions catholique du Congo belge. *La Revue Congolaise* 2(3): 286–299.

Kessler, David (1982). *The Falashas: The Forgotten Jews of Ethiopia*. Boston: Allen & Unwin.

Key, Mary Ritchie (1975). *Paralanguage and Kinesics*. Metuchen, New Jersey: Scarecrow.

_____ (1977). *Nonverbal Communication. A Research Guide and Bibliography*. Metuchen, New Jersey: Scarecrow.

Kiernan, J. P. (1976). Prophet and Preacher: An Essential Partnership in the Work of Zion. *Man* n.s. 11(3):356–366.

Kilson, Marion (1971). *Kpele Lala: Ga Religious Songs and Symbols*. Cambridge: Harvard University Press.

_____ (1972). Ambivalence and Power: Mediums in Ga Traditional Religion. *Journal of Religion in Africa* 4(3):171–177.

_____ (1976). Women in Traditional African Religions. *Journal of Religion in Africa* 8(2):133–143.

Kimpianga kia Mahaniah (1975). The Background of Prophetic Moments in the Belgian Congo. Ph.D. dissertation. Department of History, Temple University.

King, Noel Quinton (1973). *Islam and the Confluence of Religions in Uganda, 1840–1966*. Tallahassee, Florida: American Academy of Religion.

_____ (1986). *African Cosmos: An Introduction to Religion in Africa*. Belmont, California: Wadsworth Publishing Company.

Kirby, Jon P., trans. (1981). *Jesus of the Deep Forest*. Accra: Asempa Publishers.

_____ (1985). The Non-Conversion of the Anufo of Northern Ghana. *Mission Studies* 2(2):15–21.

_____ (1986). *God, Shrines, and Problem-Solving among the Anufo of Northern Ghana*. Berlin: D. Reimer.

Kitzinger, Sheila (1966). The Rastafarian Brethren in Jamaica. *Comparative Studies in Society and History* 9(1):33–39.

_____ (1969). Protest and Mysticism: The Rastafari Cult of Jamaica. *Journal of the Scientific Study of Religion* 3(2):240–262.

Knappert, Jan (1967). *Traditional Swahili Poetry: An Investigation into the Concepts of East African Islam as Reflected in the Utenzi Literature*. Leiden: E. J. Brill.

_____ (1971). *Swahili Islamic Poetry*. Leiden: E. J. Brill.

Knight, W. (1880). *The Missionary Secretariat of Henry Venn*. London: Longman, Green.

Kohlberg, Louis (1971). From Is to Ought: How to Commit the Naturalistic Fallacy and Get Away with It in the Study of Moral Development. In *Cognitive Development and Epistemology*. Theodore Mischell, ed. London: Academic Press.

Kolié, C. (1986). Jésus guérisseur. In *Chemins de la Christologie africaine*, 167–199. F. Kabasele, J. Dore, and R. Luneau et al., eds. Bruges, Belgium: Desclée.

Kopytoff, Igor (1964). Classifications of Religious Movements: Analytical and Synthetic. *Symposium on New Approaches to the Study of Religion*, 77–90. June Helm, ed. Washington, D.C.: American Ethnological Society.

_____ (1980). Revitalization and the Genesis of Cults in Pragmatic Religion: The Kita Rite of Passage among the Suku. In *Explorations in African Systems of Thought*, 183–212. Ivan Karp and Charles Bird, eds. Bloomington: Indiana University Press.

_____, ed. (1987). *The African Frontier: The Reproduction of Traditional African Societies*. Bloomington: Indiana University Press.

Kosmin, Barry Alexander (1981). *Majuta: A History of the Jewish Community of Zimbabwe*. Gwelo, Zimbabwe: Mambo Press.

Kratz, Corinne (1990). Persuasive Suggestions and Reassuring Promises: Emergent Parallelism and Dialogic Encouragement in Song. *Journal of American Folklore* 103(407):42–67.

_____ (1993). *Affecting Performance: Meaning, Movement, and Experience in Okiek Women's Initiation*. Washington, D.C.: Smithsonian Institution Press.

Kretzschmar, Louise (1986). *The Voice of Black Theology in South Africa*. Johannesburg: Ravan.

Kritzeck, James, and William H. Lewis, eds. (1969). *Islam in Africa*. New York: Van Nostrand-Reinhold Co.

Kubik, Gerhard (1987). *Nyau: Maskenbunde im südlichen Malawi*. Unter mitarbeit von Moya Aliya Malamusi. Vienna: Verlag der Österreichischen Akademie der Wissenschaften.

La Fontaine, J. S. (1985). *Initiation: Ritual Drama and Secret Knowledge across the World*. Harmondsworth, England: Penguin.

Lagerwerf, Leny, ed. (1985). Witchcraft, Sorcery, and Spirit Possession: Pastoral Responses in Africa. *Exchange* 14(41).

Lambek, Michael (1981). *Human Spirits: A Cultural Account of Trance in Mayotte.* Cambridge: Cambridge University Press.

Lamp, Frederick (1985). Cosmos, Cosmetics, and the Spirit of Bondo. *African Arts* 18(3):28–43, 98–99.

Lan, David (1985). *Guns and Rain: Guerrillas and Spirit Mediums in Zimbabwe.* Maurice Bloch, preface. London: James Currey; Berkeley: University of California Press.

Landes, Ruth (1947). *The City of Women.* New York: Macmillan.

———— (1986 [1970]). A Woman Anthropologist in Brazil. In *Women in the Field: Anthropological Experiences,* 119–139. 2nd ed. Peggy Golde, ed. Berkeley: University of California Press.

Lanternari, Vittorio (1963). *The Religions of the Oppressed: A Study of Modern Messianic Cults.* New York: Knopf.

Lapidus, Ira. (1988). *A History of Islamic Societies.* New York: Cambridge University Press.

Latourette, Kenneth Scott (1937–1945). *A History of the Expansion of Christianity.* 7 vols. New York: Harper & Brothers.

———— (1975). *A History of Christianity. Volume 1.* 2nd ed. New York: Harper & Row.

Launay, Robert (1992). *Beyond the Stream: Islam and Society in a West African Town.* Berkeley: University of California Press.

Lawal, Babatunde (1970). Yoruba Sango Sculpture in Historical Retrospect. Ph.D. dissertation, Department of Fine Arts, Indiana University.

———— (1977). The Living Dead: Art and Immortality among the Yoruba of Nigeria. *Africa* 47(1):50–61.

Lawson, E. Thomas (1984). *Religions of Africa: Traditions in Transformation.* San Francisco: Harper & Row.

Leach, Edmund R. (1954). *Political Systems of Highland Burma.* London: London School of Economics.

———— (1969). *Dialectic in Practical Religion.* Cambridge: Cambridge University Press.

Lee, Barbara Makeda (1981). *Rastafari: The New Creation.* Kingston: Media Productions.

Lee, Richard B. (1979). *The !Kung San: Men, Women, and Work in a Foraging Society.* Cambridge: Harvard University Press.

Lee, Richard B., and Irvin DeVore, eds. (1976). *Kalahari Hunter-Gatherers.* Cambridge: Harvard University Press.

Legesse, Asmarom (1973). *Gada: Three Approaches to the Study of African Society.* New York: Free Press.

Lepine, Claude (1981). Os Estereotipos da Personalidade no Candomblé Nago. In *Oloorisa: Escritos Sobre a Religião dos Orixas.* Carlos Eugénio Marcondes de Moura, ed. São Paulo: Agora.

Le renouveau: Une chance pour l'église africaine (1986). Actes du 1er congrès des dirigeants du renouveau charismatique catholique d'Afrique francophone. Kinshasa, 4–9 octobre 1985. Kinshasa: Editions du Comité Diocésain du Renouveau.

Leroi-Gourhan, André (1964). *Les religions de la préhistoire.* Paris: Presses Universitaires de France.

Lévi-Strauss, Claude (1958). *Anthropologie structurale.* Paris: Plon.

———— (1962). *La pensée sauvage.* Paris: Plon.

———— (1975). Histoire d'une structure. In *Explorations in the Anthropology of Religion,* 74, 71–79. Walter E.A. Van Beek and J. H. Scherer, eds. Leiden: VKI.

Levtzion, Nehemia (1968). *Muslims and Chiefs in West Africa.* Oxford: Clarendon.

Lewis, Herbert S. (1970). Wealth, Influence, and Prestige among the Shoa Galla. In *Social Stratification in Africa,* 163–186. Arthur Tuden and Leonard Plotnicov, eds. New York: Free Press.

Lewis, Ian M. (1966). Spirit Possession and Deprivation Cults. *Man* n.s. 1:307–329.

_____ (1971). *Ecstatic Religion: An Anthropological Study of Spirit Possession and Shamanism.* Harmondsworth, England: Penguin.

_____, ed. (1980). *Islam in Tropical Africa.* London: Oxford University Press.

_____ (1983). The Past and Present in Islam: The Case of African "Survivals". *Temenos: Studies in Comparative Religion* [Helsinki] 19:55–67.

_____ (1986). *Religion in Context, Cults, and Charisma.* Cambridge: Cambridge University Press.

Lewis, James R. (1990). Images of Traditional African Religions in Surveys of World Religions. *Religion* 20(4):311–322.

Lewis-Williams, J. David (1980). Ethnography and Iconography: Aspects of Southern San Thought and Art. *Man* 5:467–482.

_____ (1981). *Believing and Seeing: Symbolic Meanings in Southern San Rock Paintings.* New York: Academic Press.

_____ (1982). The Economic and Social Context of Southern San Rock Art. *Current Anthropology* 23:429–449.

_____ (1986). Seeing and Constructing: A Neurological Constant in San Rock Art. Paper presented at the Conference in Honour of J. D. Clark, The Longest Record: The Human Career in Africa, Berkeley, California. Volume of abstracts: 54–55.

Lhote, Henri (1966). Les peintures pariétales sur la magie et la religion. *Journal de la Société des Africanistes* 36:2–27.

_____ (1967). Gravures rupestres au Tassili n'Ajjer. *Objets et Mondes* 7:217–232.

Lienhardt, Godfrey (1961). *Divinity and Experience: The Religion of the Dinka.* Oxford: Clarendon.

Linares, Olga F. (1992). *Prayer, Power, and Production: The Jola of Casamance, Senegal.* New York: Cambridge University Press.

Lincoln, Bruce (1980). *Priests, Warriors, and Cattle: A Study in the Ecology of Religions.* Berkeley: University of California Press.

Lincoln, Charles Eric (1961). *The Black Muslims in America.* Boston: Beacon Press.

Linden, Ian (1977). *Church and Revolution in Rwanda.* New York: Africana Publishing Co.

_____ (1980). *The Catholic Church and the Struggle for Zimbabwe.* London: Longman.

Linden, Ian, and Jane Linden (1974). *Catholics, Peasants, and Chewa Resistance in Nyasaland, 1889–1939.* Berkeley: University of California Press.

Lindgren, N. E., and J. Matthew Schoffeleers (1978). *Rock Art and Nyau Symbolism in Malawi.* Zomba: Malawi Ministry of Local Government, Department of Antiquities.

Little, Kenneth L. (1965). The Political Function of the Poro. Part I. *Africa* 35(1):349–365.

_____ (1966). The Political Function of the Poro. Part II. *Africa* 36(1):62–71.

Loubser, J. A. (1990). *A Critical Review of Racial Theology in South Africa: The Apartheid Bible.* Lewiston, New York: Edwin Mellen.

Lufuluabo Mizeka (1977). *L'anti-sorcier face à la science.* Mbujimayi, Zaïre: Editions Franciscaines.

Lukanga, Dende (1983). Essai de classification des sectes religieuses de Lubumbashi. Mémoire de licence. Lubumbashi: National University of Zaïre.

Lundwall, N. B. (1966). *Temples of the Most High.* Salt Lake City: Bookcraft.

Lutz, Catherine, and Lila Abu-Lughod (1990). *Language and the Politics of Emotion.* Cambridge: Cambridge University Press.

Luzbetak, Louis J. (1963). *The Church and Culture: An Applied Anthropology for the Religious Worker.* Techny, Illinois: Divine Word Publications.

Ly-Tall, Madina (1991). *Un Islam militant en Afrique de l'ouest au XIXe siècle: la Tijaniyya de Saiku Umar Futiyu.* Paris: L'Harmattan.

MacCormack, Carol P. (1979). Sande: The Public Face of a Secret Society. In *The New Religions of Africa.* Benetta Jules-Rosette, ed. Norwood, New Jersey: Ablex.

Macfarlane, Douglas (1985). The Root of All Evil. In *The Anthropology of Evil.* David Parkin, ed. Oxford: Blackwell.

MacGaffey, Wyatt (1970a). *Custom and Government in the Lower Congo.* Los Angeles: University of California Press.

_____ (1970b). The Religious Commissions of the BaKongo. *Man* n.s. 5(1):27–38.

_____ (1976). Kimbanguism: An African Christianity. *Africa Report* 21(1):40–43.

_____ (1977). Cultural Roots of Kongo Prophetism. *History of Religions* 17(2):177–193.

_____ (1978a). African History: Anthropology and the Rationality of Natives. *History in Africa* 5:101–120.

_____ (1978b). The Physical Idiom of Kongo Art and Ritual. Typescript.

_____ (1980). African Religions: Types and Generalizations. In *Explorations in African Systems of Thought,* 301–328. Ivan Karp and Charles S. Bird, eds. Bloomington: Indiana University Press.

_____ (1982). The Policy of National Integration in Zaïre. *Journal of Modern African Studies* 20(1):87–105.

_____ (1983). *Modern Kongo Prophets: Religion in a Plural Society.* Bloomington: Indiana University Press.

_____ (1986). *Religion and Society in Central Africa: The BaKongo of Lower Zaïre.* Chicago: Chicago University Press.

_____ (1990). Religion, Class, and Social Pluralism in Zaïre. *Canadian Journal of African Studies* 24(2):249–264.

_____ (1991). *Art and Healing of the Bakongo Commented by Themselves: Minkisi from the Laman Collection.* Stockholm: Folkens Museum-Etnografiska; Bloomington: Indiana University Press.

Machuma, Shepherd (1972). Knowledge of the Past Connects Generations. *Umbowo hwe Ukristu* [*Witness of Christianity*] 55(May).

_____ (1972–73). From the Archives. *Umbowo hwe Ukristu* 55(December)–56(May).

MacLean, Una (1971). *Magical Medicine: A Nigerian Case Study.* London: Allan Lane.

MacMillan, Mona (1980). Spiritual Healing in Africa. *Tablet* 12(July): 673–674.

Maier, D. J. E. (1983). *Priests and Power: The Case of the Dente Shrine in Nineteenth-Century Ghana.* Bloomington: Indiana University Press.

Makinde, M. Akin (1988). *African Philosophy, Culture, and Traditional Medicine.* Athens: Center for International Studies, Ohio University.

Malinowski, Bronislaw (1923). The Problem of Meaning in Primitive Languages. In *The Meaning of Meaning,* 451–510. C.K. Ogden and I. A. Richards, eds. London: Kegan Paul.

Maltz, Daniel, and Ruth Borker (1982). A Cultural Approach to Male–Female Miscommunication. In *Language and Social Identity.* John Gumperz, ed. Cambridge: Cambridge University Press.

Malula, Cardinal (1977). Preface. In *L'anti-sorcier face à la science.* Lufuluabo Mizeka. Mbujimayi, Zaïre: Editions Franciscaines.

Mangat, J. S. (1969). *A History of Asians in East Africa.* London: Oxford University Press.

Marcoux, Marcene (1982). *Cursillo: Anatomy of a Movement.* New York: Lambeth.

Marett, R. R. (1909 [1907]). *The Threshold of Religion.* London: Methuen.

Mark, Peter Allen (1985). *A Cultural, Economic and Religious History of the Basse Casamance since 1500.* Stuttgart: F. Steiner.

_____ (1992). *The Wild Bull and the Sacred Forest: Form, Meaning, and Change in Senegambian Initiation Masks of the Diola.* New York: Cambridge University Press.

Marliac, Alain (1981). *Recherches sur les pétroglyphes de Bidzar au Cameroun septentrional.* Chambéry: Editions de L'Orstom.

Marshall, Lorna (1969). The Medicine Dance of the !Kung Bushmen. *Africa* 39:347–381.

Martin, Bradford G. (1976). *Muslim Brotherhoods in Nineteenth Century Africa.* Cambridge: Cambridge University Press.

Martin, David (1978). *The Dilemmas of Contemporary Religion.* New York: St. Martin's Press.

Martin, David, and Peter Mullen, eds. (1984). *Strange Gifts? A Guide to Charismatic Renewal.* Oxford: Basil Blackwell.

Martin, Marie-Louise (1975). *Kimbangu: An African Prophet and His Church*. London: Heffer.

Martin, Phyllis M., and Patrick O'Meara, eds. (1977). *Africa*. Bloomington: Indiana University Press. [1986. 2nd ed. rev.]

Marwick, Max G. (1950). Another Anti-witchcraft Movement in East Central Africa. *Africa* 20:100–112.

Marx, Karl (1962). Alienated Labor. In *Man Alone: Alienation in Modern Society*, 93–104. Eric Josephson, ed. New York: Dell Publishing.

_____ (1971a). *Early Texts*. D. McLellan, ed. London: Oxford University Press.

_____ (1971b). *Marx's Grundisse*. D. McLellan, ed. London: Oxford University Press.

Masden, Douglas, and Peter G. Snow (1983). The Dispersion of Charisma. *Comparative Political Studies* 16(3):337–362.

_____ (1987). Recruitment Contrasts in a Divided Charismatic Movement. *American Political Science Review* 81(1):223–238.

Mason, John P. (1977). *Island of the Blest: Islam in a Libyan Oasis Community*. Athens: Center for International Studies, Ohio University.

Maupoil, Bernard (1943). *La géomancie à l'ancienne Côte des Esclaves*. Travaux et Mémoires de l'Institut d'Ethnologie 42. Paris: Institute d'Ethnologie.

Maurier, Henri (1985). *Philosophie de l'Afrique noire*. St. Augustine: Anthropos.

Mazrui, Ali A. (1986). *The Africans: A Triple Heritage*. Boston: Little, Brown.

Mbiti, John S. (1970). *Concepts of God in Africa*. New York: Praeger.

_____ (1971). *New Testament Eschatology in an African Background*. London: Oxford University Press.

_____ (1972). Some African Concepts of Christology. In *Christ and the Younger Churches*, C. F. Vicedom, ed. London: Willas KMS.

_____ (1975). *The Prayers of African Religion*. Maryknoll, New York: Orbis.

_____ (1990 [1969]). *African Religions and Philosophy*. 2nd ed. Portsmouth, New Hampshire: Heinemann.

_____ (1991). *Introduction to African Religion*. Portsmouth, New Hampshire: Heinemann.

McIlwaine, John (1992). *Africa: A Guide to Reference Material*. Oxford: Hans Zell

McIntosh, Roderick, and Susan McIntosh (1986). Dilettantisme et pillage: trafic illicite d'objets d'art anciens du Mali. *Museum* 149:49–57.

McKenzie, Peter R. (1976). *Inter-Religious Encounters in West Africa: Samuel Ajayi Crowther's Attitude to African Traditional Religion and Islam*. Leicester: Study of Religion Subdepartment, University of Leicester.

McNaughton, Patrick R. (1988). *The Mande Blacksmiths: Knowledge, Power, and Art in West Africa*. Bloomington: Indiana University Press.

Meeker, Michael E. (1989). *The Pastoral Son and the Spirit of Patriarchy: Religion, Society, and Person among East African Stock Keepers*. Madison: University of Wisconsin Press.

Melland, Frank Hulme (1967 [1923]). *In Witchbound Africa: An Account of the Primitive Kaonde Tribe and Their Beliefs*. London: Frank Cass.

Mengrelis, Thanos (1963). Equisse sur l'habitat guerze. *Africa* 23(1):45–53.

Mercier, Paul (1954). The Fon of Dahomey. In *African Worlds*. Daryll Forde, ed. London: Oxford University Press.

Merleau-Ponty, Maurice (1945). *Phénoménologie de la perception*. 7th ed. Paris: Gallimard.

Messi Metogo, E. (1986). La personne du Christ dans l'oeuvre de Mongo Beti. In *Chemins de la Christologie africaine*, 43–68. F. Kabasele et al., eds. Bruges, Belgium: Desclée.

Messick, Brinkley (1987). Subordinate Discourse: Women, Weaving, and Gender Relations in North Africa. *American Ethnologist* 14(2):210–225.

Metcalf, Peter, and Richard Huntington (1991 [1979]). *Celebrations of Death: The Anthropology of Mortuary Ritual*. 2nd ed. Cambridge: Cambridge University Press.

Metuh, Emefie Ikenga (1985). *African Religions in Western Conceptual Schemes: The Problem of Interpretation*. Studies in Igbo Religion. Ibadan: Pastoral Institute.

Middleton, John (1960). *Lugbara Religion*. London: Oxford University Press.

Middleton, John, and E. H. Winter, eds. (1963). *Witchcraft and Sorcery in East Africa*. New York: Praeger.

Milingo, Emmanuel (1984). *The World in Between: Christian Healing and the Struggle for Spiritual Survival*. Mona Macmillan, ed. London: C. Hurst.

Milkias, Paulos (1989). *Ethiopia: A Comprehensive Bibliography*. Boston: G. K. Hall.

Miller, Jon (1990). Class Collaboration for the Sake of Religion: Elite Control and Social Mobility in a Nineteenth-Century Colonial Mission. [Evangelical Missionary Society of Basel, Switzerland, on Gold Coast of Africa, 1828–1917.] *Journal for the Scientific Study of Religion* 29(1):35–53.

Mission Handbook: North American Protestant Ministries Overseas (1973). Monrovia, California: Missions Advanced Research and Communication Center.

Mitchell, John Clyde (1956). *The Kalela Dance: Aspects of Social Relationships among Urban Africans in Northern Rhodesia*. Manchester: Manchester University Press.

Mitchell-Kernan, Claudia (1972). Signifying, Loud-talking, and Marking. In *Rappin' and Stylin' Out: Communication in Urban Black America*, 161–179. Thomas Kochman, ed. Urbana: University of Illinois Press.

Mitchell, Robert Cameron, and Harold W. Turner, comps. (1966). *A Comprehensive Bibliography of Modern African Religious Movements*. Evanston, Illinois: Northwestern University Press.

Miyahara, Kojiro (1983). Charisma: From Weber to Contemporary Sociology. *Sociological Inquiry* 53(4):368–388.

Mobley, Harris W. (1970). *The Ghanaian's Image of the Missionary: An Analysis of the Published Critiques of Christian Missionaries by Ghanaians 1897–1965*. Leiden: E. J. Brill.

Moerman, Michael (1988). *Talking Culture: Ethnography and Conversation Analysis*. Philadelphia: University of Pennsylvania Press.

Monteil, Vincent (1980). *L'islam noir*. 3rd ed. Paris: Editions du Seuil.

Morris, Charles (1938). Foundations of the Theory of Signs. *International Encyclopedia of Unified Science* 1(2):1–59. Chicago: University of Chicago Press.

Mortelmans, George, and René Monteyne (1982). La grotte peinte de Mbafu, témoignage iconographique de la première évangélisation du Bas-Congo. In *Actes du IVe Congrès Panafricain de Préhistoire et de l'Etude du Quaternaire. Section III. Pré- et Protohistoire*, 457–486. Georges Mortelmans et Jacques Nenquin, eds. Tervuren: Annales du Musée Royal de l'Afrique Centrale.

Morton-Williams, P. (1964). An Outline of the Cosmology and Cult Organization of the Oyo Yoruba. *Africa* 34(3):243–261.

Mudimbe, Valentin Y. (1973). *Entre les eaux: Dieu, un prêtre, la révolution*. Paris: Présence Africaine.

——— (1988). *The Invention of Africa: Gnosis, Philosophy, and the Order of Knowledge*. Bloomington: Indiana University Press.

Muga, Erasto (1975). *African Response to Western Christian Religion: A Sociological Analysis of African Separatist Religious and Political Movements in East Africa*. Kampala: East African Literature Bureau.

Mugambi, J. N. Kanyua (1989). *The African Heritage and Contemporary Christianity*. Nairobi: Longman Kenya.

Muhammad, al-Hajj (1984). *The House of Si Abd Allah: The Oral History of a Moroccan Family*. Henry Munson, Jr., trans. and ed. New Haven: Yale University Press.

Mulago, Vincent (1981). Evangélisation et authenticité. Aspects du Catholicisme au Zaïre. Special issue. *Cahiers des Religions Africaines* 14(27–28):41.

Munro-Hay, Stuart C. (1991). *Aksum: An African Civilisation of Late Antiquity*. Edinburgh: Edinburgh University Press.

Murphy, Joseph M. (1988). *Santería: An African Religion in America*. Boston: Beacon Press.

Murphy, William P. (1980). Secret Knowledge as Property and Power in Kpelle Society: Elders versus Youth. *Africa* 50:193–207.

Murray, Jocelyn (1985). *Proclaim the Good News: A Short History of the Church Missionary Society*. London: Hodder and Stoughton.

Murray, M. (1956). Burial Customs and Beliefs in the Hereafter in Predynastic Egypt. *Journal of Egyptian Archaeology* 42:86–96.

Muzorewa, Abel (1978). *Rise Up and Walk*. London: Evan Brothers.

Nanji, Azim (1974). Modernization and Change in the Nizari Ismaili Community. *Journal of Religion in Africa* 6(2):123–139.

———— (1978). *The Nizārī Ismāʿīlī Tradition in the Indo-Pakistan Subcontinent*. Delmar, New York: Caravan Books.

———— (1981). Ritual and Symbolic Aspects of Islam in African Contexts. *Contributions to Asian Studies* 17:102–109.

———— (1986). The Ismaili Muslim Identity and Changing Contexts. In *Identity Issues and World Religions*, 119–124. V. Hayes, ed. Bedford Park: Australian Association for the Study of Religions.

Nasser, Rachid Abdallah (1983). Morocco, from Kharijism to Wahhabism: The Quest for Religious Purism. Ph.D. dissertation, University of Michigan.

Neckebrouck, Victor (1983). *Le peuple affligé*. Immensee: Neue Zeitschrift für Missionswissenschaft.

Neill, Stephen (1966). *Colonialism and Christian Missions*. New York: McGraw-Hill.

———— (1986). *A History of Christian Missions*. 2nd ed. New York: Penguin.

Neill, Stephen, Gerald H. Anderson, and John Goodwin, eds. (1971). *Concise Dictionary of the Christian World Mission*. 17 vols. Nashville, Tennessee: Abingdon.

————, ed. (1967–1979). *New Catholic Encyclopedia*. New York: McGraw-Hill.

Nelson, Jack E. (1992). *Christian Missionizing and Social Transformation: A History of Change and Conflict in Eastern Zaïre*. New York: Praeger.

Newell, William H., ed. (1976). *Ancestors*. Chicago: Aldine.

Ngokwey, Ndolamb (1984). Candomblé as a Healing System. Chapter in *Medical Pluralism in Urban Brazil*. Ph.D. dissertation, University of California at Los Angeles.

Ngongo, Lois (1982). *Histoire des forces religieuses au Cameroun: De la Première Guerre Mondiale à l'Indépendance* (1916–1955). Paris: Éditions Karthala.

Ngubane, Harriet (1977). *Body and Mind in Zulu Traditional Medicine*. London: Academic Press.

———— (1981). Aspects of Clinical Practice and Traditional Organization of Indigenous Healers in South Africa. *Social Science and Medicine* 15(3B):361–365.

Niane, Djibril Tamsir (1965). *Sundiata. An Epic of Old Mali*. G. D. Pickett, trans. London: Longman.

Nida, Eugene A. (1954). *Customs and Cultures: Anthropology for Christian Missions*. New York: Harper & Row.

Nimtz, August H. (1980). *Islam and Politics in East Africa: The Sufi Order in Tanzania*. Minneapolis: University of Minnesota Press.

Nina Rodrigues, Raimundo (1935 [1896]). *O animismo fetichista dos negros bahianos*. Rio de Janeiro: Civilização Brasileira.

———— (1977 [1905]). *Os Africanos no Brasil*. São Paulo: Companhia Editora Nacional.

Nketia, J. H. Kwabena (1955). *Funeral Dirges of the Akan People*. Accra: Achimota Press.

———— (1988). The Intensity Factor in African Music. In *Performance in Contemporary African Arts*. Ruth M. Stone, ed. Special issue. *Journal of Folklore Research* 25:53-87.

Norman, Edward R. (1981). *Christianity in the Southern Hemisphere: The Churches in Latin America and South Africa*. New York: Oxford University Press.

Norris, H. T. (1975). *The Tuaregs: Their Islamic Legacy and Its Diffusion in the Sahel*. Warminster: Aris & Philips.

———— (1990). *Sufi Mystics of the Niger Desert*. Oxford: Clarendon.

North, Charles R. (1952). *An Outline of Islam*. London: Epworth Press.

Nzongola-Ntalaja, ed. (1986). *The Crisis in Zaïre: Myths and Realities*. Trenton, New Jersey: Africa World Press.

Obenga, Theophile (1985). *Les Bantu: Langues, peuples, civilisations*. Libreville: Centre International des Civilisations Bantu. Paris: Présence Africaine.

O'Connell, James (1962). The Withdrawal of the High God in West African Religion: An Essay in Interpretation. *Man* 62(109):67–69.

Oded, Arye (1974). *Islam in Uganda*. New York: John Wiley and Sons.

Ofori, Patrick E. (1977a). *Black African Traditional Religions and Philosophy: A Selected Bibliographic Survey of the Sources from the Earliest Times to 1974*. Nendeln, Liechtenstein: KTO Press.

_____ (1977b). *Christianity in Tropical Africa: A Selective Annotated Bibliography*. Nendeln, Liechtenstein: KTO Press.

_____ (1977c). *Islam in Africa South of the Sahara: A Select Bibliographic Guide*. Nendeln, Liechtenstein: KTO Press.

Ogharaerumi, Mark Onesosan (1986). The Translation of the Bible into Yoruba, Igbo, and Isekiri Languages of Nigeria, with Special Reference to the Contributions of Mother Tongue Speakers. Ph.D. dissertation, University of Aberdeen.

Okorocha, Cyril C. (1987). *The Meaning of Religious Conversion in Africa: The Case of the Igbo of Nigeria*. Aldershot: Avebury.

Oliver, Roland A. (1952). *The Missionary Factor in East Africa*. New York: Longmans.

Olupona, Jacob K., ed. (1991). *African Traditional Religion in Contemporary Society*. New York: International Religious Foundation.

Omari, Mikelle Smith (1979). New World Yoruba Aesthetics: A Socio-Historical Analysis. Master's thesis, Art Department, University of California, Los Angeles.

_____ (1984a). Cultural Confluence in Candomblé Nago: A Socio-Historical Study of Art and Aesthetics in an Afro-Brazilian Religion. Ph.D. dissertation, Department of Art History, University of Michigan.

_____ (1984b). *From the Inside to the Outside: The Art and Ritual of Bahian Candomblé*. Los Angeles: Museum of Cultural History, UCLA.

_____ (1990a). Creativity in Adversity: Afro-Bahian Women, Power, Art. *The International Review of African-American Arts* 9(1).

_____ (1990b). Critique. In *African Art Studies: The State of the Discipline,* 119–124. Washington, D.C.: Smithsonian Institution.

_____ (1991). Completing the Circle: Notes on African Art, Society, and Religion in Oyo Tunji, South Carolina. *African Arts* 24(3).

Omoyajowo, J. Akinyele (1982). *Cherubim and Seraphim: The History of an African Independent Church*. New York: NOK Publishers International.

Oosthuizen, Gerhardis C. (1986a). Islam among the Zanzibaris of South Africa. *History of Religions* 31(3):305–320.

_____, ed. (1986b). *Religion Alive. Studies in the New Movements and Indigenous Churches in Southern Africa*. Johannesburg: Hodder & Stoughton.

Oosthuizen, Gerhardis C., J. K. Coetzee, John W. de Gruchy, Jan H. Hofmeyr, and Bernard C. Lategan, eds. (1988). *Religion, Intergroup Relations, and Social Change in South Africa*. New York: Greenwood.

Oosthuizen, Gerhardis C. et al., eds. (1989). *Afro-Christian Religion and Healing in Southern Africa*. Lewiston, New York: Edwin Mellen.

Oosthuizen, Gerhardis C., and Irving Hexham, eds. (1991). *Afro-Christian Religion at the Grassroots in Southern Africa*. Lewiston, New York: Edwin Mellen.

Orita: Ibadan Journal of Religious Studies (1967–). Ibadan: University of Ibadan.

Oruka, H. Odera, ed. (1990). *Sage Philosophy: Indigenous Thinkers and Modern Debate on African Philosophy*. New York: E. J. Brill.

Ottenberg, Simon (1975). *The Masked Rituals of Afikpo: The Context of an African Art*. Seattle: University of Washington Press.

_____ (1982a). *African Religious Groups and Belief: Papers in Honor of William R. Bascom.* Meerut, India: Arcana Publications for Folklore Institute, Berkeley.

_____ (1982b). Illusion, Communication, and Psychology in West African Masquerades. *Ethos* 10(2):149–185.

_____ (1983). Artistic and Sex Roles in a Limba Chiefdom. In *Female and Male in West Africa,* 76–90. Christine Oppong, ed. London: Allen and Unwin.

_____ (1986). Two New Religions: One Analytic Frame. *Cahiers d' Etudes Africaines* 14(4):437–454.

_____ (1988a). The Bride Comes to the Groom: Ritual and Drama in Limba Weddings. *Drama Review* 32(2):42–46.

_____ (1988b). Religion and Ethnicity in the Arts of a Limba Chiefdom. *Africa* 58(4):437–465.

_____ (1989a). *Boyhood Rituals in an African Society: An Interpretation.* Seattle: University of Washington Press.

_____ (1989b). The Dancing Bride: Art and Indigenous Psychology in Limba Weddings. *Man* 24(1):57–78.

_____ (1990). Männerbunde, Geschlechtszugehörigkeit und ihr künstlerischer Ausdruck in zwei westafrikanischen Gesellschaften. In *Männerbande Männerbünde: Zur Rolle des Mannes im Kulturvergleich,* vol. 2: 283–288, plate xvii. Gisela Völger and Karin v. Welck, eds. Cologne: Rautenstrauch–Joset–Museums für Völkerkunde.

_____ (1992). The Beaded Bands of Bafodea. *African Arts* 25(2):64–75, 98–99.

Otto, Rudolph (1917). *Das Heilige.* Breslau, Germany: Trewendt and Granier. [English ed. 1923, *The Idea of the Holy.* John Harvey, trans. London: Oxford University Press.]

Otunga, Maurice (1978). African Culture and Life-Centred Catechesis. *African Ecclesiastical Review* 20(1):27–28.

Overing, Joanne, ed. (1985). *Reason and Morality.* London: Tavistock.

Owens, Joseph (1976). *Dread: The Rastafarians of Jamaica.* London: Heinemann.

Page, Jesse (1979). *The Black Bishop, Samuel Adjai Crowther.* Westport, Connecticut: Greenwood.

Pager, Harold (1971). *Ndedema.* Graz: Akademische Druck–u. Verlagsanstalt.

_____ (1975). *Stone Age Myth and Magic.* Graz: Akademische Druck–u. Verlagsanstalt.

Palmer, Spencer J., ed. (1983). *Mormons and Muslims: Spiritual Foundations and Modern Manifestations.* Provo, Utah: Religious Studies Center, Brigham Young University.

Parkin, David (1968). Medicine Men and Men of Influence. *Man* 3(3):424–439.

_____, ed. (1985). *The Anthropology of Evil.* Oxford: Blackwell.

_____ (1991). *The Sacred Void: Spatial Images of Work and Ritual among the Giriama of Kenya.* New York: Cambridge University Press.

Parrinder, Edward Geoffrey (1949). *West African Religion.* London: Epworth Press.

_____ (1953). *Religion in an African City.* London: Oxford University Press.

_____ (1969). *Religion in Africa.* Baltimore: Penguin.

_____ (1976). *Africa's Three Religions.* London: Sheldon Press.

Paul, Lois (1978). Careers of Midwives in a Mayan Community. In *Women in Ritual and Symbolic Roles,* 129–150. Judith Hoch-Smith and Anita Spring, eds. New York: Plenum.

Paulme, Denise (1948). *Organisation sociale des Dogon.* Paris: PUF.

Pauw, Berthold A. (1960). *Religion in a Tswana Chiefdom.* London: Oxford University Press.

_____ (1963). African Christians and Their Ancestors. In *African Independent Church Movements,* 33–46. Victor E. W. Hayward, ed. Edinburgh: Edinburgh House Press.

p'Bitek, Okot (1980). *African Religions in Western Scholarship.* Kampala: Uganda Literature Bureau.

Peek, Philip M. (1981). The Power of Words in African Verbal Arts. *Journal of American Folklore* 94:19–43.

_____, ed. (1991). *African Divination Systems: Ways of Knowing.* Bloomington: Indiana University Press.

Peel, John D. Y. (1968). *Aladura: A Religious Movement among the Yoruba*. London: Oxford University Press for the International African Institute.

Peirce, Charles Sanders (1931–1958). *Collected Papers*. Cambridge: Harvard University Press.

Pelikan, Jarsolav (1984). *The Vindication of Tradition*. New Haven: Yale University Press.

Pemberton, John III. (1978). Egungun Masquerades of the Igbomina Yoruba. *African Arts* 11(3):40–47.

Pérez ya Mena, Andrés Isidoro (1991). *Speaking with the Dead: Development of Afro-Latin Religion among Puerto Ricans in the United States*. New York: AMS Press.

Pern, Stephen, Bryan Alexander, and Walter E.A. van Beek (1982). *Masked Dancers of West Africa: The Dogon*. Amsterdam and New York: Time–Life.

Perrings, Charles (1979). *Black Mineworkers in Central Africa: Industrial Strategies and the Evolution of an African Proletariat in the Copperbelt, 1911–1941*. London: Heinemann.

Petersen, Paul D., ed. (1985). *Missions and Evangelism: A Bibliography Selected from the ATLA Religion Database*. Chicago: American Theological Library Association.

Philipsen, Gerry, and Donal Carbaugh (1986). A Bibliography of Fieldwork in the Ethnography of Communication. *Language in Society* 15(3):387–398.

Picot, J. (1958). *N'zérékoré*. Paris: Guillemot et Lamonthe.

Pirouet, M. Louise (1978). *Black Evangelists: The Spread of Christianity in Uganda, 1891–1914*. London: Collings.

Pitts, Walter F. (1993). *Old Ship of Zion: Afro-Baptist Ritual in the African Diaspora*. New York: Oxford University Press.

Pomerantz, Anita (1990–1991). Mental Concepts in the Analysis of Social Action. *Research on Language and Social Interaction* 24:299–310.

Post, Ken (1978). *Arise Ye Starvelings: Jamaican Labor Rebellion of 1938 and Its Aftermath*. S'Gravenhage: Internationaal Instituut Voor Sociale Studien.

Pouwels, Randall L. (1987). *Horn and Crescent: Cultural Change and Traditional Islam on the East African Coast, 800–1900*. Cambridge: Cambridge University Press.

Prandi, Reginaldo (1991). *Os candomblés de São Paulo: a velha magia na metrópole nova*. São Paulo: HUCITEL.

Pratt, Orson (n.d.). *Masterful Discourses of Orson Pratt*. Salt Lake City: N. B. Lundwall.

Pratt, Parley P. (1874). *Autobiography of Parley Parker Pratt*. New York: Russell Brothers.

———— (1978 [1855]). *Key to the Science of Theology*. Salt Lake City: Deseret Book.

Prins, Gwyn (1979). Disease at the Crossroads: Towards a History of Therapeutics in Bulozi since 1876. *Social Science and Medicine* 13(4B):285–315.

Proctor, J. H. (1987). The Church of Scotland and British Colonialism in Africa. *Journal of Church and State* 29(3):475–493.

Pye, Michael (1971). Syncretism and Ambiguity. *Numen* 18(2):83–93.

Quarterly Index Islamicus (1977–). London: Mansell. [SOAS, London. Replaces annual *Index Islamicus. Supplement*. See also *Index Islamicus, 1905–1955, ... 1665–1905*.]

Quirin, James (1992). *The Evolution of the Ethiopian Jews: A History of the Beta Israel (Falasha) to 1920*. Philadelphia: University of Pennsylvania Press.

Rabinow, Paul (1975). *Symbolic Domination: Cultural Form and Historical Change in Morocco*. Chicago: University of Chicago Press.

Rader, Dick Allen (1991). *Christian Ethics in an African Context: A Focus on Urban Zambia*. New York: Peter Lang.

Radin, Paul (1927). *Primitive Man as a Philosopher*. New York: Appleton.

Rahner, Karl (1980). Towards a Fundamental Theological Interpretation of Vatican II. *African Ecclesiastical Review* 22(6):323–335.

Ramos, Artur (1934). *O negro brasileiro: ethnographia, religiosa, e psychanalyse*. Rio de Janeiro: Civilização Brasileira.

_____ (1942). *A aculturação negra no Brasil*. São Paulo: Companhia Editora Nacional.

_____ (1946 [1940]). *O negro brasileiro*. São Paulo: Companhia Editora Nacional.

_____ (1976). *Os Africanos no Brasil*. 4th ed. São Paulo: Companhia Editora Nacional.

Rangeley, William H. J. (1953). Mbona the Rain Maker. *Nyasaland Journal* 6(l):8–27.

Ranger, Terence O. (1968). *The African Churches of Tanzania*. Nairobi: East African Publishing House.

_____ (1975). *Dance and Society in Eastern Africa 1890–1970: The Beni Ngoma*. London: Heinemann; Berkeley: University of California Press.

_____ (1984). Religions and Rural Protests in Makoni District, Zimbabwe, 1900–1980. In *Religion and Rural Revolt*. János M. Bak and Gerhard Benecke, eds. Manchester: Manchester University Press.

_____ (1985). *Peasant Consciousness and Guerilla War in Zimbabwe*. London: James Currey.

_____ (1987a). Religion, Development and African Christian Identity. In *Religion, Development and African Identity*. K. H. Petersen, ed. Uppsala: Scandinavian Institute of African Studies.

_____ (1987b). Taking Hold of the Land: Pilgrimages and Holy Places in Twentieth-Century Zimbabwe. *Past and Present* 117.

_____ (1989). Missionaries, Migrants and the Manyika: The Invention of Ethnicity in Zimbabwe. In *The Creation of Tribalism in Southern Africa*. Leroy Vail, ed. London: James Currey.

Ranger, Terence O., and Isaria N. Kimambo, eds. (1972). *The Historical Study of African Religion*. London: Heinemann.

Rappaport, Roy (1979). *Ecology, Meaning and Religion*. Richmond, Virginia: North Atlantic Books.

Rattray, R. S., and Robert Sutherland (1927). *Religion and Art in Ashanti*. Oxford: Clarendon.

Raymaekers, Paul, and Henri Desroche (1983). *L'administration et le sacré: discourse religieux et parcours politiques en Afrique centrale (1921–1957)*. Brussels: Académie Royale des Sciences d'Outre-mer.

Raymaekers, Paul, and Hendrick van Moorsel (1964). *Dessins rupestres du Bas Congo*. Léopoldville: Editions de l'Université.

Reeck, Darrell (1976). *Deep Mende: Religious Interactions in a Changing African Rural Society*. Studies on Religion in Africa 4. Leiden: E. J. Brill.

Reefe, Thomas Q. (1981). *The Rainbow and the Kings: A History of the Luba Empire to 1891*. Berkeley: University of California Press.

Reimann, Paul E. (1974). *Plural Marriage Limited*. Salt Lake City: Utah Print Co.

Religion in Southern Africa (1980–1987). Continued as *Journal for the Study of Religion*. Durban: Association for the History of Religion, Southern Africa.

Rema, Henrique Pinto (1982). *História das missões católicas da Guiné*. Braga, Portugal: Editorial Franciscana.

Ricoeur, Paul (1967). *The Symbolism of Evil*. Boston: Beacon Press.

Rigby, Peter (1975). Prophets, Diviners, and Prophetism: The Recent History of Kiganda Religion. *Journal of Anthropological Research* 31:116–148.

Roberts, Allen F. (1984). "Fishers of Men": Religion and Political Economy among Colonized Tabwa. *Africa* 54(2):50–70.

_____ (1985). Social and Historical Contexts of Tabwa Art. In *Tabwa, The Rising of a New Moon: A Century of Tabwa Art*, 1–48. Evan M. Maurer and Allen F. Roberts, eds. Ann Arbor: University of Michigan Museum of Art.

_____ (1990). Tabwa Masks, An Old Trick of the Human Race. *African Arts* 23(2):36–47, 101–103.

Roberts, Colin H. (1979). *Manuscript, Society, and Belief in Early Christian Egypt*. London: Oxford University Press.

Rosaldo, Michele (1973). I Have Nothing to Hide: The Language of Ilongot Oratory. *Language in Society* 2:193–223.

Ross, Andrew C. (1969). The Political Role of the Witchfinder in Southern Malawi, 1965–1966. Paper presented at the Seminar on Witchcraft and Healing. Edinburgh: Centre for African Studies, University of Edinburgh.

Rotberg, Robert I. (1965). *Christian Missionaries and the Creation of Northern Rhodesia, 1880–1924.* Princeton: Princeton University Press.

Rouadjia, Ahmed (1990). *Les frères et la mosquée.* [*Algérie.*] Paris: Karthala.

Roy, Christopher D. (1985). *Art and Life in Africa: Selections from the Stanley Collection.* Iowa City: University of Iowa Museum of Art.

Rubin, Arnold (1969). The Arts of the Jukun-Speaking Peoples of Northern Nigeria. Ph.D. dissertation, Department of Fine Arts, Indiana University.

_____ (1975). Accumulation: Power and Display in African Sculpture. *Art Forum* (May):35–47.

Ruesch, Jurgen, and Gregory Bateson (1968). *Communication.* New York: Norton.

Ryan, Patrick J. (1978). *Imale, Yoruba Participation in the Muslim Tradition: A Study of Clerical Piety.* Missoula, Montana: Scholars Press.

Sadek, Ashraf I. (1988). *Popular Religion in Egypt during the New Kingdom.* Hildesheim: Gerstenberg.

Said, Edward (1984). *Beginnings: Intention and Method.* New York: Columbia University Press.

Salamone, Frank A. (1974). *Gods and Goods in Africa: Persistence and Change in Ethnic and Religious Identity in Yauri Emirate, North-Western State, Nigeria.* Salem, Wisconsin: Sheffield Publishing.

Sales, Jane M. (1975). *Mission Stations and the Coloured Communities of the Eastern Cape, 1800–1852.* Cape Town: A. A. Balkema.

Sanneh, Lamin (1976). The Origins of Clericalism in West African Islam. *Journal of African History* 17(1):49–72.

_____, ed. (1979). *Muslims in non-Muslim Societies in Africa. Christian and Islamic Contributions towards Establishing Independent States in Africa South of the Sahara.* Stuttgart: Federal Republic of Germany.

_____ (1981a). Futa Jallon and the Jakhanke Clerical Tradition, Part I: The Historical Setting. *Journal of Religion in Africa* 12(1):38–64.

_____ (1981b). Futa Jallon and the Jakhanke Clerical Tradition, Part II: Karamokho Ba of Tauba in Guinea. *Journal of Religion in Africa* 12(2):105–126.

_____ (1983). *West African Christianity.* London: Allen and Unwin.

_____ (1989a[1979]). *The Jakhanke Muslim Clerics: A Religious and Historical Study of Islam in Senegambia.* Lanham, Maryland: University Press of America.

_____ (1989b). *Translating the Message: The Missionary Impact on Culture.* Maryknoll, New York: Orbis.

_____ (1991). Religion and Politics: Third World Perspectives on a Comparative Religious Theme. *Daedalus* 120(3):203–208.

Santerre, Renaud (1973). *Pédagogie musulmane d'Afrique noire: l'école coranique peule du Cameroun.* Montréal: Presses de l'Université de Montréal.

Sawyerr, Harry A. (1970). *God, Ancestor or Creator: Aspects of Traditional Belief in Ghana, Nigeria, and Sierra Leone.* London: Longmans.

Schacht, Joseph, and C. E. Bosworth, eds. (1974). *The Legacy of Islam.* 2nd ed. Oxford: Clarendon.

Schechner, Richard (1986). Magnitudes of Performance. In *The Anthropology of Experience*, 344–369. Victor W. Turner and Edward M. Bruner, eds. Chicago: University of Illinois Press.

Schiltz, Marc (1978). Egungun Masquerades in Iganna. *African Arts* 11(3):48–55.

Schmidt, W. (1926–55). *Der Ursprung der Gottesidee.* 12 vols. Münster, Germany: Aschendorff.

Schneider, Harold K. (1981). *The Africans: An Ethnological Account.* Englewood Cliffs, New Jersey: Prentice-Hall.

Schoffeleers, J. Matthew (1975). The Interaction between the Mbona Cult and Christianity. In *Themes in the Christian History of Central Africa*, 14–29. Terence O. Ranger and John Weller, eds. London: Heinemann.

_____ (1985a). Oral History and the Retrieval of the Distant Past: On the Use of Legendary Chronicles as Sources of Historical Information. In *Theoretical Explorations in African Religion*, 164–188. Wim van Binsbergen and Matthew Schoffeleers, eds. London: Kegan Paul International.

_____ (1985b). *Pentecostalism and Neo-Traditionalism: The Religious Polarization of a Rural District in Southern Malawi*. Amsterdam: Free University Press.

_____ (1986a). *Economic Change and Religious Polarization in an African Rural District*. In *Malawi: An Alternative Pattern of Development*, 189–242. William Beinart et al., eds. Edinburgh: Centre of African Studies, University of Edinburgh.

_____ (1986b). Review of *Bwiti: An Ethnography of the Religious Imagination in Africa*, by James W. Fernandez. *Africa* 56(3):352–356.

_____ (1987). Ideological Confrontation and the Manipulation of Oral History: A Zambesian Case. *History in Africa: A Journal of Method* 14:257–273.

_____ (1992). *River of Blood: The Genesis of a Martyr Cult in Northern Malawi, c. 1600 A.D.* Madison: University of Wisconsin Press.

Scholz, Piotr O., and Reinhard Stempel, eds. (1988). *Nubia et Oriens Christianus: Festschrift für Caspar Detlef G. Müller*. Cologne: J. Dinter.

Schutz, Alfred (1962). *Collected Papers I: The Problem of Social Reality*. The Hague: Martinus Nijhoff.

Schwab, George, with George W. Harley (1947). *Tribes of the Liberian Hinterland*. Peabody Museum Papers. Cambridge: Peabody Museum

Schwimmer, Eric, and Patrick de Josselin de Jong, eds. *Symbolic Anthropology in the Netherlands*. The Hague: Verhandelingen van het Koninklik Instituut.

Searle, John R. (1969). *Speech Acts*. Cambridge: Cambridge University Press.

Sells, E. L. (1936). *On Trek with Christ in Southern Rhodesia*. Rhodesia Mission Press.

Serequeberhan, Tsenay, ed. (1991). *African Philosophy: The Essential Readings*. New York: Paragon House.

Setiloane, Gabriel M. (1976). *The Image of God among the Sotho-Tswana*. Rotterdam: A. A. Balkema.

_____ (1979). Where Are We in African Theology? In *African Theology en Route*, 59–65. Kofi Appiah Kubi and Sergio Torres, eds. Maryknoll, New York: Orbis.

_____ (n.d.). *Snippets Out of Research Experience*. Mimeograph.

Shafer, Byron, ed. (1991). *Religion in Ancient Egypt: Gods, Myths, and Personal Practice*. Ithaca, New York: Cornell University Press.

Shaje a Tshilulla (1986). A la mémoire des ancêtres. Le grand art funéraire kongo: son contexte social et historique. Ph.D. dissertation, Brussels Free University.

Sharpe, Eric J. (1975). *Comparative Religion: A History*. London: Duckworth.

Shepperson, George, and Thomas Price (1958). *Independent African: John Chilembwe and the Origins, Setting and Significance of the Nyasaland Native Rising of 1915*. Edinburgh: Edinburgh University Press.

Sherzer, Joel (1977). The Ethnography of Speaking: A Critical Appraisal. In *Linguistics and Anthropology*, 43–57. Muriel Saville-Troike, ed. Washington, D.C.: Georgetown University Press.

_____ (1983). *Kuna Ways of Speaking: An Ethnographic Perspective*. Austin: University of Texas Press.

_____ (1987). A Diversity of Voices: Men's and Women's Speech in Ethnographic Perspective. In *Language, Gender, and Sex in Comparative Perspective*, 95–120. Susan J. Philips, Susan Steele, and Christine Tanz, eds. Cambridge: Cambridge University Press.

_____ (1988–89). The Ethnography of Speaking. In *International Encyclopedia of Communications*. Eric Barnouw, ed. London: Oxford University Press.

Shils, Edward A. (1958). The Concentration and Dispersion of Charisma. *World Politics* 11:1–19.

_____ (1965). Charisma, Order, and Status. *American Sociological Review* 30:199–213.

_____ (1968). Charisma. In *International Encyclopedia of the Social Sciences* 2:386–390. David L. Sills, ed. New York: Crowell.

_____ (1981). *Tradition.* Chicago: University of Chicago Press.

Shimoni, Gideon (1980). *Jews and Zionism: The South African Experience (1910–1967).* Cape Town: Oxford University Press.

Shinar, Pessah (1983). *Essai de bibliographie sélective et annotée sur l'Islam maghrebin contemporain: Maroc, Algérie, Tunisie, Libye (1830–1978).* Paris: CNRS.

Shorter, Aylward (1974). *African Culture and the Christian Church: An Introduction to Social and Pastoral Anthropology.* Maryknoll, New York: Orbis.

_____ (1975). *African Christian Theology: Adaptation or Incarnation?* Maryknoll, New York: Orbis.

_____ (1976 [1975]). *Prayer in the Religious Traditions of Africa.* New York: Oxford University Press.

_____ (1979). *Priest in the Village: Experiences of African Community.* London: Geoffrey Chapman.

_____ (1982). Folk Christianity and Functional Christology. *African Ecclesiastical Review* 24(3):133–137.

_____ (1985). *Jesus and the Witchdoctor: An Approach to Healing and Wholeness.* London: Geoffrey Chapman.

Siegmann, William, and Judith Perani (1980). Men's Masquerades of Sierra Leone. Marie J. Adams, ed. Special Issue. *Ethnologische Zeitschrift Zürich* 1:25–40.

Simensen, Jarle, ed. (1986). *Norwegian Missions in African History.* 2 vols. New York: Oxford University Press.

Simpson, George Easton (1955). The Ras Tafari Movement in Jamaica: A Study of Race and Class Conflict. *Social Forces* 34(2):167–171.

_____ (1978). *Black Religions in the World.* New York: Columbia University Press.

_____ (1985). Religion and Justice: Some Reflections on the Rastafari Movement. *Phylon* 46(4):286–291.

Smally, W. A. (1960). Anthropological Study and Missionary Scholarship. *Practical Anthropology* 7:113–123.

Smith, E. W. (1934). Anthropology and the Practical Man. *Journal of the Royal Anthropological Institute* 64:xiii–xxxviii.

Smith, Fred, ed. (1987). *Death, Ritual, and Art in Africa.* Special issue. *African Arts* 21(1).

Smith, Joseph (1938). *Teachings of the Prophet Joseph Smith.* Salt Lake City: Deseret News Press.

Smith, Joseph F. (1939). *Gospel Doctrine.* Salt Lake City: Deseret Book Co.

Smith, Mary (1981 [1954]). *Baba of Karo, A Woman of the Muslim Hausa.* New Haven: Yale University Press.

Smith, Michael G. (1974). Institutional and Political Conditions of Pluralism. In *Corporations and Society: The Social Anthropology of Collective Action.* Michael G. Smith, ed. London: Duckworth.

Smith, Michael G., Roy Augier, and Rex Nettleford (1960). *The Rastafari Movement in Kingston, Jamaica.* Kingston: Institute of Social and Economic Research.

Smith, Pierre (1979). Naissances et destins: les enfants de fer et les enfants de beurre. *Cahiers d'Etudes Africaines* 19:330–351.

Speed, Clark K. (1991). Swears and Swearing among Landogo of Northern Sierra Leone: Aesthetics, Adjudication, and a Philosophy of Power. Ph.D. Dissertation, Department of Anthropology, University of Washington.

Spiro, Melvin E. (1966). Religion: Problems of Definition and Explanation. In *Anthropological Approaches to the Study of Religion*, 85–126. Michael Banton, ed. London: Tavistock.

Spradley, James P. (1979). *The Ethnographic Interview.* New York: Holt, Rinehart, and Winston.

_____ (1980). *Participant Observation.* New York: Holt, Rinehart, and Winston.

Spring, Anita (1978). Epidemiology of Spirit Possession among the Luvale of Zambia. In *Women in Ritual and Symbolic Roles*, 165–190. Judy Hoch-Smith and Anita Spring, eds. New York: Plenum.

_____ (1985). Health Care Systems in Northwest Zambia. In *African Healing Strategies*, 135–150. Brian M. du Toit and Ismail H. Abdalla, eds. New York: Trado-Medic.

Springer, John M. (1922). After Fourteen Years. *South Africa Missionary Advocate* 1(4).

Springer, Mrs. John M. (1932). The Fallacy of Paul's Methods. *South Africa Misssionary Advocate* 11(4):3–4.

Stewart, Charles C. (1973). *Islam and Social Order in Mauritania: A Case Study from the Nineteenth Century.* Oxford: Clarendon.

_____ (1985). Introduction. In *Popular Islam South of the Sahara*, 363–368. John D. Y. Peel and Charles C. Stewart, eds. Manchester: Manchester University Press.

Stoeltje, Beverly J. (1985). The Rodeo Clown and the Semiotics of Metaphor. *Journal of Folklore Research* 22:155–177.

Stoeltje, Beverly J., and Richard Bauman (1988). The Semiotics of Folklore Performance. In *The Semiotic Web 1987*, 585–599. Thomas A. Sebeok and Jean Umiker-Sebeok, eds. Berlin: de Gruyter.

Stoller, Paul (1989a). *The Fusion of Worlds: An Ethnography of Possession among the Songhay of Niger.* Chicago: University of Chicago Press.

_____ (1989b). *The Taste of Ethnographic Things: The Senses in Anthropology.* Philadelphia: University of Pennsylvania Press.

Stone, Ruth M. (1972). Meni–pele: A Musical Dramatic Folktale of the Kpelle. *Liberian Studies Journal* 4:31–46.

_____ (1982). *Let the Inside Be Sweet: The Interpretation of Music Event among the Kpelle of Liberia.* Bloomington: Indiana University Press.

_____ (1988a). *Dried Millet Breaking: Time, Words, and Song in the Woi Epic of the Kpelle.* Bloomington: Indiana University Press.

_____, ed. (1988b). *Performance in Contemporary African Arts.* Special issue. *Journal of Folklore Research* 25(1/2).

Stone, Ruth M., and Frank J. Gillis (1976). *African Music and Oral Data: A Catalog of Field Recordings, 1902–1975.* Bloomington: Indiana University Press.

Stone, Ruth M., and Verlon L. Stone (1981). Event, Feedback, and Analysis: Research Media in the Study of Music Events. *Ethnomusicology* 25:215–225.

Strayer, Robert W. (1978). *The Making of Mission Communities in East Africa: Anglicans and Africans in Colonial Kenya, 1875–1935.* Albany, New York: State University of New York Press.

Strobel, Margaret (1979). *Muslim Women in Mombasa, 1890–1975.* New Haven: Yale University Press.

Sturtevant, William (1968). Studies in Ethnoscience. In *Theory in Anthropology*, 475–500. Robert Manners and David Kaplan, eds. Chicago: Aldine.

Sundkler, Bengt G. M. (1961). *Bantu Prophets in South Africa.* London: Oxford University.

_____ (1976). *Zulu Zion and Some Swazi Zionists.* London: Oxford University.

Swantz, Maria-Lisa (1970). *Ritual and Symbol in Transitional Zaramo Society.* Uppsala: Gleerup.

Sweet, Charles F., Thomas D. Blakely, Pamela A. R. Blakely, and Alan Roth (1977). *Project Paper: North Shaba Maize Production.* Washington, D.C.: AID.

Tambiah, Stanley J. (1990). *Magic, Science, Religion, and the Scope of Rationality.* Cambridge: Cambridge University Press.

Tamrat, Taddesse (1972). *Church and State in Ethiopia: 1270–1527.* Oxford: Clarendon.

Tasie, Godwin M. (1978). *Christian Missionary Enterprise in the Niger Delta: 1864–1918.* Studies on Religion in Africa 3. Leiden: E. J. Brill.

Taylor, John Vernon (1957). *Christianity and Politics in Africa.* London: Penguin.

_____ (1958). *The Growth of the Church in Buganda.* London: SCM Press.

_____ (1961). *Christians of the Copperbelt.* London: SCM Press.

Te Haar, Gerrie (1991). *Spirit of Africa: The Healing Ministry of Archbishop Milingo of Zambia.* London: Hurst and Company.

Tempels, Placide (1945). *La philosophie bantoue.* Elisabethville: Louvania. [English edition 1959, *Bantu Philosophy.* Paris: Présence Africaine.]

Temu, A. J. (1972). *British Protestant Missions.* London: Longman.

Tennekes, J. Hans (1982). *Symbolism en hun betekenis.* Assen: van Gorcum.

Te Rangi Hiroa [Peter H. Buck] (1939). *Anthropology and Religion.* New Haven: Yale University Press.

Tesfa, Ras J. (1980). *The Living Testament of Rasta–far–I.* Distributed by the author.

Thilmans, Guy, Cyr Descamp, and Bernard Khayat (1980). *Protohistoire du Sénégal: I. Les sites mégalithiques.* Dakar: IFAN.

Thoden van Velzen, Bono, and Walter E.A. van Beek (1988). Purity: A Greedy Ideology. In *The Quest for Purity: Dynamics of Puritan Movements,* 1–35. Walter E.A. van Beek, ed. Berlin: Mouton/de Gruyter.

Thoden van Velzen, Bono, and Wilhelmina van Wetering (1988a). *The Great Father and the Danger: Ndjuka Collective Fantasies.* Leiden: Verhandelingen van het Koningklik Instituut.

_____ (1988b). *The Great Father and the Danger: Religious Cults, Material Forces, and Collective Fantasies in the World of Surinamese Maroons.* KITLV Caribbean Series 9. Dordrecht: Foris.

Thomas, Louis-Vincent, and René Luneau (1975). *La terre africaine et ses religions.* Paris: Larousse.

_____ (1977). *Les sages dépossédés.* Paris: Univers Magiques d'Afrique Noire.

Thompson, Lloyd A., and John Ferguson, eds. (1969). *Africa in Classical Antiquity: Nine Studies.* Ibadan: Ibadan University Press; New York: Africana Publishing.

Thompson, Robert Farris (1969). Abatan: A Master Potter of the Egbado Yoruba. In *Tradition and Creativity in Tribal Art,* 120–182. Daniel Biebuyck, ed. Berkeley: University of California Press.

_____ (1971). *Black Gods and Kings: Yoruba Art at UCLA.* Los Angeles: Museum of Cultural History, UCLA.

_____ (1973). An Aesthetic of the Cool. *African Arts* 7(1):40–43, 64–67, 89–92.

_____ (1975). Icons of the Mind: Yoruba Herbalism Arts in Trans-Atlantic Perspective. *African Arts* 8(3):52–59.

_____ (1981). Kongo Civilization and Kongo Art. In *The Four Moments of the Sun: Kongo Art in Two Worlds,* 34–140. Robert Farris Thompson and Joseph Cornet, eds. Washington, D.C.: National Gallery of Art.

_____ (1983). *Flash of the Spirit: African and Afro-American Art and Philosophy.* New York: Random House.

Tienou, Tite (1990). Indigenous African Christian Theologies: The Uphill Road. *International Bulletin of Missionary Research* 14(2):73–77.

Tobias, Phillip V., ed. (1978). *The Bushmen: San Hunters and Herders of Southern Africa.* Cape Town: Human and Rousseau.

Tonkin, Elizabeth (1979). Masks and Powers. *Man* n.s. 14(2):237–248.

_____ (1983). Women Excluded: Masking and Masquerading in West Africa. In *Women's Religious Experience,* 163–174. Pat Holden, ed. London: Croom Helm.

Topan, Farouk (1974). Modern Swahili Poetry. *Bulletin of the School of African and Oriental Languages* 37:175–187.

Towler, Robert (1974). *Homo Religiosus: Sociological Problems in the Study of Religion.* London: Constable and Co.

Triad, Jean-Louis (1973). *Islam et societés soudanaises au Moyen age: étude historique.* Paris: Laboratoire d'Anthropologie Sociale.
___ (1987). *Tchad 1900–1902: une guerre franco-libyenne oubliée? Une confrérie musulmane, la Sanusiya face à la France.* Paris: L'Harmattan.
Trigger, Bruce G. (1976). *Nubia under the Pharaohs.* London: Thames & Hudson.
Trimingham, John Spencer (1962). *A History of Islam in West Africa.* London: Oxford University Press.
___ (1964). *Islam in East Africa.* Oxford: Clarendon.
___ (1965a). *Islam in Ethiopia.* London: Frank Cass.
___ (1965b [1949]). *Islam in the Sudan.* London: Frank Cass.
___ (1968). *The Influence of Islam upon Africa.* London: Longman.
Tshibangu, Tharcisse (1974). *Le propos d'une théologie africaine.* Kinshasa: Presses Universitaires du Zaïre.
Turnbull, Colin M. (1961). *The Forest People: A Study of Pygmies of the Congo.* New York: Simon & Schuster.
Turner, Harold W. (1966). Monogamy: A Mark of the Church? *International Review of Missions* 219(July):313–21.
___ (1967a). *History of an African Independent Church.* Oxford: Clarendon.
___ (1967b). A Typology for African Religious Movements. *Journal of Religion in Africa* (1):1–34.
___ (1977). *Bibliography of New Religious Movements in Primal Societies.* Boston: G. K. Hall.
___ (1979). *Religious Innovation in Africa: Collected Essays on New Religious Movements.* Boston: G. K. Hall.
Turner, Victor W. (1967 [1959]). *The Forest of Symbols.* Ithaca: Cornell University Press.
___ (1968). *The Drums of Affliction: A Study of Religious Processes among the Ndembu of Zambia.* Oxford: Clarendon.
___ (1969). *The Ritual Process: Structure and Anti-Structure.* London: Routledge & Kegan Paul.
___ (1975 [1962]). *Revelation and Divination in Ndembu Ritual.* Ithaca, New York: Cornell University Press.
___ (1986). *The Anthropology of Performance.* New York: Performing Arts Journal Publications.
Turner, Victor W., and Edward M. Bruner, eds. (1986). *The Anthropology of Experience.* Chicago: University of Illinois Press.
Twesigye, Emmanuel K. (1987). *Common Ground: Christianity, African Religion, and Philosophy.* New York: Peter Lang.

Uchendu, Victor (1965). *The Igbo of Southeast Nigeria.* New York: Holt, Rinehart, & Winston.
Udoh, Enyi Ben (1983). Guest Christology. Ph.D. dissertation, Princeton University.
Utamaduni: A Journal of African Studies in Religion (1980–). Nairobi: Department of Philosophy and Religious Studies, Kenyatta University College.
Utok, Efiong (1991). *From New York to Ibadan: The Impact of African Questions on the Making of Ecumenical Mission Mandates, 1900–1958.* New York: Peter Lang.

Valerie, Valerio, and Roger Keesing (1987). On Anthropology as Interpretive Quest. Discussion and Reply. *Current Anthropology* 28(3):355–357.
Van Avermaet, Emile, and Benoît Mbuya (1954). *Dictionnaire Kiluba–Français.* Tervuren: Musée Royal de l'Afrique Centrale.
Van Baal, Jan (1967). *Mensen in Verandering [People in Change].* Amsterdam: Arbeidenspers.
___ (1981). *Man's Quest for Partnership. The Anthropological Foundations of Ethics and Religion.* Van Gorcum: Assen.
Van Baal, Jan, and Walter E.A. van Beek (1985). *Symbols for Communication: An Introduction to the Anthropological Study of Religion,* 2nd ed. Van Gorcum: Assen.

Van Beek, Walter E.A. (1975). Religion in Everyday Life: An Ethno-Scientific Investigation into the Concepts of Religion and Magic. In *Explorations in the Anthropology of Religion: Essays in Honor of Jan van Baal*, 55–70. Walter E.A. van Beek and J. H. Scherer, eds. Leiden: Verhandelingen van het Koninklik Instituut.

_____ (1978). *Bierbrouwers in de bergen: De Kapsiki en Higi van Noord Kameroen en Noord-Oost Nigeria.* Utrecht: Instituut Culturele Antropologie Utrecht.

_____ (1982a). Les savoirs Kapsiki. In *La quète du savoir. Essays pour une anthropologie de l'éducation camerounaise*, 180–207. Renaud Santerre and C. Mercier-Tremblay, eds. Montreal: Presses Universitaires Montréal.

_____ (1982b). *Spiegel voor de Mens: Religie en Anthropologie* [*Mirror for Humanity: Religion and Anthropology.*] Van Gorcum: Assen.

_____ (1983a). Harmonie en schaamte bij de Dogon. *Prana* 32:44–53.

_____ (1983b). Sacrifice in Two African Communities. *Nederlands Tijdschrift voor Theologie*, 121–131.

_____ (1985). Cultural Anthropology and the Many Functions of Religion. In *Contemporary Approaches to the Study of Religion. Volume 2. The Social Sciences.* F. Whaling, ed. Berlin: Mouton.

_____ (1986). The Ideology of Building: The Interpretation of Compound Patterns among the Kapsiki of North Cameroon. In *Op zoek naar mens en materiéle cultuur: Festschrift J. D. van der Waals,* 147–162. H. Fokkens, P. Banga, and M. Biersma, eds. Groningen: Biologisch Archologisch Instituut.

_____ (1987). *The Kapsiki of the Mandara Hills.* Prospect Heights, Illinois: Waveland Press.

_____ (1988a). De zondebok en het kwaad: een ethnografishe kritiek, 223–252. In *Mimese en Geweld: Beschouwingen over het werk van René Girard.* Walter E.A. van Beek, ed. Kampen: Kok-Agora.

_____ (1988b). Functions of Sculpture in Dogon Religion. *African Arts* 21(4):58–66.

_____ (1991a). The Dogon Restudied: A Field Evaluation of the Work of Marcel Griaule. *Current Anthropology* 32(2):139–167.

_____ (1991b). Enter the Bush: A Dogon Mask Festival. In *Africa Explores: 20th Century African Art,* 56–73. Susan Vogel, ed. New York: Center for African Art.

_____ (1991c). Harmony vs. Autonomy: Models of Agricultural Fertility among the Dogon and the Kapsiki. In *The Creative Communion: African Folk Models of Fertility and the Regeneration of Life,* 285–306. Anita Jacobson-Widding and Walter E.A. van Beek, eds. Uppsala: Uppsala University Press.

_____ (1992a). The Dirty Smith: Smell as a Social Symbol among the Kapsiki/Higi of North Cameroon and Northeastern Nigeria. *Africa* 62(1):38–58.

_____ (1993). Processes and Limitations of Dogon Agricultural Knowledge. In *An Anthropological Critique of Development: The Growth of Ignorance*, 43-61. Mark Hobart, ed. London: Routledge.

Van Binsbergen, Wim (1977). Regional and Non-Regional Cults of Affliction in Western Zambia. In *Regional Cults*, 141–173. Richard P. Werbner, ed. London: Academic Press.

_____ (1979). The Infancy of Edward Shilonga: An Extended Case from the Zambian Nkoya. In *In Search of Health,* 19–90. Sjaak vander Geest and Klaas van der Veen, eds. Amsterdam: University of Amsterdam.

_____ (1981). *Religious Change in Zambia.* London: Routledge & Kegan Paul.

Van Binsbergen, Wim, and Matthew Schoffeleers, eds. (1985). *Theoretical Explorations in African Religion.* London: Kegan Paul International.

Van Butselaar, Jan (1984). *Africains, missionnaires, et colonialistes: les origines de l'Eglise presbytérienne du Mozambique (Mission suisse), 1880–1896.* Leiden: E. J. Brill.

Van de Loo, Joseph (1991). *Guji Oromo Culture in Southern Ethiopia: Religious Capabilities in Rituals and Songs.* Berlin: D. Reimer.

Van Dijk, Frank Jan (1988). The Twelve Tribes of Israel: Rasta and the Middle Class. *New West Indian Guide, Niewe West Indische Gids* 62(1–2):1–26.

Van Gennep, Arnold (1922). *The Rites of Passage.* Chicago: University of Chicago Press.
Van Nieuwenhuijsen, J. W. (1974). *Diviners and Their Ancestor Spirits: A Study of the Izangoma among the Nyuswa in Natal, South Africa.* Antropologisch-Sociologisch Centrum 3. Amsterdam: Hijsdrukkerij Universiteit van Amsterdam.
Van Noten, Francis (1972). *Les tombes du Roi Cyirima Rujugira et de la Reine-mère Nyirayuhi Kanjogera. Description archéologique.* Tervuren: Annales du Musée Royal de l'Afrique Centrale.
Van Onselen, Charles (1976). *Chibaro.* London: Pluto Press.
Van Ufford, Philip Q., and J. Matthew Schoffeleers, eds. (1988). *Religion and Development: Towards an Integrated Approach.* Antropologische Studies 11. Amsterdam: Free University Press.
Verger, Pierre (1954). *Dieux d'Afrique.* Paris: P. Hartmann.
_____ (1957). *Notes sur le culte des Orisa et Vodun.* Dakar: IFAN.
_____ (1980). *Orixas da Bahia.* In *Iconografia dos deuses africanos no candomblé da Bahia.* São Paulo: Raizes.
_____ (1981a). *Noticias da Bahia: 1850.* Salvador, Bahia: Corrupio.
_____ (1981b). *Orixas: Deuses Iorubus na Africa e no novo mundo.* Salvador, Bahia: Corrupio.
Verhaegen, Guy (1983). *Le renouveau dans l'Esprit.* Kinshasa: Centre d'Etudes Pastorales.
Veysey, Laurence (1978). *The Communal Experience: Anarchist and Mystical Communities in Twentieth-Century America.* Chicago: Chicago University Press.
Vilakazi, Absalom, et al. (1986). *Shembe: The Revitalization of African Society.* Braamfontein, South Africa: Skotaville Publishers.
Villa-Vicencio, Charles (1992). *A Theology of Reconstruction: Nation-Building and Human Rights.* New York: Cambridge University Press.
Vinicombe, Patricia (1972a). Motivation in African Rock Art. *Antiquity* 46:124–133.
_____ (1972b). Myth, Motive, and Selection in Southern African Rock Art. *Africa* 42:192–204.
_____ (1976). *People of the Eland: Rock Paintings of the Drakensberg Bushmen as a Reflection of Their Life and Thought.* Pietermaritzburg: University of Natal Press.
Voloshinov, V. N. (1973 [1929]). *Marxism and the Philosophy of Language.* Ladislav Matejka and I. R. Titunik, trans. New York: Seminar Press.
Von Grunebaum, G. E. (1962). Pluralism in the Islamic World. *Islamic Studies* 1(2):37–59.
Von Harnack, Adolf (1905). *The Mission and Expansion of Christianity in the First Three Centuries.* 2 vols. New York: G. P. Putnam's Sons.
Vryjhof, Pieter H., and Jacques D. Waardenburg, eds. (1979). *Official and Popular Religion: Exploration of a Theme for Religious Studies.* The Hague: Mouton.

Walji, Shirin (1974). A History of Ismali Community in Tanzania. Ph.D. dissertation, University of Wisconsin, Madison.
Walker, Sheila S. (1972). *Ceremonial Spirit Possession in Africa and Afro-America.* Leiden: E. J. Brill.
_____ (1983). *The Religious Revolution in the Ivory Coast: The Prophet Harris and the Harrist Church.* Chapel Hill: University of North Carolina Press.
Wallace, Anthony F. C. (1956). Revitalization Movements. *American Anthropologist* 58:264–281.
_____ (1966). *Religion: An Anthropological View.* New York: Random House.
Wallis, Roy (1982). The Social Construction of Charisma. *Social Compass* 29(1):25–39.
Walls, Andrew F. (1981). The Gospel as the Prisoner and Liberator of Culture. *Faith and Thought* 108(1–2):39–52.
Warren, Max, ed. (1971). *To Apply the Gospel: Selections from the Writings of Henry Venn.* Grand Rapids, Michigan: William B. Eerdman's Publishing Company.
Waters, Anita M. (1985). *Race, Class, and Political Symbols: Rastafari and Reggae in Jamaican Politics.* New Brunswick, New Jersey: Transaction Books.

Wauthion, René (1940). Crimes et superstitions indigènes. Quelques notes sur des sociétés indigènes (région de Kongolo). *Bulletin des Jurisdictions Indigènes et du Droit Coutumier Congolais* 8(11):310–314.

Weber, Max (1963). *The Sociology of Religion.* Ephraim Fischoff, trans. Boston: Beacon.

_____ (1964). *Wirtschaft und Gesellschaft. Studienausgabe.* Cologne: Kiepenheuer and Witsch.

_____ (1968a [1922]). The Prophet. In *Max Weber: On Charisma and Institution Building,* 253–267. S. N. Eisenstadt, ed. Chicago: University of Chicago Press.

_____ (1968a [1946]). The Sociology of Charismatic Authority. In *Max Weber: On Charisma and Institution Building,* 18–27. S. N. Eisenstadt, ed. Chicago: University of Chicago Press.

_____ (1968a [1947]). The Nature of Charismatic Authority and Its Routinization. In *Max Weber: On Charisma and Institution Building,* 48–65. S. N. Eisenstadt, ed. Chicago: University of Chicago Press.

_____ (1968b). *Economy and Society: An Outline of Interpretive Sociology,* 3:1111–1157. Guenther Roth and Claus Wittich, eds. New York: Bedminister Press.

Webster, James (1964). *African Churches among the Yoruba: 1888–1922.* Oxford: Clarendon.

Welbourn, Frederick Burkewood (1961). *East African Rebels: A Study of Some Independent Churches.* London: SCM Press.

Welbourn, Frederick Burkewood, and B. A. Ogot (1966). *A Place to Feel at Home: A Study of Two Independent Churches in Western Kenya.* London: Oxford University Press.

Wendroff, A. P. (1981). The Role of Traditional Divining Healers in Northeastern Malawi. Paper presented at the African Studies Association annual meeting, November, Bloomington, Indiana.

_____ (1983). Health Care and Social Change in Northern Malawi. In *Third World Medicine and Social Change: A Reader in Social Science and Medicine,* 256–284. J. H. Morgan, ed. Lanham, Maryland: University Press of America.

Wendt, W. E. (1976). "Art Mobilier" from Apollo 11 Cave, South West Africa: Africa's Oldest Dated Works of Art. *South African Archaeological Bulletin* 31:5–11.

Wengatz, Susan (1927). Back to Pentecost. *South Africa Missionary Advocate* 6(6).

Werbner, Richard P., ed. (1977). *Regional Cults.* London: Academic Press.

_____ (1989). *Ritual Passage, Sacred Journey: The Form, Process, and Organization of Religious Movement.* Washington, D.C.: Smithsonian Institution Press.

Werner, Oswald, and G. Mark Schoepfle (1987). *Systematic Fieldwork.* 2 vols. Newbury Park, California: Sage Publications.

Wescott, J. (1962). The Sculpture and Myths of Eshu-Elegba, the Yoruba Trickster. *Africa* 32(4):336–354.

Wescott, J., and P. Morton-Williams (1962). The Symbolism and Ritual Context of the Yoruba laba sango. *Journal of the Royal Anthropological Institute* 92(1):23–37.

West, Martin Elgar (1975). *Bishops and Prophets in a Black City: African Independent Churches in Soweto, Johannesburg.* Cape Town: D. Phillip; London: R. Collins.

Westerlund, David (1980). *Ujamaa na Dini: A Study of Some Aspects of Society and Religion in Tanzania, 1961–1977.* Stockholm: Almqvist & Wikgell International.

Whisson, Michael G., and Martin West, eds. (1975). *Religion and Social Change in Southern Africa: Anthropological Essays in Honour of Monica Wilson.* Cape Town: D. Philip.

Whitney, Orson F. (1917). *The Strength of the "Mormon" Position.* Independence, Missouri: Zion's Printing and Publishing Co.

Willett, Frank (1967). *Ife in the History of West African Sculpture.* London: Thames and Hudson.

Williams, Ethel L., and Clifton F. Brown, comps. (1972). *Afro-American Religious Studies: A Comprehensive Bibliography with Locations in American Libraries.* Metuchen, New Jersey: Scarecrow Press.

_____, comps. (1977). *The Howard University Bibliography of African and Afro-American Religious Studies: With Locations in American Libraries.* Wilmington, Delaware: Scholarly Resources.

Williamson, Sydney George (1965). *Akan Religion and the Christian Faith: A Comparative Study of the Impact of Two Religions.* Accra: Ghana Universities Press.

Willis, John Ralph, ed. (1979). *Studies in West African Islamic History, Volume 1. The Cultivators of Islam.* London: Frank Cass.

Willis, Roy (1985). Do the Fipa Have a Word for It? In *The Anthropology of Evil.* David Parkin, ed. Oxford: Blackwell.

Wilson, Godfrey (1939). Nyakyusa Conventions of Burial. *Bantu Studies* 13:1–31.

Wilson, Monica Hunter (1961 [1936]). *Reaction to Conquest: Effects of Contact with Europeans on the Pondo of South Africa.* 2nd ed. London: Oxford University Press.

____ (1963 [1951]). *Good Company: A Study of Nyakyusa Age-Villages.* Boston: Beacon Press.

____ (1971). *Religion and the Transformation of Society: A Study in Social Change in Africa.* Cambridge: Cambridge University Press.

Wilson, Peter J. (1967). Status, Ambiguity and Spirit Possession. *Man* n.s., 2(3):366–378.

Wiltgen, Ralph M. (1956). *Gold Coast Mission History, 1471–1880.* Techny, Illinois: Divine Word Publications.

Winter, Marlo (1983). The Balokole and the Protestant Ethic: A Critique. *Journal of Religion in Africa* 14:58–73.

Wiredu, Kwasi (1980). *Philosophy and an African Culture.* New York: Cambridge University Press.

Wolff, Norma (1982). Egungun Costuming in Abeokuta. *African Arts* 15(3):66–70.

Wyllie, Robert W. (1980). *The Spirit-Seekers: New Religious Movements in Southern Ghana.* Missoula, Montana: Scholars Press.

Yansane, Aguibou Y. (1985). Cultural, Political, and Economic Universals in West Africa. In *African Culture: The Rhythms of Unity,* 39–68. Molefi Kete Asante and Kariamu Welsh Asante, eds. Westport, Connecticut: Greenwood.

Yankah, Kwesi (1989). *The Proverb in the Context of Akan Rhetoric: A Theory of Proverb Praxis.* New York: Peter Lang.

Yoder, P. Stanley, ed. (1982). *African Health and Healing Systems.* Los Angeles: Crossroads.

Young, Brigham (1954). *Discourses of Brigham Young.* Salt Lake City: Deseret Book Co.

Young, Crawford, and Thomas Turner (1985). *The Rise and Decline of the Zairian State.* Madison: University of Wisconsin Press.

Zahala, Xavier (1974). Etude sociologique de la Jamaa. Le cas de Lubumbashi. Mémoire de licence. Université National du Zaïre, Campus de Lubumbashi

Zahan, Dominique (1979). *The Religion, Spirituality, and Thought of Traditional Africa.* Chicago: University of Chicago Press.

Zaretsky, Irving I., and Mark P. Leone, eds. (1974). *Religious Movements in Contemporary America: An Annotated Bibliography.* Princeton: Princeton University Press.

Zaretsky, Irving I., and Cynthia Shambaugh (1978). *Spirit Possession and Spirit Mediumship in Africa and Afro-America.* New York: Garland.

Ziadeh, Nicola A. (1958). *Sanusiyah.* Leiden: E. J. Brill.

Zoghby, Samir M. (1978). *Islam in Sub-Saharan Africa: A Partially Annotated Guide.* Washington: Library of Congress.

Zuesse, Evan M. (1979). *Ritual Cosmos: The Sanctification of Life in African Religions.* Athens: Ohio University Press.

Index

A

'Ábezhá Mbungú [Hêmbá creator god], 405
Abímbọ́lá, Wándé, 5–6, 12, 100–116
ablution, 251
abortion, 356
Abrahams, Roger, 441 n.14
accommodation, 139–140, 157
acephalous societies, 15, 172–174, 186, 401, 437
action-orientedness of African religion, 16–17
adaptation, 5–6, 11, 16–17
aesthetic(s): & awareness of supernatural, *388*, 389, *390*, 391–393, *393*, 394–396, *396*, 397, 412; & healing or ritual efficacy, 13, *422*, *428*, 428–429; & performance of Hêmbá oratory & song-dance, 10, 415, *416*, 419–423, *422*, *427*, *428*, 428–429, 435–438; & pilferage of art, 188; & religious ties, 10. *See also* dance; gestural art; music; *músúúsá;* oratory; performance(s); sculpture; verbal art
aesthetically framed action: emergence of religious notions during, 9–10, 435–438
affliction, 11, 14, 17; freedom from, 249; long-distance translation of, 7; & problem solving, 181. *See also* disease; healing association(s); misfortune; ritual of affliction
African Advance, 280
African Christian, 5, 16, 400, 405. *See also* Christian; church
African Diaspora, 6, 15, 87, 156, 324, 331, 333
Africanization, 5, 8, 14, *56*, *68*, 263, 275–313
African Theology, 73, 86
Afro-Bahian, 136, 141, 148, 150, 156
Afro-Brazilian, 137, 147, 156
afterlife, 10, 49, 190, *240*, 438. *See also* ancestor(s)
afterworld, 405–407, *425*, 429, 434, 442 n.17; proto-Bantu term for, 195
Àgbìgbò [an evil bird], 108–109, 116
Aghahowa, Azaigueni, 121, 123, 125, 126, *132*, 134
agriculture, 75, *75*, *103*, 282, 287–289, 293–294, 297–309, 363, 400, 401. *See also* farming
Àjàlá [human who molds heads], 111. *See also* head
ajogun [malevolent superhuman power: in Yoruba cosmology], 102, 104–106, 108–110
Akinsowon, Abiodun, 43
Aladura revival, 42–44

alcohol, 247, 319
alienation, 4, 8, 181, 315, 319–321, 327–329, 340; from self, 329. *See also* communitas; liminality; marginality; outcast(s); social change
Allah, 10, 54, *200*
Alldridge, Thomas J., 350, 360 n.6
altar, 17; in Dogon ritual, 199, 202, 209–210, 216; at Great Zimbabwe, 192; prehistoric Yoruba, 192; sacrifice on, *184*, 185
Ama [Dogon head god], 208, 220
ambiguity, 16; in plural societies, 246, 254
AMEC *Discipline*, 281
American Methodist Episcopal Church (AMEC), 8, 14, 275–309, 310 n.24, 312 n.76
American Methodist Episcopal Church (AMEC) Historical Society, 281
Amerindian, 11, 12, 136–137
Amharic, *26*, 28
anarchy, 11, 272, 437
ancestor(s), 1, 6, 90–92, 95–98, 144, 146, 156, 166, 168, 173, 175, 208, 218, 245, *253*, *398*, 402, *402*, 403, 428, 434, 436, 438, 439 n.8; aiding in health of the living, *398*, *402*, 405, *408*, *422*; appreciation for, *422*; as cause of misfortunes, 166, 436; Christ as, 73, 85; dead dwell with, 429; drumming voice of, 162, 164–165; & family, 95; influence from, 167, *200*; kinship with the living, 95, 407, 411, 436; as part of audience of ritual performance, *398*, 405, 407, *410*, 416, *422*, 422–423, 425, *425*, 429, 431, 442 n.17; protection by, 348–351, 358, *398*, *408*; protection from, 144, 146, 166–167, 206, 295, 382, 384, *408*; proto-Bantu term for, 166, *193*, 195; & rock art, 186; role of, 437; sacrifices to, 295, 384; & sculpture, *184*, *408*; shrine, 62, 65; as source of morality, 95; as tutelary spirit in music performance, 392; of Yoruba, 104. *See also* dead, the; funeral(s); healing; healing association(s); ritual; sculpture; soul; spirit(s)
Andersson, Efraim, 242–243, 248–249
androgyny, 357–358, 361 n.9
angels, 248
Anglican church, 40, 258, 275–276, 280, 291–292. *See also* Church Missionary Society (Anglican)
Angola, 136, 164, 188
Angola Candomblés, 136–137. *See also* Candomblés

484

B

L

veiled insult: among the Báhêmbá, 413, 415, 431, 434, 436–438. *See also* dirge; *músúúsá;* oratory; proverb(s); verbal art
Venda, 165–166
Venezuela, 101
Venn, Henry, 38, 40, 42
verbal art: importance of ~ in performance, 10, 419–423, 441 n.12; & verbal communication, 185, 401, 406, 407, 412, 415–419, 434–438; Hêmbá funeral provides occasion for, 407, 415, *416, 421, 422,* 424, 426, *427, 433. See also* dirge; epic; *músúúsá;* myth; oratory; proverb(s); song; veiled insult
vernacular discourses: & hierarchy of religions, 6
vernacular language: & Africanization of missionary churches, 8, 24–25, 39–42, 61; Christian translation into ~ as springboard for nationalism, 4, 25; & national identity formation, 11; spoken, 302; written, 302
Victoria, Lake, 172
Vinnicombe, Patricia, 186
virilocal residence, 400
vision, 304. *See also* dreams; trance
visionary, 320; leader of a liberation movement, 4
Visram, Allidina, 51–53
vodu, 136. *See also* Candomble
voice power, 393–394, 396, 397
Voloshinov, V. N., 416

W

Wahvuwi [Methodist men's organization], 282
Wagner, Kush, 300
Wai [Nkundo ancestor], 229
wailing: at graveside, *410*
Wallace, Anthony F. C., 315, 317, 319, 337, 340
Wallis, Roy, 334–338, 340
Wamatumbi, 54
Wanctsama, Mai, 306
war, 102, 204, 207, 212, 234, 352, 354; protection against, 207, 222, *225;* women cause of, 355. *See also* military; warrior
Wara Wara Bafodea. *See* Bafodea
Wara Wara Yagala, 364
warrior: as hero, 233–235, 237–238, 299. *See also* military; war
Warungu [spirits], 177
washing: female initiation rite, 348–349, 355–356, 380, *383. See also* cleansing; purity
washing hands, 378, 380, *381*
wasps [in Nkundo myth], 230–235
water, 81, 102, 104, 119–120, 121, 123, 125, 129, 143–144, 177, 216; in blessing, 249, 251–252, 370; in communion, 251
water god(s): Dogon, 208; Gola, 351

Wauthion, René, 439 n.5
wealth, 93, 120, 121, 126, 130–131, 133–134, 181, 271
Weber, Max, 257–259, 269, 271, 299, 315–317, 319, 334, 336–340, 340 n.2
welfare, 328
Wendroff, A. P., 82–83
Wengatz, Susan, 291
Wesley, John, 286, 287; mother of, 290
West Africa, 7, 9, 11, 15, 58–60, 71, 87, 89, 101, 116, 139, 145, 148, 150, 154, 156, 180, 343–345, 384
Westermann, Diedrich, 343
Western academia: comparison vis-à-vis cultural categories of, 4
Western Bantu, 165–167
Western Christianity: Zaïrean state plus ~: in political dualism with Kimbanguism, 8
Western-imported Christ figure, 5
Western Limba, 364
Western medicine, 179, 204
Western missionaries: performance topped by African Christians, 14
Western theological concepts: translation of ~ into Yoruba culture & vice versa, 5
white: in art, 126, 129, 145, 166, 187; Casa Branca [White House], 137, 157, 159; covering of *kendu,* 350; for funerals, 151; kaolin: for Edo shrines, 121, 129; as purity, 120, 166; in ritual, 199, 375, *402, 406;* ritual clothing, 81, 120, 131, 134, 142, 144–145, *180;* sacred color of Şàngó, 152; symbolism of, 142; "in the white", *160,* 158, 179; whitewashed shrine, 121, 144, 155
"white belly" or "white liver", 209, 219
White Fathers, 59, 401
"White man", 66, 71
Wilson, Monica, 163
witch(es), 76, 79, 84, 197, 203–204, 209–212, 215–216, 220, 245–246, 251–252, 256 n.3, 289, 345, 354–355, 357, 365–366, 382, 384; bewitch: proto-Bantu term for, 195; evil from, 211, 226; & illness, 382; Kpelle music event named for, 391, 395, 396, 397; most do not claim to observe a ~, 1; protection against, 374; religion as taming of potential, 9; Satan as, 249; "sniff out", 251. *See also* divination; healing; *nganga;* secret society(ies); semisecret society(ies); sociosomatic causes of illness; sorcery; therapy
witchcraft, 71, 84–85, 87, 148, 203–205, 215–216, 248–249, 251–252, 254–256, 264, 352, 357–359, 366, 405, 411, 415, 420, 422, 428, 430, 434–438; antiwitchcraft medicine cults, 172; cause of death, 430; cause of disorder, 430; cause of illness, 430; *músúúsá* songs